THE TANGLED WING

THE TANGLED WING

BIOLOGICAL CONSTRAINTS ON THE HUMAN SPIRIT

MELVIN KONNER

HOLT, RINEHART AND WINSTON
NEW YORK

Published by Holt, Rinehart and Winston, 383 Madison Ave, New York, New
York 10017.
Published simultaneously in Canada by Holt, Rinehart and Winston
of Canada, Limited.
Library of Congress Cataloging in Publication Data
Konner, Melvin.
The tangled wing.
Includes bibliographical references and index.
1. Emotions—Physiological aspects. 2. Human behav-
ior. I. Title.
QP401.K6   152.4   81-47464
ISBN 0-03-057062-X   AACR2

First edition

Designer: Amy Hill
Printed in the United States of America
1 3 5 7 9 10 8 6 4 2

Grateful acknowledgment is made for permission to quote
from the following works:
"Life of Galileo," from *Collected Poems, Volume 5* by Bertolt Brecht,
translated by Wolfgang Sauerlander and Ralph Manheim. Copyright
© 1972 by Stefan S. Brecht. Reprinted by permission of Pantheon
Books, a Division of Random House, Inc.
"The Hollow Men," from *Collected Poems 1909–1962* by T. S. Eliot. Reprinted
by permission of Harcourt Brace Jovanovich, Inc.
"Sea Side," from *Collected Poems* by Robert Graves. Reprinted by permission
of Robert Graves.
"Rendezvous," from *Mink Coat* by Jill Hoffman. Copyright © 1969, 1970,
1971, 1972, 1973 by Jill Hoffman. Reprinted by permission of Holt,
Rinehart and Winston, Publishers.
Duino Elegies by Rainer Maria Rilke, translated by permission of
W.W. Norton & Co., Inc. Copyright 1939, © 1967 by
W.W. Norton & Co., Inc.
"To Me That Man Equals a God," by Sappho, reprinted by permission of
Schocken Books, Inc., from *Greek Lyric Poetry*, translated by Willis
Barnstone. Copyright © 1962, 1967 by Willis Barnstone.
"Sunday Morning" and "Le Monocle de Mon Oncle," reprinted from *The
Collected Poems of Wallace Stevens* by permission of Alfred A. Knopf,
Inc. Copyright 1923 and renewed © 1951 by Wallace Stevens.
"Lapis Lazuli," from *Collected Poems* by William Butler Yeats. Copyright
1940 by Georgie Yeats, renewed © 1968 by Bertha Georgie Yeats, Michael
Butler Yeats and Anne Yeats.
"Among School Children," from *Collected Poems* by William Butler
Yeats. Copyright 1928 by Macmillan Publishing Co., Inc.,
renewed © 1956 by Georgie Yeats.
"Do not go gentle into that good night," from *Poems of Dylan Thomas*.
Copyright 1952 by Dylan Thomas. Reprinted by permission of
New Directions Publishing Corporation, New York.

ISBN 0-03-057062-X

TO IRVEN DEVORE AND
HERBERT PERLUCK, AND TO THE
MEMORY OF GERALD HENDERSON.

All bibles or sacred codes have been the causes of the following errors:

1. That man has two real existing principles: viz: a body & a soul.

2. That energy, called evil, is alone from the body: & that reason, called good, is alone from the soul.

3. That God will torment man in eternity for following his energies.

But the following contraries to these are true:

1 Man has no body distinct from his soul; for that called body is a portion of soul discerned by the five senses, the chief inlets of soul in this age.

2. Energy is the only life, and is from the body; and reason is the bound or outward circumference of energy.

3. Energy is eternal delight.

—William Blake, "The Marriage of Heaven and Hell," 1790

CONTENTS

CONTENTS

ACKNOWLEDGMENTS

Many an author, sitting with pencil stub in hand, bent over sprawled galleys, must have thought, as I did, of the first few phrases of Don Quixote: "Idle reader, you may believe me without any oath that I would want this book, the child of my brain, to be the most beautiful, the happiest, the most brilliant imaginable. But I could not contravene that law of nature according to which like begets like." If such can be said of Cervantes's brainchild, what can one possibly say about one's own?

Only that one has done one's best. And yet, if the truth be told, that "best" may prove to belong as much to certain others as to one's self. For generous conversations that proved critically important in the development of my concept of human nature, and thus of the subject of this book, I thank Rabbi Bernard L. Berzon, Nicholas G. Blurton Jones, T. Berry Brazelton, Stephan Chorover, Victor Denenberg, Nancy DeVore, Howard Eichenbaum, Marjorie Elias, Pamela English, Robin Fox, Jerome Kagan, Marc Kaminsky, Larry Konner, Jane Lancaster, Richard Lee, Miguel Leibovich, Robert L. Liebman, Kopela Maswe, Myrtle McGraw, Richard Morris, Walle Nauta, Penelope Naylor, !Xoma N!aiba, Paul Pavel, John Pfeiffer, Leonard Rosenblum, Alice Rossi, Laura Smith, Stefan Stein, Charles Super, Lionel Tiger, Robert Trivers, Dora Venit, Eric Wanner, Beatrice Whiting, John Whiting, E.O. Wilson, Richard Wurtman, and Paul Yakovlev.

Although none of the following foundations directly supported this project, they supported other aspects of my work that were relevant to it, and I am grateful: the National Science Foundation (1969–71, 1979–82), the National Institute of Mental Health (1969–71, 1979–81), the Foundations Fund for Research in Psychiatry (1973–75), the Harry Frank Guggenheim Foundation (1975–77), and the Social Science Research Council (1979–80).

I thank the administrations and staffs of the Department of Anthropology, the Peabody Museum of Archeology and Ethnology, and the Tozzer Library of Harvard University for their contributions of space and other assistance. Jerome and Edna Shostak provided the hospitality of their home in New York City, and George and Anne Twitchell that of their Vermont farm, where parts of the book were written.

Alex Gold was the first person to believe in and provide encouragement for this effort. My agent Elaine Markson was another early and generous supporter. Marian Wood, Executive Editor at Holt, Rinehart and Winston, gave the entire manuscript two separate close readings, and her detailed comments improved its stylistic and intellectual coherence markedly. Jill Weinstein did a superb job supervising the copy editing and shepherding the book through the production process.

For seven years my undergraduate and graduate students at Harvard provided a source of stimulation and criticism that made me feel privileged. They will recognize much of what is in this book as material that was delivered to them in cruder form, and I am grateful to them for inducing many refinements in it. Two, Robert Sapolsky and Michael Elias, have stood out from this group and become colleagues. I therefore asked them to read the manuscript and comment in detail on it. The resulting improvements are many.

To thank one's parents seems routine, but is not so always. Mine overcame both physical handicap and poverty to deliver to me a desire and an opportunity for a lifelong dedication to learning; this gift can never be repaid.

Marjorie Shostak is the one person of whom it can be said that without her this book would not have been written. Her companionship, support, friendly criticism and intellectual stimulation have been at the very core of it since its inception.

ACKNOWLEDGMENTS

This book is dedicated to Irven DeVore and Herbert Perluck, and to the memory of Gerald Henderson. To these teachers and friends are owed, respectively, its central ideas, its ethical and esthetic sensibility, and its guiding vision. With a sense of gratitude and affection I have tried to live up to their expectations. They and others mentioned above are the forces behind whatever is best in this book. In a spirit of rather wistful regret, I must concede that they cannot be asked to share the burden of its undoubted flaws and follies

A PREFATORY INQUIRY

> We must recollect that all our provisional ideas in
> psychology will presumably one day be based on an organic
> substructure.
> —Sigmund Freud, "On Narcissism"

Why we are what we are, why we do what we do, why we feel what we feel; these questions have been on the minds of philosophers and theologians, medical men and medicine men, actors, diplomats, poets and, of course, scientists, beginning with the first glimmer of human thought itself. From late-night TV psychobabble to the sober musings of the Sunday supplements, we are deluged with an endless supply of advice and explanation. Some of it tries to pass as science; for example, we are told that by reliving the painful experience of our own birth we can change the circuits in our brains and so find happiness. Some of it doesn't bother with explanation, but merely exhorts: pull your own strings, look out for number one, win through intimidation—succeed. So congenial are these bits of advice to our era, culture, and nature that those who offer them seem destined to find their own paths paved with gold, as life follows art and they live out their own prescriptions.

Some of what we read really *is* science. It is difficult to understand, but we know it is authoritative, so we puzzle our way through it, taking it like a rather nasty medicine. And, like much medicine, we can't quite tell if it helps. Some fragment of human behavior, normal or abnormal, is analyzed before our eyes; we are given the latest word. A shaft of light falls on it for a little while and we see it clearly. But, very often, the difficulty of integrating what we have just learned into a larger picture of ourselves, of human action, is such that the new knowledge fades before we can use it.

In the old cliché, scientists find out more and more about less until they know everything about nothing. That, amusing as it is, is not the problem. The problem is that we know more and more about more and more, and although we will never know everything about everything, the time will come when we know so much about so many things that no one person can hope to grasp all the essential facts about, say, violence, or anxiety, that are needed to make a single wise decision. Knowledge becomes collective in the weakest sense, and scientists become like men and women in a crowd, looking for one another, each holding a single piece of a very expensive radio.

Every so often someone must say: Now is a time to stop and see what we know. Without such pauses, epistemology—the process of knowing—is a bargain basement, shoppers jostling and shouting as they grab at a garment that fits and one that, momentarily, is in style. None of the knowledge we have gained, or will gain, about behavior is of any use to us if we get it piecemeal, if we cannot somehow contrive to make it whole. Scientists, including those who speak most eloquently to the public, are continually saying "We must know more." This is true, of course, but the muted conviction that this in itself will save us is false. Knowledge does not automatically order itself in human terms, and if this is true of science generally, it is all the more true of the sciences of human behavior. More startling, and contrary to the workaday beliefs of most scientists, knowledge does not even always accumulate, in the simplest, additive sense. A few years ago a colleague of mine came back from a conference on information retrieval where one of the speakers argued (using, of course, calculations) that for some of the knowledge unearthed by scientists of the past, it would be cheaper to rediscover it than to retrieve it. Imagine, if you will, the wave of uneasy movement that might have rippled through the graves of dead scientists at that argument: For some, the work to which they devoted their lives was not merely wrongheaded—this they were prepared for—it was, even when right, never absorbed in the body of human knowledge.

For those of us who do not share the conviction that bits of knowledge laid end to end lead to wisdom, the articulation of the bits becomes a challenge separate from that of unearthing them. When the knowledge in question concerns behavior, especially human behavior, the emergent image must bear a human face. If it doesn't, the mind goes blank when we look at it, irrespective of how detailed or right it is. So there are two tasks, really: first, the assessment of what we know, the assembly of the pieces; second, the discernment of a human face.

Some time ago I was being interviewed in front of a camera by Dick Gilling, a producer of excellent BBC-TV science programs. My involvement seemed to have been precipitated by a wave of enthusiasm for a new field called "sociobiology," and not through any merit or fault of my own. He was making a series then optimistically called "The Human Futures"—though perhaps by pluralizing that uncertain noun phrase, calling to mind speculation in hogs and soybeans, something less than blue-chip confidence was intended.

We were chatting straightforwardly about the family among the !Kung San, hunter-gatherers of Africa's Kalahari Desert. I was trying to look at the camera instead of at Gilling. I was supposed to be revealing something about the biological limits on the naturally occurring variation of human behavior, one of the subjects I am paid to try to know about. The overall question was: When and how will futuristic social engineering come up against this or that biological brick wall? I sat awkwardly on a hard chair in a makeshift studio in Harvard's Museum of Comparative Zoology, surrounded by strange equipment. Four or five skeptical, rather intimidating craftspeople were in the room working and listening.

"We're almost finished," Gilling said. (His remarks and questions were to be cut from the tape.) He paused and looked at a piece of paper folded in his hands. The lights hurt my eyes a bit. I was very uncomfortable. "What," he went on, "can you suggest for the prevention of future global conflict?"

There was a long pause. I believe I grunted before I burst out laughing.

"Cut," he said.

Yes, I thought, as I tried to stop laughing. Yes, indeed. Quite. *Cut.*

Gilling was very good-natured. "You don't have to answer that one," he said.

"You didn't warn me there were going to be questions like that."

"We can skip it," he said wistfully.

"Well, if you give me a few minutes to think I might be able to come up with something that doesn't sound completely ridiculous."

What I came up with after a minute's thought was that if we are ever to control human violence we must first appreciate that humans have a natural, biological tendency to react violently, as individuals or as groups, in certain situations. If we could understand the details of this response and its determinants, we might begin to grasp some hope of prevention. For example, if, as now seems clearly demon-strated, there are biological reasons why women, like other primate females, have a weaker aggressive tendency than males, then it is possible that an overall increase in the percentage of powerful positions held by women might tend to buffer political systems against violence.

"Was that more or less what you wanted?" I asked.

It was. But in retrospect it was not at all what I wanted. As I walked away, I thought of all the other things I should have added. For example, to fail to mention population growth in such a context is a serious omission, since this is perhaps the gravest threat to future world peace. Second only to it in gravity is the grossly unequal distribution of planetary wealth and power. We had been talking about San hunter-gatherers, and they provide as good an example of this as any: Among them, hoarding of wealth by some increases the likelihood of violence; sharing of wealth with others correspondingly reduces it. Beyond these problems, I might also have mentioned that vivid historical extension of tribalism into the twentieth century that we call nationalism; but that is more a synonym for global conflict than an explanation of it.

If we had had time to discuss the question at the level of individual physiology, a plethora of significant determinants could have been implicated. For example, given the procedures through which people (usually men) rise to power in every known society, and given the well-established individual variation (from genetic and other causes) in the tendency to aggressive competition, it can scarcely be supposed that the least aggressive, greedy, and competitive sets of genes in a population will come to control the deployment of that population's military might. And we could have explored the specific significance, in terms of what is now known about behavioral physiology, of the fact that most people who run the world—its politics and its armies—do so on a chronic insufficiency of sleep; with personal health declining more rapidly than that of their age-mates in other walks of life; and under conditions characterized by an unnaturally high density of social interactions (particularly with strangers), by constant extreme stress, and by fear—ranging from fear of loss of influence to fear of assassination. These and other features of their personal biological lives are not without known effects on the biological tendency to violence and threats of violence.

So much for my second thoughts, which could not have found their verbose way into Gilling's film even if they had been more timely. We prefer simple, clear explanations. This is understandable; we are busy with other things. But, of course, the answers must also be comprehensive. Otherwise, what good are they? We have no time for endless academic musings, or for a telephone-book litany of facts. We need theories that are incisive and illuminating, enabling us to grasp the solution at once; they must transcend the complexities, paring away all that is irrelevant, leaving the elegant, decisive beauty of a Euclidean proof, that first paradigm of our intellectual training.

I offer no such theories. It is my belief that the failure of behavioral science up to the present day results, precisely, from the pursuit of them. Marxism, psychoanalysis, learning theory, instinct theory, cognitive theory, structuralism, sociobiology—not a single one false in its essence, but each one false in its ambitions and in its condemnation of the others. A good textbook of human behavioral biology, which we will not have for another fifty years, will look not like Euclid's geometry—a magnificent edifice of proven propositions deriving from a set of simple assumptions—but more like a textbook of physiology or geology, each solution grounded in a separate body of facts and approached with a quiverful of different theories, with all the solutions connected in a great complex web.

The pages that follow form a sort of game plan for such a text. They deploy the problems, the playing pieces, and the rules, but they do not provide the solutions—least of all simple, clear, comprehensive ones. Yet the solutions to come in the next few decades are prefigured by these complex considerations. On the modern cardiolo-

gy ward, in confronting cardiac failure, professionals talk of everything from chemistry to anxiety, from surgery to diet, from
bioelectricity to love; and they had better, since no one theory can
save a failing heart. I believe that such problems as global conflict,
psychotic or neurotic depression, and sexual unhappiness are similar
in nature. Just as cardiac-ward professionals rely on a surprisingly
high fraction of the totality of human knowledge to find their
solutions, so will human behavioral biologists require a great complexity of knowledge to find ours.

In Bertolt Brecht's *Life of Galileo*, the great astronomer says:

> Truth is the child of time, not of authority. Our ignorance is
> infinite, let's whittle away just one cubic millimeter. Why
> should we still want to be so clever when at long last we have a
> chance of being a little less stupid?

And late in the play he says it more clearly:

> One of the main reasons for the poverty of science is that it is
> supposed to be rich. The aim of science is not to open the door to
> everlasting wisdom, but to set a limit on everlasting error.

That is the motto and hope of this book. For those who find it
insufficient to their purposes, I cannot in good conscience recom-
mend a further investment, since there are so many books that will
open the door to everlasting wisdom at a comparable cost. But for
those who share my view that "to set a limit on everlasting error" is
ambition enough, already pressing the point of human pride, I offer
an account of the first few steps on an immense journey.

PART ONE

FOUNDATIONS OF A SCIENCE OF HUMAN NATURE

Thus, from the war of nature, from famine and death, the most exalted object which we are capable of conceiving, namely, the production of the higher animals, directly follows. There is grandeur in this view of life, with its several powers, having been originally breathed into a few forms or into one; and that, whilst this planet has gone cycling on according to the fixed law of gravity, from so simple a beginning endless forms most beautiful and most wonderful have been, and are being, evolved.

—Charles Darwin, *The Origin of Species*, 1859

What a book a Devil's Chaplain might write on the clumsy, wasteful, blundering low and horribly cruel works of nature!

—Charles Darwin to Joseph Hooker, July 1856

1

THE QUEST FOR THE NATURAL

And the Lord planted a garden eastward in Eden; and
there he put the man whom he had formed.
—Genesis 2:8

Rousseau was not the first, nor even, probably, the most
naïve. But he was the most famous in a long line of credulous people,
stretching as far back as thought and as far forward, perhaps, as our
precarious species manages to survive, who seem to believe that we
have left something behind that is better in every way than what we
have now and that the most apt way to solve our problems is to go
backward as quickly as possible. Inevitably, what is past is viewed as
natural, what is present as unnatural; as if the march of history, with
its spreading plague of gadgets, had somehow distanced us from the
bodies we inhabit, from the functions we perform every day. This
nostalgia is characteristically undiscriminating. The naïve romantics
of an era often look back just a few decades to find their Eden, little
realizing that the romantics of that era also looked back, and so on,
and so on. Rousseau himself fell in love with the Swiss peasantry,
both in the person of his wife and in the object of his philosophy. He
saw in their atomized social (asocial?) life the road to happiness.
Society was the root of evil, and in this "natural" peasant condition of
supposedly complete self-sufficiency, the human atoms avoided collision by avoiding contact—strife being impossible in a vacuum. Each
person, or at least each family, kept its own counsel and went about
the business of survival with efficient aplomb, neither asking nor
giving anything, without snobbery and, of course, without gadgets.

If this sounds more like the dream of a bookish philosopher than the social life of peasants, that is probably because it is. No known society has ever been as unsociable as Rousseau's peasants, and the absence of ethnographic substance in his descriptions makes us skeptical that they are in fact descriptions and not imaginings.

But more ironic than that he should fail to *see* peasant social life is that he should settle on it as the natural, original human condition. For as we have finally come to understand, if there is any such thing as a natural human condition, peasant society is as much a distortion of it, and almost as much of a novelty, as industrial urban life itself.

What society, then, does exemplify the natural human condition? Candidates abound, but all the serious modern ones have this in common: they gather wild plant foods and hunt wild game for a living. No other sorts of societies are admissible, and this is as it should be, because the archeological record, as we know it now, speaks plainly: for 95 to 99 percent of human generations on this planet—depending on what you want to call human—our ancestors lived in this manner alone. If we could write a true "book of begats" to replace the biblical generations of Adam, the generational wheel would turn forty thousand times—hunters begetting hunters, gatherers begetting gatherers—before the first Abel or Cain appeared to plant a seed or husband a useful animal. A million years would have gone by before a few begetters would begin to scrape the earth with a view toward planting, and peasant society would still be postponed for millennia. Though the ten thousand years during which we have had agriculture seem a long time to us, it is only a minute in the hour of human life, scarcely a moment in the history of mammals. If an archeologist, a million years hence, were to stand in a trench and look at a good stratigraphic representation of human history, there would be a great thick layer holding the record of hunting and gathering, and on top of it an equal-sized layer for industrial urban life. Only on closer inspection would there appear a slender stratigraphic lens signifying agriculture, the mere transition.

Naturally (if one can use that word at all), anthropologists, absorbing at length these facts of archeology, became concerned to document the way of life of hunter-gatherers before its inevitable complete disappearance. This task wedded biological and social anthropology, in an intrinsic way, for the first time. Hunting and gathering was the crucible in which natural selection pounded at the grist for the human spirit as well as the human body; it was a matter of some importance to those who presumed to know the species to discover something about the forces that formed it.

The conditions under which humankind evolved were no better documented, and perhaps no better exemplified, than among the San of the Kalahari Desert. Made famous in the 1950s by the Marshall family—who wrote of them and filmed them brilliantly for twenty-five years—they went on to become the subjects of one of the most extensive and sophisticated interdisciplinary investigations ever made by anthropologists in a simple society, under the leadership of Richard Lee and Irven DeVore. The San weathered wave after wave of scrutiny with immense patience, persuaded that their own worth was sufficient cause for scrutiny. By the end of it they had rendered up enough of their essence—and, perhaps, the essence of life as our ancestors lived it for over a million years—to engender and in turn shatter myth after myth about the human condition.

The Harmless People was the title of Elizabeth Marshall Thomas's book about them. And so they are, harmless to oppose the advance of a technological civilization, dwarfed by the military might of sur-rounding peoples, black and white, who have borne down on them for centuries. During the white colonization of southern Africa the San were not merely massacred for convenience but also hunted for sport. They resisted bravely but feebly, ceding territory everywhere. In the end, they remained in a relatively pristine condition only in distant pockets of land unwanted by others, where ethnographers of the present era met them.

They are depicted as living in a kind of organic harmony, not only with the world of nature, but with one another. Their knowledge of wild plants and animals is deep and thorough enough to astonish and inform professional botanists and zoologists. Their transactions with wild things give them their living, but their knowledge goes far beyond necessity. Necessity itself appears harmonious. Women work three days a week at gathering nuts, fruit, and vegetables from the wild, and in so doing provide three-fourths of the food their families need to stay alive. This wide-world-as-supermarket also provides fresh meat on the hoof, in the form of some of Africa's most regal game animals: Eland, oryx, kudu, wildebeest, duiker, steenbok, and—in the days before the government ban—giraffe, to name a few, fall prey to San hunters. Those animals, such as oryx and warthog, that will stand and face dogs are hunted with dogs and spears by small groups of men. The others are usually hunted by solitary men with small bows and tiny, deadly arrows. The arrows are poisoned with toxins made from the thorax of the larva of a certain beetle, found in the sandy soil among the roots of a certain bush, in a certain season of the year. How the intricacies of this process became known to the San is only one among many remaining mysteries about them.

Men pursue game with about the same degree of intensity as women gather vegetables: three to four days a week is considered sufficient. They kill only what they can eat and remain in a balance with game populations that has persisted for millennia. They have a great respect for and fascination with the animals they prey upon, sometimes—as in the case of a man who came upon oryx copulating and was so interested he forgot to shoot them—to the detriment of their proper business of killing. Among these men (although they are far from foolhardy), extraordinary physical courage becomes ordinary. A number carry the scars of hand combat with leopards, and men and women alike, sometimes sleeping innocently, have met a grim end in the jaws of a lion or hyena.

Women, too, have their ordeal of physical courage. Childbirth is supposed to be managed by the woman all alone. The labor usually begins at night, and, after her first birth, a woman will often simply go out beyond the confines of the village-camp, deliver her baby by herself under the vast dome of Kalahari stars and, surrounded by any number of unknown dangers, cut the cord and return quietly to her hut. Often the first inkling of her confinement will reach others in the form of her baby's cry.

This deep dwelling in the world of nature is mirrored by the organic harmony of the human social world. Each village-camp consists of a small circle of grass huts. Each hut holds a family in a hemisphere just large enough to lie down in. The camp includes perhaps thirty people in all, but it is flexible. It moves from time to time, following the changes of the seasons, the vagaries of food and water availability. Or, it may move because someone has died there, and the place becomes unpleasant for people to stay in, even though the burial is far away. People join or leave more or less at will; there are other bands and camps to be with. Conflicts may be resolved by group fission. The fragments may go their own way for a time only to recoalesce months later, bygones forgotten; or they may form the social nuclei of nascent bands.

War is unknown. Conflicts within the group are resolved by talking, sometimes half or all the night, for nights, weeks on end. After two years with the San, I came to think of the Pleistocene epoch of human history (the three million years during which we evolved) as one interminable marathon encounter group. When we slept in a grass hut in one of their villages, there were many nights when its flimsy walls leaked charged exchanges from the circle around the fire, frank expressions of feeling and contention beginning when the dusk fires were lit and running on until the dawn. Surely a potent selection pressure for the evolution of language must have been the respect gained by a person whose voice commanded attention around such fires.

Equality is universal. No social or economic distinctions are known. Nor, indeed, could any be maintained, since the ethic of sharing is so powerful that it parts a person from any accumulated wealth as soon as such wealth becomes visible. Niggardliness is the chief sin in this world, punished by social ostracism; there, where mutual aid is key, no one can suffer ostracism for long. Only intractable violence is more repugnant to the San than selfishness, and the former is so incomprehensible it seems to be classified more as mental disorder than sin. The smallest guinea hen or tortoise brought back from the chase may be split into ten pieces as it comes out of the fire, and an infant in arms, its fist—closed around its tiny share—halfway to its mouth, will receive a first crucial lesson, as an adult reaches toward the morsel and speaks slowly and clearly the word "Give."

This ethic of sharing, this mutual dependence, this organic social harmony is nowhere more vividly expressed than in the trance-dance ritual, an exquisite, impassioned drama of healing. Here the line between sacred and social fades, and the people test their very unity, since only unity can engender the energy needed by healers who have to step into death to importune the gods on behalf of an invalid. The patient lies by the fire, half-conscious, feverish with malaria or pneumonia. All the friends she has in the world are near her and are needed. The women sit in a circle around the fire, preparing to sing the songs that will alter consciousness, to clap the complex rhythms that will change the shape of time. Behind them, walking in a circle, are men beginning to dance, getting the feel of their feet, adjusting the dance rattles around their legs. Will the women sing and clap well enough to inspire them? Will they dance well enough to give the women confidence? Will the women stay together, hear each other, find their harmony? Will, above all, the difficult whole be whole enough so that some of the men, on the strength of it, can drop into trance, into half-death, traverse the road to the other world, and berate the gods for causing human illness? So that, returning, they can lay hands on the sick person and, shrieking and shaking for dear life, drag the cause of the illness out of her? Nowhere more than here do the San symbolize to themselves how life and death hang upon mutuality.

According to Hobbes, that philosopher of resignation (and on as little evidence as Rousseau's in concocting his own very different fantasy of the natural state), the life of primitive human groups was "solitary, poor, nasty, brutish and short." Yet here, in the San, we view the most basic of human societies operating as it must have for millennia. Archeological evidence shows that hunter-gatherers culturally antecedent to the San lived in their present village locations for something like forty thousand years. Ancient hunting blinds have been unearthed beside seasonal pans where modern San still come and lie in wait for game. Plainly we are watching a sort of human experience with a proven viability vastly more ancient than our own. Far from solitary, it is above all things mutual. Far from poor, it is amply supplied and amply leisured; it has even been called "the original affluent society." Far from nasty, it is based on human decency, respect for others, sharing, giving. Far from brutish, it is courageous, egalitarian, good-humored, philosophical—in a word, civilized—with an esthetic so fine its very music touches the gods. Although many die in early childhood, those who do not may live to a ripe old age, and this is an old age not consigned to a ghetto or to a "home" that is not a home; rather, it is one embedded in that same intimate social world, surrounded by grandchildren full of delight, by grown, powerful children full of courtesy.

Now for the bad news.

First, there is no going back. Throughout the world, the hunting and gathering way of life supports less than one person per square mile. Since the total area of the planet is under two hundred million square miles, the human population turned its back on the hunting and gathering possibility at least several doublings ago. We are obviously committed to high technology.

More important, some features of San life, and of hunting and gathering life in general, have been lost sight of in a wave of ethnographic enthusiasm, based on the real, rather pleasant facts that I have recounted above. For example, from the champions of San nonviolence we rarely hear mention of San homicide rates. These have been measured, and are comparable to those in American cities. We hear much about San egalitarianism, including the absence of sexism. But what of the observations and reports of wife-beating, and the obvious sexist ideology evident in all-male discussions? We have much talk and print about San sharing, but little until recently of the now plain fact that almost all sharing occurs only among close relatives. We dwell on the absence of war; but the San lack the manpower to mount even the simplest war, and when they talk about other tribes, even other groups of San, they make it clear they are not above prejudice. If they could make a war, perhaps they would. We speak of their "affluence" without mentioning periods of shortage, in which they may lose 10 percent of their body weight; of their kindness to their children, without mentioning childhood illness, which kills half before they ever grow up; of their decency to the aged, without mentioning that only 20 percent of infants can expect to live to be sixty, leaving San society with an incomparably lighter burden than the elderly and infirm constitute in our own.

What must be said, then? That the emperor has no clothes? That the idyllic picture of San life is no more than another Rousseauian ruse? No. Not nearly. But I do feel strongly that the positive features of their life have been somewhat oversold, and the negative features of our own blamed, unfairly, only on historical changes that have occurred since we lived the way they do. The emperor has clothes, but the clothes show a rent or smudge here and there, amid the believable sparkle. And the suit, as it stands, is not so stunningly superior to our own.

Yet there is something in the cut of it that we might like to get, if we could only figure out just how it fits. It needs study. We cannot step out of our own clothes into those, and yet . . .

I am reminded of something the poet Apollinaire wrote in his introduction to the published version of his play *Mamelles de Tirésias* with illustrations by Picasso. It has always seemed to me the most apt guide to people like myself who wish to learn from human hunter-gatherers. Here, in Picasso's work, were mammals that looked like none anyone knew; and yet to Apollinaire they somehow revealed more of mammal-ness than had ever before emerged in two dimensions. He wrote: ". . . I thought that one should return to nature itself, but not by imitating it in the manner of photographs. When man wanted to imitate walking, he invented the wheel, which does not resemble a leg."

It seems to me, too, that we must return to nature; and for human beings this means in some sense a return to the human condition as it was lived when people were evolving. I do not see any much better proposal for discovering how to modulate the social chaos now swirling constantly around this hapless planet. But we return to learn, not to mimic. The direct study of hunter-gatherers does not, cannot mean mere imitation of them; but it can lead us to understandings that, in turn, must figure in the design of a workable world. Thus, we can learn that the ethic of sharing is not "unnatural" and try to revive it even though we dwell among nonrelatives. We can try to somehow renounce war—although we are eminently capable of making it—and be encouraged by the fact that there have been other worlds without it. We can try to relinquish our fierce hold on things, and try instead to take a better hold of people. And we can search for some ritual, some sacred social symbol that can make us whole again; that so transcends the field of conflict as to release us from our mundane limitations and, finally, heal. But I suspect that if we can make a workable social world (and I am by no means sure we can), it will resemble San life as little (or as much) as a wheel resembles a leg.

2

ADAPTATION

It should by now be obvious that there is, indeed,
a general theory of behavior and that the theory is evolution, to just the same extent and in almost exactly the same
ways that evolution is the general theory of morphology.
—Anne Roe and G.G. Simpson,
Behavior and Evolution

No one in today's behavioral sciences doubts that biology is making, and is destined to continue to make, a massive, profound impact on those sciences. The understanding of behavior that results from this impact will be as changed from what we have had before as physics was after Einstein, Planck, and Lorentz. The analogy is fairly precise. Einstein and his colleagues did not invalidate Newton; they merely found the edge of Newton's universe. Beyond this edge, in the macro- or microcosm, *their* phenomena cried out for new laws, and they invented them. Back in the middle-sized universe, among the falling apples and colliding billiard balls, Newton was still as informed as they. But, looking back from where they now stood, admitting the practical usefulness of Newton's laws in his domain, Newton's world would never again seem the same.

A similar change in the way we look at human behavior is resulting from the impact of biology. It is not invalidating prior views; indeed, it is supporting many of them, as far as they can go. But it is opening vast frontiers where the prebiological laws are useless; as we chart those unknown reaches and turn and look back, the human spirit will never again seem the same.

The encroachments of biology on behavioral science have come in two broad, separate areas: evolution and genetics on the one hand, and anatomy and physiology on the other. These two areas have a natural link in the science of embryology, but the link—biochemical genetics—has only just begun to be explored. Still, at every step in the life of every organism, the link exists, implicit, in adaptation.

Adaptation, in common parlance, is the process through which any creature adjusts to the world around it, including the world of creatures near and dear to it. We discern vaguely that this process includes physical as well as behavioral change. For example, if we insist on running around the park every evening, we can see and feel gradual changes in the body's shape and weight. We know, too, that there are changes in coordinated patterns of nerve and muscle firing and in the balance of certain biochemical pathways. Finally, there is a definite mental change: What was painful and exhausting becomes pleasurable though exhausting, partly because it comes more easily, but partly because we have gotten into the habit.

All these adaptive changes are in a deep sense biological, although they are set in motion by a choice. We *decide* to insist on running around the park in the evening, and a complex interactive causal cycle is set in motion in which behavioral and biological change act in tandem on each other until body and mind are both in a new set. "That's culture, not biology," says a traditional kind of naïve observer. "You can do anything you and your culture decide."

This is wrong on two counts. First, running is the most natural form of vigorous human exercise. Try gymnastics or pole-vaulting or dancing *en pointe* to see the sorts of biological obstacles that can confront a human decision. Second—and this count is merely the consequence of the first—we are designed by nature to respond to daily running with these changes.

Designed by nature? I permit myself this traditional phrase, but what I really mean is, designed by evolution. Still more properly, designed by natural selection, since evolution is merely the result of which natural selection is the cause—or, at least, one major cause. Darwin's presentation of the idea in 1859—he and Alfred Russel Wallace had outlined it jointly a year earlier—set off a century-long stir, but not because evolution was new. Goethe had studied it and

Darwin's own grandfather had written an epic poem about it. Charles Lyell's masterpiece, *Principles of Geology*—a treatise that fully accepted the fossil evidence for evolution—was in Darwin's trunk when he embarked on the *Beagle*. The idea had been in the air, and accepted by many people—despite vigorous opposition from some scientific quarters—for more than a hundred years. Darwin's contribution, aside from a masterly review of the then-known facts bearing on evolution, in several different major lines of evidence, was to set out in clear language the first convincing theory of how evolution could take place: the theory of adaptation through natural selection.

The title of Darwin's book was a bit misleading. In keeping with the custom of the period, it was very long: *On the Origin of Species by Means of Natural Selection or the Preservation of Favoured Races in the Struggle for Life*. It contains three misrepresentations, at least two of which he was aware of, as he shows in the body of the book. He was apparently not aware that he was not solving the problem of the origin of species. This later showed itself to be a highly specific puzzle in evolutionary biology, not to be solved fully until Ernst Mayr's *Animal Species and Evolution* was published in 1963.

The other two "errors" in the title are more interesting. First, it suggests that evolution proceeds primarily through competition among races. This viewpoint has been discredited by modern investigations; in its place is the almost universal view among biologists that evolution proceeds primarily through competition among individuals and their kindreds. The selection or elimination of larger population units is, at best, very uncommon. Beyond that, the concept has numerous difficulties, the chief of which is that no one has ever observed an animal group (other than a closely inbred lineage) in which the group functioned so much as a unit that individual competition was successfully suppressed. "Group selection," as the old idea was called, was to my satisfaction laid to rest by George C. Williams in 1967; in his book *Adaptation and Natural Selection*, he made the extreme case for individual selection and concluded it by baldly stating that every creature is engaged in a constant struggle with every other creature in its environment, however related, however closely allied.

The third "error" in Darwin's title concerns the misleading phrase "struggle for life." The goal of the struggle was not merely life, but reproductive success, or fitness. Darwin was, however, clearly aware of this problem, since he himself introduced the concept of sexual selection. The idea is basically this: While being better adapted for survival is certainly one way for an organism to be favored by selection—individuals dying before breeding could not, except in special cases, perpetuate their characteristics—it is not the only way. We can easily visualize a population in which all individuals die at the same age, but in which evolution nonetheless proceeds very rapidly in consequence of differential breeding success—differences in the ultimate number of offspring. Indeed, it is not hard to imagine a creature that "burns itself out" early by breeding very rapidly, yet perpetuates its prodigal characteristics more effectively than other creatures do their sedate ones.

Recognition of these possibilities in 1859 prompted Darwin to say "a few words on what I call Sexual Selection," a few words that are echoing to this day:

> This depends, not on a struggle for existence, but on a struggle between the males for possession of the females; the result is not death to the unsuccessful competitor, but few or no offspring. . . . Sexual selection by always allowing the victor to breed might surely give indomitable courage, length to the spur, and strength to the wing to strike in the spurred leg, as well as the brutal cockfighter, who knows well that he can improve his breed by careful selection of the best cocks. . . .
>
> Amongst birds, the contest is often of a more peaceful character. All those who have attended to the subject, believe that there is the severest rivalry between the males of many species to attract by singing the females. . . .
>
> Thus it is, as I believe, that when the males and females of any animal have the same general habits of life, but differ in structure, colour, or ornament, such differences have been mainly caused by sexual selection; that is, individual males have had, in successive generations, some slight advantage over other males, in their weapons, means of defence, or charms; and have transmitted these advantages to their male offspring.

Thus Darwin rather innocently introduced not only the theory of sexual selection, but the theory of the evolution of behavior, and also a possible theory of sex differences.

It had, to be sure, its problems. For one thing, it was obviously male-centered. As evolutionary biologist Robert Trivers was to point out more than a hundred years later, there are at least a few species in which females typically compete for males—phalaropes, for instance. Predictably, sexual selection in these species has worked to make the female rather more spectacular than the male, both in her behavior and in her body structure. Even in species where male-male competition is the rule, there is still competition for males among females, with males trying to get the best females even while they attempt to attract as many as possible. Finally, although males can usually vary much more in the number of offspring they produce—both sexes can have zero, but males can have a larger maximum number, giving selection more variation to go on—females of course vary as well. Those that raise the most offspring to maturity, by means of more clever or more dedicated care, for instance, will be favored in the fitness competition. This, too, is a kind of sexual selection, though not in Darwin's original limited sense.

This argument puts us—as it indeed put Darwin—squarely in the realm of what is now called "sociobiology." Perhaps a few well-chosen words on this latter subject will be of use at this point, since so many poorly chosen ones (both for and against) have been expended on it during the last few years. I think it is fair to say that in the parlance of those who know something about it (whether they like it or not), "sociobiology" has a quite specific meaning. It is the application of natural selection theory to the explanation of reproduction, especially the behavioral aspects of reproduction. Put another way, it is an attempt to see how far one can get in the analysis of the social behavior of animals armed mainly with the assumption that the purpose of such behavior is the maximization of reproductive success. It also deals with morphology—a technical word for anatomical structure—but usually only those aspects of morphology that play a direct role in mate selection and reproduction. The passage from Darwin quoted above is a prime example of sociobiological analysis.

Here is what it is not: It is not the whole study of animal behavior, even animal behavior in the wild. It is not the study of the effects of social life on biology. It is not the same as E.O. Wilson's fine book, *Sociobiology*, which contains much that few others consider sociobiology (for example, conventional accounts of animal communication), as well as much that many sociobiologists vehemently disagree with (for example, a daring theory of the evolution of human culture). It is not a revolutionary, decisive, all-encompassing theory of animal and human nature. And it is not a pernicious, cynical, reactionary theory of animal and human nature.

Also, it is not the same as behavioral biology, which is the subject matter of this book. Indeed, I would venture a guess that at the very most about 5 percent of behavioral biologists consider themselves sociobiologists, or do any work that anyone would be willing to call sociobiology. The vast majority of behavioral biologists, then—ethologists, neuroethologists, physiological psychologists, neuropsychologists, behavioral neurologists, behavioral endocrinologists, biological psychiatrists, comparative psychologists, biological anthropologists, behavioral geneticists, psychopharmacologists, and others not even anchored yet in the sea of science subfield gobbledygook—are nonsociobiologists.

G.G. Simpson, one of the present century's greatest evolutionists, was a perhaps unwitting harbinger of sociobiology when he co-authored the sentence that stands at the head of this chapter. It bears examining. It appears to make a very sweeping claim, particularly in its mention of morphology; but a moment's thought makes that analogy seem as much a restriction as an extension. When we raise the question, Why does the male peacock have such extravagant feathers? it is not very satisfactory to talk about how they grow, or about the chemistry of the pigments that give them color. Such morphological and biochemical answers, albeit interesting, still leave the initial puzzle nagging at us, and it is not until we say "For eons peacock females thought they were pretty spiffy" (or words to that effect), that we begin to sense the cause coming clear.

But consider now the question, Why is it that most long nerve fibers in higher animals have fatty sheaths? Well, the simple answer is, because conduction is faster. But *why* is conduction faster? Here the science of bioelectricity, the physics and chemistry of nerve conduction, provides some fairly impressive answers, and if we listen for half an hour to someone who knows what she is talking about (well enough to explain it in simple terms), we will see nerve fiber function falling into place along with the lovely laws of high school science—an impressive illumination, to say the least. A certain kind of deliberately naïve evolutionist, who will not, I fear, have been listening very carefully, will then say, "I knew the reason all along; the nerve fibers work better that way. Otherwise they wouldn't have been selected for."

If we have not shared the fellow's very parochial training, we are at pains to discover what he thinks he knows. *We* know that we have come up against one of the innumerable puzzles in morphology that yields precious little to evolutionary theory, that cries out for better explanations. It isn't that what the fellow said isn't true; it is true of everything, which is one of the reasons it offers us so little. That is the paradox of adaptation—not adaptation in the sense of common parlance, but adaptation in the sense of evolution.

Evolutionary biologists—including, alas, Darwin—rarely define adaptation, leaving us to infer for ourselves what they mean by it—as in this sentence from the *Origin of Species*:

> Whatever the cause may be of each slight difference in the offspring from their parents—and a cause for each must exist— it is the steady accumulation, through natural selection, of such differences, when beneficial to the individual, that gives rise to all the more important modifications of structure, by which the innumerable beings on the face of this earth are enabled to struggle with each other, and the best adapted to survive.

The passage sets out rather stunningly, at least by implication, the three essential features of the theory. In order for animal populations to evolve, they must have, first, a means of inheriting some characteristics from their parents; second, a source of natural variation, replenishable from generation to generation, to mitigate hereditary fixedness and to provide grist for selection's mill; and, third, a greater degree of success in becoming progenitors, observable in some of the visible variants. These latter are said to be "best adapted."

Fine. But when we define adaptation as the ability to procreate more successfully, and then go on to deduce that adaptation exists in every organism we observe in the natural world, we have involved ourselves in a circular process of reasoning. And if we know a little about the elements of logic, we begin to wonder whether the statement that the nerve fibers are adapted says anything at all about the world.

Richard Lewontin, a distinguished evolutionary theorist, has begun to believe that it does not. Spurred by the excesses of some sociobiologists, who seem to see in every bump and blemish on an animal a cleverly concocted adaptation—the best, in this best-of-all-possible worlds—Lewontin has argued that the concept of adaptation is no more than a Procrustean bed. If it fits, wear it, the sociobiologists seem to say; and if it doesn't fit, try it on a different way, stretch yourself, make it fit. It has to fit. It's the law of evolution: adaptation through natural selection. This has produced some impressive flights of fancy, among them: the theory that women's breasts evolved to mimic their behinds, which males were already quite pleased with; the theory that physical handicap was a fine thing for sexual competition, since it made your particular heartthrob at least take notice of you; and the theory that infertility—even permanent infertility—can be highly adaptive in reproductive competition, if it's the wrong time and place to have offspring.

I make fun of them, but they are all serious theories, and the trouble is they are very hard to dispose of. An organism has characteristics; they must have been selected for or they wouldn't be here now; and they must be adaptive or they wouldn't have been selected for; a completed derivation, just like in Euclid. Now think up an adaptive function for the characteristics in question—however implausible.

But there is the key; it *is* just like in Euclid. It is a logico-deductive proof that follows necessarily from the acceptance of certain elementary assumptions. Just as the Pythagorean theorem follows from the definition of a straight line, an angle, and "parallel," so the necessity of adaptation—a theorem of evolutionary biology—follows from the definitions of variation and natural selection. In the strictest philosophical sense, neither theorem tells us anything about the real world, because neither is subject to disproof by reference to that world. Neither constitutes empirical knowledge.

Nevertheless, every day, carpenters and bricklayers go out into the world (or at least they once did) carrying in their pockets a three-four-five string; a string knotted to make lengths equal to three, four, and five units, as a guide to producing a right angle. This bit of very worldly activity uses the Pythagorean theorem, which holds, inevitably, that if a square on the longest side of a triangle is equal to the sum of the squares on the other two sides, it must be a right triangle; a theorem that, strictly speaking, says nothing about the world.

In the everyday world of field biology and ethology (and increasingly, also, of anthropology), the theorem that creatures are adapted to their environments has much the same seat-of-the-pants usefulness. For example, when I was investigating the neurological status of newborn infants among the !Kung San, I was interested in the question of whether these infants—born to parents very different from ourselves in any number of ways—would exhibit the same panorama of basic nervous system reflexes as are observed in newborn infants among ourselves. (Contrary to certain prior assurances, they did.) But I was also interested, and only a bit more idly, in the possible functional meaning of the reflexes. For example, a brand-new baby, fresh from its very taxing journey, will, if held upright and carried, turn its eyes and head in the direction of movement, as if looking where it is going; if held against the body, it will push against the body with its hands, lift its head away, even make crawling movements with its legs; if support is released from its head it may grab hold as if trying to keep from falling. In most pediatrics books, these reflexes are described as signs of an immature nervous system (this they surely are) and as vestiges of an evolutionary past when some of them may have had some function.

It seemed to me that in that foraging society I was observing them to be functioning still; because it was one of a large number of human societies in which the smallest infants are carried around all day long—in this case in a leather sling. Perhaps in our advanced industrial state, where infants lie around all day in cribs, the neonatal reflexes are useless; but I couldn't help thinking that where I was studying them—where I could observe them in action in naturalistic observations, used by the infant to adjust itself in the sling—to, perhaps, prevent itself from smothering—they had the distinct look of adaptation.

Now, I wouldn't want my reputation to stand or fall on whether they were or not; I am sure that the notion will sound as silly to some people as the "breast-behind theory" sounded to me. It is easy to argue that the reflexes are the inevitable consequence of neurological immaturity, which evolved in humans for many other reasons; that they have no function except to enlighten pediatricians as to the status of the nervous system at birth. But I know a little about adaptation in general, and a fair amount about infants in that African society, and the concept seems to me to fit; it seems useful, like the three-four-five string. There are other cases where it seems more useful, still others where it seems less. I do not want it to sound like a simpleminded exercise; there are criteria for judging its usefulness, some of which are rigorous and quantitative. But, finally, either those acquainted with the organism in question find the concept useful or they don't. Adaptation is thus that most puzzling of all scientific phenomena: an inherently unprovable, yet eminently usable idea.

Darwin certainly found it useful. It is the central idea in the *Origin*, the central fact of nature that the *Origin* tries to explain. It was, indeed, what struck Darwin most vividly when, as a young man, he sailed around the world, and especially as he studied variation in the Galapagos: the remarkable fit, the suitedness, of creatures to their environments.

It is this suitedness to which ecologists and evolutionary biologists refer when they speak of "adaptation" or of creatures being "adapted." But in different contexts, scientific or not, the word "adapted" has a wide range of meanings, and the use of it in an unclear manner can be the source of much unnecessary anguish.

We can spare ourselves some of that anguish by being very clear at the outset. Individual, common-parlance adaptation—perhaps better called "adaptability"—is simply flexibility in the face of change. Learning a new job, behaving differently in different seasons of the year, coping with and, in the end, surviving the experience of grief— all show our adaptability in the context of environmental flux. To return to an earlier example, bodily and mental changes that follow the habit of daily jogging are a virtual showcase of human adaptability. Such changes cannot, of course, be passed on to offspring through the genes.

Adaptation, in contrast—in the evolutionary and genetic sense—is the fit of an organism to its environment by means of characteristics usually widely shared throughout a species. Adaptation may include adaptability, but on the other hand it may not, and it includes much more besides. It has already been said that our adaptability to the habit of jogging is something we are adapted for by nature, because of the circumstances of human evolution; but there is more to it than flexibility. Go back a mere ten million years in our ancestral line, and you will find a creature incapable of jogging, running, or walking on two legs; resurrect that creature and you would find it inflexible in the face of efforts to make it do so. It simply does not have the basic nerve, muscle and bone for it—the structure that we have, coded by our genes. In other words, major portions of evolutionary adaptation are not flexible at all and do not share in that aspect of the common-parlance use of the word "adapt." To take one more example, humans are not adapted by evolution to live in Antarctica, but are so adaptable that some do so; penguins *are* adapted to live there, but are not sufficiently adaptable to live anywhere else.

Darwin was guilty of failing to distinguish between evolutionary and common-parlance adaptation, but it must be said on his behalf that he was in distinguished company; most of the day's evolutionists did the same, with deliberation. The confusion was, indeed, the centerpiece of the theory of evolution set forth by the French naturalist Jean Baptiste de Lamarck in the year 1809, exactly a half century before the *Origin*. The idea, variously known as inheritance through use and disuse, or the heritability of acquired characteristics, was widely accepted by scientists who accepted evolution, and was explicitly—even warmly—embraced by Charles Darwin. (Alfred Russel Wallace, the co-author of the theory of natural selection, distinguished himself, among other ways, by not falling prey to this error.)

We now know (as surely as we know most things in science) that the hereditary material carried in the germ cells is subject to no such systematic change. Build your muscles as you may, your offspring will be born with the same genetic potential for muscles as if you had lain around eating bonbons. Common-parlance adaptation (the kind that occurs in a life span or less) cannot translate into evolutionary adaptation (the kind that occurs over geological time). Nevertheless, there are three different sorts of relations between the two that are worthy of attention.

First, the stricture against Lamarckian theory applies only to *genetic* evolution. Other kinds of transgenerational change—they are analogous to evolution in some ways, but are so different that I dislike calling them by that term—may not be subject to that stricture, and some of them certainly are not. For instance, if you begin life speaking Italian, and later learn to speak English and stop speaking Italian, your children can grow up speaking English, having learned it from you. Subtler changes in language, such as those that have altered English since Elizabethan times, occur in much the same way. Although this process is sometimes called language evolution, I much prefer to call it language history; there is enough confusion about the meaning of evolution without subsuming under the one rubric both genetic and nongenetic processes. Nevertheless much transgenerational change in human and animal populations, affecting the phenotype—the organism's observable characteristics—in substantial and lasting ways, can occur without genetic change.

And not only in people. For instance, rhesus monkeys on the Caribbean island of Cayo Santiago seem to inherit their rank in the dominance hierarchy—their status—by cultural transmission from their mothers. A Japanese monkey—some call her a monkey genius—invented potato washing, to get sand off the potatoes she was provisioned with; before long, the other monkeys in her troop had learned it from her, and it became a permanent fixture of group behavior into the following generations. Finally, the song of the white-crowned sparrow, sung by males to attract females, is learned by the young from their fathers. Traveling up the California coast in the vicinity of Berkeley, one hears different white-crowned sparrow songs, and they are dialects, in the strictest cultural sense, carried on by learning through imitation. Many more examples could be cited. Nongenetic transmission of phenotypic characteristics is a fact of transgenerational change—and also of transgenerational stability—in animals. And one has only to consider the implications of the fact that infants born of heroin addicts are already addicted to the drug at birth to realize that the results of nongenetic transmission—and indeed the process itself—may reach much more deeply into the function of the organism than most of what we are pleased to call culture. Clearly, then, stable transgenerational change can occur outside the genes.

Second, nongenetic adaptation seems to be able to *lead* genetic evolution, although certainly not in the mechanistic sense meant by Lamarck. In one process, sometimes called the Baldwin effect, change within the life course of some individuals in a population creates conditions that, over a longer course of time, select for genetic features that mimic the same changes. For example, consider a population of birds in which some individuals learn to like a new sort of berry—say blueberries. These individuals start nesting in blueberry patches, and their offspring learn to like blueberries just as they did. Eventually, just randomly, the genetic shuffle produces a few individuals who like blueberries right off—they don't have to go through the process of learning. These individuals may be favored by selection (the readily available food is the blueberry; their genetically coded taste for them means that they will begin eating them sooner than other nestlings; their weight gain and maturation are faster; and so on), and may reproduce so effectively that eventually we observe a generation in which all individuals have the genetic propensity to like them without learning.

In the meanwhile, selection is also likely to be proceeding in related areas. Enzyme systems for processing blueberries better, or retinal cells more sensitive to blue, may arise through chance and spread through the population—all by strictly genetic means. But the point is that the initial conditions for this genetic change will have been created by behavioral change within individual life spans; a mechanism that may be a major feature of evolution. And, in a famous experiment, the geneticist C.H. Waddington showed that something similar can happen strictly in the province of morphology. He observed that some fruit flies in a population changed the vein structure of their wings in response to a change in temperature in the environment. By selecting those that made this change most easily and breeding them, he eventually produced a population that had the new vein structure in the first place. Although this seemed perilously close to Lamarckian evolution, it was merely another example of individual life span adaptation creating conditions that can be mimicked by evolutionary change. The flies born with the new vein structure did not inherit it from their parents, despite the fact that the parents had acquired it. They merely achieved the same end through genetic mutation and recombination that their parents had previously achieved through environmental modification. The new structure was evidently a fundamental biological alternative for the species, reachable by genetic or nongenetic routes.

There is yet a third kind of relationship between individual adaptive change and evolutionary genetic change, and it is perhaps the most important. It was alluded to at the start of this chapter, in the example of the response of the mind and body to daily running; but it has much more widespread implications. It is that the ability to adapt, as an individual, has itself a genetic basis and is subject, like any other characteristic of an organism, to standard evolutionary change.

This fact has always been recognized by behavioral scientists, but in a very weak sense. They have always stressed that the hallmark of human evolution is an increase of individual adaptability. Many features of the organism, especially its behavior, that in lower animals are fixed by the genes, are in human beings labile with regard to the environment, certainly over a life span, often over a much shorter time course. To be fair, they recognized that this increased lability has itself a genetic basis and is in a sense the major product of human genetic evolution during the last few million years. Behavioral scientists were also willing to grant that nonhuman animal species differ widely among themselves in the extent to which they, too, are adapted for genetically programmed lability.

These convictions, held by behavioral scientists for many decades, are certainly not wrong; they merely do not go far enough with the concept. First, the genes must be given credit for being able to specify more about individual adaptability than just some unitary (probably nonexistent) dimension of response to the environment over the life course. For example, a creature might be more adaptable when young, or after giving birth. Second, it must be deemed possible for them to influence adaptability not only in degree but in kind—for example, unusual ease in memorizing odors. And, finally, it must be admitted that they can specify much more—the kinds of environmental change an animal will be able to respond to; the kinds of response that will be made; the nature of the links between stimulus and response; the speed of the change in various different cases; the time in the life cycle when the change can be best effected; and the degree of permanence of the change. The error of many was, to quote Julian Huxley, to "forget that even the capacity to learn, to learn at all, to learn only at a definite stage of development, to learn one thing rather than another, to learn more or less quickly, must have some genetic basis." And through this error they were led to believe that the genes have receded into the background of human behavior, whereas in fact they are very much with us still.

Let us take an example from a nonhuman creature, the redoubtable laboratory rat. If there were one creature the learning psychologists thought they understood, that would surely have been it. By the 1950s there were at least a half-dozen major journals that devoted their pages to the ever greater refinement of the laws of rat learning and conditioning. Under the now tattered banner of the then reigning psychological theorist, B. F. Skinner, hundreds of investigators observed how the rat could be made to acquire or lose certain highly restricted responses (such as bar pressing) when presented with certain highly specific stimuli (such as flashing lights), and from this it seemed possible to generate laws not only for the behavior of rats but for—as in the title of Skinner's major early work—"the behavior of organisms."

It is worth dwelling on this point for a moment. Skinner's book consisted mainly of a description of how the ordinary laboratory rat acquires a small complement of artificial behavior patterns in response to an equally small number of artificial stimuli completely controlled by the experimenter. Extraneous stimuli were ruled out and the rat's naturally occurring behavior was ignored. In fact, the book was devoted to the acquisition by the rat of bar-pressing responses in a handful of situations in which the rat was rewarded with stimuli (for example, food pellets), which were called reinforcers, because they tended to increase the likelihood of whatever responses happened to occur just before the reinforcer was given. This circular definition was deliberate. Skinner and his disciples explicitly ignored the question, What is a reinforcer, really, and why does it reinforce?

This question would have led them to the boundaries of learning where they would have had to confront the fact that the categories of stimuli that will reinforce behavior, whether positively or negatively, are determined in the first place by the genes; that they may differ quite substantially from one species to another; that reinforcement learning presumes the prior existence of behavior patterns that are there to be reinforced, some of them very complex and many of them unlearned; and, perhaps above all, that some instances of learning might follow very different laws than do others, due to the inborn preparation of the nervous system for certain kinds of learning. Skinnerians viewed the laws of learning they were establishing in the laboratory—in one species, in a few situations—as uniform and universal. For the rat especially, they believed that they had come upon laws that would apply to it in all situations, for all behaviors, and for all reinforcers.

In the 1960s a series of papers by John Garcia and his collaborators made the rat look a different creature indeed. Rejected by the major journals—*The Psychological Review*, *The Journal of Comparative and Physiological Psychology*, and *Science*—they appeared in relatively obscure journals such as *Psychonomic Science* and *Communications in Behavioral Biology*. (One editor who had rejected one of them, a distinguished learning theorist himself, later apologized for having failed to recognize the importance of the paper.) In spite of the obscurity of the journals, the papers created a scientific revolution in learning theory. The results—obvious to some, but astounding to many learning psychologists—showed that very different laws govern the learning of different kinds of associations.

The key experiment may be summarized as follows: Take four groups of genetically identical rats and subject them to a classical form of laboratory training known as avoidance conditioning. Have them drink water, and while they are drinking, give them a punishment; but precede the punishment with a signal. In no time at all they will stop drinking when the punishment occurs, unless they are desperately thirsty; but, in addition, they will gradually learn to stop drinking before the punishment, when the signal is given. When they have done so, they are said to have acquired an avoidance response.

So far this is all the standard stuff of the learning lab. But the special twist is this. We give the four groups of rats different combinations of two signals and two punishments. One group gets a noise-and-light signal followed by an electric shock. The second group gets a distinctive flavor in the water, followed by an artificially induced feeling of nausea (caused by X rays and having nothing intrinsic to do with the flavor).

Up to this point both the experiment and the results are conventional. The rats in Group One and Group Two acquire the avoidance response—stop drinking at the appearance of the noise-and-light signal or the distinctive flavor—after a usual number of "trials," or experiences with the situation. This result merely confirms what has been shown by many others before.

The surprise comes with Groups Three and Four. In those groups, the pairing of signal and punishment is reversed. Group Three gets the noise-and-light signal followed by the X ray–induced nausea. Group Four gets the distinctive flavor followed by the electric shock. *These two groups do not learn the avoidance response.* In other words, it is very easy to teach a rat an association between a taste and artificially induced nausea, so that it will avoid the taste thereafter; and it is easy to teach it to associate a light or sound with an electric shock, with similar results in avoidance behavior. But it is very difficult indeed to make the rat learn the converse associations. That is, it simply will not get the idea that the taste signals a forthcoming shock, or that the light or sound signals forthcoming nausea, given a comparable training effort. As Garcia and his co-author Robert A. Koelling suggest, the rat seems to have a "genetically coded hypothesis" when it feels sick to its stomach, which may be characterized as "It must have been something I ate." It holds that "hypothesis" strongly enough so that it ignores the true sensory signal of forthcoming nausea when that signal comes in the sensory realms of sight and sound. Similarly, when it feels external physical pain, it is not designed to "think" in terms of flavors by way of "explanation."

The Garcia experiments also showed that the association between taste and nausea could be made in spite of long lapses—up to seventy-five minutes—between the taste and the nausea. This was an extraordinarily long gap for a rat to experience between a signal and a punishment and still learn avoidance. Thus the taste-nausea association seemed to violate a long-standing law of learning, according to which lengthening the gap between a stimulus and a reward or punishment systematically and markedly weakens the learned association that can be expected from the training. Here was clear evidence that the domain of taste-avoidance learning included a violated "general" law of learning.

To give the flavor, as it were, of the difficulties these findings caused for the scientific world view of learning theorists, one investigator who had worked on similar problems for years said publicly, "Those findings are no more likely than birdshit in a cuckoo clock." They were not only likely, they were true; they have turned up many times in many laboratories.

Now while these findings may have startled learning psychologists, even to the extreme of public profanity, they came as no surprise to biologists. They are obviously adaptive in the most meaningful sense. The ancestors of rats, in the wild, must surely have gotten into situations where tastes or smells led to nausea, and where lights and sounds led to external physical pain. But natural selection very likely had no opportunity to favor rats who could associate lights and sounds with nausea. A bit more surprisingly, it evidently saw no call to produce rats that could make stimulus-response associations equally well across the board. It produced, instead, genetically based tendencies to learn some lessons better than others.

As Garcia and his colleagues pointed out in a later, more theoretical paper, general laws of learning—laws that will apply to all stimuli and all responses—are implausible not only ecologically but neurologically. The nerve path of the taste modality, for example, has its first way station in a lower brain center called the nucleus of the solitary tract; visceral sensation from the stomach reports first to the same nucleus. Why should we expect an auditory stimulus, with an input pathway relatively isolated from these, to form an equally easy link with the visceral sensation of nausea? Similarly, there is a close central nervous system association between sound and skin-surface sensations—in the thalamus and in the cerebral cortex, far from the centers where the rat senses nausea. Such major structural features of the nervous system are indisputably genetically determined.

Experimental psychologist Martin Seligman called this kind of learning the "Sauce Béarnaise phenomenon," because it explained the following set of events. One evening he had filet mignon with Sauce Béarnaise, his then favorite sauce. Six hours later he became violently ill; the cause was later determined to be stomach flu. In spite of the fact so many hours had elapsed, in spite of the fact he knew the sauce had nothing to do with the nausea, in spite of the fact there were other things—such as the dinner plates, or *Tristan und Isolde*, the opera he listened to in the interim—that he might have developed an aversion to, he acquired from this experience one and only one association: a permanent distaste for Sauce Béarnaise. He interpreted it as a clear instance of the Garcia effect, which was apparently perfectly applicable to humans.

Nowadays we call it "prepared" or "directed" learning, and it goes way beyond Sauce Béarnaise. As Seligman and his colleague Joanne Hager suggested, it is our best current bet for a reconciliation between those ancient opponents, instinct and learning. Instinct is not pure instinct, of course, and learning is not pure learning; that has been known by intelligent people for centuries. But we have in the Garcia effect and related demonstrations the beginnings of an empirically based theory, a theory that stands in the middle ground. Let us study (the theory says) the myriad kinds of prepared or directed learning—describe them, distinguish them, try our best to explain them as nervous system adaptations—and let "instinct" and "learning" go hang.

New studies have confirmed and extended the principle. For example, in the golden hamster a number of complex behavior patterns, such as digging, rearing on the hind legs, washing and scratching, are "instinctive" in the sense that they emerge without training, but modifiable in the sense that they can be trained to certain cues. However, if you reward all four of these patterns with food, only digging and rearing will increase in frequency; these are the patterns associated with the food quest in the wild.

Very recently the Sauce Béarnaise phenomenon has been studied more systematically in humans. People who eat ice cream before receiving a nausea-inducing form of chemotherapy can develop a powerful taste aversion to ice cream, despite all past positive ("rewarding") experiences. But implications for human behavior go far beyond the limited realm of taste aversions. Seligman himself, for instance, has contributed an incisive analysis of human clinical phobias based on the same principle. And learning to jog exemplifies it as well. For a million years or more, our ancestors had occasion to adapt themselves—in the individual life course—to the necessity to run long distances; the result was a sort of creature that has, coded in its genes, an elaborate set of abilities to adapt in that manner, a complex learning preparedness, centered on running. Few people can run three miles in half an hour without first practicing and getting into condition; most healthy people can do it after a few weeks of work. We are adapted, in the evolutionary sense, to adapt, in the individual sense, to running.

I won't belabor the subject of running further. I have chosen it deliberately, for its dullness. It, unlike certain other human tendencies, does not provoke cries of indignation when subjected to biological analysis. But the reader inclined to find such analysis uncongenial should now feel warned; the running example is only a model for less dull things.

In conclusion, since I have been rude enough to point out one of Darwin's major errors (these are not numerous), it seems only fair to give him the last word on a subject so close to his heart; especially since, with his usual prescience, he foresaw the subject matter of this book:

> In the distant future I see open fields for far more important researches. Psychology will be based on a new foundation, that of the necessary acquirement of each mental power and capacity by gradation. Light will be thrown on the origin of man and his history.

These are the subjects to which we now turn.

3

THE CRUCIBLE

Origin of man now proved. He who understands
baboon would do more towards metaphysics than Locke.
—Charles Darwin, "The
M Notebook," 1856

Despite the sense of inevitability that arises in certain accounts of the life of the hunting-gathering San, the notion that they represent the human way of life during the course of evolution leaves much to be desired. First, they do not represent in a biological or psychological sense anything of the sort. Biologically and psychologically, they are most closely similar to ourselves. Indeed, we have no direct way of knowing anything of the functions of brain and mind in our ancestors, even as recently as fifty thousand years ago. It is only in gross anatomical structure, in material culture, and in some of the details of their subsistence ecology, that our distant ancestors ever become known to us. Worse, the San do not represent in every detail—or even in most details—the way of life of living hunting-gathering peoples in general. These range from the arctic, igloo-dwelling Eskimo to the boomerang-throwing desert wanderers of aboriginal Australia, from the elephant-hunting Pygmies of the African tropical forest to the longbow-bearing Siriono of the Amazon. The complexities of all these worlds can scarcely be subsumed in the traditional way of life of a few thousand Kalahari San.

Nevertheless, there are ways of using our knowledge of them in an effort to reconstruct our distant past. These begin with an attempt to order all the information we have about hunter-gatherers in general—the above four cases, the San, and many others—in such a way as to extract general principles of their approach to human social and ecological life. (Much, although not all, of what was said in the first chapter in reference to the San is of the order of general principles.) Once such principles are established—for example, the fact that almost all hunter-gatherers are nomadic, whatever their continent or climate—they become reasonable candidates for possible principles governing the lives of our preagricultural ancestors.

But hunter-gatherers in general constitute only one source of critical information. Darwin, in the epigraph at the beginning of this chapter, alludes to another. Of course he does not mean that the baboon will provide all the answers. He means, presumably, that if human beings, like other creatures, are products of evolution, then the comparative analysis of such creatures will provide for us a context in which to understand our very selves. And if these creatures are near relatives of ours, then they will have so much the more to say to us. There was a time—about two decades ago—in anthropology, when baboons were thought to be as good representatives of our ancestors as any we were likely to discover; they were monkeys, they were smart, they were socially living, and they were on the African plain, facing many of the challenges that must have been faced by our ancestors something like ten million years ago. (This is, of course, a very different set of ancestors from the ones that might have resembled—in some ways—modern human hunter-gatherers; *those* ancestors lived perhaps fifty thousand years ago.) In any case, plausible as they seemed, baboons went out of fashion as model human ancestors, to be replaced in the subsequent decade by chimpanzees. These were bigger than baboons, smarter, and even more closely related to humans; all of which made them fine ancestor-models. They certainly did things differently from baboons.

If I incline to make fun of them, it is not because I find these animals uninteresting, or the people who are studying them misguided. It is merely that to pin so much responsibility on any of them is to miss the whole point about their value. As in the case of the San—who can constitute only one set of data points in a vast chart of living hunter-gatherers—either baboons or chimpanzees or any other living higher primate species can only constitute one set of data points in the panorama of higher primate behavior. Only after many data points have yielded an overall structure can we derive general principles, and only from such principles can we make any guesses about our ancestors. Baboons, chimpanzees, and people are what they are because of unique histories of evolutionary demands. Understanding will come not from a comparison of ourselves with another primate species, but from establishment of the general laws that have brought about all our uniquenesses.

Strictly speaking, the method of extrapolating backward in the realm of behavior is no different from the same method applied to soft body parts. We begin with comparative studies of living forms of known degrees of relatedness, and generalize from principles derived from the comparison, together with some elementary assumptions about the uniformity of the process of evolution.

Consider these examples. The *substantia nigra* ("black substance") is an important brain stem nucleus. It plays a role in the regulation of movement, and a defect in it is the cause of serious deficits, which we summarize as Parkinson's disease. A direct ancestor of ours of perhaps five million years ago must, like ourselves, have had a *substantia nigra* larger than that of the average mammals; larger, that is, relative to total brain size. How can this be known, when the *substantia nigra* is, in life, about the consistency of jelly—a soft part that, like the rest of the brain, is washed out of the skull as soon as the creature dies and, unlike the structures on the surface of the brain, leaves no mark on the inside of the skull?

This is a valid question, one which must be asked of any statement about parts of any ancient organism that, by their nature, do not fossilize. And the answer is usually this: that all such statements arise from the comparative study of the anatomy of living creatures, taken together with the parts that *did* fossilize from the ancient creature itself. All living higher primates have large *substantia nigras*, and the human ancestor in question was indisputably a higher primate—that we know from the bony skeleton, which we can see. We infer the existence of the soft organs from the other evidence. It would have to have been an extraordinary pastiche of an animal, arrived at by hitherto unknown biological processes, to have escaped having a large *substantia nigra*, which appears to be standard equipment for higher primates.

Equally certainly, the ancestor in question must also have used its face rather expressively to communicate emotion, and it must have had complex facial muscles to do that. There are no fossils of facial muscles, or even, usually, of their insertion on the bony part of the face. But complex facial expression used to communicate emotion is universal among Old World higher primates; and it would simply have been too great a violation of the principles of zoology for the higher primate in question to have abandoned it.

Finally—and here I will seem to be, but in fact will not be, on shakier ground—I would be really amazed if the creature in question did not have, as part of its reproductive life, competition among males for access to females, occasionally erupting into violence; infants kept in contact with their mothers and nursed freely; and males that, after maturity, rarely attempted to mate with their own mothers. If it violated any of these generalizations, it would have to have been the most freakish higher primate that ever lived in the Old World; so unusual, in fact, that I would not be inclined to believe that it existed.

All these assurances come from the now extensive literature on the comparative study of higher primates. In the realm of behavior, such studies have now at least begun, under field conditions, on virtually all Old World monkeys and apes. Laboratory studies penetrating behavioral questions more deeply are less advanced, but they are available, and there is even some good work on comparative brain structure. Some of the assurances of the old days (fifteen years ago!) have now gone by the wayside. For example, many primatologists believed that social structures of primate groups would fall in place phylogenetically, much as brain size does; apes would have complex social structures, monkeys less so, lemurs and lorises less so, and so on. Instead, on a scale of social structural complexity, Japanese monkeys clearly are closest to humans, followed by baboons; while chimpanzees, our nearest relatives, appear rather disorderly; and orangutans, also close cousins of ours, have no social structure at all—just a mother with offspring and an occasional male visitor.

A subsequent hope was that some simple ecological factors would prove to be the key, but this too was vain. No good predictors of social structure have emerged from ecology so far and, except for the centrality of the mother-offspring unit, at least while the offspring are young, no generalizations about the higher primates can be made. Variation in social structure within one species in different environments can be as great as variation across the whole primate order. It is for that reason I offer no assurances about what our five-million-year-ago ancestor's social structure was like; for all we know it could have lived like the orangutans, in isolated families, or like Japanese monkeys, in hierarchical troops of over a hundred. Probabilities can be offered; it was *probably* not at either extreme but somewhere in between. But assurances may never be available.

If they do come, it is not likely to be from living primates, but from direct study of the fossil record. Such study constitutes the central part of the picture, the most believable evidence of our ancestors. Without it, the comparative evidence I have been talking about up to now means little.

Fossil evidence gets a good, but fragmentary, press; it deserves better. The very brief treatment that is possible here attempts to convey a sense of the immense excitement that attends the unearthing of fossils that may be ancestral to ourselves, and of the feeling—akin to exhilaration—shared by all those who devote their lives to the search for them.

A*egyptopithecus*—"the Egyptian ape"—named for the country where its bones were found, as well as for its apelike teeth, is where we will have to begin the story. It would be delightful to reach down and down into the bowels of evolutionary time, to find our much earlier ancestors—into the Cretaceous, for instance, more than a hundred million years ago, where we would be looking for a furry creature that could sit in the palm of our hand and that we might come upon, at night, making a meal of a dinosaur egg; or deeper, into the Devonian, three hundred fifty million years ago, where we would try to find a fish with odd, strong, lobular fins used for crawling along the floors of shallow, muddy pools and, occasionally, for crawling through the mud from one pool to another; or deeper still, into the Precambrian, two thousand million years ago, when the atmosphere of the planet was just beginning to be rich in oxygen, and the dominant form of life on earth, blue-green algae (a sort of advanced bacteria) were generating that oxygen, by means of aerobic photosynthesis. But, appealing as it is to delve into that impressive history, to do so would constitute too luxurious a journey. We must content ourselves, then, with beginning *in medias res*, and *Aegyptopithecus* makes as good an Adam as any.

It is a small apelike monkey, discovered by Elwyn Simons in 1966, in the Fayum Oligocene of Egypt. "Fayum" locates it geographically, in a shallow dip in the landscape sixty miles southwest of Cairo that was once on the edge of the sea. "Oligocene" locates it in its era, approximately thirty million years ago. It was then quite a lovely spot, heavily wooded in places and interlaced with rivers; now it is barren, but not to the eye of the paleontologist—it is one of the world's richest lodes of primate fossils. The species name *zeuxis*—a reference to the chief Greek god—assigned to *Aegyptopithecus* by its discoverer gives some indication (at least in his eyes) of its importance. He described it as "the skull of a monkey equipped with the teeth of an ape," and later, when a limb bone was found, it became apparent that the body too was monkeylike. Superficially anomalous, this was exactly what was needed, since the emergence of apelike creatures (including ourselves) from the basic monkey body-plan was just then beginning to take place.

Aegyptopithecus was a largish, robust, arboreal climber, something like the modern-day Central American howler monkey. Its eyes faced forward in a pair of almost complete bony cases, and the arrangement and fit of its teeth were distinctly apelike. These are advanced features, with intriguing implications. The shape and disposition of the eyes, in a sense, look back to thirty million years of prior evolution. Through the Paleocene and Eocene, the "dawn epochs" of modern earth history, the primates differentiated from the fundamental mammalian plan by virtue mainly of their eyes. Relentlessly arboreal, they succeeded in adaptive terms by evolving, as a major group, the then most impressive mammalian eyes—eyes that could find a bug on a branch, even in the dark; eyes that would never misjudge the location of the branch itself, despite rapid scrambling through the trees. These skills required depth perception, which requires substantially overlapping—"binocular"—fields of vision; this in turn requires forward-facing eyes.

The consequences of these pressures are manifold. Already, by the Eocene, forty or fifty million years ago, the fossil evidence of brain evolution reflects this commitment to the eyes. The olfactory apparatus, which so many other mammals are investing so much in, is already shrunk in the most ancestral monkeys, and the region of the brain that concerns itself with vision, in the rear of the skull, is already noticeably larger. Ultimately, this commitment to vision will produce a whole panoply of characteristics distinctive of the higher primates—not only depth vision but color vision, advanced focusing capability, eye-hand coordination, and visual learning ability. Even during the evolution producing *Aegyptopithecus*, from sixty to thirty million years ago, we can observe a subtle shift of immense potential importance for the final phylogeny of mind; a shift from a sense modality for the detection of a part of the physical world—the realm of chemical signals—in which pattern is nonexistent, to a sense modality for the detection of a part of the physical world—the realm of light—in which pattern is infinitely realized.

The shape and disposition of the teeth of *Aegyptopithecus* look forward. It is not absolutely clear that this species itself is in the direct line of human ancestry (although recent new evidence strengthens its candidacy), but it is clear that it is at least quite close to the line. It, or something very like it, gave rise, during the subsequent ten or fifteen million years, to an immense variety of apelike creatures destined to give rise in turn not only to the apes but to ourselves.

The Miocene epoch, from roughly twenty-five to roughly five million years ago, saw the differentiation, at least at the genus level, of all the major forms above the monkey stage of adaptation. It is likely, from many lines of evidence, that the line leading to gibbons diverged from the others first. Thereafter some conflicts arise as to whether the Great Apes and hominids—the bipedal higher primates—had a joint common ancestor until all diverged from each other, or whether the orangutan left the common lineage earlier than the other apes. Molecular evidence—similarities and differences among species in the structure of complex molecules such as DNA and proteins—suggests that humans, chimpanzees, and gorillas are more closely related to each other than any of them is to the orangutan. The fossil picture may one day bear this out.

In the meanwhile, we must be content to grope around in the Miocene for forms ancestral to ourselves and to the various apes, without being absolutely certain which is which. We can take comfort in the fact that the confusion arises from an embarrassment of riches—a great many different Miocene apelike fossils, together with increasing molecular evidence as to the relatedness of modern forms. All the Miocene apelike forms were descended from *Aegyptopithecus,* or at least from a group to which this creature belonged. One of them, *Ramapithecus,* has long been considered to be the best candidate for direct human ancestry, and it is illuminating now to see why.

Named—like its contemporary *Sivapithecus*—to recall a Hindu god, it certainly seemed godlike against the backdrop of the other Miocene apes, at least to the extent that all our gods must be in the image of man. The main thing about it was, it had a small face; although much else may be said about it, this summary feature stands out. Its contemporaries, whether specialized with prominent, extended canines for tearing, or with massive cheek teeth for grinding, had all committed themselves too far in the direction of prognathism—the condition of long-snoutedness—to be candidates for our ancestral lineage. Looking into its face, after having done the same with its competitors, we would probably have experienced a shock of recognition.

Ramapithecus-like fossils have been found in the middle Miocene of Europe, Asia, and Africa, an impressive range indicating an equally impressive success. It is likely—from consideration of its jaws and teeth, which, by being small themselves, allow for its modest face—that it was capable of comfortable adaptation in the tropical forest or on the open savannah, and that it was, during this period, making a transition from the former to the latter. It was already capable of utilizing, by grinding, the small, tough seeds of grasses that cover the open plain, and it may have relied mainly on these for its food. As pointed out by Clifford Jolly, a physical anthropologist and authority on primate feeding ecology, a seed-eating phase this early in human evolution would probably have resulted in preadaptations for upright posture. Like modern seed-eating baboons, *Ramapithecus* may have spent much of its day sitting upright in a grassy field grazing with its hands. Its hand, from indirect evidence, was in all likelihood general-ized—committed in basic form neither to the long-fingered, short-thumbed brachiating plan of the apes, nor yet to the prominent human thumb, neatly opposed to the four fingers to make the precision grip. But if it was, indeed, spending most of its time searching for tiny seeds, grasping them, and bringing them to its mouth, then it may have entered upon a new phase of selection pressure for visual acuity and eye-hand coordination, beyond that achieved by the early primates, setting the stage for all that was to follow.

It was also rather small, even smaller than the pygmy chimpanzee; this is part of the reason we can accept it as ancestral to later humanlike creatures no bigger than four feet tall. But its size must have made it very vulnerable to predation as it made the transition from the relatively protected forest to the dangerous open savannah. In this circumstance it is quite likely that it developed social groups of substantial size—say fifty or more individuals—and that these groups had a fair amount of hierarchical ordering, especially among males, who would have to have cooperated efficiently in defense. This was the model, for one phase of protohuman evolution, that anthropolo-gists Irven DeVore and Sherwood Washburn proposed twenty years ago, and that led them to study baboon social behavior.

In baboon troops living on the African savannah, the generation-to-generation social structure of the group depends for continuity on a solid core of closely related females. But on a day-to-day basis, the most prominent arbiters of social life are dominant males. One of the interesting things about savannah baboon-troop structure is that if you match males on a one-to-one basis—as DeVore did, instigating fights over food—you get a linear hierarchy of dominance, but it is different from the actual troop hierarchy observed in practice. De-Vore showed that this discrepancy is explained by coalitions. At the top of a troop will be not a lone enduring tough, but a sort of troika in which the members reliably come to each other's defense. This enabled an elderly male who remained "politically" capable to exercise dominance over other males who could easily defeat him in individual combat. (Such coalitions have sometimes been observed to function in defense against predation, protecting females and young at the center of the troop, while younger males ["subdominants"] deployed themselves strategically at the periphery—but this aspect of the pattern is controversial.)

This coalition-based dominance structure contrasts markedly with the more rigidly linear structure of lower primate groups. Furthermore, it is not limited to baboons; other ground-living monkeys have similar arrangements, and so may savannah-living chimpanzees. But unfortunately for simplicity, the same species that is an intricate piece of political clockwork on the savannah may be a quite disorderly hodgepodge in the forest. Among forest baboons, the largest males may be the first to flee, scrambling up a tree when a leopard appears. This difference is, presumably, an instance of the principle of species adaptation for guided flexibility. The "range of reaction" of the social organization of the savannah baboon includes both these polar possibilities, and much else in between as well.

The facts thus enable us to guess that our ancestor that pioneered on the ground—something very like *Ramapithecus*—was probably capable of a baboonlike social order when on the savannah, with all its attendant dangers. But they also constrain us to accept the possibility that the very same creature, ranging into the forest, would adopt a much looser, less hierarchical structure; and they require, too, that we turn our backs on the notion that social hierarchy is in any direct sense "wired in." Nevertheless, a range of reaction is not ultimate freedom. It is an equation provided by the genes to relate the environment to the creature's characteristics. The species-specific, "hard-wired" equipment includes if-then statements even in the purely physical realm: "If the environment's rich, then grow large; if poor, grow small." Similar if-then statements exist for behavior.

Our middle-Miocene ancestor thus leaves us in some confusion, but not as much as we are soon to encounter. Between about eight and about four million years ago, we have no fossils of our ancestors or of closely related animals. One would not want to call what is missing *"The* Missing Link" since that phrase implies a creature crucial to the transition to human status; candidates for *"The*

Missing Link" come later and are no longer missing. However, there is certainly *a* missing link between eight and four million years, because what we have at the close of this gap is stunningly new indeed.

As if Mary Leakey had not already contributed enough to our knowledge of fossil humans, she and her research group in 1977 stumbled upon one of the most spectacular finds in the history of the field. At Laetolil, in Tanzania—not far from Olduvai Gorge, where she and her husband, Louis Leakey, had spent decades collecting fossils—were found, in fossilized mud dated at more than three and a half million years, footprints of a pair of upright-walking animals. Imagine, if you will, what Mary Leakey must have felt, after a lifetime of searching, occasionally exhilarating, usually very dull, with the most spectacular discoveries coming to you in the form of the edge of a tooth peeking from a rock; imagine, then, strolling across a mud you know to be almost four million years old, frozen solid for all that time as rock, and looking down, and seeing the imprint of an unmistakably human foot, and another, and another, making a passage across the mud just like yours.

In fact there were two individuals who walked across the mud that day in the early part of the Pliocene era—an adult (much smaller than ourselves) and a juvenile. Many bones were also found in the vicinity, and they match, in most respects, the bones found at the same time level elsewhere in Africa. The footprints and the bones belong to a genus known as *Australopithecus*, "the southern ape," named generations ago when it was first identified in South Africa. The species that made the footprints was named *Australopithecus afarensis* by Donald Johanson, who found, in 1974, in the Afar region of Ethiopia, the most complete skeletal specimen of the species, that of a small female biped known as "Lucy."

There has been some argument—there always is—about whether the group of *Australopithecus* fossils dated at three and a half million years or so really merit a separate species name. But the resolution of that conflict will not alter the facts that all are agreed on—namely that the small female biped from Ethiopia and the creatures that made the Tanzanian footprints represent an unprecedentedly early collection of evidence for the immediate ancestry of our species. And what they show is that by just under four million years ago we had become fully upright walkers. The missing fossils between *Ramapithecus* and *Australopithecus afarensis* (or whatever we end up calling it) notwithstanding, we know that during that period bipedal locomotion emerged. The long, slender pelvis of the Miocene apelike creatures had given way to a short, sturdy, weight-bearing arrangement. The foot is unmistakably weight-bearing, and although it is possible that the stride was not fully human (it may have been more like a half-run, half-walk), the use of the forelimbs in locomotion had been decisively left behind.

The implications of these facts are powerful. First, this creature clearly must have had more difficulty with birth than its Miocene ancestor. Among our modern relatives, apes have much easier deliveries than we do—partly because we have "cephalopelvic disproportion" (heads too big for our hips) and partly because fully erect posture and locomotion have turned the human pelvis into a sturdy, bulky, clumsy affair that holds up most of the body—not at all the sort of setup that an infant would most like to pass its head through. The latter problem was already faced by Lucy and her children, and the process of delivery was already increasing in importance as a focus for natural selection. It is likely, too, that this change played a role in the evolution of women—so far a little-studied subject—and in the evolution of human physical courage.

Second, Lucy's hands were free. Unnecessary for walking, they were available for carrying, one of the most distinctively human of behaviors. Even chimpanzees have been seen walking bipedally for short distances with armfuls of bananas; for Lucy, such an enterprise would already have been easier. Orangutans have been photographed walking bipedally while supporting their infants with their hands. This seemingly innocent posture suggests a nexus of pressures and possibilities for Lucy that are worthy of attention. Did she have long body hair? If not, then she was one of the first members of the primate order whose infant was not able to cling to her as she walked. Even if it could, it is likely that (like modern apes, perhaps even more so) the infant's clinging ability in early infancy was imperfect, and some support from its mother's hands necessary. Among Lucy's contemporaries and descendants, then, there would have accrued considerable advantage to the individual or lineage that conceived of using an animal skin, tied around the infant, to give the needed support, leaving the mother's hands free.

But, unfortunately, there is no evidence whatever that Lucy and her contemporaries used tools. Somewhat later, at about two million years before the present, we have clear evidence not only of tool use but of tool making, in the form of the pebble-tool industries of the next phase of human evolution. While evidence for tool making is usually clear, evidence for tool use is more difficult to obtain—it is difficult to prove that an unworked, unmodified piece of rock has been utilized by a hominid, as opposed to having been damaged by natural causes. Nevertheless, there are strong reasons for believing that Lucy belonged to a tool-using species. These reasons are indirect, but still compelling. They come from investigations of the modern-day chimpanzee, studied in the wild by Jane Goodall—at the instigation, interestingly enough, of Louis Leakey, whose main interest in them was in what he thought they would tell him about human evolution.

Wild chimpanzees in the Gombe Stream Reserve in Tanzania not only use tools but make them. Approaching a termite mound, they will strip the small branches from a twig and then use the twig to fish out termites, an important food. Young chimps closely observe their parents in this activity and so learn to do it themselves. Adults will also crumple leaves by moderate chewing, and then use the resulting leafy mass as a sponge to extract water from the crux of a tree, or for cleaning out the inside of a baboon skull after a kill. In other areas of Africa, other tool-using and tool-making behaviors have been observed and these, together with extensive observations of chimpanzee groups in captivity, lead to the inescapable conclusion that chimpanzees exhibit a rudimentary form of cultural tradition (and variation) in tool use and tool modification. On the rougher side of human and animal nature, there is a fascinating experiment by ethologist Adriaan Kortlandt, who introduced a convincing life-size model of a leopard—complete with roaring and head-turning—to a group of chimpanzees in the wild. The chimps made a group assault on the "leopard," using large sticks as weapons. They attacked both simultaneously and alternately, and put their arms around each other excitedly after scoring a successful blow.

It is likely, although far from certain, that Lucy and her contemporaries—*Australopithecus afarensis*—exhibited at least such a range of tool modification and tool use. And they did so, it must now be admitted, with no more brain capacity, relative to body size, than the modern chimpanzee. That is, although some of the most distinctive features of the human organism had already emerged by Lucy's day, the supremely distinctive feature—an oversized brain—had not even begun to take its place. It was once thought that all the major human characteristics evolved in concert, but this view has gone by the wayside; erect posture preceded, by at least a million years, the *beginning* of human brain evolution.

I have said little about Lucy's male counterpart. This is partly because males have already gotten too much attention in the study of human origins, but also because of the confusion that surrounds him. Timothy White, a paleontologist who has studied extensively the hominids from this period, has concluded that they are best understood as male and female of one species, with a substantial size difference between them. This is consistent with the chimpanzee model, and with the degree of sexual dimorphism—gender differences in body size and shape—in a number of other ground-living higher primates. If this is correct—or if, indeed, any of our direct ancestors had substantially more sexual dimorphism than we do—then we must probably prepare ourselves to accept certain characteristics of their behavior as highly likely. Following Darwin and others, Irven DeVore has pointed out that among known species of animals, a large difference in body size between males and females almost invariably signals the existence of intensive competition among males for females, which, over time, has produced the size difference. Since species in which the pair-bond is the basis of reproductive behavior usually have minimal size difference between the sexes, substantial dimorphism makes the pair-bond less likely for any of our ancestors that were highly dimorphic; and it makes some form of competition among males for females more likely.

Another characteristic of chimpanzee males that may have been applicable to the earliest human ancestors is that they jointly hunt, slaughter, and eat small mammals—the Thomson's gazelle, for instance, or infant baboons. The temptation to rush forward with a "killer ape" hypothesis of human evolution has often been succumbed to historically, and we must guard against it here. For one thing, such arguments always involve a tendentious and false suggestion that killing members of one's own species is somehow a natural outcome of predation. In fact, there is no such connection. Many vegetarian animals exhibit within-species violence, and the predation of carnivores may have more in common, psychologically, with play than with anger. Nevertheless, we must accept the fact that at some point, probably early, our ancestors incorporated into their diet the flesh of creatures killed mainly by males.

The stage is now set for the next act of the drama, and the scene shifts to the east of Lake Turkana, in northeastern Kenya. Here Richard Leakey and Alan Walker have been working for more than a decade, carrying forward the life work of Leakey's parents, begun hundreds of miles away at Olduvai. Like the South African sites of Swartkrans and Sterkfontein before them, Olduvai and now Lake Turkana have steadily yielded up to the patience of paleontologists a treasure trove of ancestral bones—direct and indirect, but hominids all—between three and one million years old. And if there is one thing that can be said about this latter group, to distinguish it from what went before, it is this, and with certainty: Some of these creatures made tools. The earliest pebble tools are more than two million years old. They are modest—no more than oval rocks with one rough edge made by two or three blows of another rock. Nevertheless, they are tools, and, as Louis Leakey personally and dramatically demonstrated in 1955, such bits of sharpened stone make the butchering of a carcass a very different proposition indeed. It is not beyond the realm of possibility that several million years of chimpanzeelike, spur-of-the-moment mammal hunting led very gradually, through natural selection for tool-making ability, to the introduction of the pebble-tool culture. It was perhaps directed first at the process of butchering. But it must be remembered that none of the tools of the modern chimpanzees—the termite-stick, the leaf-sponge, and the log-as-club—would, if they had indeed been used by our ancestors, have fossilized. Moreover, some of the most important tools used by modern hunter-gatherers—the digging stick, for example, no more than a sturdy, smoothed, pointed stick for getting at roots in the ground; or the sack for carrying vegetables; or the infant-carrying sling—being made of perishable materials, can almost never come to archeological light. It is probable that such tools were as important or more important in the first halting steps toward human culture than the stone tools and weapons that have survived. It is also possible that the low profile of women in the study of human origins is as much a consequence of the fragility of their artifacts as it is of the natural sexism of scholars.

The notion that tool use and tool making are a cause more than a consequence of human brain evolution is an old one. It was hinted at by Darwin in *The Descent of Man*, and made explicit (although in a Lamarckian cast) by Friedrich Engels in his essay "The Part Played by Labor in the Transition from Ape to Man." Recently it has been most closely associated with the views of anthropologist Sherwood Washburn, who cogently argued that the use, manufacture, and design of tools conferred unprecedented selective advantage on the more intelligent, and so led to larger brains.

The only difficulty (and it is not an enduring or serious one) is that at the moment the fossils of manlike bipeds from the next crucial horizon of human evolution are so numerous and so variable that it is virtually impossible to associate the known tool industries with the known skeletal specimens to put together a single convincing story. Walker and Leakey, confronting only the specimens from the eastern shore of Lake Turkana, and at only one time depth—around two million years—have to come to terms with a range of variation in skull form alone that would not have been believed possible a decade ago. Indeed, at that time it was still possible to argue that there was only one species of hominid in Africa, or indeed on the earth, at any given time depth. This theory is no longer tenable.

It was not entirely surprising to find specimens at East Turkana corresponding to *Australopithecus africanus* and *Australopithecus robustus*. These two species designations summarized the previous evidence very nicely, with the exception of an advanced form at Olduvai. They represented, respectively, the gracile (small and lithe) and robust (larger and thicker-boned) forms of the genus, and were presumed to range over large portions of Africa, before one of them, the gracile form, gave rise to our own genus, *Homo*. Both have small brains for their bodies (about 400 to 500 cubic centimeters of volume), but the robust form has much more massive jaws and teeth, for grinding and crushing, with a crest on the top of the head for muscle attachment.

The difficulty was that there appeared in the earliest time depth at East Turkana, essentially contemporaneous with the small-brained robust and gracile forms of biped, a third form, also with a small face, but with a much larger brain. The third form, represented by the now famous catalog number 1470, had a cranial capacity estimated by Ralph Holloway, an authority on such measurements, at 775 cc. This made it incapable of membership in either of the two species of *Australopithecus*, and at the same time, a better candidate for the making and using of stone tools found in the region—as well as for direct ancestry to ourselves.

It is most likely that 1470 belongs to a species named by Louis Leakey to describe a similar specimen at Olduvai: *Homo habilis*, or "capable man." It is also likely that this is the African hominid directly ancestral to us, at a time depth of two million years. A half-million years later at East Turkana, we have, again, three forms; but while the gracile and robust small-brained forms have changed little, the large-brained form has already changed dramatically. The cranial capacity has increased only 75 cc, but the facial form has become much more modern, and the accepted species designation is now *Homo erectus*, the same species as "Java man" and "Peking man." This was the last member of our own genus before the emergence of *Homo sapiens*. It was a species with a worldwide range, a cranial capacity of 800 to 1,000 cc, and an exceptional penchant for making stone tools—now no longer the simplest pebble tools, but the vastly more articulate hand axes, stunningly uniform in design throughout the Old World.

There are arguments with this scheme, of course; but they are more likely to be about names than about specimens. Few in the field now doubt that something very like *Ramapithecus* (at ten to fifteen million years) gave rise to what has been called *Australopithecus afarensis* ("Lucy," at around four million years), which gave rise to *Homo habilis* and then *Homo erectus* (by about one and a half million years). Some would like an extra species between Lucy and *habilis*; others would like *habilis* to be deemed an early *erectus*. But these are irrelevant quibbles. The history of protohuman life is a continuum, in which the line between a species and its successor must be arbitrarily drawn. The known fossils may punctuate the continuum in such a way as to make it seem segmented, but—at least for higher animals—it is not, and the better the fossil record gets, the more apparent will be the arbitrariness of the line-drawing. As the great taxonomist and evolutionist G.G. Simpson used to say, the transitional forms are argued over because they are transitional, and that is why they are interesting. It is best to think of them as transitional instead of wasting time about labeling.

The rest of the story is fairly straightforward. At a million years the single-species hypothesis is confirmed again. The robust and gracile forms of small-brained hominids, whether one species or two, are gone from the scene, and we have only *Homo erectus* with a range throughout the Old World and a uniform brain size, facial form, body form, and culture. Hunters and gatherers with a fairly simple, if very useful tool kit, they evidently hunted large mammals, and they could only have done so by advancing greatly the degree of cooperation involved in hunting. They probably had a low population density, with flexibly organized nomadic groups. They had—like all higher primates, and especially apes—slowly developing offspring requiring intensive care and prolonged dependency, almost undoubtedly the responsibility of women. In all likelihood women were also responsible for the gathering of wild fruits and vegetables. By this time in human evolution, brain size was large enough so that childbirth was probably already a matter of the gravest risk and difficulty.

Over the last million years we observe a steady, gradual increase in brain size to the modern average of 1,350 cc. Why? Although in modern living humans the large range of normal brain sizes—1,000 to 2,000 cc—is almost impossible to correlate with any measures of intelligence, the prediction of intelligence from brain size is to some extent possible when comparing different animals. This is especially true when the ratio of brain size to body size is taken into account, so that we focus only on "extra neurons"—brain tissue beyond what a larger animal needs to manage a larger body. Most important of all, the brain, during human evolution, is not only increasing in size but is being reorganized neurologically.

Ralph Holloway, who has devoted his career to the study of human brain evolution, argues that the reorganization is fundamental to our human status, while the increase in *relative* brain size is unimpressive. He has observed the pattern of convolutions and blood vessels of the brains of our ancestors indirectly, through the impressions they left on the inside of their owners' skulls. Although one cannot see much, and nothing at all of the deeper structures, it is clear that some of the distinctly human features of the surface of the brain—features not present in chimpanzees—were characteristic of the genus *Australopithecus*. These specimens are humanlike rather than apelike, and this is true even of the one found by Raymond Dart at Taung, South Africa, in 1924. A six-year-old juvenile with a naturally formed and exposed cast of the inside of its skull, it was the first *Australopithecus* fossil found. The frontal lobes, the parietal (upper side) lobes, and the poles of the temporal (lower side) lobes of the cerebral cortex—all of which have been shown to be crucial in higher human intellective function, subserving association, delayed response, language, and memory—are larger and more human in convolutional form in this cast than they are in the brains of modern apes.

It is thus possible that even the small-brained forms among the early hominids were capable of substantially greater intellective function than apes, and that we have in the past been led astray by the absolute size of their brains. In any case, their large-brained contemporaries and the descendants of the latter, up to and including modern humans, were under substantial selection pressures leading to more complex brains with more complex functions. Many proposals have been made as to the specific functions creating those pressures; among the more plausible are: the problem-solving capacity needed for hunting effectively without a good sense of smell; the information-storage capacity needed for gathering; the various cognitive functions needed for making and designing tools; the linguistic functions needed for cooperative hunting and for passing down tool-making traditions; general intelligence needed for the protection and training of an offspring dependent for an exceptionally long time; and the abstract thought needed for the reckoning of complex ties of kinship and economic exchange. What is certain is that brain size and cultural complexity—as seen in stone tool industries—increased over the last million years, and did so gradually and in concert.

Fire, under human control, appears, at Choukoutien in China, at a time depth of half a million years. The roasting of meat by creatures who were still *Homo erectus* is proven by unmistakably charred bones of many prey species littering the floor of the Choukoutien caves. If their taste apparatus was anything like ours, such cooking must have greatly increased the appeal of the meat in their diet. It must have made certain parts of the carcass digestible for the first time, and it must also have relaxed selection pressure on the teeth, jaws, and face, allowing them to shrink even further. But the appearance of controlled fire has even larger implications.

If these creatures responded to fire the way modern humans do—especially in hunting-gathering and other nonindustrial societies—then the advent of controlled fire resulted in a quantum advance in human communication: a lengthy, nightly discussion, perhaps, of the day's events, of plans for the next day, of important occurrences in the individual and in the cultural past, and of long-term possibilities for the residence and activity of the band. Of course, such discussions can go on during the day. But the day must generally serve more urgent purposes, and anyway there is something about the night: the terror of solitude, and the deep need for social life; the longing for light and warmth; the soothing, even mesmerizing effect of the flickering burning. "Look not too long into the fire," says Melville's Ishmael in *Moby Dick*, a warning against the lapses of pragmatism—the lapses, even, of self—that such gazing may occasion. One can visualize a group of these prehuman creatures—one wants to call them people—huddled together, touching, perhaps talking, and gazing into the fire, safe from the night outside; one can even visualize the attainment of a new plateau of human consciousness—a distinctively *social* consciousness—and, perhaps, the emergence of an impulse, both individual and collective, that we might feel inclined to call religious.

A hundred thousand years later, and halfway around the world, in what is now the vicinity of Nice, we have not only hearths, but houses built around them. Huts we may call them, but they are as much houses as are lived in by many of the world's extant peoples.

They are oval—20 to 50 feet long and 12 to 18 feet wide—and could shelter between ten and twenty people. They have postholes for large branches, a wall of stones, and odd slabs of limestone for sitting or working at. There is much debris on these house floors, but immediately around the hearths are places cleared—perhaps for sleeping, as is done by native Australians today. There is also clear-cut evidence of repeated brief occupation. From the pollen in the coprolites (fecal fossils), which comes from spring and early summer plants, it appears that the occupation of these sites was seasonal, much in the style of modern, seminomadic, gathering-hunting peoples. Thus, the French Riviera, circa 400,000 B.C.

In Spain, at the same time depth, at Torralba and Ambrona, we have the most unmistakable evidence of collective and very brutal big-game hunting. To view the situation from the vantage point of the archeologist, we have the bones of too many elephants in too short a time period, associated clearly with human killing and butchering. Together with the evidence of grass fires, quite possibly deliberately set, these characteristics of the Spanish sites point to collective elephant-driving—one of the most dramatic, dangerous, cruel, and potentially wasteful of all hunting methods. These suggestions violate many misconceptions about "natural conservation" by primitive peoples, and about the presumed humaneness of their hunting methods; whole herds of elephants were apparently driven by grass fires to their deaths, stampeded over a cliff, in much the way recent inhabitants of the American Great Plains stampeded bison. Unless the population density was much higher than other evidence leads us to believe, a great deal of elephant flesh was wasted.

In another hundred thousand years, or at most two hundred thousand, we have the earliest specimens that most authorities will agree to call *Homo sapiens*. At Swanscombe in England, at Steinheim in West Germany, and undoubtedly elsewhere as well, there appeared skulls that had shorter, more tucked-in faces, smaller brows, and a thinner but higher vault than was the case for the typical, earlier *Homo erectus* skull. While one might not have had, as one's first inclination on confronting these creatures, the impulse to engage them in a solicitous embrace, they must be deemed members of our own species: people.

According to prevailing current opinion, these European fossils were to lead, in another hundred thousand years, to the "Classic" Neanderthals. The latter have been the subjects of extreme controversy since the discovery of the first specimen in the Neander valley, near Düsseldorf, by quarry workers, in 1856. It was not only the first Neanderthal, but the first human or protohuman fossil of any kind, and it occasioned the almost too evidently delighted remark of Darwin's that stands at the head of this chapter. We need not be detained by the heated argument of that early day, in the first flush of passion about evolution; nor, indeed, by the much more recent arguments about the Neanderthals' correct taxonomic placement, raging until the 1950s and now serving mainly to embarrass. It must suffice for us to accept the Neanderthal people as fully human. Whether or not it is true, as one authority has said, that a Neanderthal man dressed up in a business suit and hat would not be taken notice of on the subway (I think this unlikely), it is very evident that in the general shape of the face and in the volume of the brain, the Classic Neanderthals were fully human; and some other skeletons that occur in the Near East, also clearly Neanderthal in type, are even more similar to modern skeletons.

Two things, however, remain distinctive about them. The first of these is exceptional robustness. The cross-sectional areas of the long bones and the size of the points of insertion of various muscles indicate a body designed to bear enormous stresses. The legs seem adapted for running, climbing, and weight bearing, and the arms seem adapted not only for vigorous activity, but for controlled vigorous activity, as in throwing objects or striking blows. The face can pretty much be accounted for as a transition from the very robust form of Homo erectus to the very gracile form of modern people.

Neanderthal robusticity is evident in children's skeletons, at least by the age of five years; thus it was not adaptation in the individual sense, a response to the environment during the life course, but adaptation in the genetic sense, fixed in the body's maturational plan. The only exception is in the bones of the pelvis; in both sexes, these are gracile, even in adults. It is probable that this is due to the necessity to pass a large head during delivery, a problem that had, by the Neanderthals' time, been increasing in seriousness for several million years; it is possible that in the male the slender pelvis resulted from a kind of evolutionary economizing—building both genders on the same basic plan. In the Neanderthal case the slender pelvis may be the opposite side of the coin of the robustness of the rest of the skeleton, which could have rendered even more costly the treacherous passage through the birth canal.

The sorts of activity that would help to explain such a robust skeleton include the hunting of big game, many other kinds of vigorous physical work, and, it cannot be denied, combat. The various categories of activity mentioned could also, any of them, account for the second highly distinctive feature of the Neanderthal people's skeletons: the exceptionally high frequency of injuries. This is especially true at Shanidar, a rich Neanderthal site in a cave in Iraq. There are simply too many healed fractures and unhealed broken bones to give us a picture of life as very like that of any modern "primitive" people. We cannot tell the source of most of the injuries; most could easily have been caused in any number of ways. However, we do have one unmistakable sign of the cause of not only an injury but a death.

In a Shanidar man there is a partially healed scar in the bone on the top of the left ninth rib, a scar unmistakably caused by a sharp object thrust between the ribs. By far the most likely explanation is that of a spearpoint wound in close combat. The man may have suffered a collapsed lung, and it is evident from the extent of healing around the wound that he lived not more than a few weeks. It is possible, although less likely, that such a wound could have occurred accidentally, during the excitement and confusion of a game kill; wounds occur in this way among modern-day hunter-gatherers. If it is evidence of combat, it is the only such evidence pertaining to the Neanderthal people; but, together with the exceptional rate of injury, it points to the possibility that violence was part of their everyday life.

But what had they accomplished? There is, first, the Mousterian stone-tool industry, a quantum advance in complexity and refinement over the hand axes of *Homo erectus*. This technology, although in some places associated with post-Neanderthal people, is also characteristic of all the Neanderthals. It is gradually becoming possible, through advanced statistical techniques, to assess the complexity of these tool assemblies quantitatively and, through advanced microscopy, to determine how the tools were being used. The more we know about these people, the less they seem in any way peculiar to anyone familiar with modern hunter-gatherers—except, again, for the robustness and the injuries.

But what is most impressive about their culture, when compared to all earlier ones, is the first apparent evidence of ritual. In the Cave of Witches, west of Genoa, Neanderthal people had penetrated 1,500 feet into the murky depths, and habitually threw pellets of clay at a certain stalagmite vaguely shaped like an animal. In the cave of Drachenloch—the "lair of dragons"—8,000 feet high in the Swiss Alps, in a carefully built cubical stone chest, are seven skulls of then-common bears, larger than grizzlies; six more skulls are set in niches along the walls. Since the Ainu of northern Japan, and other hunting peoples of northern Asia, have had bear cults in modern times—and witness the cultish pursuit in Faulkner's story "The Bear," set in early twentieth-century Mississippi—it did not seem farfetched to propose the existence of a Neanderthal bear cult. Finally, in yet another cave in Lebanon, with an estimated age of fifty thousand years, there is evidence that a dismembered fallow deer carcass was laid on a bed of prearranged stones and sprinkled with red ocher.

These tantalizing hints do no more than establish a possibility. But taken together with yet another set of facts about the Neanderthal people, their significance is enhanced. These latter facts concern the practice of burial.

It is among the Neanderthal people that deliberate burial of the dead occurs for the first time in human history. As early as 1908, in the cave of La Chapelle-aux-Saints, there was evidence of this practice. A Neanderthal hunter was laid out in a shallow trench, a bison leg set on his chest, and the trench strewn with tools and other animal bones. The similarity to the burial rites of many recent peoples, speeding the soul of the deceased on its way in the next world, is unmistakable. At La Ferrassie, also in France, over the course of the subsequent twenty-five years, there emerged the shape of a rock shelter that had been used as a family cemetery. Sixty thousand years ago, a man, a woman, two children about five years of age, and two infants were buried here, and with some ceremony. The man and woman were buried head to head, the children neatly laid at the man's feet; one of the infants, newly born, had been interred together with three beautiful and valuable flint tools. This infant was in a small earth mound adjacent to eight other similar mounds of unknown significance. In the Crimea, in Israel, and elsewhere in the Near East, a number of burials occur with the legs pulled up tightly to the body, and the one exception is still intriguing—it is a forty-five-year-old man with the jawbone of a boar held in his arms. In yet another Near Eastern site, a boy's grave is surrounded by pairs of goat horns.

But the most astonishing find among these is the Shanidar flower burial. Here, at a time depth of sixty thousand years, in the grave of a hunter with a fatally crushed skull, were found the remains, in fossil pollen, of a multitude of flowers. Analysis shows them to have been brightly colored—related to hollyhock, bachelor's button, groundsel, and hyacinth. The man had evidently been laid on a bed of such flowers, perhaps woven together with soft pine boughs; more flowers were apparently strewn over him. There are speculations by experts, of course, as to what the flower burial may mean; I am of the opinion, however, that such speculations offer no more, and perhaps they offer less, than what each of us may privately do with this knowledge. It is a stunning and beautiful piece of knowledge indeed.

What the Neanderthals did not accomplish, aside from the usual advances in technology—these are inevitable in the sense that they always come—was any significant form of plastic art. We cannot accuse them of lacking a musical culture or a literary one (in the oral mode, of course); but on the other hand we cannot credit them, or any other prehistoric people, with either of these supremely important achievements, and we never will be able to. The only inroad we have into the aesthetic world of our early ancestors, the only reflection we have of their aesthetic faculty, is in the plastic arts.

Of these the Neanderthal people left none. They disappeared from the earth by roughly thirty thousand years ago—later in some places, earlier in others. What is clear is that, by evolution's standards, they disappeared quickly. They evolved gradually, both in physique and culture, over the course of about fifty thousand years; but they were replaced, in Europe at least, in only about five thousand.

The specter of mass slaughter by a technologically superior race, which was repeatedly raised by early theorists, need not be invoked; five thousand years is still quite a long time. Nevertheless, it is probably not long enough for the Neanderthal people of Europe to have evolved through the usual processes into the Europeans of subsequent vintage. Consequently, the most widely accepted theory for the facts as they now are has the later European population evolving from an undetermined non-European Neanderthal population, and then migrating to Europe, gradually overtaking—absorbing, conquering, squeezing out, and also perhaps killing—the technologically more primitive European Neanderthal people. These migrants are usually called Cro-Magnon, after a hermit who lived in a rock shelter high in the limestone cliffs of the Dordogne. This rock shelter housed a few of the perhaps hundreds of thousands of new people, about thirty thousand years before the hermit, Magnon, was born. The migratory process, and the attendant process of replacement—partly brutal, partly merely selfish, energetic, inadvertent—seems very easy to understand, and indeed very human, if we note in comparison the almost continual sequence of essentially similar processes in many parts of the planet, throughout the domain of well-recorded history up to the present day.

This is not by way of exoneration, but merely to apprehend rather than judge. What the Cro-Magnon people had was simply the most impressive array of lithic (stone) tools and weapons—not to mention others of bone, antler, and ivory—that had ever been brought together before by any human culture: spearpoints, lances, knives, chisels, needles, tools for scraping, perforating, sawing, whittling, pounding, even iron pyrite for making fire, and much more.

But, while these items of superior technology must surely have seemed the central facts about them to the people who became their inevitable victims, they cannot seem so central to us. What we, on the contrary, see as so distinctive about these people—and what may have had consequences that we are in no position to judge just yet—are certain items of probably little practical value that they left on some of the walls of their various caves.

At Altamira, a raucous herd of polychrome bison tumbling around the ceiling of the gallery—walking, standing, crouched, charging, in warm rich reds and browns, with a horse, two hinds, and a few wild boar thrown in for good measure; at Font de Gaume, a pair of exquisitely executed reindeer, also painted in color, the hart almost tenderly sniffing the head of the kneeling hind; at Trois Frères, a collection of puzzles—an utter chaos of masterfully engraved big-game fauna, superimposed on each other on a series of rock panels; a pair of sketchy snow owls with their chick; and the poignant, eerie figure called "the sorcerer," presiding over the animals, with antlers, with staglike ears and body, with human hands and feet, and with a prominently human male sex beneath his horselike tail—none of which match the impression made by the all-too-human eyes, shocked, plaintive, sad, set in the midst of a mouthless, bearded face.

But none of these holds a candle to Lascaux. Called by one of its early students "a paleolithic Sistine Chapel," it was unknown until 1940 when a pair of boys discovered it and thought to alert some expert. It rarely fails to impress the observer of sensibility—whether religious or not, whether expert or not—with a strong sense of the holy. Its halls, naves, and galleries, as they are justly called, twisted though they may be, have walls and ceilings covered with beautiful animals, masterpieces of realism, although by no means merely zoological. A bistre yellow and black horse surrounded by flying arrows, a herd of ornately antlered, graceful little stags, a horse with a fluffy mane, a "Tibetan" antelope, a pair of bison tail-to-tail, a big red dappled cow, a fire-eyed five-meter-long black bull—among these and other paintings at Lascaux are several that art historians with no particular brief for prehistory readily accept as some of the greatest works of art of all time.

No, we do not know what they "mean," what they "were for." We know that many of the friezes in these caves were physically accessed with only the greatest difficulty; they are literally in the bowels of the earth. They can only have been approached with torches, and some of them only by crawling through cramped spaces. John Pfeiffer, a noted archeological writer who has devoted several years to viewing and thinking about them, now believes that they are best understood as part of a kind of theater, perhaps religious theater, in which the torch-lit, strained approach was a critical, spellbound prelude to the drama. Among the other proposed explanations are hunting magic, for either propitiation or restitution; totemism; shamanism; initiation ritual; and decoration. As Ann Sieveking has said of Paleolithic works of art, "They are simply a language for which we have no vocabulary," and it is not likely that we ever will.

But suppose the simplest case—that they are merely decorative. Auguste Renoir said, "The purpose of a painting is to make a wall pretty," and in his mouth those words give dignity enough to the "merely" decorative. In the long voyage of humankind on the surface of this planet, these are the first "objets" for which the question "But is it art?" must be answered unequivocally in the affirmative. As the dedication of his book about Lascaux, Fernand Windels wrote: "To our distant ancestors who worked in the silence of the caves some two hundred centuries ago in belated honor of genius never surpassed." It is significant, I think, that we begin to speak of centuries, as if welcoming these women and men at the boundary of the realm of the recent past. The fact that some of them could execute such paintings, engravings, and carvings is impressive enough in itself; but more impressive is the fact that the undoubted majority who could not evidently could appreciate, even support, those who could. I can think of no more significant single advance in the whole course of human evolution; and I can think of no more convincing demonstration of the final, decisive emergence of the utterly, distinctively human brain.

4

THE FABRIC OF MEANING

After every foolish day we sleep off the fumes and
furies of its hours; and though we are always engaged with
particulars, and often enslaved to them, we bring with us
to every experiment the innate universal laws.
—Ralph Waldo Emerson,
"Nature"

Anatomy may not be destiny, but it is all we bring into this
world and all we can take away with us when leaving. Not that we
are endowed at birth with a fixed and changeless structure; it is dying
and being reborn continually. But in this intricate, dense, moist web
of cells we carry around with us (and not in any airy thing attached to
it) lies the substance of all the love and hate, joy and grief, hardhead-
ed analysis and excited imagination we experience during our sojourn
on this planet. And it is only because certain cells make signals,
chemical and electrical, to communicate with each other, that we are
able to think and feel at all.

Take, for instance, that crowning glory of evolution, the pyramidal
cell of the new, outer crust of the brain. Named for its shape, it sits
like an ancient symbol in a gel-like sea of cells, tentacles motionless
but intricately poised, waiting for messages. All these messages it
swallows into its steady, electric rhythm, modifying in its tiny,
supremely important way what it says to other cells. It, in its millions
of incarnations all over the cortex, is the centerpiece of "higher"
brain functions. As the incoming messages course around the skin of
its cell body, falling together, they may add up to a single trigger

impulse in the axon—the main outgoing trunk. This impulse affects cells in remote parts of the brain and body. To control movement, it may have to run a course from the motor cortex to the base of the spine. In the giraffe this is no small distance; in the blue whale it's a far cry indeed.

For ourselves, more important even than motion-controlling signals, leaving the brain bound for the body by the billions, is the vastly larger number of signals within the brain. It is mainly because pyramidal cells are pestering each other, connected together in a great web of circuits, that we are able to have these lofty thoughts about them.

The design of this web cost many millions of years. Entrusted as it is with much of what we need to get through life, even to reproduce, in a brain-ridden species, one would not expect its assembly during growth to be left to the mere vagaries of experience. Growth cones of axon trunks—the tips of developing nerve cells in the embryo—grope like snakes through the jelly, sniffing at chemical gradients and climbing along them blindly. They reach at length their private, ultimate anatomical destinies while the infant is in the womb, before the lure of bright lights or the warmth of mother love can make any impression. Once in the vicinity of the cells they are to talk to, axons begin to make synaptic connections—direct chemical bridges to the tentacle-like dendrites of the receiving cell.

At least this far the process is run entirely by genes. Nutrients and energy are supplied from the outside, and minimal conditions of warmth and protection must be met. But the organizing is all automatic. It is fast, it is orderly, it is infinitely complex, and on the whole it is really rather miraculous. Critics are right in saying that little is now known about how the genes get the job done; but they will be right for only a few more decades. What is already clear is that the genes are in charge at this stage. When a growth cone is recruited the sign says *No experience necessary.*

Brain growth after birth is also embryological, in the sense that it is largely inner-directed. But now the brain, for which experience counted relatively little in the womb, must swallow large doses of it, in addition to doses of oxygen and milk-derived sugar.

In a stunning experiment on experience and the brain, rat pups were raised in rich or poor environments. The favored pups, selected at random, grew up in a world full of toys and other pups. A control group grew up under ordinary laboratory conditions. A third group was impoverished; even the relatively low level of stimulation available in the ordinary laboratory was withheld from them.

These different conditions stamped differences in the brain. In the visual part of the brain, where patterns taken from the eye are converted into usable thought, those same pyramidal cells so crucial to higher mental life appeared changed under the cold eye of the microscope. Not changed in their basic placement or overall structure; in rats as in ourselves these are determined by the genes, mostly before the time of birth. But in the finer aspects of structure the impact of experience was evident. Animals raised in a rich environment had more small branches far out along the main trunks of the dendrites. And on these branches, each of which has countless tiny spines for the insertion of contact points for incoming messages, more spines could be counted for each unit of length in the rats that had stimulation during growth.

There are other differences, but these suffice to convince. Everything from learning ability to brain chemistry has been shown to be changed by experience. But somehow it is structure—that most ancient of biological subjects—seen and drawn or photographed through the microscope—that most classic of tools—that persuades at last. For me, it was something I wanted so to believe that I had to see structure with my eyes, mistrusting every other form of evidence. Look, I remember thinking when I first saw the photographs, see for yourself. Experience changes the brain.

Those same spines can be changed in number by a gene. In Tay-Sachs disease, a dreaded form of profound mental retardation that strikes selectively at East European Jews, the dendrite branches become stripped of all their spines during the course of the first year of life. As if to compound the tragedy, the child is normal at birth. The Tay-Sachs gene causes an enzyme deficiency that allows a usually harmless chemical to build up to poisonous levels in the brain. This in turn gradually distends the dendrites and causes them to become bare of spines. Since being bare of spines is tantamount to being bare of incoming messages, the cells become gradually functionless, while parents and physicians stand by, helpless, watching.

There is no known treatment, and death is inevitable, usually before age two. Certainly the rapidity and relentlessness with which the Tay-Sachs gene devastates brain cells could never be opposed by mere experience, and when there is a treatment it will be chemical. Yet there is something so illuminating—even comforting—in knowing that there are visible, real structures in the brain—the spines along the dendrites—which we now know can be changed by a gene, or changed by experience as well. When I sit around listening to tedious, barren arguments about nature and nurture, heredity and environment, I think of the spines on the dendrites. How amused they would be if they could listen to the pronouncements: "Genes have no known effects on complex behavior!" and "Most of mental function is determined by the genes!"

Recent studies of experience and the brain have begun to produce some very intriguing details. For instance, age is no object. While it was natural to try the experiment first with very young rats, enrichment was later tried with rats of all ages. Even elderly rats show brain changes in response to experience, contrary to the adage about old dogs and new tricks. Also, since most of the changes in structure, at all ages, were in the visual part of the brain, it seemed possible that merely seeing more could make the difference. Rats were kept in small cages within the larger "enriched environment" cages, from which they could watch the toys and other rats but not participate. Their brains showed no changes. Evidently, we must grapple with the world to change the brain, not just sit back passively watching.

In the wake of such findings it is conventional to suggest that if brain modification in response to experience is demonstrable in rats (even in aged rats), this must be all the more true in humans. Aren't we, after all, vastly brainier? Don't we show, in plain, irrefutable view, many times the little learning known in rats? If environmental enrichment can cause a sprinkling of new dendritic spines to sprout on a rat's brain dendrites, imagine what must go on in the human brain, where such dendrites are thousands of times more numerous. Learning must be thousands of times more possible.

There is a good deal of truth in this argument, but what is treacherous about it is that it can lead us into temptation—the temptation to believe that such learning (with its attendant brain modification) somehow liberates brain structure and function from the influence of the genes. No one, of course, believes that the genes do nothing; but many behavioral and social scientists today would like (at least a little) to believe that the known facts of brain modification, multiplied to a larger, human scale, reduce the effects of the genes to the crudest aspects of gross brain structure. The genes, according to this view, sort of start the ball rolling, in the recesses of the womb, during the early weeks of gestation; after some unspecified early point, the embryonic human brain somehow gels into rough outline of its destined ultimate form, and thereafter, beginning with the pregnant mother's diet, drugs, habits, and moods, experience does the work of brain design.

It is said that Michelangelo's view of the work of carving was that it was merely that of liberating the figure from the marble that imprisons it—that in effect one had merely to chip away the excess stone. If this were true, it would be a better analogue of the process of neural and behavioral development than is the usual view of sculpture, according to which very little is inherent in the marble and everything is imposed from the outside, making allowance only for the nature of the material. This latter perspective, although undoubtedly a more realistic view of sculpture, is completely unrealistic as a view of brain and behavior development, and this fact is unchanged by the complexity of the human brain. Indeed, it can be said that the massive new burden of size and complexity represented by the human brain lies much more with the genes and their maturational process than it does with the forces of experience—even while it provides a vast new field of action for experience.

Reconsider what has happened in evolution. "Encephalization," a complex ratio of brain size to body size that indicates how brainy a species is, has not changed in reptiles in a good two hundred million years; yet even the initial transition to mammals, over a hundred million years ago, involved a fourfold increase in this measure, requiring a major genetic reconstruction. In the last fifty million years of mammal evolution, another four- or fivefold increase in relative brain size has occurred—a twentyfold increase in all for the average mammal compared to the average reptile.

"Average" mammal, of course, leaves a lot to be desired, and when we begin to distinguish among them, we find that even our very earliest primate ancestors had moved ahead of the "average mammal" pack. *Necrolemur*, which was not even much of a primate, but was very near our ancestral line, had a brain-to-body weight ratio of 1:35 as early as the Eocene epoch, sixty million years ago. Meanwhile, one counterpart, an ancestral rhinoceros, had at the same time period a brain-to-body weight ratio of 1:2,000. This disparity has since increased substantially.

The initial increase in encephalization during the transition from reptiles to archaic mammals probably, judging from modern comparative data, attended a major shift in the stimulus world from one predominantly visual (although not yet *analytically* visual) to one dependent on hearing and smell in addition to the visual mode. Harry Jerison, who is responsible for much new knowledge about the evolution of the brain, believes that the initial mammalian brain expansion was essentially a solution to "a packaging problem." In the visual mode, there is room in the retina of the eye itself to "package" enough neural units for considerable integration. Similar integration in the auditory and olfactory systems has to take place at higher (more central) nervous system levels—perhaps partly because it is temporal rather than spatial integration, perhaps only because of lack of room. It seems likely that the archaic mammals were driven from daylight adaptive niches by the much more successful contemporary reptiles (this may have occurred only after a long struggle), and that the evolution of greater auditory and olfactory capacity was part of their adaptation to the twilight or night world. The usual processes of natural selection operating on the genes that code for neural structures are all that are needed to explain this impressive, protracted transition, completed over one hundred million years ago.

Interestingly enough, it is *possible* that experience played a key role in this transition. Imagine an archaic mammal, living in a twilight niche, with a brain responsive to experience much as the brains of the rats described above. (Since such responsiveness of pyramidal cell dendrites to experience has been shown even in the brain of the jewelfish, similar processes in the brains of archaic mammals are highly likely.) Let us say that during the course of its individual life cycle this archaic mammal finds itself forced to rely on auditory stimuli for finding food and eluding predators, more so than another member of its species—say in a southerly part of the geographic range, where the daylight hours are longer, and vision is still more useful. We can expect transformations in the distribution and shape of the spines and thorns on the dendrites of the nerve cells in the auditory system of the animal that is relying on hearing. It cannot, we know, pass this hard-earned advantage on to its offspring. However, it can force those offspring to grow up in an environment where the same alteration is likely to happen to them because of exposure of the brain to similar forces.

More important, in the long run, it can force the offspring to grow up in a situation where the inevitable differential reproductive success will favor those with *genetically* better hearing, even if it is only slightly better. This would be a clear case of the Baldwin effect: environmental modifications accomplished during the individual life cycle can bring a population under new selective forces, which can in turn produce genetic change that tends in the same direction as the original environmental modification.

Yet no *inheritance* of acquired characteristics is involved. Experiential modification merely *pilots* genetic change. The overall evolutionary transition, requiring millions of years, is fundamentally, relentlessly genetic. It is likely that the brain of the archaic mammal is more responsive to environmental influence than that of its reptilian ancestor, merely because of the increase in brain mass (more neurons, more dendrites, more dendritic spines, more opportunity for change). Yet the fundamental change is not one of increased mass but of reorganization. What is interesting about it is the introduction of new possibilities of sensory processing (in the auditory and olfactory modes) and, subsequently, some changes in the nature of central nervous integration that must have eventually followed the sensory changes. No experience, however rich, however powerful, could, in the course of an individual life, begin to produce the sorts of changes that make the brain of the archaic mammal so different from that of the reptile.

Similar generalizations can be made about all subsequent evolutionary changes. In the next phase of mammalian brain evolution, it is the disappearance of a reptile group, the dinosaurs, and the reoccupation by mammals of the daylight niche, that provide the impetus; and the reorganization consists in a return to the visual mode—at least to some extent, at least in some mammals—but in a manner much more advanced than that of reptiles. Using the advances of the archaic mammals as a "base for operations," the newer mammals evolved a system of visual processing in the brain that became the key to subsequent brain evolution. Compared to the reptile visual system, it is highly patterned in both space and time, highly integrative, highly analytic, highly responsive to environmental modification, and, perhaps above all, highly open to communication with the systems that process information from the other sensory modalities. And it is this latter characteristic that made possible the evolution of the great associative systems—in essence, the systems of thought—of the higher mammalian brain.

All these characteristics were accomplished to a more impressive extent in the primate lineage than in any other mammals. They relied more on analytic vision, they expanded their brains more, and they did both things earlier. They certainly carried brain evolution further in the end than did any other lineage, entering an adaptive niche that was tool-using, then tool-making, and finally linguistic—the last step toward culture. All of this required progressive, continual reorganization of the brain. This evolution through natural selection was again fundamentally a change in genes and in the way they interact to generate the structures of the brain.

The culmination, which we carry around in our heads, is, for all its flaws, an impressive result. It weighs more than three pounds—an enormous load for a middle-size mammal, making one sometimes wonder how we hold it up. It contains between 10^{10} and 10^{11}—that is, between ten and one hundred billion—nerve cells. (The uncertainty is caused by the so-called granule—"grainlike"—cells, tiny neural components of certain brain structures, of which there are probably billions, and which are very hard to count.) Only a few million of these are sensory cells, the real points of input in the various sense organs; and only about one or two million are motor neurons, the "final common pathways" directly controlling the contraction of muscles and the secretory activity of gland cells. The phrase "final common pathway" is important because there are roughly ten thousand nonmotor, nonsensory nerve cells for every motor neuron, ten thousand units converging on one. The potential for integration is enormous. Known to neuroanatomists as "the great intermediate net," these billions of central—nonsensory, nonmotor—neurons account for the vast majority of the mental, emotional, and spiritual functions of the brain.

Seventy percent or so are in the cerebral cortex, an intricately patterned, usually six-layered structure, designed above all for integration. A vast, sheetlike structure of fairly uniform thickness, it is folded and refolded on itself, according to genetically determined patterns that are unique to the human species. Thus convoluted and shoved into a smallish, roundish skull, it occupies most of the space given up to the brain. Without it we cannot speak, comprehend, see patterns, learn associations, anticipate, remember, think, or—at least in the *human* sense—feel. It is the most highly evolved, newest, largest, most interesting, and, possibly, most highly ordered structure in the brain.

At the other extreme, in almost every sense, is a concourse of neurons (to call it a "structure" might be to dignify it beyond its just deserts) known as "the reticular activating system." Located in the core of the brain stem, it is as vague as the cortex is ordered, as old as the cortex is new. Yet, as primitive as it is, it is enough; remove it, and death occurs, whereas removal of the entire cerebral cortex is perfectly compatible with survival, under protected conditions. Its function is the regulation of arousal; or, in the felicitous phrase of the great neuroanatomist Walle Nauta, it provides "the posture of the internal milieu." It occupies the core of the brain stem, and, through short connections made by unspecialized multipolar neurons—neurons, as Nauta points out, made for listening—as well as by longer direct connections, it can communicate with virtually all higher and lower regions of the central nervous system. It regulates sleep and waking and all the manifold cyclical activities associated with them, including the briefer cycles within sleep and within waking. It modulates alertness and arousal, two distressingly vaguely defined but nevertheless real patterns of wakefulness. It is in a pivotal position for mediating between the emotional functions of the limbic system ("the emotional brain," cradled in or near the fringes of the cortex) and the physical functions of the spinal cord and the autonomic nervous system. Impulses travel in both directions, upstream or down, meandering slowly but surely from one multipolar neuron to another. Because of their starlike—or really asterisk-like—shape, these neurons are in an excellent position to listen widely and to communicate an integrated message. Collectively they belong to a vast population of similar starlike neurons hidden deep in the core of the brain, a continuous river of fairly unstructured gray matter running up from the spinal cord, through the brain stem, and into the very hub of the higher brain.

This course, in a sense, recapitulates an evolutionary history. In the brains of the lamprey and the shark—close to the ancestral forms of the vertebrates—just such a river of undifferentiated small neurons, relatively unstructured, dominates the remaining neural formations. It now seems very likely that the earliest ancestors of the vertebrates—creatures a bit like the lamprey—had central nervous systems that consisted largely of what in our brain is the reticular gray core. Phylogenetically, we have piled many new structures, most of them much more orderly, on top of this ancient system, but the core still regulates the rest. It seems at times almost to be looking on skeptically at the antics, as it were, of the Johnny-come-lately rest of the brain. In the exquisite words of Paul Yakovlev, one of the greatest neuropathologists of this century, "Out of the swamp of the reticular formation the cerebral cortex arose, like a sinful orchid, beautiful and guilty."

This highly ordered cerebral cortex, and its relatively less ordered "swampy" counterpart in the brain stem, are alike the products of millions of years of evolution through natural selection. The Baldwin effect notwithstanding, the overwhelmingly crucial events in this process took place in the chemistry of the genes, genes that control the structure of the brain. Of course, the brain does not spring into being, least of all *orderly* being, by some instant genetic magic; this would indeed seem most implausible and leave us groping for some environmentalist guidance. But whether one is a brain-burdened human being or a neurologically undistinguished little lamprey, one's nervous system is the product of a course of intrinsic growth, and, miraculous as it sometimes seems, it no longer seems magical; indeed, it now seems miraculous only in the sense that many natural phenomena do that are in large part readily explainable—a cloud, say, or the colors of a sunset. It would be unfair to suggest that all the answers are in, or that their forthcoming appearance will be a quick or simple matter. They depend on some of the most appealing and, at the moment, most awkward unsolved problems in biology. Nevertheless, some of those answers are to hand, and we have reached the stage, so very exciting in science, at which we can specify rather nicely the sorts of knowledge we have to gain if we are, in a generation or so, to paint a readable picture of brain genesis.

In a crude sense, much was already known by the turn of the century. At that time, descriptive embryology occupied the attention of many of the best-known biologists, and the use of the increasingly sensitive light microscope to describe where organs come from in early embryonic life was a major part of the explicit agenda of nineteenth-century biology. During the twentieth century's opening decades, description was carried further, in ever greater detail, and the discovery of the origins of organs and suborgans of various species continues to some extent today. Particularly in the nervous system, which can be so exquisitely differentiated into separate cell fields by reference to orderly cell architecture, there has been room for continuing light-microscope description. The studies of Paul Flechsig, J. Leroy Conel, Paul Yakovlev, and others throughout the first eight decades of this century have vindicated the process of "mere" description by continuingly raising its level of sophistication and by carrying it forward through the latest stages of fetal development and, ultimately, through the course of postnatal life. With the advent of the electron microscope, and now the scanning electron microscope, which reveals in a magnificent three dimensions things that we have long seen flatly with transmitted light, the descriptive process is yielding still more.

Nevertheless, it must be acknowledged that the field of nervous system development, now larger and more vigorous than ever, has shifted massively away from description. Description largely answered the question, What? just as adaptive teleology addressed the question, Why? Until the last few decades, however, the key intermediate question, How? remained a mystery. Answers to this last category of questions—the central questions of developmental biology—will remove all remaining doubt about how the genes effect the "miracle."

Consider what must be accomplished during the course of fetal brain development. In effect, in a few months, the entire work of hundreds of millions of years of evolution must be reachieved, though not necessarily recapitulated. Tens of billions of neurons must be born before the time of birth, an average of over a hundred thousand a minute, as the result of the division of parent cells. These new nerve cells must find their way to their anatomical destinations, sometimes moving over substantial distances, in an embryo that is constantly changing in form. Countless millions of these cells must then die at predestined times, leaving surviving other millions behind, like a living sculpture. Each must develop a shape that is highly peculiar to itself (or at least to its category), and that shape must above all include a highly designed set of processes or outgrowths: dendrites, generally shorter and predominantly the receivers of information, and axons, usually longer (sometimes very long), predominantly the transmitters of information.

Once the cell is fixed in place, the axon must find its way to its own destination. The organs of the nervous system are unique in this regard; it is especially there that connections among cells, even remotely separate cells, constitute the very basis of function. Even the dendrites are not still, and we can properly visualize the cell as slightly motile in its place—especially its processes—doing a long, slow, twisting dance throughout life; but it is the axons that bear the great burden of making connections, which they do by traveling, sometimes over a great expanse of brain. They must not only get where they are going and make a connection, but they must avoid making any number of other connections that they might wrongly make in places they pass.

Each nerve cell must develop one or more of at least a dozen neurotransmitters—the chemical substances nerve cells use to "speak" to neighboring nerve cells—and it must be the right one. A number of appropriately disposed synapses—the interfaces between one nerve cell and the next—must be formed, be architecturally correct, and be between the right pair of cells. Cells must begin functioning, carrying electricity, and so make circuits function too. Some of the hard-won connections in many parts of the brain must die, for "sculptural" reasons connected with streamlining the system, just as millions of hard-won neurons have died earlier. Finally, supporting systems of all kinds must develop in the nonneural tissue surrounding the nerve cells. For example, the myelin sheath, a fatty wrapping around the axon, must form on many nerve cells, as a result of the action of nearby nonneural supporting cells, by one of two intricate processes different for central and peripheral nerves; without that sheath, the nerve will never reach its mature level of function in terms of conduction velocity, consistency of responsiveness, and the intricate timing of action of the circuits to which it belongs.

All these processes are now under study, and the beginnings of understanding are in our grasp. Much is yet to be learned about virtually all of them, but a few impressive facts can be set forth here. Since genes are mere chemicals, and since all they can do is turn one another on and off, or just make more chemicals, the understanding we are groping for must in the end be chemical; and the difficult routes of approach must seek to explain the operating mechanisms rather than merely describe the events as they look under the microscope. The overall question is: How can the fabulous intricacies of the brain's many billions of neural connections get themselves arrayed in orderly circuits?

Fancy chemical experiments can now give answers that go far beyond mere description. This is, in effect, what has happened in a subfield of brain development research started by Richard Sidman, a neuropathologist at the Harvard Medical School. Sidman began, around 1960, to apply the technique known as autoradiography to the study of the timing of the birth of nerve cells. Simply stated, autoradiography is merely the injection of radioactive chemicals, followed by what is in effect a photographic development procedure that allows the investigator to visualize the specific location of the radioactive "label" in the tissue. This technique has been turned to many purposes, but none more intriguing than the method of "tritiated thymidine," a specific type of radioactive tracing linked to DNA and designed to identify cells that are in the process of dividing. It is widely used to study the growth of the brain, especially in its earliest embryonic stages.

The result of this powerful technique has been to describe a whole new dimension of brain development: the pattern and sequence of nerve-cell birthdays. This pattern is presumably ruled by regulator genes that tell a cell when to divide and that are responsive to cues of position and signals from neighboring cells. It proves very important in determining brain structure. The relationship of structure to the sequence of cell birthdays differs in different places in the brain. For example, in the cerebral cortex, earlier-born cells deposit themselves in the first, inner layer, and latecomers must then bypass them, migrating farther to form the outer layers. In most other parts of the tube-shaped early brain, the reverse is the case; that is, early-born cells migrate farthest, with later-born cells, as it were, lining up behind them. It is not known why the cerebral cortex differs in this, but it is known that a violation of its unique pattern can be a disaster.

That disaster occurs in the reeler mutant mouse. The reeler has a genetic defect: a recessive alteration of a known gene at a known locus on a known chromosome (chromosome 21, in fact)—a tiny chemical change in an otherwise perfectly normal mouse. This change, through a still unknown metabolic pathway, causes profound abnormalities in behavior, including obvious mental retardation and locomotor incapacity. Many of these abnormalities are traceable to equally profound abnormalities of structure in the cerebral cortex and the cerebellar cortex. The reeler, like many other mouse neurological mutants, is under intensive study by neuropathologists, who hope that a grasp of these genetically simple malformations will lead to inroads into devastating forms of inherited mental retardation in humans—some of which, genetically at least, are not intrinsically more complicated (although they are probably different) than the disorder of the reeler mutant mouse.

In the reeler, the beautiful laminated structure of the normal cerebral cortex is totally violated—literally turned upside down. Cells that belong on the bottom are on top, in the outermost layers, and cells that belong on top are on bottom. Initial speculations as to how the reeler cortex gets that way pointed to cell birthdays as a possible answer. Perhaps, so the hypothesis went, the genetic defect simply alters the timing of birth of cortical cells, so that their characteristic inside-out pattern of laying down is tragically mocked. An autoradiographic experiment in Sidman's laboratory proved this wrong; cell birthdays in this mutant were normal, and the earliest born cells were the size and shape they should have been, but were in very much the wrong place—on top instead of on bottom. This meant that the genetic defect could not be affecting, primarily, the timing of cell birth, but must rather mainly distort the migration path itself—or, perhaps, the "stop" signal. That is, we have narrowed the field of acceptable hypotheses somewhat, to the process of how the neural connections are specified.

This, of course, is only one obscure disorder in the mouse. But it has parallels in humans, if not exact ones, and it is hoped that the complete understanding of the process of brain development in mouse neurological mutants will lead to solutions of the puzzles posed by some forms of human mental retardation. Beyond that, it will also give us an understanding of how the genes of all mammals carry out their architectural plan for the building of the brain.

It is certainly far from clear how the cells of the early brain find their way in the morass of neural matrix, but here too the answers are dimly visible. The field of immunology, oddly enough, has spawned a rash of experiments in developmental biology, including the subfield of nervous-system growth. Immunology, dealing as it does with the capacity of cells to recognize other cells so as to either destroy them (if they are foreign) or leave them alone, suggests a whole range of hypotheses about the earliest differentiation of embryonic organs. If the body's cells can be genetically programmed to recognize tissue foreign to the host (as they do in graft rejection), then why not different populations of cells among themselves? Such recognition need not result in destruction, but it might well result in rejection, attraction, even adhesion; and to different degrees, so that many of the dramatic cell movements, the orderly mass migrations that make the brain and body what they are, could in fact be caused by an elaborate matrix of positive and negative mutual valences. As in immune reactions, the cells could recognize and attract or repel each other by virtue of chemical markers on their surface membranes, where they are most likely to come into contact with other cells. These markers, in turn, are easy to understand as products of the genes. Many laboratories are now focused on this problem of cell-cell recognition in the early embryo, so we can expect to find out a good deal about it soon.

The thoughtful reader, especially one suspicious of genes, may now be wondering how it can be that the cells of an embryo can produce such a variety of cell-surface markers—strong enough to produce adhesion, repulsion, and everything in between—when all the cells are genetically identical. Indeed, this flaw in our understanding continues to plague developmental biologists, as it has since the early days of twentieth-century embryology. All that can be said with confidence is that something about the physical disposition of cells, even after very few divisions of the fertilized egg, causes them to express, chemically, different aspects of their identical sets of genes. Once thus chemically differentiated, they have presumably committed themselves to distinctness and can influence one another chemically in a myriad of marvelous ways, among which are repulsion and adhesion.

This grows technical, I know, but there is method in it. We hear so much about the effects of genes on behavior, on intelligence, on emotions; this book is peppered with such generalizations. In order to escape, for once, from the terrible sense of "hand waving"—the sense we have, while listening to certain explanations, that some things happen by magic, or, at the very least, that the explainer has no idea how they happen—we have to get down into the abstruse mess of mechanism. For the genes to affect behavior or intelligence or emotion, they often must affect a bodily structure and how it grows. Most frequently that structure is the brain. It is in the earliest events of brain development that we are likely to see most clearly the effects of the genes on structural design in that organ; and to remove finally the sense that their work is magical, we must focus on the physical and chemical events of those early stages. It is there that we are likely to find points for the genes to get a handle on, and there, in consequence, that we are likely to see them in action, in a very specific sense, in the next few decades.

One area where the work of the genes may soon become apparent is the study of how these early cells get around. Much of the movement occurs in blocks; cells are dividing frequently, perhaps a bit faster at one pole or side of the embryo than the other, and shape changes are inevitable, with most of the movement caused by sheer mechanical shoving—guided, yes, but shoving nonetheless. Within such block movements, the chemical surface markers causing cells to adhere or repel can modify and direct the physical forces. Later, cell movement can become much more individualized; although whole populations are moving, each cell is moving on its own, and such movement is generally amoeboid. That is, the cell is soft, even jellylike; part of it slops in a certain direction and adheres until more of the cell follows.

Such amoeboid, migrating nerve cells can be thought of as chemically guided; it is probable that they have cell-surface markers that urge them along chemical gradients, toward higher and higher concentrations of an attractant, until they have reached their destined places. But they are also guided physically, and not just by being shoved en masse; some of them, at least, are guided by inching along structural tracks already laid in place. This is the case, for instance, in the cortex of both the cerebrum and cerebellum, where newborn nerve cells cling to elongated radial fibers—nonneural cells stretching through the cortex from the inner margin, where the nerve cells are born, to the outer cortical surface, where they must finally find their way.

Pasko Rakic of the Yale School of Medicine has described the long, slow climb of such cells along the radial fibers late in the embryonic life of the rhesus monkey, and Sidman and his colleagues have found that in another mouse mutant—the weaver—abnormalities in these "guide" fibers in the cortex of the cerebellum (a key motor control center) are the key to the disorder. If even one of the pair of genes at the critical locus on the chromosome pair is defective, the guide fibers will be enlarged and irregular; the adult mouse will have a cerebellum reduced in size by 5 to 10 percent. If both genes in the pair are defective, the guide fibers are almost absent, and the grossly abnormal cerebellum results in an animal with severe movement dysfunction, tremor, and general weakness. In the case of the single gene dosage, there is impaired migration of the nerve cells of the cortex and a resulting death of some of them; with a double dose, the failure to migrate is widespread, and nerve-cell death ubiquitous. Although the chemical links between the molecular structure of the defective gene and the abnormalities of the "guide" fibers have not yet been found, the gene dosage effect makes the pattern more comprehensible and real. More important, it raises the possibility that we will soon have a grasp of the mechanism of certain brain and behavior disorders that are subtle—that is, caused by a single, not-quite-recessive gene, with minor but measurable effects—not just the gross defects of mental retardation syndromes. And this step will bring us considerably closer to a behavior genetics of individual differences in the normal range.

Some progress has been made in the exploration of the chemical gradients that cause migrating nerve cells to go in one direction or another. Experiments on that set of problems constitute the first steps in cracking the chemical code by which migrating cells find their destined places. And when that code is cracked, it will be a short step to the genes that specify the signals in the code.

But beyond being attracted in a certain direction, the cells must of course actually make their destined connections. Some do so by trailing a long cell process behind them as the central cell body moves; this strategy removes the necessity for the cell process to find its way in a separate step. Others form connections that are purely local, so that cell processes don't have far to go. Some, however, must put out processes that are destined to become long axons. These will not have to cover a distance comparable to the length of the longest axons in the adult, because the embryo is of course much tinier; nevertheless, it can be thousands of times the length of the cell itself. Here the challenge to neuroembryologists is comparable to that of the pattern of cell migration itself: How does the growing axon move, how does it find its way, and how does it know when to stop?

These questions formed a central conflict in brain science until the mid-1960s. Briefly summarized, the conflict concerned the role of "chemospecificity"—the guidance of growing axon tips by highly specific chemical gradients—in the building of nervous system circuitry. The older (though not the oldest) view was that of Paul Weiss, who maintained through the middle decades of this century that the dominant forces were mechanical, involving the orienting effects of physical stress lines—something like the "shoving" referred to earlier; or to put it in a more dignified light, a sort of historical geology of submicroscopic structures. The "new" view, really a revival of the classic view of the early years of the century, is that of 1981 Nobel laureate Roger Sperry of the California Institute of Technology, who insisted, and gradually showed, that chemical affinities had much more to do with the guidance of nerve cell growth cones than Weiss would have liked to believe.

Sperry chose to study frogs and salamanders—phylogenetically simple enough to have substantial capacity for nerve regeneration (which the experiments required), yet complex enough and close enough to mammals so that upward generalization might be made with some confidence. In a long series of experiments, repeatedly challenged by the mechanical guidance school and repeatedly redesigned to meet the challenges, Sperry and his colleagues detached the eye from the brain and scrambled the connections. As time went on, the goal of each experiment was to make it increasingly difficult for regrowing axons to find their way, even to the point of mixing up the retina like a jigsaw puzzle. Regenerating fibers unerringly found their way to their correct sites of previous connection, even though the eye as a result functioned inappropriately (for instance, a flying insect appeared in one part of the visual field, and the tongue of the frog flicked out in another). This was viewed as strong evidence in favor of specific chemical labels, unresponsive to the scrambled cues of anatomy and experience.

As in the case of the migration of whole nerve cells, these facts about the role of chemical gradients in guiding the axons that grow out from those cells by no means rule out the possibility of a role for purely physical forces and other mechanical guides. For example, one means by which axons find their way is by following other axons, although to be sure this leaves an obvious question. In some parts of the brain—the hippocampus, for example, a structure that seems to play a role in memory and in integrating various forms of incoming sensory information—the timing of growth seems to be critical for the correct establishment of connections. Axon tips can evidently find their way by chemical means to the general vicinity where they must make their hippocampal connections, but not to the final local destination—unless they arrive at the right time. Altering their arrival time alters the circuits that will be formed, presumably because the hippocampus itself is at a different stage of development when the slower or faster connecting fibers arrive.

Another strategy, which plays its role after the connections are made, seems to be trial and error; some connections are made that are somehow later seen to be wrong, and these die off, leaving the more useful ones. Yes, *useful*. From the earliest moments of embryonic development, cells crucially influence one another, are of *use* to one another and to the embryo. Genes may do much of the guiding from within, but cells are keenly responsive to other cells. These cues from other cells may be cell-surface markers or purely mechanical forces, caused by the genes or just by the geographic layout and the movements entailed in growth. Some of the most fundamental events of development depend entirely on the juxtaposition of different tissues at critical moments. To take an example familiar from basic biology—and one of the oldest bits of knowledge in this field: the optic cup, which is destined to become the eye, is lensless in the early embryo. As it touches the epidermis—the outer shell of embryonic cells—it triggers the breaking off of some of the epidermal cells, and these become the rudiment of the lens. Any epidermal cells will do, so that an optic cup planted under the skin of the developing foot will also produce a lens; yet without some such epidermal contact, the lens of the eye will fail of its development. Before this event, eye growth proceeds more or less under its own steam; after it, reimplantation of the organ virtually anywhere in the body will still give you a more or less normal eye, though of course functionless because it lacks connections to the brain. Thus the developing eye is set up by evolution and, more immediately, by the genes, to do a good deal of the work on its own and yet to require, at a strategic moment, a key intervention by an outside tissue.

Thanks to a remarkable experiment in the laboratory of Stanley Crain, at the Albert Einstein College of Medicine, we know that it is possible for nerve cells to build themselves into most elaborate networks, with fully mature connections between cells, in the *absence* of any use. In Crain's ingenious strategy, explants—tiny fragments—of the cerebral cortex of the early fetal mouse were grown in tissue culture and, beginning at a time during development substantially before synapses (functional neural connections) are made, kept under anesthetic. The local anesthetic Xylocaine was applied to the fragments, because it was known to suppress all normal electrical functions of cultured nerves, whether spontaneous or evoked by stimulation, without causing the nerves permanent damage. In spite of total absence of stimulation or spontaneous electrical activity, the explants continued to develop under the anesthetic and produced organized neuronal assemblies—the basis of circuitry—including the characteristic substructures of the synapse as seen under the electron microscope. Reviewing their own work in relation to that of Sperry and others, Crain and his colleagues concluded: "Thus there is by now considerable evidence suggesting that specific interneuronal contacts are determined by genetic mechanisms during development, and that organized neuronal assemblies are formed in forward reference to their ultimate function."

Yet, for all the importance of internal structures in brain development, experience still affects neural connections. We encountered some of these phenomena earlier. Mark Rosenzweig, Marian Diamond, Edward Bennett, and others at the University of California at Berkeley showed that impoverishing or enriching the environment of rats, even aged rats, can affect the weight and thickness of the cerebral cortex, the ratio of supporting cells to nerve cells, the number and size of synapses, the amount of synaptic transmitter chemicals and their enzymes, the complexity of higher-order branching of dendrites, and the number of spines crowded onto a unit length of dendrite. Richard Coss and Albert Globus of the University of California at Davis have further shown that the *shape* of the dendritic spines is different in jewelfish reared in isolation and those that are community reared. The latter, evidently receiving much more stimulation, have spines that in cross-section look like squash racquets, with large, long heads and shorter stems, while cross-sections of the isolates' spines look more like badminton racquets, with small heads and long stems.

To be sure that this alteration did not apply only to the jewelfish, Coss and Globus reexamined the spines in photomicrographs from a similar study by Francisco Valverde of the Instituto Cajal in Madrid. This material, from mice reared either in light or in darkness, showed similar shape changes in the spines on the dendrites. Finally, Coss and Globus reviewed neurophysiological studies showing, again, similar shape changes in spines following intensive short-term stimulation of individual cells; these studies also demonstrated that such changes in structure are accompanied by functional changes. They reasoned that short-stemmed, fat-headed dendritic spines would provide less electrical resistance to incoming stimulation than would long-stemmed, small-headed ones (this follows from elementary principles of physics) and that such adaptive modification of structure would modify the responsiveness of the neural circuits, and thus the practical functioning of the brain.

How can these dramatic findings of structural change in response to experience be reconciled with the weight of evidence in favor of circuit-building in the absence of stimulation or even function? One thought that comes to mind is that embryonic events might proceed, in the absence of stimulation, to carve out gross circuit structure, and then postnatal refinements of this structure would be left to experience. Unfortunately for this neat theory, however, we have ample evidence that stimulation can play a major role in some aspects of embryonic brain growth, and that, conversely, some major events of postnatal brain development can proceed very nicely without the sorts of specific experience that might be expected to be relevant.

The fact of the matter is that no simple construct will ever subsume even what we know already, much less what we will soon know, about how the various tasks of brain design and construction are partitioned between the genes and the environment. Now that the discussion of heredity versus environment has transcended the "versus," passing beyond the question, Which? and the only slightly less useless question, How much? to the mature question, How? we must prepare ourselves to face the fact that this last is not one question at all, but thousands. For each system, for each moment in development, we may have on our hands a different balance, a different division of labor, a different integration of the functions of the genes and of the world. The roaring torrent of argument between the hereditarians and the environmentalists, narrow-minded bigots of different stripes, will undoubtedly continue; and, for the unsuspecting listener, it will obscure the complexity of the issues, and so in effect sabotage understanding. Meanwhile, a few individuals will continue to press forward the genuine scientific frontier of the field. Things have come far enough, though, so that any analysis of the causes of human nature that tends to ignore *either* the genes *or* the environmental factors may safely be discarded.

5

THE SEVERAL HUMOURS

The thoughts to which I am now giving utterance
and your thoughts regarding them are the expression of
molecular changes in that matter of life which is the
source of our other vital phenomena.
—Thomas Huxley, c. 1870, as quoted
by Charles Sherrington, *Man on
His Nature*

When I listen to intelligent people deny the importance of
the effects of genes in the causation of complex behavior, I sometimes
feel moved to take them kindly but firmly by the elbow, and escort
them to Las Ventas, the big *plaza de toros* in Madrid. After the
opening fanfare, after the deliberately arch parade of the *toreros* in
the sun, after the few quiet moments staring down at the empty ring,
a gate would be swung open and back, and there would prance or
stumble or plummet into view approximately four hundred kilos of
herbivorous mammal, masculine gender, not in a very pleasant frame
of mind. Ideally, seated on the environmentalist's other hand would
be an older, seasoned, dedicated follower of *toreo*, or better still,
perhaps, a former *torero*.

Now, not even the most extreme environmentalist would attempt
to explain the difference between the animal in view and the average
bovine of the male sex without referring to genes. No thoughtful
person would dream of denying that the dozens, possibly hundreds of
generations of careful breeding for the bullring that have preceded

our afternoon have produced a set of genes that is somehow critically "behind" the behavior of the fighting bull. But what might be less readily acknowledged—although it is equally evident to those who know the first things about bullfighting—is that each breeding ranch produces a strain with a characteristic set of behavioral tendencies and abilities. In one of the few books in English on the subject, it is summarized as follows:

> In a period of thirty-five years in the eighteenth century, the four great bloodlines that made modern toreo possible came into being: the Cabrera, in 1745; the Gallardo, about 1750; the Vistahermosa, in 1775; the Vazquez, in 1780. For a century, the Cabreras, an Andalusian strain developed from many localities in the Seville region, were noted for their size and bravery. They also became noted for sentido, the ability to distinguish the torero from the lure, thus diminishing their popularity. In 1852, Don Juan Miura bought the Cabrera stud and combined it with other Andalusian strains to produce the magnificent and murderous Miuras that we still see occasionally today.

The details of the behavior of specific strains can be specified much more precisely and for a larger number of strains. Indeed, the knowledgeable aficionado beside us at the *barrera* will feel quite confident in checking the ranch and strain of the six bulls on the card and predicting not only some features of their size and muscular strength, but many features of their behavior, including not only "bravery" and *sentido* but, for example, how straight and far they will charge under the lure before turning, how tightly they will turn, how inclined they will be to charge the horses, how many times they will accept the picador's lance, how tired they will be after fifteen minutes in the ring, how they will carry their heads after six *banderillas* have been placed in their neck muscles, how they will hook with their horns, how much they will tend to hook upward when the matador goes over their horns with the sword, and even how easily they will die.

Of course, it will not be possible to predict all this about each ranch or strain, and in any case these various features are not independent of each other or of the size and shape of body and horn and the distribution of muscle over skeleton. Furthermore, no prediction will apply in a simple or trivial way to every specimen of a strain, however famous it may be for a given characteristic. Finally, no scientific studies have validated these predictions. Nevertheless, the expert follower of the bulls will be able to say a few things about the most distinctive tendencies of the members of a strain. He or she will be right more often than not, and will be justified in feeling disappointed if those expectations are violated. The next day's newspaper reviews may vindicate that disappointment by specifically criticizing the breeding practices of the ranch, and, occasionally, by warning that the quality of the strain may be in danger.

There is no reason to believe that any important contributions to the predictability described above come from sources other than the genes. Fighting bulls are not trained for the *plaza*; they are merely bred. Meticulous precautions are taken so that they will rarely if ever have seen a man on foot before they enter the ring and see the matador. They see ranch hands on horses as they are growing up, but these do not engage them in any unfriendly intercourse. There is opportunity for a playful or perhaps serious locking of horns with other bulls; but at no time are there experiences of the sort that the animal will have during the last fifteen minutes of its life, in response to which it will exhibit the behaviors that must either contribute to or detract from the prior reputation of the strain. At no time will there have been an opportunity to observe and copy models of behavior in that situation.

It is remotely possible that intrauterine effects—resulting from the chemical environment acting on the fetus, created by the mother's hormones—play an important role in the development of some behavioral tendencies. But such effects are poorly understood, and at the moment are more speculative than are genetic effects. Learning, too, must play some role in these behaviors. It is likely that aggressive play with other bulls on the ranch makes possible the maturation of the behavioral tendencies of interest; still, the inclination to learn certain things at a certain pace in a certain way is of great professional interest to the geneticist—as great as the interest in the emergence of behaviors that require essentially no learning. Indeed, *sentido*—the ability to distinguish the man from the lure—is something that a fighting bull learns rather quickly at the end of his life, in his only arena episode. That is why it is deemed essential to prevent developing bulls from seeing a man on foot. Such experience would increase the tendency to ignore the lure and go directly for the man, making *toreo* impossible; it is intended not as fair fight, but as skillful, graceful, courageous ritual slaughter. What *sentido* describes, then, is the ease with which the various strains carry out this process of learning under conditions of stress and pain; the differences in *sentido* among the strains are genetic differences in learning ability—specific to a narrow range of behavior and a spectacularly peculiar situation.

Of course, this is not science, it is only common sense; and, at that, the common sense of members of one particular subculture to whom most of the rest of the world—or, at least, the Anglo-Saxon world—feels superior. A place where common sense and science converge beautifully is in the analysis of the behavior of breeds of dogs. Take, for example, the cocker spaniel and the English bulldog. No one would think of suggesting that the distinctive stamp of face and body on these two very-different-looking animals results from anything but differences in the concatenation of their genes, created by hundreds of generations of deliberate and very restrictive breeding. By this point in the history of behavioral science we should have no more difficulty in admitting that the equally distinctive stamp on the behavior and "personality" of spaniels and bulldogs is also—perhaps equally—the product of genes, operating during the course of development on the nervous and endocrine systems, rather than on bone, muscle, and skin.

John Paul Scott and John L. Fuller were, in the 1950s and 1960s, taking this possibility very seriously. At their kennel-laboratories at Bar Harbor in Maine, using the standard methods of laboratory genetics for physical traits, they investigated the genetic control of distinctive behavioral characteristics in five pure dog breeds: the wirehaired fox terrier, the American cocker spaniel, the African basenji, the Shetland sheep dog, and the beagle. Each breed has special behavioral features, and all were subjected to Scott and Fuller's genetic analyses. But much of the work focused on two of the breeds—the cocker and the basenji—and on hybrids between them, since it is hybrids of the first and second generation that provide crucial clues to the mode of inheritance. They proceeded very much as Gregor Mendel did in his classic experiments on the inheritance of height and color in pea plants.

Although not the two most different breeds of the five, the cocker and the basenji are very different. The first is, of course, the favorite American family dog, good with children, friendly, tame. Its history involves breeding as a hunting aid, but primarily for use in retrieving, not for assault or chase. The basenji is a hunting dog used by the Central African Pygmies. Although we have no details of its breeding history, the short-haired, short-eared dog (it resembles a spaniel-size boxer) has been used by the Pygmies and other Africans as a general-purpose hunting dog. Expectations for it probably included chase and attack, either alone or in groups, and the likelihood that it received or expected the sort of kindness that we lavish on cocker spaniels is, given the general attitude of rural African people toward dogs, nil. On the contrary, those basenjis that lived to breed were probably tough survivors, able to cooperate with humans without depending upon or offering affection. In the laboratory they are obviously wilder than cockers, struggling against restraint more and vocalizing and avoiding more in response to handling. They are very timid and fearful of humans at five weeks of age, yelping and snapping when cornered, running away, and generally acting like wild animals. At thirteen to fifteen weeks of age, they show more playful aggressiveness to human handlers than do cocker spaniels, and throughout life show less tendency to be quiet when weighed.

From what is known of the cocker spaniel breeding tradition, it is likely that their behavior results largely from two key criteria in breeding selection: crouching in response to an upraised hand and the highly restrained biting—"soft mouth"—essential for good retrieving. For at least dozens of cocker spaniel generations, owners preferentially bred those dogs that exhibited those features most clearly. Other differences, perhaps incidental to deliberate breeding history, are that basenjis bark much less, producing instead a wailing or yodeling sound, and breed only once a year, while cocker spaniels breed semiannually.

Scott and Fuller's analysis of the trait of playful aggression in the two breeds provides a representative example of their approach. In the test, given at thirteen to fifteen weeks of age, basenji puppies are much more likely to leap playfully at the handler, nipping at or wrestling with his hand. First-generation hybrids between the breeds are intermediate; they are equally likely to show any of the nine measured levels of playful aggressiveness. The second-generation hybrids (products of matings between male and female first-generation hybrids) are, like their parents, very variable, showing the whole range of levels of playful aggressiveness.

But the backcrosses (first-generation hybrids mated with pure basenjis or pure cocker spaniels) tend strongly back to the characteristics of the pure breeds. These findings are *consistent with* the hypothesis that the trait of playful aggressiveness in dogs is controlled by two genes that somehow regulate the threshold for aggressiveness, with neither gene locus allowing much dominance or recessiveness. That is, at each of the two loci in the first-generation hybrids, the basenji and cocker traits will coexist without either dominating the other. I emphasize "consistent with" because these findings do not prove that the situation is not more complicated than the hypothesis suggests; merely that it is not more simple. It is common practice in these experiments—and good science in most cases—to propose the simplest theory consistent with the data, until the data force a more complex hypothesis upon us.

Tests run on a second trait, fearfulness, contrast with the findings for playful aggression while confirming the simple hypothesis. In this instance, avoidance and vocalization in reaction to human handling at five weeks were tested. A majority of cocker spaniels showed no fearfulness, while all basenjis showed some. The first-generation hybrids, which had equal doses of basenji and cocker genes, behaved very much like basenjis. This suggests the action of one or more genes for which basenjis carry dominant versions. The distribution of the second-generation hybrids (three-fourths fearful, one-fourth tame) and of the cocker backcrosses (half and half) support and perhaps constrain us to a very simple hypothesis. Unlike playful aggressiveness, fearfulness—avoidance and vocalization in reaction to handling—in the dog is controlled by a single gene locus for which basenjis, the traditional dog of African Pygmy hunters, carry an "allele" or variant that is chemically dominant over the variant carried in the corresponding locus of the gene complex of the American cocker spaniel.

How could it be that such a simple chemical change—perhaps a substitution of only one nucleotide base of a vastly long chain of DNA—could effect such a specific change in so complex a behavior? It would be disingenuous to suggest that the answer to this question is near at hand. In fact, little is known of the developmental genetics of dog behavior—the process by which a minor change in a molecule of DNA can produce changes in chemical reactions in the nervous or endocrine systems, in the developing organism or the adult, which can plausibly account for corresponding observed behavioral changes. But there is much evidence from other species, including humans. At present it applies only to abnormal behaviors, including the profound abnormalities of the mentally retarded. It is both sensible and useful to begin with these abnormalities, since research on them may lead to improved treatment or prevention programs. But it is also assumed that the links between these and the more subtle processes of the normal range of human variation will gradually begin to become clear.

As noted in the last chapter, extensive and distinguished scientific attention has been devoted to the genetics of mouse neurological disorders. The examples of the reeler mouse and the weaver mouse have already been considered. There are literally dozens of other mouse neurological mutants under study, and several laboratories are slowly approaching the point at which they will be able to give a complete account of the chemical reactions that cause the abnormal behaviors, beginning with the simple single-gene mutation, going through the biochemical steps of structural development, and terminating with an established theory of how the altered brain structure produces the behavioral abnormality.

This is already nearly possible for at least two human mental disorders. In phenylketonuria (PKU), a severe form of mental retardation that is now treatable, much of the chemical story is in place. We know that there is a defective enzyme, and that the defect is caused by a single gene mutation; we even know what chromosome the mutation is on. The fact that a baby must have a double dose of the gene—one from each parent—to have the disorder tells us that the normal variant of the gene, if it appears beside the abnormal one, will somehow chemically dominate, and no disorder will appear. (The abnormal variant of the gene is said in such a case to be *recessive*.) We do not know the precise structure of the enzyme that is defective or of the gene itself—the molecule of DNA—that ultimately generates it. But we know much about the functions of the enzyme, and how a simple defect in it can cause a child to lose that most precious of human possessions, a normally functioning brain. While the normal human behaviors, emotions, and intellective capacities considered later in this book bear little resemblance to the profound malfunctions of the mind of the child afflicted with phenylketonuria, they and variations in them will one day be seen to result, in part, from similar genetic and enzymatic mechanisms.

The enzyme that is defective in phenylketonuria is called phenylalanine hydroxylase. Like all enzymes it is known by what it does: changing a molecule called phenylalanine to a slightly different structure with very different functions, called tyrosine. Phenylalanine is an amino acid; we get it by eating protein. Its conversion to tyrosine, and thereafter to other compounds, is perfectly normal and simple except in the phenylketonuric child. In that child, the defective pair of genes causes all molecules of the critical enzyme, phenylalanine hydroxylase, to be abnormal in chemical sequence and thus, inevitably, in shape. The shape change impairs its ability to do its principal work: the facilitation of the reaction by which phenylalanine is transformed. The phenylalanine, ingested in large amounts along with the rest of the protein in the diet, instead of being converted to tyrosine, builds up behind the enzyme block. A major normal mechanism for its removal is lost, and it simply stays in the brain. Tragically, it is poisonous to nerve cells, simply kills them. It can be treated with almost complete success by keeping phenylalanine out of the diet, and many states now require universal screening of newborn babies for high levels of phenylalanine in the urine—a key sign of abnormal phenylalanine hydroxylase—so that the diet can begin almost at birth.

In another condition of severe human mental retardation, an enzyme known as beta-galactosidase is defective, also due to a recessive single-gene mutation. This causes a metabolic block in another fundamental chain of biochemical synthesis, with the result that a compound normally removed builds up to toxic levels. Thanks to long-term, elegant studies by Dominick Purpura of the Albert Einstein College of Medicine in New York, we now have some idea of the neuropathology of this syndrome, down to the level of the nerve cell as observed under the electron microscope. Cell processes take on an extremely abnormal shape in this condition and distort the normal functions of electrical transmission to the point where competent mental abilities are lost. The abnormal shape is caused, in turn, by the toxin.

In effect, the link from gene to enzyme defect to toxin to abnormal cell is clear in these two disorders. Furthermore, in each case, the functional defect—the defect in how the brain works—can be plausibly derived from the abnormalities of cell structure; by the very laws of electric conduction, such cells must malfunction badly. It may all seem obvious in retrospect; it may seem, indeed, that medical science should have figured out so simple a system very long ago. But in fact most of these links rest on discoveries made in the last two decades. Given the advances of the last few years in the analysis of the genetic materials and their chemical mechanisms, it will only be a matter of time before every detail of the process is filled in, beginning with the outline now in hand. We are thus on the verge of complete explanation of certain disorders of the human mind, beginning with a chemical change in a gene.

But we can't get away quite so easily. Phenylketonuria, by far the best understood of such conditions, is caused by a poison in the diet; remove the poison and you get no disorder, despite the fact that the genes are still in place and still abnormal. Of course, the "poison" is no poison to most people; only to those with the gene defect. But the fact remains that this is a disease of the mind that is totally genetic and totally environmental at one and the same time. No more impressive evidence can be brought to bear against the folly of trying to partition mental and behavioral characteristics into percentages of genetic and environmental causation.

Nor can one find a better proof of the fact that the discovery of a genetic determination for a disorder may provide the best hope for an environmental treatment of it. Only the knowledge of the *genetic* determination of the disorder gave us a chance to identify, at birth, those infants who would be poisoned by phenylalanine; and only that identification could lead to a change in the *environment* that would save them.

And in this era of genetic engineering it is only fair to point out that the discovery of genetic determination of a disorder now holds out another hope—albeit one that will not be realized in the immediate future. That is the hope of intervening to alter the genetic machinery with the techniques of recombinant DNA. It is at this stage a dream, but not an empty one.

Now such studies as these of severe mental retardation syndromes (and the earlier mentioned ones of profoundly disabling single-gene neurological defects in the mouse) are accepted as evidence of genetic influence on the brain and on the mind by even the most skeptical opponents of biological theories of behavior and mental competence. What they do not accept is the notion that this has anything to do with behaviors within the normal range, or even with less severe abnormalities such as emotional disturbances and mental illnesses. They would never concede that the perfectly clear research we now have on some severe disorders of mice and men provides suggestive evidence for less abnormal behavior. And they insist that there is little or no evidence of similar metabolic effects on normal behaviors.

For example, in the above-mentioned case of the apparent single-gene control of fearful reaction to handling in two dog breeds, skeptics will remain skeptical until it can be shown that underlying fearfulness there is a metabolic chain leading to a structural difference in the neural or endocrine systems; or, at least, leading to a stable difference in the level or rate of production of one or another of the behavioral molecules—hormones, neurotransmitters, and their related enzymes. Furthermore, skeptics will require us to show an enzymatic difference between cockers and basenjis, resulting *from* the proposed single-gene difference and resulting *in* the structural or "behaviorochemical" difference. That would begin to substantiate the hypothesis of continuity between severe disorders and normal differences, at the level of genetic control.

No such account exists, or is likely to exist soon, in the case of the fearful behavior of basenjis and cocker spaniels. But the extreme environmentalists are being shaken from their complacency by a good deal of research on other animals, from the fruit fly *Drosophila melanogaster* to the peculiar bipedal primate *Homo sapiens*. Let us consider some of this evidence, beginning with the simplest of the systems.

When Seymour Benzer (now professor of biology at the California Institute of Technology) became interested in brain function, he took a crash course in neuroanatomy from a famous and excellent teacher—Walle Nauta of M.I.T. He was already widely known for his work on the genetics of viruses and for his role in the elucidation of the elegant code by which the simple language of the sequence of DNA is translated into the different language of protein sequences. He concluded from his course of study of the mammalian brain that "everything in the brain is connected to everything else," and determined to find a simpler, more tractable system.

This he found in the common, well-studied fruit fly, and he has now devoted about fifteen years to the analysis of its behavior genetics. Unsatisfied with single-pronged research approaches, he and his colleagues have set themselves a task no less than that of completely characterizing the determination of behavior in a wide variety of fruit-fly mutants, beginning with the gene and ending with the behavior. For an increasing number of behavioral mutants of this fly, it can now be specified on which chromosome (and where on the chromosome) the single gene responsible is located; where on the map of the developing embryo, in its earliest phases, the gene first finds expression; what structural change in nerve cell, sense receptor, or muscle accounts for the behavioral feature in question; and how, in a chemical sense, the gene produces the causative structural change. This, incidentally, is the advantage of studying simple systems, as Benzer well knew when he gave up on mammals; one group of scientists, in about the length of a lifetime, can perhaps hope to arrive at a global characterization of how the system works. It is a level of knowledge that cannot be hoped for in complex systems without a much greater outlay of scientific manpower, and it has dividends of its own for understanding.

Some of the fly mutants have grave disorders, like the mouse neurological mutants. One, half-jokingly called the *drop-dead* mutant, emerges from the pupal state and behaves completely normally for a day or two, after which, within a few hours, it becomes less active and uncoordinated, and finally falls on its back and dies. The syndrome begins with a recessive gene on the X chromosome and can be traced thereafter to a part of the early embryo that is destined to become the brain. At the point at which the disorder appears, the brain becomes rapidly full of holes, due to a factor intrinsic to itself, caused by the gene. Of course, this *drop-dead* mutant is no more interesting from the viewpoint of normal behavior—probably less—than the severest of mouse neurological mutants. But it is only the most extreme case.

Among the other single-gene mutants under study in this manner are much more complex behaviors of much subtler adaptive significance. These include alterations in many fruit fly fixed action patterns ("instinctive behaviors") such as the tendency to approach the light, the tendency to climb away from gravity, and the ability to regulate behavior on a twenty-four-hour cycle. (Mutants with nineteen-hour and twenty-eight-hour cycles have been found, and Benzer speculates—not too seriously, I suspect—on the possible implications for human "early birds" and "night owls.")

One mutant is more sluggish in its movements than the normal, another faster. The *easily shocked* mutant has a seizure in response to a mechanical jolt, recovering after a few minutes to go about its business. *Paralyzed* is only paralyzed when the temperature goes above 28°C (82°F) and promptly revives as soon as the temperature drops; while *comatose*, also normal except at high temperatures, takes much longer to recover, depending on how long it was exposed to the heat. (Electrical function in the motor nerves is depressed and revives only slowly.) Most intriguing are the mutations affecting courtship and sex, highly stereotyped behavior in the fruit fly: One type of mutant male courts, but with less than normal vigor; another pursues males as enthusiastically as females; another—called *stuck*—gets stuck during copulation and fails to disengage, while yet another—*coitus interruptus*—needs no introduction.

What is particularly interesting about this series of investigations is that mutants range from the most severe abnormalities through milder disorders to behavioral differences that might conceivably be within the normal range in the wild. They include several behavioral syndromes that only appear under certain environmental conditions and are responsive to varying degrees of environmental manipulation, and they even extend to genetic differences in learning ability. Yet they are all single-gene changes—operating through a wide variety of body systems and chemical mechanisms, but fundamentally similar in principle. For the fruit fly, then, the existence of continuity between the way severe behavioral disorders are controlled and the way at least some subtler differences are controlled, has been effectively established. This is not to say that other fruit-fly behaviors are not controlled differently; for example, a behavior may be a complex result of many genes acting in concert rather than one acting alone; or primarily the result of diet or temperature during growth; or the result of learning. It does not even say that the behaviors shown to be simply controlled are not subject to many other influences. What it does show is that some relatively subtle behaviors, such as would be of great interest to the natural historian, are in large part the result of causes that are genetic in the simplest, most concrete sense.

In the case of the laboratory mouse, a creature with thousands of times the brain capacity of the fruit fly, we have already glimpsed one end of the subtle-severe continuum. Can we do anything to extend the range of genetically influenced behaviors toward the more normal, for this much more interesting animal? The question has an emphatic affirmative answer. In many experiments it has now been shown that mouse strains that classically differ genetically exhibit differences in behavior that are correlated with, and perhaps result from, differences in metabolism. For example, thyroid gland activity is correlated with locomotor activity in four strains; differences in brain serotonin (an important neurotransmitter) are correlated with differences in "emotionality" (measured by defecation in a strange environment) in two strains; differences in the neurotransmitters serotonin, norepinephrine, and dopamine in the brain have been reported to explain strain differences in reaction to shock; strain differences in the activity of the liver enzyme alcohol dehydrogenase are believed at least by some investigators to explain strain differences in alcohol preference; strain differences in susceptibility to seizures produced by a noxious noise seem to be under the control of two separate gene loci, one affecting ATP metabolism (basic to energy generation) in the brain structure known as the hippocampus, the other affecting glutamic acid metabolism; and strain differences in sensitivity to androgens (male sex hormones) seem to account for some observed differences in copulatory behavior. The strains of mice in these experiments are raised in the same environments and differ, essentially, only in their genes.

One need not accept with a high level of certainty every item on this list to conclude that in the mouse, as in the fruit fly, many relatively subtle behavioral differences are under genetic control (this has been known for a long time) and (newer and more important) plausible physiological mediators can be proposed as links between the genes and the behaviors. Most interesting, perhaps, is that these studies of varieties of normal mice offer a much more subtle behavioral physiology than do those of the mouse or fruit fly neurological mutants. Far from the fairly obvious corruptions of brain anatomy that were seen in those cases, what we have here in each case is a chemical difference: the level of a neurotransmitter; the turnover of a hormone; the activity of an enzyme; the availability of an energy-generating molecule; the sensitivity of receptors for a humoral factor from the gonads. It is possible that close observation will reveal some obvious structural pathology determined by the genes, but it is not likely. More probably we will remain in the realm of the messily, actively chemical, the realm in which altered tendencies to action of various nerves and muscles, due to various chemicals, is the order of the day. Subtle behavior, subtle physiology—yet still partly determined by the genes.

Thus in a creature as complex as the mouse, one quite closely related to us as the world of animals goes, we have the outline of a genetically caused physiology of behavior, without even leaving the province of single genes. There is less extensive information of this kind available for rats, dogs, and other mammals. But the next higher creature for which information becomes substantial is none other than ourselves.

Human behavioral genetics is the most dreadfully controversial of all pursuits in behavioral biology, even more so than the study of sex differences. Skeptics are justified in their skepticism by past failings and excesses of the field. Most dramatically, we have the use of behavior-genetic-like theories (although they have really been very ignorant) to support political repression and mass extermination. Such efforts extend from the distant past up to the present day.

Less dramatic, but equally indicative, is the sloppiness of what has often passed for respectable research in this field. In the twin studies on which so much of recent theory is based, the statistical procedures of inference have usually been simply inappropriate to the task, and given the relatively small numbers of twin pairs, findings could easily have arisen by chance. Also, it may turn out that genetically identical twins are more similar than nonidentical twins because parents treat them more similarly, and in fact there is now some evidence that this is in part the case. Moreover, some famous studies of identical twins reared apart did not insure against separate but highly similar rearing, and in some cases "separated" twins went to the same school and were in frequent contact.

Statistical procedures drawn from the experimental literature on heritability make assumptions (for example, random assignment of genetic strains to environments) that certainly do not apply to humans, yet these procedures have been relied on as if they did. (Resulting estimates, for instance, of the heritability of IQ range from about 45 percent to about 80 percent, which in itself should be sufficient to make us doubtful.) These estimates are also based on the assumption that a given genetic endowment A will compare with another endowment B in a consistent way regardless of the environment, an assumption that has already been shown to be false, both in animals and humans.

Finally, and worst of all, some of the most famous twin data on the inheritance of IQ were simply faked. As shown recently by a reluctant historian of British psychology, L.S. Hearnshaw, the famous psychometrician Sir Cyril Burt either made up twin correlations, or at the very least repeated the same ones several different times, claiming they were from different studies (exact to three decimal places!) and even, astoundingly, invented co-workers and co-authors for papers written (and "researched") entirely by himself. It is difficult to interpret this history of sloppiness and misrepresentation except by reference to a long-standing human prejudice in favor of the belief that blood is destiny.

Better twin studies are now being done; but it is likely that future advances in human behavioral genetics will not be made in the old manner in which identical twins, fraternal twins, and siblings are compared on some measure and a questionable statistical operation produces a percentage estimate of heritability. Twin studies can be indicative, but the real advances will come from metabolic studies of the sort described above for nonhuman animals, and for severe human disorders.

One extensively studied problem is schizophrenia, a human psychosis characterized by emotional withdrawal and thought disorder, among other symptoms. The chronic form often required chronic hospitalization before the advent of antipsychotic drugs; there is also an acute form with long periods of remission to normal behavior between attacks; and there are a series of syndromes that may be related but are much less serious, known as the schizophrenia spectrum disorders. From many studies it was known that the identical twin of a schizophrenic has an average of 50 percent probability of being or becoming schizophrenic, whereas a randomly chosen person of the same age and sex in the general population has a probability of less than 1 percent of contracting this illness, and a nonidentical twin or a sibling has a probability somewhere in the neighborhood of 15 percent.

Dissatisfied with the twin studies for the usual reasons, Seymour Kety, a physician-scientist at Maclean Hospital in Massachusetts, mounted an elegant and conclusive study that demonstrated to the satisfaction of almost everyone that an important part of the basis of schizophrenia is traceable to the genes. He and his colleagues (David Rosenthal, Paul Wender, Fini Schulsinger, and Bjørn Jacobsen) hit on the strategy of studying adopted children in a large population. They had access to excellent Danish records that included the adoptive population between the ages of twenty and forty-five in Greater Copenhagen at the time of the study, a total of more than 5,000 individuals. Of these, 33 were diagnosed as schizophrenic (a typical incidence level) and 28 of the 33 had been adopted away from their biological parents before the age of six months. These 33 were carefully matched with 33 nonschizophrenic adoptees for demographic and economic characteristics, and several hundred relatives (adoptive and biological) of the two groups were identified and interviewed (participation by identified relatives was 90 percent).

Several different ways of breaking down the data, using several different levels of severity of schizophrenia as the criteria, all resulted in the same conclusion, always highly significant statistically. Taking only one representative breakdown, that of the relatives of individuals adopted away *before the age of one month*, the results were as follows: The incidence of schizophrenia in the biological relatives of nonschizophrenic adoptees was 0 in 92; the incidence in the adoptive relatives of the same nonschizophrenic adoptees was 1 in 51; the incidence in the adoptive relatives of schizophrenic adoptees was 2 in 45. None of these three incidences was significantly different from the others. The incidence in the *biological* relatives of schizophrenic adoptees was 9 in 93, an incidence of almost 10 percent, much higher than in the other groups of relatives or the general population, and comparable to the levels in the biological relatives of schizophrenics who are not adopted away.

This study, conducted by excellent and scrupulous investigators, using every care and control that had been absent from many earlier studies, demonstrated beyond doubt that a significant part of the basis of schizophrenia is genetic. In fact, it is the best study so far in the whole field of human behavior genetics, and as close as human studies are likely to come to experimental rigor. But it remained for other investigators to satisfy the need for a convincing metabolic story, a series of links from the gene to the disturbance of feeling, thought, and behavior—links that must be chemical, physiological, and perhaps structural.

Hundreds of investigators have been in pursuit of this possibility, and while it would be wrong to say that a conclusion is available— schizophrenia may in any case turn out to be a final common pathway for the operation of several separate causes, including several genes— it is possible to point to some very promising inroads.

Many of the studies have focused on brain neurotransmitters. Drugs that are successful in the treatment of schizophrenia, although they have a variety of actions, share one action in common:

All block the receptors for dopamine in the synapses (gaps between nerve cells) that use dopamine as their neurotransmitter. The effect is thus to reduce the communication between dopamine-secreting neurons and the next cells in the circuits they participate in. Amphetamine, which usually exacerbates the symptoms of schizophrenia, and which in large doses can produce a full-blown psychosis resembling schizophrenia in major features, has the effect of stimulating dopamine receptors, the opposite of the effect of antischizophrenic drugs. These and many other pieces of evidence have led investigators to focus attention on the functioning of the neurotransmitter dopamine, even though the mechanism by which it could cause psychotic symptoms is poorly understood and despite the fact that, in small quantities, neither dopamine nor amphetamine can cause hallucinations.

This latter reservation is not true of some other compounds—the hallucinogenic or "psychotomimetic" drugs—and consequently there have been theories suggesting that the psychotic brain might somehow be making such compounds from its own sources. Since we know of several classes of drugs that cause hallucinations, and since some of these are closely related to chemicals used by the brain as neurotransmitters, it has not seemed farfetched to reason that the brain itself might generate such chemicals. These might resemble LSD, which would suggest some disorder of the neurotransmitter serotonin, a chemical relative of LSD (close enough, in fact, so that LSD seems to have its effect by fooling certain receptors for serotonin). Or they might resemble mescaline, the active hallucinogen in the peyote plant; this could implicate either dopamine or norepinephrine, two neurotransmitters similar in chemical structure to mescaline.

Finally, there has even been a theory that an error of norepinephrine production might result in a toxin that could poison the nerve cells responsible for the experience of pleasure and reward in the brain, which might in turn give rise to the psychosis. This would be partly analogous to the well-understood mental retardation syndromes discussed earlier; but no such structural defect has been seen in the brains of schizophrenic patients.

None of these biochemical analyses is proven, but each is plausible, respectable, and the subject of much serious investigation. In addition, there are other neurotransmitters, hormones, and brain chemicals that modulate nervous activity and that have been implicated in schizophrenia in even more complex ways. Wherever a molecule is implicated—its level, its rate of production, its rate of removal, or the sensitivity of receptors for it—there lies an opportunity for a gene. A small change in a single gene, causing a change in a single enzyme, could, by altering these factors, be responsible for profound abnormalities in behavior—or, for that matter, for subtle ones.

This possibility has not been lost on investigators, and their enthusiasm was if anything heightened by the recent conclusive demonstration by Kety and his colleagues that schizophrenia is partly genetic in basis. For every molecule thought to be a serious candidate for a mechanism of schizophrenia, there are enzymes of production and removal that can be and have been studied. For example, an enzyme called monoamine oxidase (MAO) is responsible for removal, by oxidation, of a wide variety of brain neurotransmitters, including dopamine, norepinephrine, serotonin, and related molecules. The activity of MAO is reduced in the blood of schizophrenic patients compared with nonschizophrenic controls. Although its level in the brain is more difficult to measure, there is indirect evidence that there too its activity is reduced. The effect of this might be to leave an excess of one or more of the above neurotransmitters, which might then cause hyperstimulation itself or be converted to something toxic. A defective version of the enzyme MAO could be produced by a single gene or pair of genes, leading to reduced MAO activity.

Another enzymatic candidate for producing schizophrenia is related to the LSD-type theories: A little-known enzyme in the blood, it is capable of forming the molecule dimethyltryptamine (DMT), a hallucinogen related to LSD. This enzyme has been shown to be more active in the blood of schizophrenics than in normal controls. Theoretically, it could generate levels of DMT in the brain high enough to cause the delusions or hallucinations experienced by many schizophrenics.

But perhaps the best possibility of this kind is dopamine beta hydroxylase, the enzyme that converts dopamine to norepinephrine.

For one thing, this enzyme, known as DBH, has been found in postmortem examination to have lower activity in several regions of the brains of schizophrenics than in the same regions of the brains of normal controls. And in the acute form of schizophrenia, patients have been shown to have higher levels of DBH activity during psychotic states than after those states have passed.

But undoubtedly one of the most interesting things about DBH activity is that it has been shown to be heritable. At least in blood, very low levels of DBH activity imply that one's siblings and other primary relatives will have much lower levels than the general population. Also, genetically identical twins have more similar levels than do nonidentical twins. Although more complex explanations are possible, the simplest explanation consistent with the facts is that very low serum DBH activity is the result of a single recessive gene—that is, it is usually masked by a normal gene in the pair, but only partly—and it is not sex-linked. Carefully studied family pedigrees and other lines of investigation support this analysis.

It is not known as yet whether families carrying this gene have a greater or lesser chance of having schizophrenia than do other families; the samples are still too small. But the fact is that a specific body chemical, perhaps involved in schizophrenia in one of several possible ways, has been shown to be subject to a simply inherited change. This should make us hopeful about the prospect of a genetic account in the future, at least for some subgroup of schizophrenics.

It may seem that we have strayed far from the genes, but in fact we are near to them. The knowledge that an enzyme is defective in some way is strong evidence that the gene that makes it has an error: a mutation that alters its own sequence and, in turn, alters the sequence that it codes for in the enzyme. An enzyme is a protein, and it takes on an intricate three-dimensional shape of piles and coils and folds related to its function. It catalyzes—speeds up—a chemical reaction in the body, such as the conversion of dopamine to norepinephrine, by attracting the key reactants to its complicated surface in such a way as to urge them into position to work on each other. Changes in shape affect their ability to do this; changes in sequence change shape; and changes in genes change sequence. Thus it comes about that without a major structural manifestation, such as damage to a nerve cell or hormonal organ, a genetic alteration changes the rate of production of a molecule that affects the way we act, think, or feel.

We have at least one other provisional account of such a process in human behavior, aside from those in the grossly abnormal range. It begins with a single-gene recessive defect that alters an enzyme called "steroid 21-hydroxylase." The steroids, small but intricate molecules, are important hormones affecting behavior. All are made from cholesterol and have a beautiful four-ringed structure with various side chains added or deleted. All the main links are carbon atoms, and, depending chiefly on the side chains, the molecule in question can be, for example, testosterone, the male sex hormone; estradiol, the female sex hormone; progesterone, another female sex hormone, which is also the hormone of pregnancy; or cortisol, a hormone broadly useful in response to stress. All the metabolic paths start by changing cholesterol into progesterone, but after that, different things happen in the testis, ovary, placenta, and adrenal cortex, which make the four hormones, among others. These different metabolic routes depend on the presence of different enzymes, which add or clip off various steroid side-chains.

The enzyme we are concerned with here is one of three responsible for changing progesterone, one of the early products in the chain, to cortisol, the main human stress hormone. This takes place in the cortex or outer portion of the adrenal gland, and cortisol is normally the major product of that portion of the gland. But because of the genetic defect in steroid 21-hydroxylase deficiency, the pathway of cortisol production is blocked, with the result that the progesterone is forced into a different production path—one that normally takes place only in the gonads and that leads to the male hormone testosterone and other androgens. If the individual is a girl, she will have higher levels of androgens during early development than other girls. There is evidence that this may result in a higher level of aggressive behavior in childhood, even if corrected at birth. This is a first example of a demonstrable single-gene effect on a behavior that can be considered to be in the normal range.

Finally, recent investigations have identified a gene or group of genes on human chromosome 6 that correlate with familial depressive disorders. This finding has opened a new frontier of research in the biology of depression, and has given new weight to the study of specific genetic influences on human behavior.

But how does all this apply to the variations we see and feel in ourselves and others around us, in the basic human emotions and their attendant behaviors, in everyday life?

The Elizabethans had the view, acquired from the ancients, that human behavioral dispositions, and even character, were the result of four body substances, which they called "humours." While no one had one or another of them exclusively, each person was believed to have a unique balance of humours, and some individuals had so great a predominance of one bodily fluid as to cause unfortunate consequences for behavior and mood. A "sanguine" temperament, reflecting a predominance of blood, might in moderation be warm, cheerful, lively, and hopeful, even associated with a healthy, ruddy complexion, but carried to excess would be too animated and passionate. The "phlegmatic," who had a predominance of phlegm, could be sluggish, apathetic, and dull, although phlegm in a normal person could make him simply cool, calm, imperturbable. There were two types of bile, one producing the "choleric" or angry temperament, the other producing the "melancholic" or depressed, and these completed the array of four types. A wide variety of intermediate temperaments could be produced by an appropriate subtle mixing of the four fluids, but only an ideal balance could result in an ideal person with ideal moods.

While we can smirk at these notions today, they have a piece of the truth that has been missing from analyses of human behavior for some decades; a piece that has two separate components.

The first has to do with what psychologists call motivation. Since the turn of the century most of psychology has been under the influence of the concept of "drive," according to which behaviors are energized (driven) by specific forces, innate or acquired, that cause the organism to eat, or have sex, or explore the environment. These "forces"—as psychological concepts—began as analogies to the mechanical forces that exist in a hydraulic pressure system, and the "consummatory acts" (say, drinking or copulating) were believed to resemble the driving of a piece of machinery or the letting off of steam. The analogies were reinforced by the subjective sense we sometimes have of being "driven" to eat, or copulate, or sleep. These notions, however, were really merely analogies, and nothing in the neural or hormonal systems of the body corresponds to them in a useful way.

Indeed, it can now be said that the "humour" metaphor of the Elizabethans is intrinsically closer to the truth as we understand it than was the "drive" metaphor of the early twentieth century. Contrary to drive theory, the nervous system is not a hydraulic system. No fluid in it builds up under pressure, forcing or urging us to do this or that action, so that it can relent after "letting off steam." Of course, no fluid corresponding to the Elizabethan humour exists either; yet that concept is closer to current ones. Behavioral scientists, especially outside of psychology, but also within it, are turning to concepts like "state," "arousal," and "excitation," which can refer either to a general condition of the organism or a specific tendency to activation of a specific behavioral system (such as sex). Rather than building up pressure until release occurs, these activation tendencies rise and fall according to various causes, often without deprivation or release. The terms used to describe them are nonmetaphoric and epistemologically very conservative, merely describing what can be seen and measured in behavior. But they have the great advantage of having plausible correlates in the neural and endocrine systems, for which "state," "arousal," and "excitation," are highly meaningful terms.

As behavioral arousal, specific or general, can vary with respect to time of the day, day of the month, month of the year, and year of life, as well as with respect to many specific environmental cues, so neural or hormonal arousal varies too, and the day may come when we realize the hope of the Elizabethans by being able to characterize not only stable aspects of temperament but also short-lived changes and long-term "personal growth" by reference to a subtle mixing of fluids. We will have, of course, to give up the simple calculus of blood, phlegm, and bile in favor of at least a few dozen hormones and neurotransmitters, but the Elizabethans would probably forgive us.

Meanwhile, we cannot hope to get to that point without relinquishing the much more recent metaphor of the brain as a sort of pressure cooker. It was helpful for a while, generating, as a good theory does, a veritable multitude of important observations; but it must now go by the wayside, not because it is useless or silly but because we have something better. In the words of the neuroanatomist Walle Nauta when lecturing on this subject: "I am often puzzled by some of the remarks made by my psychologist colleagues on the topic of motivation. It seems to me that, etymologically at least, motivation is what moves us, and I believe that what moves us is moods." When we have characterized the biology of moods we will have characterized the major forces behind behavior.

The second component of the foresight of the humour theory goes beyond transient motives and has to do with accounting for stable temperaments. The Elizabethans believed that the temperaments were largely innate, that you were "given" this or that predominance of fluid. Many obstacles confront acceptance of even a weak modern version of that belief. First, it is not clear that any aspect of temperament is really very stable over the life course. There is some evidence to support such stability, but not very much, except in specific areas. Second, human behavior genetics is only just beginning to emerge from its sad history of sloppiness, and good studies supporting the heritability of a wide range of normal temperaments are only now entering the literature. In the meantime, we have the animal research and the evidence of human single-gene defects affecting behavior. These latter work through a small number of metabolic pathways in the neural and endocrine organs, but they will undoubtedly prove to be only the tip of an iceberg.

That said, it must be emphatically added that every genetically caused alteration discussed in this chapter is subject to reversal by an appropriate change in the environment that is already known or that can be found out. They can also be produced in a normal individual by nongenetic environmental means that mimic in one way or another the chemical effect of a defective gene. The contrary belief, which holds that genes are destiny and that the demonstration of a genetic effect is tantamount to throwing up one's hands about the prospect of intervention for change, would be ludicrous were it not both persistent and pernicious. It is false, of course, as countless eyeglass-wearers and insulin-takers can testify. The demonstration of a genetic effect through a metabolic pathway to a feature of the observable phenotype, behavioral or otherwise, says nothing whatever about the possibility of subsequent change, except that the understanding of the genetic and metabolic path can only help in the identification and treatment of the alteration, and ultimately provide a solution of the problem. In other words, genetic analysis of behavior can lead to an increase not only in human welfare, but in human freedom.

What can be said on the basis of the evidence sketched in this chapter (and much other evidence besides) is that two individuals who differ genetically in metabolic characteristics controlling behavioral tendencies will, if raised in identical environments with identical resources and training, grow up to act and think and feel differently. The effort, engaged in by millions in modern times, to ignore these facts and to trace every aspect of character, personality, or behavioral tendency, desirable or otherwise, in themselves or in people they know, to some or other feature of their experience—especially early experience, and especially in the intimacy of the family—is a vain one. This approach can explain a good deal, but far from everything. There is in each of us a residue of characteristics of heart and mind that we brought with us when we entered the womb, a mere few days from conception. The denial of this, as liberal as it usually sounds, is really a denial of individuality, in the most fundamental sense, and it is every bit as dangerous as the most rigid forms of genetic determinism. Extreme environmentalism had its magnificent heyday when the excesses of genetic determinism were threatening, for decades, not only human dignity, but human survival. It served a noble purpose and was for very many years an objectively respectable position. But the sands of scientific time are shifting beneath that position, and those who tend it had best look to a foothold.

6

THE BEAST WITH TWO BACKS

The beast with two backs is a single beast. . . .
—Robert Graves, "Seaside"

Anke Ehrhardt, Patricia Goldman, Sarah Blaffer Hrdy, Corinne Hutt, Julianne Imperato-McGinley, Carol Nagy Jacklin, Annelise Korner, Eleanor Emmons Maccoby, Alice Rossi, Dominique Toran-Allerand, Beatrice Blyth Whiting. These are the names of some distinguished women scientists who devote their lives to the study of brain, hormones or behavior, human and animal. They range from the world famous to the merely well known. Each, within her discipline, has a reputation for tough-mindedness. All have in common that they have given considerable attention (most of them many years) to the question of whether the sex differences in behavior each has observed—in the field, in the clinic, and in the laboratory—have a basis that is in part biological.

Without exception, they have answered this question in the affirmative. One cannot imagine that they did so without difficulty. Each has suffered, personally and professionally, from the ubiquitous discrimination against women that is common outside the academy and within it. Each has worked with some man who envisioned her—in his heart of hearts—barefoot, meek, pregnant, and in the kitchen. Each has sacrificed more than the average brilliant man to get into position to work on a problem that troubles her intellectually, and the payment of that sort of price makes the truth more compelling than comfortable. Nevertheless, each is wise enough to know that over the long course of time, the very sorts of oppression she has experienced are bulwarked and bastioned by theories of "natural" gender differences.

These women are doing a balancing act of formidable proportions. They continue to struggle, in private and in public, for equal rights and equal treatment for people of both sexes; at the same time, they uncover and report evidence that the sexes are irremediably different—that after sexism is wholly stripped away, after differences in training have gone the way of the whalebone corset, there will still be *something* different, something that is grounded in biology. They have, undoubtedly, to endure the smirks of the "I knew it all along" sort of men—and they are not people who suffer fools gladly. At the same time, they must contend with the assaults of feminist critics who, in many cases, will not or cannot read their papers. What these women think about—how they reconcile these difficulties—in the privacy of their libraries and laboratories, is not something we can know; probably it is none of our business anyway. But we can at least do them the courtesy, before turning to their discoveries, of acknowledging the complexity, even anguish, of their position. They are among the most estimable people in science.

Like many stories in modern behavioral science, this one begins with Margaret Mead. Mead was one of the greatest of all social scientists, and if she had become the first such scientist to win the Nobel Prize in Medicine and Physiology (she could have been cited, for instance, for her contributions to pediatrics and psychiatry, as well as for her almost single-handed formulation of our present, flexible concept of human nature), the choice would have done credit to the Swedish Academy. Perhaps her flamboyant style, perhaps her gender . . . well, these speculations are always pretty useless. For present purposes it will suffice to say that in a world in which all odds were against it, she established a concept of human differences as more flexible, more malleable, more buffeted by the winds of life experience—as delivered by our very different cultures—than anybody had then thought possible. And this concept has stood the test of time.

No question so engaged her interest as that of the role of gender in behavior. In trip after stubborn trip to the South Seas, enduring hardships rare for a woman in any era, she gathered information impossible to come by otherwise. Among headhunters and fishermen, medicine men and exotic dancers, in steamy jungles, on mountaintops, on vivid white beaches, in bamboo huts, in meetinghouses on stilts high above water, in shaky-looking seagoing bark canoes, she took out her ubiquitous notebook and recorded the behavior and beliefs of men and women who had never heard of American sex roles. By 1949, when *Male and Female* was published, she had done this in seven exotic, remote societies. There could be no doubt that by this time she knew more about the human variety of gender roles than any person ever had in history. And with that knowledge—it, too, for the most part, has stood the test of time—she justly clobbered every smug, sexist male in America:

> The Tchambuli people, who number only six hundred in all, have built their houses along the edge of one of the loveliest of New Guinea lakes, which gleams like polished ebony, with a back-drop of the distant hills behind which the Arapesh live. In the lake are purple lotus and great pink and white water lilies, white osprey and blue heron. Here the Tchambuli women, brisk, unadorned, managing and industrious, fish and go to market: the men, decorative and adorned, carve and paint and practice dance-steps, their headhunting tradition replaced by the simpler practice of buying victims to validate their manhood.

And among the Mundugumor, river-dwelling cannibals of New Guinea, men and women seemed to be equally masculine:

> These robust, restive people live on the banks of a swiftly flowing river but with no river lore. They trade with and prey upon the miserable, underfed bush-peoples who live on poorer land, devote their time to quarreling and headhunting, and have developed a form of social organization in which every man's hand is against every other man. The women are as assertive and vigorous as the men; they detest bearing and rearing children, and provide most of the food, leaving the men free to plot and fight.

One may imagine, perhaps, an at least slightly startled readership in the United States. In the wake of World War II, fresh from complete victory, full of a sense of the rightness of the American way of life, and experiencing that vivid apparent proof of the gap between the sexes that only a victorious war can deliver, this readership was treated to men who primped, gossiped, and danced all day while their down-to-earth female counterparts, reluctant mothers at best, attended to serious business. Moreover, these ways were being touted as perfectly workable and valid, and some had gone on for a thousand years.

Judicious, or perhaps merely skeptical readers may have noticed, however, a rather important chink in Mead's armor. In all her cultures there was homicidal violence, and in all, that violence occurred at the hands of men. Tchambuli men, as the first passage indicates, may have been effeminate in relation to certain American conventions, but they were still very devoted to taking victims—and, more traditionally, hunting heads. Mundugumor men were evidently unthreatened by having their women provide for them, but that was because it freed them to plot and fight.

This part of the pattern may be traced in a like manner through all the world's thousands of different cultures. In every culture there is at least some homicide, in the context of war or ritual or in the context of daily life, and in every culture men are mainly responsible for it. Among the !Kung San of Botswana, noted for their pacifism as well as for equality between the sexes, the perpetrators in twenty-two documented homicides were all men. Fights over adultery or presumed adultery were involved in several cases, and a majority of the others were retaliations for previous homicides. In a sample of 122 distinct societies in the ethnographic range, distributed around the world, weapon making was done by men in all of them. There are of course exceptions, certainly at the individual level and, in rare cases—such as modern Israel or nineteenth-century Dahomey—transient partial exceptions at the group level. What we are dealing with, to be sure, is a difference in degree, but one so large that it may as well be qualitative. Men are more violent than women.

Even in dreams the distinction holds. In a study of dreams in seventy-five tribal societies distributed, again, around the world, men were more likely to dream of grass, coitus, wife, weapon, animal, death, red, vehicle, hit, and ineffectual attempt, while women were more likely to dream of husband, clothes, mother, father, child, home, female figure, cry, and male figure.

The dreams raise, incidentally, a related point about gender universality. The women among Tchambuli and Mundugumor may have been disgusted with child bearing and rearing, but they did it. So do women everywhere in the preindustrial world. There are, of course, individual exceptions; but there is no society in the ethnographic or historical record in which men do nearly as much baby and child care as women. This is not to say anything, yet, about capacity; it is merely a statement of plain, observable fact: men are more violent than women and women are more nurturant, at least toward infants and children, than men. I am sorry if this is a cliché; that cannot make it less factual. And for the moment at least, there are no inferences to be made from it. It is nothing but plain, dull fact.

Of course, it is ethnographic fact, and that raises some eyebrows. Although the cross-cultural surveys quoted above are quantitative in nature, they are based on individual studies consisting mainly of mere description. As such, they are the victims of "hard science" snobbery. That snobbery is most ill founded. Ethnology is in its earliest phase as a science. As in botany, zoology, anatomy, histology, geology, astronomy, that phase must be descriptive. Indeed, the pages of professional journals in histology and anatomy to this day abound with nonquantitative papers. Just as "mere" description of the look of a new brain nucleus or a type of liver cancer as they appear under the microscope is a first step on a new path in science, so, equally, is the description of a society; description, using the human eye, the human ear, the human mind, given, at least at first, without computers.

Nevertheless, we recognize quantification as necessary, and, at least until recently, such quantification was more usual in the work of psychologists than of anthropologists. For many years now, psychologists in the Western world have studied gender differences and they have done so with an exactitude very difficult to match in the tropical jungle. Eleanor Maccoby, an elder stateswoman of American psychology, and Carol Jacklin, a younger scientist trained in part by Maccoby, have, after years of work on the problem, written a major book, *The Psychology of Sex Differences*. It not only summarizes their own work but, more important, systematically reviews and tabulates hundreds of carefully described and annotated studies by other investigators. They review studies of sex differences on scores of different dimensions—tactile sensitivity, vision, discrimination learning, social memory, general intellectual abilities, achievement striving, self-esteem, crying, fear and timidity, helping behavior, competition, conformity, imitation, to name only a sprinkling.

For most of these dimensions it may be emphatically stated that there is no consistent pattern of gender difference. For almost all there are at least some studies that find a gender difference in either direction—usually both—and many studies that find no difference. Indeed, the main thrust of the book is to demolish cliché after cliché about the differences between boys and girls, men and women. There is no evidence that girls and women are more social, more suggestible, have lower self-esteem or less achievement motivation than boys and men, or that boys and men are more analytic. Just taking the sample list in the above paragraph, only in the realms of tactile sensitivity and fear and timidity is there even weak evidence of a gender difference—girls show more of these. There is also weak evidence that girls are more compliant than boys and less involved in assertions of dominance. In the realm of cognitive abilities, there is good evidence for superiority of girls and women in verbal ability, and of boys and men in spatial and quantitative ability.

But the strongest case for gender difference is made in the realm of aggressive behavior. Out of 94 comparisons in 67 different quantitative studies, 57 comparisons showed statistically significant sex differences, and in only 5 was the difference in favor of girls. Fifty-two of the 57 studies that showed differences showed boys to be more aggressive than girls. The specific measures ranged from hitting, kicking, and throwing rocks to scores on a hostility scale, and included such things as fantasy and dream material, verbal aggression, and aggression against dolls; the subjects ranged from age two to adulthood. Of 6 different studies in which actual physical aggression between peers, of a nonplayful sort, was measured, 5 found that boys exceeded girls, with 1 showing no difference.

Maccoby and Jacklin do not report on studies of nurturance per se, but in an earlier book, published in 1966, Maccoby summarized 52 studies in a category called "nurturance and affiliation"; in 45 studies, girls and women showed more of it than boys and men, while in only 2 did males score higher, with 5 showing no difference.

While it is difficult to get accurate information in nonindustrial cultures on such measures as verbal and spatial ability, a number of excellent studies have been done on child behavior, using techniques of measurement and analysis that live up to a high standard of rigor. Beatrice Whiting has been a leader in this field, originating techniques of study, and sending students out to remote corners of the earth (as well as making field trips herself) to bring back accurate knowledge about behavior. She is one of the most quantitatively oriented of anthropologists, and may be said to have built an edifice of exactitude on the foundation that was laid by Margaret Mead. She has been at it for about forty years.

In a series of investigations that came to be known as the Six Cultures study, Whiting, together with John Whiting and other colleagues, studied children's behavior through direct, detailed observation, in standard settings, distributed throughout the day. These observations were made by teams in a New England town—called "Orchard Town," its identity is still a mystery—and in five farming and herding villages throughout the world. In Mexico, Kenya, India, Japan, and the Philippines, as well as in New England, hundreds of hours of observations were made on children of all ages, using uniform methods. Children were scored on twelve small units of behavior, such as "seeks help," "offers support," "touches," "reprimands," and "assaults." In a sophisticated statistical analysis called multidimensional scaling, all the data on these small units were aggregated and the children were seen to vary on two large dimensions called, respectively, "egoism versus altruism" and "aggressiveness versus nurturance."

In all six cultures, boys differed from girls in the direction of greater egoism and/or greater aggressiveness, usually both. The difference varies greatly from culture to culture, presumably in response to different degrees of inculcation of gender role. Even more interesting, the girls in one culture may be more aggressive than the boys in another. But the direction of the difference within any culture is always and tediously the same. In other words, studies of children who are not fully socialized to their cultures, using methods more exact than most anthropologists have used, underscore rather than jeopardize the hypothesized gender differences in the areas of aggressiveness and nurturance.

It may be argued that the children in Whiting's studies had nevertheless been trained; they ranged in age from three to twelve. Furthermore, all six cultures may be sexist. There is in fact evidence that cultures around the world are quite consistent in their efforts to *train* gender roles: 82 percent of a sample of 33 cultures attempted to get more nurturance out of girls than boys, and none attempted the reverse, according to ethnographers' descriptions; 85 percent of 82 cultures gave boys more training in self-reliance than girls, again with none reversing the preference. Might it not be that the universal difference in aggressive and nurturant behavior stems from an equally universal, albeit unexplained, sex-role training, rather than biological factors?

It may be useful to look at younger children separately. In Maccoby and Jacklin's list, 27 of the 94 comparisons involve children under six. Of these, 14 showed boys to be more aggressive, and only 2 showed girls to be more aggressive. In one of these two cases the difference was reversed when the sample was expanded. In a separate cross-cultural study, not part of Whiting's analysis and not in Maccoby and Jacklin's review, three- to five-year-old children were observed in social interaction in London and among the !Kung San, noted, as mentioned before, for egalitarian sexual politics. Two separate observers using two different techniques both found boys to be more aggressive in both cultures.

Although we cannot identify aggressiveness at ages much younger than three years, we can certainly look at sex differences in behavior. At three weeks of age, for instance (in middle-class homes in the United States), boy babies have been found to be more active, to cry more, to look at the mother more, and to sleep and vocalize less than girl babies.

But, unfortunately for simplicity, mothers of boys three weeks old hold them, burp them, rock them, stimulate them, arouse them, stress them, look at them, talk to them, and even smile at them more than do mothers of girls, and have probably been doing so since they were born. What is the first question we ask when we hear of the birth of a baby? Right; we need that piece of information so that we know how to act, how to feel, even toward a newborn baby. Gender is a key to proper behavior. (Even among higher primates, the monkeys and apes that are our closest animal relatives, the first reaction to a birth in some species is a visit from adults in the troop for inspection of the neonate's genitals.) That knowledge of gender influences the adult's behavior toward the child. It has been shown that the same baby will elicit very different responses from adults depending on whether it is dressed in pink or blue; and a tape recording of a child's mischievous utterances will draw amusement and encouragement from adults who are told that the child is a boy, but negative reactions from otherwise similar adults who think it's a girl.

These facts make it very difficult, for any age child, to make the case that boys and girls are so different in their behavior and responsiveness that they constrain their parents to treat them differently. Even at age three weeks we have the chicken-and-egg problem; we cannot justly say that it is the differences in the infants that are prior. Still, we can go younger. Annelise Korner has spent many years studying newborn infants, and one of her central interests has been sex differences. She, as well as other investigators, has found that at birth boys show more muscle strength—greater head lift in the prone position, for example—while girls show greater skin sensitivity, more reflex smiles, more taste sensitivity, more searching movements with their mouths, and faster response to a flash of light—the response being measured by evoked electrical potentials recorded over the visual part of the brain.

It is not easy to relate such differences to aggressiveness, and perhaps it should not be tried. Nevertheless it could be argued that individuals with greater skin sensitivity might be conditioned by life experience to be less aggressive. In one good study following children from birth to age five, those with less skin sensitivity at birth were more likely to attack and surmount an inanimate barrier at the age of five years, and this correlation held within each sex, not just between sexes. Degree of muscle strength at birth is also a plausible precursor of aggressiveness.

But before we resort to this indirect kind of accounting, it behooves us to consider another category of evidence; the sort of evidence that comes from studies of hormones, behavior, and the brain.

The idea that humoral factors secreted by reproductive organs influence gender differences in behavior is very old; castration has long been used in attempts to reduce aggressiveness in animals and men, and systematic experimental work demonstrating that this works has been available since 1849. By the present time so many studies have been done in so many species of animals—including humans—that to call the case convincing is to put the matter mildly. The question is no longer whether hormones secreted by the testes promote or enable aggressive behavior, but *how*, and also: What else goes on in a like manner?

The principal male gonadal hormone in mammals is testosterone. It belongs to a chemical class known as steroids, a class that includes the remarkable and justly famous cortisone—a nearly natural compound with widespread medical uses, the chief of which is in the realm of wound healing. The steroid class also includes the two principal female reproductive hormones: estradiol—the key estrogen in humans—and progesterone, the gestation-promoting substance secreted in massive quantities by the placenta, and in lesser quantities, in the nonpregnant woman, by the ovaries. Estradiol and progesterone, together with the pituitary hormones that regulate them, participate in the determination of the monthly cycle, a spectacularly intriguing system with a still incompletely solved mechanism. Although nothing so fabulous as that exists in males, there is much in common between testosterone's mode of action and that of the two female sex steroids.

Steroids are small, as biological molecules go—yet not as small as the best-known neurotransmitters. Although they have many important actions on nonneural organs—testosterone, for example, promotes muscle growth in teenage human males, an effect with clear importance for behavior—the most direct, and probably the overwhelmingly important route by which a steroid hormone (or for that matter any substance in the blood) can affect behavior is by transfer from blood into nerve and brain. The brain is the main regulatory organ of behavior, and behavior is that organ's major output; for a molecule to affect behavior it must generally first affect the brain, or at least the peripheral nerves.

Sex steroids are no exception. But in addition to the more typical means of influencing nerve cells—direct, immediate action on neural activity—shared by drugs, diet, and neurotransmitters, steroid hormones have a special access route that is well established, though little understood. They combine with receptor molecules in the body of the target cell, and the steroid-receptor complex goes to the genes. That is literally true: One of the major modes of action of the steroid hormones is by direct influence on DNA, altering its patterns of manufacture of RNA and protein, and thus the most basic functions of the cell. They do not apparently interfere with the machinery of heredity in the sense of replication, making an impact that could alter daughter cells; but they do interfere with that machinery in terms of regulation, which is to say that it is the most intimate example of the gene-environment interaction described in the chapter on adaptation. Here are genes whose effect on the organism—perhaps on the very cell they inhabit—is so little fixed that it is vulnerable to the merest winds of blood-borne humoral factors. That means anything in the environment that can influence, say, testosterone—diet, stress, temperature, seduction, even fantasy—can potentially toss a molecular wrench among the delicate cogs of the hereditary machinery; so much for the fixed effects of the genes.

Of course this characterization is a bit improper; the genes are, as it were, expecting such interventions. Nevertheless, it is fair to say that knowledge of this mechanism has added a new dimension to our concept of gene-environment interaction, and has done so in just the last few years. Nerve-cell genes are no exception to this "fifth column" assault, and so far we know little of how they respond to it. One thing we do know is that it is slow-acting and long-lasting. Unlike the mechanism of a compound—say, amphetamine—that acts quickly and, for the most part, transiently, on the response tendencies of nerve cells, steroid hormones bound to their receptors may land in their target cell nuclei—presumably in contact with DNA—hours before they make their effect on function. For example, giving a rat a systemic injection of estradiol (radioactively labeled for tracing) will produce a high concentration of this hormone in certain brain cells—specifically, in their nuclei—within two hours. Twenty-two hours after that, and no sooner, there will be a correspondingly massive increase in the tendency of the rat—if female—to respond to stimulation with sexual posturing. What happens in those twenty-two hours will tell a tale not only about hormone action but about gene action that may change the way we look at cell biology; but the tale cannot be told without at least a few more years of research.

Meanwhile, we know, as children like to say, for sure, that sex steroid hormones affect behavior, and we know they get around quite well in the brain. Using radioactive labeling it has been very easy to show not only that they pass from blood to brain, but that they make their passage selectively; or, more properly, they concentrate selectively in certain brain regions. These concentrations are highest in the hypothalamus—at the base of the brain—and in other regions of the limbic system (the "emotional" brain)—in short, exactly where theory would like them to be. That is, concentrations occur in brain regions that play an important role in courtship, sex, maternal behavior, and violence—just the behaviors in which the sexes most differ and the ones most subject to influence by testosterone, estradiol, and progesterone.

Although the way the system works is scarcely understood, there are clues. For instance, injection of testosterone lowers the threshold for firing of nerve fibers in the *stria terminalis*; this pathway leads from the amygdala—the "almond," near the sides of the base of the brain—to the hypothalamus. As such in all likelihood it mediates an excitatory influence of the limbic system (the "emotional brain" to which both the amygdala and hypothalamus belong) on sexual and aggressive behavior. This finding gives substance to the action of testosterone on behavior. It is one thing to say that the hormone probably influences sex and aggression by acting on the brain; it is quite another to find a major nerve bundle deep in the brain, likely to be involved in sex and aggression, that can fire more easily when testosterone acts on it than when it does not. A key link in the story has been formed.

But we don't even need to reach so deeply into the brain. Peripheral nerves have now been shown to concentrate these hormones. In songbirds in which the male of the pair is the singer, testosterone is concentrated in the motor nerves to the syrinx—the bird's voice box—and this is almost certainly part of the reason testosterone promotes song, a male courtship pattern. In female rats, injection of estradiol increases the size of the region of sensitivity of the nerve to the pelvic region, even when that nerve is detached from the brain; this is presumably part of the mechanism that makes the female susceptible—some of the time, anyway—to male advances.

Such is the view of the physiologist, which is, not surprisingly, pretty unrelenting. What is a bit surprising is that someone like Alice Rossi has accepted it. Rossi is a family sociologist. After years of distinction in her field, she became dissatisfied with Durkheim's dictum that only social facts can explain social facts, and began to take seriously the notion that some social facts at least might be explained in part by biological ones. She has become adept in reading the biological literature, and when she reviews it for her sociologist colleagues, she does not attempt to conceal from them her belief that some of the observed gender difference in social behavior—for example, in the realm of parenting—is attributable to causes in endocrinology.

Rossi has done more than review the literature. She has done some of the most interesting research to date on behavioral effects of the human menstrual cycle. Using precise methods of measurement and a complex mathematical model borrowed from econometrics, she showed that there are mood cycles in college women that can be predicted from the menstrual cycle. For example, she identified a rise of negative feelings in the women during the luteal phase of their cycles —the period beginning four or five days after ovulation, when the steroid hormone progesterone is at its monthly peak. More interesting and more unusual was Rossi's inclusion of a group of men as comparison subjects. While she did not discover a male cycle—no one else really has either, despite some clues pointing in that direction— she did find that men have the same number of days per month of physical discomfort as women, but that some, at least, of the women's discomfort days were predictable from the menstrual cycle; they usually occur during menstruation. (For the reader who still believes that menstrual distress disqualifies women from such positions as airline pilot and President, consider whether you would want your plane—or your country—piloted by someone who has a few days a month of distress that come around like clockwork, or someone with the same number of days of distress arriving randomly.)

Systematic changes in hormone levels, occurring in all normally cycling women, may thus affect complex human emotions. In reviewing the well-known sex difference in nurturing behavior—obvious particularly within the family, and in all cultures—Rossi has accepted the possibility that it may have its roots partly in hormonal differences, although probably not cyclical in nature. She has defended this viewpoint in several recent articles, in the scholarly as well as semipopular literature.

But from a hormonal perspective, nurturance itself has not been as well studied as aggressiveness, which in some ways is the antithesis of nurturance. In many studies of humans and other animals, it is clear that testosterone at least enables and perhaps directly increases aggressiveness. While no one with any experience in this field thinks that there is a simple ("push-pull, click-click" is the way it is often derisively referred to) relationship between testosterone and aggression, most people now accept that some such relationship does exist. Not only does castration reduce aggression and testosterone restore it in many animals, but there are fascinating correlations between aggression and testosterone level in group-living and normally behaving animals. For example, when two groups of monkeys fight, the winners experience an increase in blood level of the hormone, and the losers experience a decrease.

To take a second example, although repeated studies of aggression and testosterone in prison inmates have produced a confused picture, one intriguing discovery stands out: among male prison inmates, in one very good study, the higher the adult testosterone level, the earlier the age of the first arrest. That is, the men who had the highest levels had been arrested youngest, in early adolescence. In another study, the level of testosterone in male juvenile delinquents was correlated with their level of observed aggressive behavior.

This finding brings us to one of the most central facts about the gonadal hormones: they rise very dramatically at adolescence. From very low levels during early and middle childhood, testosterone (especially but not exclusively in males) and estradiol and progesterone (both especially but not exclusively in females) all rise to adult levels over the course of a few years, and the female monthly cycle is instituted. Few studies have measured hormones and behavior in the same individuals, but it is likely that adolescent behavior—and its gender differentiation—is influenced by these massive hormonal changes. Gender differences in fat, muscle mass, and the pitch of the voice, all of which contribute to gender-specific behavior, are determined essentially completely by the teenage boy's rise in blood testosterone.

One could conceivably leave the picture here—allude, say, to the Graves epigraph at the head of this chapter, stress the overwhelming similarity between the sexes in neurobehavioral plan, and suggest that evolution made "a single beast" with a single twist: an infusion of different hormones, coming from the gonads, just at the moment of reproductive maturity; in other words, just when we would expect the genders to begin to be really different.

The difficulty with this neat picture is that we have overwhelming evidence that the sexes differ in their behavior long before puberty, when there are not enough circulating sex steroids to make the difference. For example, we have the evidence mentioned above from psychological and anthropological studies that preschool-age boys and girls exhibit different degrees of aggressiveness. Still, it would be fairly easy to explain this without invoking a biological basis for their behavior. If we accept, say, that the parents of these children behave in a gender-appropriate way because of their own postadolescent hormones—and accept further that small children identify with and model themselves on the behavior of the parent of the same sex—that will be all we need to explain the sex difference in the children, and it should still give us cross-cultural regularity.

But consider now the following experiment. Rhesus monkeys, that favorite object of laboratory scrutiny—because of presumed similarity to humans—are raised in total social isolation. Subjects are of either sex, and they not only have no sex role training, and no opportunity to identify with the parent of the same sex; they have no social experience of any kind. At about age three—corresponding, roughly speaking, to human ten-year-olds—each monkey is put in a room with a monkey infant, of randomly chosen sex, and its behavior with the infant is recorded. The result is that female juveniles take care of the infant more, and male juveniles hit the infant more, and the difference is highly significant statistically. With no differences—as yet—in hormones actively circulating, and with no differences in rearing experience, what can possibly account for such impressive differentiation of gender?

There is increasing evidence that the accounting may lie deep in the brain. In 1973 it was shown for the first time that male and female brains differ structurally. In the most forward portion of the hypothalamus, the deepest nucleus of the brain, male and female rats differed in the density of synaptic connections among local neurons. Furthermore, castration of males just after birth would leave them with the female brain pattern, and injection of testosterone into females—likewise just after birth—would give them the male pattern.

To say that this study—done by G. Raisman and P.M. Field—"rocked the neuroscience community" seems an extreme statement, yet it is not much of an exaggeration. For one thing, it was the first demonstration that the brains of the sexes differ, in any animal. For another, the difference was in a region where it should have been—a region concerned with the brain's regulation of the very gonadal hormones we have been looking at. But most impressive of all, to those who knew the field, was the demonstration that sex hormones, circulating *at birth*, could change the brain. For years, studies of mice, rats, dogs, monkeys and other animals had shown that testosterone and related male gonadal hormones, given to female young at birth or a little earlier, suppressed their normal female sexual posturing, and in some species suppressed sexual cycling. In males, castration or administration of an antitestosterone compound at birth would suppress normal male sexual behavior later in adulthood, even despite replacement therapy with testosterone later in life. One of the most impressive experiments of the kind produced "pseudo-hermaphrodite" monkeys by administering male gonadal hormones to female fetuses before birth. As they grew, these females showed neither the characteristic low female level of aggressive play nor the characteristic high male level, but something precisely in between.

For these reasons, investigators had, before 1973, already begun to talk about "neonatal androgenization of the brain"—which means a change in the brain by male sex hormones around the time of birth; to put it crudely, a masculinization of the brain. But the involvement of the brain was only speculative until the report of Raisman and Field, which gave the phrase its first genuine meaning. It also gave real credence to the possibility that the frequently observed preadolescent gender differences in aggressiveness were as biological in origin as the more easily comprehended postadolescent ones.

That, it now appears, was only the beginning of the story. A few years later, Dominique Toran-Allerand did a tissue-culture experiment—with brain slices in petri dishes—in which she was able to watch the process in action. She made thin slices of the hypothalamus of newborn mice—of both sexes—and kept them alive long enough to treat them with gonadal steroid hormones, including testosterone. Her brief paper, published in *Brain Research*, shows the stunning results in photomicrographs. Many cells in the mouse hypothalamus are growing at that age—putting out neural processes that will finally form connections to other cells; but the cells in the slices treated with testosterone show more and faster-growing neural processes than those treated only with the "vehicle"—the oil suspension the testosterone was dissolved in. Thus, the treatments only differed in the presence or absence of the hormone. In effect, she was able to watch as testosterone changed the newborn brain. Her work did not imply that this faster, more florid growth made the testosterone-treated hypothalamus *better*. But it required the conclusion that the hypothalamus would be different, if only because the connections in the brain are in part determined by the rate of growth of various nearby nerve cells.

For these and a variety of other reasons, the community of scientists working in this field concluded that the basic plan of the mammalian organism is female and stays that way unless told to be otherwise by masculine hormones. That this was not a necessary arrangement was shown by the sexual differentiation of birds, in which the opposite seems to be true; the basic plan is male, and the female course of development is the result of the action of female hormones. Nevertheless, the mammal story was becoming clear: the genetic signal for masculinity, coming from the Y chromosome, did its work on a basically female structural plan, through masculine hormones, including steroids.

It is only natural to doubt whether such generalizations are applicable to that most puzzling of all mammals, the one that does research on its own nature. My own doubts in the matter—formidable at the time—were largely dispelled by the investigations of Anke Ehrhardt and her colleagues, first at the Johns Hopkins School of Medicine, later at the Columbia College of Physicians and Surgeons. Ehrhardt has spent years studying the condition and clinical treatment of certain unfortunate "experiments in nature"—anomalies of sexual and psychosexual development. In one such set of anomalies, known as the adrenogenital syndrome, a genetic defect results in the absence of an enzyme in the adrenal cortex—the outer portion of the crucial adrenal gland—so that instead of secreting normal amounts of the stress steroid cortisol, it produces abnormally large quantities of the sex steroid testosterone. For girls with the syndrome, masculine levels of the latter hormone are floating around in the blood throughout gestation, until the time of birth. Shortly after birth the condition can be corrected, so that it is presumably only in the prenatal period that the hormone can have its effects.

At age ten these girls are psychologically different from their sisters and from unrelated controls. They are described by themselves and by their mothers as doing less doll play, being more "tomboyish," and expressing less desire to be married and have children when they grow up. Whatever value judgment we choose to place on these phenomena—I am inclined to place none—they seem to be real. They have been repeated by different investigators with different samples and even with different syndromes that amount, hormonally, to much the same thing. Taken together with the increasing animal evidence, these findings suggested to Ehrhardt and her colleagues—and to many others as well—that humans too could conceivably experience psychosexual differentiation, affecting both behavior and the brain, as a result of masculinizing hormones acting near or shortly before the time of birth.

This possibility received stunning confirmation in a series of discoveries made by endocrinologist Julianne Imperato-McGinley of the New York Hospital–Cornell Medical Center. These had to do principally with the analysis of a new syndrome of abnormal sexual differentiation that defied all previous rules. It was confined to three intermarrying rural villages in the southwestern Dominican Republic and, over a period of four generations, afflicted 38 known individuals from 23 interrelated families. It is clearly genetic, but has arisen only recently in the population due to mutation and intermarriage.

Nineteen of the subjects appeared at birth to be unambiguously female, and were viewed and reared as completely normal females by their parents and other relatives. At puberty they first failed to develop breasts and then underwent a completely masculine pubertal transformation, including growth of a phallus, descent of the testes (which had previously been in the abdominal cavity), deepening of the voice, and development of a muscular masculine physique. Physically and psychologically they became men, with normal or occasionally hypernormal sexual desire for women and with a complete range of sexual functions except for infertility due to abnormal ejaculation (through an opening at the base of the penis). After many years of experience with such individuals, the villagers identified them as a separate group, called *guevedoce* (penis at twelve) or *machihembra* (man-woman).

The physiological analysis undertaken by Imperato-McGinley and her colleagues revealed that these individuals are genetically male— they have one X and one Y chromosome—but lack a single enzyme of male sex-hormone synthesis, due to a defective gene. The enzyme, 5α-reductase, changes testosterone into another male sex hormone, dihydrotestosterone. Although they lack dihydrotestosterone almost completely, they have normal levels of testosterone itself. Evidently these two hormones are respectively responsible for the promotion of male external sex characteristics at birth (dihydrotestosterone) and at puberty (testosterone). Despite the presence of testosterone, the lack of "dihydro" makes for a female-looking newborn and prepubertal child. The presence of testosterone makes for a more or less normal masculine puberty.

But for present purposes, the most extraordinary thing about these people is that they become, completely and securely, men of their culture in every sense of the word. After twelve or more years of rearing as girls, with all the psychological influences encouraging that gender role in a rather sexist society, they are able to completely transform themselves into almost typical examples of the masculine gender—with family, sexual, vocational, and avocational roles. Of the 18 subjects for which data were available, 17 made this transformation, the other retaining a female role and gender identity. The 17 did not make the transformation with ease. Imperato-McGinley reports that it cost some of them years of confusion and psychological anguish. But they made it, without special training or therapeutic intervention. Imperato-McGinley and her colleagues reason that the testosterone circulating during the course of growth in these men has a masculinizing effect on their brains—an effect "that appears to contribute substantially to the formation of male gender-identity," when combined with the transforming effect of the further testosterone surge at puberty.

> These subjects demonstrate that in the absence of sociocultural factors that could interrupt the natural sequence of events, the effect of testosterone predominates, over-riding the effect of rearing as girls. . . .
> Our data show that environmental or sociocultural factors are not solely responsible for the formation of a male-gender identity. Androgens make a strong and definite contribution.

In studies with laboratory animals, there were further findings and complexities reported during the late 1970s. For example, it was found that in songbirds in which the male is the singer, there is a gender difference in the area of the brain controlling song that is so large that it is readily visible under the microscope without subtle statistical techniques. A bit closer to home—in mammals—it was found quite recently that the same region of the brain in which Raisman and Field, by meticulous counting, showed a sex difference in the density of synapses, exhibits a much more striking size difference that somehow eluded them. The region—the "sexually dimorphic nucleus of the preoptic area"—is three to six times larger in male rats than in females, and this difference is, once again, a function of the presence or absence of testosterone around the time of birth. It is so striking that the seasoned observer, holding the microscope slide up to the light, can tell the sex of the brain with the naked eye.

What are we to make of these extraordinary facts? For the immediate future, at least as far as I am concerned, nothing. It is simply too soon; there is too little information to make inferences about human behavior at all responsibly. Given present knowledge, for instance, it is not beyond the realm of possibility that the observed differences between the brains of the two genders serve only physiological functions; that is, the brains must be different to exert different control over different reproductive systems, having nothing at all to do with behavioral subtleties. However, I think this unlikely. If not now, then, my guess is, in the very near future, it will be extremely difficult for an informed, objective observer to discard the hypothesis that the genders differ in their degree of violent behavior for reasons that are in part physiological. And physiological determinants may prove to extend to some other behaviors as well.

If the community of scientists whose work and knowledge are relevant should come to agreement on this point, then it seems to me that one policy implication is plausible: Serious disarmament may ultimately necessitate an increase in the proportion of women in government. Reviewing the record of past female rulers is, in this connection, a useless exercise. Such women have invariably been embedded in and bound by an almost totally masculine power structure, and have gotten where they were by being unrepresentative of their gender. Some women are, of course, as violent as almost any man. But speaking of averages—central tendencies, as the statisticians call them—we can have little doubt that we would all be safer if the world's weapons systems were controlled by average women instead of by average men.

I think it appropriate to end where we began, contemplating the women who have helped unearth these facts. Visualize them in their offices and laboratories, trying to sort out what it all means; how do they handle the dissonance their findings must engender? I suspect that they do it by making a reconciliation—not a compromise, certainly not that—but a complex difficult reconciliation between the idea of human difference and the ideal of human equality. It is one that we must all make soon.

7

THE WELL OF FEELING

I wish that I might be a thinking stone.
The sea of spuming thought foists up again
The radiant bubble that she was. And then
A deep up-pouring from some saltier well
Within me, bursts its watery syllable.
　　　　—Wallace Stevens, "Le Monocle
　　　　de Mon Oncle"

What is the anatomical location of grief? In which bodily organ is the warmth we feel at the approach of a loved child? Where is pain? Although these questions may reveal substantial misunderstanding, they are not meaningless. Philosophers, for millennia, have groped their way toward answers; but most of these well-meaning individuals, many of whom were of course brilliant and wise, were burdened to the point of bafflement with the notion that feelings are not to be found in the body. Human feelings, the most faultless and fine indicators of the state of the human spirit, must be sought instead (so they believed) in the soul; and by soul they meant no metaphor for substantive qualities of heart and mind but, on the contrary, a separate entity, completely insubstantial, coterminous with the body and linked to it during life, but surviving it very nicely after death. In Dante, the souls of the dead may be seen to exhibit almost every nuance of feeling they could have been capable of during life; it is only their experience that is different. To experience damnation, one must be sensible of pain; to reap the reward of heaven, pleasure. Purgatory and limbo depend in part upon anxiety, and the bemused poet's interlocutors on every platform of heaven and hell give vivid testimony of the wide-ranging, exquisite sensibility of figures presumed to be made of airy nothing.

The relationship between mind and body, whether as a philosophical or biological issue, can scarcely be said to be resolved. But it is fair to say that the philosophers of the nineteenth century—at least those who were independent of theology—were already taking what biologists would consider a more mature approach to these questions; and in the twentieth century, particularly in and near the movement known as analytic philosophy (the mainstream of modern academic philosophy in England and the United States), it is evident from implicit as well as explicit reference that philosophy regarding the mind-body problem is under the influence of at least the fundaments of biological and psychological research. This is not to say that philosophers are merely reacting to such research. They are engaged in the clarification of the use of language (an innocent-sounding occupation that has resulted, among other things, in an undermining of the basis of religion and metaphysics) and in the description and explication of subjective experience, an exercise behavioral and biological scientists are either not inclined toward or, if they are, do very badly. Still, it must be admitted that some of the best philosophers of this century—Russell, Moore, Ayer, Ryle, and others—have also been engaged in an effort to explain the attainments of modern science to their less enlightened, more metaphysical colleagues.

To be sure, there is a skeptical, contrametaphysical thread that runs through Western philosophy from its Greek beginnings. Aristotle (and for centuries some of his followers) denied the insubstantiality and immortality of what is usually translated as "soul," but granted both to "mind." This stance, although ambiguous, would make Dante's world of the spirits impossible. Epicurus, a younger contemporary of Aristotle's, carried skepticism much further, and in a letter written around 300 B.C. he wrote plainly: "The soul experiences sensation only when enclosed in the body; and the body receives from the soul a share in this sensation. Sensation may survive the loss of parts of the body, but it ceases with the destruction of the soul or of the whole body." Realizing that this statement was made in the context of a complete natural science, including a theory of cosmological, organic, and cultural evolution, makes it seem almost uncannily modern. But, although its aim was to comfort (through acceptance of what is necessary and transcendence of irrational religious fears), it was viewed as a comfortless philosophy. In an age charged with religious conviction it languished, despite the eloquent discipleship of the poet Lucretius, whose epic *On the Nature of Things* expressed similar views two centuries later. It is only at the end of the eighteenth century—at the time when Blake wrote the passage of verse that appears as the epigraph to this book—that we can discern the beginnings of a steadily growing skepticism and rationalism that has had, and promises to continue to have, historical continuity of the widest significance.

In philosophy, the thread of skepticism characteristic of twentieth-century logical analysis can be traced back to Blake's contemporary David Hume. Like Blake, Hume was also something of a lone voice. His major early work, *Treatise of Human Nature*, which attacked all the reigning philosophies of his day, was resoundingly ignored, and his *Dialogues Concerning Natural Religion* he considered too dangerous to publish in his lifetime. But over the course of the next hundred years there were empirical and theoretical advances that really constituted the foundations of a future treatise on human nature. These advances removed all doubt of at least the possibility of a nonmetaphysical account and, incidentally, fleshed out the sketch given by Epicurus twenty-one hundred years previously.

Just to mention the names—Charles Lyell in earth history, Darwin in organic evolution, Claude Bernard in general physiology, Pasteur in pathogenesis, Marx, Engels, Herbert Spencer, Lewis Henry Morgan and others in social science, Hughlings Jackson and Charles Sherrington in neurophysiology, Paul Broca and Carl Wernicke in neuroanatomy, Santiago Ramón y Cajal and Camillo Golgi in neurohistology, and James and Freud in psychology, these a mere prominent few—conveys vividly the changed climate of thought. With so much of "the nature of things"—previously most easily explained by reference to religious and metaphysical entities—now brought firmly under the banner of common sense, it could come as no surprise that "soul" was ripe to be cannibalized by science.

The viewpoint of A.J. Ayer, representative of a large segment of late-twentieth-century philosophy, is that a "prudent theory" would be "one that does not attempt to explain away the occurrence of experiences, or to maintain that our descriptions of them are logically equivalent to descriptions of physical events, but still claims that they can be factually identified with states of the central nervous system." In other words, our subjective experience of neural and neuroendocrine events within us cannot be satisfactorily accounted for by a full objective description of those events, for the simple reason that the language of neurobiology is not suitable for the communication of subjective experience; but neither can it exist in the absence of them. Soul is at best a metaphor for our subjective experience and for what we presume by analogy to be the subjective experience of others. Some such metaphor is needed; that is why the word "spirit" appears in the subtitle of this book. But the subjective sense in question, whatever it be called, cannot transcend in space or time the mundane activity of the body.

The most prominent modern theorist of the nature of the "soul" was Sigmund Freud, a neurologist by training and, at least until his middle years, by inclination. Through the 1880s, he was involved in such enterprises as brain anatomy, clinical neurology, and investigations of the psychotropic and other medicinal effects of cocaine. It was only in the 1890s that he began to write on psychology per se; by this time he was over thirty-five and well known as a medical scientist—a fact that undoubtedly helped make possible his leadership in his newly adopted field. A reading of his papers of the early 1890s leaves a strong, often surprising impression that Freud was completely conversant with the neuroanatomical and neurophysiological knowledge of the day and seemed satisfied with the possibility of accounting for much of the human mind by reference to it. (Although this will come up again later, it is worth noting here that the most important non-Freudian psychologist of the same period, William James, was also a physician conversant with neurobiology and also put it to use in his psychology.)

Freud's neuropsychology is best represented by two long papers from this period, both of which show what he expected to gain *in psychological analysis* from brain science, as well as his emerging sense of frustration with it. The first, "On Aphasia: A Critical Study," completed in 1891, gives a highly detailed account of the neuroanatomy of aphasia—the loss of speech or comprehension or both—

and related cognitive disorders attributable to brain damage, as these subjects were then understood.

"On Aphasia" summarized Freud's reading and thinking about the neural basis of language function, a subject he had been occupied with throughout the late 1880s. The monograph consists mainly in a critique of the then reigning (and, in modified form, still widely accepted) theory of localization of language in the cerebral cortex, which was established by Paul Broca and Carl Wernicke, and extensively reviewed in a paper of Wernicke's published in 1886. Briefly, this theory held that the cortex contained two major centers for language, a speech production center and a speech reception center; it was based on evidence that each of these two functions could be lost by specific differential damage. The result would be one or another form of aphasia. Other disorders could result from damage to the fiber pathways that link the speech reception and the speech production areas ("conduction aphasias"). Still other areas of the cortex were believed to control such functions as reading and writing.

Freud mounted his critique of the cortical localization theory of aphasia on the basis of a careful review of the published clinical case studies and also on the basis of then recent advances in neuroanatomy. But his most serious source of objection came from his reading of the neurophysiology that was then being shaped by Hughlings Jackson, Charles Sherrington, and others. One suspects Freud of having deliberately underestimated, at least to some extent, the intelligence, open-mindedness, and breadth of knowledge of Broca and Wernicke. But we must recognize that the monograph was written at the close of a century during which claims regarding the cerebral localization of function had been carried to extremes of specificity (not by Broca and Wernicke, but by many others) that became in the end ludicrous. Also, the 1880s and 1890s were a heady time for neurophysiology, when knowledge of the function of individual nerves was being organized for the first time into larger units and producing the first theories of brain *function*. It is not surprising if these developments inspired the young neurologist into an excess of zeal against the neuroanatomy he had given his youth up to learning.

His strategy was to identify what he saw as the soft underbelly of the localization theory, and then try to explain what was needed to improve it. He noted, for example, that aphasics may retain the ability to swear, to sing a song, or to repeat a phrase spoken just before their injury. He discussed the pattern of recovery of mental functions after epileptic seizures, which was known to sometimes include a phase of transitory word deafness. He was aware of the existence of individual variability in the loss following a given lesion ("Different amounts of nervous arrangements in different positions are destroyed with different rapidity in different persons," a quotation he gives from Hughlings Jackson) and, following his own teacher, the French neurologist Charcot, he attributes this variation not to individual differences in anatomical organization but rather to the vagaries of personal experience—that is, to the individual's history of function. For example, a literate and a nonliterate person could be expected to suffer different losses from the same lesion separating the visual areas of the cortex from the speech-perception areas.

Freud's understanding of these clinical phenomena, which he saw as inconsistent with the Broca-Wernicke view, was that they resulted from differences not of structure but of function, and he argued from them that language is best comprehended not just by references to the anatomical structure of the cerebral cortex, but to the level of neural energy expressed in that organ and in other brain systems in various functional states. He accepted Hughlings Jackson's view that loss of function, whether transitory or permanent, reversed the sequence of acquisition of function in normal childhood development—you would lose your most adult functions first—and that recovery of function recapitulated the childhood sequence. He believed that the explanation of the retention of swearing, of simple oft-repeated words like "yes" and "no," of singing, and of phrases learned in extreme stress, all pointed to a powerful role for neural excitability in language function; and, with that, to a role for emotion.

The clinical evidence to which Freud referred holds good, for the most part, to this day—and in greatly expanded volume. More surprising, a modern explanation would parallel Freud's own arguments in many important ways, criticizing localization theory by reference to physiological function, particularly as the latter relates to emotion. But what is perhaps more interesting about the monograph is that it marks the merest beginning of a transition that, in less than a decade, was to leave Freud involved in function alone, and at that not neurophysiological but psychological function. In all his most famous works published after the late 1890s, there is virtually no reference to the neuroanatomy and neurophysiology that had once been a consuming preoccupation for him. In most of the mature Freud's canon, the only reference to structure within the nervous system is to purely metaphoric "structures": *unconscious, preconscious, conscious*; or *id, ego*, and *superego*. While it is not correct to say that there is no relation between these and his earlier anatomical and physiological notions, they make it obvious that he was trying to distance himself from the language of biology, and his twentieth-century writings, which extend through most of the 1930s, give little evidence of his having followed the growth of neurobiology with even a fraction of the attention he had given it until 1890.

Much in the aphasia monograph prefigures the later, wide-ranging genius: the emphasis on the role of emotion in thought, on the relationship between trauma and later adaptation, on the significance of states of nervous-system excitation, and on the idea that recovery was somehow bound up with or parallel to the course of normal development in childhood. But it is only four years later, with the completion in 1895 of *Project for a Scientific Psychology*, that we can really see how the theoretical transition to psychoanalytic theory was effected.

In the terms of the nervous system, the basic features of Freud's understanding of the biology of psychological function as of 1895 are easily summarized, and in essence each is still valid today:

First, the central nervous system can be divided into two basic sectors, a division with important functional consequences: namely, a sector containing projection systems—long fiber tracts carrying impulses (for example, pain) from the peripheral body organs to higher brain centers such as the cerebral cortex, where the periphery is in some way represented; and a second sector containing "nuclear" systems, located in the core of the brain, made up of short neural elements with many connections, and responsible for the monitoring and regulation of the body's internal milieu.

Second, there are neurosecretory elements in the nervous system that produce chemicals that circulate in the body; furthermore, these chemicals can excite the neural elements of the brain, giving rise to the possibility of a positive feedback cycle. (The modernity of this viewpoint is uncanny.)

Third, the function of the brain consists of electrical activity of the neural elements, which, when sufficiently excited, can discharge.

Fourth, the neural elements are separated from one another by "contact barriers," and in order for one in a circuit to excite the next, this contact barrier must be traversed. Thus Freud accepted and made central use of the concept of the neuron and of the barrier between neurons—the synapse—at a time when the existence of these features of the nervous system ("the neuron doctrine") was still hotly contested, dividing followers of the great neurohistologist Santiago Ramón y Cajal, who believed in it, from followers of the equally respected Camillo Golgi, who did not. (On the basis of the fact that gaps in the nervous system had never actually been observed under the microscope, Golgi wrongly believed that they did not exist, and that the nervous system was one vast gapless interconnected web. A decade after Freud's acceptance of the neuron doctrine in his *Project*, Cajal had won wider—if incomplete—acceptance, and Sherrington was preparing to publish *The Integrative Action of the Nervous System*, which gave the synapse a central place in neurophysiological theory.)

Finally, the neural elements are capable of a level of excitation that is below that required for discharge and transmission across the contact barrier. Freud thus prefigured by half a century or so the establishment of the existence of subthreshold levels of electrical activity in neurons.

These features of brain function—mostly presumed, but nonetheless correctly so—were articulated in the monograph into a theory of the mind. In it, we can recognize much of what was to become psychoanalysis. It is fair to say (and has been said by a number of Freud's recent biographers and disciples) that although the theory of neural function outlined in the *Project* was rarely specifically referred to in later works, it influenced his thinking throughout his life. A crude sketch of the theory follows.

Primary transactions with the external world, including sensation, pain, and muscle action, are concluded by the long, fast-acting projection systems from the periphery to the cortex. The core sector responds more gradually. It can be influenced by the projection systems through collateral fibers, but is also critically subject to influence by circulating humoral factors in the internal milieu of the body; these latter it could in turn also influence, giving the core sector an important role in what we would now call homeostasis (and its disturbances). The core sector is full of diffuse connections—either complex or messy, depending on how one looks at them—and it can be excited not only from without but from within, through spontaneous activity of its elements. If this excitation were subthreshold and widespread among the neural elements, a condition of potential for relatively diffuse firing could be said to exist in the core. Significantly, such firing might sometimes be maladaptive. Moreover, either in the core or in the projection systems, repeated discharge of impulses over a pathway could be expected to result in easier future transit over that pathway: in other words, in learning.

So far, there is nothing here that would raise an eyebrow in the modern neurobiological community; most of it is textbook fact. As for what follows, much of it would raise eyebrows, some of it would be viewed as pretty speculative, but none of it could be simply said to be beyond the realm of possibility.

Subthreshold excitation of elements in the core sector—"cathexis"—could, if widespread, cause "strain" (in German, *unlust,* or unpleasure). Such widespread cathexis in the core could result from a positive feedback cycle between the neural or neurosecretory elements on the one hand and the blood-borne humoral factors on the other; these processes might be expected to go on during a state of hunger or unsatisfied sexual excitement. If transmitted to the cortex, this cathexis would be subjectively perceived as strain or unpleasure. (Pain would consist in a larger and more sudden increase in both cortical and subcortical excitation.)

The cortex, perceiving strain, would activate transactions with the world, such as eating or sexual intercourse, which would bring the blood-borne factors and the neural elements back into balance, producing a decrease in overall cathexis, or pleasure. Pleasure has the tendency to reinforce; that is, to lower the resistance of the contact barriers to discharges along the same pathway the next time. When this has proceeded enough to effectively prevent the strain that results from accumulated cathexis in the core, learning is said to have taken place.

Thereafter the structure of the core is no longer random, and the specific distribution of more and less reinforced pathways within it constitutes the ego structure or personality of the individual, which consists of memory traces (reinforced pathways) selected by prior experience from all possible pathways within the core. These include *motives* (pathways of core excitation), *wishes* (perception of the motive by the cortex), and *mechanisms of defense*—literally defense against excessive cathexis by lateral dispersal of the excitation over pathways not plainly related to the satisfaction of the motive. *Emotion* is patterned change, whether increase or decrease, in the distribution of cathexis in the cortical system, and *thought* is the result or process of comparison of the patterns of cortical activity produced by excitation from the core (*wishes*) with those produced by excitation over the long projection systems from the periphery (*perceptions*); in other words, the product of the mismatch between the way things are and the way we would like them to be.

In subsequent years, Freud made a variety of transformations in many of these concepts and replaced his anatomical conception of the structure of the human soul with various others of a more metaphoric nature. Many of his later contributions were of the greatest importance, both clinically and scientifically, and must not be minimized or even slighted. Nevertheless, it is a pity that he did not continue to follow in an active way the developments relevant to the neurobiology of emotion during the last four decades of his life and attempt to relate them to his growing, flowering theory. If he had, it would perhaps not now be as difficult as it is to bridge the gap between psychoanalysis and neurobiology—a difficulty that arises in part from the fact that few practitioners of either discipline share with Freud the inclination and ability to follow both.

If we leave his career after the publication of the *Project*, it is not because his later work is irrelevant; indeed, it casts a notable shadow over even neuroanatomical thinking about the emotions to this day. It is rather because after that monograph he leaves us as we endeavor to follow the mainstream of thinking about the neuropsychology of the emotions.

William James, Freud's fellow physician and older contemporary, had also mastered the elements of brain structure and function as they were then understood. But in lieu of Freud's experience and training in neurology, he exposed himself, during extensive travels in Europe, to the experimental psychology of the day, which was rigorous and good and which concerned itself with the elements of human sensation and perception in different modalities; and to the philosophy of the day, which in many respects was vague and bad and which provided for James an unfortunate distraction in his effort, carried out over many years teaching physiology at Harvard, to found a comprehensive scientific psychology.

His attempt, the two-volume *Principles of Psychology*, begun in 1878 and completed in 1890, is remarkable in its range, its organization, and its similarity to the subject matter of the modern textbook of psychology, for which, for generations, it has been the model. Compared with the major works of Sigmund Freud, it shows greater balance and modesty of claims, greater knowledge of experimental psychology, even greater grasp of the structure and function of the sense organs. One does not have the feeling, in reading, of being cast about in the intellectual grip of a powerful personality, and genius does not intrude, either to inspire or to cause disorder. But philosophy does—in a didactic, dull, distracting way that makes it difficult to judge what is psychology (which for James is based on evidence) and what is philosophy (which seems to come from his own rather commonplace self-observations). The work foreshadows his later complete abandonment of psychology and physiology in favor of pragmatist philosophy. But before doing so he left behind a theory of the basis of the emotions that, despite the fact that it was wrong, held the field for many years.

Called the James-Lange theory (named in part for its Danish co-discoverer, Carl Lange), its only virtues were that it was an attempt to ground the emotions in physiological functions, and that it recognized the importance of visceral and peripheral organs in the subjective experience as well as in the expression of the emotions. In James's words (the italics are his):

> *The feeling, in the coarser emotions, results from the bodily expression.* Our natural way of thinking about these coarser emotions is that the mental perception of some fact excites the mental affection called the emotion, and that this latter state of mind

gives rise to the bodily expression. My theory, on the contrary, is that *the bodily changes follow directly the perception of the exciting fact, and that our feeling of the same changes as they occur is the emotion.* Commonsense says, we lose our fortune, are sorry and weep; we meet a bear, are frightened and run; we are insulted by a rival, are angry and strike. The hypothesis here to be defended says that this order of sequence is incorrect, that the one mental state is not immediately induced by the other, that the bodily manifestations must first be interposed between, and that the more rational statement is that we feel sorry because we cry, angry because we strike, afraid because we tremble. . . .

The obvious objection that we may feel those things without performing the corresponding actions is met with the answer that while we are restricting ourselves from these actions they still exist in restrained or potential form and create sensations at the periphery of the body for us to perceive centrally. James recognizes that this is counterintuitive: "Stated in this crude way," he says, "the hypothesis is pretty sure to meet with immediate disbelief." The only efforts he makes to dispel that disbelief are of the order of argument, not evidence.

Despite its inherent improbability, the lack of evidence to support it, and the fact that enough information about the central aspects of emotion was available to make possible Freud's vastly richer account a mere ten years later, the James-Lange theory remained the accepted outlook in the United States; so much so that when Walter B. Cannon, the leading American physiologist of his day, proposed a critique and an alternative in the pages of the *American Journal of Psychology* in 1927, he had to begin it apologetically, "with some trepidation." This, despite the fact that his critique was based on decisive evidence from the physiological laboratory, his own as well as that of others.

Referring to the work of Sherrington, Bechterev, Langley, and others, Cannon noted methodically the experimental points against James and Lange. First, total separation of the viscera from the brain by severing of neural connections has little or no effect on emotional behavior, despite the absence of visceral reactions usually accompanying the emotions—and believed by James and Lange to cause them. Second, the same visceral reactions occur in very different emotions, leaving causation inadequately specific in the James-Lange theory. Third, the viscera are relatively insensitive organs, and we have a lot of trouble feeling what is going on in them, making them poor candidates for a medium of emotional sensitivity. Fourth, visceral responses such as James and Lange presumed to be causative of emotion actually are too slow for this task; they occur more slowly, in fact, than the emotional responses in question. Finally, artificial induction of those same visceral changes generally produces various forms of irritation or malaise, but rarely causes any recognizable emotion. "The processes going on in the thoracic and abdominal organs," Cannon concludes, "are truly remarkable and various; their value to the organism, however, is not to add richness and flavor to experience, but rather to adapt the internal economy so that in spite of shifts of outer circumstance the even tenor of the inner life will not be profoundly affected."

This negative side of Cannon's attack was only the half of it. More interesting and more important, he tried to pull the supports out from under James's argument that there were "no special brain centers for emotion," by proposing a plausible group of such centers. In doing so (although he was largely wrong in his specifics), he began a course of historical development that was to result in our present and future knowledge of the central nervous control of the emotions. It is difficult to overestimate the importance of this step. It not only transcended James and Lange by proposing a theory of the emotions that located them in the brain rather than in the peripheral organs; it transcended Freud as well, because Freud's appropriately brain-based theory of the emotions was deliberately ignorant anatomically, except for his almost clumsy twofold division into "nuclear" systems with visceral functions, and "cortical" systems with sensory-motor functions. Where James and Lange had located emotion in the periphery, Cannon brought it back into the brain; where Freud, who had long before accepted the brain location, based his theory on function more than on structure, Cannon took a chance on a functional theory full of architectural detail.

It should be noted yet again that in the 1880s and 1890s of James, Lange, and Freud, thoughtful people had had their fill of brain centers. It was the end of a century charged with reckless, even ludicrous claims about the location in the brain of specific mental functions and tendencies. The extreme to which this was carried can be seen in the relatively short-lived but very popular pseudoscience, phrenology, which involved the reading of character through feeling bumps on the head (the bumps were supposed to reflect the degree of development of specific brain regions). People even designed their child-rearing methods to counteract undesirable tendencies in the child that they believed they had "read" phrenologically. Small wonder, then, that Freud challenged even the prevailing theory of language centers in the cortex, which was certainly the best-supported theory of the kind, and that his increasing skepticism led him to abandon anatomical detail almost completely in the *Project*. This skepticism finds almost universal sympathy among the brain scientists of the 1980s, as in this summary quoted by one distinguished neuroscientist from another: "I find singularly little in all the vast volume of stimulation studies of subcortical structures that would promote the notion of 'centers.' There seems to be the need to introduce the notion of complex cortical-subcortical interrelations, rather than the autonomy of activity in the sense of centers."

In other words, emotions, like other mental and behavioral phenomena, must be located in the brain not primarily in the simple static geography of centers, but in the complex dynamic commerce of circuits. Thus when Cannon, in his 1927 paper, located the seat of the emotions in the thalamus, a pair of ovoid neural organs lying deep along the midline of the brain, he was proposing a model too limited for the facts. He did refer to some fascinating pieces of evidence. For example, laboratory animals with the thalamus intact, but with all higher brain centers removed, showed much of the range of emotional expression found in the normal animal; removal of the thalamus abolished these capacities. More interesting, some human victims of tumors in the thalamus (on one side only) were perfectly capable of assuming two-sided smiles, voluntarily, on command, but in the normal situations in which involuntary, spontaneous smiling and laughter occurred, their faces responded only on the side without the tumor. This suggested to Cannon that on-command smiling was regulated from the higher cortical centers, but true emotional expression from the thalamus; in effect, he thought, the tumor victims were emotionless on one side of the face and body.

To be fair to Cannon, he did give some small perspective on the *circuitry* involved by speculating that emotions are produced *through a relay* to the thalamus. Either impulses from the sense organs at the periphery passed through the thalamus on the way to the cortex, or they went to the cortex first and then down to the thalamus. In either case, Cannon wrote (the italics are his): *"the peculiar quality of the emotion is added to simple sensation when the thalamic processes are roused."*

At present we would be inclined to say that the tumor results are best explained by the hypothesis that damage to the thalamus interrupted the functioning of a complex circuit mediating the emotions—a circuit passing through the thalamus among numerous other brain organs. But it was to be left to the next decade to propose such a complex emotional circuit.

This was done by James W. Papez (it rhymes with "tapes"), a fairly obscure physician-neuroanatomist working independently in Ithaca, New York, in the year 1937. His paper—"A Proposed Mechanism of Emotion"—presented a disarmingly simple abstraction of a welter of anatomical details; but it was as revolutionary as it was elegant, and it set the tone for thought and research about emotional physiology ever since.

In a sense, one might have predicted that this would have to be done by an anatomist. Neither a psychologist like James, nor a neurologist like Freud (who was growing disappointed with anatomy) nor even an outstanding systemic physiologist like Cannon would be likely to have sufficient mastery of neuroanatomical details to think through a theory of how the brain might handle emotion. Papez located the emotions and their expression in a *circuit*—sufficiently complex to be plausible—not a center, and he chose for the circuit in question a set of interrelated structures we now call "the limbic system."

This system, located where Freud would have wanted it—in the core of the brain—included parts of the thalamus, but also parts of the cortex and, most important, the hypothalamus, which, situated below the thalamus, just about in the center of the head, is an organ through which the brain regulates the hormones of the pituitary and, in turn, those of the body. The system described by Papez had been thought by the classical anatomists to be mainly concerned with olfactory function, but this notion had been overthrown by subsequent evidence; for example, animals with little or no sense of smell, like dolphins, may still have prominent limbic systems. There was, by 1937, already substantial evidence (from lesion studies in animals and tumors in people) to support a strong relationship between this circuitry and the emotions. Papez proposed a theory involving three "streams" of impulses corresponding to three broad categories of psychic life, all three beginning with the sense organs, and each involving some part of Cannon's thalamus.

The first—"the stream of movement"—relayed the sensations through the thalamus to the *corpus striatum*, a larger structure forming the central mass of each cerebral hemisphere and long known to cause movement disorders when damaged. The second— "the stream of thought"—relayed the sensations through the thalamus to the major portions of the cerebral cortex. The third—"the stream of feeling"—the one that was the subject of his paper, relayed the sensations through still other thalamic regions to the hypothalamus and the parts of the cortex located in the midline of the head, between the two hemispheres, near the core of the brain. "In this way the sensory excitations . . . receive their emotional coloring." And in a fine rhetorical summary: "Is emotion a magic product, or is it a physiologic process which depends on an anatomic mechanism? . . . The evidence presented is mostly concordant and suggestive of such a mechanism as a unit within the larger architectural mosaic of the brain."

The extent to which these notions have survived the test of time (as well as the test of increasing complexity) is remarkable. Papez's contribution was a quantum advance beyond that of Cannon (as Cannon's was beyond that of Freud) and stands today as an outline of most of what we know about the neuroanatomy of the emotions. But before reviewing its modern vindication, we need to digress to a separate "stream of thought."

As pointed out by the great evolutionist Ernst Mayr, biology has thrown down two separate reductionist gauntlets before the poised figure of modern psychology. The first is the physiological-biochemical, which threatens to replace the language of act, thought, and feeling with another that is entirely mechanical. The second is the evolutionary-adaptive, which threatens equally with a historical and functional account that seems more powerful than psychological process. To put it in the crudest terms, biology chips away at the lofty human soul by, first, showing how easily its processes can be explained physiologically and, second, showing how much it shares, both in structure and in purpose, with the corresponding phenomena we see in other animals.

All the students of the emotions so far mentioned gave some evidence, usually explicit, of having been influenced by Darwin; but none of them took sufficiently seriously his major contributions on the subject. The first contribution was that he wound up, as it were, and set in motion the study of social behavior as adaptation. This approach has recently spawned the vigorous new subfield of behavioral biology known as sociobiology. To the extent (surely great) that social behavior and emotion are interfaced categories, this is also a contribution to the study of emotion.

Darwin, however, also addressed emotion very directly in a book called *The Expression of the Emotions in Man and Animals*, first published in 1872. It might be said that the theory of evolution by natural selection took something of a backseat in this work, although it certainly provided a background for Darwin's comparisons of humans with other animals and for theorizing about the functional importance of the expressive movements. But it is really as if Darwin did not want arguments about the *process* of natural selection to become an issue, as if he wanted the book on emotional expression, published more than a dozen years after the *Origin*, to stand on its own merits.

I think it is fair to say that if he had written nothing else his place in the history of science would have been secured by the quality and originality of the later book. It is strange, then, that it has had so little impact; perhaps it is an irony of scientific leadership that a person's most impressive work must obscure much of the rest of it, however fine it may be. In any case, *The Expression of the Emotions* has been ignored by most students of the emotions (and of social behavior), but not, at least, by one important tradition. That tradition, which arose in Europe and England during the first decades of this century—grounded firmly in the soil of zoology, not psychology—now flourishes all over the world. It culminated in a 1973 Nobel Prize for three of its living proponents, and along the way it evoked from several major American students of animal psychology papers that were at once both capitulations to it and attempts to incorporate it into the comparatively impoverished American research tradition.

I refer to the field of behavioral biology known as ethology, the comparative study of animal behavior. Although since 1973 it has been eclipsed in the popular press by the newer, more controversial field of sociobiology, it is ethology that is indisputably more mature, more substantive in its findings, and more secure in its formulations. These are as follows: that the comparative study of animal behavior must be carried out across the broadest possible range of species; that observation of the behavior of each species must be studied first of all under natural conditions—"in the wild"; that many aspects of the behavior of a species are as fixed as its morphology, and equally as attributable to the genes; that fixed and plastic components of a species' behavior are appropriately distinguished through deprivation experiments, in which relevant aspects of experience are withheld from the growing animal and its behavioral competence later examined; that once established, the fixed components of a species' behavioral repertoire are so reliable that they can become, along with anatomy, part of the basis on which its evolutionary relationship to other species is discerned; and that, whatever they are, these behaviors have evolved to serve adaptive functions (that is, in response to selective pressures) in the natural environment of the species.

The importance of these now seemingly obvious formulations may perhaps best be seen by noting that not one of them played a significant role during the heyday of animal psychology in the United States—the psychology of John B. Watson, B.F. Skinner, Clark Hull, and their disciples and colleagues. In fact, the European ethologists—both the senior trio that shared the Nobel Prize (Karl von Frisch, Konrad Lorenz, and Niko Tinbergen) and the leaders of the subsequent generation (Robert Hinde, Paul Leyhausen, Irenäus Eibl-Eibesfeldt, and others)—have paid much more attention to the work of the American animal psychologists than the latter have to them, at least until recently.

Since Darwin's initial contribution to ethology was published in 1872, lack of opportunity for influence cannot be the explanation. Indeed, Darwin's book approaches behavior with a range of strategies remarkably similar to the modern ethological ones. Although he did not do field observations himself, he referred extensively to such observations by others. He also personally canvased numerous missionaries and other amateur ethnologists for firsthand descriptions of patterns of emotional expression in human beings living in the most remote simple societies all over the world; he thus established the first proposed categorization of universals of human emotional expression. He then set these in the context of detailed descriptions of emotional expression in a wide variety of animal species, especially mammals—observed in zoological gardens, as pets, and in the wild.

He approached the question of the role of experience by comparing expressive movements in infants and adults of the same species, including our own, where part of the evidential basis was his detailed diary of the development of his own firstborn infant. He speculated on the adaptive significance of many of the movements, from communicative (as in the erection of the hair to make the body seem larger to an opponent) to physiological (as in the dilation of blood vessels for the delivery of blood-borne factors to the muscles preparing for action). He even proposed a neurophysiology of the emotional expressions and actions, albeit a crude one; it concentrated on the control of peripheral organs by the nerves from the spinal cord, and incorporated a theory (attributed by Darwin to Herbert Spencer) whereby emotional expression was held to be the result of an "overflow of nerve-force" from the central nervous system, with the course followed to be determined by a combination of nature and habit—a very simple form of the theory that was to be proposed by Freud in the 1890s.

Many of the findings of the modern ethologists are described in the second part of this book. For the moment it must suffice to say that

Darwin's approach, and the more refined ethological formulations of the first half of the twentieth century, have been very largely vindicated. Such ethological concepts as the fixed action pattern (an inherited complex motor action sequence), the innate releasing stimulus (a perceptual pattern reacted to in a predictable way *with or without* prior experience of it), and the ethogram (a catalog of the fixed components of a species' behavior) are all very viable. And these concepts apply to the behavior of "higher" animals (including humans) as well as to that of "lower" ones. There are no ethological concepts of emotional expression—except, perhaps, the "drive" model still accepted by some ethologists—that can be said to be currently useless; even the concept of instinct, even applied to humans.

The two kinds of reductionism—the physiological and the evolutionary—are joined in the developing subfield "neuroethology." Most of the work in this area, devoted to tracing out the neural basis of fixed action patterns and innate releasing mechanisms, has been done in invertebrates and lower vertebrates, where both behavior and nervous system are simpler. But some very good work has been done on an animal quite closely related to humans, the squirrel monkey, *Saimiri sciureus*, and the collaboration that produced the work is as interesting as the discoveries themselves.

The senior member of the team was Paul MacLean, an American with a distinguished, long-standing reputation in neuroanatomy. In the late 1940s and early 1950s, MacLean was the major heir to the tradition of neuroanatomical modeling of the emotions that was established by James Papez in 1937. He has carried this work forward in a way that has been steady and marked by many significant contributions. In a 1949 paper titled "Psychosomatic Disease and the Visceral Brain," he reviewed the Papez circuit, rescuing it from relative obscurity, extending it, and naming the resulting circuitry "the limbic system"—referred to as such for the first time. It has by now won almost universal acceptance as the central neural network of the emotions. In the same paper, he began to attribute separate emotional functions to different parts of the circuitry (this remains much more controversial) and, as suggested by the title, proposed that the limbic system is the major circuit that would have to be involved in psychosomatic diseases, such as gastrointestinal ulcers caused by social or psychological stress (a now widely accepted hypothesis, since limbic system control of the pituitary and the autonomic nervous system, which in turn control the viscera, has been repeatedly shown).

In a 1952 paper reviewing more detailed lesion and stimulation studies, he proposed that the famous frontal lobes, long known as the seat of some of the highest human faculties, such as foresight and concern for the consequences and meaning of events, may have these functions and others by virtue of intimate connections between the frontal lobes and the limbic system. Thus the "highest" and certainly the newest portion of the human cerebral cortex does not serve its functions by remaining aloof from older, "lower" portions of the brain but, on the contrary, precisely by virtue of its relationship to the old emotional circuitry. MacLean's bold hypothesis about the anatomical relations of the frontal lobes to the limbic system was to be decisively confirmed in the 1970s by neuroanatomist Walle Nauta, who has referred to the frontal lobes as "the neocortex of the limbic system," thus suggesting that their principal function may lie precisely in this relationship. That is, just as other parts of the cortex have been identified as the highest report-and-control centers for vision, hearing, tactile sensation, and movement, so the frontal lobes have emerged as the highest report-and-control center for the emotions.

Over the course of three decades. MacLean gradually elaborated his theory of overall brain structure and evolution, which has become known by his interesting phrase, "the triune brain." Briefly, it holds that the brains of humans and our closest relatives, the primates and other advanced mammals, contain within them three important evolutionary levels, which are to some extent functionally separable but which, at least ideally, act in concert.

The first is the "reptilian brain," which in lizards and other reptiles is the dominant and controlling circuitry, and which corresponds to the *corpus striatum* and related structures in the human brain—the circuit that figured prominently in Papez's "stream of movement." But MacLean's contribution has been to show that this structure, whether in reptiles, birds, or mammals, is not concerned with mere control of movement, but with the storage and control of "instinctive" behavior: the fixed action patterns and innate releasing mechanisms of the ethologists. This helps explain why reptiles and birds, in which the *corpus striatum* is the most highly developed part of the brain, seem (much more than mammals) to have behavioral repertoires consisting of stereotyped behaviors and responses: a lizard turning sideways and displaying its dewlap as a threat, for instance, or a bird repeating over and over again the same territorial song. It isn't that mammals have no such behaviors, but rather that birds and reptiles have so little else.

The second collection of circuits is called "the old mammalian brain," a designation that comes from evidence that it arose with the evolution of the earliest mammals. This, in effect, is the limbic system, and corresponds to Papez's "stream of feeling." In primitive mammals such as rodents and rabbits, it occupies a much higher percentage of the cerebral mass than it does in higher mammals such as monkeys. According to MacLean, it is this circuit that, without replacing the "instinctive" functions of the striatal or "reptilian" circuitry, gives those functions an emotional coloring they would otherwise not have.

The third and last set of circuits is the "new mammalian brain," corresponding to the "stream of thought" proposed by Papez and achieving its evolutionary culmination in the complex mental functions of the human brain.

MacLean and his colleagues Michael Murphy and Sue Hamilton have neatly demonstrated the roles of the three levels in a recent study. Removal of hamsters' neocortex at birth leaves them with no impairment of instinctual behavior patterns. Thus these are handled by the old mammalian brain and the reptilian brain. Further removal of the limbic structures damages maternal behavior and play behavior, these evidently being functions of the old mammalian brain specifically. The remaining unlearned species-typical behaviors— sex, aggression, food getting, and so on—can apparently be conducted in hamsters that have the reptilian brain alone. This finding, astonishing to some, has vindicated the "triune brain" model. It may also be applicable to higher mammals.

MacLean's collaborators have often been people trained in the methods and discoveries of European ethology. One of these is Detlev

Ploog, an ethologically oriented German psychiatrist. MacLean's knowledge of neuroanatomy and brain evolution, as well as his training as a physician, together with Ploog's ethological and psychiatric background, make an intriguingly apt set of preparations for exploring the physiology of the emotions. Their chosen species, the squirrel monkey, is a tractable laboratory subject with complex emotional behavior—behavior controlled coordinately by all three parts of the "triune brain."

Consider a behavioral pattern known as the genital display. The monkey lifts its leg and spreads its thigh out to expose the genitals, while making a characteristic vocalization. It does this as a threat in aggressive encounters that may or may not lead to violence, and dominant animals are more likely to do it to submissive ones, even to the point of, as it were, sticking it in their faces. Males do it much more often than females in these dominance encounters, and also do it to females as a prelude to sexual intercourse. It is present in both sexes in essentially adult form from within a few days of birth, but the context is readily influenced by experience; one female who had a dominant position in a group exhibited it frequently, just as do males, although whether she had the anatomical analogue of the male phallic erection is not known.

This display is firmly within the category of species-typical fixed action patterns as defined by the ethologists. Lesion studies have shown conclusively that it is controlled by a circuit passing through the *globus pallidus*, a key part of MacLean's "reptilian brain." Lesions of the limbic system itself do not affect the display, but it is of interest that the *globus pallidus* has intimate structural relations with the limbic system; it is possible that what is interrupted is a circuit mediating some crucial interplay between the emotional arousal of the aggressive or sexual encounter and the concatenation of fixed motor impulses that constitute the display. In any case, it is clear that the display behavior is associated with emotional experience and expression in the normal monkey, and that such expression and experience must be largely mediated by the "old mammalian brain" or limbic system. Finally, although no neural evidence of this is as yet available, it is likely that the ability of context to influence the display in ways more complex than would be possible for a "lower" mammal indicates involvement of the "new mammalian brain" or neocortex in the regulation of its exhibition. Thus, the three levels all participate in the control of this instinctive yet flexible emotional behavior.

It will not have been lost on the reader that some similar considerations might apply to some aspects of human behavior. For example, smiling in greeting is a human fixed action pattern universal (despite contextual variations) to all cultures. It appears early in infancy as a result of events in brain development rather than as a result of learning, and it frequently appears involuntarily from that point on. It clearly has concomitants, and perhaps also causes, that lie in the limbic system, but it is possible that its principal output control network—in the sense of coordinating the many muscle contractions involved—lies in the oldest, "reptilian" part of the brain and works in much the same way as control of the squirrel monkey genital display. Finally, it can be dissimulated—that is, exhibited voluntarily without the emotion of pleasure generally associated with it. And we know from anatomical work previously summarized that this ability is regulated from the newest, neocortical part of the brain, while involuntary smiling is controlled by lower, older circuitry.

Thus, the human smile—a gesture of joy, a gesture of greeting, a gesture of submission, a gesture of deception, occasionally even a gesture of contempt—involves, or at least can involve, all three portions of the triune brain. The sudden smile in greeting a welcome acquaintance toward whom we feel very little may be no different in neural control from the friendly or aggressive displays of lizards and robins. The slowly spreading smile on the face of a parent watching a loved child take its first steps depends, in all likelihood, on a normally functioning limbic system, that invention of the early mammals. And the presumably less authentic, endlessly repeated "stewardess smile" could probably not be effected without the more advanced portions of the cerebral cortex.

But most interesting for present purposes is the smile that comes over us as we are sitting, aware of thinking nothing at all, in silent, solitary reverie. Somehow the flow of feeling catches a favorable wind and releases neural energy in a certain set of circuits, and without a conscious thought we find ourselves smiling. In the title of this chapter, the physiological sources of feeling are symbolized as a well.

The suggestion is that our thoughtful, conscious, higher, and more noble selves can dip down into this "well" and bring up a bucket full of warmth, or joy, or sadness. This is undoubtedly a part of what is happening when we respond to the complexities of poetry or theater. Indeed the metaphor of a well—which stretches reality somewhat— seems even more appropriate now than it would have in Papez's day; the limbic structures, we realize, lie on the banks of the fluid-filled ventricles of the brain, and these are capable of carrying chemical factors that help to mediate the emotions—including, but not exclusively, neurotransmitters and hormones.

But the wording of the analogy is liable to be misleading if we visualize the emotional brain as a cistern; for far from being a static, tepid well, it more closely resembles an artesian spring, upwelling sometimes forcefully, and of its own accord. And even this analogy may still lead us astray. since it suggests only a bubbling of sweet water; whereas in reality this particular spring, however benign it usually is, is perfectly likely to spew forth poison.

8

LOGOS

> . . . the consciousness of the human organism is
> carried in its grammar.
> Or the unconsciousness of the human organism.
> —Joan Didion, *A Book of*
> *Common Prayer*

Although E.O. Wilson is maligned as a reductionist who can
scarcely tell the difference between human beings and ants, although
his book *Sociobiology*, published in 1975, was viewed by its critics
(wrongly, of course) as a transparent attempt to rob us of the last
shred of our humanity, rendering us incoherent half-apes—that book
by that man contains this sentence: "The development of human
speech represents a quantum jump in evolution comparable to the
assembly of the eucaryotic cell." This is tantamount to calling the
emergence of human language one of the three or four most important events in the history of life; more important, perhaps, than the
evolution of multicelled animals or the conquest of the land. It is a
viewpoint that places Wilson squarely in a tradition that is at least as
old as history—namely, that human language is absolutely unique in
the animal kingdom and that it distinguishes us absolutely and
irrevocably from any other creatures around, from any other creature
that came before us.

"In the beginning was the Word, and the Word was with God, and
the Word was God." So begins the Gospel According to John. In the
Book of Genesis, man's first task is the naming of all other creatures,
to gain dominion over them. And the first great cooperative human

effort—the Tower of Babel—is foiled by a failure of human speech. These convictions about the importance of language echo in our own day among intellectuals far removed from religious faith. In a sense they are, for some, the last vestige of such faith. In past ages, men and women had no difficulty specifying the source of the separation between themselves and animals: People had souls, animals did not. With the death of the soul—at least in the old sense—engineered by nineteenth-century intellectuals, referring to language was about the best that the average agnostic could do to maintain the conviction of human uniqueness. Anthropologists have been among the greatest enthusiasts of this view, and to this day every student in Anthropology I can recite a catechism about symbolic speech as the moat around humankind that keeps all lesser zoological lights at bay.

Is it true? It may yet be. But it cannot escape our notice that the last fifteen years have seen a frontal assault on this position, launched by people who study our closest animal relatives. At least four different teams in four different universities using widely varying methods claim to have taught chimpanzees the elements of language. And another team, led by F.G. Patterson, claims to have taught the infant female gorilla, Koko, more than four hundred words, leading Patterson to say, in print, in a distinguished scholarly journal, "language is no longer the exclusive domain of man."

The validity of these claims depends, of course, on an agreed-upon definition of language. "Language is a purely human and non-instinctive method of communicating ideas, emotions, and desires by means of a system of voluntarily produced symbols." This seemed to the famous anthropological linguist Edward Sapir a "serviceable" definition of language; but since it involves us immediately in a challenge to say what we mean by "instinct," by "voluntary," and by "symbol"—tasks if anything worse than the one we started with—I think we may be permitted to conclude that it is for our purpose insufficiently serviceable. Also, as reasonable as it seems, it includes the phrase "purely human," thus excluding from consideration by fiat the very claims that interest us.

If the point seems belabored, let me say that virtually every definition of language suffers from flaws like those, so that the tacit conviction that we know what language is is based—unless we happen to be theoretical linguists—really on very little. This is not the case for those students of anthropology who have read the excellent work of Charles Hockett. Fed up with the vagueness of prior definitions, Hockett advanced the most precise and exhaustive definition up to that time—the early 1960s—and one that, if flawed, still stands as the best. It includes thirteen features, clearly defined in observable terms, and a true language must include all of them. Briefly, they are: (1) the use of the vocal-auditory channel for the communicative act; (2) broadcast transmission and directional reception; (3) rapid fading of the signal; (4) interchangeability of speakers for a given signal; (5) feedback, or subjective comprehension of the signal by the signaller; (6) specialization of the communicative act for the function of communication alone; (7) semanticity, or meaning; (8) arbitrariness of the relationship between a given signal and a given meaning; (9) discreteness of the elements, change in which can signal a change in meaning; (10) displacement, or the ability to refer to things remote in space and time; (11) productivity, or the openness of the system to, and generativity of, novel signals; (12) traditional transmission, extragenetically, by teaching and learning; and (13) duality of patterning, or the possibility of shuffling the same elements to make different signals (as in "team" and "meat").

By this definition it is absolutely clear that only human speech can meet the challenge. While each of the thirteen characteristics may be found in one or another animal communication system, and some— such as numbers 2 and 6—in a great many of them, only human speech has, or at least can have, all without exception. The definition is precise and, as definitions of complex phenomena go, well operationalized—that is, its applicability is fairly easy to determine empirically. Nevertheless, it has problems, and serious ones.

For one thing, it is so exhaustive as to exclude some things that most of us would like to call language. For instance, the sign languages of the deaf, whether alphabetically based or not, do not use the vocal-auditory channel; nevertheless, they have been shown to be the complete structural and functional equivalents of vocal-auditory human speech. To exclude them would be to hold a definition of language that contains something seemingly inessential. Along the same lines, we can visualize a deaf person learning to read and write without learning to speak; this would violate not only the first but also the second and third items in the definition. Would we really want to cast it out of court?

Worse, the list, as thorough as it is, omits something that we experience as closer to the "essence" of language than some of the things it includes: syntax, or the organization of communication above the level of the individual meaningful signal. While Hockett was working on his definition, and considering various animal communication systems in relation to it, the great theoretical linguist Noam Chomsky was designing his theory of syntax. This theory would bring to the fore the higher level of organization as perhaps the most central feature of language; and one which would make the attainment of language capacity seem more remote from the ken of the apes than ever.

One of Chomsky's famous examples—*Colorless green ideas sleep furiously*—served to illustrate the higher level of organization. Although essentially meaningless, it is easily recognizable as a grammatical sentence—contrast it with *Furiously sleep ideas green colorless*. Our ability to choose from these two the one that is grammatical, in spite of the fact that it too is largely meaningless, shows that we have knowledge of rules of how words are organized, knowledge that is to some extent at least independent of meaning.

Syntax, like phonology—the sounds of language—has its own capacity for duality of patterning—*Jim hits Bill* or *Bill hits Jim*—and for productivity—the invention of never-before-seen forms. Indeed, it could be argued that the infinite capacity of syntactic rules for generating new forms is the most crucial feature of human language. In any case, these features of higher-level organization must certainly be added to Hockett's list.

Chomsky argued, as many anthropologists had done before him, that all human languages perform the same functions, and that these functions reflect some basic capacities of the human mind and brain. For every human sentence produced or understood, there is a deep structure, and the deep structures of sentences in different languages that tend to the same purpose would be isomorphic. The rules for the relationships of elements in the deep structure would constitute a universal grammar, shared by all people of all cultures, and these rules would arise from brain function. The crucial thing to know about a language would be the generative, or transformational, grammar—the rules for getting from the universal deep structure to the specific surface structure of the language. The knowledge of deep structure, together with the knowledge of some specific transformational grammar, is known as competence—it is the abstract knowledge of the speaker. Performance is what we hear, the fully realized, practical speech act, and it depends upon much else besides competence—at least competence as defined formally above.

Chomsky's theory of syntax, together with Hockett's features of semanticity, productivity, displacement, and arbitrariness as key characteristics of signal capacity, began to approach what we might be willing to consider the essence of language, without including unfair strictures. These definitional achievements set the stage for the reception of Eric Lenneberg's major life work, *Biological Foundations of Language*, published in 1967. This magnificent book summarized the then available evidence—it has by now reached overwhelming proportions—for the view that language is a fundamental feature of human biology, and that its emergence during the life course of each individual is primarily the result of a genetically coded maturational plan, particularly in the growing nervous system.

The obvious challenge to this viewpoint, stemming from the immense diversity of human languages and from the undoubted role of learning in the acquisition of any specific language—a challenge that had stood for more than a century—was effectively cleared away by the concept of competence, implicit in Hockett's definition and explicit in Chomsky's. Genetically determined neural structures would account for the "deep structure" of languages, as well as for mental capacities for semanticity, productivity, displacement and the generation of surface structure from deep structure. The learning environment would merely fill in the gaps; its impact on language, superficially impressive, would be of small formative importance.

I accept this argument in virtually all particulars and I consider it very difficult for anyone who knows the facts to do otherwise. But I hasten to add what is obvious: It is undoubtedly true that normal language development depends on the learning environment, and that language performance is responsive to it in many subtle and not-so-subtle ways. I have not said that it is of small importance but that it is of small *formative* importance. The human skeleton, to resort to analogy, has a genetically coded structure that unfolds in a quite rigid maturational plan. Without a supply of nutrients, that plan is useless, and the unfolding stops. More specifically, placed in an environment poor in calcium or phosphorus or vitamin D, the plan will go badly awry—the resulting structure may be so deformed that it is difficult to recognize as the characteristic, species-specific human skeletal structure; it may be functionally useless. Varying the sheer number of calories certainly can alter the size and rate of growth of the skeleton, and it is even possible that such vagaries of the outside world as lighting and psychological stress can do the same. Conceivably, variations in diet composition within the normal range for human societies account, in part, for the subtle variations observed in normal skeletal structure; the amount and nature of exercise certainly do.

Nevertheless, it would not occur to any knowledgeable scientist to doubt that the basic structure of the human skeleton is produced under the aegis of the genes during a very largely rigid course of development, and that in what is usually called "the normal expectable environment" of a growing human being in any population, the characteristic species-specific human skeletal structure will always reliably emerge.

A similar conviction, stated in very similar words, may now be responsibly held concerning language. But giving credence to this conviction requires that we specify some details of the maturational plan; and that in turn requires a return to the fundamentals of the functional anatomy of the brain.

Perhaps the first specific piece of evidence for language localization in the brain was provided by the anatomist Paul Broca in 1861. He noticed that in cases in which a patient was unable to produce any speech, there was frequently a brain lesion on one side in the area just forward of and adjacent to the region controlling the muscles of the face and throat—roughly halfway between the top of the ear and the edge of the eyebrow. This area, now known as Broca's area, was not involved in direct control of muscle action; but it was involved in giving adjacent muscle-control centers linguistic direction. A few years later, in 1865, Broca presented the further observation that in the vast majority of these cases of aphasia, or language loss, the lesion in question was on the left side; the notion of lateralization of brain function, and the attendant notion of cerebral hemispheric dominance, had been fully born.

"Broca's aphasics," as they are generally called, can make with great effort a very telegraphic version of speech. "New York . . . go" may stand for a whole idea about a trip to New York that would normally be expressed in a complex sentence. Most difficult of all for these patients are small transitional words. However, they often give every evidence of understanding what is said to them—for example, by carrying out instructions. Very different aphasia syndromes are possible.

In 1874, Carl Wernicke, a then obscure twenty-six-year-old neurologist, described a new aphasic syndrome characterized by fluent and rapid but largely meaningless speech, with most of the content words missing, and by almost total loss of comprehension of speech, despite normal hearing. These patients often had lesions in a quite different region—now called Wernicke's area—behind and adjacent to the area of the cerebral cortex involved in the first-level interpretation of auditory patterns. (Wernicke's area would be approximately above the ear, although this association with hearing is purely coincidental.) In his impressive paper on the subject, Wernicke went on to advance a theory of the brain mediation of language, taking into account his own findings as well as Broca's. According to this theory, the area he identified, adjacent to the primary higher processing center for hearing, was responsible for the analysis of sound patterns at the level of speech comprehension, while Broca's area controlled the translation of thought into speech. For a patient to, for example, repeat a sentence spoken by the physician, both Wernicke's and Broca's areas would have to be intact; further, there would have to be some connection between them.

This connection in fact exists, in the *arcuate fasciculus*—a fiber bundle running between the two areas under the surface of the brain. As if designed to confirm Wernicke's theory, there appeared much later a description in the literature of yet a third form of aphasia—conduction aphasia. It is characterized by the presence of both comprehension and fluency, but by an inability to repeat what has been heard; and the lesion is where it is expected, in the *arcuate fasciculus*, disconnecting the faculty of comprehension from the faculty of speech.

We are far from the 1870s, but this outlook has held up rather well. Many refinements have been made on these early accounts, but none that require major revision of the outline. For example, the loss of the ability to read and write, without deficit in the vocal-auditory channel, is often associated with a lesion in the area just behind Wernicke's area—a transitional zone between speech comprehension and visual pattern processing. Also, we now have a greater sense of the complexity of things—Broca's aphasics can sing rather well, even songs with words, and they can swear much better than they can speak. But this merely indicates that presently unknown or partly known brain functions can make an "assist" when Broca's area is damaged; in the case of singing, it may be the right cerebral hemisphere; in the case of swearing, the limbic system. Finally, consistent with all that we know about the way the brain works, we can abandon the Broca-Wernicke notion of functional "centers" in favor of a more complex notion of circuits.

In recent years, the part of the picture that has received the greatest attention is cerebral dominance and lateralization of language function. It has been repeated so often that one begins to wonder about the truth of it, but this is a case of a fact-based legend. A 1981 Nobel Prize went to Roger Sperry for his work on this problem, rather than for his earlier work on brain development. Handedness, language, music, space perception, and certain aspects of the emotions are among the human functions that have been shown to be handled better, if not localized, in one or the other cerebral hemisphere. Each side of the brain controls the opposite side of the body, so that in right-handed people the left hemisphere is dominant. In the vast majority of right-handed people, the left hemisphere is also where language is localized—in the manner described above—while musical ability, spatial perception, and some emotional functions appear to be handled better in the right hemisphere. In left-handed people the situation is much less clear, but it tends to be the reverse of that for right-handers. In how these relationships are demonstrated there lies, of course, a tale, but the procedures need not detain us. Suffice it to say that few people in behavioral and neural science today doubt the existence of hemispheric specialization, pretty much along the lines I have outlined—although there is much controversy as to how it grows and why it evolved.

One of the most impressive demonstrations of hemispheric specialization is anatomical. Norman Geschwind and his colleagues at the Harvard Medical School have repeatedly shown that in normal adult human brains, there are bilateral asymmetries in a region corresponding to Wernicke's area, and that the left side is usually larger. On the average, the left side is one-third larger than the right; a full centimeter longer in absolute terms. The difference can be observed and measured in the gross anatomical specimen with the naked eye and it can be confirmed by detailed microscopic analysis defining the region according to its distinctive cell structure. It is real.

What is more, it exists in the newborn infant, fresh from the womb, having had no experience of language. Sandra Witelson, Juhn Wada, and others have measured it in neonates, and it has even been found in fetuses thirty-one weeks of gestational age. It is evidently coded from conception. Experimental settings designed to expose subtle aspects of hemispheric specialization have shown that it exists in the youngest infants. Language is unfolding, gradually, in the infant in the most fundamental sense of metamorphosis.

Eric Lenneberg, were he alive, would be delighted by these discoveries. "Why do children normally begin to speak between their 18th and 28th month?" he wrote in his 1967 book. "Surely it is not because all mothers on earth initiate language training at that time." Although little systematic cross-cultural work on language acquisition had been done up to that time, his answer to his own rhetorical question, with its assurance of universality, proved to be very close to the mark. Language *training*, if it exists, is very difficult to identify in any culture. Mothers everywhere speak something called "motherese," which is a simplified version of grown-up language; they repeat the child's near-words and make them words; they respond to a baby's pointing hand, accompanied by a high-inflection grunt, by naming something. If this is training, then it certainly exists in the environment of children of language-learning age, and I saw as much of it among the !Kung San of Botswana as I see among the parents of my own daughter's friends. However, I do not believe it to be coincidence that mothers (and other people) act this way to one-and-a-half and two-year-olds. On the contrary, I think it is precisely the universal and natural behavior of those tiny linguophiles that makes adults behave the way we do to them.

Among the !Kung San of Botswana, among Indian peasants of Guatemala, among the Luo of Kenya, in Samoa, Korea, Japan, Russia, Israel, and virtually every Western European country, we now have evidence showing the rapid onset of true linguistic capacity during the age period specified by Lenneberg. Roger Brown has reviewed this work and evaluated it in relation to his own masterly work on the acquisition of American English. For many, though not all of these languages, the evidence is good enough so that it is possible to show that not only the overall timing but even the sequence of acquisition of linguistic functions is similar in widely disparate languages. More impressive, perhaps, is the recent demonstration that deaf children acquiring American Sign Language show the same rapid increase in the mean length of utterance during that age period.

Lenneberg himself had an inkling of this last fact from informal observations of deaf children. He presented data showing that normal hearing children with deaf parents show little difference from those with normal parents, except that they quickly learn to use "deafisms" with their parents and normal speech with others. He studied Down's syndrome children (mongoloids) and showed that language develops in them, albeit more slowly, in much the same way as in normal children, and that an IQ of 50 at age twelve or 30 at age twenty does not rule out grammatical mastery of English. He reviewed the literature on nanocephalic ("bird-headed") dwarfs and found that these individuals, grossly subnormal in body weight, brain weight, brain/body weight ratio, and IQ, usually attain verbal skills comparable to those of a normal five-year-old.

At the conclusion of these and many other explorations he decided, sensibly enough, that a behavioral pattern that would unfold in the face of such obstacles had to be very deeply engrained in human biology. He concluded, in fact, that language is as much a species-specific behavioral capacity of human beings as bipedal walking is; and that not even the very grossest distortions of environment seemed to be able to derail its development. He was interested, of course, in the characteristics of brain maturation that might explain linguistic metamorphosis—what developmental psycholinguists were then calling the Language Acquisition Device, or LAD. He didn't find it, but he did make some inroads, and many more have been made since.

He appears to have realized, to begin with, that overall brain maturation is astonishingly rapid during the first two years of life, after which it slows almost suddenly. Stephen Jay Gould, in his superb book *Ontogeny and Phylogeny*, has pointed out that this pattern of brain growth is one of the most distinctive features of our species. A brief period of rapid brain growth followed, almost suddenly, by a long epoch of slow growth is characteristic of apes and monkeys too. But there is this important difference: In even our closest higher primate relatives, the time of sudden slowing coincides roughly with birth. In humans, it is postponed almost two years after birth, and to Gould, this change in maturational plan may explain a great deal about our species—including, perhaps, its capacity for language acquisition.

But, as Lenneberg realized, overall increase in brain size, however distinctive, however rapid, cannot go very far toward explaining the specific sequence of behavioral changes we observe universally in human infants. For such explanation we must turn to differential growth in specific brain systems.

Referring to the work of J. Leroy Conel at the Harvard Medical School on the maturation of the cerebral cortex, Lenneberg noted that, in a region of the cortex roughly corresponding to Broca's speech production area, there are massive increases in the density of the web of fiber connections during the first two years of life, including during the period from fifteen to twenty-four months. Although the birth of new nerve cells is finished throughout the cortex—and perhaps throughout the brain—by the time the infant is born, there is ample room for maturation in other ways. New dendrites, the receiving processes of neurons, form and make new synaptic connections with the axons of other cells. The area of synapses changes, and nerve cells increase in size. Most interesting, perhaps, because its function remains puzzling, is the great increase observed in number of non-neural cells in the brain; this accounts for most of the doubling of brain weight in the first year of life, and it has in addition the seemingly paradoxical effect of thinning out the density of nerve cells in the cortex—a well-known effect with unknown meaning.

Part of the non-neural cell proliferation consists of the development of myelin—the sheath of fatty white matter surrounding many nerve fibers. Nerves can function without myelin—many normally do—and, even in myelinated nerves, function begins before myelination. Nevertheless, myelin alters function dramatically; it increases conduction velocity, increases the maximum possible rate of firing, allows the nerve cell to work longer without fatigue, and protects it from irrelevant stimuli. For these reasons, neurologists have been interested for decades in the possibility that myelination sequences in the brain would help to explain the growth of function.

In the early part of this century, a number of neuroanatomists, particularly Paul Flechsig, described the pacing and sequence of myelination in the cerebral cortex. Primary sensory areas—such as for vision, touch, and hearing—and primary motor areas acquire myelin first, followed by adjacent association areas. Both Broca's area and Wernicke's area would fall into the latter category. Flechsig's descriptions, which were purely anatomical and did not concern themselves with the origin of language, suggest that Wernicke's area myelinates somewhat earlier than Broca's. This is consistent with the fact that comprehension precedes fluency throughout language growth. It also helps to explain why a one-and-a-half-year-old seems a bit like a Broca's aphasic: understanding a good deal, but talking only in halting telegraphic utterances made up of one or two content words. (Even the ability to sing seems as true of the toddler as of the Broca's aphasic, although swearing, at this age, does not appear to be a part of the picture.)

In 1975, André Roch-Lecours, drawing on work he had done under the great neuropathologist Paul Yakovlev, advanced materially the understanding of what might be the anatomical LAD. He confirmed Flechsig's observations on the myelination of the cortex, but went way beyond them by describing the myelination of subcortical portions of the brain. He noticed that the lower, subcortical portions of both the visual system and the auditory system were myelinated shortly after birth, consistent with the fact that in simple reflexive aspects of visual and auditory function, the six-month-old resembles the adult. However, the two sensory systems differed markedly in the rate of myelination of their "higher" bundles—those connecting their respective subcortical regions to the cortex: In vision, myelination was rapid, consistent with the mature visual pattern processing and visual learning of the infant; but in hearing, the complete myelination of the highest bundle to the cortex was stretched over the course of several years. This latter finding was beautifully consistent with the long, slow growth of language comprehension.

Can it not be that these myelination sequences are the result of experience and training, rather than the cause of the child's behavior? Almost certainly not. There are one or two studies, not well confirmed, that suggest that the process of myelination is to some extent responsive to experience. But even if true, this responsiveness will be quantitatively minor compared to the massive growth changes. These latter transformations are coded, in an as yet unknown manner, by the genes, and they account for the universal facts of infant and child language.

The phrase "origin of language" has a very different meaning for the student of evolution than it does for the student of child development, and in the evolutionary sense as well it has received much attention. Here, however, I must be less enthusiastic about the results. It is a field which now, as always, suffers conspicuously from a dearth of data and a surfeit of speculation. It is said that in the early part of this century the Linguistic Society of Paris established a standing rule barring from its sessions papers on the evolutionary origins of language. At the moment, I am half inclined to think that such a moratorium may once again be a good idea.

As an example of the sorts of information people in this field are forced to rely on, consider the work of one group of investigators who have combined anatomical evidence with computer simulations to try to show that Neanderthal people were incapable of speech because they were incapable of certain vowel sounds ("ay," "ee," and "oo"). Apart from the fact that the anatomical judgments themselves were subject to great error, there was the very impressive demonstration that a letter written to a scientific journal criticizing this hypothesis omitted those three vowel sounds completely—it used only the vowel sound "eh"—and yet was perfectly comprehensible. It read in part: "Et seems emprebeble thet ther speech was enedeqwete bekes ef the lek ef the three vewels. . . . The kemplexete ef speech depends en the kensenents, net en the vewels. . . ." That letter laid to rest for me the notion that pharynx morphology was the key to language—or at least it made me doubtful that the Neanderthals, with their very impressive brains and not much less impressive culture, could have been alinguistic.

The study of brains themselves, alas, cannot offer much help, since brains do not fossilize. We often have what are called endocranial casts—either natural or laboratory-made impressions of the inside of the skull. These reflect to some extent the impression made by the brain during life, and so the surface anatomy of the brain. But in humans and our ancestors, the skull is sufficiently flexible during growth so that the brain doesn't make a very strong impression on it. Ralph Holloway of Columbia University, and others, are going to considerable lengths to measure and analyze fossil endocasts, but I doubt that they will come up with subtle findings.

Speculations about the possible *functions* of language during human evolution have been more amusing but not very much more helpful. It is reasonable to suppose that language in early hominids functioned in the planning of hunts, the teaching of young, the mutual teaching of adults, and the modulation of emotional arousal; it certainly functions that way in modern hunter-gatherers. It is possible that some selection pressure for its emergence came from sexual selection operating on the courtship behavior of males—that is, to put it bluntly, the male who talked the best line got the girl.

Probably any thinking about the matter should take into account the fact that women have better verbal ability than men; it may mean that females led males in the evolution of this characteristic. (Considering the great philosophical weight we give to the linguistic capacity of our species, it is a wonder that we don't take more notice of the fact that women have more of it.) One could visualize an evolutionary course in which language capacity began to evolve first in females, who then produced it in males through sexual selection. But one would then have to get away from hunting and tool making as the key selection pressures for language. It is possible that storage and transfer of information about the location of plant foods required increasing linguistic ability. It is also possible that the key lies in the mother-infant relationship. Peter Marler of Rockefeller University has made a wonderful film of chimpanzee vocalizations in their natural context, and when I saw it I listened carefully for sounds remotely resembling human language. As many people have pointed out, there is very little in chimpanzee or any other natural communication in animals that resembles human language in the slightest. However, I did notice that a mother-infant pair lounging on the forest floor cooing at each other made the only sounds relaxed enough, low enough, and continuous enough to resemble even remotely human speech. I couldn't help thinking that perhaps somewhere in our ancestry just such cooing mother-infant pairs were the crucible of language evolution.

Which brings us back to the question of talking apes. How good are they? I for one have been very much impressed with them. They have done any number of things that I—or almost anyone else interested in language—would have insisted, in 1965, was impossible. They have learned at least 150 different words—as many as 400, if we are to believe the investigators working with the gorilla Koko—and use them fairly accurately and effectively. They generalize well and meaningfully among objects not obviously in the same class, and even from objects to pictures. For instance, Washoe, the first chimpanzee to learn Ameslan—American Sign Language—spontaneously used the word "hat" to refer to a nightcap that didn't look anything like the hats she was used to. They clearly show displacement, the ability to discuss things remote in space and time, and they have mastered the elements of languages that have all of Hockett's characteristics except the use of the vocal-auditory channel, which I think we can now agree is a side issue.

They also have the rudiments of syntax. They have produced, spontaneously, combinations of words they have learned individually, and these combinations, often highly inventive, clearly follow simple grammatical rules. They use the visual equivalent of a questioning intonation, represented by a symbol in each of their languages, and they formulate more complex questions as well. They use language in everyday life to get what they want from the experimenters, which is not surprising; but they also use it in other contexts. For instance, Washoe was observed to talk to herself in Ameslan—or at least to practice signs—on a number of occasions when she couldn't have known anyone was watching. Recently two chimpanzees, Sherman and Austin, using the visual-symbolic language "Yerkish," have talked to each other and communicated successfully their wants and needs. And Washoe, fully grown, is at present beginning to communicate to her infant in Ameslan.

They are even creative. Washoe, the first time she saw a duck, invented the name "water bird," and spontaneously called Brazil nuts "rock berry." Lana, who was learning Yerkish and knew the symbols for apple and the color orange, produced, after a few false starts, the question "Tim give apple which-is orange," to get an orange. And Lucy, learning Ameslan, called radishes by the generic term "food" for three days, whereupon she spontaneously began calling them "cry hurt food." We may be forgiven, I think, the slight inclination to deem these utterances poetry.

It is not surprising, then, that as early as 1973 Roger Brown, a leading student of human language development and a leading skeptic of chimpanzee language capacity, was willing to concede that Washoe at least, the only ape at that time that had learned a natural language, had attained a level of language comparable to that of a two-year-old child.

The question since then has been, How much further can it go? It was granted by even the skeptics that the ultimate ape linguistic achievements could not be predicted from a few pioneering studies that put apes at a great disadvantage compared with children. It was even possible that the wrong species was chosen—witness the much larger vocabulary attained by the gorilla infant Koko, compared with any of the chimps; and studies by Marjorie LeMay and Norman Geschwind of the degree of anatomical lateralization of the brains of the apes found the greatest difference to be in orangutans, suggesting that they might be the best linguists.

At least one group of investigators that has devoted years to this question has concluded that it has gone about as far as it can go—and that isn't much further than where Washoe was in 1973. Herbert Terrace leads the ape language group at Columbia University, and the group's ape is Nim Chimpsky—named in wry homage to Noam Chomsky, in the hope that Nim would be as bright a linguistic light in his own species as his namesake is in ours. At first, while he was immersed in his work with Nim, Terrace was very impressed. But after the data-gathering phase, going over and over the videotapes, Terrace reversed his earlier conclusion.

First, he noticed that while Nim's mean utterance length progressed to a point at which it was greater than one sign, it didn't grow beyond that. At age three and a half, when a human child (even one learning Ameslan) would be racing toward sentences, Nim was still hovering between one- and two-word phrases, where he had been for two years. Nim never produced utterances longer than two words that could be said unequivocally to be grammatically rule-bound. His percentage of imitations of trainer utterances remained high when it should have been declining. He rarely expanded on his caretakers' utterances, something human children do frequently, and he never learned turn-taking—necessary for true conversation. Finally, Terrace's reevaluation of the abilities of the other linguistic apes makes it seem as if they have all been overrated.

This controversy will undoubtedly go on for some time, and in the course of it we will learn a lot about language and about mind. In the meanwhile, apes in the wilds of Africa seem to get along very well without language, whereas humans in the wilds of New York and Boston seem to need it. Do we really? I suppose we do, although it seems to me that all the conventional wisdom as to *why* is pretty useless. But of all the off-base conventional wisdom about language, the most useless, the most egregious, the most pigheaded, is undoubtedly the conviction that it makes us morally superior to other animals. This is not an idle conviction; it is based on a sort of logic, and it goes something like this: Language enables us to keep our emotions, our baser instincts, in check. We have animal motives, of course, but we think about them, are conscious of them, a consciousness carried in language. Language thus enables us to master them, divert them, resist them, and that is what we do every day.

False, totally false. I don't know what, if anything, dampens human enthusiasm for the pursuit of motives arising from baser instincts—perhaps nobler instincts, perhaps learning, perhaps the desire to gain the high regard of others—but as far as I can tell it certainly isn't language. Language, to the contrary, may have as one of its major functions *deception*—the covering up of base motives or the distortion of them to make them look pure. This, indeed, may be one of the major adaptive purposes of communication systems in many animals, in an evolutionary sense. And we may have carried it to its most exotic realization—a communication system so complex and flexible that it raises to utter perfection the self-serving enterprise of lying.

I am reminded of the ape-turned-human in Kafka's "Report to an Academy." Having recounted his forcible training away from ape-hood, and showing his utter contempt for the moral aspect of the transformation, he says, "I repeat: there was no attraction for me in imitating human beings; I imitated them because I needed a way out, and for no other reason." He means this literally—a way out of his cage. This particular declaration comes just after his description of how he learned his first word—"Hallo!"—which came out of a drunken stupor while he was learning to drink schnapps. This, too, is the point of the epigraph from Didion. If I read her right, and Kafka right, what both are saying is that language is merely our way of carrying forward the same base motives—if they are, indeed, base—that are carried forward in every other animal; perhaps even baser ones.

From my vantage point in behavioral biology, I would have to say much the same thing. What we do with language is very like what all other creatures do without it; we do it more complexly, more gradually perhaps—we certainly do it on a grander scale. But we do it all the same and nevertheless. If language doesn't give us, then, the mastery of emotion, what does it give us really? Anything?

> Strether sat there and, though hungry, felt at peace; the confidence that had so gathered for him deepened with the lap of the water, the ripple of the surface, the rustle of the reeds on the opposite bank, the faint diffused coolness and the slight rock

of a couple of small boats attached to a rough landing place hard-by. The valley on the further side was all copper-green level and glazed pearly sky, a sky hatched across with screens of trimmed trees, which looked flat, like espaliers; and though the rest of the village straggled away in the near quarter the view had an emptiness that made one of the boats suggestive.

In this, the most important, or at least the most pregnant passage in Henry James's *The Ambassadors*, we have a glimpse of an exceptionally conscious creature, slightly hungry, resting, at home in the surround, and about to discover the existence of an illicit love affair between two other creatures he cares about, one that has up to now been concealed from him. His situation, and his impending shock, would be not unfamiliar to any number of nonhuman creatures.

But the words they are cast in are something else again. If the words elevate us above all those other creatures, it is not for moral, but for esthetic reasons; it is because they are beautiful. The music, the echoes of metaphor and meaning, the painterly quality of the phrases, the evident homage paid to a great tradition of language all combine to produce something unique in the animal world; unique, not because of its moral superiority, but because of its beauty.

Dorothy Hammond, a professor of mine at Brooklyn College, used to wave away the question of the origin of language by saying "What would we talk about, sitting around the fire at night, if we didn't have language?" It was meant as at least a half-joke, but I take it seriously. Sitting around the fire at night among !Kung San hunter-gatherers one sometimes—not often, but sometimes—will hear passages of speech as beautiful as the written one quoted above. The music is different, the echoes of meaning are different, the visual surface is not the same, and the whole tradition is another world of its own. But the aesthetic achievement is similar; I would be inclined to say, equivalent. "What would we talk about, sitting around the fire at night, if we didn't have language?"—it is the sheer useless joy of it, the time-filling, the loveliness, the grandeur.

Of course, language has functions, or else it wouldn't be here; but these are the least interesting things about it. Many of the functions are achieved by other organisms in other ways. Social cohesion is a

function, but monkeys and apes achieve that through mutual grooming, a behavior with many functional parallels to human talking.
Communication of emotion and of bits of information critical to
survival are also carried in speech, but other creatures accomplish
this in many other ways, from the dance of the bees to the song of the
lark to the wail of the howling monkey. Traditions are borne in
language, but other creatures carry them without it.

Of course, there is more than this, too. All these functions are
greatly expanded by the use of human speech. Vastly greater amounts
of information can be stored and transferred to others, concerning
everything from the location of food sources to the behavior of
predators to the movements of migratory game. Not only stories, but
great stores of knowledge are exchanged around the fire among the
!Kung; and the dramatizations—perhaps best of all—bear knowledge
critical to survival. A way of life that is difficult enough would,
without such knowledge, become simply impossible. As for cultural
traditions, those of other animals are so rudimentary in comparison
with human culture that the difference seems at least categorical.
This difference is largely owing to the human capacity for using
symbols, both verbal and nonverbal, and to the access symbolic
signals have not only to information but to the emotions. It is the use
of this information transfer capacity, not only horizontally but vertically in time, that has made possible the uniquely wide range of
ecological adaptations we see even in hunting and gathering commu-
nities.

But to list such functions and stop there would be like talking
about the functions of sex without mentioning pleasure. We would
know all about why sex evolved but not why people do it, especially
not why people will go so very much out of their way for it. As surely
as we are naturally endowed with the capacity to feel pleasure in sex,
so we are naturally endowed with a capacity to hear beauty in
language, not only in the articulation of the sounds but in the echoes
at level upon level of meaning: imagination, suggestion, challenge,
appeal, innuendo. A sentence creates in the mind of the speaker as
well as the hearer not merely a picture but a realm of intricate mental
events encompassing all five sense modalities. Say what you will
about nonhuman creatures—their admirable capacities, their behav-

ior, their consciousness—there is not a thing like it in the whole of the animal world.

In a wonderful study of the verbal exchanges of three-year-olds, the following occurs, in the context of a longer talk, between a boy and a girl: "Hello, Mr. Dinosaur." "Hello, Mr. Skeleton." These three-word utterances seem to me to contain enough complexity, enough levels of meaning and enough imagination so that I feel confident in predicting that comparable things will never be said by even the most brilliant talking chimpanzee.

But even simpler utterances can be distinctively human. Consider a ten-month-old pointing at a butterfly: "Dat!" she says, emphatically. She has gotten into the habit, of late, of pointing at things in just that way, saying "Dat, dat!" either questioningly or indicatively or emphatically or thoughtfully. She sometimes gives you the impression that she is trying to drag a name out of you, and sometimes, when you offer it, she is satisfied. At other times, when she points and speaks, she seems to be announcing the existence of a relationship between a piece of the great world and her own presumptive mind, a relationship that has evidently surprised her.

This utterance, produced by a creature who is as yet the indisputable mental inferior of the various talking apes, is already in some respects distinctively human. This behavior, very common in human infants, is very rarely observed in talking apes. Beyond that, we know what is going to happen next, and that makes it seem different. We are, after all, looking at a creature who is going to, in effect, suck a language out of the air around her during the course of the next two or three years. She has that potential, and much more; she may even, conceivably, make sentences as beautiful as those of Henry James. But I suspect there is even more distinction. I suspect that what we are looking at is the most rudimentary form of what may be the key to being human: a sort of wonderment at the spectacle of the world, and its apprehensibility by the mind; a focusing, for the purpose of elevation; an intelligent waking dream. In that capacity, it seems to me, we find our greatest distinction, and in that, and that alone, may be our salvation.

≡ PART TWO ≡

OF HUMAN FRAILTY

We live in an old chaos of the sun,
Or old dependency of day and night,
Or island solitude, unsponsored, free,
Of that wide water, inescapable.
Deer walk upon our mountains, and the quail
Whistle about us their spontaneous cries;
Sweet berries ripen in the wilderness;
And, in the isolation of the sky,
At evening, casual flocks of pigeons make
Ambiguous undulations as they sink,
Downward to darkness, on extended wings.
—Wallace Stevens, "Sunday
Morning"

9

RAGE

Many of our intellectuals rush to quell our fears
by telling us that theoretically none of this has to happen,
that violence is not part of human nature, that it occurs
only because of evil intentions and circumstances that we
can eradicate. They are the Christian Scientists of sociology; and they have not as yet solved the paradox: if we are
not by nature violent creatures, why do we seem inevitably
to create situations that lead to violence?
—Lionel Tiger and Robin Fox,
The Imperial Animal

On July 8, 1977, Richard James Herrin, a twenty-three-
year-old Yale senior, went to the bedroom of Bonnie Jean Garland, a
classmate and sometime girl friend in whose home he was then a
guest, and bludgeoned her to death in her sleep with a claw hammer.
He then fled from the scene in a car, driving from White Plains, New
York, where the slaying took place, to Coxsackie, New York, where
he surrendered himself to a priest and confessed his crime. He told
the arresting officer that he had planned to kill the young woman and
then commit suicide. The precipitating cause was romantic rejection;
Garland had evidently broken off with Herrin.

At the trial, he pleaded not guilty by reason of temporary mental
defect or disease. Evidence concerning the relative poverty he lived in
as a child was introduced (by his mother) as a mitigating factor.
Herrin testified that he did not know why he committed the slaying.
Two psychiatrists testified that he was psychotic at the time of the

alleged murder, and two other psychiatrists testified that he could not be considered to have been psychotic at the time of the alleged murder. It became evident during the trial that Herrin was a well-brought-up, well-behaved, even religious young man who had never done anything that would in the slightest way suggest that he was capable of homicide. Because of this, there was support of his defense in the Yale community. On the third day of deliberation by the jury, Herrin was convicted of manslaughter, and he was subsequently sentenced to the maximum term of eight and one-third to twenty-five years. The jurors, confused by conflicting psychiatric testimony among other complex matters, had almost reported to the judge that they were deadlocked—three of the twelve had been holding out for a second-degree murder verdict; instead, they requested that they be allowed to go to mass on Sunday in the hope of "some divine inspiration." However, they reached their verdict without this source of inspiration. Citing Herrin's evident premeditation, they also took into account the depth of his and Garland's dependence on and love for each other (as evidenced by their love letters) and the extreme emotional disturbance influencing Herrin during his crime: his two-year intimacy with Garland was to have ended in marriage, but instead she decided that she wanted to date other men and broaden her social life, plunging him into despair and the belief that "I could not live without her." The judge, in delivering the maximum sentence, said, "Even under the stress of extreme emotional disturbance, the act of killing another is inexcusable," therefore, in effect, refusing to consider the argument of the defense attorney that Herrin's crime had been "totally inconsistent with his conduct before and after the act."

On November 18, 1978, while Richard James Herrin awaited trial, Wang Yungtai, a twenty-four-year-old warehouse worker at the Materials Recuperation Company in Peking, sought out Hu Huichin, a fellow worker whom he had wanted as his girl friend, and, near their lockers at the factory, struck her seven or eight times in the head with a hammer. She was to survive this assault, but barely, after months of intensive care and with permanent brain damage. Wang Yungtai left the scene of his crime on foot, but only after swallowing a substantial amount of mercury, which he had prepared for his planned suicide attempt. He became ill, but not seriously so, and the next day confessed to his father. His father recommended that he go to the police, but withdrew this recommendation when he realized that if the victim died his son would get the death sentence. He was arrested several months later and subsequently confessed. The precipitating cause was romantic rejection; Hu Huichin had refused to become his girl friend, after he had requested her to do so several times, with all due respect, in writing.

At the trial, the defendant was asked by the judge what he was thinking while he hit the victim with the hammer. He said, "I was thinking that she made me lose face by telling everything to someone or everyone. . . . I was very angry and I wanted revenge. I wanted to teach her a lesson, to let her suffer. I didn't think of the consequences." The defense attorney pointed out that the defendant showed every sign of contrition, including contributing a substantial sum of money to aid in the victim's recovery, and that he had been, prior to his crime, a model worker guilty of no other criminal acts. After summary by the defense and prosecution, Wang was permitted to make a summary statement of his own, and he reiterated sentiments he had expressed earlier in the trial: "I would like to repeat that when I struck her I did not intend to kill her. I only wanted to vent my anger. I had no other thoughts. The cause of my crime is my low political consciousness. I didn't study very much; I knew nothing about the rights of citizens and of the law and I have very bourgeois thoughts." In his previous statement, a reply to a patently leading question from the judge, he added that he had come under the influence of Lin Biao and the Gang of Four during the Cultural Revolution. "I don't know what the law is and I have bourgeois ideas. Because I could not achieve my personal aims, I did not consider the interests of the state or of other people, so I threw everything to the wind and did what I wanted." In the final statement by the judge, "in order to implement the law, preserve revolutionary order, protect the safety of all citizens, insure the smooth progress of socialist modernization and strike at criminal activity, in order to strengthen the proletarian dictatorship," Wang was sentenced to life in prison.

The juxtaposition of these two cases makes them striking—even more so than each is on its merits. Two modern societies professing completely different beliefs and, indeed, acting on those beliefs with different systems of child training, education, work, and justice, confront in effect the same crime and respond to it in the same way, while giving radically different explanations of the crime and the punishment. In one, the individuals sitting in judgment listen to expert testimony by psychiatrists as to whether the criminal was capable of controlling his actions and distinguishing between right and wrong; they are impressed by the romance between the criminal and his victim, take into consideration his impoverished childhood, and attempt to consult "divine inspiration" to aid in their decision. The defendant says "I could not live without her," and gives himself up to a priest after his crime. In the other, the defendant says "She made me lose face," and confesses his crime to the head of his family, his father. The judges appear to believe that the crime can be explained by ideological inadequacy on the part of the defendant, particularly his "bourgeois ideas" and the influence of the Gang of Four, a viewpoint with which the defendant, after some encouragement, concurs.

But consider the similarities. In each case a young man is enamored of a young woman, is rejected, "loses control" of his emotions, and, after at least some premeditation, brutally bludgeons his beloved to death or near death with a hammer held in his hand, striking many hard blows. One contemplates, one attempts suicide, each relates his crime to a culturally appropriate confessor, each is very contrite, neither has ever committed a crime or "lost control" in an unusual way before. Both report having acted under an extreme of emotional agitation, despite relatively calm preparations. Both introduce culturally appropriate explanations at the respective trials and both receive the maximum sentence allowable given the nature of the charge. Both face judges who react, finally and primarily, to the brutality and injustice of the assault, giving all other factors minor consideration. Both end up in prison, not because anyone believes they are likely to commit such crimes again, but because of the sense of justice common to the social orders to which the young men and their victims belong, and as a warning to all others to respect and fear the law.

This is, of course, not an everyday series of events. Nevertheless, in many societies, including so-called primitive ones, young women occasionally meet death at the hands of men who supposedly love them, and in a wide range of these societies such crimes make up a substantial percentage of homicides. Frequently there is a motive of rejection and/or jealousy, there has been no other criminal behavior, there is suicide or attempted suicide, and there is contrition. Certainly it is not the only, or even the principal course of events leading to homicidal or near-homicidal violence, but it is interesting because, of all situations that tend to violence, this one covers and exemplifies the widest range of human—or, indeed, nonhuman—emotions.

The young man experiences lust, of course; he has had, and/or wants to have, sexual intimacy with the young woman who is to become his victim. But in these cases, to be perfectly fair, the lust is held in check within the context of a much more respectful feeling, one which, except with the easy wisdom of hindsight, we would not be able to distinguish from what we usually are willing to call love: a desire to be close, a desire to stay with, a desire to care for, a desire to share with, a desire, we may suppose, to possess. In the context of this feeling, and as a product of it, there must usually be a deep sense of joy that attends the thought of the prospect of shared life, the contemplation of the innumerable rewards of that life. When the young woman's affections begin to be alienated, or when she is disinclined to return those of the man, he experiences fear—of loss, of loneliness, of humiliation—a fear that must sometimes be close to terror. There arises from this fear a feeling of rage, a desire to take revenge upon, to punish the object of the fear; in these cases, the rage is sufficiently strong to produce homicidal violence. And mixed with the fear and rage, supplanting them in the end, is grief, a mourning for the losses—after the rejection, the loss of love, companionship, pride, sexual release, hope; and, after the crime, the loss of the very person of the beloved.

It is only because this gamut of the emotions is run that such cases compel our interest more than does many another homicide. Conflict is more moving than unalloyed motive—however horrible—and we are able to sympathize with the conflict in question because we have, however moderately, shared it. It touches every corner of the human unconscious.

I feel a great impatience with behavioral and social scientists (or for that matter, lawyers) who try to explain away acts of selfishness or brutality by reference to psychological facts and principles. Except in the rare cases of psychotic derangement or real mental incompetence, such principles have little place in a court of law. The law is not an instrument of explanation, it is an instrument of justice, of protection, of redress of grievances, and of punishment of wrongdoing. Behavioral and social scientists may analyze these functions, and even point out flaws in them—judges, lawyers, and jurors are after all only human—but if the overall competence of the law is granted in a given instance, then what counts thereafter is the legal evidence and the moral and legal sense of the judge and jurors, tempered by human decency of a pretty straightforward sort. Expert opinions should be used to rule out a clearly established psychosis or a condition of mental retardation, and when this is done the experts should withdraw and offer no further opinion on the behavior of the defendant; not, at least, in connection with the trial. The defendant should then be judged by his or her nonexpert fellow human beings, according to the evidence and the law.

The purpose of this digression is to prevent the misconception that my attempts throughout this chapter to explain acts of violence have anything at all to do with condoning them. The law should judge, but the scientist should still explain, irrespective of what the law may do. To explain is not to explain away, and to understand, in my opinion, is not necessarily to forgive. But to understand *is* to get a better grasp on things, and that is an inevitable advantage.

The "unconscious" described by Sigmund Freud is indeed a marvelous metaphoric organ. With its ebb and flow of emotion, its stored record of salient experience, its concourse with the body, and its well-blazed trails of feeling and expression, it can generate dreams, errors, beliefs, symptoms, lifelong patterns of word and deed, while its mechanisms remain unbeknownst to us. Freud did not discover the unconscious, but he and his colleagues certainly added immensely to our knowledge of it; and yet they did not go far enough. For the unconscious processes of the mind are by no means subsumed by the characterization of powerful, submerged currents of feeling that was provided by psychoanalysis. Among the things we may do without consciously thinking—without, that is, awareness of what we are doing—are driving sixty miles an hour along a highway and suddenly acting to avoid a collision "before we know it"; decoding the meaning and grammar of a complex sentence even as we become aware that someone is speaking it to us; walking or talking during sleep; and shouting a grave insult at someone we love, one of many acts we regret as soon as they reach conscious awareness. It was said of one recent American President by another that he could not walk and chew gum at the same time; most people, however, can walk, chew gum, carry a package, scratch themselves, and daydream about sex all at the same time and still avoid walking into a lamppost—all without real conscious awareness. It was in the context of facts such as these that two psychiatrists testified in a court of law that Richard Herrin was not responsible for his actions when he bludgeoned Bonnie Jean Garland to death with a hammer.

Whatever we may think of such testimony—I personally reject it because of its failure to distinguish between awareness and responsibility, which, in some cases at least, seem to me separable— it is not ridiculous. It rests on a firm basis of knowledge about the enormous range of actions, thoughts, and feelings that the human brain can generate without bringing them into conscious awareness. Some of them, like the prevention of urination during sleep, are relatively simple reflexes that are relatively trivial from the point of view of mind. Some, like returning a fast serve in tennis while we watch ourselves, "as if from the outside," are vastly complex muscle contraction patterns, concatenated rather marvelously in space and time, but without important, specific emotional content. Some are self-protective, such as the raising of the arms and hands to protect the face from a blow. Some are designed to hurt other creatures.

What most behavioral biologists would now do with these "functions of the unconscious" would be to drop the use of that term as a noun, but preserve its use as an adjective. Replacing the unknown brain functions formerly denoted by the word "unconscious" (noun) are a great variety of increasingly well-known circuits throughout the central nervous system, the functioning of which is often "unconscious" (adjective). Many of these circuits have been discussed earlier in this book. Suppression of urination during sleep involves control of the autonomic nervous system from the brain stem, which happens to regulate much of the rest of sleep as well. Returning the tennis serve engages the cerebellum and the *corpus striatum* in regulating different aspects of coordinated muscle action, and probably also the motor portion of the cerebral cortex, which at the least must inhibit irrelevant movements. Decoding a sentence involves primarily Wernicke's area, a substantial portion of one—usually the left—human cerebral hemisphere. Self-protective flinching could bypass the cerebral cortex, using other connections between the visual system and the motor coordination mechanisms in the cerebellum and *corpus striatum*, and it might or might not involve simultaneously activated limbic system circuits mediating fear. Shouting a grave, immediately regretted insult could begin in limbic system circuits mediating rage, and would probably involve both cortical circuits controlling speech and striatal circuits controlling facial and bodily gestures.

Several things about these unconsciously functioning circuits are worth mentioning. First, they are not limited to any one level of brain structure by any definition *except* that of the dimension of consciousness. In terms of evolutionary antiquity or novelty, place in the sequence of individual brain development, or degree of complexity of internal circuitry, all brain levels can involve themselves in unconscious actions. In MacLean's terms, the "reptilian brain," "the old mammalian brain," and "new mammalian brain" can all operate, at least at times and in part, unconsciously, and this is true even of the newest portions of the new mammalian brain in humans, controlling speech. In Papez's terms, the stream of action, the stream of feeling, and the stream of thought can each proceed to some extent without our conscious awareness, either separately or together.

Second, the processes in question, whatever level they are on, may be learned or unlearned, or include components of both. Sequences of action, thought, and feeling that are the products of the most complex and protracted processes of learning can be carried out unconsciously just as can the simplest of unlearned reflexes.

Third, unconscious processes may be sanctioned or unsanctioned by society, considered normal or abnormal by physicians, viewed as desirable or undesirable by the conscious mind, however strict the particular mind may be.

What then, and where, is consciousness? As to the "what,"

Webster's Twentieth Century Unabridged Dictionary defines "conscious" as "aware of oneself as a thinking being; knowing what one is doing and why," and I don't know of a behavioral science definition that is much more informative. The anatomical seat of consciousness is a slightly more tractable matter, however, and if it is unwise to suggest a "center" for it—like the rest of brain function, it must be thought of in terms of circuits—it is at least possible to specify what sorts of damage to the brain will tend to abolish it.

This has been a major preoccupation of the famous neurosurgeon Wilder Penfield, of the Montreal Neurological Institute, throughout the course of a long, distinguished career. To begin by subtraction, vast areas of the cerebral cortex—the "new mammalian" brain—can be removed without disturbing consciousness per se, corresponding to the fact that many cortical functions—such as the decipherment of sentences—are carried out unconsciously. To go to the other extreme, damage to major portions of the peripheral nervous system, whether involving action or sensation, leave the faculty of consciousness unharmed, as does damage to the cerebellum and *corpus striatum*. Severe damage to the lower portion of the brain stem causes life functions to cease, making its role in consciousness moot. The one brain region that typically produces loss of consciousness if damaged, while allowing life to continue, is the upper portion of the brain stem, the diencephalon; this includes the thalamus, the major way station of incoming sensation, and the hypothalamus, the center of the limbic system and the major switching center for brain-body relations. These structures, or at least parts of them, are at the head of the "reticular formation" of the brain stem, the central core of the three-dimensional web of short, complexly interconnected, slow-acting neurons that regulates the sleep-waking cycle. These structures, acting in concert, somehow light up the brain with mind.

The purpose of this long digression from the theme of the chapter—rage—has been to establish that vast realms of behavior, thought, and feeling are regularly outside of awareness. Keeping in mind that "out of awareness" is not synonymous with "out of control," whether the control is personal or social, we may now proceed to consider the problem of rage.

Rage is the name we give to the emotion that sometimes underlies the behaviors we call aggressive, although each can exist without the other. In characterizing such behaviors and emotions and their causation, it is generally useful to begin descriptively. To get an idea of the magnitude of the problem, consider the following pattern of behavior. Many species in the cat family exhibit a sequence of predatory behaviors that are as close to constituting an instinctive sequence of motor action patterns as mammals are likely to get. It includes lying in wait, crouching, stalking, pouncing, seizing between the paws, and directing a "killing bite" quite specifically at the nape of the neck of the prey, where it will do mortal damage to the brain stem. A cat with no experience of prey will not do this properly at first, but with a few repeated opportunities, especially under conditions of playful excitement, the sequence "clicks into place" and it does so in a tiny fraction of the time required for cats to learn comparably complex sequences that do not draw on phylogenetic preparation.

The gulf between the acts of these cats and the human acts described at the beginning of the chapter is vast, the list of differences long. First, the behavior just described is normal for all wild cats, the behavior described for humans, rare and abnormal. Second, the cat behavior necessarily involves the motor action sequence described, with little variation, while the specific motor action sequence in the human cases of homicide, though they happened to be parallel, was incidental. Third, the cat behavior serves the obvious adaptive purpose of food getting, while the human behavior, if it is functional in any sense at all, is certainly much more obscurely so, and perhaps is a case of function gone awry; in any event it has nothing to do with food. Finally, the cat sequence is carried out in a spirit of playful excitement, even in a subdued mood, while the young men who attacked their friends did so in a mood of intense rage.

Nevertheless, behavioral scientists, sometimes with important and confusing consequences, classify both these very distinct sequences of behavior under the general rubric of "aggressive" because they both have the effect, in some sense intended, of inflicting damage upon another creature. The category "aggressive behavior in animals" includes at least the following: serious fights that can inflict real damage; play fights, or rough-and-tumble play, that generally cannot; dominance hierarchies that eventually result from a settling out of winners and losers into a temporarily stable social pattern; threats of violent action, which can begin fights, play a role in them, or prevent them; and predation. Threat, attack, and fighting can serve a wide range of adaptive functions: competition between individuals for mates, food, and other scarce resources; play and exercise; enforcement of sexual intercourse, and defense against such enforcement; defense of the young; elimination of the young, either one's own or those of others, for purposes relating to the reduction of competition; competition between groups for territory and other scarce resources; exploitation of prey species, for the purpose of obtaining food; and action against members of another species, one's own species, even one's own family, for purposes of self-defense. To these must be added an unknown quotient of functionless aggression that surely must emerge, the inevitable misfirings of so complex a system of hurtful acts.

Some distinctions of kind must now be made. Playful fighting, or perhaps more properly "rough-and-tumble play," is a universal characteristic of the mutual behavior of young mammals and also occurs among many mammalian adults. It is not violent, it is usually not damaging, and it involves different behaviors of threat, attack, defense, and especially expression from those involved in real fighting. Nevertheless, it can sometimes grade into real fighting, it provides exercise for real fighting, and it helps to establish the dominance hierarchy that will regulate real fighting.

Predatory "aggression" involves members of another rather than one's own species, is usually done in a playful mood or a mood of skilled challenge, and is motivated by hunger rather than anger or competitiveness. Nevertheless, it inflicts mortal damage using at least some of the same motor actions and fighting apparatus that the predator may use against conspecifics—members of its own species.

To further complicate matters (or perhaps to help explain some of the complexities) rage and fighting behavior can be dissociated from one another in experimental animals in the laboratory, using appropriate different brain lesions. Cats may have real rage, as shown by expressive signals under sympathetic nervous system control—widening of the eyes, growling and hissing, arching of the back, and erection of the fur—which appears as a prelude to attack; but after an appropriate brain lesion they will have only "sham rage," the same expressive signs never followed by attack. Cats may kill their prey with all expressive signs following stimulation of one part of the midbrain, but stimulation of another midbrain location produces only quiet-biting attack, the unemotional killing characteristic of cat predation in the wild.

The various forms of aggressive behavior and their emotional concomitants, if any, may have varying degrees of unlearned and learned components. Every such behavior, in every species without exception, has some of both. But in some, genetically determined fixed action patterns and releasing mechanisms play a powerful role, in others little or none, with the innate factors reduced to some characteristics of motive and mood. Adapting for our purposes a scheme originally put forward by the Dutch ethologist Niko Tinbergen, we may say that to ask the question, What causes aggressive—or indeed any—behavior? is really to ask a series of questions, and we will be greatly aided in our attempt to provide an answer if we make ourselves aware of the different questions in advance, and indeed organize our explorations in accord with them. This is not the series of questions engendered by our usage of the word "aggressive" to denote so many categorically different behaviors, but rather by the variety of things we can mean by the word "cause."

First, we mean, What events in the individual's environment immediately or recently preceded the behavior, and seem to have precipitated it? These are called by ethologists "releasing stimuli" and they may be learned or unlearned. Second, we are asking about fast-acting physiological causation: the neural circuitry and associated neurotransmitters whose activation preceding or concurrent with the behavioral output produced it. Third, slower-acting physiological determinants within the organism, such as hormone levels or disease processes, must be considered. Fourth, environmental events of fairly recent vintage, such as training or observation, though not the immediate precipitating factors, may have had a strong influence on the behavior by altering the organism's response tendencies, just as hormones and disease do.

Fifth, we want to know the events of gene coding and embryonic development—really a sort of remote physiology of the behavior, which tells us something about the raw materials of the organism—in relation to the particular behavior. Sixth, we are interested in environmental causation of a remote sort: "sleeper effects" that may arise from experience, nutrition, or insults in early life, including life before birth or hatching. Seventh, Why did the organism do that? can mean, What adaptive function does it serve? To a pre-Darwinian such as Goethe, this might have meant, Why did God give it that behavior? but to us it means, What were the forces of natural selection that favored it, given the environment inhabited by the creature and its recent ancestors?

Eighth and finally, we want to know the phylogenetic history of the animal. The wings of flies come from the thorax; those of birds, from forelimbs; of bats, from fingers; and the "wings of man" from Eastern Airlines. In each case the same adaptive function is served: flight, which in various ways enhances survival. But these very different creatures must solve this problem in very different ways, each consistent with its own unique phylogenetic history. That history directs and constrains the animal in its evolutionary response to the adaptive problem posed by the environment.

In this framework, and only in this framework, is it possible to give a more than partial, more than trivial account of the causation of behavior, including aggressive behavior. It would be misleading, perhaps even dangerous, to suggest that behavioral biology can provide a satisfactory explanation for the homicides described at the start of this chapter. Although it might do better than the court psychiatrists, its findings would be no more useful to the court, which in the end must decide on the basis of simpler, more human, and perhaps more brutal principles. Indeed, I doubt whether another hundred years of research in behavioral biology will make possible the prediction or control of individual acts of passionate homicide.

What I do expect from such research, however, is a more comprehensive understanding of anger and violence in general; an understanding of the sort that could lead to a better prediction, management, and prevention of conflict of a more ubiquitous sort, from marital fights to child abuse to international warfare. Many of the components of these latter forms of conflict reflect those of the two homicides discussed. But to approach the sort of comprehensive explanation of human conflicts that we will need, we must first proceed to a much more detailed kind of analysis—one that carries us from the physiological laboratory through the field setting of the natural historian to the annals of human history. These components will give us, in the end, at least an outline of what will one day be a nearly complete explanation of violent and other conflict-related behavior, drawing on all the eight categories of causes mentioned earlier—from the immediate precipitating cause, through the physiological mediators, to the phylogeny. And in the process we will have evolved a method for explaining behavior that is more balanced and eclectic than any that has been previously devised; an outline for the understanding not only of rage and conflict, but all human emotional behavior. We begin, quite arbitrarily, in the brain, with the understanding that this is only a beginning.

The short-term physiological causes of aggressive behavior, unknown until a few years ago, have now become a subject of active study. Inroads have come from investigators in neuroethology, physiological psychology, psychopharmacology, and, most controversially, neurosurgery. The latter has produced both knowledge and controversy in this area for the same reason: the recent use of a type of neurosurgical practice called "psychosurgery" in the treatment of violent epileptic fits. The vast majority of cases of severe epilepsy are characterized by seizures involving massive but uncoordinated muscle contractions, dangerous only to the seizure victim. In a very small percentage, the seizure is directed outward and can result in violent attacks on another person. A few of these cases in the United States (where public opposition to psychosurgery is strong), and more in Japan and in some European and Latin American countries, have received surgical treatment for the disorder. It should be noted in passing that these cases do not come to surgery, at least in the United States, unless the disorder is very severe—indeed disabling and dangerous—and other treatment methods, including a variety of drugs, have been tried without success. Nevertheless, the ethical problems entailed in such a decision must make any thoughtful person feel cautious, and the results of such surgery (like, admittedly, most new surgical methods) have not been unreservedly encouraging.

By the 1950s it was known that lesions of the hypothalamus—the basal brain structure that is the "hub" of the limbic system—could produce violent behavior in rats in the laboratory. Different hypothalamic lesions could reduce violent behavior, and stimulation of appropriate regions of the intact hypothalamus, using implanted electrodes, could either increase or reduce such behavior. These findings were consistent with both the central role postulated for the hypothalamus in the limbic system and the central role postulated for the limbic system in the emotions. Earlier still, it had become evident that other limbic system structures played an important role in aggression.

In the late 1930s, Heinrich Klüver and Paul Bucy had done experiments in which they removed the end of each temporal lobe (a part of the cerebral hemisphere above and behind the temples) in monkeys. This procedure caused extensive damage to a variety of brain structures, including the limbic system structures called the amygdala and hippocampus. There were various changes and abnormalities in the behavior of the monkeys, but the one we need to know about for present purposes is that they became tame, a characteristic very hard to find in laboratory rhesus monkeys. This was not the result of general debilitation (they were very active) or of fearfulness (they in fact showed less fear than they had before surgery). Later studies, mostly in the last two decades, showed that the tameness would result from removal of the amygdala alone.

Meanwhile, some experiments in some species indicated that lesions in another limbic system structure, the septal area, would have the opposite effect; that is, they would cause rage, although in an undirected way inefficient in combat. This controversial effect combined with the more accepted effects of large amygdala lesions led several investigators to think in terms of hypothalamic regulation of rage and aggression, with the hypothalamus in turn regulated by higher limbic system structures; for example, the amygdala could under normal conditions enhance rage and aggression by exciting the hypothalamic regions to which it projects fibers, and the septal area (or other limbic areas) could reduce rage through the hypothalamic regions receiving *its* neural projections.

Some of the specifics of this picture remain controversial, but the general theory has been provisionally accepted: Rage and, indeed, many other aspects of emotional and motivational excitability, are, or at least can be, regulated from the hypothalamus, which integrates messages from various parts of the limbic system, producing a balance either for or against a behavioral output associated with the excited condition.

To produce muscle action such as that involved in aggressive behavior, or indeed to produce the activation of the circulatory system and visceral organs involved in the emotion of rage, the hypothalamus must communicate its integrative summary of limbic system activity down to the spinal cord and out to the periphery. It evidently does so through way stations in the midbrain, and here the work of John Flynn and his colleagues at the Yale University School of Medicine has been of great importance. It is these investigators who established the brain localization of the distinction between "affective" and "quiet-biting" attack. In essence, stimulation of the medial hypothalamus—the part near the midline of the brain—causes affective attack, and stimulation of the lateral hypothalamus—more outlying portions on either side—causes quiet-biting attack. Through studies involving lesions and stimulation of the midbrain—the brain stem region just behind and below the hypothalamus on the way to the spinal cord—Flynn and his colleagues showed that the hypothalamus exerts its effect on attack, whether with or without rage, via circuits running through different parts of the midbrain. These midbrain regions must in turn communicate with parts of the spinal cord that produce, respectively, the attack itself and the expressive emotion of rage.

The various forms of psychosurgical intervention that have been used to attempt to control violent fits have focused on different parts of this circuitry. One intervention that has been used to treat extreme and frequent violent fits in patients in Japan and Argentina is destruction of an area 3 to 5 millimeters in diameter in the posterior portion of the medial hypothalamus. As might be expected from the Flynn studies, this procedure usually reduces violent rage. (But it does have problematical side effects that are beyond the scope of this discussion.) Another approach used in Japan, India, and the United States has been to destroy large portions of the amygdala, and this too is freqently reported to have the desired effect of reducing or eliminating violent fits.

Because of the experimental nature of these procedures, their side effects, and their still uncertain results on the syndromes in question, it is proper for thoughtful people to view them skeptically and for physicians using them to proceed with caution. But, as pointed out by Walle Nauta in an address to the 1973 Neuroscience Society meeting (he was then president of the Society), the experience of the severest critics of psychosurgery (he prefers the term "psychiatric neurosurgery") does not always include firsthand knowledge of the degree and kind of suffering that leads patients, their families, and their physicians to consider this very drastic and uncertain form of treatment.

It should be emphasized that such procedures could not conceivably be justified, or even ethically contemplated, in cases such as the homicides discussed earlier in this chapter. The only justification for them has been in cases of relentlessly repetitive violent fits that are closely related to an underlying epilepsy and that are unresponsive to other forms of treatment. As pointed out by physiological psychologist Stephan Chorover, the danger of misuse of them in strictly criminal or even political cases is real and must be guarded against carefully.

Still, it is fair to say that the experience of these cases provides a useful dimension in the study of the neural control of violence, one dimension among many. Another line of investigation relating to the neural circuitry of aggression and rage is psychopharmacological. This research involves experiments in which laboratory animals are given drugs that in one way or another influence the functioning of neurons, or of neurotransmitters in the junctions between neurons, within the circuitry of the central nervous system.

Two research paradigms are worthy of mention, although the direct relevance of either to human aggression is questionable. One involves fighting between two male mice; it has been shown, for example, that homogenates of the brain of a male that has been in such a fight have a higher rate of uptake of norepinephrine than do those of a male that has exercised in another way. Mice that have been kept in isolation for several weeks have an increased tendency to fight; they also have changed levels or rates of turnover of several neurotransmitters in the central nervous system, and drugs directly affecting those neurotransmitters can increase or decrease the likelihood of fighting. (It is not yet known whether similar effects occur before or during fighting in human neurotransmitter systems.)

The second paradigm involves "muricide" or mouse-killing by rats, a normal predatory activity of the latter species. This behavior can be influenced by psychoactive drugs that act through the neurons, affecting the neurotransmitters serotonin, norepinephrine, dopamine, and acetylcholine. (As we have seen, the connection between predatory aggression and interindividual aggression is weak and obscure at best, and perhaps nonexistent; a problem that some pharmacologists using the mouse-killing paradigm seem unaware of.) It is clear that exploration of the neurotransmission aspects of the central nervous circuitry of aggression is only just beginning. But it should be mentioned that these paradigms, unlike the ones using brain lesions in animals and humans, deal with less drastic and more reversible interventions. They hold out a long-term hope for pharmacological agents that may be able to modify aggression within and near the normal behavioral range—an approach that would not, of course, be without ethical problems of its own.

The slower-acting physiological agents—particularly the hormones affecting behavior—have been the objects of longer and more detailed study than is the case for neurotransmitters, particularly in relation to aggression. All the classical hormones of stress—adrenaline from the central portion of the adrenal gland, cortisol from its outer portion (secreted in turn in response to a pituitary hormone, ACTH), and several others—are secreted in abundance in a "fight or flight" situation, the classic setting recognized by the physiologist Walter B. Cannon as producing a critical adaptive demand for energy for muscle action. Accordingly, the stress hormones tend to cause release of energy from stored cellular forms to free blood-borne forms and/or to constrict and expand blood vessels selectively, in such a way that more blood will flow to the muscles and less to the rest of the body, bringing along the needed energy for contraction.

The limbic system is affected by these hormones, but that effect is somewhat delayed relative to central neural events and also relative to the beginning of the muscle action involved in attack and expression of rage. The fastest hormonal event would be release of adrenaline (also called epinephrine) because a neural signal controls that release. The signal may be initiated in the higher centers of the limbic system and pass through the hypothalamus, the midbrain, and the spinal cord to the sympathetic nervous system, which has nerves reaching out directly to all the blood vessels and internal organs, as well as to the cells in the adrenal gland that release adrenaline. New synthesis of more adrenaline would be yet another, more slowly acting effect, and one that would be promoted by the secretions of the outer portion of the adrenal gland.

The principal secretion, in humans, of that part of the gland is cortisol, and its secretion is caused by the pituitary hormone ACTH. ACTH, in turn, is regulated by a chemical signal from the hypothalamus, which, again, is integrating information from all over the limbic system. This set of events, all requiring blood-borne chemical agents, is necessarily slower than direct neural communication, but is essential for the sustained muscle action involved in protracted fight or flight.

As indicated in the chapter on sex differences, reproductive hormones, especially testosterone, have been repeatedly shown to have specific effects on aggression. This is in some ways more interesting and relevant than the effects of such hormones as adrenaline and cortisol, which are more general in their action and are called up in all stressful circumstances. Testosterone promotes aggression, certainly in males and possibly in females, in a much more specific way. Indeed, generalized stress is likely to decrease the level of testosterone. Yet, in members of various species, especially in males, testosterone injections can increase aggressiveness in various situations and male castration can decrease it. Naturally occurring variations in testosterone level can accompany fighting behavior, and fighting can in turn affect that level. For example, in an experiment in which two groups of rhesus monkeys were made to fight, the losers experienced a large decrease after the fight (actually in two stages, the second perhaps corresponding to final acceptance of the loss), while the winners did not. In a similar study of members of the Harvard wrestling team, all men competing experienced a rise of testosterone level during the fight, but the winners experienced a significantly larger rise than did the losers, with those who fought to a draw having levels exactly in between.

It is a paradox of testosterone activation during fighting that elevation seems to promote aggressiveness but stress seems to oppose elevation—thus testosterone is not a stress hormone. The solution may be suggested by other studies that show that dominant individuals in a monkey hierarchy are physiologically less responsive to basal (prefight) levels of stress than are monkeys at the bottom of the pyramid. Another clue comes from studies of humans that do not involve aggressiveness directly: Performance on skilled tasks is enhanced by some, but not too much, subjectively experienced stress. If we visualize a highly stress-responsive individual beginning a fight with a less stress-responsive one (though not to the point of apathy!) we can imagine the calmer one performing better (to the extent that fighting is a skill) and also experiencing a greater or at least more efficient mobilization of stress hormones during the fight. Testosterone may even have the unfortunate effect, for the lower-ranking animal, of getting him into fights that he can't finish.

Adrenaline and cortisol, the two major stress hormones, act to mobilize energy, an indisputably critical purpose, and testosterone probably acts through effects on the neural circuitry involved in aggression and rage; for example, it lowers the threshold for firing of the stria terminalis, a major fiber tract linking the amygdala to the hypothalamus, in rats; and it affects the nerves controlling territorial singing in male birds. But why these slow-acting physiological mechanisms when neural circuits are so much more efficient? Probably there are many reasons, but a major one is that hormone levels have a life of their own. They are not mere servants of the limbic system, called into play whenever the individual decides to fight. Each has its own ebb and flow that is tied to daily, monthly, annual, or other cycles, as well as to a set course through the life span.

Animals are not equally likely to encounter stress at any randomly chosen hour of the day or night, so it makes good sense for stress-related hormones to have different levels at different hours of the day, which they generally do. Breeding in many animals takes place only at certain times of the year, and an annual rise in testosterone level at those times serves a dual function: It increases the male's tendency to court and copulate, and it renders him a more apt combatant in any conflict that may arise, whether with another male over a female or with the female herself over the object of his desire. The actions of the hormones affecting behavior on the one hand, and the limbic system of the brain on the other, are mutual. The latter can, through the hypothalamus and the midbrain, produce hormonal secretions to service the behaviors it "decides" to become engaged in; but the hormones, to the extent that they can transcend the blood-brain barrier, will bathe the brain and the rest of the nervous system, making firing more or less likely in some very specific circuits, as well as making energy available for continued nerve and muscle action.

Going much further back in the life history of the organism, the processes I have grouped under the rubric of "remote physiological causes" are also quite easy to exemplify, but since they have been treated in previous chapters in relation to the problem of aggression, they will be dealt with only briefly here. The events of "fetal androgenization" of the mammalian brain—and indeed, also the mammalian body—which were considered in some detail in chapter 6, fall in the subcategory of embryogenesis; they show that the tendency to aggression in adulthood is influenced by the amount of testosterone circulating in early life (before birth in monkeys, just after birth in rats), and, furthermore, that this effect is almost certainly the result of long-lasting changes in the brain. As to the other category of "remote physiology," the genes themselves, their action on aggression has been treated in chapter 5, anecdotally in relation to fighting bulls, and systematically in relation to dog-breeding experiments. In these species, the genes have a strong and predictable effect on aggression, and it can be emphatically stated that taking two individuals that differ genetically on this dimension and rearing them in exactly the same way will give you two adults that differ significantly (and importantly) in aggressive behavior.

This experiment has in fact been done, at least in mice, by Charles Southwick of the Johns Hopkins University. In each of fourteen purebred strains of mice, four males were grouped together after a period of social isolation, and the number of occurrences of chase, attack, and fight were simply counted and added together. The scores for several of the strains were highly significantly different, ranging from less than 10 to 80, an almost tenfold difference. Cross-breeding experiments blending different strains suggested that the genes for higher aggressiveness are dominant over those for lower aggressiveness (the offspring were as aggressive as the more aggressive parent) and that heterosis, a genetic interaction effect in which genes affect each other in unexpected, nonadditive ways, is operating in some crosses (offspring much more aggressive than either parent).

Since, as is proper in cross-breeding experiments, crosses sometimes used a given strain as the mother and other times as the father, some consideration of the problem of preweaning or even intrauterine effects by the mother was possible. In some cases such effects were evident, in others nonexistent. Systematic study using cross-fostering of infants of one strain to parents from another gave support to both these possibilities. In some cases the foster mother could alter the level of aggressive behavior of the offspring, in others she could not. To summarize the genetic side, then, there was clear evidence that *some* highly significant strain differences in the summary score of chase, attack, and fight were the result of genetic effects alone and not of genetic effects in combination with or in subordination to the effects of nongenetic maternal influence.

We will return shortly to the evidence of maternal influence that emerged from this experiment. But it will first be useful to review in general terms the evidence that the likelihood of rage and aggression is affected by environmental factors—other, that is, than the most immediate precipitating ones. The evidence in favor of such influences is overwhelming; indeed, in discussing them we are if anything on much firmer ground than is the case for genetic influences. This is particularly true of events in the environment preceding the aggression by some, but not too much time—effects that are recent enough so that they cannot be said to have occurred at an earlier stage of the individual's life cycle.

A large number of experiments have shown that pain, irritation, frustration, and fear increase the likelihood of aggression in a wide variety of situations in animals and humans—confirmations of the "frustration-aggression hypothesis." Of course, fear and pain, appropriately introduced, can be used to decrease the likelihood of aggression, although usually only temporarily and in a situation-specific manner. But in a number of more general experimental paradigms, the opposite occurs. For example, two rats are placed near each other on an electrified grid and shocked; one typical response is to attack each other, particularly if both are males. In other experiments, pain is not directly involved, but motivational behavior of various sorts is aroused in the animal and then deliberately frustrated. This situation also typically increases the likelihood of aggressive behavior.

Many have seen in these simple, effective paradigms experimental models for the frequently high levels of aggression observed within impoverished urban ghettos—and this could apply to violence at the individual as well as at the group level. In animals, the often observed and well-studied phenomenon of "redirected threat," or "redirected aggression," which occurs in natural and experimental situations in a wide variety of vertebrate species, is a closely related process. Dominant individual A attacks or threatens less-dominant individual B, who does not return the attack or threat, presumably for fear of the consequences. But B is in a state of arousal that presumably has elements of fear and rage. Sometime soon after, C, even less dominant than B, comes into the latter's vicinity and, for little or no provocation, is threatened or attacked by B. The implications for human behavior are to some extent obvious, and we will return to them in the next chapter, on fear.

In several experiments on rat or mouse fighting already mentioned, it was noted in passing that the animals were usually male and that they were housed in social isolation for a period preceding the pairing or grouping for induced fighting. This latter factor is a door to a whole separate realm of environmental causes of aggression. It is not clear to us what social isolation means to a mouse, but we know that several weeks of it, beginning after weaning, for males of almost any strain, will greatly increase the likelihood of fighting when the males are paired. In rats, the effects are more ambiguous, but similar.

Fighting can also be trained. German shepherd attack dogs are shaped through a process known in the laboratory as operant conditioning—reward of naturally occurring behaviors progressively more similar to the desired ones—and this is quite successful. Pets can usually be trained to inhibit chase, attack, and fighting responses, at least most of the time and in most situations, by a process that utilizes both negative and positive reinforcement, as well as the animal's capacity for association and generalization. And attack dogs as well as other pets can be brought through fairly complex processes of discrimination learning to a point at which they will exhibit very different behaviors on the continuum of aggressiveness and rage depending on the situation and the individual confronting them. All these processes have been studied systematically and quantitatively in the animal psychology laboratory.

Finally, modeling, imitation, and identification—an emotionally complex focusing of imitation on one model or class of models—can play a critical role as environmental influences altering the likelihood of violent behavior. Many psychological studies of modeling and imitation have been done with laboratory animals, and many ethological field studies have indicated its importance in wild species. (Significantly, the ethologists like to distinguish between imitation and what they call "social facilitation"; the latter refers to a spread of behavior from individual to individual that seems too fast to be explained by imitative learning, and which seems to be better accounted for by a shared tendency that is given a "permissive" atmosphere by its prior occurrence in other individuals. Yawning or coughing in a theater would be a good simple example in human beings, but the violence of a lynch mob might well belong to the same category.) Some of the best studies of the effects of modeling and imitation on subsequent aggression have been done in human children, by psychologist Albert Bandura and others. These clearly show that when a child is permitted to watch an adult, either live or on film, committing aggressive actions, the likelihood of the child's performing similar actions shortly thereafter is increased.

A more complex, less well-understood category of environmental effects is the "remote" ones: the effects that result from rearing conditions or other circumstances dating to an earlier period in the life of the individual. Such effects have been repeatedly demonstrated in many species, and while their mechanisms are still obscure, it is clear that they can contribute something to the prediction and explanation of violence in individuals and populations. It has been noted already that a few weeks of social isolation prior to pairing will greatly increase the likelihood of fighting in males from fish to mice;

but in monkeys there is another, more interesting effect of a specific form of social isolation. It is that early rearing in social isolation—for six months to a year, in the case of rhesus monkeys—will produce a lifelong tendency to social hyperreactivity, unaffected by the usual sorts of later social experience. In males, such hyperreactivity frequently results in a high level of threat, attack, and fighting behavior, often inappropriate and unsuccessful. To a lesser extent, the same behavioral abnormalities occur in rhesus monkeys that have been raised normally with their mothers in the first year of life, but without contact with peers. As little as twenty minutes a day of play in a peer group during this early period of life is sufficient to prevent the development of hyperaggressive behavior in these monkeys.

Not surprisingly, given the above evidence, dominance ranking in monkeys—really little more than a summary of how the animal has modulated its aggressive behavior—is also affected by early experience. In free-ranging rhesus monkeys it has been shown by primatologist Donald Sade and others that high-ranking females have female infants—and possibly also males—that grow up to be high-ranking themselves, and probably not just for genetic reasons. Infants of such mothers are frequently observed to imitate their mothers' threat-and-chase behavior, even in relation to adult animals. Obviously they are not capable of defeating the adults in individual combat, but the infants make their moves in the mother's shadow—even if she is not in the immediate vicinity—a phenomenon called by ethologists "protected threat." In this context, the infant has innumerable conventional learning experiences and opportunities for imitation and social facilitation that lead eventually to effective dominance behavior and high rank. The implications for status and power hierarchies in human societies, including our own, are almost too obvious to mention.

Even predatory aggression, if it indeed is aggression, is influenced by early experience. For example, rats reared with mice show a greatly reduced tendency to prey upon mice. And among the !Kung San, young children are not discouraged from cruelty to small animals or, for that matter, to the hunting dogs that are the closest things in that society to pets. In fact, children have a great deal of fun chasing, torturing, and killing small animals while adults watch approvingly. Since !Kung behavior toward infants and small children is among the most generous and tender in any human society, it can only be concluded that early cruelty to animals represents no general tendency to cruelty but merely specific early experience that is probably of preparatory value in relation to hunting.

Finally, to return to the mouse cross-breeding experiment described earlier, Southwick produced evidence that maternal behavior toward the young alters their later aggressive behavior in some strains. There is some evidence that a mother that spends more time off the litter—giving the pups shorter feeding sessions in which they have to compete with each other for access to the nipple, and also generally lowering their body temperature—can thereby raise the level of aggressiveness of the young when grown. Cross-fostering a nonaggressive strain onto an aggressive one (aggressive mothers, nonaggressive young) can raise the level of aggressiveness of the non-aggressive strain by 80 percent, but the reverse procedure cannot change the behavior of the aggressive strain. This was consistent with previous laboratory findings that training programs designed to increase aggressive behavior were more successful than those designed to decrease it and, furthermore, that once such behavior was acquired, it was very difficult to extinguish by the usual methods for reducing the level of acquired behaviors in the laboratory.

Enough has been said to demonstrate convincingly that there are powerful genetic effects on aggressive behavior and rage, and powerful environmental effects on them. Any answer to the question, Why did that act of aggression occur? must include both. It would trivialize the bitter experiences of Richard James Herrin and Wang Yungtai—and even more, that of their victims—to presume to explain what they did on the basis of what has been learned in all these studies. Nevertheless, one can see certain common threads of causation. Both were men, and such crimes are overwhelmingly committed by men rather than women—partly, at least, for genetic and hormonal reasons. Both were well bred in the moral sense, but both also lived in societies that traditionally glorified violence, including violence by men against women designed to make them submit. Both were exposed to one of ordinary life's worst stresses, that of romantic rejection, and both were young enough perhaps to be experiencing this stress for the first time. Both were probably exposed to the activation of testosterone in connection with their sexual feelings toward the women they attacked, but this is of course much more speculative. All of these factors are at times present in millions of individuals who do not commit homicide, and so do not help very much in explaining these cases. Nevertheless, the presence of such factors makes them slightly more comprehensible—not, I must stress, more excusable—than, say, the random shooting of motorists on a highway.

But what of the remaining whys, those of adaptation and phylogeny? Psychiatrist David Hamburg has devoted a great deal of serious effort to the study of aggression and other emotions as expressed in wild chimpanzees and other higher primates under natural conditions. He has found much to confirm the notion that we and our nearest relatives are emotionally similar. Aggressive behavior emerges early, is common, shows sex differences (males do more of it), and plays a critical role in the maintenance and alteration of social hierarchies. Imitation and other forms of learning play a role in it, but not an overridingly important role—although the use of tools in aggression by wild chimpanzees improves with practice, and suggests some unpleasant hypotheses about the role of violence in the evolution of human intelligence.

I would only add to this account a brief summary of a recent shift in outlook affecting many behavioral biologists, a shift owing largely to a successful challenge to classical ethology by the newly developed field of sociobiology. According to the classical view, identified especially with the name of Konrad Lorenz, a principal function of aggressive behavior is to distribute members of a group over an area of resource availability. This way, the group as a whole benefits, and individuals are not getting in each other's way. Furthermore, the existence of aggressive displays, such as threats, serves to reduce actual violence by spacing individuals and arranging them in a hierarchy.

Field observations of wild animals for a long time seemed to support this view. It used to be said that humans are almost unique among animals in that they kill members of their own species; this was explained by reference to the fact that our use of weapons renders less effective our normal mechanisms for limiting the damage we do to each other.

This is now known to be simply false. It was pointed out by some observers that if a troop of baboons had the same homicide rate as people in New York City, the baboon troop would have to be watched constantly for hundreds of years before the observer would be likely to see a homicide with his or her own eyes. It was only after thousands of person-years of field observations were logged by animal behaviorists that it became clear that intraspecific (within-species) homicide exists in many species other than humans—and this is now an incontrovertible finding. In other words, "natural" mechanisms for the limitation of violence do not work much better in nonhuman animals than they do among humans.

Animal homicide takes many forms in many species, but the grimmest and most fascinating is "competitive infanticide." This has been most extensively observed in Indian monkeys known as Hanuman langurs (*Presbytis entellus*) and is described by Sarah Hrdy and others as following a consistent pattern. Langur troops consist of a hierarchy of female relatives with their young (this is true of almost all monkeys) and a small number of males attached to the group, often for a year or more. From time to time new males appear, drive the old males out of the troop, and take over as the resident males. Within a few days they generally kill all infants under six months of age and reimpregnate the infants' mothers soon thereafter. Similar patterns have appeared in lions and various other species.

The existence of such a pattern of violence is a key piece of information. Einstein's general theory of relativity had to predict that light would bend around the sun, and, when this was found to be so, that theory was much more widely accepted. So sociobiological theory, with its emphasis on individual selection and competition rather than on group selection, would have to predict the existence of something like competitive infanticide; and its discovery lays group selection pretty much to rest, at least for higher animals. Here is a pattern—and it is not unique—that has obvious serious disadvantages to the group while giving a strong evolutionary advantage to a few individuals. This latter principle certainly seems to be true of many human groups. Group selection—the proposed process by which a population as a whole wins out over another population—has never been shown to occur. And appealing as it is in certain ways, it simply does not produce as logical a picture of how evolution has happened as does individual selection. The burden of proof is now on the proponents of group selection. In the meantime, we must accept the position of George C. Williams and other proponents of the newer view, that each individual is in competition with every other individual in its environment, at least in an evolutionary sense and in the long run. Aggression evolved to serve the interests of individuals, and that is why some individuals use it so much more successfully than others.

As for human phylogeny, we can say very little at present. A few years ago it was a common belief that the evolution of human hunting had important implications for the nature of human aggression. This is not likely. As we have seen, there is little or no evidence, physiological or behavioral, to suggest that predatory aggression has much in common with intraspecies aggression. All over the animal world are examples of vegetarian species whose members fight violently among themselves and have the natural weaponry with which to inflict great damage. Even our closest relatives, the chimpanzees, for whom meat makes up a trivial portion of the diet, have intraspecies aggression of the severest sort, including violence between groups at territorial boundaries, violent attacks on females by much larger males, and competitive infanticide committed by females against the infants of other females. A full range of violent behavior and violent expression exists in that usually gentle species.

The problem of violence among humans, of course, looms darkly over any such discussion as this one. Since it is obvious that I believe in the existence of innate aggressive tendencies in humans, the easy way out for me would be to describe the most violent of human societies: the Yanomamo of highland Venezuela, the Dani of highland New Guinea, the Plains Indians of the United States, the Zulu of southern Africa, the Germans of the Third Reich. But it will be more interesting to look at the least violent. Differences in the degree of violence among cultures and societies are real and large, and an understanding of the basis of those differences will help us to develop a strategy for reducing violence. But it is first important to abolish the myth that there are societies in which people are incapable of violence.

The !Kung San of Botswana are frequently used as a textbook example of the least violent end of the human cultural spectrum. They are. But this is very far from being equivalent to total nonviolence. They have a homicide rate shown by Richard Lee (who had originally subscribed to the view that they were nonviolent) to be equal to or greater than the rate for most American cities, and not very different in character. Most people among the !Kung are perfectly capable of violence, and there are many nonlethal acts of violence in addition to the recorded homicides. While the !Kung, like most hunter-gatherers, do not have war or other organized group conflicts, their explicitly stated contempt for non-San people, for San people speaking languages other than !Kung, and even for !Kung in other village-camps who are not their relatives, makes it perfectly clear that if they had the technological opportunity and the ecological necessity to make war, they would probably be capable of the requisite emotions, despite their oft-stated opposition to and fear of war.

The Semai of Malaysia are a society almost as simple as that of the !Kung. They have been the subject of a study by anthropologist Robert Knox Dentan. Violence is said to be virtually nonexistent among them and abhorrent to them. "Since a census of the Semai was first taken in 1956," Dentan writes, "not one instance of murder, attempted murder, or maiming has come to the attention of either government or hospital authorities."

> People do not often hit their children and almost never administer the kind of beating that is routine in some sectors of Euro-American society. A person should never hit a child because, people say, "How would you feel if it died" . . . Similarly, one adult should never hit another because, they say, "Suppose he hit you back?" . . .

It should be clear at this point that the Semai are not great warriors. As long as they have been known to the outside world, they have consistently fled rather than fight, or even than run the risk of fighting. They had never participated in a war or raid until the Communist insurgency of the early 1950's, when the British raised troops among the Semai, mainly in the west. Initially, most of the recruits were probably lured by wages, pretty clothes, shotguns, and so forth. Many did not realize that soldiers kill people. When I suggested to one Semai recruit that killing was a soldier's job, he laughed at my ignorance and explained, "No, we don't kill people, brother, we just tend weeds and cut grass." Apparently, he had up to that point done nothing but grounds duty.

But when the Semai were lured by the British into counterinsurgency activities against Communist rebels in the 1950s, they gave evidence enough of violent capability. Dentan goes on:

> Many people who knew the Semai insisted that such an unwarlike people could never make good soldiers. Interestingly enough, they were wrong. Communist terrorists had killed the kinsmen of some of the Semai counterinsurgency troops. Taken out of their nonviolent society and ordered to kill, they seem to have been swept up in a sort of insanity which they call "blood drunkenness." A typical veteran's story runs like this. "We killed, killed, killed. The Malays would stop and go through people's pockets and take their watches and money. We did not think of watches or money. We only thought of killing. Wah, truly we were drunk with blood." One man even told how he had drunk the blood of a man he had killed.

Astonishing as this description is, it is in some respects less astonishing than the adaptation that followed the Semai experience with warfare:

> Talking about these experiences, the Semai seem bemused, not displeased that they were such good soldiers, but unable to account for their behavior. It is almost as if they had shut the experience in a separate compartment, away from the even routine of their lives. Back in Semai society they seem as gentle and afraid of violence as anyone else. To them their one burst of

violence appears to be as remote as something that happened to someone else, in another country. The nonviolent image remains intact.

Despite this bleak reversal of a nonviolent cultural tradition, there is some evidence that cultural contexts can be constructed so as to reduce the likelihood of certain kinds of violence. One finding of anthropologists John Whiting and Beatrice Blyth Whiting is of interest here and strikes a much more positive note. They discovered in a wide-ranging cross-cultural study that husband-wife intimacy is apparently not compatible with organized group conflict. Societies in which husbands and wives eat together, sleep together, and take care of children together are among the least violent; while the ones that have organized themselves around constant or at least intermittent warfare find it necessary to segregate men away from influence by women and children, in separate men's houses for eating and sleeping, and in men's societies in which even young boys are severely stressed and actively trained for warfare. The Whitings' study established on a quantitative basis a set of hypotheses put forward in a different form by Lionel Tiger in his book *Men in Groups*. Something happens when men get together in groups; it is not well understood, but it is natural, and it is altogether not very nice.

The Whitings' version of the theory gives substance to the popular slogan "make love, not war"; and actually it improves it, giving it new and interesting depth, since that slogan probably did not mean "love" at all.

Whatever cultural conditioning we may do, we must remain cognizant of the fact that human beings who have been trained and conditioned to be nonviolent retain the capacity for violence; as constrained as that capacity may be in certain contexts, it can come out in others. It is subdued, reduced, dormant, yes. But it is never abolished. It is never nonexistent. It is always there.

This is the lesson of the experience of the Semai, the nonviolent people of Malaysia; and in a more personal way, that of Richard James Herrin and Wang Yungtai. Yet to recognize the impossibility of erasing the tendency to violence is not to throw up our hands and let the blows fall as they may. The Semai have returned to nonviolence;

perhaps if they had never been recruited and trained by the British, or if their relatives had never been killed by the Communists—if they had never been exposed to the whole horror of modern war—they would have remained nonviolent permanently. Perhaps, just perhaps, if the two young men who so violently attacked their lovers had not been exposed to folk traditions in which violence done by men against women was deemed at least understandable, they would have swallowed their pride—and grief—and not taken up their hammers.

What seems certain to me, though, is that no cultural training, however designed, can eliminate the basic core of capability of violence that is part of the makeup of human beings. The continued pretense by some social scientists and philosophers that human beings are basically peaceable has so far evidently prevented little of human violence—which latter achievement would be the only possible justification for its benighted concealment of the truth. Perhaps we could let it go for a while and see if the other assumption gives us a better understanding; if it does, it will give us a better chance at control.

10

FEAR

Of the world as it exists, one cannot be enough afraid.
—Theodor Adorno, *The Authoritarian*
Personality

Fear is what quickens me. . . .
—James Wright, *The Branch Will*
Not Break

We have dropped into the bowels of the beast, where the snarl curls, poised to provocation. What provocation? Lust thwarted, love rejected, thirst unslaked, hunger lingering, the frustration that chokes the gorge at practically any motive blocked, the example of creatures one admires, pain at the hands of those one hates, or simply being brutalized through a long, slow course of growth—but one cause, perhaps, above all: fear.

"Nociception"—the sense of pain—is the first function of nervous systems, and the nociceptive reflex—the flinch from pain—is well within the ken of creatures with one nerve cell. The nociceptive reflex aids them neither in eating nor drinking nor reproducing nor finding prey, but enables them to withdraw, to flee.

It has been said that every creature is in competition for survival with every other creature in its environment; if this is so, it surely has much to fear from them—from each of them, however close, however similar, however, ordinarily, allied. Creatures that threaten run the gamut from the tiger at one's hut door through the man in one's bed and the infant at one's breast, to the virus in one's blood.

But the threats do not end with living creatures. Light, darkness, heat, cold, heights, depths, rock falls, water, storms, earthquakes, wind, mere time spent without food or drink, mere distance from the things one knows—any of these may spell an abrupt end to the course of life, or an end to reproductive success, which (from the viewpoint of natural selection) amounts to the same thing. Creatures are therefore equipped—amply equipped—to detect and rebuff or withdraw from potential threats.

Pain, stress, fear—subjectively quite distinct perceptions, though often combined—all serve the purpose of notifying the organism of a potential threat to survival or reproduction. Pain and fear suggest an immediate threat; stress, a slower acting one. But paradoxically, all three signals have to be distrusted. Potential threats are so ubiquitous that if every detection of one produced a full-blown species-specific motor action pattern, animals would spend their lives in flight or hiding, unable to eat, drink, play, sleep, copulate, or care for their young—any of which activities may involve pain, stress, and fear *without* fleeing. Thus we may watch a herd of caribou feeding calmly on a wolf-dotted stretch of tundra, a zebra nuzzling a foal just in striking distance of a pride of lions, a human mother cooing at a contagious, dying child.

Fear may govern, but its aegis is overridden by any one of a number of other motives. What are we to suppose, then, that the caribou is feeling? A continuous clench of fear that persists and is felt, but transcended? A transient fear when the wolf appears on the horizon, which subsides, to be followed by calm? A continuous mild fear below the surface of action, quickly intensified by certain of the wolf's movements?

And what tells the human hunter to persist, in spite of the pain in his legs and chest, in pursuit of the caribou? What persuades the young girl whose hymen is breaking, prefiguring a later, greater pain, to stay instead of fleeing? What makes the human animal (and other, much less prescient ones) bear and transcend certain pains while other comparable pains are run from?

Comprehension of these balances struck among pain, fear, stress, and other feelings requires first of all an account of the motor output that may ultimately resolve them: escape and flight. Escape and flight, which we can measure, form a final outward manifestation of the subjective feelings in question, which we cannot measure, at least not very directly. Following the paradigm of the ethologists we can characterize (and they have done so) the species-specific motor action sequences resulting in escape and flight in various animals. As might be expected, caribou escape by running, Canada geese by flying, stickleback fish by swimming. Not very interesting.

But other details of the picture engage our attention. For example, there are *releasing stimuli* that reliably produce escape and flight, and many of these are highly species-specific. In the caribou we were considering, flight may not be released until its *flight distance*—the distance from which it can still be confident of escaping should pursuit begin—is violated by the wolf. But this distance is variable and uncertain. Consider an ill, aged, or disabled caribou grazing with its herd near wolves that are outside the flight distance of healthy herd members but well within its own. It can stay with the herd or detach itself and move farther away, but either way it is exceptionally vulnerable and, in fact, most likely to be taken.

The extent to which such releasing mechanisms are innate will be taken up shortly. But despite the extensive individual and circumstantial variability they exhibit, it is evident that the anatomical substrates of many of them—from perceptual pattern recognition through simple or complex neural networks to the effector neurons that produce hormones or motor actions—are essentially fixed by genetic plan resulting from thousands of generations of selection.

What of the motor action itself—a coordinated, delicately timed firing sequence involving up to billions of nerve and muscle cells, not to mention synthesis and release of an array of complex hormones that energize and regulate those cells, brought into play in a matter of seconds to save an animal's life. What stretch of the imagination could lead us to suppose that such a system could be built up through experience in the course of a single lifetime? We must suppose, on the contrary, that such sequences—*fixed action patterns*—like their companion releasing mechanisms, are laid down long in advance, though with substantial amounts of leeway. But this insight does not absolve us of the responsibility to account for the specific details of each pattern or mechanism: its function; its development through the life cycle; and, most interesting, its variability through situations and individuals.

It also leaves a myriad of less dramatic responses that cluster around escape and flight in the animal's array of motor actions—preceding them, or following them, or occurring in similar circumstances, but yet not constituting escape or flight themselves. One of the great contributions of Tinbergen and the other classical ethologists was to identify *intention movements* as potential or actual communications. Their outlook, simply stated, is this: When two members of separate species confront one another, they may ignore each other or engage in some attack and flight activity in a straightforward way. It is generally unnecessary for them to communicate their intentions to each other, and it may well be disadvantageous for them to do so. But when two members of the same species confront each other, they may find it necessary to maintain proximity—because they are going to engage in courtship, or because they are likely to join in alliance against an enemy, or merely because they are sharing, willy-nilly, the resources of a niche or territory. There is no vertebrate species that is so solitary that its members do not have to be phylogenetically prepared for such confrontations. The crux of the problem is, how can two creatures capable in every sense of inflicting damage on one another avert such damage without running away?

For many species, one answer seems to lie in the evolution of appeasement signals that let the other individual know (or at least make the other individual think) that no harm is intended. Tinbergen and others have shown that in many cases these signals are most easily understood as expressions of simultaneously aroused intentions (and motivations) to attack and flee; hence the term "intention movements." However, during the course of evolution, the movements in question seem capable of becoming "emancipated" from the motivations—whether fearful or aggressive—that initially gave rise to them, at which point they are said to have become "ritualized."

For example, the zigzag dance of the male three-spined stickleback is interpretable as an attack intention alternating with a flight intention; the displays of some ducks combine wing movements identical to those that initiate flight with head movements and body postures related to attack; and dogs and other canids face each other, bare the teeth, and lay the ears back flat—the former a potential threat and the latter a protective component of flight. These combinations, whether alternating or simultaneous, seem to be saying, "I am afraid of you, but not enough to run from you; and, although I do not want to fight, if you insist on it I am ready for that too."

These signals clearly influence the motivational state of the other animal watching, as indicated by the frequency of attack or flight following them. It is not clear in individual cases whether or how much of the motivation originally associated with these movements is present when the display is activated, but there are probably cases of greater and lesser emancipation. If both animals give such displays, the likelihood of mutual damage is, at least for the time being, lessened, and continued proximity is possible—along with all the other motivations and behaviors that proximity facilitates.

Here we have two complications to confront. First, not merely attack and flight tendencies, but approach, feeding, courtship, copulation, and many other tendencies may be simultaneously aroused, with the result that displays may combine intention movements from any pair, triad, or more complex combination of intentions. Second, each combination is really a continuum. For example, in the attack-approach-flight triad, different degrees of each tendency or motive will produce different displays. Even though the animal stays in one place in all cases, the predominance of an attack tendency may produce a threat display (identifiable by a consistently greater likelihood of attack by the actor or flight by the recipient following it); the predominance of approach tendency may produce a courtship display (identifiable by the sex of the actors and the likelihood of pair formation); and the predominance of the flight tendency may produce an appeasement or submission display (identifiable by the greater likelihood of flight by the actor or attack by the recipient). In the case of the squirrel monkey genital display, discussed in an earlier chapter, we have elements related to sex (such as genital exposure) combined with facial expressions related to attack and vocalizations variously and perhaps ambiguously expressing high arousal. It is thus not surprising that this display is sometimes used as a sexual approach but can also be used as an aggressive or defensive threat—its interpretation by the recipient evidently contingent not only on the display configuration but also on the relative ages, sexes, and sizes of the animals in confrontation.

In consequence of this continuum, it is inevitable that two individuals, each with some combination of the attack-approach-flight tendency triad, will often begin or at least end the encounter with somewhat different displays. Animal A may be exhibiting what is more usefully called a threat display, while animal B exhibits an appeasement or submission display. If this is their first such encounter, and if most subsequent encounters end the same way, then it may become useful to speak of them as having a dominance relationship, in which A is dominant over B. If in a subsequent encounter B should challenge A with an escalation of threats, there may ensue a fight that confirms or alters the original direction of dominance in the relationship. To some extent—and the extent, but not the fact, is controversial—important resources will be distributed differentially according to the direction of dominance. Such resources include territory, food, and, especially during breeding season, access to members of the opposite sex.

The evidence that dominance strongly influences reproductive success poses what has become a classic question for evolutionary theory: How are appeasement and submission displays and behaviors preserved and transmitted by natural selection? The initial answer depended on group selection theory—the notion, previously discussed, that not merely individuals and lineages but larger social groups can be units of selection, and can be in competition with one another in such a way that characteristics beneficial to a group will be preserved despite the disadvantage they may confer on individuals that exhibit them.

It has now become evident that group selection theory is at least unnecessary to solve the problem. As pointed out by the English behavioral ecologist David Lack, the most dominant animal can never get all the members of the opposite sex; so appeasing, submissive, and other fearful expressive movements and displays can be transmitted to future generations by the second most dominant animal. Other factors might include the likelihood that the most dominant animal will still find use for appeasement at some time or other, especially at early and late stages of the life course. There is no theoretical necessity to invoke benefits to the group, such as efficient spacing of individuals or general reduction of conflict; there is great and evident individual advantage to the less strong animal and its descendants to feel fear, appease or submit, and live to fight and reproduce another day.

It has been known since Darwin's *Expression of the Emotions*, and confirmed and extended recently by the work of the German ethologist Eibl-Eibesfeldt and the American psychologist Paul Ekman, that the facial expression exhibited by people in situations that evoke fear is quite consistent cross-culturally. Furthermore, photographs of that facial expression, which surely must be harder to interpret than the real thing, are labeled as fearful by individuals in widely disparate cultures and populations. The mouth is half-open, the corners strongly retracted, the teeth mostly covered, the ears drawn back, the eyes wide open, and the brows raised and perhaps also furrowed. The point-by-point similarity to the facial displays indicating fear in many other mammals is unmistakable, and it is likely that the phylogeny, physiology, and genetics in the human case follow the pattern for mammals generally, just as does the phenomenology. Presumably, the degrees of teeth-baring and brow-furrowing reflect to some extent the admixture of attack tendency, as is the case with other mammals.

Somewhat more difficult to place phylogenetically, perhaps even anomalous, is the principal human appeasement display, the smile. Even in this case, though, there is a clear continuum from the submissive grin of many nonhuman primates to the human smile in the presence of a superior. The fact that we so often smile, even in the presence of a superior, without feeling fear, is no obstacle to the hypothesis of homology—a common structure, function, and evolutionary origin—with the monkey's submissive grin; in many species, appeasement displays are believed to have become, during the course of evolution, emancipated from the emotions to which they were originally connected. Nevertheless, it is likely that the uncomfortable, even nervous smile a person exhibits when passing the boss in the hall is parallel in every respect, including physiology and genetics, to the grin a baboon exhibits when passing a more dominant baboon in the savannah equivalent of a narrow corridor.

What may we suppose is going on inside the organism during fearful displays? What is the neural and endocrine accounting for the observable behaviors and the subjectively felt emotion? As for all complex emotions, it is impossible at this date to describe such causes fully, but we do have a number of interesting leads.

At least since the time of Cannon, it has been known that the sympathetic portion of the autonomic nervous system is aroused during fear and flight as well as during rage and attack. This set of nerves regulating the viscera and the circulation is responsible for the increase in heart rate, rise in blood pressure, increased flow of blood to the muscles, and decreased circulation to the viscera that accompany fear and flight in many animals. It is also responsible for the reflexive emptying of the bladder and bowel that helps to prepare an animal for flight from a predator and that can humiliate a human being on the verge of a battle or an execution.

However, as we have seen, these reactions, important as they are, do not constitute the emotion itself, and they certainly do not account for the complex motor action patterns involved in flight and in fear-related displays. The neural control of these latter must be sought in the central nervous system. A first clue comes from research by neurophysiologists H. Ursin and B.R. Kaada involving the stimulation of the amygdala—the almond-shaped nucleus about an inch inside the skull behind the temples; to be exact, the basal (lower) and lateral (outer) portions of that nucleus, a prominent switching center of the limbic system. It has been shown in cats that stimulation of this region with a very small electrical pulse can cause alertness and orienting—a bright-eyed looking around at the environment and postural changes indicating a sort of aware readiness. The same electrode, in the same spot, with a larger pulse of current, will cause fear, with all its facial and postural indicators.

This is a fascinating finding for several reasons. First, it implicates the amygdala in the normal regulation of fear—a place to start, at least, with the neurology of it. Second, since other studies have implicated the amygdala in connection with rage, it suggests that the intimate relationship between fear and rage that we observe phenomenologically is meaningful in the stark structural terms of the nervous system. Finally, it raises the possibility that there is a continuum of arousal, and that alertness and fear are mere points on it, a suggestion with powerful potential consequences for the study of intelligence as well as of fear.

But the amygdala, of course, can be no more than a part of a circuit, and the other parts are of equal interest. It was noted in the last chapter that one view of violence holds that the amygdala and the septal-hippocampal circuit are in competition for the control of the hypothalamus; and that when the amygdala dominates, violence may be potentiated, but when the septal-hippocampal circuit dominates, it may be inhibited. Although this theory is controversial, it is elegant, and it applies about equally well to the control of fear. As in the case of rage, it is the central, lower portion of the hypothalamus that seems to inhibit fear, and the amygdala seems to enhance it indirectly, by inhibiting the inhibitor. (Such "double negatives" are not uncommon in neural circuitry.) The final way station in this proposed system is the central gray region of the midbrain, just as it was in the case of rage. The "inclination" of this region is to promote the motor actions (and, perhaps, the feelings) associated with fear or rage; most of the time, the central, lower ("ventromedial") portion of the hypothalamus prevents the midbrain from proceeding with that inclination; and the amygdala, probably integrating signals from many, including higher, parts of the brain, from time to time prevents the hypothalamus from doing its preventing.

It is quite likely that other portions of the central nervous system, especially the limbic system, figure in the causation of fear. The cingulum, for example, a major limbic system fiber bundle that relates the cerebral cortex to the hippocampus, has been severed in a psychosurgical procedure designed to reduce incapacitating phobias, and there are claims that the results have been successful. Some laboratory experiments also support a relationship between this fiber bundle and avoidance or escape reactions.

Remarks made in chapter 9 concerning the endocrine physiology of rage are all directly relevant to the physiology of fear. Since both emotions (and their associated behaviors) involve activation of the body's general stress response, the series of stress hormones released in the two cases is very similar. There was for a time a hypothesis that norepinephrine, the neurotransmitter secreted by the nerve terminals of the sympathetic nervous system (and in some species by the adrenal gland), is primarily related to the facilitation of aggression, while its sister hormone epinephrine (adrenaline, produced by the adrenal in all species that have it) is more closely associated with fear. Although these two "catecholamines" differ by only one methyl group—one carbon and three hydrogen atoms, which are added to "norepi" to make "epi"—that is more than sufficient to give them opposite actions; often a nutrient and a poison differ by much less. But this hypothesis has not been holding up very well. In fact, it now seems likely that norepinephrine, epinephrine, or both can be released under varying conditions of arousal and stress to produce a more specific pattern of activation or inhibition of bodily functions. In other words, as usual, the body's functioning turned out to be more complex than our simple theory.

Some fascinating and now almost classic experiments by Stanley Schachter, a physiological psychologist at Columbia University, throw light on the controversial role of these hormones. Schachter administered epinephrine to volunteers in three distinct settings, one calculated to produce anger, one to produce excited happiness, and one neutral setting not emotionally loaded in any way. Compared to volunteers who received the placebo, subjects receiving epinephrine felt *either* more angry or more happily excited, depending on the situational setup. Subjects in the neutral situation responded to the hormone, but only with a generalized agitation or even nausea, not with any recognizable emotion. It seems possible then that a single stress hormone is to some extent a common servant of several different states of arousal.

There is no good candidate for a fear-enhancing hormone in any specific sense. However, it is possible that testosterone is facilitating to aggression but antagonistic to fear. It is almost certain that it is antagonized *by* fear; fear and gonadal function have something of a competitive relationship, in the sense that the former can interfere with the latter. Since testosterone is known to facilitate aggression in various species when two males are paired for a possible fight, it reduces fear almost by definition, at least in that situation.

The emergence of fear during the life course has received extensive research attention, in humans as well as in many other species. In mice, rats, dogs, and other mammals it is perfectly clear that the degree of fearfulness in an individual, a strain, or a breed is in important ways a function of genes. We have already reviewed some of the evidence pertaining to the inheritance of timidity in dogs.

Rodents have been studied more extensively and systematically. Rats, for example, are tested in a situation known as the "open field," simply a strange large shallow box into which they are admitted and allowed to behave as they will. Fear in the open field (also called "emotionality" or "reactivity") is measured by observing the exploratory activity (the less exploration, the more fear) and the amount of defecation during the test, a simple indicator of autonomic nervous system mobilization preparatory to flight.

Beginning with rats that have identical scores on these measures, and then selectively breeding the ones that are more reactive and less reactive in each generation, it is easy to arrive at two distinct genetic strains, one of which is ten times more reactive than the other, in approximately ten generations. Relaxation of selection at fifteen generations leaves the strains stably far apart for at least the subsequent five generations. Cross-fostering at birth leaves the differences between the strains unaltered, showing that maternal behavior toward the young does not play a significant role in this disposition. Mating reactive or fearful males with nonreactive females produces offspring with intermediate fearfulness, and so does the reverse mating of fearful females with fearless males. The offspring from these two converse types of mating do not differ, which seems to rule out the possibility that much of the strain difference is the result of intrauterine effects. Genes alone would seem sufficient to account for the results in this particular set of experiments, and this is but one set of experiments among many that point to the same conclusion.

Nevertheless, it is equally well proved that experience strongly affects fear. Several simple types of learning that relate to it have been extensively studied: (1) habituation, in which fear is reduced by simply presenting the fear-inducing stimulus or situation over and over again with no adverse consequences; (2) classical Pavlovian conditioning, in which a fear-causing stimulus is paired with a neutral one, and the neutral one eventually becomes frightening; (3) passive avoidance conditioning, in which the individual is signaled that a painful stimulus (such as a shock) is on the way, and gradually learns to flee the vicinity; and (4) active avoidance conditioning, in which the escape is blocked but the subject can avert the painful stimulus by pressing a lever or performing some other action that turns the shock off in advance.

These conditioning strategies involve generating or reducing fear by manipulating it in relation to pain, to other fears, or to other consequences over an appropriate course of experience. The withdrawal (nociceptive) reflex in response to a pinprick on the foot occurs in the human fetus at least by fourteen weeks of gestational age, and some time before birth habituation is already possible. This, in a sense, is the first glimmer of learning. The other forms of learning related to fear cannot occur until after birth, but it is clear that learned enhancement and reduction of fear play a role in this dimension of human experience throughout the life course.

In what was and is perhaps the most famous demonstration in the history of learning theory, John B. Watson, the colorful founder of American Behaviorism as a psychological school, gave a toddler named Albert a secure place in intellectual history by making him insecure about furry objects. Albert was easily frightened by the noise made by the striking of a steel bar; this became the unconditioned stimulus in the experiment—the one that worked without training. When the noise was paired with a furry object, Albert formed a classical association, responding fearfully to the furry object itself after sufficient training. This process was almost exactly like Pavlov's famous experiment in which a bell was rung when food was presented, and the canine subjects eventually salivated in response to the bell alone. But it was not clear before Watson's experiment that an emotional response, much more complex neurologically than salivation, could be conditioned in the same way. Albert also generalized the new fear to furry objects of all kinds, including several he had never seen, and to furry animals. Watson argued that not only children's fears, but fears and phobias at all ages, could be accounted for by classical conditioning processes such as the one he had successfully carried through with Albert.

The difficulties with this notion are essentially two. First, how many children have arrived at their fears through a process of classical conditioning even remotely resembling the one that made Albert frightened of animals? Second, what made Albert afraid of the steel bar?

This latter question is the interesting one, because it conceals the whole complex matter of innate fears. In the late 1940s, the Canadian psychologist Donald Hebb showed that infant chimpanzees, with no experience of the objects before and with no prior deliberate conditioning of any kind, would exhibit extreme fear when presented with a snake, or the death mask of an adult chimpanzee, or the cadaver of a chimp fetus, as well as with a number of other objects. There was no reason to believe that these fears were the result of the usual learning processes, and Hebb wrote a famous paper about them in which he speculated on a mechanism for their development. He suggested that they were the result not of experience with the objects themselves, but of experience with other objects. Against the background of knowledge the infant chimps had accumulated, the new objects were discrepant; they aroused many perceptual schemata—patterns stored in the brain—but they fitted into none, and thus caused arousal to the point of fear. The brain, he argued, was somehow designed to generate fear as the result of such a cognitive mismatch.

In the meanwhile, in Europe, the ethologists were proceeding with their own investigations of innate fear. As might be expected, they used an animal model that was both simpler and more natural—the reflexive, fearful crouch response of the chicks of many birds in response to the sight of a hawk flying over the nest. Tinbergen and Lorenz themselves studied this phenomenon and arrived at the conviction that it constituted a classic innate releasing mechanism, a reflexive response, both in muscle contraction and emotion, to a stimulus configuration for which there was a genetically "wired" representation in the brain.

They were able to show that the full response occurred when a silhouette of a vaguely hawklike shape was passed over a nest of chicks. Passing the same silhouette over the nest in the opposite direction—tail first—did *not* elicit the response, however, and they reasonably argued that the latter movement more closely resembled a goose- or ducklike shape (long neck, short tail) to which the chicks were not "preprogrammed" to respond. But they carried out these studies on wild birds, so that a role for experience could not be ruled out. When experimental studies were done by a younger ethologist,

Wolfgang Schleidt, it was discovered that the hawklike movement caused fear because of discrepancy: If the chicks were made to experience repeatedly the sight of the gooselike movement over the nest, they crouched in response to the "hawk"; if, however, they were accustomed from hatching to the sight of the hawklike movement, they then crouched in response to the "goose" and let the "hawk" pass without reacting.

Thus there seemed even in this simple system to be an operating principle similar to the one proposed by Hebb for the infant chimpanzees, namely, departure from a previously established perceptual schema. But three qualifying or at least augmenting remarks are necessary. First, if the brain is designed to generate fear from cognitive mismatch, that may be less mysterious and easier to believe than that it should be programmed with a specific response to a specific shape (I for one am not sure that this *is* less mysterious); but such a design need be no less innate and genetically "hard-wired" than is the design of more classic ethological releasing mechanisms— it is merely less specific.

Second, it is evident that there are some fears that *are* highly specific. This is particularly true for lower vertebrates. But a looming object (or a simulation of one) can cause startled crying in even the youngest of human infants; and the edge of a cliff (or an optical illusion that looks like one) will cause fear not only in human infants but in a wide variety of vertebrate infants, including those with no experience of heights. It is not at all difficult to imagine a wiring diagram in the brain that could be constructed by the genes in early embryogenesis and that would produce fear in response to these relatively simple visual stimulus configurations.

But it is the third proviso that is most interesting. If the brain is designed to acquire certain fears with selective strength or rapidity, or if the normal environment in which the infant of the species must (or at least almost always does) grow up gives rise to certain fears more or less automatically, then an equally sure adaptive result can be had without neurological specificity. That is, if you wire the brain of the turkey chick for reaction to mismatch, you will achieve, in the normal environment of that creature, a guaranteed fear of hawks. And you will have done so without having to specifically and specially wire in an innate hawk schema. At the same time, you will have wired in a general mechanism—reaction to mismatch—that can serve the creature in many other ways.

Both possibilities apply to the growth of social fears in human infants. These include the fear of separation from a trusted caretaking figure and the fear of strange people, particularly if either of these is confronted in the context of a strange environment. Systematic study of these phenomena is now most closely associated with the reputation of Mary Ainsworth, a psychologist at the University of Virginia and a leading American authority on infant social behavior. She has developed and applied a simple test of infant fearfulness that involves placing the mother and infant in a strange but nonthreatening environment; introducing a friendly strange woman who converses with the mother, attempts to play with the infant, and remains with the infant when the mother leaves; and then having the mother return to the setting after a three-minute separation. There is subsequently a separation without the presence of a stranger, followed by another reunion. This test admittedly confounds the two responses by arousing the fear of strangers and the fear of separation simultaneously. But the results obtained in *this* standardized setting have been obtained by many other investigators using *other* settings, most of which keep the testing of the two fears distinct.

Those results are essentially as follows: In every sample of infants, in widely separated social classes and cultures around the world, the percentage of infants who fret, cry, or show other signs of distress when the mother leaves or when a strange person appears rises markedly after the age of six months. In each sample, some or even many infants do not show obvious fear at all, and some respond positively to strangers. But the growth change is universal in this sense: Before the age of six months, and especially between birth and four months of age, signs of either fear are for all intents and purposes nonexistent, whereas after seven or eight months of age they are quite common, and in many samples predominate. In infants from the professional class and the working class in the United States, in infants in an Israeli kibbutz where mother-infant contact is by our standards quite limited, in rural and urban Guatemala, and among the !Kung San of Botswana, who have the closest, most intimate, and most indulgent mother-infant relationship ever systematically described, the rise of separation fear and stranger fear occurs during the same age period. There are large cross-cultural variations in the percentage of infants who cry at any given age, in the age at which the percentage reaches its peak, and in the steepness and duration of the subsequent decline with further growth. But the variations in the shape and timing of the rising portion of the curve between the ages of six and fifteen months are minor or nonexistent; cultural training does not much accelerate or decelerate the change.

It is thus most likely that the change is a result of growth and that, like the rise of social smiling during the first few months of postnatal life, it is primarily the result of maturation in the nervous system— changes most of which are not in principle different from those that go on prenatally. They are of many different sorts, but one reasonable and easily examined index of all of them is the formation of myelin around the fiber axons that are destined to have myelin, an index that has been extensively studied by Yakovlev, Flechsig, and others.

During the period represented by the rising portion of the fear curve, the brains of human infants go through a rapid process of myelin deposition in all the major fiber tracts of the limbic system: the fornix, connecting the hippocampus with the hypothalamus; the mammilothalamic tract, connecting the hypothalamus with the anterior nucleus of the thalamus, and thence with the cerebral cortex; and the cingulum bundle connecting the cortex with the hippocampus. These large fiber bundles—the fornix is as massive as the optic nerve, which brings one-third of all external sense impressions into the brain—constitute the key paths of the Papez circuit, the core of the limbic system or "old mammalian brain," and there is thus a real sense in which the "stream of feeling" cannot be said to be properly functional until they are at least substantially myelinated. Another myelination event at this age, which is outside the limbic system and might have relevance to the growth of the social fears, occurs in the striatum, a principal portion of the "reptilian brain" believed by MacLean and others to account for much of the neural causation of fixed action patterns generally. To the extent that crying at separation and at the appearance of strangers constitutes a fixed action pattern triggered by an innate releasing mechanism, striatal myelination may play a role in its onset.

What of the mismatch theory? If such flexibility applies to chicks, surely humans must be at least that flexible. In fact, there is good reason to believe that the mismatch theory applies to human infants as well. Since human strangers do not fit a perceptual mold the way hawks do, the possibility of wiring in a specific pattern is moot in any case. The mechanism must be generalized, and mismatch is a good candidate; the infant stores the images of known persons, and the stranger (any stranger) activates these "person schemas," but matches none of them, whereupon the circuitry generates fear. What, then, is the role of maturation? No smaller than it would be in the simpler case of a wired-in special schema; it is just that in this case what is maturing is the capacity to experience mismatch, and to generate actions and emotions from it. This too requires functional neural wiring, and that wiring too must grow into place.

There is evidence of the maturation of the mismatch capacity from other experiments distinct from the stranger studies. Jerome Kagan and his colleagues at Harvard University have produced much evidence in support of the theory that human infants attend to stimulus patterns that are intermediate in discrepancy from ones they are familiar with—patterns that are neither too similar nor too different. But it is clear that some forms of intermediate discrepancy—like a mask, for example—can cause fear. Similarly, it is likely that if we were to take Hebb's chimpanzee infants (the ones that showed fearful responses to discrepancy) we could easily find less intense or less specific forms of discrepancy that would elicit only attention and not fear.

Although these experiments on human and chimp infants involve perceptual mismatch, whereas the cat experiments done by Ursin and Kaada involved direct stimulation of the brain, the two processes have this important feature in common: low-level stimulation gives rise to alertness, arousal, or interest, and high-level stimulation gives rise to fear or flight.

If we consider the fact that perceptual mismatch is, in a manner of speaking, a form of indirect stimulation of the brain, we may begin to understand more about this process. But this statement is only a form of "hand-waving"—that is, it is insubstantial—unless we get more specific about how mismatch in perceptual patterns might actually stimulate the brain.

From several lines of evidence it is now fairly clear that the hippocampus—a larger structure adjacent to the amygdala—is involved in the process of comparing newly presented perceptual configurations with those already stored in memory. The report of a mismatch to the arousal-fear mechanisms of the hypothalamus would thus almost have to involve the hippocampus and its major fiber bundle, the fornix. Thus the ability of human infants to respond to perceptual discrepancy from an established schema, known to increase as the brain grows during the first year, may be in part dependent on the myelination of the fornix. One can visualize, for example, that the approach of a stranger to the infant at twelve months of age might occasion a rapid "filing through" of the faces stored in the infant's memory (a process that would involve the hippocampus and fornix) followed by the reporting out of a mismatch. At four months of age, with no myelin in the fornix, such a process would perhaps be so slow as to be ineffective in generating arousal at the level of fear.

It is, however, most unlikely that mismatch detection capacity is the whole of the infant fear story; we need now an emotional output from the mismatch. If Papez and his numerous intellectual descendants are at all right, then the myelination of the major fiber tracts of the limbic system during the second half-year of life could result in a quantum advance in the capacity to *feel*, above and beyond the parallel advances that may be occurring in cognitive capacity and in the regulation of innate behavior patterns. The very cingulum bundle that has little or no myelin at four months of age and a great deal at twelve is the bundle that is lesioned by psychiatric neurosurgeons to treat some intractable cases of phobia. It is difficult to imagine that the "lesion" caused by the absence of myelin at four months can have nothing to do with that age-group's relative fearlessness. More generally, it is evident that the four-month-old's emotional capacity is rudimentary compared with that of the twelve-month-old, even though the latter has none of the subtleties of emotion and its expression that are made possible by the advent of language. These developmental changes are primarily maturational and under fairly close control by the genes.

But it is not true that there are *no* cross-cultural differences. The percentage of fearful infants at a given age, the age of the peak of fearfulness, and the shape of the declining portion of the curve are, as noted above, subject to substantial variation. While it is not well understood how the experiences of the infant can influence the known differences in fearfulness, it is likely that the large differences in the infant's social context in the different cultures—including the amount of mother-infant contact and separation, the amount of experience with other caretakers, and the amount of contact with strangers—play a role in their causation.

Many studies of laboratory animals have demonstrated the influence of critical early experiences on the later likelihood of fearfulness. Schleidt's work on the response of chicks to hawk silhouettes has been mentioned, but there are many other lines of investigation. The same open-field situation that has been used to test fearful and nonfearful genetic strains of rats has been used to show the existence of strong early-experience effects on fear in the same species. Mostly owing to the lifework of comparative psychologist Victor Denenberg and his colleagues, we have a clear picture of these effects. A continuum of different experiences given to different experimental groups of rats in the first twenty-one days of life—ranging from what might be called stimulation, such as petting by a human handler or being placed for a few minutes a day in a tin can filled with sawdust, to what would certainly be called stress, such as being shaken in the tin can, or given electric shock, or placed for a few minutes on a block of ice—will reliably produce a series of changes that include faster growth, greater adult body weight and length, longer survival times under various regimes calculated to be difficult for a rat to live through, and, most pertinent to the present subject, less fearfulness in the open-field test, whether assessed by exploration, of which they do more, or by defecation, of which they do less.

Some clues are available as to a possible physiological mechanism for the results of this early stimulation. Rats stimulated or stressed in infancy—only a few minutes a day are required—have lower levels of secretion from the adrenal cortex in the open field, as indicated by smaller amounts of corticosterone, the rat equivalent of the human stress hormone cortisol. Other evidence suggests that the whole activity of what is sometimes called the "pituitary-adrenocortical axis," the control system from the hypothalamus to the adrenal cortex via the pituitary, is altered in the stimulated rats. What seems to happen is that during repeated stress or stimulation in infancy, the pituitary-adrenocortical axis becomes habituated or exhausted, making it less responsive later and throughout adulthood. But this is only one hypothesis, and it is possible that there are neural as well as endocrine changes in the hypothalamus or in other parts of the brain.

While this phenomenon can perhaps be interpreted as a salutary effect of early stress (it certainly reduces fearfulness), other stresses in other species can have the opposite effect. Isolation-reared monkeys develop a syndrome resembling autism in which they withdraw from social contact and rock or bite themselves rather than making normal forays into their environment. They are more, not less, reactive to stimuli coming their way than are normally reared monkeys, and their already mentioned hyperaggressiveness is probably partly an overreaction produced by fear.

But more impressive than such consequences of the extreme stress and deprivation of isolation rearing is the demonstration, by Robert Hinde and his colleagues at Cambridge University, of long-lasting effects of short separations in the same species, rhesus monkeys. Separating a rhesus monkey infant from its mother twice, for six days each time, during the first six months of life, results in significantly greater fear of entering a strange environment at the age of two years. To most investigators familiar with the experimental work on rearing of laboratory monkeys, this was a surprisingly large and long-lasting effect of what would be considered a relatively minor intervention. (It was in fact designed as a model for what might happen to a human mother-infant pair separated for hospitalization.)

There is even evidence—and this will be of interest to women who have worried about the emotional strain they have been under during pregnancy—that rat pups will show different degrees of fear in the open field, depending on the amount of fear experienced by their mothers during pregnancy. In an ingenious experimental paradigm designed by the psychologist W.R. Thompson, prospective rat mothers were trained, before they became pregnant, to avoid an electric shock after presentation of a warning signal. During pregnancy, they were placed in the shock apparatus, given the warning signal, and not allowed to escape, but were given no shock. This produced a condition of fear in the mother that communicated itself to the fetus in various physiological and endocrinological ways. In experiments by Thompson and subsequently by another psychologist, Justin Joffe, this treatment could alter in complex ways fearfulness in the open field and speed up the acquisition of a learned avoidance task, perhaps an indication of increased fearfulness.

Thus the animal experimental literature confirms three common notions about the effects of early experience on fearfulness. First, there are stresses in early life, probably mild ones, that can decrease fearfulness. Second, there are other stresses, mild or severe, that can increase it. Third, these early experiences do not necessarily have to occur after birth to have significant effects. These findings provide indirect support for the belief, common to New England Yankees and Plains Indians, among other cultures, that letting an infant cry will toughen it up; for the belief of psychoanalysts that phobias or even neurotic timidity may be traceable to early psychological trauma; and—although this may be stretching things—for the folk belief that a calm pregnancy will produce a calm child. It is possible that there is a continuum of effects, with mild to moderate stress having a salutary effect and severe stress having a detrimental one, but this is probably a great oversimplification. None of the links, in any case, is strong, and much more direct evidence is needed on all these points before such generalizations can be made with confidence. What the experimental evidence does show is that these beliefs are basically consistent with processes known to occur under controlled conditions in nonhuman mammals.

It will by now be obvious that fear is entirely normal in the experience of humans and other animals, both in the biological senses (adaptive and physiologically inevitable) and the psychological senses (ubiquitous and universal) of the word "normal." But given the variation that must attend virtually every characteristic of living things—whether the main source of the variation is genetic or environmental or, as in the case of fear, both—it can come as no surprise that some abnormal variants will appear.

Plainly, fear plays a major role in many important syndromes of mental illness. Since it is so ubiquitous in human experience, being nearly activated in every instance of alerted arousal, it will of course appear in the phenomenology of psychiatric disorders. Explicitly paranoid fantasies are prominent in many cases of schizophrenia, and social withdrawal, a possible consequence of social fear, is present in virtually all cases. Childhood autism, sometimes called childhood schizophrenia because of the similar nature of the withdrawal symptoms, exhibits a phenomenology that in social contexts frequently looks fearful. Depression has as one of its consequences a protective social withdrawal and, in the manic-depressive syndromes, it may be caused in part by fears generated in the rush of activity and emotion of the manic phase. Of the neurotic disorders, fears of course constitute the content of phobias, but they are also believed to underlie the strange rituals of obsessive-compulsive neurosis; and the anxiety neurosis, which is as much the neurosis of our time as conversion hysteria was the neurosis of Freud's, has as its major symptom a mild form of unfocused fear.

While this is no place to trace out properly the role of fear as cause or symptom in any of these conditions, it may be useful to review three examples of special interest. One involves what is perhaps the first serious blending of ethology and psychiatry. Niko Tinbergen, one of the leaders of modern animal-behavior research, turned his attention in the late 1960s to the problem of childhood autism. Together with his wife and colleague, Elisabeth Tinbergen, and using methods and theory drawn from ethology, he closely observed and analyzed the social behavior of autistic children and arrived at the conclusion that fear might be at the base of some cases of the disorder in a causative sense. After demonstrating that autistic behavior could be intensified by intrusive (not necessarily threatening) social behavior on the part of an adult toward the child, they reasoned that exceptionally timid children might be at risk for developing the disorder if they grew up in a sufficiently threatening—or perhaps for them, merely a very intrusive—social environment. While it cannot be said that this view has met with wide acceptance among the relevant psychiatric authorities—and while it is almost certain that childhood autism is a diagnostic "wastebasket" for several distinct disorders with different developmental histories—it is conceivable that the Tinbergen theory is applicable in some cases.

A second example involves the problem of phobia. One of Freud's famous published cases was the analysis of Hans, a five-year-old boy with an extreme fear of horses—a serious problem in turn-of-the-century Vienna. Freud analyzed and in fact treated the case without direct contact with the boy, through the boy's father, a concerned physician interested in psychoanalysis. There had been no direct child analysis at that time, and Freud considered the case to be of special interest since it would give direct access to processes that he had presumed to have occurred during the early childhoods of his adult patients.

Analysis of Hans did not require much delving to turn up thoughts and feelings of the sort that were uncovered only with difficulty in adults. Hans explicitly and spontaneously talked about a keen interest in penises and women's lack of them, about intimacy with his mother, about fears of his father, about jealousy of his baby sister for his mother's affection, even about his desire to have his mother touch his penis. After his sister's birth he became steadily and increasingly anxious, and gradually developed intense fear of and interest in horses that prevented him from going out on the street or thinking about much else. He talked explicitly about horses' large penises, about beatings of horses he had seen, and about various imagined similarities between his father and horses. His father entered into regular written communication with Freud, and together they analyzed Hans's talk, behavior, and dreams. Their strategy was for the father to bring the entire complex of associations concerning horses, genitals, sex, and the strong emotions of love and rage that Hans felt toward his mother and father into conscious awareness in conversation. Gradually the boy's fears abated and disappeared, and both Freud and the parents attributed the improvement to the analysis.

Quite a few years later, Freud had a visit from Hans, age nineteen, who was obviously healthy and happy and who

> declared that he was perfectly well, and suffered from no troubles or inhibitions. Not only had he come through his puberty without any damage, but his emotional life had successfully undergone one of the severest of ordeals. His parents had been divorced and each of them had married again. In consequence of this he lived by himself; but he was on good terms with both of his parents, and only regretted that as a result of

the breaking-up of the family he had been separated from the younger sister he was so fond of.

Remarkable (although not from Freud's viewpoint surprising) was the young man's complete amnesia for the phobia and all the associated emotions and events of his early childhood. When he read the case history "he did not recognize himself." Thus (although Freud forbore mentioning this in his "Postscript" describing the later meeting), if Hans had come to analysis at age nineteen, and the analyst was unaware of the earlier events, the procedure would have been constrained to the usual efforts of anamnesis through association and dream analysis—deliberate attempts to recover the lost memories. Worse, if the adult Hans in this hypothetical situation had at last remembered the early phobia in accurate detail (and we cannot know whether he could have), it would have had the same ring of implausibility as do the memories of early childhood sexuality and fear in many another adult analysis.

In other words, Freud was quite correct in thinking that a child analysis would be inherently more plausible than any other. We can in no way be sure that the analysis was correct, or that it had anything to do with the disappearance of the phobia—many childhood phobias go away "by themselves," through growth and experience, or aided by more conventional desensitization through learning. But one psychoanalytic hypothesis that is indisputably and brilliantly confirmed by the case of Hans is that central emotional preoccupations of our early childhood—including not only sex and love, but even fears strong enough to be called traumatic and disabling—can be so relegated to some back-room storage space in the brain that they will be inaccessible not only to our ordinary adult conscious awareness, but even to an effortful remembering.

As the third, and for now last example, we have "the problem of anxiety." Freud's brief book by that name, originally published in German and sometimes translated as *Inhibitions, Symptoms and Anxiety*, is perhaps his most mature and elegant account of his central theory of the causation of neurosis. It will be necessary for us to return to it in trying to understand pleasure, but it cannot be omitted in any account of fear.

He reiterates and develops here the hypothesis introduced in the much earlier case study of Hans; namely, that anxiety is the result of a wish, arising from instinct, that is at least temporarily incompatible with survival, or is viewed as such by the conscious mind. We should note in passing that this definition, if true, must render anxiety a nearly constant component of everyday life, since the appraisal and laying aside of such instinctual wishes happens all the time. He restates his hypothesis of Hans's fear of horses, but this time generalizes it to include "infantile zoöphobia" as a category. A deeply felt fear—that of castration, occasioned by strongly sexual wishes—is diverted and masquerades as a strong but comparatively easy to accept fear of animals. Thus does he establish a continuum between anxiety and phobia, and he subsequently makes clear that he intends for it to apply to adult as well as childhood phobias and to many irrational fears besides fears of animals.

But, most interesting, he also emphatically answers the question of the relationship between anxiety and fear, as follows: "The anxiety in zoöphobia is thus an affective reaction of the ego to danger, the danger which is in this case warned against being that of castration. *There is no difference between this anxiety and the reality fear normally manifested by the ego in situations of danger,* other than the fact that the content of the former remains unconscious and enters consciousness only in distorted form" (emphasis added). Freud accepts the existence of a continuum from real fear of real external danger through the anxiety occasioned by potentially dangerous strong wishes to the irrational fear attached to external objects that are not really that dangerous.

A perspective guided by current knowledge of behavioral biology could accept, I think, a surprising amount of this. One might quibble about the "irrationality" of fear of animals, for instance, which were certainly something to be afraid of during most of human evolution, but one would still have to explain why Hans experienced more of such fear than other children in Vienna. One might balk at giving a central place to fear of castration when it seems only one of many imaginable dire consequences of failing to control one's instinctual wishes. But on the whole Freud's view is consistent with the notion that a steady, or at least steadily recurrent, measure of fearfulness, whether of external dangers appearing spontaneously or of possible

external consequences of our desires, is a salutary adjunct to survival. And it is not difficult to accept the hypothesis that this persistent
murmuring of fear will sometimes lead us to recoil from or even
attack objects that pose us no real danger.

Most of us, at all ages, do not respond to this murmuring very
much more maturely than did Hans. The second most frequently
prescribed drug in the United States is Valium, an "anxiolytic"
(anxiety-reducing) compound. (The most frequently prescribed drug
is now the new anti-ulcer drug Cimetidine, which may in fact be
replacing Valium in certain kinds of cases.) Valium (generically
called diazepam) has been recently found to have its effect by
potentiating the release of gamma-aminobutyric acid (GABA), an
inhibitory rather than excitatory neurotransmitter that controls
about one-third of all synaptic junctions in the cerebral cortex.

One of the side effects of Valium is a depressive effect on alertness,
not surprising in view of the fact that alertness and fear are on a
continuum of arousal. Very recently it has been shown that ethanol
(ethyl alcohol), the psychoactive principle of wines, beers, and
spirits, has (among other probable chemical effects) a potentiating
effect on GABA synapses similar to that of Valium. An estimated five
to ten percent of Americans are alcoholics, but a number many times
larger would be necessary for an estimate of those who use alcohol
regularly to reduce anxiety or fear (it has been a battlefront staple
since ancient times). Estimates of vodka consumption in the Soviet
Union do not suggest that "the New Soviet Man" is substantially less
in need of anxiety-reduction than his Western counterpart. And, in
the United States at least, we have a newly burgeoning teenage
drinking problem, suggesting that even the tensions and tremors of
the routine departure from childhood now require the potentiation of
GABA by artificial means.

But such psychic alchemy is scarcely the most threatening consequence of ubiquitous anxiety, or the worst solution to universal fear.
What we really need to worry about is the strategy of little Hans, writ
large. At various times and places in human history vast numbers of
people have allowed their natural fears to be turned outward and
focused upon others, whom they then victimized. Christians, Jews,
blacks, immigrants, "witches," Communists, "reactionaries," and

"capitalist-roaders"—to name a tiny fraction of the categories of people so, at various moments, singled out—have become, for millions in the majorities around them, the psychological equivalents of Hans's horses.

Except that Hans of course did not, indeed could not, hurt the horses. Take the same emotional process from Hans's innocent, weak little spirit, isolated in its confusion, and paint it onto a canvas depicting multitudes, with the objects of their fears few and weak among them; it is not difficult to imagine a degeneracy of human decency such as history has shown us many times. Discouragingly, these episodes are abetted by the most natural of the human social fears. Xenophobia draws upon the natural fear of strangers; conformity—the fear of *appearing* strange—draws upon the fear of separation; and obedience to authority, including illegitimate authority, draws on the fear of stepping out of one's place in the dominance hierarchy. Fears that served us adaptively during our phylogeny constitute a perfectly good basis for these reprehensible, terrifying episodes.

Imagine now, if you will, this alternative situation. Instead of placing the human objects of the refocused fear in a small minority living among the multitude, we place them in a geographically separate but juxtaposed arena and number them a comparable multitude. Now we allow the turning outward of natural fear to become mutual. Soon, to be sure, the fears will cease to be completely irrational; each multitude, precisely because of its fear, will pose a threat to the other. But the irrational component can always be depended upon to distort the threat upward; thus the familiar "positive feedback cycle" that always, so far, has resulted in war. There is much to be said of that, of course, but this is not the place. Let it suffice to remark that no reasonable analysis of human behavior can fail to grant that the situations that most seriously jeopardize human survival and human dignity, past, present, and future, owe much more to irrational fear than to irrational rage.

As for the personal dimension, it is not more encouraging. Natural selection has poised us on a knife-edge of uncertainty, destined to tumble, luckily, into knowing or, oftener, unluckily, into trembling. We awake and cringe, stir and cringe, eat and cringe, strive and cringe, even love and cringe in the midst of loving. Unlike other animals, we must knowingly look in the face of death, to find it a maw, insatiable. Aside from that, we are—not metaphorically, but precisely, biologically—like the doe nibbling moist grass in the predawn misty light; chewing, nuzzling a dewy fawn, breathing the foggy air, feeling so much at peace; and suddenly, for no reason, looking about wildly.

11

JOY

. . . that they are endowed by their Creator with certain unalienable Rights; that among these are Life, Liberty and the pursuit of Happiness. . . .
—Thomas Jefferson and
colleagues, 1776

It is a tradition in the United States to recognize in the words "pursuit of happiness" a great measure of Thomas Jefferson's wisdom. It was certainly forward-looking for him to guess that happiness would become a major preoccupation for the inhabitants of the newly conquered continent. It had not been a major explicit goal for most past societies, which, when they were not preoccupied with survival, had to muster together under such banners as Purity, History, Destiny, and Glory in order to keep on going. But given that the bounties of the American continent seemed to permit such a preoccupation, it nevertheless seemed the better part of valor to insist upon no more than the pursuit.

And "pursuit" certainly seems to be the word. Ask people who trust you, "Are you happy?" and when you don't get a "No," you very frequently get a "Yes, but . . ." The but may consist of no more than a facial expression; it usually means "I'm not sure I know what happiness is," or "I certainly ought to be happy," or "I'm trying hard, I'm almost there," or "Who are you to suggest that I'm not happy?" Of course, there are always the ones who grab you by the shoulders and shout at you about how happy they are: They have usually just been married, or just been born again in God, or just bought a new set of driving clubs, or just become very drunk. They do not enter much into our thinking about happiness, because they give so much the impression that they are riding for a fall, a fall one does not want to be in the way of.

From an evolutionary viewpoint, it is clear that creatures are endowed by natural selection with the tendency, if not the right, to pursue happiness. But that leaves two questions: Why and how are they endowed with the capacity to *experience* happiness; and to what extent are they able to know it when they feel it?

The subject of the previous chapter presents a part of the difficulty. To the extent to which nature is "the war of all against all" (and this extent is significant although not utterly tyrannizing), creatures must be on the alert for danger. Alertness for danger may be a source of martial elation, but for most of us outside the ranks of battlefield officers (and, except momentarily, probably for most of those within them), this is not what we mean when we speak of joy. As for the threats that come from within—the ones posed by our own wants— they engender an unease of mind that can scarcely lead to elation of any kind, at least until those wants are either discarded or more or less satisfied.

And yet, both the external and the internal threats can lead us into a state of joy, or at least of pleasure. This paradox is fairly easily resolvable when we consider that a creature must know when the external threat has been eluded or destroyed, or the internal threat laid aside through some satisfaction of the want. External events in general occasion a set of organismal responses, which, as indicated in the last chapter, appear to lie on a continuum between what we call alertness and what we call fear. The internal wants produce a state called by the psychologists "motivated," by the ethologists "appetitive," and by the psychoanalysts "unpleasure." Whether externally or internally generated (or both), these various internal states can be subsumed under the term "arousal," although this designation for them omits a quality of agitation that must be joined to it.

Agitated arousal, then. This does not mean to suggest that it must be punitive. Even the psychoanalysts' "unpleasure" does not mean literally that we must dislike the condition. We may like it and seek it in the course of normal life. However, when we enter into that condition, whether inadvertently or deliberately, the usual main exercise that follows is to do something to get ourselves beyond it. There is some suggestion in the current literature of neurobiology that, in terms of neural circuitry, all these states of arousal have a good deal in common. That is, the arousal caused by hunger, by the slow approach of danger, or by the helpless needs of one's young may involve very different circuitry of input and output, but overlap a lot in the depths of the brain. By the same token, the assuagement of these different forms of arousal—which we usually call pleasure and which occasionally, incomprehensibly, become joy—involves, to an important extent, a common neural circuitry in the limbic system. But before we turn to consider that circuitry, it will be useful to consider the phenomenology of arousal, and its counterpart, satisfaction, in the realm of observable behavior.

Freud's fascinating 1920 monograph, *Beyond the Pleasure Principle*, begins with the words,

> In the theory of psychoanalysis we have no hesitation in assuming that the course taken by mental events is automatically regulated by the pleasure principle. We believe, that is to say, that the course of those events is invariably set in motion by an unpleasurable tension, and that it takes a direction such that its final outcome coincides with a lowering of that tension—that is, with an avoidance of unpleasure or a production of pleasure.

With characteristic brilliance and aplomb, Freud plunged forward from these words to a major revision of the theory mentioned in them. He did so by adding, in a comprehensive way, the concept of "death instinct" as an independent motivator of behavior. He ranged over many then new fundamental discoveries of invertebrate reproductive biology, embryology, and animal behavior, and tied them together in a sweeping instinct theory.

While this effort was well-meaning, no modern biologist can follow believingly its leaps and spins; they are superficially impressive but intrinsically impossible. It is as if Freud felt that it was time for him to return to the fundamentals of biology after more than twenty years away from them; but instead of reviewing and incorporating into his thinking the intervening discoveries in neuroanatomy and neurophysiology, those beloved subjects of his youth, he tried, at once too hard and not hard enough, reaching out into irrelevant territory. The result was one of those confused, pseudobiological theories of the purpose of all of life—they still crop up occasionally today—from the crawl of the amoeba to the diplomacy of a nation; the kind of theory that, by explaining everything, explains nothing.

But, again characteristically, it was impossible for him to write a book full of blunders without also making a valuable contribution. This came in the analysis of a psychiatric disorder that had recently presented itself vigorously to his attention and that he badly wanted to explain. It was called the "traumatic neurosis." It had long been known, but only obscurely, as a sequel to certain railway disasters and other accidents; but "the terrible war which has just ended gave rise to a great number of illnesses of this kind." This category of traumatic neurosis, called war neurosis, had forced its way into the consciousness of Freud and other psychoanalysts, and there had been sufficient numbers of documented cases to rule out the possibility of organic brain damage in many. The chief symptom was a tendency to repeat the experience of the trauma, with all its attendant frightful emotion, in memory, and especially in dreams.

From which definition Freud proceeded immediately to a lengthy account of child's play. A baby of his acquaintance, just on the verge of acquiring language, made a habit of playing games of disappearance. That is, the child would hide and recover objects, or hide himself in front of a mirror and make himself reappear, over and over again, especially when his mother was out or had recently returned. Obvious signs of pleasure were associated with the return of the object or the mirror image, however many times the game was repeated.

Such childhood games, of which hide-and-seek is a great one from infancy onward, were linked to traumatic neurosis through the concept of repetition compulsion. According to this concept, a prospect that generates great anxiety or fear is awakened and reawakened, deliberately, by the mind, for the purpose of allowing the sense of mastery; or if mastery is not possible, at least allowing the sense that survival *is*—in itself, a kind of weakened mastery. This sense of mastery, in the case of the infant and child at least, is a joyful one.

There were clear echoes here of Freud's conception of humor, elaborated in his book *Jokes and Their Relation to the Unconscious.* According to his notion there, the listener deliberately places herself in the hands of the joke-teller—she is in the mood to laugh—and the teller brings her into a condition of arousal by creating uncertain anticipation; the punch line has an economizing effect in the mind, making it clear that the built-up tension was unnecessary, and causing a discharge of that tension through laughter. An ethological addendum to this analysis would note the similarity between human laughter and the aggressive hoots made by some of our nonhuman relatives when involved in conflicts, and also note the fact that many jokes are obvious acts of verbal aggression. This would suggest the possibility that some of the mental tension or arousal we feel—even in jokes apparently innocent of aggressive content—has strong components of fear and/or anger. The laughter at the end of the joke subsumes the discharge of this anger, together with the pleasure we feel at the cessation of fear.

The elation of having just passed through danger is well known if not common in our experience. It is felt in sports—more purely, perhaps, since anger is largely bypassed, in those sports that pit human beings against nature rather than against each other; and it is felt by people who have survived serious illness, and by some women who experience childbirth. It can be, really, an almost ecstatic elation. Even aesthetic contemplation and awe partake of that elation. The emotion of joy that overcomes us while walking on mountain ridges or while sailing in a small boat on a great expanse of water or while resting in a beautiful garden at night must surely have, in some measure, the transcendence of fear in it. And no less an aesthetic authority than Rilke wrote:

> Then beauty is nothing
> But the start of a terror that we're still able to bear
> And the reason we love it so is that it blithely
> Disdains to destroy us.

We even have some evidence for a biological link between fear and joy. In the famous experiment by Stanley Schachter of Columbia

University, either elation or anger could be produced by an injection of epinephrine, a hormone secreted under conditions of stress or fear. The subject's emotional response depended on whether the person sitting next to him was behaving happily or angrily.

But it is probable that so elaborate a hormonal mechanism as the secretion of epinephrine need not become involved in lesser instances of such emotions, and that a mechanism intrinsic to the brain is sufficient. This mechanism may be fundamental to the very processes of perception and cognition.

Freud himself referred to such processes in summarizing the work of G. T. Fechner, the nineteenth-century perceptual psychologist and founder of psychophysics, the most quantitative branch of perceptual psychology. Fechner began the process, which Freud and others were to continue, of identifying aesthetic appreciation and even pleasure itself with the intensity of incoming stimulation and its relation to internal expectations. He thought—wrongly, as it happens—that pleasure was caused by the crossing into consciousness of sensations approximating stability, and unpleasure by sensations causing deviations from stability, while between the two there was said to be "a certain margin of aesthetic indifference." This view has been superseded, but the important thing about it was that it opened a path of investigation and a way of thinking about pleasure: namely, as a sort of epiphenomenon of the degree of discrepancy between external input and internal expectation; in effect, a perceptual theory of pleasure.

In present-day perceptual-cognitive psychology, the relationship between perceptual processing and pleasure is more complex, more carefully studied, and more interesting. In the cognitive psychology of Jean Piaget—the polymathic Swiss genius who personally invented about half of that field of study—a smile occurs when a problem is solved or when a stimulus configuration is recognized. This "smile of recognitory assimilation" has been studied extensively by Jerome Kagan, Philip Zelazo, and others, especially in infants and children, and there is no doubt that it is real. To rephrase Fechner (and Freud): The condition of unpleasure in relation to cognition is caused by the perusal of a stimulus that is not well represented in the memory store.

More precisely, to give unpleasure the stimulus must evoke *something* in the memory store in order to produce attention; but the pattern configuration of the stimulus must be such as to fail to match the schema stored in memory. That is, the stimulus must be "moderately discrepant from an established schema." If sufficient visual or auditory attention to the stimulus pattern is able to produce a mental reconciliation of the mismatch—by creating a new schema or extending the old one—then a smile occurs. For the older child intent on solving a problem, the theory is parallel: If the problem is too unfamiliar, it will not evoke attention; if it is difficult but doable, it will evoke interest, attention, and arousal and, when solved, it will evoke pleasure, often signaled by a smile.

If the problem is too easy, these events will not occur because arousal will not occur. The same is true for four-month-old infants who see a stimulus pattern with which they are completely familiar. It may be remembered that Donald Hebb's fear theory was also based on evocation of arousal by moderate discrepancy. It is probable that moderately discrepant stimulus configurations with which the organism has no previous experience produce alertness, attention, and arousal—until they are assimilated and produce pleasure. But if they should prove unassimilable after some cognitive effort, they produce fear.

It thus seems possible that the smile of recognitory assimilation is a pleasurable discharge of arousal comparable, although on a smaller scale, to the discharge of laughter at the end of a joke. To use and revise Fechner's exact language, as adopted by Freud, pleasure is caused by the crossing into consciousness of sensations that first deviate from, and then reapproximate stability.

It follows from this that work tasks and learning tasks that are either too simple or too repetitive can rarely be interesting or pleasurable. For this generalization we must of course add a caution relating to age, prior experience, and individual differences. A retarded person might find both challenging and pleasurable a task that would bore a normal person to tears. An orderly person might see in certain routines a challenge that would be missed by someone else. Finally, there may be some truth to the notion that some people can reach a kind of Zen *satori* state while doing repetitive tasks, a state said to be serene and even pleasurable.

But, for most of us, engagement in an activity that is endlessly repetitive must lead to estrangement or alienation from what we are doing, instead of to joy in it. And this in fact was one of the four kinds of alienation that Karl Marx referred to in his essay "Estranged Labor," in the *Economic and Philosophic Manuscripts of 1844*. Since it is likely that this alienated condition results primarily from technological mode rather than from economic organization, it is not surprising that socialist and Communist countries have not had more success in combating it. But it may be that it can be influenced even in assembly-line situations by giving working people substantial emotional stake in and control over the quality of the product they are working on.

In the realm of learning, joy is as fragile and as easy to destroy as in the realm of work. It is also likely that childhood experiences produce "learning sets"—attitudes about how to learn—that may last a lifetime. And Daniel Stern, a psychiatrist at the Cornell University School of Medicine, and John S. Watson, a psychologist at Berkeley, have independently explored a region of human mental life in which the joy of learning (or, if you like, of cognitive activity) is very nearly joined to the joy of love.

That region is the experience a three- or four-month-old infant has of transactions with its primary social world. Stern, having extensively observed (and measured with innovative, complex quantitative methods) the interaction of infants of this age with their mothers, has been able to bring the joy infants take in such interaction squarely in line with the theory behind the "smile of recognitory assimilation." In a paper titled "Mother and Infant at Play," he and his colleagues proposed a sort of ideal mother (not ethically but cognitively ideal) who, in the course of facial interaction or "play," would make expressions and sounds designed to arouse the infant, within limits, by challenging his or her established social schemata. Probably this play also taps into mechanisms of perceptual arousal that are genetically encoded and require a certain level of brain maturation but no prior experience; loudness and pitch of voice, sudden raising of the brows and widening of the eyes, and vigorous physical stimulation are likely to belong in this category.

In any case, the "ideal" mother or caretaker is carefully monitoring the infant's arousal level, attempting to bring it to a threshold at which discharge and smiling or laughing can occur—not too high but just high enough. Repetitions and variations on this theme—of course, the "threshold" level of arousal as well as the conditions for eliciting it may vary even within one session—constitute the resulting "game." Gazing, smiling, laughing, and cooing indicate that the stimulation is in the right realm; while gaze aversion, fussing, or crying indicate that the play has lapsed into boredom or fatigue or that it has escalated into distress.

Watson has focused on the same relationship at the same age with a different theory and with equally rigorous methods, although his are experimental rather than observational. Consider this ingenious experiment: A three-month-old infant is lying in a crib looking at a stationary mobile. Under its pillow, on either side, are levers that, when tripped, make the mobile move. Thus, by turning its head from side to side, the infant can generate for itself a spectacle that delights it, as evidenced by persistent gazing and by smiling and cooing. After a few weeks of such opportunity, such infants are, not surprisingly, more adept at learning similar control tasks than are others the same age without such experience. They have become accustomed, in Watson's terms, to "response-contingent stimulation"—stimuli that do not merely occur and change and pass, intriguing by the power of complexity and discrepancy to draw attention, but change in response to the infant's own actions. And, in addition, the infants obviously like it.

More surprising, however, is the result for another experimental group—infants that had mobiles that moved on their own. These infants were not only less adept at learning control than were the infants who had had controllable mobiles all along; they were also less adept than infants who had had no mobile experience whatever. In other words, they had learned, to some extent, to consider the world as outside their control.

Although we must not underestimate the capacity of infants and children to behave differently in different learning contexts, one obvious warning that emerged from this line of work was against too much passive cognitive activity—such as most of television-watching. We might call to mind in this connection that fact that enriching the environments of rats does not affect their brains unless they grapple actively with those environments. A second warning is more intriguing: Watson theorized (in a manner converging independently on Stern's thinking) that the mother or primary caretaker would be, if loving enough, an "ideal" response-contingent stimulus pattern, changing, like the controllable mobile, in a way that both challenges and responds to the infant's own cognitive apparatus. So far, so good.

But the caution was this: If the infant was set up biologically to delight in and perhaps grow to love contingently responsive stimuli, then some ingenious toy manufacturer might come up with a convenience device, based on Watson's own research, that could fool the three-month infant's attachment-formation system and destroy a part of its capacity for human social life. We do not know whether this has ever happened to an infant, but it is likely that the strong attachments formed nowadays between some young adults and computers (the more extreme among these dependencies cease to be amusing as soon as they are seriously scrutinized) belong in the same category, although to be sure they are of more complex causation.

As for later learning, and love of learning, the last few decades have seen changes that some consider to be as significant as the initial commitment to universal education. The name of A.S. Neill, whose *Summerhill* became a model and guide for emotionally aware teaching and learning, as well as those of John Holt and Joseph Featherstone, who helped initiate the "open classroom" movement in the United States, arc among many associated with these changes. Although they were not conceived as such, they may be viewed as attempts to do for the schoolchild what Stern's or Watson's "ideal mother" would do for the infant: challenge the child's arousal system in a way that would bring the child along at its own best pace, based on careful individual monitoring.

This intriguing experiment has not yet been vindicated, but neither has it proved unfeasible. It has made some impact on teaching and learning from the preschool nursery to the great professional training centers, but the results are far from clear. Attempts to blame on it the recent decline in college entrance examination scores are simplistic at best.

Nevertheless, it has been misinterpreted at times to mean that learning must be nothing but pure unadulterated pleasure, pandering in every way to the merest and most solipsistic whims of the learner. Thus does watching television substitute in the curriculum of some secondary schools for the reading of the classics, or rap sessions on petting for the study of biology; thus may the challenge of a curriculum be reduced by half or three-fourths in capitulation to a collective teenage whimper. The joy of learning is destroyed as much or more easily by such antics as it is by excessive rigidity and repetition. Even in infancy, even in animals, joy in learning requires challenge, and challenge, up to a point, entails, and may be synonymous with, distress.

This applies even to what we call play, which has long been one of the central concerns of ethology. To summarize a great deal of print about how to define play, I think that to say that it is an expenditure of energy that looks both impractical and pleasurable would not, despite its brevity and vagueness, do violence to the literature on the subject. But the fact that it looks impractical does not mean that it is adaptively useless. The evidence suggests that it serves the functions of exercise, of learning about the environment and about one's fellow creatures, and, in some species, of sharpening or even acquiring fundamental subsistence and social skills. In some mammals it is clear that the deprivation of opportunities for play in early life have major deleterious consequences for social and reproductive skills in adulthood.

In reviewing the data it soon becomes apparent that, for most animals that have play, it serves functions that make it difficult to separate the playful from the educative. Not surprisingly, it turns out that, broadly speaking, the most intelligent mammals—the primates, the Cetacea or whales and porpoises, and the terrestrial and aquatic carnivores—are the most playful; these two characteristics of complex mammals probably have evolved in concert, each strengthening the other. Also, if an animal is very short-lived, the young do not appear to play very much, perhaps because there is too little time for them to gain very much from it. Play in mammals is typically engaged in among juveniles, and in this context there is ample opportunity for observational learning, particularly if, as in many species, the juveniles are of somewhat different ages and developmental levels. Opportunity for observation of a task while or before trying to do it has been shown to improve the rate of learning it in a number of mammals in experimental settings.

The playlike features of prey-catching behavior in the cat family, which make it difficult to classify such behavior as aggressive, have already been described. These features become the basis of an almost unique system of communication between adults and young that is perhaps properly called teaching. Feline mothers bring back half-dead prey, which their young then kill and eat. They lead cubs and kittens on expeditions whose main purpose seems to be to acquaint the young with stalking. And they partially kill prey on the hunt, leaving the young to finish the job and intervening only if the prey is about to escape.

Hunter-gatherer subsistence and cultural learning resembles much more "the open classroom" on the one hand and the learning of nonhuman mammals on the other than it resembles the traditional setting of Western education. Yet to some of the educators of the nineteenth and early twentieth centuries, the rigors of the old-style schoolroom must have seemed very benign compared with the daily chores or full-time work lives of children in most of the world's cultures—including especially the one into which their mass education was being introduced. Indeed, the literature of anthropology shows that intermediate-level societies—the ones that have left the hunting-and-gathering subsistence mode behind in favor of gardening, agriculture, or pastoral means of production—bring much more work and drudgery into the lives of children than do hunter-gatherers. Thus the lenient modern educational philosophy might be viewed as in some respects restoring the hunter-gatherer playful-learning pattern.

But even play involves serious challenges. The social play among juveniles in all mammals includes a common pattern of rough-and-tumble play, which can be very vigorous and highly arousing, and which contains some components—behavioral and physiological—of aggression. Although it usually does not, it *can* result in injury. In our species, this among other playful behaviors is carried forward into adulthood, supplying one of several justifications for the interesting designation *Homo ludens* ("playful man") given to our species by the Dutch historian Johan Huizinga. Rough-and-tumble play, whether in childhood or adulthood, can be rough. People who find bullfighting repulsive usually ignore the fact that some American boys and youths are killed each year while playing football, and even in baseball the incidence of serious, including deliberate, injury is not trivial. To stand one's ground in or near the path of a ball that is hard and fast enough to break one's skull must surely be regarded as arousing.

Much has been learned about arousal and pleasure as they are processed by the brain, owing especially to the genius of the late James Olds, a physiological psychologist who at the time of his death was teaching at the California Institute of Technology. In 1953, he and his colleague Peter Milner made an observation that has changed the subsequent history of psychology. A rat with an electrode implanted in its brain was, while roaming the open-field apparatus, stimulated with a small electric shock for experimental purposes having nothing to do with what happened. It responded by returning to the place where the shock had been delivered.

Taking advantage of this serendipitous event, Olds and Milner abandoned their previous line of research in order to explore the rat's behavior. They discovered that rats would indeed return repeatedly for stimulation of certain parts of the brain; would stimulate themselves this way if given a lever controlling the shock; would work to get that opportunity; and would neglect other aspects of their lives—including aspects essential to survival, such as eating—in order to pursue that stimulation. Since delivery of the shocks could reinforce (increase the likelihood of) normal behaviors occurring in association with them, Olds came to refer to the shocks as "brain reward," or "rewarding brain stimulation"; but later investigators could not resist the expression "pleasure centers of the brain." It has been seen in animals from fish to higher primates, including human ones.

The findings of this line of research have become so fundamental to our current knowledge of the physiology of pleasure, of arousal, and of reinforcement, that it is worth recounting them at some length, following Olds's own account in a late and masterly review paper published in 1976.

The parts of the brain found to be susceptible to "rewarding" stimulation were fairly wide-ranging, but centered upon the hypothalamus, as though on the hub of a wheel. The "spokes"—neural pathways not necessarily very symmetrically arranged—radiated primarily to the olfactory and limbic systems, including the olfactory bulbs and olfactory cortex, the septal area, the amygdala, the anterior nucleus of the thalamus, the cingulate cortex, the hippocampus, and pathways radiating down to the limbic portion of the midbrain and related lower brain-stem centers. The list reads almost like a modern definition of the limbic system, and it contains the whole of the Papez circuit of the emotions.

It proved possible to evoke rewarding effects by stimulating other areas, but with much more difficulty than within the central reward system. Furthermore, these main reward areas were not all equally useful in producing the effect. In the lateral hypothalamus, spreading backward to the midbrain, electrodes evoked the highest rates of self-stimulation. Rates in the central hypothalamus, near the midline of the brain, were lower, and rates in the hippocampus and cingulate cortex were lowest of all. This seemed to confirm the notion, familiar from limbic system anatomy, of the hypothalamus as the central organ of motivation.

Rats made to work for brain reward will press the lever up to twenty times for one brain stimulus, but no more than that; if, however, the rat is given a signal before the stimulus comes on, it will press the lever up to two hundred times for a single stimulus. This puzzling finding suggested that brain stimulation is much more rewarding if it is anticipated. Still other experiments suggested that the same stimulation could produce escape reactions if delivered into the brain at random intervals and produce reward (the opposite effect) if the rat could control the timing. In other words, the same stimulation could be very desirable, slightly desirable, or quite undesirable depending on the degree of subjective control experienced by the animal. (Echoes of the human infant's joy in controlling *external* stimulation are clear.)

The relationship of brain self-stimulation to arousal was explored in several experiments, with ambiguous but fascinating results. Depending upon electrode location, rewarding stimulation could be either arousing or quieting. A stimulus near the septal area slowed or arrested normal behavior and had a physiological pattern describable in terms of parasympathetic dominance of body functions: lowered heart rate, blood pressure, and respiratory rate. But a stimulus in the lateral hypothalamus, *also* rewarding, caused sympathetic arousal, raising respiratory rate and blood pressure, and also increased general behavioral activity. This paradox is perhaps resolvable when we consider that pleasurable experiences in the normal course of human life may be either arousing or quieting.

There has in fact been direct study of similar brain-stimulation effects in humans. Brain surgeons, operating for reasons having nothing to do with psychological theories, often must stimulate the brain to find their way. That is, the anatomy they see on the brain's surface is ambiguous, and the best way to map it—and avoid a cut in the wrong place—is often to stimulate various spots and record muscle activity and other responses on the part of the patient. Since there are no sensations coming from inside the brain, patients may be conscious during these procedures. Physiological psychologist Elliot Valenstein, who has also done extensive work on brain self-stimulation in rats, described several patients as follows:

> A patient who had just attempted to commit suicide by jumping off the roof suddenly started to smile when the electrode in his septal area was activated. It was difficult for him to verbalize his experience more explicitly than, "I feel good. I don't know why. I just suddenly felt good." Upon further questioning the patient implied that there might have been sexual overtones to his experience as he said: "It's like I had something lined up for Saturday night . . . a girl." Given an opportunity to press a button controlling a portable stimulation unit worn around his belt one patient reported: "When I get mad if I push the button I feel better. . . . that's a real good button. . . . I would buy one if I could." A woman with intractable pain said during the stimulation: "I'm feeling fine . . . feel like I could clean up the whole hospital." In several instances it has been suspected that a patient reached an orgasm during stimulation.

There has been insufficient work of this kind on human beings to justify many generalizations. But it is clear that there are individual differences in responsiveness and that a variety of different kinds of positive experience may be reported. It appears that brain stimulation has its most clear and dramatic effect on patients who start in a circumstance of psychological or physical pain. For others, the experience is often pleasurable but not compelling. In one patient, the desire to self-stimulate with the implanted electrode was very strong and an embarrassment to her, and she tried (usually successfully) to conceal it or distract herself by reading, listening to music, and helping other patients. The resemblance to strongly motivated "bad habits," such as smoking, seems evident.

The relationship between brain reward and specific motivated behaviors has been explored and is fascinating. There are brain locations where self-stimulation rates will increase when the animal is hungry, others where they will increase when the animal is satiated. Furthermore, at the sites at which hunger decreases self-stimulation, sex drive increases it, and vice versa. In one human patient who had an implanted electrode for some time, and who resumed menstruation during that time, stimulation produced sexual overtones after menstruation occurred, but not before. This among other findings suggests that the subjective effect of stimulation of brain locations is influenced by hormonal background.

A series of experiments by Valenstein using rats showed that some of the reward centers also produced various motivations of the animal's behavior. Stimulation of the lateral hypothalamus, which is highly effective as a reward and which, if controlled by the animal, will lead to high rates of self-stimulation, also causes the animal to eat, to hoard food, and to perform other activities. Electrodes planted in the same site in rats could produce food hoarding or maternal retrieving depending upon whether food pellets or rat pups were in the cage with a stimulated subject. To make matters more complicated, some of the sites elicited satiation of driven activity rather than enhancement of it.

To summarize the phenomenon of brain self-stimulation, the findings are consistent with our subjective sense that pleasure can be arousing or quieting, and either general or specific in one of several ways. They suggest that the animal receiving potentially pleasurable brain stimulation will much prefer to know about it in advance, and will prefer to control it actively; this is consistent with much that has been said about the relationship of joy to the sense of mastery. They suggest too that the brain is designed to pursue pleasure, but that it defines pleasure in a pretty vague way; this may mean that it is not ideally suited to distinguish among the various sources of pleasure and to choose the one the animal (or person) really needs. It may even mean that it is not ideally suited to detect the existence of organismal satisfaction.

Finally, it has been shown that animals deprived of REM (dream) sleep will increase their rates of feeding, sexual behavior, and brain self-stimulation in brain regions known to produce reward. Furthermore, REM-deprived animals that are allowed self-stimulation of the brain will not "catch up on" REM sleep when they are allowed to, as other REM-deprived animals will. These findings give rise to the utterly fascinating suggestion that rewarding self-stimulation of the brain is somehow a substitute for dreaming; this apparent equivalence, if true, would seem to confirm both the notion of self-stimulation of the brain as pleasure and the notion of dreams as wish fulfillment.

"Woe to you, my Princess, when I come, I will kiss you quite red and feed you till you are plump. And if you are froward you shall see who is the stronger, a gentle little girl who doesn't eat enough or a big wild man with cocaine in his body." So wrote the author of that same notion of dreams, Sigmund Freud, in a letter to his fiancée in June 1884. He was then on the verge of achieving international recognition with a series of reports on his studies of the medicinal uses of the coca plant and its alkaloid derivative, cocaine. He was at least ten years from the first steps into psychoanalysis, and his interest in cocaine pharmacology preceded even his work on the neuroanatomy of language disorders. He had eagerly reviewed the published literature on the subject—then very limited—and he soon began experimenting on himself and others with cocaine. In a manner similar to that used by modern pharmacologists, he requested a sample of the drug from the Merck company and began to explore its properties.

The procedure of self-experiment with drugs was not as unusual then as it is now, and Freud's first paper, "Über Coca," was favorably received and was reprinted, quoted, and translated. With the meticulous method characteristic of his early period, he reviewed the history of cocaine use, the botany, the known pharmacology, and the labora-

tory and clinical evidence of its effects. Like many drugs of fundamental medical importance, it was discovered by a "primitive" people,
in this case the Incas of Peru, who habitually chewed the coca leaf, a
"divine plant which satiates the hungry, strengthens the weak, and
causes them to forget their misfortune." Prior experience with the
drug both among the Indians and among soldiers in Europe suggested
its possible use to make brutal work tolerable and to combat the
natural effects of fatigue.

Freud gave an excellent account of the animal research, and it
could be summarized similarly today; cocaine causes a general sympathetic activation with increases in respiration, heart rate, and blood
pressure, and at higher doses causes poisoning, with motor agitation
leading to convulsions and finally to death. He cited evidence that
this sympathetic activation is carried down from the brain to the
spinal cord through the medulla oblongata in the brain stem. At low
doses, he reported, "dogs show obvious signs of happy excitement and
a maniacal compulsion to move." He gave an almost correct chemical
formula for the compound, although without drawing its structure,
then unknown. And he ended the paper by recommending further
exploration of its use as a stimulant, aphrodisiac, digestive, antiasth-
matic, local anesthetic, and substitute for morphine during withdrawal.

But most interesting were his remarks on his own and his friends'
experience with self-administration:

> The psychic effect . . . in doses of 0.05–0.10g consists of
> exhilaration and lasting euphoria, which does not differ in any
> way from the normal euphoria of a healthy person. . . . One
> senses an increase in self-control and feels more vigorous and
> more capable of work. . . . One is simply normal, and soon finds
> it difficult to believe that one is under the influence of any drug
> at all. . . . Long-lasting, intensive mental or physical work can
> be performed without fatigue; it is as though the need for food
> and sleep . . . were completely banished.

Freud was to be heavily criticized for his championing of cocaine,
and was eventually to regret it despite his quite adequate self-defense
in a later paper. Among other things, cocaine was implicated in the

death of a friend of Freud's who was a morphine addict. More important in his change of mind perhaps was his final firm conviction that psychologically active chemicals are ultimately useless in, and perhaps also interfere with, the process of real psychological change.

Interest in cocaine (in the laboratory, not just on the street) has surged in the last decade, and some of Freud's fears have been confirmed. It is certainly toxic, seriously habit-forming (Freud at first believed it was not), and at high doses causes a florid psychosis similar to some forms of schizophrenia. But it also appears that he may have been too hard on himself, because potential positive medicinal uses are also evident; not to mention some psychic effects that would sound familiar to him.

We now know cocaine to have a three-ringed chemical structure closely resembling that of the "tricyclic" antidepressants. It is not, however, an effective treatment for depression, probably because it has widespread other effects. Yet it does share with them one major effect: It blocks reuptake of the neurotransmitters norepinephrine and serotonin at the nerve endings. This is the major means of inactivation of those neurotransmitters, so that more of them will be around, following cocaine ingestion, to stimulate the next cell in the circuit.

These findings form part of the basis of the neurotransmitter theory of mood. It is undoubtedly oversimplified, but very likely to constitute part of the truth. As for cocaine, recent studies have vindicated many of Freud's findings. Appropriate doses taken under controlled conditions indeed produce the "high" described on the street, and in a dose-related manner that declines neatly with the clearance of the drug from the blood. The four items most frequently checked on one scale given to subjects under the influence of cocaine were: "I feel as if something pleasant had just happened to me"; "I am in the mood to talk about the feeling I have"; "a thrill has gone through me one or more times since I started the test"; and "I feel like joking with someone."

In a study of three monkeys given a continuous choice between food and cocaine, "the drug was almost exclusively chosen. Periods of low drug intake did not coincide with increased food intake. . . . This exclusive preference for cocaine persisted for 8 days. Concern for the health of the animals prohibited extending the testing period." Amphetamine is also a stimulant, and probably works in part by inhibiting reuptake of norepinephrine, but it typically produces an agitated kind of euphoria, whereas one of the most frequent spontaneous remarks of human subjects in cocaine studies is, "I feel more relaxed."

The monkey cocaine study is reminiscent of the work already described on self-stimulation of "rewarding" brain regions: Rats in some experiments neglected food to press the lever. It would be helpful to be able to localize the brain's capacity for "reward" (or pleasure, or euphoria) more than was done by Olds and Valenstein and their colleagues, but experiments in which various brain regions were specifically destroyed did not eliminate the reward capacity. One important line of research begun by psychopharmacologists Larry Stein and David Wise showed that use of a drug that poisons norepinephrine-containing nerve cells throughout the brain pretty much abolishes a rat's capacity to experience reward, and perhaps even pleasure. This finding is consistent with the notion that cocaine, amphetamine, and the tricyclic antidepressants now in use in psychiatry all exert their effects *partly* by enhancing the transmission of norepinephrine. In another study, injection into the ventricles of the brain of the same norepinephrine-depleting substance used by Stein and Wise—this time in free-ranging monkeys—produced a behavioral syndrome phenomenologically resembling human depression.

But recent activity in the study of the chemistry of mood has decisively found a second major focus, away from the small neurotransmitter molecules norepinephrine and serotonin. This focus is on the class of brain chemicals known as peptides—chains of several amino acids that, if built up the same way until they became very long, would be proteins. Discoveries relating to brain peptides have revolutionized the study of brain function in just the last few years. They add several new dimensions to previous possibilities. First, they are five or ten times the size of the previously known neurotransmitters, and thus provide a dimension of added complexity. Second, they may resemble or even be identical to some hormones of the pituitary and hypothalamus, suggesting the possibility that hormones from those organs flow up into the brain, not just down into the body.

Third, they may frequently be the breakdown products of proteins, the long, complex molecules only one step removed from the genes; this allows for the possibility that they may be involved in a vast assembly and reassembly system of hormones with interchangeable parts and with great information-carrying capacity.

Of all the newly studied peptides the most interesting by far are the endorphins. Known by structure before they were known by function, they moved to center stage in brain science during the late 1970s because of work on a completely different class of chemicals—the opiates. Candace Pert and Solomon Snyder of the Johns Hopkins University, among others, spent the early years of the 1970s characterizing and locating in the brain "the opiate receptor"—the then hypothetical chemical site where morphine and heroin land and start their effects. They, Roger Guillemin, and many other investigators gradually showed that the endorphins and related peptide molecules could mimic the effects of morphine on pain. They subsequently came to be called "morphinomimetic" or "opioid" peptides. Equally significantly, in 1976 two separate laboratories came to the conclusion that tiny doses of opioid peptides—less than one one-hundredth of those required for pain reduction—produced in rats dramatic behavioral symptoms, including body rigidity, immobility, and unresponsiveness.

The most important fact about these effects is not that they occur at such low doses—although this is impressive enough—but that the chemicals that cause them are naturally occurring in the human brain. Through various lines of evidence it has begun to seem very likely that they constitute part of a natural system for control of pain from within—or, in the words of some investigators active in the field, "the brain's own morphine."

In his *Optimism: The Biology of Hope*, anthropologist Lionel Tiger of Rutgers University ties together a vast number of ethnographic and sociological findings in a biological theory of how we view the future. According to Tiger, religious beliefs, beliefs about progress, the desire for children, the search for money and power, the belief in social utopias, and even such things as gambling and shopping sprees all share in common an attempt to dull the pain of the present with a usually false but dedicated focus on the future. He reasons that an animal—especially one aware of its own death—simply cannot go through the drudgery, fear, difficulty, and pain of daily life without some system of self-tranquilization. He speculates that natural selection has produced the opioid peptides to serve this function—that animals release them within themselves when the going becomes too rough to bear; the consequent mild sedation or even dulling of pain makes it possible to go forward. Finally, he proposes the possibility that the above-listed human behaviors and beliefs are ancillary products of such sedation, or attempts to control it, or both, in an animal so eminently capable of keeping one eye upon the future. It is an idea that should get much more attention than it has. I suspect it has suffered the fate that was early on accorded to psychoanalysis: It is almost intrinsically impossible for ideas about how we are fooling ourselves to gain an adequate hearing. We are good enough at it to keep them nicely at bay.

And yet, these mental tricks upon ourselves seem somehow more acceptable than the increasing resort to molecular elixirs. Booze, 'ludes, dope, coke, smack, speed, angel dust—a whole pharmacopoeia of fake happiness. Children are not only eager to try them, they are making them a way of life, a way of growing up. By adulthood, we are experts, even if we remain within the law. Here a recharge of norepinephrine to put the blush back on the mood; there a little GABA potentiation to dampen the faceless fear; over there a little ionic trickery to kick the brain's own morphine into action, and dull the long, terminal pain of life. "Reality," we are heard to say, just about half-jokingly, "is only a crutch, for people who cannot learn to cope with drugs."

What ever happened to that school of thought according to which the pain of life was a part of the joy of life, or at least a place on the path to it? The belief that the embrace of, and triumph over, difficulty, is more exhilarating than denial? In "California," that fabulous state and state of mind, this is called the "beat-your-head-against-the-wall-because-it-feels-so-good-when-you-stop" school. But for those of us in the "Northeast," whether physically or figuratively, for those of us who do not absolutely reject all that has gone before us, the triumph-over-adversity theory stills seems a good hypothesis of happiness.

There is even evidence. It comes from a summary of thirty-five years of research on the adult development of ninety-four men who were in college in the Northeast in 1940—a sample chosen to be broadly representative of at least that group of young American men. In his 1977 book *Adaptation to Life*, psychiatrist George Vaillant of the Harvard Medical School summarized the lifetime findings on these men, many of whom were successful and happy (by their own reports as well as objective criteria) and some of whom were unhappy and/or failures. Ample information was also available concerning the men's childhood and family life, as was direct information obtained throughout their adulthoods. Nothing can make such a study objective in the same sense and degree that a study of hormone levels is objective. But it is a mistake to think that the latter is very exact, and in fact hormone-and-behavior studies are also subject to major errors of interpretation. The Vaillant study meets reasonably high criteria of method for research of its kind.

Its conclusions are simple. First, a stable, loving family in early life is a great advantage. Men with bleak childhoods usually continued to be unhappy, permanently, despite all the objective trappings of external success. Some of them were well adapted to life's challenges, but insusceptible to the special happiness that comes with intimacy and the risks it entails; at least one such man was aware of his plight, and disliked it, and could do nothing about it. In summary of this part of the study's findings, Vaillant quoted the words of Joseph Conrad in the novel *Victory*: "Woe to the man who has not learned while young to hope, to love, to put his trust in life."

Second, stress is not necessarily bad for you. One-third of the men in this study spent at least ten days in continuous combat in World War II. All of them suffered major personal griefs, setbacks, disappointments, and losses during adulthood. None of these, per se, predicted poor later adjustment. About a famous man who was not in the study, Vaillant writes: "How can I give a logical explanation for the growth of Roy Campanella, a great Brooklyn catcher who at thirty-six broke his neck, was paralyzed in all four limbs; yet at fifty the crippled Campanella seemed a greater man . . . than Campanella the baseball star had seemed at thirty." He quotes the results of another lifetime follow-up study of normal adult Americans in California whose director, Jean MacFarlane, wrote, "Many of the most outstanding mature adults in our entire group, many who are well integrated, highly competent and/or creative . . . are recruited from those who were confronted with very difficult situations and whose characteristic responses during childhood and adolescence seemed to us to compound their problems." And finally, at the end of the Vaillant study: "It is not stress that kills us. It is effective adaptation to stress that permits us to live."

When my daughter, Susanna, was twenty-one months old, and just upon the verge of discovering sentences, she was left for a couple of hours with grandparents while her mother and father took a needed rest from her. She was accustomed to that situation and it didn't usually bother her, but on that particular evening it made her unhappy. She had been crying for some time when we returned, and she fell into her mother's arms, but was unable to stop sobbing miserably. Her mother sat down with her and held her, and in a little while she looked up and there came, out of her still-heaving chest, through the sobs, through the expression of dejection on her face, through the tears, the words "Zana happy." I felt as if I were witnessing the dawn of her human consciousness. Such a gesture would have to give an ethologist pause. Here was a typical mammalian creature, juvenile version, having given a beautifully predictable response to maternal separation, including the species-specific cries and facial displays that go with dejection; and in the midst of it all, contradicting every animal gesture, two human symbols, pressing forward the claim that she was happy.

"There is more happiness in one real tragedy than in all the comedies ever written." So said Eugene O'Neill, who could move with either. It is true, and in thinking about why it is true, one stumbles immediately across the possibility that it is good to watch somebody else's misery. But that isn't it. It is that what we are watching is a reflection of our own: our losses, our dismally failed good intentions, our chaos, our inevitable dying. It is watching a reification of the triumph of the spirit in the midst of such adversity that moves us; and if we come out of the theater exhilarated, it is because we feel that we have lost, but won; we feel we have, vicariously, come through.

On the same subject in his poem "Lapis Lazuli," Yeats writes:

> Hamlet and Lear are gay;
> Gaiety transfiguring all that dread.

The lapis lazuli of the title is a carving in stone of three men; they stand on a mountain in ancient China, and a long-legged bird, a longevity symbol, flies over them. Yeats imagines them, after a long climb, staring down from the place on the mountain upon the whole "tragic scene" of awkward humanity.

> One asks for mournful melodies;
> Accomplished fingers begin to play.
> Their eyes mid many wrinkles, their eyes,
> Their ancient, glittering eyes, are gay.

12

LUST

If sex were all, then every trembling hand
Could make us squeak, like dolls, the wished-for words.
But note the unconscionable treachery of fate,
That makes us weep, laugh, grunt and groan, and shout
Doleful heroics, pinching gestures forth
From madness or delight, without regard
To that first, foremost law. Anguishing hour!
Last night, we sat beside a pool of pink,
Clippered with lilies scudding the bright chromes,
Keen to the point of starlight, while a frog
Boomed from his very belly odious chords.
— Wallace Stevens, "Le Monocle
de Mon Oncle"

Among many biological and behavioral scientists nowadays it is popular to use the word and the concept "system" in a manner somewhat more complex and specific than that of everyday parlance. In effect, it is a concept and definition borrowed from engineering, where "systems" are often elegant, resilient, precise, predictable, and responsive to mathematical manipulation. In one classic example, the thermostat, a commodity (temperature) is given a set-point (say, 22°C) and the system detects deviations from the set-point and corrects them. This is a simple negative-feedback control system. In another, the antimissile missile, the system detects distance from a goal (the heat source of the target missile's engine) and generates reductions in that system until contact is made; this is a "goal-corrected feedback control system." It is perfectly clear that *some* aspects of human biological and behavioral functioning follow one of these or a few other simple engineering system models—the regulation of body temperature, for instance, or (although less precisely) the cessation of eating upon satiety. But a very large number of others do not.

Consider, for example, two individuals—adults, humans, and of opposing genders—becoming adjacent and interacting (under our careful, watchful eyes) in the manner formerly known as courtship and marriage, latterly as "coming on" and "making it." It is at least possible, perhaps even legitimate, to view the two individuals as interacting systems. Before, each "system" received many "inputs," some of which brought them together. Now the "output" of each system is part of the input of the other, increasing the complexity of the problem considerably.

What is each regulating, in the sense that the room regulates its temperature by means of the thermostat? Emotions? Perceptions? The level of some hormone? The quantity of general arousal? And how and where could this "emotional thermostat" be set? Could it change its setting, cyclically, by day and night, the way some clock-controlled thermostats do? Could the system "cool itself down" as well as heating and turning off, like a combined air-conditioning/heating system? Could the basic setting change, as an economizing measure, in response to a changing energy supply? Will the two individuals have different settings, because of genes, early training, and previous experience? Can they tamper with each other's basic settings?

The complexity becomes quickly overbearing. Some observers have tried to simplify the problem by treating the two individuals as one larger system, designed to attain the goal of mating and reproducing. This outlook was satisfactory in an era of evolutionary biology when the concept of "survival of the species" was considered a valid way of thinking about the aim of mating. If species were designed by nature to perpetuate themselves, then of course each should have evolved a courtship and mating dance that was a system in itself, getting the two principals into intimate juxtaposition, willy-nilly, for a higher goal separate from themselves. And, if this were true, the two individuals engaged in the courtship process could validly be viewed as one smoothly functioning system.

They are not validly viewed as such, however smooth they look, because they were not designed by nature in that way. The era of "species survival" as an independent goal of mating has come to an end in modern biology, and the vast majority of present-day students of evolution view *the individual organism* as the most, if not the only, useful, reliable, and logical unit of analysis in the study of natural selection. This is equally true of the process of mating, which was classically—and wrongly—viewed as independent of individual adaptive purpose. And if, as suggested in the chapter on adaptation, the individual adaptive purpose is nothing but a gene's way of making another gene, then there is no good reason to think of the two individuals in the courting pair as really sharing one simple goal.

In other words, in no case should we view two mated or potentially mated individuals as making up one system with one goal. Their respective purposes are exquisitely individual and—I choose the phrase carefully—are not happily wedded by the design. Neither, of course, are they at desperate odds with each other in every conceivable instant. But they are individual, complex, poorly matched, and, to the observer as well as the participants, guessed at but unknown.

Even accepting their separateness, is the systems model of use? Each person (or system) in the pair would be regulating some quantities tightly around an intermediate set-point, like the thermostat, but minimizing others (disappointment? fear?), cyclically varying others (arousal?), and maximizing still others (attraction?). Even accepting the long-term goals in the way I have just outlined them, what are the immediate, closely regulated ones? "Scoring"? Orgasm? A few flirtatious minutes of arousal? A few hours of physical intimacy? A year of companionship? A lifetime of loyalty? A family?

And consider what must be transcended for this intricate dance to occur. Whenever two creatures come together for any reason, there is fear; it may be irrational or rational (I have trouble with this distinction, since it is very often a matter of opinion), but fear nevertheless. In the case of courtship, among the fairly reasonable things to fear are rape, other physical injury, venereal and other infectious diseases, the humiliation of unrequited affection, unwanted pregnancy, seduction and desertion with the attendant pain and grief, and, simply, making the most colossal mistake of one's life—wedding one's destiny to that of the wrong person.

The intricacies of the model become unmanageable, as system. Complex internal commodities are being regulated; uncertain goals are being approached; and numerous fears are modulated and minimized (or at least weighed against the fear of loneliness) as the dance goes on. Even with what little we have said so far, it will be seen how very trivial are such concepts as drive, instinct, habit, imitation, ritual, and others like them in the face of these complexities of subjective human experience. And it will be seen as well why intelligent, sensitive people who have some understanding of the human emotions throw up their hands in exasperation at the simple-minded world of behavioral science, where stick figures dance around on all-too-visible strings.

Some of the tragedy inherent in human relations, particularly in the presence of desire, is inaccessible to behavioral and social scientists because, either tacitly or explicitly, they believe in the systems model. That is, they think that human intercourse was designed to run smoothly. Thus the large gap observable between the assessment of human relations that is found in the classical literature of every language and the one usually purveyed by behavioral and social scientists. Literary artists of stature have tended, almost universally, to perceive and record the very nasty illogic of the system (I now use the word loosely), usually with no attempt to explain; whereas behavioral and social scientists—not all, but most—have tended to build models of human experience in which everything turns out okay, and if it hasn't yet, it soon will. This, I think, is as much or more a product of their penchant for systems logic as it is of a pollyanna disposition. Systems should work—whether they are individual people, or interacting pairs of them, or small groups of them, or large masses of them, or even groups of these latter large masses. If they don't work, something is wrong with them; fix them, and then they will. If they haven't yet, keep working at it; they will, finally, eventually.

I call this outlook the "tinker" theory of human behavior. Its practitioners, however, far from being itinerant, are very well established, and in every field of behavioral and social science. From the psychotherapists to the economists, from the marriage counselors to the social revolutionaries, the tinker theory is their bread and butter. They work along as if on a beautiful, intricate jigsaw puzzle, fitting a piece here, a piece there, and they truly believe it is only a matter of time before the immense picture becomes whole.

They are working on a puzzle in which the pieces do not fit. Or if they do, it is in a third dimension, one the tinkers are almost never aware of. That dimension is evolutionary time. A jigsaw puzzle is logical and doable because it is designed by a mind like that of the hopeful solver. Unless the designer is perverse, the pieces will all be there, will fit, the picture will come whole. But in evolutionary time—a stream in which not only Methuselah's life span but even his temporal distance from us is not even a drop—there is no designer. There is only the blind action of natural selection, sifting genes.

"A person is only a gene's way of making another gene." I do not even know who said it first, but it doesn't really matter. It is a thought that enters the mind of everyone who comes to an understanding of the genetic basis of evolution. Of course, it is oversimplified. The gene, even if it is in a virus, does not act alone; it "cooperates" with other genes, at least temporarily. Together, they make a person, or any other creature. That creature, to be sure, has subsidiary purposes. It wants to eat a meal, to learn, to embrace another creature, to tear a mouse limb from limb, to sniff mustard, to feel safe from harm, to get out of a cage, to empty its bowels, to bomb a city, to see a sunset, to get a reward in heaven, to ejaculate, to win the Nobel Prize.

That is all right with the gene. It is not distressed by the existence of such purposes, nor by the creature's unawareness of *its* purposes, nor even, should the creature be aware of them, by a denial of those purposes. How should it be? It has no machinery of awareness itself. It doesn't know anything. It simply arranges the chemicals of life around it, simply organizes protoplasm in such a way as to provide one or another kind of container. If this container carries the gene around, protects the gene from disintegration, and facilitates, at crucial moments, the gene's effort to organize some of the chemicals around it into a replica of itself, then the gene will remain part of the stream of DNA—the conduit of the material of life since life, by definition, began.

The stream has, of course, innumerable meanders, eddies, tributaries, deltas, dams, branches. It is the central fact of life in evolutionary time, but it is constantly changing. The changes can be point mutations—alterations in the chemical structure of the gene itself. Or they can be rearrangements of the genes in relation to each other, at least as important for the shapes the "gene carriers"—the organisms—will take as are point mutations. But the most trenchant and powerful process of change is the change in gene frequency. And the fundamental contributor to that change is natural selection—that is, change in gene frequency that is contingent on the adaptive success of the gene "carrier."

Or in the human case, us. Time was when all reproduction on the planet was asexual. It sounds boring, but the creatures that practiced it did not much care. They were invertebrates, impressive in their way and seemingly successful at reproducing without sex—a feat carried forward in any number of present-day organisms. In effect, there were at that time only females. They were the only DNA carriers, and they all participated equally and directly in the generation of young. The question—and it is an unsolved one that occupies some of the best theoretical minds in evolutionary biology today—is: *Why did they ever invent males?* Which is a tongue-in-cheek way of saying, To what advantage did males in fact evolve?

Males are on the face of it highly impractical. If you have an equal sex ratio (and it can be easily shown that sexually reproducing populations will tend toward equal numbers of the two sexes) and if the males are about as big as females (frequently they are that big or bigger), you are wasting half the biomass of your population on the ground in creatures that can't make eggs. One traditional explanation, that sexual reproduction increases variability, seems unequal to the challenge that asexual species find other ways to increase variability. Another, that males can help with the young and provide for the common defense, has trouble with the fact that in many sexually reproducing species the male doesn't hang around long enough to say thanks, much less help.

One intriguing suggestion, made by Irven DeVore, Robert Trivers, and others, is that males were a breeding experiment. In fact DeVore has said that the whole history of sexuality has been "one vast breeding experiment" in which females were the breeders and males the gradually "improving" breed. According to this view, the first sexually reproducing organisms may have had the advantage that the basic sex (the females) had alienated half of the DNA away from themselves and located it in expendable creatures—namely, males. The females could then reduce competition among themselves while intensifying it among the males; more males could be discarded without reducing egg-production capacity, and a relatively elite group of "chosen" males, with more desirable characteristics, could father the females' offspring. Meanwhile, the females could concentrate on producing more offspring.

This latest version of sexual selection theory, which began with Darwin, now rests on a fairly large body of evidence. The "origin of sex" part of it will always be speculative; but to whatever extent it is meaningful to pose the question, What are the sexes for? this outlook comes close to furnishing answers.

In all sexually reproducing species and especially among vertebrates, several facts about males can be predicted from the degree to which they participate in or abstain from direct care of the female's offspring. In what have been called "pair-bonding" species—including about eight thousand species of birds, the small South American monkeys called marmosets, the gibbons or lesser apes, and a few members of the dog family such as coyotes and bat-eared foxes—the male tends to contribute substantially to the care of the young. In these species, males and females tend to be approximately the same size, approximately the same colors, without fancy appendages, and growing at about the same rate. They mate in pairs on a long-term basis, sometimes for life. Male marmosets may carry the young, usually twins, 70 percent of the time, giving them to their mother only to nurse. Males of many species of pair-bonding birds—the ringdove, for example—have elaborate physiological adaptations for infant feeding that rival those of the female. So much for one end of the spectrum.

At the other end there is a quite different story. Males differ markedly from females. They take little interest in infants and juveniles. They are either larger than females, or more floridly conspicuous, or possessed of more dangerous weapons, or more slowly maturing, or some combination of these. They may be triple the weight of the female, as in the elephant seal, or have fantastic display coloration, as in the peacock, or have antlers for prancing and battering, as in white-tailed deer. These species are often called "tournament species" because competition for females among males varies from intense to fierce and may be concentrated in an annual breeding "tournament" or lek, as in the Uganda kob antelope or the elephant seal. Such competition results in extreme variation in reproductive success among males, which is achieved partly through a much higher mortality rate for males than for females, a fact of life for most known species at all stages of the life course.

But in tournament species it is made more extreme through tournament reproductive competition. In one breeding season among the elephant seals off the coast of California, studied by ecologist Burney LeBoeuf, 4 percent of the males accounted for over 85 percent of the copulations, and these few males almost certainly impregnated the large majority of females. The rest of the population's males (96%) were left to compete for the attention of the remaining few females. This is sexual selection with a vengeance.

It is characteristic of such species that males do little or nothing to care for the young. In elephant seals, fights among the enormous, dangerous males in the breeding colony frequently result in injury and death to newborn pups. Theory says that only in pair-bonding species do males "know" where their genes are. Of course, they do not know in any cognitive sense, but they have been selected during the course of evolution to behave as if they did. In a pair-bonding species, the male has the female more or less corralled. She has him corralled as well, but for this issue that is beside the point; no female can be "in doubt" of the fact that the offspring she cares for carry her genes. Whereas no male, in any species with internal fertilization, can ever "be sure" he has not been cuckolded. In tournament species where males career around taking copulations wherever they find them, and females may be almost as willing in one place as another, a male investing heavily in any offspring of any chosen female would be running a high risk of spending energy on genes not his own. And he would be wasting valuable time that he might have spent seeking copulations. Thus his own genes—including the ones that led him to choose that questionable strategy—would be unrepresented in future generations. None of these actions assumes conscious recognition, by the animals, of the forces at work; evolution has merely designed them so that they act, however blindly, to enhance their own reproductive success.

All this does not explain, of course, how species get to be pair-bonded or tournament in character. Behavioral ecologists have produced some interesting ideas about this, but they are beyond the scope of this discussion. What seems to be reliably the case is that pair-bonding species will tend to have sexes that resemble each other, relatively low variability in male reproductive success, relatively high male investment in offspring, relatively low promiscuity, and relatively unspectacular competition among males. Tournament species tend to have large, florid males, high variability in male reproductive success (some garnering all the females, some losing out entirely), little or no direct care of offspring, high promiscuity or polygamous mating, and intense male-male competition. Furthermore, it is a case in which the exceptions prove the rule. In species such as phalaropes, birds in which females are larger than males, it is males that take on the major part of the caretaking burden, and they consequently become a scarce resource competed for among females.

But these are rare exceptions. For the vast majority of species of birds and mammals, males are at least somewhat larger or more conspicuous, more competitive, more variable in reproductive success, and less generous with their offspring, than females. In pair-bonding species (most birds), the differences are small; in tournament species (most mammals), they are large. Almost always, they are there, and most species fall somewhere in between the two extremes.

Consider, for example, the humble bank swallow, known to zoologists as *Riparia riparia*. Male and female resemble each other in size, form, and behavior. Mated pairs form and persist in large colonies, each pair digging and nesting in one of hundreds of burrows in a sheer sandbank above a natural waterway. Both sexes subsist by foraging for insects, but in the first week after pair formation, the male follows the female every time she leaves the nest, chases her, and remains within one meter of her, which puts him through some impressive acrobatics. He does this up to one hundred times a day. It is always male-chase-female, never the reverse. The female is never allowed to leave without being followed. The pair often attracts a third chaser. In more than one hundred such instances studied, the interloper was always male.

They may number up to five at once. In the words of the investigators, Michael Beecher and Inger Mornestam Beecher, "all the males follow the intricate maneuvers of the female, giving the chase its spectacular appearance." The male mated to the female "will loop back and attempt to fight off the chasers," bumping or attacking them. When the odds are against him he attempts to chase the female back into their burrow. Both the chasing behavior of the interlopers and the guarding behavior of the mated males is restricted to the fertile period of the female in question. Some of the interlopers involved in the chase are males mated to other females that are not in their fertile period. Interlopers sometimes succeed in completing copulations.

Or take, as another example, the ringdove, *Streptopelia risoria*. This beautiful bird's courtship and reproductive behavior has been the subject of some of the most impressive research in the history of behavioral biology, mainly due to the efforts of the late Daniel Lehrman of Rutgers University, and his students. Under natural conditions a strongly pair-bonded, tree-living African bird in which the male participates extensively in parental care—and is fully adapted physiologically for that purpose—the ringdove has been studied mainly in the laboratory. Here, under controlled conditions, it has been shown that pair formation requires an elaborate, prolonged courtship period in which the male bows and coos to the female. Watching this behavior—or for that matter a film of it—directly stimulates the pituitary gland of the female (through an unknown brain pathway) to secrete luteinizing hormone, which in turn stimulates the ovary to produce increases in the blood level of progesterone and estradiol, the hormones that will prepare her, physically and behaviorally, for breeding. After that they build a nest together and copulate, and the female gestates and lays the eggs.

The male's initial behavioral gestures are a function of his own testosterone level, which when it rises presumably alters the responsiveness of neural circuits controlling bowing and cooing. But the female's physiological changes depend on the male's movements. As pointed out by Leon Eisenberg, a distinguished psychiatrist who has taken a keen interest in ethological studies, the weight of the female's oviduct can be plotted as a function of the male's testosterone level, a powerful physiological effect in which the intervening variables are behavioral. Both male and female sit on the eggs, and this experience stimulates each of them to develop "crop milk," a specialized baby food produced in the crop, a side chamber of the esophagus. This they regurgitate in response to the newly hatched young. Males are thus investing almost as much in their offspring as are females.

One of Lehrman's students, Carl Erickson, has taken the laboratory ringdove studies in a direction suggested by sexual selection theory. He has found that males can detect females that have already been courted by other males, and will reject them. Furthermore, if the male of a mated pair is separated from the female and brought back to her, there is little effect, but if the female is in the interim exposed to another male, her returning mate will assault her with a severe pecking attack.

Or take the redwing blackbird, *Agelaius phoeneceus*. Like many marsh- or tree-nesting passerine (perching) birds, this species is highly territorial. Males do not participate directly in care of the young to any great extent, but they do establish and defend territories, advertise them with a species-typical spring song, and attract a female whose young will be fed from the resources of the territory. Males intruding in an established territory are attacked by the resident male, and studies of wild-caught males of this species have shown that the attack involves rapid and large changes in levels of lutcinizing hormone—the pituitary hormone that stimulates the production and release of testosterone and other androgens—as well as changes in the levels of the androgens themselves. In locales where resource density varies greatly among territories, it is quite possible for a male on a superior territory to attract and keep more than one female, or for a male on a particularly poor territory to attract and keep none. In experiments in which males of a mated pair were vasectomized, the female still often managed to lay fertile eggs, demonstrating under natural conditions the threat to a male's paternity from unseen strange males; thus, the selective pressure for territorial defense.

These three patterns are fairly typical for the behavior of pair-forming species. As mentioned before, there are exceptions. Three species of phalaropes—sandpiperlike shorebirds—have females that are bigger, have bolder, brighter plumages, and show more aggressive behavior than the male. In Wilson's phalarope (*Steganopus tricolor*), the female arrives first on the breeding ground, where the pair will nest amid marshy vegetation. *She* picks a male from among the arrivals and jealously guards him as they swim together, feeding from the surface of the water. *She* threatens and drives away other females. Males may fight among themselves, but they are less aggressive than females. In this species as in the other two phalaropes, all post-hatching care of the eggs and young is done by the males. Thus males are the sex that invest most in offspring, and they are the resource that must be fought over.

These exceptions are important, since they demonstrate that the observed patterns are not wedded, in some obligatory phylogenetic sense, to the two sexes. Evolution has reversed the roles in a few cases. However, it must be noted that these are three among eight thousand species of pair-forming birds. They have already taken up a proportion in this discussion many times larger than their role in nature. The three examples previously given above—bank swallows, ringdoves, and redwing blackbirds—are much more typical of the behavior of males and females in pair-forming species. Males are adapted for greater aggressiveness, whether toward other males or toward females, and the physiological changes underlying sexual behavior also increase their tendency to fight. Males use this aggressiveness to prevent the female they have mated with from cuckolding them, at the same time attempting to copulate outside the pair or to attract other females to their side. They behave as if they want it both ways; and theory holds that they should, since they produce sperm at much lower cost than females produce eggs, and since they can never be sure that the offspring of the female they mate with are really theirs.

The female has much less "doubt" that she is the mother, and has little to gain, in number of offspring produced, by ranging away from her territory for stolen copulations. She can gain in the quality of the male and in self-protection from desertion, particularly in species in which pairs may reform differently in successive seasons. These potential gains suffice to make her a participant, albeit a much less active one, in stolen copulations initiated in the absence of her mate by intruding males. Males have evolved various mechanisms to protect themselves from such cuckoldry, including an aggressive policy of defense, corralling of the female, detection of cheating followed by abandonment, and the indirect policy of "casting their seed upon the wind." Females, having somewhat less to lose by male cheating, have evolved correspondingly less dramatic mechanisms of prevention.

It must also be noted here that all these are examples of the more well-behaved end of the continuum of male sexual habits in birds and mammals—what I have called the pair-bonding end. Males in non-pair-forming species (a minority of birds but a majority of mammals) are typically more aggressive, more brutal, and more neglectful toward each other, toward females, and toward young than are males in pair-forming species—although to be sure they are not all as bad as elephant seals.

Humans, from all available evidence, seem to belong in the part of the continuum occupied, among birds, by bank swallows, ringdoves, and redwing blackbirds. We are clearly pair-bonding and, equally clearly, imperfectly so. Males and females develop at slightly differ-ent rates, with girls reaching maturity a year or two earlier. Males are somewhat larger than females, and in most populations have conspicuous hair on the organ that is the seat of most human social displays: the face. Females have breasts and other secondary sex characteristics, but, as mammals go, human males and females are quite similar in form.

Of 849 human societies in the ethnographic record, George Peter Murdock—one of anthropology's great systematizers—found the marriage form called polygyny (one man married to two or more women) in 708 of them (83 percent), these about equally divided between those with usual and those with occasional polygyny. Most hunting-gathering societies have occasional polygyny. As in redwing blackbirds, males with the best resources are likely to garner extra females. Monogamy is characteristic of 137 (16 percent) of the societies, but it must be remembered that in most of these a single individual may have more than one mate in succession, and because of the starkly different reproductive life spans in men and women, men who choose this option are much more likely than their female counterparts to have more than one family. Polyandry—a marriage of one woman to more than one man—occurs in 4 of the societies (less than half of one percent), and in all of these there are special conditions that make the pattern much less than a mirror image of polygyny. The human species can thus be said to be pair-bonding with a significant polygynous option and tendency.

In a larger sample of 860 societies, Murdock reported the exchange of goods or services at marriage. In 553 (64 percent) of the societies, the groom or his family gave goods or services to the bride's family; in 27 (3 percent) women were exchanged directly between the families of the two grooms; in 258 (30 percent) there was either no exchange or an equal exchange of gifts between the bride's and groom's family; dowry, the custom in which the bride's family gives gifts to the groom's family, existed in 22 (2.5 percent) of the societies, or less than one-twentieth of the number that had the reverse custom. These data seem to suggest strongly that in most human matchmaking females are the scarce resource being competed and often paid for.

The "double standard," according to which women and girls are more strongly punished for infidelities than men and boys, is very widespread in human societies. In many societies, women adulterers are punished by death. According to the Kinsey reports on sexual behavior among Americans during the 1940s, men in most age groups were at least twice as likely to have had extramarital intercourse as women. There is definite evidence that permissiveness has increased markedly since that time, and that the sexual revolution is real; with that change, the double standard has probably weakened, but it still exists, at least in the United States.

Human males in every society are more aggressive than human females, and the former account for the overwhelming majority of homicidal violence in all human groups. Such violence is often occasioned by sexual infidelity. Among the !Kung San, noted for gender egalitarianism, men have been known to commit homicide over adultery, and in one case to kill the wife herself. Wife-beating of a severe but sublethal sort often follows the discovery of adultery; whereas women's response to their husbands' infidelity, while equally angry, is much less effective.

Among the Yanomamo, "the fierce people" of the Venezuelan highlands, groups of men in a village attack other villages with a view toward seizing land and wives. If they succeed, they kill the men in the village and take the widows as wives. If these women have infants, the infants may be killed as well. For the Yanomamo and for the Xavante Indians of the Mato Grosso in Brazil, there is good genetic evidence of enormous variability in male reproductive success. Among the Xavante, one man had sired twenty-three children by various wives while sixteen men in the same group had one or none—a disparity in reproductive success three times as large as that of Xavante women. And in all known human populations, male mortality is higher than that of females at all ages, which means that males will be more frequent at the zero end of the scale of reproductive success, as well as at the extreme high end.

Only men commit rape. It seems obvious, but is it? Could not homosexual women launch sexual attacks on victims that attract them? They do not, or if they do it is in such small numbers as to make no impression on the statistics. As for heterosexual rape that might result in conception (and this is the sort most likely to become grist for natural selection's mill), only men are capable of enforcing it, regardless of the relative strength of rapist and victim. The successful act rests on the man's whim; thus, one physiological result of eons of biased sexual selection.

It is not the only one. There is much to celebrate about the famous *différence*, but the well-known gender differences in latency to arousal and latency to orgasm do not seem to constitute cause for elation. For most mammals there is no evidence that females have orgasm. Recent studies of our closest relatives, the higher primates, have begun to suggest that their females do, but this is still controversial. There can be no such controversy regarding males, since orgasm is for most purposes synonymous with ejaculation, and without ejaculation there is no reproduction. The genes of males that do not ejaculate are quickly culled from the stream of DNA.

Females that do not have orgasm are missing something, to be sure. Perhaps they will be less inclined to copulate; perhaps orgasm even plays a minor role in promoting fertilization. But it is perfectly possible for females to achieve high reproductive success without orgasm. If they are reluctant, they can be urged; if they are very reluctant (in some species), they can be forced. And in many species there is a moment—annually or semiannually in most birds and mammals, monthly in monkeys and apes—when the female is overcome with a rush of hormones that effectively precipitate at least cooperation, at best enthusiasm: the behavior known to pet lovers as estrus, or "heat."

Human females do not have "heat," one of the supremely distinctive facts about this species. The theoretical notion that human females are continuously receptive—very popular in anthropology textbooks—is surely mostly a product of male optimism. Still, it is true that the moments at which they are likely to feel sexually inclined are distributed more or less randomly over the days of the month or year, with the exception in many cultures of lowered receptivity during the days of menstrual flow, for a variety of reasons. This is an impressive evolutionary change, viewed against the background of the adaptation of our relatives. In most monkeys and apes, there is a clear monthly surge of female sexual posturing and invitational behavior directed toward sexually active males. In some, such as the savannah baboon (*Papio cynocephalus*), there are distinctive physical manifestations as well—color changes and/or swelling of the genital region. Many monkeys and apes also have annual breeding patterns, and in some, like the South American squirrel monkey (*Saimiri sciureus*), annual sexual activity is accompanied by physical changes even in the male.

All these cycles are regulated by neuroendocrine clocks. The annual cycles in most animals seem to depend upon the activity of the pineal gland, a small organ between the cerebral hemispheres that Descartes apparently thought was the seat of the soul. The activity of the pineal has been found to be partly controlled by light. In some lower vertebrates, it is right under a thin skull, and light affects it directly—a fact that may also be true of some mammals. In higher primates and humans, it lies too deep, under too many tissues; but it still responds to light indirectly. It is under the control of a neural pathway beginning at the retina of the eye and passing through the sympathetic nervous system. It in turn secretes into the bloodstream a hormone called melatonin—made with a few chemical changes from a neurotransmitter, serotonin. Melatonin affects gonadal activity in a way that is not yet precisely clear, and some other secretions of the pineal also affect the gonads. In any case, what is clear is that the pineal is indeed the seat of annual breeding rhythms, or part of it. It detects the changing length of the light of day and translates that information into altered reproductive physiology.

The monthly rhythm of monkeys and apes seems a good deal more complex. Only females have it (this is not true of annual rhythms) and it depends on multiple interactions among the hormones of the hypothalamus, the pituitary, and the ovaries, at a minimum. At the foundation is the fact that the hypothalamus secretes infinitesimal amounts of a small peptide hormone—usually called LHRH—into the tiny local circulation leading down to the pituitary. There it stimulates the secretion and/or release of two large protein hormones: LH, or luteinizing hormone, and FSH, or follicle-stimulating hormone. Although both of these are named for their role in changing the female gonads, the story up to here is the same for males. But in males the responding gonadal hormones are androgens—especially testosterone and dihydrotestosterone, which together account for many of the physiological effects we know as masculinity. And in males the "hypothalamo-pituitary-gonadal axis" is not cyclical in its functioning.

In females—and this includes humans—the system has a clock. The ovaries do not produce constant or randomly distributed amounts of their two principal hormones, estradiol and progesterone, nor does the pituitary secrete constant amounts of LH or FSH. Both pituitary hormones, especially LH, rise markedly about fourteen days following the onset of menses in human females. Before this time, estradiol has been rising gradually in the blood, reaching its first monthly peak several days earlier. Progesterone rises slowly after the fourteenth day, reaching its peak about a week later, a period when estradiol, which has fallen, rises to its secondary peak. (The pituitary hormones fall about as rapidly as they rise, so that their high level is really confined to just one or two days.) Estradiol and progesterone both fall during the fourth week after the onset of menstrual flow.

Meanwhile the reproductive organs are metamorphosing, both as cause and result of this changing chemical cocktail in the blood. In the ovary, during the first two weeks, an egg-containing follicle is growing and secreting estradiol. In response to the surge of pituitary hormones, the follicle bursts, releasing the egg, and this results in a couple of days of exceptional fertility. The egg leaves behind a small organ called the corpus luteum (hence the name "luteinizing hormone"), which secretes progesterone, building up to the twenty-one-day peak in that hormone. The latter increases the vascularity of the wall of the uterus (among other effects) in preparation for the implantation of a fertilized egg. If fertilization or implantation do not occur, progesterone and estradiol have their typical monthly fall, and their withdrawal causes the uterine wall to, in part, slough off; hence, menses, and the start of the next month's cycle.

The hypothalamo-pituitary-gonadal axis is of interest here because every hormone mentioned has been shown to have some effect on behavior, especially sexual behavior, in animals and/or humans, male and female. LHRH, in addition to its effect on pituitary hormones, has its own direct effect on brain tissue. If appropriately delivered into the brain, it potentiates the female lordosis response in rats, a fixed action pattern in which the body is arched downward and the rump raised in response to the male. (This is a typical laboratory model for studying the enhancement or suppression of sexual function.) LHRH has also been used (in the form of a nasal spray) in a few clinical trials as a treatment for male impotence, and it looks as if it may have some success.

There is evidence too that LH and FSH, the pituitary hormones controlled by LHRH, have direct effects on sexual behavior; they have "target" cells in the brain, and a recent major revision of the function of the blood vessels connecting brain and pituitary suggests that these vessels carry things both ways. But the most powerful hormonal effectors of sexual function in vertebrates are the gonadal hormones: testosterone and other androgens in males, and estradiol and progesterone in females. All are steroid hormones built from the basic four-ring structure of cholesterol. All are synthesized and manipulated, at least in small measure, in other organs besides the gonads, most notably in the outer segment of the adrenal gland. And all are present in measurable quantities, in some tissue, in both sexes.

The effects of these hormones have already been discussed, but it may be useful to briefly review them here. Testosterone removal by means of castration causes a decline, rapid or gradual, of sexual activity in the males of many species, although extensive experience before surgery and patient partners after it have been shown to slow the decline in complex animals. Testosterone replacement therapy reverses the decline, and testosterone enhances normal sexual behavior in unoperated males of some species. Estradiol correspondingly potentiates female sexual activity in various species. Ovariectomy typically reduces it, although as in the case of male castration experience plays an important role in higher animals. Progesterone appears to have the paradoxical effect of enhancing sexual activity at some times or at low doses, while inhibiting it at other times or at higher doses. Its enhancing actions seem to depend upon the presence of estradiol, and are most evident at low estradiol levels. Finally, there is a little evidence that testosterone, which occurs at low but significant levels in females, may also potentiate female sexual activity.

Androgens in males, and estradiol and progesterone in females, rise markedly at the time of sexual maturation, and are responsible for many events that we associate with puberty. The cyclic activity of the female hypothalamo-pituitary-gonadal axis, described above, begins at this time in all females of higher primates, including humans, who are normal, not pregnant, and not starving. This cyclicity depends on the intactness of the hypothalamus. There is good reason to believe that it is a basic part of the body plan of all mammals (both sexes) but that testosterone circulating normally around the time of birth in male mammal fetuses or infants permanently abolishes the cycling capacity of the male hypothalamus.

Since human females have a hormonal cycle comparable to the monthly cycles of other higher primates, and since the latter have obvious behavioral consequences associated with the changes of the cycle, it has seemed intriguing to many investigators to explore the possibility that human females might also be subject to such consequences. To summarize a great deal of information very briefly, there is strong evidence of a weak effect. In populations as widely separated as Americans and !Kung San, there has been shown to be an increase of sexual interest or activity at mid-cycle (the time of the pituitary hormone surge and of ovulation). The cross-cultural evidence makes it difficult to attribute this phenomenon to cultural factors. Taken together with other evidence, there is every reason to believe that it is the result, at least in part, of hormonal changes.

However, and this is a critical qualification, the effect is small in every sample studied. It has been shown to be subject to external cultural influences (such as the day of the week) and subjective psychological influences (such as false beliefs about what part of the cycle you are in). If all other things were equal, we might see an important (rather than just a statistically significant) effect of mid-cycle hormonal changes on women's sexual activity. But all other things are not equal, and external forces such as cultural events, aesthetic suggestion, availability and behavior of partners, and even the weather, or internal forces such as fear of pregnancy, fatigue, illness, imagination and mood, have effects powerful enough to swamp the smaller effects of the mid-cycle or other cyclic changes in women's hormones.

How then do these other forces have their effects? External effects are of course delivered into the body and brain over the usual routes of sensory access. But what happens next—as well as many self-starting components of the system's sexual activity and responsiveness—are due to events in an arrangement of neural circuits with which we have already become familiar.

The functions of the limbic system have been committed to memory by at least one generation of students of brain and behavior as "the four f's": feeding, fleeing, fighting and . . . the subject matter of this chapter, sex. The same regions and circuits come up over and over again in the experiments: the hypothalamus, the amygdala, the hippocampus, the limbic midbrain, the septal area, and the regions of the neocortex associated with these lower structures. All these and the fiber paths connecting them have been implicated to some degree in the motivation and regulation of sexual activity, just as they have in the performance of the other three "f's." Stimulation of the lateral hypothalamus, under the right conditions, can enhance it, just as it can, under the influence of other environmental stimuli, enhance feeding, fighting, fleeing, hoarding, and even maternal behavior, at least in rats. Lesions in the forward portion of the midbrain—an important final common pathway of emotional behavior—can decrease the time between ejaculation and subsequent erection and intromission in male rats. Evidently a significant and selective depletion of the forebrain neurotransmitter norepinephrine is involved in this surgically decreased sexual inhibition.

Lesions in the amygdala, or in the stria terminalis—the fiber pathway that connects the amygdala to the hypothalamus—or in the hypothalamic region known as the bed nucleus of the stria terminalis, where that connection is made, all have the effect of altering sexual activity in male rats. Typically, such lesions increase the time elapsed between the first intromission of the penis and the ejaculation. Enough other information is available about the amygdala-hypothalamus circuit to suggest that it may play an important role in sexual activity—partly via the pathways from the hypothalamus to the midbrain, partly via the hormonal influences of the hypothalamus on the pituitary and the gonads. All the brain structures mentioned have been shown to garner and concentrate sex steroid hormones, as have some of the nerves outside the brain that mediate the sensation or action involved in sex. Thus emerges a picture of limbic system circuits that can respond to and also influence the hormones of reproduction, even while they respond to and influence—over more rapidly acting neural pathways—the stimuli and motor action patterns that constitute sexual behavior.

Some of the most interesting suggestions about the role of limbic system structures in human sexual behavior have come from studies of epileptics whose seizure focus is in the temporal lobe, in or near the amygdala or hippocampus. Although systematic study of the phenomenon is recent, clinical observers have long held that temporal-lobe epileptics often have modified sexual behavior. In a study by Dietrich Blumer of 50 such patients, 29 were found to be hyposexual: they described low levels of desire, imagery, and activity, reporting that they were aroused less than once a month (20 of them less than once a year). They found it difficult or impossible to experience orgasm. The obvious objection that generalized effects of epilepsy or the drugs used to treat it may have caused the dampened sexuality is easily met with the fact that epileptics with their seizure focus in other brain regions are not hyposexual.

Twenty-four of these patients were operated on in a standard procedure attempting to remove the epileptic focus. All but 1 of the 8 patients whose seizures were successfully stopped also showed increased sexuality; all but 1 of the 16 patients whose seizures continued showed continued hyposexuality. This study, added to much other evidence about the role of the limbic structures in the temporal lobe, underscores their key role in emotional behavior.

It was indicated above that the neurotransmitter norepinephrine was depleted in one experiment on increased sexual activity. This is only a small part of the knowledge we are rapidly gaining about the role of brain neurotransmitter molecules in sexual behavior. According to one theory that has received considerable support both experimentally and clinically, an increase in dopamine transmission in brain circuits enhances sexual activity, while an increase in serotonin transmission dampens it. Research of this kind is fraught with problems, not the least of which is that it is usually very difficult to get any idea of the anatomical location of the brain circuits that are affected by the neurotransmitter chemicals administered; but it is also extremely important, since it can lead to drug treatments much less dangerous than surgery.

Drug molecules—at least those that get into the brain—can have easy access to regulation of neural activity by invading the synaptic cleft, the window of communication between each neuron and the next. It has been observed, for example, that many patients suffering from Parkinson's disease experience increased sexual desire when they receive dopamine replacement therapy, and that this increased desire follows a pattern suggesting that more is involved than just generally feeling better. Neurotransmitter stimulants and antagonists may thus one day play an active role in the modulation of our sexual emotions. Furthermore, although no traditional aphrodisiacs have been shown to *specifically* enhance sexual desire (some help, but by reducing anxiety and inhibition generally), there has recently accumulated a small body of experimental evidence that seems to support the idea that food can affect sexual desire on a short-term basis.

In principle, there is no reason why it should not; food is made up of molecules, and some of these find their way into the brain, just as do the molecules of some drugs. Well studied, just in the last decade, has been the hypothesis that neurotransmitter levels and activities in the brain can be altered in a specific manner by the consumption of foods containing large amounts of the chemical precursors of brain neurotransmitters, or other chemical combinations that play a role in brain chemistry. (The present credibility of this hypothesis owes most to the work of Richard Wurtman and his colleagues at M.I.T.) Eat enough eggs, which contain choline, and the amount of acetylcholine in brain synapses rises; eat enough cereal, which contains tyrosine, and there is an increase in brain dopamine, which is synthesized from tyrosine.

Eating a large carbohydrate meal increases the uptake of the amino acid tryptophan by the brain, by altering the balance of amino acid competition at the blood-brain barrier. This has significance for brain function because increasing brain tryptophan increases brain serotonin, the neurotransmitter made from it. Since there is good evidence that increasing serotonin activity inhibits sexual behavior in laboratory animals, this finding about carbohydrates lends credence to the bit of culinary folklore that says that if a woman wants a man to perform she should not fill him up with a potful of starch at dinner.

But these, as far as we know, are minor factors. The most direct and dramatic enhancement of sexual behavior is caused by signals coming from sexual partners, or potential ones. Courtship and mating signals, displays and rituals have been studied in hundreds of animal species. In the fruit fly the developmental genetics of courtship are now being unraveled. In the stickleback fish the zigzag dance of the male causes courting displays in the female, which cause the male to go to the nest, which causes the female to follow, and so on, in a manner so automatic and intermeshed that at each step a model can be substituted for the real fish and still keep things moving. And in the common laboratory rat the male and female dance together in a similarly alternating but much less rigid way, for which much of the physiology—for instance, the increase in sensitivity of the female's pelvic sensory nerves, caused by estradiol—is already known. In rats, the crucial signals are not only visual and tactile but also olfactory, and abolishing a rat's sense of smell markedly reduces its sexual responsiveness.

This is also true of the rhesus monkey (*Macaca mulatta*), a much closer relative of ours. Owing to an impressive series of experiments by Richard Michael and his students and colleagues, we know a great deal about this phenomenon in this species. Plug up the nose of the male of a courting pair, and you effectively abolish the male's interest. Take out the ovaries of the female, this time leaving the male's nose *un*plugged, and he still shows no interest. But take a female long since ovariectomized—one who has not been able to stir a male's interest for months or even years—and smear her rump with secretions taken from the vagina of a second, intact female at the time of ovulation, and an experienced (unplugged) male will once again take an interest in her. The secretions in question have been analyzed, and the active principle is a cocktail of five simple, small, straight-chain fatty acids. When this cocktail is artificially synthesized, mixed in the right combination, and smeared on the rump of a female without ovaries, it has the same effect as the real thing: The male is roused.

Naturally, great interest has been shown in the possibility that some similar effect might be observable in humans. Three pieces of evidence are suggestive. First, human females have these same five fatty acids in their vaginal secretions, although in a different balance. Second, when allowed to smell (in a test tube) vaginal secretions taken from women at different times of the month, men rate midmonth secretions as "less unpleasant." Third, the five fatty acids in human vaginal secretions rise and fall with the monthly cycle just as they do in monkeys, peaking around the time of ovulation. Given the fact that the test-tube study was surely biased *against* anything resembling male arousal, it seems possible that there is a pattern here similar to that of rhesus monkeys.

But I am inclined to be skeptical about this matter for several reasons. First, in the stumptailed monkey (*Macaca arctoides*), a near relative of the rhesus monkey, odors play little or no role in courtship. Second, one of the major trends in human evolution has been the reduction of the olfactory apparatus of the brain and the corresponding increase in size of the visual system. Third, subjectively, in everyday life (and objectively, in psychological experiments), most of us are aware of powerful responses to *visual* stimuli of a sexual nature. The pictures in *Playboy* (or for that matter, the ads in *The New York Times Magazine*) arouse well enough, but do not give off odors. I think, then, that the rhesus monkey courtship model has been somewhat overplayed.

This may be one of the cases when the fact that an animal is quite closely related to us does not necessarily make it the best guide to investigating our own behavior. The ringdove, for instance, whose courtship and reproductive behavior was mentioned earlier, is similar to us in several ways. It uses primarily visual stimuli in courtship, and these are powerful in eliciting arousal; it tends to form pairs that stay together (unlike rhesus monkeys); and the male stays to help with the care of the young. This bird, separated from us by perhaps two hundred million years of evolution, may have more to teach us about our own courtship and sexual behavior than the much more closely related rhesus.

Other studies of true romance and naked lust in the laboratory have ranged from "homosexual rape" in flatworms to "the ultrasonic postejaculatory song" of the male rat. But none have been more entertaining (or for that matter more informative) that the studies of rhesus monkey sexual development carried out by psychologist Harry Harlow and his colleagues. What they add up to is that doing what comes naturally does not come so naturally if you have been brought up under abnormal social conditions. This is true whichever sex you belong to, but particularly true if you are male.

In a series of colorful papers (one is called "Lust, Latency and Love: Simian Secrets of Successful Sex"), the ineptitude of males who in early childhood were motherless, or reared on surrogate mothers, or even reared with normal mothers but without any opportunity to play with peers, is mercilessly detailed. Unlike most adolescent rhesus monkeys, who seem to get the idea fairly quickly, males socially deprived as infants may try to copulate with the female's side (Harlow calls this "working at cross-purposes to reality") or even her face ("the head-start program"). Such damage may be remediable with an extremely patient, well-experienced female, but even so will require long practice. It is easy to visualize such males as having their reproductive success reduced to zero in anything resembling normal conditions of competition in the wild. In fact, it is easy to visualize such serious behavioral damage as effectively culling a male's genes from the next generation's pool.

Indeed, everything we know about higher primates points to a crucial role for experience in the growth of normal behavior, and this is no less true of sexual than other forms of behavior. Juvenile social play, which includes playful mounting, is a universal characteristic of monkey and ape groups, and it evidently provides what is called "the normal expectable environment" without which the genetically coded innate responses and fixed action patterns, even those most critical to reproduction, may not emerge in normal form. Chimpanzees, our closest animal relatives, have been raised in the laboratory by Roger Davenport and others at the Yerkes Regional Primate

Center, under conditions similar to those imposed by Harlow on rhesus monkeys. The results:

> Of the five males who reached sexual maturity and were given sufficient opportunity to engage in copulatory behavior, all but one have done so. For these animals, considerable learning appeared to be involved. Initial attempts at copulation were very poorly coordinated. For example, males with erections might mount the side or head end of the female and thrust against her, but with experience, particularly with the helpful tutelage of sexually proficient females who assisted with positioning and penetration, these animals have improved in frequency and style to the point that they are approaching normal species typical sexual behavior, except that they lack the usual signalling systems exhibited by wild-born males. One (now fully adult) restricted male has neither attempted nor solicited copulation, and females rarely approach him. He masturbates frequently, sometimes to ejaculation, and occasionally uses a 55-gallon drum for thrusting.

The lessons we may derive for our own sexual growth are several. First, in order for normal sexual behavior to develop smoothly, certain critical experiences are necessary during the long course of early life. Second, deficits are remediable in many cases—at a cost. This is a tribute not so much to the flexibility of the behavioral program (the usual explanation) as to the fact that the behavioral patterns sought are deeply "canalized"—engrained in the nervous system by the genes. Third, some individuals do not seem to be able to recover from early social restriction, at least in the complex realm of sex.

All these assertions will seem unsurprising to followers of psychoanalytic literature, past and present. Animal studies—and not only those quoted above—give much credence to the idea that early experiences are crucial to the development of normal sexual behavior in adulthood, and even to the idea that early psychological trauma can leave, in some individuals, an incurable emotional and behavioral disability. However, it is essential that we develop a new, more flexible, and better informed notion of the "normal expectable environment" for the social maturation of our species.

Indeed, there is reason to believe that the middle-class nuclear family of the turn of the century in Europe, which was Freud's notion of "normal expectable," was most unrepresentative of our species as a whole, especially throughout most of history. Subtly, deeply, persistently, it continues to serve as a yardstick for us, and this has to stop, especially in view of the dramatic changes now under way in the structure of the family in the United States. Compared with the extended family of many nonindustrial societies, including hunting-gathering ones, the Freudian "normal expectable" nuclear family was (and is) a veritable pressure cooker of emotions. Isolated from the extended family and the wider social world, it was unusually severe in the training of children in all areas, including oral dependency, toilet training, modesty training, and other typical early-childhood themes. Fathers were relatively distant from children, more authoritative than in many societies, and much more powerful, compared to mothers, than in hunting-gathering societies. (Indeed, in a 1940 study of Chicago middle-class families, studied in relation to a wide range of other cultures, the only realm of childhood in which fathers and mothers could be rated as more indulgent with children than the average nonindustrial society was aggressive behavior.)

Most important for present purposes, the Western family, including that of the United States at mid-century as well as that of Freud's Vienna, afforded children much less experience and information regarding sex, playful or serious, than did the average nonindustrial society. Little wonder, then, that the most recent generation of Americans has made for itself a sexual revolution, spearheaded by teeny-boppers who found out what you do after you kiss.

Little wonder, too, that unprecedented numbers of adults are seeking professional help for complaints relating to sex. This is, perhaps, partly a fad, but it is also partly the result of real problems that were previously unrecognized. Direct study of human sex (as opposed to study of what people say about sex) was, not surprisingly, a very late development in our until recently prudish culture. But it has made up for lost time. Perhaps the most important contribution in this newly developed field is the work of William Masters and

Virginia Johnson. Their first book, *Human Sexual Response*, is one of the medical masterpieces of our era, and one of the most courageous intellectual efforts of any era. It simply and brilliantly turned the searchlights of modern behavioral and physiological research upon the dark, ancient acts of sex; and what it illuminated stands as a relatively unassailable edifice.

Among the facts clearly established in it: that in spite of the differences in male and female sexual response, there are many similarities, including similar patterns and sequences of skin flushing, increase and release of muscle tension, increased breathing and heart rate, and increased blood pressure; that while males are aroused and brought to orgasm faster, females are capable of having several orgasms in close succession, or one very long one, and as such are probably capable of greater sexual pleasure; that there are no detectable physiological differences between female orgasms caused by clitoral as opposed to vaginal stimulation; that there is no significant effect of penis size on women's sexual satisfaction during intercourse, other factors of male and female capacity and responsiveness being much more important; that the dangers of sexual intercourse during most of the average pregnancy have been greatly exaggerated in traditional medical opinion; and that the decline of sexual interest and capacity during old age (to the extent that it is observed) is largely the result of a self-fulfilling prophecy.

They subsequently originated several treatment methods, involving problem-oriented counseling and techniques of conditioning and desensitization to be used in the conjugal bed. Although these methods do not always succeed, they have worked in a sufficient number of cases to be in widespread use today, even by former critics. Their success, however limited, gives the lie to some prior expert opinion according to which sexual inadequacy always requires treatment of deep psychodynamic disorders by means of protracted psychotherapy. Their findings about pregnancy and old age have had a salutary effect on many people. Their findings about clitoral orgasm have liberated millions of women from centuries (at least) of phallic dominance in the bedroom. And for many who suffer sexual inadequacy, Masters and Johnson opened the hope of a relatively easy modification of behavior, without shame and without colossal expense. There is every reason to expect that the scientific revolution they began will produce still more benefits in this realm of emotional behavior.

But we must end on a more somber note. It has been said that a basic response of women to sex is fear. This should not be surprising, since one basic response of any creature to the approach of any other is fear; especially if (as may be the case with sex) the other is not yet the object of intimate trust. The wiring of the autonomic nervous system supports the sense-data of daily life: In sympathetic activation (such as fear would promote), ejaculation is precipitated, and it is the calm parasympathetic branch of the system that promotes erection of penis or clitoris. Natural selection can be expected to have favored a system that could detect conditions jeopardizing either survival during copulation or survival of the resulting young, and to terminate sexual activity in the face of such conditions. This mechanism has even been proposed as a "density-stat"—a route to population limitation in crowded locales.

However, one must go beyond the general antagonism of sex and fear to suggest that women have special reason to respond to the former with the latter. In our species, as in most mammals and birds, males are better equipped to inflict damage than females. And women are of course risking much more in any act of sex than men are, even taking only the reproductive consequences. But beyond this it must be considered possible that males have evolved a system in which aggressive and sexual tendencies are compatible if not mutually enhancing.

In a large number of bird and mammal species, male gestures of courtship and sexual invitation are similar or identical to those of agonistic threat and dominance. This is particularly the case in species that do not form pair bonds. In squirrel monkeys, the genital display acts as either threat or sexual plaint. In baboons and macaques, a male shows his dominance over a lower-ranking male by mounting him from behind, as he would a female for copulation. In orangutans, more closely related to us than monkeys, the female and young are usually alone, and the dominant style of male sexual advance during the male's infrequent, brief visits, is rape.

There is also evidence that some of the same conditions that might be expected to elicit fighting behavior can elicit male sexual behavior. For example, painful electric shock to a male rat will cause him to fight if he is in the presence of another male, but will enhance his sexual activity if he is in the presence of a female. Considering the many situations in nature in which males have to fight for the sex they want, this association is not surprising. From another intriguing experiment with male mice, there is evidence that removal of a female, after the male has spent a week with her, and introducing a strange female, will cause a large immediate rise in testosterone in the blood of the male—a hormonal change that could probably enhance either fighting or sexual behavior.

In humans, it is males who rape; males who support a vast pornography industry, much of which involves fantasies of violence or coercion; males who, overwhelmingly, pay hard cash for sex—including sex with humiliation, bondage, and sadomasochism. Although it is difficult to get good-information on this subject, there is evidence that male and female sexual fantasies are significantly different, and there is separate evidence that male sexual fantasies—at least those volunteered through the mail to a woman writer who was not a social scientist—are heavily laden with the themes of violence, dominance, and submission; more so than the fantasies of women volunteered in a similar way.

It must be remembered that humans are a moderately pair-bonding species. In such species, courtship rituals often involve demonstrations by the male that he is capable of caring for young; he may build the female a bower, or bring her a morsel of food and feed her, or show a very meek, submissive side. But this is in the service of formation of the pair bond. It enables the female to assess what kind of father he will be. In other sexual situations in moderately pair-bonding species such as ours, swagger, bluff, threat, and even force may edge out the romantic gestures of courtship.

It is very far from my mind to suggest that such tendencies, however natural, are admirable, desirable, or unchangeable; but I must reiterate here my belief—described more extensively in chapter 6—that insistence upon the nonexistence of significant biological bases for the different behaviors we observe in the two genders can only obscure the path to understanding, amelioration, and justice. The truth may not be helpful, but the concealment of it cannot be.

13

LOVE

The soul selects her own society,
Then shuts the door;
On her divine majority
Obtrude no more.

Unmoved, she notes the chariot's pausing
At her low gate;
Unmoved, an emperor is kneeling
Upon her mat.

I've known her from an ample nation
Choose one;
Then close the valves of her attention
Like stone.

> —Emily Dickinson,
> *Selected Poems*

When my firstborn daughter was six weeks old we went to
the pediatrician with her for the usual scheduled visit. My general
impression as a scientist—that newborn babies all looked the same
and were quite unappealing, much less appealing, say, than a Barbie
doll, or a pony—was confirmed by my experience as a father. Not
only that, but this one was one of those that did not sleep. (I became
convinced at the time that colicky babies are a small coterie of
otherworldly spirits sent to certain new fathers to punish them for
prior unnamed sins.)

Anyhow, there we were, the three of us, in the bosom of medical
wisdom, and I wanted an answer to a question. So I held the baby up

to the light, squinted at the physician out of one bloodshot eye, and made my statement starkly and clearly: "Tell me, Doctor" (I said). "You've been in this business a long time." (I now glanced meaning-fully at the baby.) "She's ruining my life. She's ruining my sleep, she's ruining my health, she's ruining my work, she's ruining my relationship with my wife, and . . . and . . . and she's ugly." (Here the reader may well imagine that my usual professorial reserve was doing battle with other forces on the strained and tiny field of the vocal cords. And yet, swallowing hard, I managed to compose myself for my one simple question and peroration.)

"Why do I like her?"

The physician, a distinguished one in our town, and a wise and an old and a virtuous man, seemed most unbaffled by the problem.

"You know"—he shrugged his shoulders—"parenting is an in-stinct and the baby is the releaser."

"Doctor," I said. "That's one of the worst clichés from one of my own worst lectures!" Suppressing a shudder over the fact that the language of so new an enterprise as ethology was already the common coin of the consulting room, I took my leave of the doctor (without giving vent to any violent feelings) and sank back into my misery of love: a desperation of affection for a tiny, whining monster that was making a constant assault upon my nerves.

The adoptive parents of another newborn we knew (they went through the same feelings in almost exactly the same way) found a wonderful way to describe it. It was, they said, like nothing so much as the short end of a one-sided adolescent love affair. You whined, you gazed, you mooned around, you dreamed orgies of tenderness, you saw, in your mind's eye, decades of future mutual love, dignified, courtly, publicly known. Meanwhile, you suffered every known variety of emotional abuse, neglect, rejection, anguish, and humilia-tion. If you managed somehow to steel yourself for an hour, to become convinced that you could stay on an even keel, you were thrown a scrap—here an appropriately timed belch, there a split second of eye contact—and you tumbled back down into the well with the glazed walls, stewing in your damned affectional juices. This set you up nicely for the next diaper change when, almost literally, you would have more offal dumped on your pitiful head.

The question that the doctor could not answer gives echo upon echo of fascination. Here is a fairly complex creature—a grown-up male college professor in his calm, intelligent thirties, full of experience, including various loves, large and small, as boy and man. He is not a recently parturient mother, rocked with hormonal changes, filled breasts urging from within. He is not a tiny baby with a fairly simple brain, clinging for blind comfort and protection. He is not even a teenager surging with rough humours, growing apace in too many different directions. He is, in short, no easy mark for any of the usual push-pull, click-click explanations that behavioral biologists love to give. Yet there is also little here to give comfort to the confirmed social determinists. Would they really think that these crazy emotions are the product of cultural nudging—that he feels these things because someone told him he should be a good father? Do we see any evidence of the sort of training during early life that might build up, through a process of conditioning, not just the acts of love, but the love?

I hardly think so. Not, that is, in the sense that pigeons are trained to play Ping-Pong; more, perhaps, in the sense that cocks are trained to fight. That is, with greater ease, by more rapid processes, and drawing upon a deep well of ancient, stereotyped emotion, thought, and action; a well that is in the nervous system, its depths extending down to the gene code.

Since the newborn infant human is incapable of love, it is essential that its mother and father make up for its deficit; if they don't, the infant will lose its life, and the parents, their reproductive success. Later in infancy, the child's emotional capacities grow, and the parent starts to get something out of the deal. But this waiting period does not by any means exist for all animals. In precocial (fast-maturing) birds such as ducks and chickens, where the hatchlings leave the nest almost immediately, natural selection has produced an infant that can hold up its end of the attachment bond almost from the very first day. The parent, to be sure, must be designed to defend and protect it (and, of course, to want to). But she does not have to chase her offspring all over the landscape, because it will shortly use its active walking ability to do not much else besides follow her. This behavior of following—and of vigorously protesting against removal of the mother—is not, primarily, the result of genetically coded images of the mother, although these may play a small role. It is the result, primarily, of *imprinting*, a process by which the one-day-old chick or duckling forms an indelible penchant for some object or other in its environment. Normally this turns out to be the mother.

But not always. In fact, the man who made imprinting famous by studying it objectively, also made himself famous by becoming the imprinting object for some ducklings. Konrad Lorenz, who later won the Nobel Prize for his work in behavioral biology, described imprinting (*Prägung* in German) in a 150-page monograph published in 1935, "Der Kumpan in der Umwelt des Vogels," usually translated as "The Companion in the Bird's World" (although *Kumpan* evidently has connotations resembling "partner" or "buddy," and *Umwelt* in ethology means "stimulus world" or "subjective world," the world as it is seen by the creature itself). It is a magnificent paper, not only informative and convincing, but sweeping, incisive, beautiful. Reading it gives an impression very similar to that gained by reading Freud's early anatomical writings: that one has been very wrong to judge Lorenz only by his late popular writings, or worse, secondhand, by the opinions of his critics.

The paper introduces the subject, the concepts, and the methods and proceeds through an orderly and comprehensive treatment of all the possible strong relationships systematically observed among birds up until that time. These are organized according to the significant figure as the bird might see it: the parental companion, the infant companion, the sexual companion, the social companion, the sibling companion. In each case, a number of species are covered, and the various expectations with which their nervous systems are apparently "wired" are discussed: what the "companion" may look like, what it is likely to do, what one can count on it for, and what one is supposed to do for it. What is important here is not the intriguing details but the fact that such relationships are real, ubiquitous, reliable (up to a point), strong, long-lasting in many cases, and in most cases easily shown to be essential for survival or reproduction. Furthermore, they are highly patterned ("stereotyped"), and although experience plays a key role in their emergence, there are major components of each of them that in no way depend upon learning; or, to put it as Lorenz does in another book, to say that they are innate is about as much of an exaggeration as to say that the Eiffel Tower is made of metal.

Take imprinting. The object to be followed by the infant bird is under some influence by genes and by prehatching experience, and that influence makes it tend to pick the mother bird of its own species if she is anywhere around. But in the absence of the mother, some of the ducklings imprinted on Lorenz; some imprinted on inanimate objects, like a big orange ball; some, in later experiments in other laboratories, even imprinted on the stripes painted on the wall of the box in which they were housed after hatching. This is a powerful effect of experience and, as we will see, it can last a lifetime. And the fact that it is caused by abnormal conditions does not much change for me the general importance of this formative environmental input.

However, and this is crucial, the rest of the phenomenon is close to being wired-in. The chick or duckling comes out of the egg, gets on its feet, and begins walking around. For a few hours it will tend to approach any object that is salient (easily discernible in relation to the external background). If one such object is highly salient, especially if it has certain characteristics of the mother—a certain call, say, or a certain shape or style of movement—the hatchling will tend to approach and follow it preferentially. The more it follows (this has been carefully shown), the more it wants to follow, and, after a certain point, punishing it for following tends to increase rather than decrease its following behavior—exactly contrary to the predictions of learning theory. Meanwhile, it becomes gradually less inclined to approach other objects in the environment, including animate ones, and finally it shows clear fear of them.

This process takes a matter of a few days at most. The pattern of attachment to the mother or other imprinting object, and of fear of other objects, will persist through much of the growth period. We do not need to rely on Lorenz for most of these assertions, since many laboratories around the world have extended and confirmed his observations, most notably those of Eckhardt Hess at the University of Chicago and Patrick Bateson at Cambridge University. Thanks to these and other investigators, it is clear that the phenomenon is more flexible than previously thought; but it is still quite rapid and mysterious. We now have some information about the basis of it in the brain, from neurochemical, pharmacological, and anatomical evidence. There is no question that the brain changes during imprinting, and we may soon understand how it has been prepared by its structure and pattern of growth to do so.

But is it love? No, of course not; yet I for one am inclined to think it is relevant to love. We have difficulty enough in making proper use of the word "love" in describing our own emotions and behavior, or those of other human and nonhuman creatures we know well. This fact should give ample pause to any effort to extend the concept to ducklings; but, on the other hand, the very difficulty we have gives us a certain freedom. All we have to go on, except in humans, is behavior; so if dogs love their masters, then ducklings, perhaps, love their mothers.

It is not a trivial issue, nor one that is completely unresolvable. I think that explorations of the neurology of imprinting, the neurology of mammalian attachments, and the comparative brain anatomy of birds and mammals, will one day test and perhaps bear out the hypothesis of similarity. If it is borne out, then two things will follow. First, we will have an elegant and simple laboratory model for the study of attachment and its disorders; second, we will know, as we already strongly suspect, that this emotion and its associated behaviors arise, to a large extent, from some of the oldest parts of the human brain.

But what of the rest of life? How much are we going to pin on the infant's attachment to its first *Kumpan* when there are at least four other kinds of companions in the world of the bird alone? And how do we know that this first relationship has anything to do with any others?

There are several arguments, both theoretical and practical, in favor of the existence of common processes. In the words of John Bowlby, the great modern theorist of attachment, all love is seen as inextricably intertwined with fear:

> In the theory here advanced it is, of course, that very archaic heritage that is placed at the center of the stage. A tendency to react with fear to each of these common situations—presence of strangers or animals, rapid approach, darkness, loud noises, and being alone—is regarded as developing as a result of genetically

determined biases that indeed result in a "preparedness to meet real dangers." Furthermore, it is held, such tendencies occur not only in animals but in man himself and are present not only during childhood but throughout the whole span of life. Approached in this way, fear of being separated unwillingly from an attachment figure at any phase of the life-cycle ceases to be a puzzle and, instead, becomes classifiable as an instinctive response to one of the naturally occurring clues to an increased risk of danger.

By this definition, the imprinting of hatchling birds falls squarely among many other forms of love.

Harry Harlow, another great student of love in humans and animals, draws his theory not from evolution primarily but from observed similarities of different kinds of attachment behavior during the life cycle. Like Lorenz, he begins by enumerating the various forms of companion-feeling—he calls them "affectional systems"—and, like Lorenz and Bowlby, sees them as linked by a thread of continuity:

> The first of the affectional systems is maternal love, the love of the mother for her child. The second is infant love, the love of the infant for the mother. . . .The third is peer, or age-mate, love, the love of child for child, preadolescent for preadolescent, and adolescent for adolescent. . . .The fourth love system, heterosexual love, is one in which age-mate passion is augmented by gonadal gain. . . .The fifth love system is that of paternal or father love.
>
> Our description of five separate and discrete love systems is not to imply that each system is physically and temporally separate. Actually, there is always an overlap . . . affectional motives are continuous . . . each love system prepares the individual for the one that follows, and the failure of any system to develop normally deprives him of the proper foundation for subsequent increasingly complex affectional adjustments.

The categories of Lorenz and Harlow can be made parallel by adding the sibling system to Harlow's and the paternal *Kumpan* to Lorenz's.

This will give six central relationships in the animal world. But it must be understood that the major theorists of attachment do not consider the six to be functionally distinct. Rather, they share much in common, and various combinatory and intermediate forms are clearly possible, although such forms may not occur as often in nature. The evolution of the brain would have to be considered unparsimonious if it were not able to draw upon the same basic capacities of emotion and action in the various settings where strong attachment is called for.

Clear evidence of such continuity is present even in the simple case of imprinting. Some of the birds that had imprinted on Lorenz as infants were raised to an age at which courtship and mating were possible. At this time they relentlessly courted Lorenz. This phenomenon even works with inanimate objects, and easily works with adult birds of the wrong species. Finally, the young of a variety of birds will imprint, including those that develop slowly and imprint only as fledglings, in adolescence, as well as those that imprint in the first days after hatching. Some birds—zebra finches, for example—that have been imprinted on the wrong species when young will court their own species if no other choice is available; but a zebra finch raised by (and imprinted on) a society finch female, given a choice, will choose a society finch rather than a zebra finch mate—even if he has already produced a clutch of eggs with a female from his own species. These findings suggest that the early experience of attachment, however inappropriate, makes an indelible impression on the brain systems responsible for affection and affiliation, producing tendencies that surface again at a much later, adaptively crucial moment.

This conclusion would come as no surprise to the clinical psychologist, whose bread and butter come from a serious effort to help patients find just such continuities that may underlie romantic (or other) affectional maladjustments. But it would be nice if we could support the conclusion from experimental work on animals more like us than birds.

The work of Harlow provides a nearer model. It consists of studies of the normal and abnormal development of the rhesus monkey (*Macaca mulatta*) as studied in the laboratory, concentrating on its affectional systems. Harlow began his work on affection in the 1950s with an effort to determine "the nature of love." What this meant to him and his co-workers was something like, "What does the rhesus monkey really see in its mother?" Or, to put it another way, what are the minimal conditions that will enable the infant monkey first to become attached and then to develop normal affectional competence?

The first part had a dismally minimal answer. The infant monkey would become attached to a sloping cylinder of wire that was covered with terry-cloth and warmed. If the cylinder also had a nipple as a source of milk, the monkey's clinging and contact time increased slightly. But given the choice between a milkless terry-cloth surrogate and a wire cylinder with a milk-dispensing nipple—both continuously available—the monkeys spent almost all their time on the cloth model, going to the other only to feed. When a frightening object was introduced into the cage, they invariably went to the cloth model, not to the wire model with the nipple.

This seemed to put aside in a fairly decisive way the Freudian idea that nursing and oral gratification were the essential bases for attachment formation in infancy (at least for rhesus monkeys). Leonard Rosenblum, in Harlow's laboratory, showed further that equipping the cloth model with a device that gave the infant a periodic blast of cold air—a negative reinforcement, or punishment—had the effect of increasing, not decreasing, the infant's time in contact with the "mother"; the fact of its being hurt was evidently more salient than the source of the hurt and so, paradoxically, it sought comfort from that source, exactly as imprinting birds had done in a parallel situation.

Thus the bond of attachment in infant monkeys. As for the second part of the question—the minimum requirements for normal *later* development—monkeys raised on cloth surrogates grew up with fewer of the abnormal behaviors—rocking, self-clasping, self-biting, and so on—than monkeys raised in social isolation without surrogates. But they showed higher levels of those behaviors than did monkeys reared by normal mothers. This was especially true in social situations, where they showed strong tendencies to withdraw into such "autistic" states of activity. At adolescence, the time of sexual florescence in normal rhesus monkeys, both males and females were inept. In social situations as adults, males were more likely to threaten or attack other individuals than were normally reared males. And females, if they could be forcibly inseminated, were inept, negligent, or even brutal in their behavior toward their infants.

These are only a few of a large number of experiments in which conditions of social rearing in monkeys have been modified. Some of Harlow's students and associates now run active laboratories of their own, and many of them have made major contributions—Leonard Rosenblum, William Mason, Gene Sackett, Gary Mitchell, and Stephen Suomi, to name a few. It was shown, for example, that opportunities for contact and play with peers are also essential for completely normal development—in some respects as important or more important than normal mothering; that there are species differences in response to social deprivation, even among closely related species within the genus *Macaca*—differences that must make us very cautious about generalizing the findings to humans; that with sufficient encouragement, males can provide "mothering" to isolated infants; that rocking the cloth surrogate significantly reduces the behavioral and emotional deficits usually associated with cloth-surrogate rearing; and that infants raised to the age of six months or even a year in total social isolation can, by being placed for a few months together with a *younger* infant monkey, be rehabilitated into socially normal juveniles. So strong is the tendency to form attachments that even placing a previously isolated monkey infant with a long-haired dog will result in a strange lasting relationship in which the infant clings to, rides, and otherwise interacts with the canine "surrogate mother."

These and many other findings can be summarized as follows: Powerful neural and neuroendocrine control functions insure the development of some forms of affectional behavior even in the most abnormal circumstances. Even a year of total social isolation beginning at birth—which essentially abolishes affectional behavior in rhesus monkeys—can be largely remediated, although by a difficult and costly method. The affectional emotions and the affectional behaviors apparently depend on an underlying set of common structures, despite obvious phenomenological differences that suggest some differences in underlying physiology. These structures are responsive to experience, in both enduring and transient ways, and affectional competence at any stage of life, in any relationship, depends to some extent on prior affectional experience.

It remains for us to turn from consideration of animal to that of human attachment and affectional systems. Considering the varieties of human relationships in the thousands of known cultures, it would seem all but impossible to characterize them in any useful general way. But a perusal of these varieties shows, on the contrary, both a surprising amount of uniformity among human populations and a lawful aspect to the still great variation that does exist beyond the uniformity. As in the case of birds and monkeys, the simplest approach is the life-span approach; that is, to begin with the capacities of the infant and build the nested affectional systems upward. Emphasis will be laid upon two cases, the !Kung San hunter-gatherers and a modern industrial society, the United States. But these will be considered in the context of the broad range of human variation. Since the preceding chapter had so much to say about sexual and romantic relationships, this discussion will be weighted toward relationships in infancy and childhood; these are in any case the bedrock of the others. And, of course, there is in some of them an adult at the other end of the bond; an adult who, as seen in the anecdote of the pediatrician, may become quite passionately involved.

There are several reasons for taking an interest in !Kung infancy, in terms of behavioral science strategy. Like any cross-cultural research, it broadens the variability available to us for study. It has the effect of giving us more variation with which to address any theoretical issue, and, occasionally, may disabuse us of false notions, explicit or tacit, of the universality of some Western infant behaviors or caretaking procedures. However, unlike most cross-cultural research, it adds a historical or evolutionary and (potentially) causal dimension to the extent that we can guess, by extrapolation from modern hunter-gatherers, what adaptations in infant care and development must have characterized *ancestral* populations of hunter-gatherers. That is, we reason from what we know of hunter-gatherer sociology and subsistence ecology and how they appear to affect infancy. Finally, it gives us leads, to be checked in an appropriately broad cross-cultural context, on possible universal features of human infant care, infant behavior, and development. And this in turn gives us a basis for cross-species comparisons.

Data from observation and testing of !Kung infants, still undergoing further formal analysis, have made possible several broad generalizations concerning *this particular group* of hunter-gatherer infants.

From the first few days of life (and continuing through at least the first year) infants are carried in a sling at the mother's side. This device positions them vertically and insures continuous physical contact with the mother's body. In this context it is possible to see naturally occurring instances of certain newborn reflexes, such as placing, stepping and crawling responses in the legs, use of the arms to move and free the head, and grasping responses in the hands. By these adjustments the infant accommodates to the mother's movements and may even protect itself from breathing stoppages caused by her skin and clothing. Equally important, these reflexive movements serve as signals of the infant's state changes, making it possible for the mother to learn to anticipate its waking, hunger, or defecation.

From the sling position on the mother's hip, infants have available to them her entire social world, the world of objects hung around the mother's neck or work held in her hands, and the breast; and the mother has immediate manual and visual access to the infant. When the mother is standing, the infant's face is just at the eye level of keenly interested ten- to twelve-year-old children, who frequently approach and initiate brief, intense, face-to-face interactions, including mutual smiling and vocalization. When not in the sling, infants are passed from hand to hand around a fire for similar interactions with one adult or child after another. They are kissed on their faces, bellies, genitals, are sung to, bounced, entertained, encouraged, and addressed at length in conversational tones long before they can understand words.

Indulgence by the mother of the infant's dependent behavior throughout the first year is absolute, and in the second year it slacks off only slightly. Nursing can best be described as continual, occurring over and over again throughout the day on a demand basis, and any slightly fretful signs may be interpreted as hunger signals. (It is as if the burden is on the infant to tell the mother when it is *not* hungry, by extruding the nipple, rather than when it is, by crying.)

Urination or defecation on the mother or on her clothing is met with no response during the early months except for moving and cleaning the infant after the elimination is completed. Intense physical proximity throughout the first two years makes possible a much more fine-grained responsiveness on the part of the mother with respect to the infant's needs than can be attained in a situation where the mother and infant are frequently separated by considerable distance. For example, during the first year the average amount of time elapsed (based on the data in timed, coded observations) between the onset of an infant's fretting and the mother's nurturant response was about six seconds.

When not asleep or in the sling, infants are typically held sitting in the lap of the mother or another child or adult, with whom they interact in close face-to-face exchanges, or whom they use as a base for interaction with other people in the immediate vicinity. (Thanks to the subsistence ecology and the resulting structure of the band, other people are almost always available.) The frequent nursing bouts are not, in observable terms, passive events connected only with the satiation of hunger, but active behaviors in which, increasingly as the infant grows, the time, setting, choice of breast, and length of the nursing session are managed entirely by the infant. This continues to be true until the time of weaning, usually some time during the fourth year. Nursing often occurs simultaneously with active play with the free breast, languid extension-flexion movements in the arms and legs, mutual vocalization, face-to-face interaction (the breasts are quite long and flexible), and various forms of self-touching, including occasional masturbation.

The process of separation is initiated by the infant and carried forward languidly for two or more years with very little urging from the mother. Remarkably steadfast and receptive, she rarely leaves the infant's immediate vicinity until the later part of the second year, and then only occasionally until the birth of her next, usually during the fourth year. However, the infant begins to move away from the mother as soon as it is mobile, using the mother, who remains sitting in the same spot, as a base for exploration. Although the prospect of becoming lost in the bush is extremely dangerous, this is very rare and is prevented both by the infant's consistent return to the mother and by the intensity of fearfulness of strangers and strange situations—an intensity much stronger than that observed in Western infants. Again, because of the subsistence ecology and the nature of the band, there is usually a dense network of possible relations with children of all ages; the infant passes fairly gradually from an intense attachment to the mother to the receptive context of a group of children—children who range in age from near-peers to adolescent caretakers, with whom the infant is both familiar and safe.

The process of weaning from the breast begins at the time the mother becomes aware that she is pregnant again, and weaning from being carried (which means the child, until old enough to keep up with the mother, will cease to accompany her on her gathering rounds) occurs around the time of her delivery. While neither of these processes is very abrupt or punitive, both are relatively firm and often result in an extended period of depressed and fretful behavior. However, there remains the consolation of a constantly present and accepting group of children who, within about a year of the infant's weaning from being carried, become a major focus of the latter's social behavior.

Considerable attention has been given in recent years to describing the specific behavior patterns that make up infant attachment. These patterns, covering a broad span of levels of development and levels of behavior description, include the following: visual-postural orientation; rooting to the breast and sucking; crying and stopping of crying; smiling; non-cry vocalization; grasping and reaching; separation anxiety; approach; following; greeting; climbing and exploring; burying of face; use of the mother as a base for exploration; flight to the mother; and clinging. When these behaviors occur more often in relation to the mother than anyone else, attachment has begun.

All these patterns have been observed in !Kung infants during the second half-year. But listing all these behaviors and giving them a label does not make an explanation of them. In this context it is gratifying to refer to at least one serious attempt to bring together a large volume of research data in a theoretical framework that is at once reasoned, elegant, and testable—the three volumes of John Bowlby's *Attachment and Loss*. Bowlby's great work has the added advantage of taking a clear stance in relation to the history of psychoanalytic theories of development, and, further, is derived from a body of work concerned directly with the making of child-care policy.

Briefly, his position is as follows: The human infant, like infants of many species of birds and mammals, is born with a set of reflexive perceptuomotor mechanisms. Although they can be blocked under experimental conditions of deprivation, given the normal, expectable environment of a newly born member of the species, they will inevitably result in the formation of attachments to caretaking figures and, subsequently, to other individuals. The emphasis for Bowlby, in the first half-year, is on mechanisms involving communication through distal receptors—mechanisms such as visual-postural orientation, smiling, crying and the cessation of crying, and non-cry vocalizations. The rooting and sucking reflexes connected with feeding, and the tendency for various forms of tactile stimulation and/or suckling to be very effective in bringing about the cessation of crying and other discomfort signs, are seen as important, but not overridingly important, components of the initial attachment propensity.

Specifically, Bowlby is critical of "secondary drive" theory (theory that stresses the role of satiation of hunger and the pleasure of suckling as primary reinforcers for attachment behavior) common to many psychoanalytic conceptions, including Freud's. Later in the first year, in association with the development of effective locomotion, proximity-maintaining mechanisms and other attachment behaviors come into play. These include grasping, clinging, and scrambling and climbing on the mother and, later, following behavior and use of the mother as a base for exploration.

In lieu of either learning or drive theories of the growth of love, Bowlby proposes an ethological unfolding of attachment behavior in accord with an imperfectly understood genetic program. This behavior system is, as it were, "seeking" an object, in something like the way the neural mechanisms underlying imprinting in precocial birds are "seeking," at a certain period, a suitable object for following behavior—with the important difference that in humans and our close relatives the process is much longer (some seven months in human infants) and very much more gradual. (What is meant by "seeking" is that the behaviors in question—attachment behaviors—will fully emerge, change, and function in certain predictable ways only after an appropriate object is found, and that the organism will experience considerable discomfort until that happens.) Because of the need immature organisms have to maintain close physical proximity to more mature members of the species, as protection against death by exposure or predation, these underlying neural mechanisms have been under powerful selective pressure during the course of evolution.

It is worth mentioning that Bowlby, in his earlier work, thought of the function of attachment primarily as a basis for healthy adult social behavior, which he saw as the result of a healthy early attachment to a mothering figure or suitable substitute. Despite this change of emphasis, it is apparent that Bowlby views the mass of new information on human and animal behavior development as generally supporting his earlier view with an evolutionary justification: Due to the long-standing causal relation, throughout human evolution, between the threat of predation and the intensity of attachment, it is now essential to child mental health for infants to have a prolonged and close relationship in early life to a single mother or "permanent mother substitute."

The implications of the !Kung findings for Bowlby's formulation and for the problems with which he is concerned are apparent. The emphasis on early attachment to a nurturant caretaking figure, common to Bowlby, Freud, Erik Erikson, and others, is a sensible one. If anything, this position is strengthened by the facts about !Kung infancy, which reveal a mother-infant relation considerably closer, more delicately responsive, and more nurturant than the Western pattern, and one that begins taxing "proximal" (contact) mechanisms in attachment at birth rather than, as Bowlby suggests, only in the second half-year.

Now consider the American context for the same growth process. In the latest edition of *Baby and Child Care*, Dr. Spock advises mothers to become suspicious of possible "spoiling" of babies by the age of three months, to exercise "a little hardening of the heart"; if, by five or six months, the baby still expects to be picked up every time he cries, the mother is advised to follow a program of "unspoiling," including pretending she is busy when she really is not in order to "impress the baby" with the impossibility of responding to his fretfulness. In an apparent reversal of his position in the earliest editions, Spock thus encourages the tendency of American mothers to begin shaping self-reliance in the early months of life.

His advice was faithfully paraphrased to a !Kung mother in her own language; she reacted with a mixture of surprise, amusement, and contempt. "Doesn't he realize it's only a baby?" she asked. "It has no sense, that's why it cries. You pick it up. Later on, when it gets bigger, it will have sense, and it won't cry so much." In other words, she had confidence in the process of growth, and was not concerned about the possibility of "spoiling" the baby; also, she considered the "unspoiling" procedure ethically unacceptable.

Should we abandon Spock and model ourselves after the !Kung? In considering these child-rearing methods, the !Kung social and ecological situation must be taken carefully into account in the comparison. An American mother is not surrounded by a network of relatives and friends who can help absorb some of the practical and, even more, the emotional burdens of baby care. More important, perhaps, her child is not surrounded by a network of continuously available children of all ages who will provide an attractive alternative to attachment to the mother when the need for separation inexorably arises. In other words, the dangers of "spoiling" *may* indeed be greater given the social context of American baby care in recent decades.

There are also many other societies of ethnographic record that differ from the !Kung model to no noticeable ill-effect. Under different conditions of social ecology, they are able to provide a variety of forms of multiple-mothering or multiple-caretaking. As Margaret Mead has pointed out in a cogent critique of Bowlby's position, many studies of multiple-caretaking, from polygynous traditional cultures to modern Israeli kibbutzim, have failed to show that multiple-caretaking has any objectively detectable unfortunate consequences, provided that the two or three or several caretakers offer an adequately nurturant and uninterrupted human environment. The same conclusion was drawn more recently in a major review of cross-cultural studies of child development by Robert LeVine.

Finally, it must be said that in societies such as ours, where the risk of infant death is small, there is no evidence of ultimate biological advantage in leaving infant care exclusively to women. Insofar as mothers have a several month head start on fathers at the time of birth, insofar as fathers are never quite sure that their offspring are really their biological offspring, and insofar as there are still certain advantages to breast feeding, mothers and infants will always be, on the average, more disposed toward each other. But that in individual cases it would be detrimental for a man and woman to participate equally (or even in a proportion favoring the man) in the care of an infant—detrimental, that is, to the infant's psychological health and growth—has never been supported with believable evidence.

It should now be interesting to consider the social context of infancy in broader perspective, by mentioning the relevant facts about higher primates living under natural conditions, and about human societies in the ethnographic record, other than the !Kung.

Nicholas Blurton Jones, an ethologist (trained by Tinbergen) who turned from birds to children, has analyzed comparative data from a number of mammals on patterns of infant care and concluded that those in continuous proximity to their young differ from those that cache or nest their young in certain predictable ways. Most important are that the "cachers" feed their young at widely spaced intervals, have high protein and fat content in their milk, and high sucking rates, whereas "carriers" (including followers) feed more or less continuously, have milk with low protein and fat content, and low sucking rates. Humans, along with all other higher primates studied, have the milk composition and sucking characteristics of continuous proximity, or "carrier" species. And, to round out the picture, !Kung hunter-gatherers nurse their infants about four times an hour. Considering the comparative picture, it makes sense to suggest that such contact was close in our species during most of human evolution.

In *non*-hunting-gathering human societies, the range of variation is very great. The key determinant here appears to be mother's work load. In many agricultural societies, the organization of work and nurturance results in several-hour separations of mother and infant, which precludes the possibility of a !Kung-like pattern of attachment.

In the typical situation, the mother might be working in the garden during part of the day, while her infant is with a young girl or young woman (often an older sibling of the infant), at a remove from the mother in the home village compound.

Mother-infant sleeping distance is one of the most neglected features of the caretaking environment, even though bedtime protest and night-waking are two of the most common problems of infant care in the United States. In all higher primates and among !Kung hunter-gatherers, mother and infant sleep in immediate proximity (if not direct physical contact) in the same bed (or nest). Almost all !Kung mothers report that their infants wake during the night to nurse, two to many times nightly, until the age of weaning. It is likely that some additional nighttime nursing bouts take place while one or both partners in the nursing relationship is in a sleeping or half-waking state. This pattern was probably selected for early in higher primate evolution. An infant sleeping alone, even among most human hunter-gatherers, would be subject to almost certain death by predation.

As for human societies other than hunter-gatherers, on this dimension there is surprisingly little variation in the whole range of nonindustrial societies (although there is considerable variation in father-infant sleeping distance). Of 90 societies in a worldwide sample for which information was available, the mother and infant slept in the same bed in 41, in the same room with bed unspecified in 30, and in the same room in separate beds in 19. In none of the 90 cases did mother and infant sleep in separate rooms. This feature of the mother-infant bond evidently did not vary much against different ecological backgrounds, until the coming of the industrial state.

Our own dominant culture in the United States derives from that of the agricultural peoples of northern Europe for whom the use of cradles and swaddling was the rule. As compared with !Kung hunter-gatherers and with the more indulgent of the intermediate-level societies, amount of contact between mother and infant is low and its regulation rests much more with the mother in the modern United States; the infant has to adapt as best it can. This is nowhere clearer than in sleeping arrangements. Departing from the universal pattern for nonindustrial societies, we often have infants sleeping in separate rooms from their mothers (and fathers), alone or with siblings too young to nurture them. It may be that the "syndrome" of bedtime protest that afflicts so many infants and toddlers and the "syndrome" of night-waking that afflicts a third of English (and probably American) one-year-olds are mere artifacts of our sleeping arrangements—that is, without mother-infant separation, bedtime protest might not occur, and night-waking might occur, but not become a "problem."

Western European and American cultures have throughout their histories devoted great energy to combating what would seem from the foregoing account to be a natural tendency on the part of infants and mothers to, as it were, fall into one another's arms. This has not been easy, and it is not at all clear what precisely motivated these cultures to do so. Recent works on the history of childhood and child care in Europe reveals common patterns, varying from strict withholding of love to isolation, neglect, and brutality, that are astounding to read of. If true, then the soil in which the emotion of love was expected to grow in the hearts of our ancestors was hard and dry indeed. In this context, the patterns of child care of Europe and America in the twentieth century seems indulgent, loving, and child-centered. Yet, compared to the child-care patterns of the average society in the nonindustrial ethnographic record, these latter-day child-rearing customs of ours seem, on the contrary, a bitter pill for a child to have to swallow.

Readers familiar with Dr. Spock and his reputation will perhaps be surprised to see him cast here as a sort of hardhearted fellow adjuring parents to stand back from indulging their babies. He is no such villain, of course. He is properly known for liberalizing the advice about baby care that was formerly standard. A review of that advice is not possible here, but an excerpt from John B. Watson's 1928 book *Psychological Care of Infant and Child*, which was widely influential, will give the flavor of it:

> There is a sensible way of treating children. Treat them as though they were young adults. Dress them, bathe them with care and circumspection. Let your behavior always be objective and kindly firm. Never hug and kiss them, never let them sit in your lap. If you must, kiss them once on the forehead when they say good night. Shake hands with them in the morning. Give them a pat on the head if they have made an extraordinarily good

job of a difficult task. Try it out. In a week's time you will find how easy it is to be perfectly objective with your child and at the same time kindly. You will be utterly ashamed of the mawkish, sentimental way you have been handling it. . . .

In conclusion won't you then remember when you are tempted to pet your child that mother love is a dangerous instrument? An instrument which may inflict a never healing wound, a wound which may make infancy unhappy, adolescence a nightmare, an instrument which may wreck your adult son or daughter's vocational future and their chances for marital happiness.

It should be noted that this 1928 advice came not from some extremist on the fringes, but from the dean of American behaviorist psychology; the same man who had trained little Albert to fear furry animals, and who later had a successful career in advertising. One wonders what he would have advised in a marriage manual.

As for the liberalization, it has had its limits. Because it is now widely reputed to have already gone too far, it is worth focusing on how nonindulgent it is in cross-cultural perspective. The standard, indeed virtually universal current pediatric advice in the United States concerning "chronic resistance to sleep in infancy"—whether of the "going-to-bed type" or the "waking-in-the-night-type"—is the same as that offered by Dr. Spock: Let them cry it out. For some infants and children, this works easily; but for some others, it may take several nights of crying for half an hour or more. Spock's counsel:

It's hard on the kindhearted parents while the crying lasts. They imagine the worst: that the baby's head is caught in the slats of the crib, or that she has vomited and is lying in a mess, that she is at least in a panic about being deserted. From the rapidity with which these sleep problems can be cured in the first year, and from the way babies immediately become much happier as soon as this is accomplished, I'm convinced that they are only crying from anger at this age. . . .

If the several nights of crying will wake other children or anger the neighbors, you can muffle the sound by putting a rug or blanket on the floor and a blanket over the window. Soft surfaces of this kind absorb a surprising amount of the sound. . . .

Some babies (and young children) vomit easily when enraged. The parent is apt to be upset and shows it by anxious looks, by rushing to clean up, by being more sympathetic afterward, by being quicker to come to the baby at the next scream. This lesson is not lost on children, and they are likely to vomit more deliberately the next time they're in a temper. . . . I think it is essential that parents harden their hearts to the vomiting if the baby is using it to bully them. If they are trying to get the baby over a refusal to go to bed, they should stick to their program and not go in. They can clean up later after the baby has gone to sleep.

This advice is to be found in the latest (1976) edition of a child-care manual that is said by its publisher to be the bestselling new book published since 1895, when best-seller lists began. Previous printings, most of them carrying the same advice, had sold 28 million copies before the 1976 version.

Most parents in the traditional nonindustrial world would place this advice squarely in the category of public advocacy of child abuse and neglect. There is no basis for the inference that the infant is crying from anger, and there is little basis for the inference that the procedure is harmless. These may be true, for all we know, but on the other hand, at least for some babies, they may not. I suspect that the experience of night-waking that most mothers outside of our society have had, whether in the distant or the recent past, would have been something like the one described in Jill Hoffman's poem "Rendezvous":

> Summoned from a dream of your summoning
> by your cry, I steal out of bed and leave
> my doting husband deaf to the world.
> We meet, couple, and cling, in the dim light—
> your soft mouth tugs and fills and empties me.

We stay that way a long time it seems, till
on your brimming face, where milky drops glide,
I see my body's pleasure flood and yawn.
We turn each other loose to sleep. Smiling
your smile of innocence, I return
to the bed of your begetting, and a man's warm side.

The prediction of "spoiling" theorists that products of such indulgence will grow up "tied to their mothers' apron strings" is easily shown to be false, at least for the !Kung. Comparative studies of preschool-age children in London and among the !Kung under roughly comparable conditions—outdoors, with both mothers and playmates available—showed that the !Kung children strayed significantly farther from their mothers than did their London counterparts; they also had more interactions with other children and were less often nurtured by their mothers or other adults. At fourteen, a !Kung boy may go out walking alone or with a friend, drive lions from an antelope carcass with sticks, and carry the meat home to his parents. A !Kung woman in her early twenties may go out into the desert in labor, alone or with a four-year-old, deliver her infant and afterbirth entirely without assistance, and, having cut the cord, bring the baby back to the village. However inadvisable these acts may be, they are scarcely what one expects to see in young people lacking in independence. If early indulgence fosters later extreme dependency, it must do so in a way that is pretty subtle.

These facts would not be surprising to John Bowlby or, for that matter, to a psychoanalyst like Erik Erikson who, in a more traditional manner, urged that the establishment of "basic trust" in infancy is necessary for the growth of independence. This proposed relationship between early indulgence of dependency and later reduced dependency runs so contrary to classical notions of reinforcement learning (responding to distress signals should theoretically increase their frequency) that it is hard to believe, however much evidence is adduced to support it. But in a major review of the literature done in 1970 by Eleanor Maccoby and John Masters, this hypothesis was shown to be supported by numerous studies. A more recent review by Mary Ainsworth and her colleagues supports it as well. Among the studies of the last decade in this area are one in Ainsworth's group showing that infants whose mothers respond to them more in the first three months of life cry less in the second three months than do infants of mothers who were unresponsive in the early period; and another study by Alan Sroufe and Everett Waters showing that toddlers who have had close mother-infant relations tend to respond more maturely to separations than do other toddlers.

Some theoretical adjustment to these findings may be in order. An ordinary reinforcement model would predict that indulgence of dependency—that is, reward of dependent behaviors with responsive caretaking—would increase the incidence of the behaviors. Actually the reverse may be the case. If we assume, as Bowlby has tried to show, that attachment behaviors are part of the normal *biological* functioning of the infant—instinctual, if you will—then it makes sense to propose that they will be very difficult to extinguish, without disrupting the basic homeostasis of the organism. Attachment behaviors are not randomly occurring Skinnerian behavioral "operants." Some at least, such as crying and contact seeking, are behavioral manifestations of organismic distress. It may be as inappropriate to try to extinguish them by ignoring them as it would be to try to extinguish cold-induced shivering by ignoring it. Ignoring attachment signals simply increases the distress, and so increases the manifestations of the distress.

I am not completely convinced of the veracity of the "basic trust" theory, but there is at least as much evidence in favor of it as there is against it. As for the spoiling theory, I think there is enough evidence at hand to be very skeptical of it, at least where indulgence of dependency *in infancy* is concerned. This has no bearing on the effects of indulgence of dependency in later childhood or adolescence, or of the sort of spoiling we are so good at in our culture, namely the indulgence of the child's (or teenager's) desire to consume selfishly, to disrupt, or to destroy.

I must reiterate also the difference context makes for the parent-infant relationship. Social support for the mother, and the lure of the child group, as seen among the !Kung, are both without parallel for mother-infant pairs in our own culture—or, rather, the parallels are very much weaker. The multi-age child group fosters the growth of separation from the mother and the emergence of innumerable behaviors associated with independence. Above all, perhaps, it fosters the growth of affectional competence in a warm and supportive environment. This includes some competition, some real fighting, and some rough-and-tumble play. But in early childhood at least, it also includes one pattern that deserves special mention. It might be called "gentle-and-tumble play." It consists of mutual touching, tangling of legs, clinging and rolling while lying on the ground. Unless it proceeds to explicitly genital activity (which also occurs in play during this age period), this behavior is ignored by !Kung adults. Its derivation from infant attachment behavior is apparent from the shared components and from the fact that this play may take an imaginative form in which the older child takes the role of parent.

The influence of parents as models is pervasive and extends to the sexual realm. While !Kung parents try to conceal their actual acts of sexual intercourse from children, they do not always succeed, and for this and other reasons young children in that culture have more awareness of sex than they do in ours. Their play includes role-taking in sexual relationships, even to the point of simulating intercourse, but almost certainly without intromission. Interview studies by ethnographer Marjorie Shostak confirm that such play occurs and remains vivid in memory until adulthood. At the time of puberty, it may still occur and the transition from such play to real sex may be (although it is not always) gradual. The hormonal changes of puberty undoubtedly transform the emotions and the physiology involved in the heterosexual affectional bond among the !Kung as among ourselves, but—just as Harlow suggested—the playmate-to-playmate bond forms a natural basis for it.

Marriage among the !Kung, however, is arranged, as it has been in most human societies throughout most of history. If the young people have strong inclinations, they may be respected, but most marriages are formed without benefit of romantic love. Once, when I was lecturing on the evolution of affectional competence, I expressed puzzlement at the adaptive function of romantic love, since it has so rarely in history been the way people got into the pair-bond. One of my more cynical students came up to me after class and explained (dismally, but, I suppose, correctly) that its obvious adaptive function is to get people *out* of a previously established pair bond—to make possible abandonment or betrayal. The !Kung, in any case, frequently divorce in these early marriages, although they rarely do so once a child has been born to them. Thus they seem to have something approaching the "trial marriage" idea once proposed by Bertrand Russell (for which, among his other "reckless" ideas in those timid days, he was barred from teaching mathematics and logic at City College), and this leaves room for romantic and sexual compatibility to play some role in pair formation.

The physiology of love is poorly understood, to say the least. Where romantic love is concerned, little progress has been made beyond what Sappho knew in the fifth century B.C.:

> To me that man equals a god
> as he sits before you and listens
> closely to your sweet voice
>
> and lovely laughter—which troubles
> the heart in my ribs. For now
> as I look at you my voice fails,
>
> my tongue is broken and thin fire
> runs like a thief through my body.
> My eyes are dead to light, my ears
>
> pound, and sweat pours down over me.
> I shudder, I am paler than grass,
> and am intimate with dying . . .

Barbaric though it must seem to point this out, these are mainly signs of autonomic nervous system turmoil. Sappho also implicates explicitly the emotion of fear, which, as I have argued, forms a part of the basis of love; and which, incidentally, may be responsible for some of the autonomic arousal she describes. It is a circumstance in which the fear is associated with the absence of a certain person, and which can be quieted by that person. As such, it is reminiscent of infant attachment, but unlike it in that the provenance of the beloved in romantic attachment is baffling. Why him (or her)? And why so much arousal, so much fear, so much, if the object is lost, grief?

The autonomic nervous system cannot explain much of that. It is likely that some explanations lie in the limbic system, the same system that mediates various other emotions, but when one explanation is given for so many different things, it becomes automatically unconvincing. There must be something specific about the structure or function of this system or of others in the brain that will make attachment and affectional behavior, whether strong or moderate, more comprehensible. Arthur Kling and Horst Steklis of Rutgers University have shown that the affiliative behavior of monkeys can be abolished by removal of the basal portion of the frontal lobes or the tips of the temporal lobes of the cortex; but this is a crude intervention and a very general effect, and so it cannot tell us much. It has already been noted that the deposition of myelin in the major fiber tracts of the limbic system occurs at such a time as to make it a possible basis of the social fears in infancy; one of these is the fear of separation, and the converse of it is attachment. It is possible that study of those structures in animals would lead to a firmer understanding of what might be called the physiology of love; but to make matters more complex, affection and attachment are of course different emotions, and we know little about what makes the former deepen into the latter, the hallmark of which is perhaps the intensity of the fear of separation. It is clear, too, that the florescence of the gonadal hormones and their hypothalamic and pituitary control systems at adolescence transforms the affectional competence of both sexes, enhancing it in some ways and damaging it in others, but it is not clear just what these changes do.

Much more work has been focused on the physiology of parental behavior in various species. We know that the hypothalamus is involved, both as a hormonal regulator and as a part of neural circuits mediating caretaking behaviors such as retrieval and protection of the young. But here the sexes must part company. The only species of higher vertebrates in which males have been shown to have physiological adaptations for parenthood elaborate enough to rival those of the females are the Columbiforms, a group of birds that includes pigeons and doves. There is little evidence of special physiological adaptations for caretaking by males in any other species of bird or mammal; they must be there, since the caretaking is there, and it isn't done by magic. But we have absolutely no idea what they are.

As for maternal behavior, it has been a focus of a great deal of research. Much is known, but there is much variation. Estradiol, progesterone, and prolactin are known to play some role in the nest-building and caretaking behaviors of rats, mice, rabbits, hamsters, ringdoves, and canaries, a fairly wide range of species, but they do so in different combinations and according to different schedules in the reproductive cycle. Prolactin, which causes milk formation in mammals and the equivalents—crop and brood patch formation—in birds, was at one time thought to be critical for maternal behavior in some species, but this no longer seems to be the case. At least in rats, all three hormones seem to play a role and, in a series of experiments by Howard Moltz of the University of Chicago, it was shown that the best way to get a virgin female rat to respond positively to pups was to put her through a course of hormone treatments identical to the one she would have gone through if she had become pregnant and given birth; that is, a gradual rise in estradiol and progesterone, an abrupt fall in both of these (such as normally occurs just before delivery), and a rise of prolactin.

But it was also shown, by psychologists Joseph Terkel and Jay Rosenblatt of Rutgers University, that if you hooked up the circulatory systems of a rat that had recently given birth and a virgin female, the virgin would be induced to behave maternally toward pups. This raised the possibility that going through all the hormonal changes of pregnancy was after all unnecessary, and that the changes immediately following parturition, combined with exposure to pups, would be sufficient. Later a student of Moltz, Michael Numan, and others showed that the "media preoptic area" of the hypothalamus is essential for maternal behavior in rats, and that estradiol promotes maternal behavior by influencing this region. This is the same area of the hypothalamus that is known to be structurally different in males and females.

There are also species differences, even among rodents, that are not trivial. Comparative psychologist Elaine Noirot has conducted a series of studies showing that exposure to pups alone ("priming") can induce maternal behavior in a matter of hours in virgin female mice, with no hormonal or neurological treatment. Similar priming in rats studied by Rosenblatt took six to seven days, by which time the pups would have to have been kept alive artificially. And in hamsters the process, as studied by ethologist Martin Richards, took even more prolonged and repeated exposure, usually requiring replacement of several litters killed by the female.

Testosterone, whether administered to females around the time of birth, during pregnancy, or after delivery, is antagonistic to maternal behavior in various mammal species. Castration of males at various points in the life cycle improves their caretaking behavior in various species. But the few species of mammals in which males play a significant caretaking role under natural conditions have not been studied. It is possible that such study would reveal intriguing new physiological adaptations.

As for humans, females go through, during pregnancy, delivery, and lactation, a series of hormonal changes much more protracted but otherwise quite similar to that of rats: a slow rise of estradiol and progesterone, an abrupt fall of both of these before delivery (as well as a rise in the ratio of estradiol to progesterone, which is falling faster), and a rise of prolactin after delivery. Putting the infant to the breast, if the woman is nursing, causes a rise in prolactin and oxytocin in the blood, and these in turn suppress the level of estradiol and progesterone, so that the entire profile of reproductive hormones, as well as the likelihood of resuming monthly cycling, is altered. It is quite possible that these extensive changes influence mood and behavior.

None of them occurs in adoptive mothers, yet the latter are often as good or better than biological mothers. Why then attribute significance to the hormonal changes? Simply put, the cultural and social preparation for motherhood, which plays an important role for any woman, is usually much greater for adoptive mothers, who have often waited eagerly for a long time. It is likely that at least a significant minority of first births throughout human history have been unwanted at the time they came; for those countless instances during our evolution, hormonal preparation may have been crucial.

Men go through no such changes, yet it is obvious that as a group they have considerable caretaking capacity, even for infants. In the abstract it is possible that they have as much inherent caretaking ability as women, given equivalent environments of rearing. This is a viable hypothesis; I personally would not put my money on it, but that doesn't make it wrong. As an assumption, however—especially one on which to base policy decisions—it is, at this moment in the history of behavioral science, not acceptable. But science cannot legislate policy; its laws constrain not through the social contract, but through practical consequences. If a certain town, for example, in the year 1985, were to pass a law saying that 50 percent of each infant and child's time must be spent with its father, or that 50 percent of the children must be cared for by men, that would perhaps be more equitable than what we currently observe in any town chosen at random. But the facts of behavior as we now understand them would predict that such a law would bring the interests of women and children in conflict with each other, much more so than they are now. That is to say, on the average, the children would be better off with the women. Of course, if the women in the town were to grow sufficiently unhappy with their more usual unfair share of the child care, it might become more or less of a toss-up for the child whether to have a grumbling mother or a bumbling father.

Neither Lorenz nor Harlow nor even Bowlby has made much of the affection we direct at family members outside the immediate ones. Focusing on animals is not a good way to have that affection brought to one's attention, although it is increasingly evident that they not only have it, but live by it. The problem is they don't talk about it; and since they don't, if the animal is at all long-lived, you have to hang around watching for quite a few years before you find out who is whose uncle or grandma or second cousin. Most *people,* on the other hand, at least in traditional settings, will talk a blue streak about kin, to each other and to any anthropologist who is strange enough to listen.

Kinship systems have been a central concern of anthropology because they are a central concern of most of the cultures that anthropologists have tried to understand. Kinship generates most of the rules of the social system in such cultures, including rules of marriage, group membership, exchange, inheritance, authority, and descent. Yet it has never been quite clear just what is the basis of the kin tie, or of the feeling that "blood is thicker than water." Some theorists have long held that it is merely a dilute form of parent-child,

child-parent, sibling-sibling, or heterosexual affection. More recent-ly, structural theorists have claimed that kinship systems are just a way of ordering the social world: You can't, after all, give gifts to or marry or take orders from everyone. Both of these explanations surely have a piece of the truth. But recent advances in sociobiology have thrown some new light on the matter.

J.B.S. Haldane, the famous English geneticist, put the problem this way: Suppose I had a brother who was drowning. How great a risk could I run in saving him, before natural selection would begin to work against me? Or rather, work against the "altruistic gene" that made me inclined to go after him? Well, all other things being equal, I could run a 50 percent risk, because the likelihood that my brother carries the same gene is 50 percent. That is, over the very long run of evolution, considering very many such acts of heroism, the frequency of the gene for altruism would not decline at that risk. If the unfortunate drowner were only my nephew, however, I could only run a 25 percent risk of losing my own life without acting so as to reduce the frequency of the altruism gene. And if he were, alas, only my first cousin, I could only afford to take a 12.5 percent chance of dying to save him.

One can go a surprising distance—easily too far—with this theory, in an effort to explain away every act of human or animal courage or generosity as based on nothing more than enhancing or reducing the future frequency of the "altruism" gene. No such gene exists in complex animals, of course, but it doesn't need to, really; all we need is a gene that enhances altruism in some way or other, and this is not difficult to imagine. But the problem here is that the theory seems to tell us about the proximal mechanism when it really doesn't; that is, it obscures the fact that there are many possible paths to the goal of achieving the distribution of generous acts that adaptation demands. For example, suppose an organism such as a human hunter-gatherer were programmed by nature to save from drowning according to how well he loved; this would result in a distribution of risk across drowning victims that might be a quite good approximation of what adaptation requires according to kin selection theory. Yet the love guiding his efforts might result from none other than the usual processes of affectional maturation, learning, and generalization.

Still, it has recently been shown that some insect species have a specific chemical signal enabling them to recognize their kin by smell. It is not beyond the realm of possibility that a simple signal exists in humans as well—although I would be inclined to expect a visual rather than olfactory signal. Indeed, this may be the original adaptive basis of our keen interest in faces: the "are you related to so-and-so" reaction. That same intense interest and fine discrimination ability might have served to help males detect cuckoldry in the faces of their alleged offspring. It may also play some role in our strong sense of what constitutes facial attractiveness, and, negatively, in our capacity for bigotry; but these may be incidental consequences rather than adaptive functions.

While we are on the subject of faces, it would be inexcusable to leave the subject of the affections without some mention of the natural equipment the former have for communicating the latter. There is of course the smile, and laughter, provided the joke is on someone or something else; there is the suitably timed blush; there is dilation of the pupils, an automatic sympathetic nervous system reaction to what might be called sympathetic attention; and there is the properly timed look away. Anthropologist Irven DeVore used to say that if two people look into each other's eyes for more than about six seconds they are either going to kill each other or make love together. (I would just add that if one of them is very small they are probably mother and infant.) As for the earlier stages of courtship (it used to take more than six seconds), the German ethologist Eibl-Eibesfeldt has filmed, in a number of widely separated societies all around the world, what he believes to be a universal flirtation display in humans: The gaze alternates from the face of the person being flirted with to the side and down according to an expectable pattern, a classic example of an approach-avoidance display. It is possible that this and all the other items above are part of a set of species-specific human fixed action patterns for displaying the affectional emotions.

But it does leave one with the unsatisfying sense of the simplistic. To escape it we turn again to that past master of affectional communication, Henry James. We are in a novel called *The Golden Bowl*. Adam Verver, a rich, decent, and generous middle-aged art collector, long since widowed, has become enamored of, and tendered an offer of marriage to, Charlotte Stant, an exquisitely beautiful, well-bred, and charming person about half his age, who happens to be his daughter's best friend. Charlotte has said yes, but; the but being erasable only by the daughter's—the friend's—and her husband's consent. Charlotte will not contravene her best friend's wishes. We see them as they are about to open a telegram from the daughter and her husband, with their answer.

What he could have best borne, as he now believed, would have been Charlotte's simply saying to him that she didn't like him enough. This he wouldn't have enjoyed, but he would quite have understood it and been able ruefully to submit. She *did* like him enough—nothing to contradict that had come out for him; so that he was restless for her as for himself. She looked at him hard a moment when he handed her his telegram, and the look, for what he fancied a dim, shy fear in it, gave him perhaps his best moment of conviction that—as a man, so to speak—he properly pleased her. He said nothing—the words sufficiently did it for him, doing it again better still as Charlotte, who had left her chair at his approach, murmured them out. "We start tonight to bring you all our love and joy and sympathy." There they were, the words, and what did she want more? She didn't, however, as she gave him back the little unfolded leaf, say they were enough—though he saw, the next moment, that her silence was probably not disconnected from her having just visibly turned pale. Her extraordinarily fine eyes, as it was his present theory that he had always thought them, shone at him the more darkly out of this change of colour; and she had again, with it, her apparent way of subjecting herself, for explicit honesty and through her willingness to face him, to any view he might take, all at his ease, and even to wantonness, of the condition he produced in her. As soon as he perceived that emotion kept her soundless he knew himself deeply touched, since it proved that, little as she professed, she had been beautifully hoping. They stood there a minute while he took in from this sign that, yes then, certainly she liked him enough— liked him enough to make him, old as he was ready to brand himself, flush for the pleasure of it.

Here do we have, I think, as complex a rendition of the affectional burdens borne by the human face as we are ever very likely to require. Despite the fact that the thirteen (they prove unlucky) words of the telegram are in a sense the center of the piece, words have virtually no place in it. The telegram is a mere token, a scrap of information transferred, like almost all human verbiage. Other than it, all the communication of the scene is in the faces, and indeed the very absence of words heightens the emotion. The subtlety of communication is all but inexpressible in words—would be for most writers other than James. The scene could be played on the screen but not on stage; the face is for private communication. Yet it seems to me that some of the most important of all human expression is made in just this way, with language playing just this dry—however critical—a role.

For Freud, the goal of a healthy mental life was twofold: to love and to work. Knowing Freud, the order is probably not accidental, and it is surely not psychological inability to work that causes the greater distress in our own time. Yet Freud also, we know, had some strong notions about how love must be achieved that have not stood the test of time, and that are reasonably attributed to the constraints of his own culture upon his own mental life. We should take care not to repeat such errors in a more modern guise.

Let me be more explicit. It is not so easy to find love that we should look askance at those who find it where we ourselves might not feel inclined to look. For example, Adrienne Rich has written a series of romantic and erotic verses—"Twenty-One Love Poems," in *The Dream of a Common Language*—that, on a recent re-reading, seemed to me the most beautiful love poems written in English in the mid-twentieth century. But what sets them apart from most previous such work is that they record an erotic romance between two women. In other words, a relationship profoundly baffling to almost every notion of orderliness in affection that we have touched on in a rather long chapter. It is a fitting way, I think, to end a chapter about love; and I must hasten to assure the reader that I have nothing useful to say about it, except, There it is. And to all such mysteries, to all such incomprehensible possibility, I say, Bravo.

14

GRIEF

To have in general but little feeling, seems to be the only security against feeling too much on any particular occasion.

—Mary Ann Evans (George Eliot), *Middlemarch*

In the August 15, 1980, edition of *The New York Times*, there appeared on the same page in the "Living" section two articles that seemed to me to say much about our time. The first reported that in Darien, Connecticut, a priest of the Episcopal Church, together with a local clinical psychologist, had written and begun offering a new church ceremony, complete with original liturgy, for divorce. The article indicated that the service was primarily for the children: to reiterate parental love toward them, which presumably continues, and to mitigate their deep sense of loss. They have, after all, lost one parent, or lost each of them some of the time, and in any case they have lost a family, at least an illusion of their parents' affection toward each other, and a certain sense they may have had of the basic reliability of the world—although, to be sure, this latter loss is one we incur somehow sooner or later.

Just below this piece on the divorce ceremonial was an article describing an organization that explains to people how they may take their own lives: as expeditiously, as quietly, and as painlessly as possible. This rather dismal club, which grew rapidly in England, has now won many adherents in the United States. They approve suicide only for terminal patients, especially those in great pain, and they claim to be providing information that will prevent people from making a mess of it; but obviously they believe in the "right to die." What they are doing is said by some critics to be against the law, but they seem confident that the law is more or less unenforceable, or that at least there is legal change in the wind.

We seem to be accustoming ourselves to at least these two kinds of losses: the loss of marriage and the loss of life. As one indication of patterns of marital breakdown, the percentage of all women who are currently divorced has about tripled since 1950. Taking a different statistical angle—divorced women as a percentage of those ever married—demographers have observed an increase from less than 1 to almost 6 percent in women between thirty-five and forty-five from the year 1910 to 1970. The most dramatic historical trend has been in the life-span slope of the curve in this latter statistic: Divorce is increasing much faster in older age groups of women than in younger ones. All these trends are expected to continue over the next decade.

As for the loss of life, fewer of us than ever are dying unexpectedly, or before our allotted threescore and ten. Because of this and many other reasons, it has become increasingly common for educated people—a majority, perhaps, of the readers of this passage—to go through most of life without belief in the immortality of the soul. I would guess that if this could be reliably measured it would show as impressive a change since the turn of the century as do the divorce and mortality statistics. Suicide itself is at present on the rise, and, perhaps, alarmingly so among teenagers—it is awful to think of them putting an end to life just at the moment when they first come to grips with it—but on the whole the suicide rates for the United States are about the same now as they were at the turn of the century. (There were major decreases during each of the two wars, but these were made up for with subsequent increases.) Still the *Times* article does indicate a change in direction, at least a cultural change, that permits public advocacy—not out of melancholy or derangement, not to save face or honor after failure, but to reaffirm the dignity and decency of life, destroyed in the course of a terrible illness. As the inscription on the Japanese suicide blade says, "It is better to die than to live without honor," so these latter-day Britons and Americans believe that it is better to die than to live in pain, completely without dignity; that they have a right, in the words of

Charlotte Perkins Gilman in her own suicide note, to "prefer chloroform to cancer."

But to say that we have become accustomed to these two kinds of
losses, and others as well—the separation of family members, the
departure from neighborhoods, the abandonment of traditions—is
not to say that we have come to grips with the feelings they engender.
Elisabeth Kübler-Ross, a psychiatrist who in the early seventies was
famous for her ability to face up to death (her characterization of the
mental processes of the dying person and of possible treatment modes
virtually founded a new field) became by 1980 almost a figure of
ridicule by committing herself (body, as it were, and soul) to the
service of a typical home-grown Midwestern clairvoyant, the sort
whose séance antics the late Harry Houdini used to delight in
exposing. Thus did a near-great psychiatrist confirm (among others)
the old adage according to which there are no atheists in foxholes.

To be fairer to her, though, we might recognize that few people
have attempted to dwell on the process of dying in so concentrated a
way as she did; no one, perhaps, ever focused so much on the
emotions people go through when they are dying. The dying do, of
course, but they only do it once, and they do not have to go on living
afterward. Kübler-Ross did it vicariously many times, and she ended,
essentially, with denial.

Which is where most of the rest of us begin. Even if we do not
participate in the typical religious sort of denial that most of our
species have embraced throughout most of history, we usually manage it by simply not thinking about it. Ernest Becker's *The Denial of
Death* not only details this process but places it at the center of a
theory of human behavior. Carrying forward the work of Freud's
Civilization and Its Discontents, Norman O. Brown's *Life Against
Death*, and Herbert Marcuse's *Eros and Civilization*, Becker—an
anthropologist who taught at Berkeley—attempted to account for
much of human action as a response to the presence of death; not
merely in the sense that it is usually in the nature of life to try to keep
on living, but in a more specifically human sense that gives the
central place to awareness of death, and to the concomitant fear and
anticipatory grieving. For Freud and his followers, it was the "death
instinct"; for Søren Kierkegaard and some later existentialists, it was
"dread" or "the sickness unto death." Since recognition of the

possibility of death must in some sense intrinsically accompany all acts designed by nature to avert it, it is obviously adaptive. But in the human condition such "recognition" can be heightened to the point at which it interferes with normal functioning. To understand how this may happen it will be useful to consider an organism's response to the possibility of its own death in relation to its response to many other possible losses.

Many animals respond to losses with unusual, yet to us understandable, behavior. It was observed by Lorenz and others that in ducks and geese the death of one member of a pair may result in systematic and repetitive searching followed by maladaptive behavioral impairment for at least a few days. In a related instance, a mother goose lost one of her four goslings and searched so persistently for the lost one as to endanger the lives of the other three.

It has often been observed, too, in free-ranging monkeys that a mother whose infant dies will clutch it to herself for several days, probably exposing herself and others in the group to infection. This phenomenon has been studied systematically under laboratory conditions by Leonard Rosenblum, who anesthetized either the infant or the mother of a mother-infant pair. It was perfectly apparent that neither would abandon the other for quite some time, despite the extreme abnormality of the situation and the total lack of reinforcing responsiveness. These situations call to mind the findings about punishment and infant attachment recounted in the last chapter, and suggest the possibility that mere proximity to a certain individual can be reinforcing for an animal in certain situations. They contrast vividly with (also valid) reports of animals that immediately abandon or even eat a recently deceased individual.

They also call to mind the possible existence of animal grief. This possibility has been known since Darwin's *Expression of the Emotions in Man and Animals*, where evidence of grieflike reactions in animals (as well as in a variety of human cultures) is presented. But nowhere is the point made more clearly than in Jane Goodall's observations of chimpanzees of the Gombe Stream Reserve in Tanzania. An old female, called Flo, had already had several young when her last infant, Flame, was born. Flame's next older sibling, a male called Flint, was just under five years of age when his mother, six months pregnant with Flame, stopped nursing him because her milk dried up. Flint whined, moaned, followed on her heels, clambered on her and threw tantrums if she did not respond. After Flame's birth, Flint's behavior improved, and he was very solicitous of his younger sister, but he still occasionally showed the tantrum behavior of the typical chimpanzee (or human) weanling.

Flame died quite suddenly at six months of age of an apparent infection. Her death was not observed and her body was lost, but it was likely from many other observations of wild chimpanzees that both her mother Flo and her older brother Flint experienced some emotional impact of the loss. In any case, they appeared to take solace in each other. Flint returned to his status as a nursling, although his mother was now quite elderly and he was six years old, the approximate equivalent of a human nine-year-old. His mother never became pregnant again and she proceeded to treat Flint like a baby, a situation that apparently suited him very well. In Goodall's 1971 book, *In the Shadow of Man*, she expressed concern for his future as follows:

> Whatever the reasons for Flo's failure [to wean Flint], there can be no doubt but that Flint, today, is a very abnormal juvenile. Will he gradually lose his peculiarities as he grows older, or will some traces of infantile behavior characterize him when he is mature? This question . . . can only be answered by continuation of our research at the Gombe Stream.

The question was indeed answered two years later. When Flint was eight years old, still "tied to his mother's apron strings" although no longer nursing, she became ill and died. He remained with the body, moping around with a dejected expression and incapable of doing anything else. When the body was removed for autopsy by the investigators, Flint returned repeatedly to the place where it had lain. His activity was severely depressed, and although he had by this time learned to feed independently quite well, he was not taking care of himself. A few days later he too died, and a veterinary autopsy revealed no obvious infection or other physical cause of death. It seemed necessary to the investigators at least to consider the possibility that Flint had died of grief.

The study of similar phenomena in human children has a long

history, but what might be called the modern phase of investigation begins with René Spitz, a psychiatrist who studied the fears of infancy. Spitz became interested in the response of infants to the loss of a parent; his study population was infants brought to foundling homes for a variety of reasons. He observed that such losses in the first few months of life, while they require adjustment on the part of the infant, do not usually, if the care is good, engender serious problems. In vivid contrast to this, however, was the response of infants eight to ten months old. These might respond to the loss of their primary caretakers with a protracted behavioral depression resistant to the most assiduous substitute care. Some of them developed a condition he called "marasmus," a gradual, steady, life-threatening wasting away. It was obvious that this entailed several physical complications, but there was good reason to believe that the initial precipitating factor was the loss.

Since previous chapters have detailed the substantial changes in emotional capacity that occur during the second half-year of life, especially in the areas of attachment and fear, it will come as no surprise that the response to permanent loss is altered during this growth phase. But Spitz was the first to clearly identify this period of infancy as the time of emergence of the capacity for grief. Since this capacity could be life-threatening for some infants, Spitz and his followers recommended that if there was any choice about when to effect a major or permanent separation from a primary caretaker, it should preferably occur in the first rather than in the second half-year of life.

John Bowlby, the great modern theorist of attachment, also inherited Spitz's mantle as a theorist of attachment's inverse, loss; and, at this writing, the third volume of his masterwork, *Attachment and Loss* (titled simply *Loss*), has just appeared. Bowlby, together with his colleague John Robertson and others, has been studying the infant and child's response to separation and loss for more than thirty years. One of the major contexts of these studies has been the situation in which infants and children have to undergo prolonged hospitalization and suffer a concomitant separation. (Since the work of Bowlby and his colleagues, some hospitals have instituted a pattern of rooming-in for the mother or primary caretaker of a hospitalized child.) It is possible to describe a series of four stages in the response to prolonged separation or permanent loss as experienced by most children. A very similar sequence of events follows the reverse type of separation—for example, when a mother has to leave a child to embark upon a hospital stay herself—but in this case the sequence can be greatly mitigated or even prevented by the judicious application of a well-planned, subtly executed system of substitute caretaking.

The first stage is that of protest, which usually lasts for a number of days. Its onset is observed in the Ainsworth experiment described in chapter 10, designed to assess protest against a separation of three minutes or less. It is the phase of active resistance to the separation, active searching for the lost mother or primary caretaker, and complete refusal to accept the long-term quality of the loss. Indeed, at this stage, the loss may not *be* long-term, and the protest may prove to be highly functional. In addition, it is frequently no abstract wail of dissent but specific intense hostility: at the mother for leaving or declaring her intention to leave, at anyone trying to substitute for her while she is away, and at the mother again when she returns. So common are hostile reactions that Bowlby titled the second volume of his series on attachment and loss *Separation: Anxiety and Anger*, thus emphasizing that rage is second only to fear as a child's basic response to such a loss.

The second stage is grief proper, in which the energy of protest has been exhausted, the futility of searching accepted, the behavioral activity generally very depressed, and the mood severely dejected, as indicated by facial expression, quiet whimpering, inability to experience pleasure, and other signs.

The third stage is one of a sort of affectless adaptation. The mood of dejection has disappeared, and there is superficial evidence of recovery, but subtle experience with the child demonstrates an inability to experience emotion, especially affiliative emotion. The child seems clearly to be in a self-protective psychological mode.

The final stage is that of real recovery, in which the loss has been accepted and the capacity for affiliation and attachment reemerges.

This is of course a great oversimplification of what is going on even in a child who more or less conforms to these four sequential phases. They are obviously not so clear cut, and much overlap and individual variation is possible. Some children may skip one phase or another, or become stuck in the phase of grief (as in the Spitz babies) or, perhaps more commonly, in the phase of affectless adaptation. Probably there is no child for whom the recovery, however good, does not include some measure of at least occasional protest, grief, and affectlessness.

Many studies have been done on the effects of prolonged separation on infant monkeys in an effort to generate an animal model for the phenomena just described (as well as of other forms of grief) and in the hope of finding suitable modes of prevention and treatment. The majority of these studies, the reader will not now be surprised to learn, were inspired by Harry Harlow. But it is important to draw a clear distinction between the studies of infant monkey separation and loss and the studies of infant monkey isolation rearing described earlier. These latter interventions begin at birth. The monkey has had no opportunity to develop normal or even abnormal social relations with the mother, caretaker, or other individuals. The absence of social contact, or at least the severe reduction of it, is the intervention being studied, and the result is a syndrome of social, communicative, and emotional incompetence; the mildest forms of it are ineptitude, while the most severe are properly called autism. Fortunately, such deprivation is very rare in human life, and most cases of human autism—total social withdrawal and inability to communicate—do not result from early deprivation.

The studies of early separation are something else again. Here the infant has been given an opportunity to form a strong emotional bond, and that bond is deliberately broken. The infant's capacity for the affectional emotions has up to this point developed normally, and is intact. The response to the disruption in some species at least is very like what Bowlby and others have described in human children; protest followed by grief is characteristic. And the latter response has become the object of active study of some investigators interested in a severe and widespread psychiatric disorder, depression.

The species differences in the response to maternal loss are not trivial, and they must make us cautious about our inferences for human losses, even in infancy. Leonard Rosenblum, who gave the first serious attention to such differences, has emphasized the affectional systems of two species closely related to the rhesus monkey (and to each other), the bonnet monkey (*Macaca radiata*) and the pigtail monkey (*Macaca nemestrina*). Bonnet monkeys habitually maintain close physical contact among adults and juveniles, and growing infants have many opportunities for interaction with adults other than the mother. In consequence of this pattern, the infant responds to removal of the mother with protest and sadness, to be sure, but also with initiation of affectional relations with other adults, one of whom usually becomes central, in effect adopting the infant.

In pigtail monkeys, on the other hand, the infant is not picked up by a solicitous adult. Adults have little direct physical contact by comparison with bonnets, and the mother-infant pair is relatively isolated. The infant whose mother is removed curls up into a ball in the middle of the cage floor, ignoring and ignored by other individuals, going through a cycle of protest, grief, and readaptation. It may recover, but this will be little thanks to other occupants of its cage, who might, it would seem, have been of great help to it.

Further systematic study of species differences in a number of other kinds of monkeys has led to the view that selecting any one species as the model for human reactions would be inappropriate. What we need is a broad framework that will place the reactions of various species, including humans, in a comprehensible perspective of cause and effect, genetic and environmental. In the meantime, we know that for human children the loss of the mother frequently has effects comparable to those in the monkey species where the effect is more, rather than less, dramatic, and this should suffice to keep us interested in them. But we should keep in mind such species as bonnets, which may be more appropriate models of what happens when a human child who has close relations with other adults loses its mother.

How do we know, anyway, that these monkey infant reactions represent grief in any specific sense—that the image of the lost mother or caretaker *as a specific individual* plays an important role? This is a legitimate question, since the infant is losing a wide variety of things it relies on, and we may be giving it too much credit in thinking that it is grieving for a lost loved one. It must be recognized that the same problem applies to the analysis of grieving reactions in very young human children and, to a much lesser extent, in all such losses. However, Rosenblum has provided evidence that specificity of the grief in monkey infants may exist.

It consists of the response of the infant to the mother's return, after the completion of recovery. It is playing happily, having gone through protest, grief, and (perhaps) a phase of suppressed affect, and it is engaged in normal social relations with other cage residents. It certainly has had restored to it much of the nonspecific loss occasioned by the mother's departure. Yet when she is returned to the cage at this point, the infant does not go to her, but has an immediate relapse to the grief phase of the response to loss; it curls up in the middle of the cage floor with a dejected facial expression and severely depressed behavioral activity. This response is so specifically tied to the mother at this stage of the recovery that it seemed to Rosenblum (and seems to me as well) to constitute clear evidence that it is *she* the infant has missed, she that has made the infant feel its grievous pain. That, in short, it is she the infant has loved.

Some general idea of the physiology of these reactions—of what is going on inside the organism—has also been gained in recent years. A group working under psychiatrist Martin Reite at the University of Colorado Medical Center has repeated the separation study using infant pigtail monkeys, but this time adding extensive physiological monitoring. The protest and grief phases of separation response observed by Rosenblum were observed again in four infants. The protest phase, lasting several hours, included increased physical activity, plaintive distress calling, and also elevated heart rate and body temperature, indicating that the agitation was physiological as well as behavioral.

During the first night following the separation, all four infants suffered marked sleep disturbances. Since Reite and his colleagues were measuring the infants' electroencephalograms, they were able to identify sleep stages with accuracy. The infants showed a marked decrease of rapid eye movement (REM) sleep—dream sleep in humans—to less than a fourth of the amount seen on average nights before separation (100 minutes). One of the infants showed no REM at all. Meanwhile, during this same night, body temperature was down from the usual nightly level and heart rate was down as well in several different sleep stages. These heart rate and body temperature responses were just the opposite of those that had occurred during the day, in the hours immediately following separation.

They turned out to prefigure the onset of the depression phase the next morning. The lowered levels of heart rate and body temperature persisted, but added to them now were some behavioral measures that could be apparent only in the light of day. Of the four infants, the two older ones showed a diminution of play and an increase in interaction with inanimate objects. The two younger ones showed all manifestations of the classic grief phase, including slouching or curling up, depressed behavioral activity, impaired motor coordination, and dejected facial expression.

It is of more than passing interest that all four had the same physiological reactions even though the older infants did not show the most obvious behavioral manifestations. It is possible that higher primates gain with growth a dissociation between physiological and behavioral responses to losses, so that dissembling is possible even in the midst of strong physiological reactions. But before considering the possible importance of this phenomenon, we must turn now to the general phenomenon of depression in human beings.

The first major treatise on this subject, and still in some ways the most comprehensive, is Robert Burton's *Anatomy of Melancholy*, long considered a classic of nonfictional English literature, and called by Sir William Osler, the great twentieth-century clinician, "the greatest medical treatise written by a layman." First published in 1621, it went through many editions and revisions during the subsequent few decades, when it was one of the bestselling of all books. It is more than a treatise on melancholy, giving a comprehensive account of then current knowledge and belief about much of the subject matter of this book. The sections "Anatomy of the Body," "Anatomy of the Soul," and "Diseases of the Mind" give what might be thought of as a seventeenth-century introduction to behavioral biology.

But most of the book is organized around the subject of melancholy, from which Burton was an occasional sufferer. He provides the common definition, "a kind of dotage without a fever, having for his ordinary companions fear and sadness, without any apparent occasion." But he makes it clear that he is not completely satisfied with this, and that melancholy can only be defined quite precisely by enumeration. This he does in a magnificent four-page synoptic chart worthy of the most obsessive of modern textbook writers. The symptoms enumerated include: fear and sorrow without a just cause, suspicion, jealousy, discontent, solitariness, irksomeness, continual cogitations, restless thoughts, vain imaginations; bodily symptoms, including much waking, heaviness and palpitation of the heart; and excessive humours, among many other more specific symptoms. The causes can be supernatural, coming from God or the devil either directly or through messengers, or from magicians or witches; or from general natural causes, such as old age, heredity, temperament, nurses, education, terrors and affrights, scoffs, calumnies, and bitter jests, loss of liberty, servitude, imprisonment, poverty, want, "a heap" of other accidents, physical diseases or bodily inflictions, death of friends, and loss; or from one of a vast quantity of more "particular" causes, including "Love of learning, study in excess, with a digression on the misery of scholars," a subject that must have been close to Burton's heart.

It becomes gradually clear that what Burton and his age meant by melancholy is something much broader than what we mean by it, or even than what we mean by depression. It includes mental symptoms ranging from schizophrenia to a lover's moping; really the book is a general treatise on mental illness and its prevention and treatment. But two things are clear from even a brief consideration of it. First, the list of "general natural causes" given above is perfectly acceptable today as an account of possible causes of depression and other mental illnesses; indeed, it can only be admired for ranging as broadly and open-mindedly as it does over the now realistically possible causes— more so than do some narrowly partisan modern authors. Second, most of the causes, other than the predisposing ones of heredity and temperament, have something to do with loss.

The form of mental illness in the present-day nosology that is most often associated in our minds with loss, grieving, and the common modern meaning of melancholy, is depression. This is partly because severe depressions can be precipitated by losses, and because of the high rate of suicide and suicide attempts in depressed persons. But this association is probably an oversimplification. Schizophrenia, the other major psychosis, does *not* characteristically involve depression, but rather thought disorder; yet it is also a condition of heightened suicide risk. More interesting, the acute-onset form of schizophrenia can result from events of life very similar to those that provoke depression in other individuals. As noted in a recent review of schizophrenia by psychiatrists Max Day and Elvin Semrad, "Acute onset is triggered by an event with critical intrapsychic meaning for the patient. In our experience, this catalyst is most often a loss, especially that of a person to whom the patient has been close." Day and Semrad tentatively question the classic current categories of mental illness, presenting various lines of evidence to show that they are not as different from each other as most psychiatrists believe them to be. If they are right, then Burton's seventeenth-century notion of "melancholy," a single vast general protean mental disorder, may need reviving.

But to limit ourselves to more securely known facts, we should concentrate on the psychiatric phenomenon of depression and its relationship to normal grief for loss. Depression is involved in various neuroses (milder mental illnesses that can usually be treated without hospitalization) and in the affective psychoses. The latter appear to fall into two groups, unipolar affective psychosis (also called involutional psychosis), characterized by continuous incapacitating depression, and bipolar affective disorder (or manic-depressive psychosis), in which the depression is periodically interrupted by a short-lived phase of (usually exaggerated or inappropriate) elation.

Distinction among these syndromes, or between normal and pathological depression, is not always easy. In the words of Gerald Klerman, a noted authority on affective disorders, "Feelings of sadness, disappointment, and frustration are a normal part of the human condition. The distinction between normal mood and abnormal depression is not always clear, and psychiatrists disagree about what affective phenomena should be diagnosed as pathological." Still, he is able to list the following features of a psychopathological state:

> . . . impairments of body functioning, indicated by disturbances in sleep, appetite, sexual interest, and autonomic nervous system and gastrointestinal activity; reduced desire and ability to perform the usual, expected social roles in the family, at work, in marriage, or in school; suicidal thoughts or acts; disturbances in reality testing, manifested in delusions, hallucinations, or confusion.

But when we turn to the broader symptom picture, the continuum with normal experience is much more apparent:

> . . . depressed mood characterized by reports of feeling sad, low, blue, despondent, hopeless, gloomy, and so on; inability to experience pleasure (anhedonia); change in appetite, usually weight loss; sleep disturbance, usually insomnia; loss of energy, fatigue, lethargy, anergy; agitation (increased motor activity experienced as restlessness); retardation of speech, thought, and movement; decrease in sexual interest and activity; loss of interest in work and usual activities; feelings of worthlessness, self-reproach, guilt and shame; diminished ability to think or concentrate, with complaints of "slowed thinking" or "mixed-up thoughts"; lowered self-esteem; feelings of helplessness; pessimism and hopelessness; thoughts of death or suicide attempts; anxiety; bodily complaints.

Few and far between are individuals who never experience any of these symptoms—or indeed most of them—some time or other. Most people do not experience them continuously, but then neither do bipolar depressives. Indeed, Ronald Fieve, a psychiatrist at Columbia University, in his *Moodswing*, makes a not very successful but still intriguing attempt to see all mood swings as symptoms of a mild form of manic-depressive disorder.

Perhaps someday such a case can be made properly. For the present, it is useful to consider the real disorders as separate. Both categories of affective psychosis occur about twice as often in women as in men: 8 to 10 percent of men and 16 to 20 percent of women can be expected to develop what Klerman calls "severe affective disorder" at some time in their lives. Using only well-defined psychotic disorders as the criterion, the incidence is closer to 1 or 2 percent for men and women respectively. In contrast, the incidence in first-degree relatives (parents, children, full siblings) of diagnosed affective psychotics is 15 percent, or about ten times the risk for the general population. This fact, combined with the fact that the concordance rate is estimated at 68 percent for identical twins and 23 percent for nonidentical twins (concordance is the chance of twin B having the disorder when twin A is known to have it), makes it necessary to accept the existence of genetic determinants of the disorder. And recent studies have linked depressions that run in families to a gene or group of genes on chromosome 6. Although it is not known how the gene works, and although there will surely be other genes that affect depression, the discovery of the location of this one is an important clue to its function. It is also impressive new evidence of the role of genes in human behavior. However the 68 percent concordance rate for identical twins also makes it necessary to accept the existence of powerful environmental effects. Here we have two individuals with identical genes, one of whom has an affective psychosis; yet the other has a 32 percent chance of escaping it. Why?

Stressful life events have been shown in various studies to be capable of precipitating depressions, particularly if the stress consists of the loss, through death or departure, of a loved one. In one study, 25 percent of depressives and only 5 percent of controls had experienced such losses immediately or shortly prior to the onset of the illness. There is also evidence of remote environmental influences of a similar nature; psychiatrist Aaron Beck, a noted authority on depression, found that the percentage of individuals who had lost a parent before the age of sixteen was higher in depressed than nondepressed adults, and higher in severely depressed than moderately depressed adults, despite the fact that many years had elapsed between the loss of the parent and the illness. This was echoed in later studies of rhesus monkeys, in which it was shown that the response to separation from a peer at adolescence was worse in individuals that had experienced separation from the mother in infancy. Rather than inuring the subject to separation, it seems possible that early separation and loss increases the severity of later responses to loss. (Since young children may react to their parents' divorces with varying degrees of depression and other disturbance, it is possible that the currently rising divorce rate will have an unfortunate "sleeper" effect on future rates of depression in adults.)

During the 1960s and early 1970s, the reigning biochemical theory of the depressive disorders was the catecholamine theory, according to which the neurotransmitter norepinephrine (a catecholamine by chemical structure designation) was high in level and/or rate of turnover during manic or elated episodes and low during depression. There were (and are) several lines of evidence to support this outlook. For one thing, the drugs that are effective in depression treatment interact with norepinephrine in the brain. One early series of effective agents had in common the action of inhibiting the activity of monoamine oxidase, the enzyme that removes norepinephrine from the vicinity of the synapse. This presumably increased the amount of the neurotransmitter available to stimulate the next nerve cell in the circuit, an effect that would tend to elevate the depressed mood. Amphetamine and related compounds, which among other effects cause release of norepinephrine, had been used in the past, but were less effective.

Because of the side effects of these other categories of drugs, the preferred class of drugs at present is a group called "tricyclic antidepressants," named for their chemical structure and their effect. They seem to work at least in part by interfering with the reabsorption of norepinephrine from the synapse by the nerve cell that secreted it in the first place. Since this is the normal means of removal of about 90 percent of norepinephrine that has been released by nerve cells, the slowing down of reuptake by the "tricyclics"— Elavil (amitriptyline) and Tofranil (imipramine) are common examples—substantially increases the amount of norepinephrine in the synapse, stimulating the next cell.

Some other lines of evidence also underscore the possible role of norepinephrine. For example, electroconvulsive shock therapy, which despite its bad name is the most effective treatment for severe depression (as well as a surprisingly safe one) has been shown to elevate norepinephrine levels in laboratory animals. Salts of the metal lithium, a remarkably simple and effective drug treatment for the manic phase of manic-depressive psychosis, also may produce their effect by altering norepinephrine metabolism. Finally, compounds that deplete norepinephrine in the brain, or that interfere with its synthesis, or that poison neurons that make norepinephrine, have been shown to cause obvious symptoms of depression in monkeys, rats, and other laboratory animals.

In the last few years, the picture has become considerably more complicated. Several of the drugs that have known effects on norepinephrine also affect the neurotransmitter serotonin in similar or other ways. One of the more interesting findings relating to serotonin was the discovery that the tricyclics increase the responsiveness of certain brain neurons to this neurotransmitter, and that they do so at a pace that is consistent with the rather slow response of many depressed patients to the drugs—unlike the effect of norepinephrine blockade, which is much faster. It has become common in the last few years in biochemical psychiatry to speak of the possibility that patients suffering from depression can be partitioned into a group that has a disorder of norepinephrine metabolism and another that has a disorder of serotonin metabolism, treatable with two different tricyclics that specifically block the reuptake of one or the other. Direct measurement of these neurotransmitters and their metabolites in the cerebrospinal fluid, the blood, and the urine of depressed patients is now under way, and may soon lead to a biochemical test that will point the way to a specific effective treatment for a given patient.

But it is not surprising to find that as complex a phenomenon as depressed mood may involve more than one neurotransmitter system, even in the same individual. Since the long list of symptoms, or even the central mood change, must involve a great many neural circuits— probably centering in the limbic system—and these neural circuits undoubtedly use more than one neurotransmitter at one stage or another, it is almost self-evident that drugs could modulate the circuitry at different intervention points by interacting with different neurotransmitters. There may even be others besides norepinephrine and serotonin implicated in this disorder.

Direct intervention in these circuits by means of psychiatric neurosurgery has also been tried in cases of extreme and intractable depression, just as it has in some cases of intractable violent fits and intractable extreme phobia. These interventions usually involve interruption of one limbic system circuit or another, but they are very uncertain in their effects—positive or negative, short or long term— and their use must proceed with caution. As neuroanatomist Walle Nauta said at a Neuroscience Society meeting at which this subject was debated, "Our tools are so crude . . . we are digging around with a hand spade among the bulldozers, trying to figure out what the bulldozers are doing." What I understood him to mean was that the treatment methods—or even the research methods—of brain science are so weak as to be almost ludicrous when compared with the forces that act on the brain to cause mental illness.

It is possible that the future will bring methods that combine the best of neurotransmitter and other neurochemical manipulation with a greatly improved version of psychiatric neurosurgery. One can visualize a surgical intervention for the delivery of a drug to a small set of nerve cells in a strategic part of a circuit—better than lesions because it would not destroy a piece of a circuit indiscriminately, and better than systemic drug treatment because it would not deliver a potentially harmful chemical to irrelevant and innocent parts of the brain and body.

But it is also possible that some interventions may have to begin with systems outside the brain. Certainly, in order to understand some important cases and aspects of depression, it is essential to do so. A case in point is postpartum depression.

A large minority of women who have recently given birth experience a syndrome of dysphoria or depression often called "postpartum blues." In one good study by psychiatrist David Hamburg and his colleagues, two-thirds of the sample of women had one or more crying episodes—often with no evident cause—during the first ten postpartum days (an episode was defined as at least five minutes of crying) and 28 percent had an episode longer than one hour. This was a much higher incidence than existed during the pregnancies or later in the postpartum periods of these same women.

In general, it is known from epidemiological studies in mental hospitals that the risk of psychotic and other mental breakdown is five or more times higher in the three months postpartum than in the last trimester of pregnancy. While there are a large number of social and cultural factors that could help to explain this phenomenon, the hormonal changes occurring around delivery should be given consideration. Progesterone in the mother's blood can fall 90 percent from its late-pregnancy high in a few days. This hormone is known from studies of laboratory animals to decrease the excitability of nerve and muscle tissue. The fall at this time changes the ratio of estradiol to progesterone in such a way as to perhaps increase nerve and muscle excitability, and the irritability of the nervous system in general. It must also be noted that a similar (although much smaller) drop in progesterone and rise in the estradiol-progesterone ratio occurs each month in a cycling woman just before menstruation. If there is such a thing as depression or irritability associated with this period of the menstrual cycle, then it is possible that similar but less extreme hormonal changes can in part account for it.

Another hormone frequently studied in relation to depression is the stress hormone cortisol, secreted by the cortex or external portion of the adrenal gland. Psychiatrist Edward Sachar of the New York State Psychiatric Institute extensively studied severely depressed patients and concluded that there is a subgroup that is characterized by excessive cortisol secretion. Their pattern involved secreting higher levels than in normal persons during most of the day and night, but especially during the night. Depressed patients also experienced more daily variation in cortisol, with their early morning values dropping nearly to the levels of the control group. Finally, in patients responding successfully to treatment, cortisol secretion levels decreased toward normal.

These and other findings suggest the possibility that there is, in some depressed patients, a fundamental abnormality of hormonal balance, or of neurotransmitter balance, caused by an intrinsic genetic cause. There is also, however, much evidence on behalf of the proposition that these hormonal imbalances are the result of *environmental* causes; or, in the words of one authority, Edward Senay, that "it would be correct to speak of an affective theory of catecholamine disorder rather than the reverse." This notion is certainly supported by many monkey studies, which show that separation and other forms of deprivation can induce in these close relatives of ours syndromes that mimic human depression not only behaviorally but physiologically and biochemically. In fact, the same symptoms that have been produced in monkeys by means of norepinephrine depletion have been produced in them by separation from an attachment figure, and the same psychoactive drugs can be used to treat the syndrome in both cases. Sleep disorders and cortisol elevation are among the other symptoms that intrinsically and extrinsically caused monkey depressions have in common.

One of the major and most interesting sources of information about the physiological consequences of loss is research in the field of psychosomatic medicine. It is now clearly established that psychological stresses, including the stress of bereavement, play a role in at least the exacerbation if not the causation of some serious medical diseases. Among the diseases that have received considerable attention in this regard are peptic ulcer, essential hypertension, bronchial asthma, Graves' disease of the thyroid, rheumatoid arthritis, and ulcerative colitis. All these diseases are important components of the clinical populations of practitioners of internal medicine. All are largely or partly mysterious in causation, in spite of much knowledge about the physiological and biochemical factors playing a role in the disease. And for each of the six conditions there is some evidence implicating loss and other psychological stresses. In addition, there is evidence implicating loss in flare-ups of skin disorders, certain heart conditions, and susceptibility to certain infections such as the common cold.

It is inconceivable that bereavement or any psychological stress alone could account for all cases of any of these disorders. Nevertheless, a role for such factors is perfectly consistent with the known facts about the physiological and biochemical effects of loss, and the skepticism of some physicians about such factors is more to be wondered at than credited. We can expect to be finding out much more about them during the next few years, and some of the findings will come from animal models. For example, it is well established that psychological stresses can cause stomach ulcers in rats, and although it is difficult to say for certain, it is possible that the particular stress is a condition similar to human depression. It is called "learned helplessness." The initial experiments were begun by experimental psychologist Martin Seligman, using dogs as subjects; they were carried forward, using rats, by physiological psychologist Jay Weiss and his colleagues.

The basic principle is simple. If you give dogs a series of electric shocks with no opportunity to escape them whatever they do, then subsequent experience with such opportunity will find them very slow to learn. They have, in effect, given up. They are convinced that they can do nothing to affect their environments and they proceed to do nothing even when they can. Weiss has shown that there are clear physiological consequences of shocking rats without allowing them to escape (as compared with rats getting the same shocks but being allowed to turn them off). The former have more gastric ulcerations (indicating more stress) and also have depleted brain levels of norepinephrine, just as is thought to be the case with human depressives. It is tempting to postulate that what infant monkeys or humans go through during the first, or protest, phase of separation from the mother is a learning of helplessness comparable to that observed in Seligman's dogs in his more controlled learning paradigm.

Indeed "learned helplessness" is almost guaranteed to be one product of the period of adjustment to any loss, whether it be a loved person, a job, or some of our own faculties. In one of the most moving and tragic studies in all of behavioral science, David Hamburg reported on the parents of children who were dying of leukemia. He was involved in one of the first systematic efforts to provide psychiatric care for such people, who after all must go on living, taking care of their other children and of each other, and who are at obvious risk for mental breakdown. He found that their reactions included universal initial shock, with subsequent intellectual but not emotional acceptance of the facts. Many sought to disbelieve the diagnosis, to doubt the doctor's description of the future course of the disease, and/or to hope for a dramatic curative medical breakthrough that they had been urged not to expect. Many experienced an awakening or reawakening of religious feeling; others insisted on acceptance of doubtful scientific explanations—some of which led them to partial self-blame—rather than accept the illness as random or meaningless.

As the disease progressed, hope diminished. . . . As the child became increasingly ill, they hoped only for one further remission. They no longer made long-range plans but lived on a day-to-day basis. They would, for instance, focus on whether their child would be well enough that evening to attend a movie. . . .

The amount of grieving in anticipation of the forthcoming loss varied greatly in the individual parents. . . . Grieving . . . gradually evolved as the child's condition worsened. The death of another child on the ward had an exacerbating effect on the sense of loss in other parents.

The process of resigning oneself to the inevitable outcome was frequently accompanied by statements of wishing it was all over. The narrowing of hope and the completion of much of the grief work was described by one mother: "I still love my boy, want to take care of him and be with him as much as possible . . . but still feel sort of detached from him." She continued, however, to be very effective in caring for and comforting the child. This anticipatory mourning appears to be very useful in preparing for the eventual loss; the few parents who did not display such behavior experienced more severe distress after the child's death than did parents who had largely worked through the loss in advance.

All these parents had high rates of excretion of 17-hydroxycortico-steroid, a major urinary metabolite of cortisol, suggesting that they were under prolonged, measurable physiological stress. These physiological indications were correlated with the severity of expressed grief, and those parents who grieved primarily in anticipation had their highest levels during that early period.

With the exception of anticipatory grief, which was not applicable, all the above psychological and physiological indicators also occurred in prior studies by Hamburg and his colleagues of victims of polio and of disfiguring burns. Thus the process of response and adjustment (to whatever extent this is possible) to the loss of part of one's own physical capacity or body image has much in common with the loss of a very close loved person such as a child.

Not surprisingly, these processes also have much in common with the response and (partial) adjustment to one's own terminal illness. Kübler-Ross identified five phases or stages of response in terminally ill people who knew they were dying. These stages are *shock and denial* ("No, not me"); *anger* ("It's not fair, why me?"); *bargaining* ("Yes, it's me, but at least if I can get or do or see X first"); *depression* (characterized by weeping, brooding, withdrawal, despair, and suicidal thoughts); and *acceptance* (a restful, weary period almost devoid of feeling).

These phases were satirized in a recent film (*All That Jazz*), as well they should be if taken too literally. There has been some evidence of crude attempts by hospital personnel to lead patients through these stages, one after another, as if they were written on the sky and every dying person had to go through all of them in order. Nevertheless, their characterization represents a significant contribution. Their resemblance to the processes previously described by David Hamburg for parents of dying children and victims of polio and disfiguring burns is unmistakable. So is their resemblance to the process of response to loss of the mother in infant monkeys and human children.

It is probably most valid to think of them as aspects of the process of adjustment to loss, whether imminent or recent, and to expect them to appear in a jumble of cycles, orders, and combinations, with some of them left out for many people. Many die in a state of denial, or anger, or depression, despite a lengthy process of dying and intervening periods of apparent acceptance. It is not even clear that acceptance is an ideal goal for every person. Studies show that most terminal patients want to know that they are dying, but some do not. Some, including some who are highly intelligent, virtually insist upon dying in a state of complete denial. The poet Dylan Thomas in effect lauded his father's final anger in the villanelle that ends with the words,

> Do not go gentle into that good night.
> Rage, rage against the dying of the light.

Given all these individual feelings, it can scarcely be left to psychiatric authorities to prescribe a spiritual method of dying. But they can identify for us some common or even universal features of the process that are essential to our grasp of human behavior.

Because we are, after all, all dying. We are, each of us, long-term terminal patients. We exhibit, at various moments of life, all the known symptoms: shock, denial, anger, bargaining, affectlessness, acceptance. Like the terminal cancer patient or the parent of that patient, but much more slowly, we are engaged in a seventy- or eighty-year-long jumble or repetitive cycle of expression and reexpression of these phenomena. And, just as for those patients, the death or illness of another heightens the conflicts that engender these expressions.

In every known society there is and always has been grief and mourning of some kind in response to the death of a beloved person. In the words of Paul Rosenblatt and his colleagues, who made a comprehensive cross-cultural study of ethnographic record, this is one of the few situations in ethnology where "an ethnocentric perspective has often been productive. . . . People everywhere expe-

rience grief . . . people everywhere experience the death of close kin
as a loss and mourn for that loss." Among their findings, drawn from
careful rating and statistical analysis of ethnographic material from
seventy-eight representative nonindustrial societies: Tendencies
toward anger and aggression, as well as of grief, are universal or near-
universal components of bereavement; in most cases, men and wom-
en respond similarly, but where there is a gender difference in
bereavement behavior, women tend to cry and mutilate themselves
more, and men tend to direct anger and aggression away from
themselves; ghost beliefs and cognitions are "probably universal" and
"arise from the normal psychological residues that remain after a
close social relationship is terminated" (and, furthermore, the occurrence of such beliefs in the modern United States has probably been
underestimated); societies tend to have *either* ritual professionals to
help bereaved persons control their anger *or* approved ritual methods
of expressing that anger; societies tend to have rituals that approve
but limit the expression of grief, and that knit up the tear in the
social fabric; some societies have "final funeral ceremonies" weeks or
months after the death occurs, and those that do not tend to have
more prolonged grieving than those that do.

Beliefs about illness and healing involve, for many societies, not a
rational or scientific analysis of disease process, but a concourse and
bargaining with death. Among the !Kung San, the healing ritual
requires the healer to enter a state called "like death," and may even
require him to leave his body, enter the world of the spirits, and win the
soul of the ill person back by insistent advocacy. The trance dance,
which is the central healing event, involves active expression of hostility
against the spirits, who are thought to be observing on the sidelines.
Even the highest gods are not immune from vituperation. Indeed, the
hostility that appears in trance is so dangerous that it may sometimes be
directed against human beings, and the control of that tendency is a
major goal of the training of healers. Even the most advanced healers
sometimes in effect assault themselves, by running through the bush in
the dark or by heaping glowing coals on their bare heads.

In our own tradition, we have little provision for such overtly
hostile expression of discontent with the gods, and indeed when Job
curses God it is understandable but far short of the cultural ideal. In
moments of impending or actual loss and grief, we are supposed to

remind ourselves (if we are religious) of the ancient Hebrew saying, "The Lord gives, the Lord takes away" or (if we are not) of the inevitability and orderliness of all events in the universe. If it is true that grief almost always includes anger, one has to wonder what it is we do with it—the anger.

The relationship between anger and grief has been a central unsolved problem throughout the modern history of psychology. Late in his career, Freud actually identified them as expressions of one and the same "death instinct," an inevitable component of fundamental human and animal biology. Other present-day depth psychologies of various stripes appear to accept some version of the belief that the two emotions are intimately conjoined; for example, by holding that neurotic depression may really be "anger turned inward," or that it may be treatable by encouraging the identification and expression of suppressed anger. What basis is there for these assertions in the evidence and outlook of behavioral biology?

The chapter on rage reviewed instances, both experimental and anecdotal, of anger provoked by loss. The most dramatic examples offered there were those of the two young men who murdered or assaulted their young women companions; certainly grief was entwined with rage in their homicidal emotions. The first phase of response to loss, even in small children, is protest, which is an agitated condition; the impulse to do *something* concrete is frequently very strong, and the feeling of helplessness that enhances the despair can only be intensified by doing nothing.

"Fight back" is certainly something to do, and it comes very readily to mind, even in situations where it is quite inappropriate. The reason it does come to mind so easily must in turn have to do with the circumstances under which we, and indeed most animals, have evolved. There have always been situations in animal life—predation, for example, or aggressive competition—which would sometimes give concrete advantage to those individuals that would fight during or immediately following the experience of a loss. And, in humans, vendetta has always been a dark option in the context of loss through violence, and has paralleled legal systems in many societies. Among the !Kung, it is a mainstay of social control, and many of the known homicides recorded there have revenge for another homicide as the main motive.

Why such violence might be a cure for depression or grief is another question, and the answer involves presently unknown mechanisms. Violence is thrilling and involves a total systemic mobilization of an organism, a transcendence of social rules, and, perhaps, a triumph over danger. It usually involves at least the secretion of adrenaline and the activation of the sympathetic nervous system, a flood of blood and nutrients to the muscles, a flushing of the skin—there is every physiological reason for it to be invigorating. It is one of the intrinsically easier ways to activate human beings: National economies are often at their most vigorous when preparing for war, and *economic* depressions have sometimes been ended by such preparations.

It is thus easy to believe that a depressed or grieving person might feel better after being stimulated to feel angry and to express that anger openly. That does not prove, however, that depression in fact consists of "anger turned inward" or that it is causally related to anger in most cases. It may be that many potentially depressed individuals who do not show up in psychiatrists' offices are treating themselves by expressing anger at the wrong targets at the wrong times and in the wrong places; this may be invigorating for them but also counterproductive and dangerous.

In any case, we all have to deal with grief somehow; because we are not only dealing with all the losses, large and small, of the normal course of life; we are also, being conscious creatures, dealing with the loss of ourselves, of our own lives, gradually but inevitably. However sedate our lives may be, we have a constant if subconscious flirtation with death and loss, which can come at any time and, in some sense at least, come all the time. Most societies show constant awareness of death and its relationship to life. For example, the !Kung healing ritual in which the gods are castigated may take the healer out of his body into death itself and back again.

Similarly, among the Australian aborigines, a person's life is a continuing relationship with the "sky world" or "sacred dream time" that he or she left temporarily at the spiritual moment of conception. At initiation, at the time of his or her own parenthood, and during various rituals, the relationship with the sacred dream time is reconfirmed, as is the purely transient character of profane existence. Finally, at death, the burial ritual allows a return to the sky world, more natural than life itself.

Among the Bororo of central Brazil studied by Claude Lévi-Strauss, several weeks of funeral ceremonies follow a death; during this period, "every day is the pretext for negotiations between Society and the physical universe," by which they really mean the *spiritual* universe.

> The hostile forces which compose the physical universe have done harm to Society, and that harm must somehow be put right: that is the role of the funerary hunt. Once the dead man has been at once avenged and redeemed by the hunters, as a group, he must be admitted to the society of spirits. That is the function of the *roiakuriluo*, the great funeral dirge.

And in some societies, the promotion of the most fundamental events of life requires an intimate concourse with death. Among the Ndembu, an agricultural people of northwestern Zambia, a woman who is infertile or who gives birth to several stillborn children must be cured by means of a ritual called *Isoma*. Studied in brilliant detail by the distinguished ethnologist Victor Turner, it requires the patient to pass through a tunnel from a blocked place in the earth near a fire that resembles the grave, to a cool place near a river that symbolizes life. The existence of rituals like these in many societies suggests that most people experience the boundary between life and death as indefinite, and that progress through life requires a periodic or even constant coming to grips with death.

Children, at least in our society, come to grips with it only slowly. Several studies show that at the age of three to five they consider it reversible, resembling a journey or sleep. After six, they view it as an inevitable fact of life, but a very remote one, and they may deal with it by personifying it as a person or ghost. By the age of ten or so, they have accepted its irreversibility and universality with a somewhat gloomy finality indicative of genuine realization.

By fifteen, they are at significant risk for suicide, which is certainly one way to cope with death. The average annual risk for this event seems to grow throughout life, but the steepest increase with age occurs before age twenty-five. Thus it rises most rapidly during the formation of the adult human consciousness and the first independent encounter with life's realities. Flirtation with suicide, like flirtation with violence, is one way of acknowledging from day to day the slender boundary between life and death.

Suicide certainly is related to grief and depression. Mourning in many cultures entails a suicide risk, and some even encourage the bereaved person to follow the beloved. Many, although not a majority, of clinical depressions that come to psychiatric attention involve a greatly elevated suicide risk. In any case, the act of inflicting this ultimate loss upon oneself is frequently initiated in an attempt to respond to or offset other losses. And it always involves an exploration of the boundary between life and death. Critics of suicide for terminal cancer patients say that the distinction between them and the rest of us can never be clear enough to draw a believable line. To some extent this must be true. Certainly the suffering of the severely depressed patient can be very great. It is not surprising that suicide rates are exceptionally high among them, especially since suicidal thoughts are part of what leads to the diagnosis of depression. In the seventeenth-century words of Robert Burton, "In such sort doth the torture and extremity of the melancholic's misery torment him, that he can take no pleasure in his life, but is in a manner enforced to offer violence unto himself, to be freed from his present insufferable pains," or in the more plain and modern words of Isaiah Berlin, "The logical culmination of the process of destroying everything through which I can possibly be wounded is suicide."

It is not an easy phenomenon to understand, if one takes seriously all the known facts about it. They simply do not fall into any simple pattern. They defy all the clichés. Nevertheless, a brief focus on them may be useful. Some do form a comprehensible pattern relating to the argument of this chapter, namely, that grief is fundamental, inescapable, and risky. As for the other, less-obvious parts of the pattern, well, at least they let us know how little we know.

Of a randomly selected group of ten thousand adults in the United States, about one will die by his or her own hand in any given year, using the most conservative definition of suicide—probably a substantial underestimate. This exposes each of us to a lifetime risk of about half a percent—lower for some groups, much higher for others. The most common methods, again in the United States, are firearms and explosives, poisons and gases, and hanging and strangulation, in that order.

It is much more common among men than women, despite the fact that both depression and suicide *attempts* are much more common among women. Durkheim knew in 1912 that married persons are at much lower risk for suicide than single, divorced, or widowed persons, and that is still true in a variety of cultures. Americans of Chinese and Japanese descent have steeply increasing rates among the elderly, while Americans of European descent experience more gradual increases. Scandinavian suicide is often pointed to as an outcome of their low homicide rates, but in fact their excess of suicides over ours does not even begin to balance our excess of homicides over theirs. During this century, in the United States, suicide rates have fluctuated considerably, especially for males; there were major declines during each of the two World Wars and a peak during the Great Depression. The rate has increased in recent years but does not approach the Depression level. There is little evidence that suicide prevention strategies work, but no final conclusions about them should be drawn as yet.

Perhaps the whole business may seem less of a puzzle if we change the focus of the problem: Given the tribulations of human life, given our consciousness of the inevitable end of it, given the relatively available opportunities for self-release, why aren't there more suicides than there are? "What youthful mother," wrote William Butler Yeats in "Among School Children,"

> Would think her son, did she but see that shape
> With sixty or more winters on its head,
> A compensation for the pang of his birth,
> Or the uncertainty of his setting forth?

In other words, to paraphrase T.S. Eliot, it might not have been worth it after all.

Most of us treat ourselves to similar doubts about our own futures on at least some occasions. And we may be thinking them, even when we are saying something quite different. All those lame remarks on those inexorable birthdays: Quarter-century, whew! Well, now it's half of those threescore and ten. Forty, that's the big one. Never thought I'd make it. Here we are half a century. How'd that happen? Two-thirds. Still get it up? Sure. You ain't changed a day. Never felt better in my life. Enjoy this one and many more. Still, not getting any younger.

Not exactly. Each birthday a little death, each *rite de passage* another passage toward it. There is a sense in which life consists of a continual condition of grief and bereavement, during which we mourn the loss of ourselves. Think of the anger; think of the affectless acceptance; think of the denial; think of the shock; think of the colossal, ineffable sadness. Is it any wonder that the young person who does not take her own life frequently becomes more selfish as she grows older, abandons certain youthful ideals, and comes to believe that living well is indeed the best revenge? Is it any wonder that the world's religions, great and small, with their venerable, mutually contradictory fictions and their insatiable taste for holy war, have such a grip on so many excellent minds?

Of course, I am overstating the case. The birthdays are also celebrations. One must think, too, of the growth, the gains, the strengths, the learning, the tests passed, the challenges mastered. The circle of loved ones can enlarge throughout life, and even death is marked by a rite of passage that, whatever else it may do, has the function of sealing the tear in the social fabric, of bringing those who remain together to comfort one another.

And religion is more than fictions and holy war. Even the great, organized, and frequently dangerous religions have much in common with the small-scale "primitive" religions mentioned above. Their functions for individual emotions are manifold. At least, they offer balm in the face of great pain; at best, they can lead to humility, and to a concomitant concern for something outside of and larger than oneself.

In his magnificent poem "Sunday Morning," Wallace Stevens attempts yet another sort of stand on the relationship between death and life and on how we may progress through life in the shadow of death. The argument of the poem is that life has its own validity in the absence of a belief in God or heaven, and that that validity is paradoxically enhanced by our knowledge of loss.

> Death is the mother of beauty; hence from her,
> Alone, shall come fulfilment to our dreams

And our desires. Although she strews the leaves
Of sure obliteration on our paths,
. . . .
She causes boys to pile new plums and pears
On disregarded plate. The maidens taste
And stray impassioned in the littering leaves.

The poem makes it clear that it is heralding the birth of a new
religion. It is Sunday morning, and the heroine, unashamedly not at
church, is relaxing in her nightgown with "late coffee and oranges in
a sunny chair." "Why," the narrator asks, "should she give her
bounty to the dead?"

Shall she not find in comforts of the sun,
In pungent fruit and bright, green wings, or else
In any balm or beauty of the earth,
Things to be cherished like the thought of heaven?
Divinity must live within herself:
Passions of rain, or moods in falling snow;
Grievings in loneliness, or unsubdued
Elations when the forest blooms; gusty
Emotions on wet roads on autumn nights;
All pleasures and all pains, remembering
The bough of summer and the winter branch.
These are the measures destined for her soul.

There follows an exquisite, slightly sardonic meditation on how very
boring life in heaven must be, without death:

Is there no change of death in paradise?
Does ripe fruit never fall? Or do the boughs
Hang always heavy in that perfect sky,
Unchanging, yet so like our perishing earth,
With rivers like our own that seek for seas
They never find, the same receding shores
That never touch with inarticulate pang?

And then the proposed "religion" takes shape:

> Supple and turbulent, a ring of men
> Shall chant in orgy on a summer morn
> Their boisterous devotion to the sun,
> Not as a god, but as a god might be,
> Naked among them, like a savage source.
> . . . .
> They shall know well the heavenly fellowship
> Of men that perish and of summer morn.
> And whence they came and whither they
>   shall go
> The dew upon their feet shall manifest.

A primitive, even a "savage" religion, but one without fictions. A religion that takes as sufficient for an orderly, decent, human life the particulars of life itself: the experience of nature in its changes; human moods; the human affections—indeed, even the acknowledgment of loss and finally death becomes part of what makes life so eminently worth living. It is in this context that one can take the risks of loving, acting, losing, and going forward, even in the absence of convictions about heaven.

But the acknowledgment of ultimate loss is dangerous. Freud, we saw, came to believe that death and violence were the same, that both resulted from the death instinct, violence turned inward. The true relationship between them is, I think, at once less intrinsic and more terrible: Violence is what we do from our virtually bottomless anger against death. If we can kill or hurt someone else, especially at risk to ourselves, it takes us out of our selves for a while, and for that little while we don't have to grieve.

What we must hope for, with Stevens, is some sort of recognition that the grieving is part of what makes life precious, that we would not love life nearly so well without it. We could perhaps be less angry at it. We could try, at least, to stop taking it out on each other. Perhaps we could get together sometime and shout turbulent praises at the sun.

15

GLUTTONY

You citizens named me Ciacco, the Hog; and for
the gross crime of gluttony I languish, as you see me, in
the rain. . . .

—Dante, *Inferno*,
Canto VI

There is only one way to lose weight, and that is to grow
accustomed to feeling hungry. This simple fact, known to everyone
who has ever battled overweight (and this means most people in
civilized countries), seems somehow lost on the authors of every fad
diet, every weight-loss or exercise plan that finds its lucrative way
through the drugstore book racks. The two questions that arise at once
are, Why should they fail to mention it? and Why should it be so?

The first is easily answered. One can't ordinarily make money or
reputations telling people something simple they already know. Since
there is little that is new in weight loss, the art of writing about it
becomes that of making what is old seem new, or what is new and
trivial seem new and important. After decades of such writing, as
well as serious research, Americans are, in the early eighties, fatter
than ever, and the problem has worsened measurably in the last ten
or twenty years. On an individual basis, successful assaults on body
fat are often followed by what has been named "weight rebound,"
leaving the problem as bad or worse than it was before the diet began.
On a national basis, we are fatter in every age-group than we were
twenty years ago; in some age-groups, the gain is over ten pounds.
This, despite all the research, all the fads and crazes, all the tennis

and jogging, all the diet schools and yoga classes and obesity encounter groups, all the sugar substitutes, all the appetite pills, and all the determination of the various government agencies responsible for keeping an eye on our health. One can almost hear the fat molecules laughing up their sleeves at us; it is almost as if each effort to dissolve them succeeded only in making them stretch and multiply.

This is not, of course, the case. Nor is it true that all these solutions are illusory; most of them have a piece of the truth. To understand where they succeed and why they fail, it is necessary to review some of our knowledge about appetite, what turns it on and off, and the destiny of nutrients in the body.

Something signals living creatures to start eating; something else signals them to stop. We use the words "hunger" and "satiety," but these have become ambiguous, since we may say, "I ate it although I wasn't hungry." Much research in overweight is directed at giving scientific meaning to that sentence. Or to phrase it another way, What makes us eat when we don't need food?

A sort of organism that stopped eating too soon would not be around long enough to cause even a stumble in the path of evolution. Nevertheless, an animal must stop eating eventually, and any animal does, abundance notwithstanding. The behavior of eating, like all behaviors, is the product of the brain, and the brain must experience a clear signal that enough has been eaten before it brings the behavior to a halt. What is the nature of the signal, and why doesn't it work more reliably?

During eating, a stream of messages, first neural and later humoral, go from the mouth and gut toward the brain. Theoretically, any of them could participate in letting the brain know how much has been eaten; actually, almost all of them do. One clue of importance is that we feel satiated and stop eating long before a meal is digested. This is as it must be, since digestion takes hours, and were we regularly to eat for that whole period we would become grossly obese in no time. It suggests a search in the laboratory for signals that can work on a short time basis during and after the ingestion of food, rather than signals that depend on the body's total nutritional needs. Another clue is that after an enormous meal we may feel stuffed, and the thought of another slice of roast may leave us numb, but we may be tempted by and eat a dessert that has as many calories as the extra slice of roast. This suggests that whatever the satiety signals are, they can be contravened by the right stimuli; or to put it another way, satiety may mean different things to different parts of the brain.

Some of the animal experiments that have elucidated mechanisms of hunger and satiety are not very pleasant; but if they contribute to possible solutions to such problems as extreme obesity or anorexia nervosa—the psychological inability to eat that afflicts some (usually young) women—then they will have helped to combat conditions that pose a real and present danger to the lives of those afflicted by them. That such experiments may lead to treatments and solutions for the much more widespread problem of moderate obesity seems obvious; but less obvious and more interesting is the possibility that they may throw light on the whole mechanism of human motivation in general.

Factors controlling the onset and offset of eating are located throughout the gut, from the mouth to the small intestine, and beyond, to the chemical balance of the body, as reflected in the blood. These factors in turn send signals by means of transmission over nerves or via chemicals crossing the blood-brain barrier. An animal pressing a lever for food to be delivered into its mouth will press longer than for food delivered directly into the stomach; this is consistent with the fact that in the early stages of a meal especially, factors of taste and smell enhance the tendency to eat. On the other hand, it is possible for an animal to be prepared in such a way that the food it eats is not delivered into the stomach; a tube from the esophagus draws the food out of the body as soon as it has been normally eaten and swallowed. Such an animal, which is said to be "sham-eating," will eat a larger than ordinary meal, but it will not continue to eat indefinitely. It will stop and organize its food-intake into meals, but with shorter intervals between them. These studies show that sensory input to the brain from the mouth and gullet can enhance hunger under some conditions and terminate it under others; but that the satiety resulting from such signals alone is short-lived and insufficient to stop eating for very long.

Since an animal pressing a lever to deliver food directly to the stomach will stop sooner than one eating in the normal way, it would seem that there must be strong signals of satiety coming from the stomach itself, and perhaps from the first part of the small bowel. These suppositions prove to be true. The "hunger pangs" we feel in the stomach when it is empty are real, consisting of thirty-second-long contractions much stronger than the usual variations of tone in the stomach wall. Injections of nonnutritive fluid, or even the pumping up of a balloon within the stomach, will stop an animal from eating, suggesting that mechanical filling by itself can produce the subjective sense of satiation. Nevertheless, it takes a greater quantity of nonnutritive fluid than nutritive fluid to stop eating, and the balloon experiment produces a degree of stomach distension that does not occur in eating unless we really gorge ourselves. Therefore, the mechanical signals cannot be all there is to it—a conclusion underscored by the fact that people who have their entire stomachs removed to prevent the spread of cancer still get hungry and still do not eat without stopping.

Chemical signals account for most of the rest of the story. The candidates are both direct and indirect. Relatively little digestion and absorption take place in the stomach, which is above all a reservoir (hence the ability of some cancer patients to live without it). In the small intestine, where the vast majority of digestion events take place, the major nutrients are broken down into small absorbable molecules—carbohydrates into glucose and other simple sugars, proteins into amino acids, fats into fatty acids—which are removed into the bloodstream, first and most especially to the liver. It seemed, and with reservations continues to seem possible that the brain detects the level of these breakdown products directly in the blood as they pass across the blood-brain barrier.

The first theory of this sort was proposed by Jean Mayer, a physiologist and authority on nutrition. Called the "glucostatic" theory (modeled on the word "thermostat"), it suggested that there are receptors in the brain that can sense the blood level of glucose and signal the cessation of feeding when glucose is high enough. Mayer suggested that the central portion of the hypothalamus at the base of the brain could sense *high* glucose levels and send neural signals tantamount to satiety, and it was later proposed that the lateral (side) portion of the hypothalamus on either side could respond to *low* glucose levels with signals that constitute hunger. This theory was consistent with already available evidence that destruction of the central portion would produce a rat that became steadily and grossly obese through overeating (a condition mimicked by some people with central hypothalamus tumors), whereas destruction of the lateral hypothalamus produced an animal that neglected food and lost weight, as if it had lost the capacity to feel hunger.

It was in fact shown that the central hypothalamus has special receptors for glucose, but unfortunately for simplicity, the poisoning of those receptors did not destroy the capacity for satiety in the way that total destruction of the hypothalamus did. Worse for the glucose theory, the variations in the behavior of eating and stopping show little correlation with the level of glucose in the blood or its availability to the brain. This seemed to rule out the prospect of regulation based mainly on brain glucose sensors, at least in the short-run regulation of meal size. A closely parallel theory based on fat-detection by the brain (called "lipostatic" for lipid control) was added by later investigators. It seems that mice are capable of detecting their total amount of body fat in various organ stores and of adjusting their food intake when the total fat is too small or too large. If a piece of fat is transferred from one mouse to another, it will normally wither away; but if some of the recipient's own fat is removed first, it will be accepted. A mouse with damage to the central hypothalamus, however—having a severely impaired mechanism of satiety—will accept the fat graft yet continue to gain weight. This suggests the possibility that this portion of the hypothalamus is involved in the detection of total body fat and in the "lipostatic" effect.

Finally, there is a bit of evidence for an "aminostatic" theory—a proposed monitoring of protein intake—as well. A high-protein meal rich in amino acids produces satiation despite low levels of fat and carbohydrate. More interesting, it seems likely that specific amino acid deficiencies will result in increased intake of foods containing those amino acids—the beginnings of experimental support for the notion of specific hungers. Ample direct evidence exists to support the notion that the brain can detect levels of specific amino acids in the blood. This comes from the laboratory of Richard Wurtman at the Massachusetts Institute of Technology, among others, where it has been shown that if an animal is given a diet loaded with some amino acids that are precursors in the synthesis of neurotransmitters, the level of activity of these specific neurotransmitters is increased both inside and outside the brain. Such effects could easily form part of the mechanism of specific amino acid hungers or, in fact, of feeding regulation in general. Add to this the fact that some neurotransmitters in the mammalian (and human) brain may *be* amino acids, and the brain's response to protein intake becomes even more plausible and more complex.

But it has become evident that most of the chemical signals of satiation and hunger probably act indirectly. Two overall mechanisms for these indirect actions have been identified. The first, studied by Mauricio Russek among others, involves glucose detection by the liver. Because of the preferential circulation of nutrient-rich blood from the small intestine and stomach to the liver, the latter organ is "first to know" that a meal is being consumed, as well as first to know that it has ended. A variety of experiments with laboratory animals now show that the liver itself is capable of detecting glucose coming from the stomach and small intestine, and that it responds to this glucose level by varying the density of neural impulse transmission over the nerves leading from the liver into the brain. These nerves fire more frequently when glucose is *low,* and so when their firing is frequent they seem to cause hunger. Severing them causes a long-lasting reduction of food intake to about a third of its normal level, whereas injecting into the liver circulation a drug that suppresses glucose activity will cause an immediate tripling of food intake. As long as the nerves are intact and glucose is coming into the liver, the sense of satiety will evidently continue.

The second indirect mechanism, now a target of very active and exciting investigations, involves the hormones of the gut. These hormones, mainly peptides, were long thought to be involved only in stimulating digestion—either directly or indirectly by altering other gut secretions. Now it is known that they play a role in feeding regulation by responding to the presence of food and in turn signaling the brain. One such hormone, enterogastrone, inhibits gastric acid secretion; its structure is unknown, but it is known to inhibit feeding by a mechanism that remains unclear. Another, cholecystokinin ("CCK"), is a gut peptide hormone that has direct effects on the brain as well as probable indirect effects. Recent evidence suggests that it may help to terminate feeding by way of nerves from the gut that eventually inhibit the central part of the hypothalamus. The role of these gut hormones in satiety and feeding constitutes a whole new line of research activity, and exciting findings are coming from the laboratory of Gerard Smith and James Gibbs at the Cornell University School of Medicine, that of R.D. Myers at the University of North Carolina, and others.

The goal of this exercise so far has been to review the findings concerning the regulation of one mammalian motivational system. Of all the motives considered in this book, the impulse to eat is by far the best understood in terms of behavior, physiology, and evolution. The story of feeding regulation as now understood is among the most elegant in behavioral biology. Furthermore, it is obvious that the mechanisms designed to respond to adequate food intake by causing satiety and cessation of eating are highly developed and "overdetermined"—that is, there are a number of different ways for the body to accomplish feeding regulation, and even if something is wrong with one of them, others can often take over. This elegant, overdetermined system leaves us, then, with the vivid puzzle of why it so frequently seems to fail.

First, it is evident that various factors can override the satiety produced by all the best efforts of the system. One of these is taste for variety; given an ordinary single-flavor rat diet, a rat will regulate its body weight; but given the same diet artificially flavored in four different ways, it will increase its intake markedly, in some cases eating more than twice as much as normal. Second, social factors such as seeing another animal eat have been shown to enhance eating after normal satiety in various species. Social eating evidently enhances false hunger signals. Thus a round of dinner parties is ideal for wrecking a diet, in at least two different ways.

Another factor that is of greater interest than any of these is stress, which has been shown in various experiments in laboratory animals to increase food intake to abnormal levels in several different species. This fascinating finding evokes the possibility, already reviewed in the chapter on joy, that mammals have been provided by evolution with a motivational system that is not entirely specific; that is, we do not always know what we want. In particular, various different motivations seem to be handled in part by a generalized arousal system in the lateral portion of the hypothalamus. Stress produces arousal, so it is not completely surprising that some kinds of stress can enhance the motivated behavior of eating, even though severe stress such as grief can diminish it. In a context-dependent way, other highly motivated behaviors, such as hoarding, may also be enhanced by stress. And, since anxiety is a form of arousal produced by vaguely perceived or imagined stresses, it becomes perfectly comprehensible that people should feel like eating when they are anxious.

It is not clear that studies of the very obese tell us much about ordinary overweight; but these studies certainly are interesting. Stanley Schachter of Columbia University has noted a series of similarities between human sufferers from obesity and the rats that become obese after lesions in the central portion of the hypothalamus. For one thing, both human obese persons and hypothalamically damaged rats are more finicky than normals. They will eat much more of good-tasting food, but much less of food adulterated with a slight touch of quinine, than will normals. For another, obese humans and rats will eat less than normals if they have to work to get their food, but much more if they do not. There is a known syndrome of hypothalamic damage in humans, Froelich's syndrome, which has among its effects increased appetite and obesity. This syndrome probably is quite parallel in a real, anatomical sense to the syndrome of rats with hypothalamic damage, but it is very rare, and it is unlikely that there is any abnormality of the hypothalamus in more than a tiny fraction of the obese or overweight population.

The stress experiments in animals are more likely to be related in a meaningful way to human overweight. It is a strange fact of the epidemiology of obesity that in the United States and other advanced industrial countries, rich people tend to be thin and poor people tend to be fat, whereas in the poor countries of the underdeveloped world exactly the reverse is the case. The explanation of this paradoxical inversion could conceivably be an intersection between the stress-and-overeating phenomenon on the one hand, and a seemingly obvious fact of life on the other. The latter fact is aptly summarized by the first sentence of the section "Obesity" in the *Merck Manual of Diagnosis and Therapy*, a standard desk handbook for physicians: "The incidence of obesity coincides with the availability of food, obesity being conspicuously absent during famine." It seems obvious, but isn't quite. If obesity were the result of an overwhelmingly strong drive, one would expect at least some obese people to manage somehow to stay that way by procuring extra food even in famine. Or, if the condition were the result of a physiological defect—the making of much fat out of little food, compared to the average person—then, too, we would see some obesity even under food-deprived conditions. But if Stanley Schachter is right about the peculiar paradoxes of the obese, then the latter will be even less inclined than ordinary people to make heroic exertions to get food; and, being more finicky than nonobese people, they are likely to tolerate less of the probably poor-tasting food that is available.

So of course poor people in the poorest countries are not going to be overweight, at least not for very long, since they will experience periodic famine. I suspect that two of the three remaining groups—rich people in poor countries and poor people in rich countries—are motivated to eat, in part, by very similar anxieties. The food is amply available, but, perhaps unconsciously, they are not quite sure how long it will be. Other stresses, coming from the general economic instability in the one case and the condition of subordination in the other, probably enhance the syndrome of anxiety-induced overeating.

Of course, this must be an oversimplification. The quality of the diet must play a role in both cases. Both those groups eat very starchy diets—starchy grains or tubers supplemented in many cases by alcohol and junk foods. Also, unlike the poor of poor countries, their diets are usually low in bulk or fiber. They might be striving to eat enough protein, vitamins, or other specific nutrients to maintain minimum requirements, and in the course of this effort putting away enough fiberless starch to grow obese. But there have been few or no convincing demonstrations of such specific hungers, so other factors must be operating as well.

It is also true that there are cultural factors that enhance or countermand the general rules about social class and obesity. It has been shown that the poor are fatter than the rich in most industrial countries in the west, but in Germany this is true only of women; rich German men are fatter than poor ones. In West Africa, in certain traditional kingdoms, the ideal of "fat is beautiful" for tribal noblewomen was carried to the grossest extremes of incapacitating obesity. But in the absence of better and more specifically predictive explanations, it seems reasonable to postulate the anxiety theory as a provisional model for the obesity of the industrial poor and the agricultural rich.

Rich people in rich countries do not escape overweight entirely, but they keep it under control more successfully. They certainly suffer anxieties, but these are perhaps less strong or assuaged in other ways. And, unlike the West African nobility, these rich are faced with two strongly countermotivating cultural forces. First, and probably less important, they are nowadays made continually aware of the increased risk of disease and death associated with overweight, especially serious overweight. Second, once the poor can afford to be fat, then a "healthy plumpness" is no mark of social distinction; a wealthy person had best stand out by slimming.

Can everyone do that? Evidently not. In a study in England carried out by D.S. Miller and Sally Parsonage and published in the distinguished medical journal *The Lancet*, 29 women who claimed they could not lose weight were isolated in a country house and fed on a restricted diet. They ate only 1,500 calories a day for three weeks, little enough for any of them to lose weight on the basis of predictions from their body size and activity level. Nine of them did not lose weight.

The subjects who could not lose weight had in common a long previous history of dieting, a low basal metabolic rate (the body's rate of fuel-burning under the least active conditions), and a low daily metabolic rate during normal activity. In other words, for a significant minority of this sample, the characteristic complaint that the body seems to be adjusting its metabolism to contravene the dieter's best efforts may be true. The authors conclude, "that among a group of would-be slimmers who claim to be unable to lose weight there will be some who have become metabolically adapted to a low-energy diet and others whose inability to lose weight is illusory." And the very title of their paper, "Resistance to Slimming: Adaptation or Illusion?"

proposed the two main possibilities, each of which they showed to be very real.

More recently, Mario De Luise, George Blackburn, and Jeffrey Flier of the Beth Israel Hospital in Boston reported in the *New England Journal of Medicine* that obese persons show reduced energy use at the cellular level. As measured by the ion-transport-pump activity of the red blood cells—presumably representative of all cells in the body—the cells of the 21 obese subjects were utilizing energy at less than 80 percent of the efficiency level of the nonobese controls. In other words, they were burning less and storing more. This provided the possibility, for these particular obese people, of eating the same amount as the controls and still getting fatter, while the controls maintained normal body weight. This, along with several other studies, has begun to give a plausible ring to the metabolic theories of obesity, at least as a partial explanation.

Thus for some of us who can't keep slim the difficulty is primarily behavioral, whereas for others it is both behavioral and metabolic. But the reader will now be taking me to task. Surely after all these pages of behavioral biology he doesn't expect us to swallow such a distinction? No, I don't; certainly not a distinction between behavior and biology. However, there is a distinction here that is real: For many who try to lose weight there is a physiological system that contravenes their best efforts by motivating them to eat when food is superfluous; for some there is instead or in addition a physiological system that slows their body's fuel usage to prevent a diet from working. Those who have neither problem are, I suspect, in a small minority of the human species—they can live in the midst of abundance without conscious dieting and without a tendency to overweight. Those who have both problems are in a sort of physiological double jeopardy.

A person with training in evolutionary biology now must be beset with a furrowed brow. One way or another—and probably in several ways—the system seems maldesigned. Here we have a species—so far a highly successful one—in which one of the most basic of regulatory systems typically malfunctions; it does not regulate body weight, or, to be precise, it regulates it at a level too high to be compatible with ideal health and ideal readiness for activity. Unwilling to accept malfunction on such a broad scale except as a last resort, our evolutionary biologist begins to rack her brains for a logical adaptive explanation: Something, in a long-ago time, must have rendered this messy system advantageous.

She does not have to look far. There has been much talk about "natural" diets, mostly by people who are ignorant of what anthropologists mean by the term. But there is in fact a quite considerable body of information that can raise that notion above the trivial. It is the ethnographic record of what people ate (and eat) in hundreds of nonindustrial societies—hunters, gatherers, fishers, gardeners, herdspeople, and larger-scale agriculturalists. In a representative sample of 186 such societies around the world (out of about 1,200 believed to be adequately described by anthropologists or historians), 13 subsisted primarily by gathering (collecting wild plant food), 14 primarily by hunting (including shooting, trapping, fowling, and mounted hunting), 17 primarily by fishing (including fishing by line, net, and spear, shellfishing, and aquatic mammal hunting), 15 by pastoralism (keeping domestic animals for meat, milk, or both), 51 by simple cultivation (slash-and-burn or shifting agriculture with annual clearing and fallowing), 19 by horticulture (semi-intensive gardening or orchard-keeping), 56 by advanced agriculture (using irrigation, fertilization, crop rotation, et cetera to eliminate fallowing), and one by exchange.

With the exception of the last society, the mode of subsistence in all these preindustrial social worlds also describes their food base, although this does not preclude exchange or sale of produced or collected food as part of the economy. Ninety-two percent of these economies were described by ethnographers between the years 1800 and 1965, so that the above distribution of economic types may be taken to represent world variation in nonindustrial economies during that time period. It is not representative, of course, of human economic activity during most of human evolution; at say, fifteen thousand years ago, a comparable sample of the world's societies would have been at least 99 percent gathering, hunting, and fishing, and twenty-five thousand years ago, 100 percent. But the broader sample is of interest for two reasons: first, ten to fifteen thousand years of nonforaging subsistence activity is sufficient to produce at least some significant adaptational change in our species; second, for the purposes of the present discussion, there turns out to be common-ality in the effects of the various subsistence modes.

Marjorie Whiting, a nutritionist with anthropological training, studied 118 nonindustrial societies for which information about diet and nutrition was sufficient; 69 of these societies actually had been the subjects of professional nutrition studies, and the others were general ethnographies with good information on diet. After examin-ing Whiting's data, one cannot be as alarmed about the adequacy of "primitive" peoples' diets as some nutrition experts, past and present, would have us be; yet neither does one feel very inclined to accept uncritically the sanguine view of it purveyed by some anthropologists. Of the 116 societies for which ratings were available on the quantity of food, only 4 (3.4 percent) are classified as having "minimal" food, the only rating in her scale that is below subsistence. As might be expected, infant health is classed as "poor" in all 4, and adult health as "poor" in 3 of the 4. Fourteen more (12.1 percent) are classed as having "subsistence" levels of food quantity, or barely enough to go around. However, removing these two categories still leaves 98 societies (84.5 percent) with food supply considered adequate or plentiful.

Dietary *quality* in the sample, at least as far as the three major components are concerned, is extremely high, with the sample averages for fat and carbohydrate falling within the recommended ranges and the percentage of protein exceeding the recommendations by a factor of approximately two. Note especially that the percentage of fat in the U.S. average greatly exceeds recommendations (as well as the sample average), while the U.S. protein percentage matches recommendations, falling considerably below the average for the sample of societies. In the 84 percent of societies whose food supply is adequate or plentiful, then, the diet seems to be superior to that in the United States. Some other aspects of U.S. diet (e.g., high intake of refined carbohydrates, excessive food quantity, and low intake of fiber) underline the superiority of the "primitive" societies' diets. Questions about minor essential nutrients and trace elements present a more serious data quality problem, but some data are available and we will consider them shortly.

Let us turn our attention first to the question of shortages, the major flaw in "primitive" diet adequacy. All 115 of the societies for which ratings on this question are available do have shortages. In 33 (28.7 percent), these are rare (every 10 to 15 years); in 28 (24.3 percent), occasional (every 2 to 3 years); in 27 (23.5 percent), annual ("a few weeks preceding harvest, anticipated and expected, recognized as temporary"); and in 27, more frequent than annual. Annual and frequent shortages are mild, and occasional and rare shortages are more severe, generally speaking. For the 113 societies for which severity of shortages could be rated, 33 (29.2 percent) had severe shortages ("comparable to a famine, deaths occur . . . many persons are desperate for food, emergency foods are exhausted"), 39 (34.5 percent) had moderate shortages ("real suffering and deprivation, a few persons are hungry and incapacitated, weight loss may be considerable, food stores exhausted, emergency foods sought"), and 41 (36.3 percent) only mild shortages ("fewer meals per day than usual . . . less activity, no great hardship experiences, people may lose weight, food stores are used").

In considering the data on shortages we would do well to remember that the more severe are the more rare, and that twice in this century several modern European countries have experienced moderate or severe shortages. Nevertheless, the data demonstrate what is fundamentally wrong with "primitive" economies: They are subject to serious shortages. The shortages do not negate the advantages of the periods of plenty, but they do dull the edge of romanticism with which these matters are sometimes addressed.

The shortage data also give us our first glimpse into the evolution of obesity. Since shortages from mild to severe were absolutely ubiquitous for humans under natural conditions, natural selection obviously favors individuals who can effectively store calories in times of surplus. For three-fourths of the societies, such stores would be depleted or at least called on every two to three years, or more frequently, up to several times annually. Selection could not provide for the eventuality of continuous surplus because, since it had never existed, there could be no obesity and no adaptive disadvantages for those tending to become obese. The "control centers" for satiety in people in industrial societies "think" that the surplus is going to end and are storing up against that eventuality. It never arrives; hence, endemic obesity. We are stocking up for a famine that never comes.

Two things, then, stand out about these subsistence economies, as valid generalizations, when comparing their diets with our own. First, their food is harder to get, and for the most part harder to eat and to digest, than ours. Second, their diet is affected by periodic shortages almost always serious enough to cause weight loss, and in many societies much more serious than that.

The !Kung San are not exceptions to these generalizations but rather exemplify them. There has been much controversy about the adequacy of their diet. In the early 1960s, economic anthropologist Marshall Sahlins (now at the University of Chicago) made a habit of referring to them as "the original affluent society," a rather questionable way to designate a population with a 50 percent childhood mortality rate and a life expectancy at birth of about thirty years. But, to be fair to Sahlins, what he was referring to was their apparent dietary adequacy; their apparent adequacy of leisure time; and above all, their apparent sense of satisfaction with their lives.

Studies by Richard Lee and Irven DeVore in the middle and late 1960s seemed to confirm these findings. They showed that the !Kung spent only a few hours a day and a few days a week in the food quest, that they had many leisure activities, that their diet was well balanced, that they did not exhaust the food-supply potential of their environment, that their caloric intake was just above the minimum for people of their size and weight as recommended by the United Nations, and that they did not aspire to the more well-to-do herding and agricultural life of their Bantu neighbors.

Other studies have since called these findings into question. Spending a few hours a day and a few days a week in the food quest is impressive, but many more hours and days are spent in the work of making tools and weapons, curing skins, preparing and cooking food, making clothing, and actively planning future hunts and gathering expeditions. None of these was included in the studies of !Kung work that made them seem leisured. One might go on to other activities that, I think, are not legitimately viewed as leisure. If what lawyers and judges do is work, then when the !Kung sit up all night at a meeting discussing a hotly contested divorce, that is also work. If what psychotherapists and ministers do is work, then when a !Kung man or woman spends hours in an enervating trance trying to cure people, that is also work. The early studies produced figures that made the !Kung seem quite leisured compared to ourselves, but only by excluding much that they do from the category "work" while including the same activities in that category when viewing our own society.

We must also take into consideration the fact that the !Kung are frequently ill; their physical complaints cannot be lost on any anthropologist who spends more than a few days among them. They suffer from endemic subclinical infectious disease processes from malaria to gastrointestinal infections to tuberculosis and many others, and in most individuals one of these conditions will emerge at some time or another with full-blown clinical manifestations. The !Kung appear to escape the "diseases of civilization"—ulcers and high blood pressure, for instance—but there are plenty of other diseases they do not escape.

Leaving illness aside, most !Kung women spend the entire period from age nineteen to age forty-five either pregnant or nursing, placing a further constant and major physical drain on themselves. Taking all these facts about physical condition (irrespective of the mortality rates) into consideration, we must not only recognize how profoundly their quality of life is hurt by such physical strains; we must also wonder whether some of what has looked like leisure to earlier investigators was not in fact morbidity. When people are feeling ill, they may not work, but that hardly gives us the right to consider them leisured.

Their diet *is* well balanced, but its sufficiency has again been called into question. Stewart Trusswell and John Hansen, two physicians who studied them, viewed their diet as adequate in almost all trace elements and well distributed among the major categories of carbohydrate, protein, and fat, but they considered the !Kung to be mildly undernourished in a blanket caloric-intake sense. They also viewed the small size of the !Kung as resulting from early undernutrition, caused by failure to supplement nursing with other food after six months of age. (My own observations confirmed their impression that such supplementation was inadequate, probably at least until eighteen months of age.)

Recent evidence has suggested that the undernourishment they observed in adults is probably seasonal. Edwin Wilmsen of Boston University has been studying !Kung diet throughout the 1970s and has concluded that there are annual shortages resulting in significant weight loss (five to ten pounds). If Wilmsen turns out to be right (it is possible that his finding is the result of acculturation), then the !Kung will in this respect seem more like the wide range of nonindustrial societies, and less like "the original affluent society" of earlier characterizations.

As for the food that is not utilized but is available in the environment, that argument too leaves much to be desired. We have seen that palatability and ease of access enhance eating, especially in the obese but also in normal individuals. Mongongo nuts are very tasty and nutritious—they are the !Kung staff of life—but even a !Kung can eat only so many of them. If a !Kung woman who has eaten little else for a week straight declines an opportunity to take yet another ten-mile trek to the farther mongongo groves in the heat, carrying a child, and even chooses to go hungry that day instead, I for one would not be inclined to accept that as evidence that she is affluent; she has merely made a cost-benefit analysis that allows the nuts to lie and rot on the ground.

Nancy Howell, a distinguished demographer now at the University of Toronto, has recently concluded her analysis of the !Kung population, and she believes that food shortages are in part responsible for the very slow population growth of the !Kung. In her 1979 book *Demography of the Dobe !Kung,* she presents an analysis based on a theory of infertility most closely associated with the name and reputation of Rose Frisch, of the Harvard School of Public Health. According to this theory, which is quite widely accepted, fertile ovarian cycles are unlikely below a certain minimum level of body fat. Although the !Kung picture is probably much more complicated than this, it is likely that caloric insufficiency—together with highly frequent nursing and late weaning—plays some role in lowering the fertility of their population, by helping to lengthen the time period between births to four years.

And then there are those terrible mortality figures. These too Howell and Richard Lee have documented in detail and beyond doubt. How anyone can call such a population affluent seems difficult to understand, but the argument goes something like this. The !Kung have lived in these same circumstances for thousands of years;

their culture and society are adapted to death; indeed their continued existence in their present social and ecological situation would be impossible without those high mortality figures; and, furthermore, they are used to it.

I do not buy this argument, and neither, I might add, do the !Kung. A recently published book by Marjorie Shostak documents the life of a !Kung woman from her own narrative, given at age fifty-five, supplemented by Shostak's annotations. Titled *Nisa: The Life and Words of a !Kung Woman*, it is perhaps the most moving and intimate life narrative ever collected from a "primitive" person in any society, and it reveals much about the !Kung that has never come to light in any other form. It makes clear that the !Kung are not satisfied with their lot; that they are neither at peace with or inured to the many losses those bleak mortality curves deliver to them; and that they are more or less continually envious of people who are better off, both within and outside their own society.

Nevertheless, they are tough, good-humored, resilient, self-possessed, and generous people. They are not self-pitying, and they do not allow their poverty or the conditions of stress they are under to destroy their joy in life. This far I can go with Sahlins: The !Kung with nothing generally whine and groan much less than the average upper-middle-class American did under the inflation of 1979 and the recession of 1981. To provide some idea of the absolute differences in these circumstances, there is little doubt in my mind that, perhaps not the poorest 5 percent of Americans, but the next poorest 5 percent, would appear to the !Kung possessors of fabulous wealth, comfort, and safety. The average !Kung family, if given that opportunity, would enter that class of Americans without a moment's thought; they are that poor, and more.

Imagine, sleeping in a bed! Imagine, eating fruit in which the fleshy part is larger than the pit! Imagine, a 95 percent or higher chance that your child will live! For the first few months after I came back from living with the !Kung, there used, every once in a while, to go through my mind a phrase in the !Kung language, a phrase that would surely have often passed through the mind of a !Kung, if one had been with me: "Rich people, everywhere rich people!" I remember one particular occasion in Harvard Square on an ordinary day—it is one of the busiest corners in the world—I was watching someone get out of a very ordinary car in very ordinary clothing and I stood and stared and shook my head and the words came to my lips, "Rich people, everywhere rich people." For years, every time I scraped a plate into the garbage—from the most modest of meals, and meals that were quite thoroughly eaten—I would hear one of my !Kung friends asking me from a dark part of my mind, "Are you the sort of person who destroys food?" One of the hardest things was throwing out orange peels; !Kung women save them to make perfume.

And yet, if they were to change places with the American poor, or even for that matter with the American rich, there is more than a grain of truth to the thought that they would not know what they were giving up. They would be trading a life of resilience and mutual support under the hammer of environmental exigence for a life of relative safety and of relative human isolation in which the quintessential social act is comparing oneself to someone else. As for the notion that because of their cultural background and upbringing they would not be utterly changed by the economic transformation, I do not believe that for a single moment. Just as the utterly peaceable Semai of Malaysia could become bloodthirsty killers in the service of Her Majesty's overseas army, so the !Kung family, transplanted to Cambridge, would be capable of forgetting the difference between their new and their old life, focusing their hopes and dreams instead on the difference between themselves and the lives of movie stars, capable, even, of "keeping up with the Joneses."

My reason for this assurance is that the !Kung gave every evidence of such capability in their very own traditional cultural circumstance. Selfishness, arrogance, avarice, cupidity, fury, covetousness, all these forms of gluttony are held in check in their traditional situation in the same way simple alimentary gluttony is: Namely, it doesn't happen because the situation does not allow it. Not, as some suppose, because the people or their culture are somehow better. I will never forget the time a !Kung man—the father of a family, about forty years of age, well respected in the community, a good and substantial man in every way—asked me to hold on to a leg of antelope he had killed. He had given away most of it, as one had to. But he saw a chance to hide some of it, for later, for himself and his own family. Ordinarily, of course, there would be no place in the entire Kalahari to hide it; it would either be unsafe from scavengers or unsafe from predatory distant relatives. But the presence of foreigners presented an interface with another world, and he wanted to slip the meat, temporarily, through a chink in that interface, into the only conceivable hiding place. I let him know that I disapproved, but, even knowing all I knew and sharing his own feelings of guilt, I could not refuse him.

I think that the !Kung situation tells us much about gluttony, both the literal and the figurative kind. Natural selection could not provide us with an effective mechanism for keeping our weight down in times of abundance for the simple reason that it was carefully providing us with the opposite: a mechanism for piling on substantial amounts of excess weight during times of abundance, so that one could draw on them in times of shortage. Since there were probably almost never conditions of continual abundance during the whole course of human evolution—and certainly not combined with the opportunity for physical indolence—natural selection cannot be expected to have prepared us for such conditions.

Similarly with all the metaphoric forms of gluttony; we were designed by evolution to pursue targets of opportunity—to recognize our "id cathexes," our instinctual wishes of the soul, for what they were: dangerous and impossible of attainment ninety-nine times out of a hundred, but perhaps doable once in a blue moon. And what can we expect to see happen when they become doable ten or twenty or thirty times in a hundred? Exactly what we see now: the most brilliant florescence of narcissism since the time of imperial Rome. The obesity epidemic is merely the most obvious result of self-stuffing; your wish fulfillments pile flesh on your body. As a type of instinctual wish fulfillment, it seems to me much the least dangerous. The dangerous gluttons are of course the ones who blindly stuff themselves with land, with money, with power, with other people's happiness and safety.

To read Robert Coles's book *Privileged Ones*, volume five of his epic *Children of Crisis*, is instructive in several ways. It gives glimpses into the childhood psychic lives of the scions of some of America's richest families. Coles is an insightful man, a compassionate psychiatrist, a sensitive observer, and a brilliant writer to boot; so the glimpses are good and real. Perhaps they are not surprising; we see the richest children in the United States wishing for things they do not have; we see them in difficult moments consoling themselves with a fabulous array of toys and the sense that they will one day have better ones; we see them comparing themselves to others who they presume may be wealthier than they are, and experiencing anguish at that thought; we see them—expectably, yet somehow unbelievably—unhappy; and we see them growing into the deeply seated, engrained sense of superiority—Coles calls it "entitlement"—that allows them in the end to suppress outward signs of greed. Above all we see them wanting more, and encouraged to do so.

Coles quotes a black maid in one of the families who feels sorry for her employers; Coles evidently feels sorry for them too, and wants the reader to. I don't, and I am puzzled at Coles. As they say in Hollywood, it is better to be unhappy and rich than to be unhappy and poor. Coles had a responsibility as a physician to those children that obligated him to express, even feel, compassion toward them; but as a social critic, following four volumes about children stressed and sometimes broken by poverty with one volume about the very rich, his transition is baffling, especially since he seems to believe that the riches of the few are part of the explanation of the poverty of the many. As children, they are taught to believe that they are better. They are taught to believe that they deserve all they have. They are taught to want more. And they are taught how to get it.

They are taught compassion for other people the way they are taught compassion for animals. A statement by a twelve-year-old girl about one of her family's servants is typical:

We had one maid, and she said we spent more time with the animals than she does with her children. I felt sad when she told me that. She has no understanding of what an animal needs. She was the one who was always telling me I was beautiful, and so I didn't need any lotion on my skin. I wanted to give her the lotion. She needs it. Her skin is in terrible shape. It's so dried and cracked. My mother says you can be poor and still know how to take care of yourself. If our maid stopped buying a lot of candy and potato chips, she could afford to get herself some skin lotion. And she wouldn't be so fat!

It may sound like the screenplay from an inexpensive remake of *Gone with the Wind*, but it is the statement of a twelve-year-old in the "new" South in a recent decade. Of course, she is only twelve, and she may be her mother's darling, and this routine may just be an imitation. She could grow out of it. But Coles's follow-ups on some of these children suggest that their sense of entitlement, far from diminishing, grows with the debutante balls and the secure places in good colleges and the long-destined right jobs and the proper marriages. As they grow farther from the bosom of the family, they become more the children of their parents, not less.

The vast American middle class is now giving a pretty good imitation of these child-rearing practices of the very rich. All have a sense of entitlement, and many parents who do not teach it to their children directly, transmit it by the example of their own narcissistic behavior. With the approval of our physicians we may divorce at will, demand round-the-clock care for our children (by other people, while we pursue our interests and ambitions), withhold physical comfort, responsiveness to distress, even love from small children, for fear of "spoiling them." When the same children are eight or ten, we spoil the very sense out of them with a cascade of privileges, things; we destroy the sense of proportion without which life is a mere chaos of desperate wantings. Then when they are fifteen, and pregnant, or stealing, or drunk, or stoned, or contemplating suicide, or simply not caring about anything, we consider their behavior to be bizarre.

Nature has endowed them with a system for judging the difference between want and need, between fear and need, between anger and need, but those systems are subject to malfunction for reasons connected with the circumstances of human evolution. By substituting privileges, entitlement, and things for love and the logic of human decency, by encouraging children to want more, by giving them whatever they want, by leading them to believe that they are superior and that there is no end to what they deserve, we remove almost all hope that they will be able to learn such subtle motivational distinctions. And we thus leave them languishing, eternally, like Ciacco, in the rain; a vividly Dantesque fate in which the very source of life's plenty becomes an instrument of torture without end.

PART THREE

THE MODIFICATION OF BEHAVIOR

Freedom does not consist in the dream of independence of natural laws, but in the knowledge of these laws and in the possibility this gives us of systematically making them work toward definite ends. . . . Freedom therefore consists in the control over ourselves and over external nature which is founded on the knowledge of natural necessity.

—Friedrich Engels,
Anti-Dühring

Effects vary with the conditions which bring them to pass, but laws do not vary. Physiological and pathological states are ruled by the same forces; they differ only because of the special conditions under which the vital laws manifest themselves.

—Claude Bernard, *Introduction to the Study of Experimental Medicine*

16

CHANGE

. . . behavior can be changed by changing the
conditions of which it is a function.
—B.F. Skinner, *Beyond
Freedom and Dignity*

Consider a system that is constantly changing, according to laws both known and unknown, from causes both internal and external, in a manner both cyclical and progressive, by processes both reversible and irreversible. Allow it to pass through an infinitude of states, substates, and combinations of states, and to come to rest, for varying lengths of time, in many of them. Give it a multiplicity of potential reactions to a given input, including the modulation and termination of input. Enable it to reproduce itself through certain functions, which have entered the design exclusively because they serve that purpose efficiently, though often indirectly. Endow it, further, with a trajectory of fixed maximum length in time (say ninety years), which carries the system, predictably, through a more or less fixed series of potential or actual states from nonexistence to final cessation of functioning; but makes possible an abrupt cessation of functioning at an earlier time. Incorporate, finally, in the design, a sensor that can detect the point the system has reached in the trajectory, assess the probability of continued adequate functioning, and react, as far as possible, so as to change that probability for the better; except—and this is a crucial *but*—where that goal conflicts with the goal of reproduction.

We now have something approaching in complexity, at least in its major outlines, the human behavioral system. We must add, of course, the potential for malfunction that is common to all systems, whether because of design flaws or unanticipated stresses; although a correct conception of the process of design—and of the corresponding real goals of the system—can make malfunction seem a much less frequently necessary explanation that it has to many previous observers.

And we must add, too, of course, the expansive prospect of change. If I did not believe in change, I would not write books—especially not difficult ones with exhortative perorations. I would find myself a more lucrative, less taxing line of work. This book is, of course, tendentious; I think that is fair, because the viewpoint it represents has not yet been given a serious hearing—not, at least, in its fullest sense in the current climate of thought. Nevertheless, the book is not one-sided. I believe it is impossible to read even a single chapter without coming away with a strong sense of the flexibility and modifiability of human behavior.

The question is, How? "Behavior can be changed by changing the conditions of which it is a function." Fine, and true enough. But, contrary to the narrow credo expressed in Skinner's book, in behavioral science those "conditions" range far beyond the tiny dot that is reinforcement conditioning. For it is not only the dolloping out of appropriately scheduled rewards that shapes behavior, but also a host of other forces that can in a trice, and under the right "conditions," swamp the effects of years of careful conditioning.

The processes outlined by Skinner and his colleagues and teachers and disciples from Pavlov to the present are real, widespread, and powerful. The fundamental one is, perhaps, associative or perceptual learning; in the simplest laboratory situation, an animal orders a set of stimulus elements frequently presented together—constructs them together, as it were, in its brain. Thus does a melody become recognizable to us, or a perfume evocative of a certain woman. A second is classical conditioning, the process we refer to casually every time we mention Pavlov's dogs; in that experiment, an instinctual, or at least very well-established reflex—the production of saliva in response to the smell of food—was modified by associative learning to produce salivation in response to the sound of a bell, the bell that had initially been rung only when food was presented. This is the same conditioning process that brings a woman to the point at which she may, after a few days of nursing, find she has wet her blouse with milk upon merely hearing her baby cry, or the process that brings a man to the point at which he may be able to ejaculate in response to fantasy alone. Or, to take a less exotic example, if a person has consistently approached us with tenderness, that person's mere approach may in time become sufficient to make us feel what, in the beginning, only the tenderness itself could make us feel.

Yet another sort of learning—the one studied especially by Skinner—is the vast realm of operant conditioning. Here we begin not with a stimulus or even with a response caused by a stimulus but with a naturally occurring act. Called by the Skinnerians an "operant," it is simply whatever the animal may do. A rat in a box will walk around, will lift its head, will sniff, will occasionally rear—all operants. If there is a lever around, it will sooner or later press it. What has been shown beyond a shadow of a doubt is that any of these behaviors can be increased in frequency or decreased in frequency by following their occurrence with certain stimuli, called "reinforcers" merely by virtue of that effect. Those that increase the frequency of operants are called positive, those that decrease it, negative reinforcers. Moreover, much is known, and with a beautiful precision, about how various schedules of reinforcement affect the rate of permanence of learning. Some of these findings are relatively obvious, such as the fact that more consistent reinforcement will produce a more rapid learning of the response. Some of them, however, are not so obvious, such as that less consistent reinforcement produces a behavior pattern that is much more difficult to extinguish—lasts longer after reinforcement is no longer given. Psychologists often use this latter fact as a model for the behavior of addictive gamblers.

There are volumes of evidence to show that such processes apply to humans as well as to rats and pigeons. Some of the first really successful treatment programs for the severely mentally retarded have been based upon such knowledge: The patients do not become mentally normal, but they become capable of toileting and feeding themselves often for the first time. Behavioral psychotherapy, which is derived from Skinnerian principles (although usually more flexible and eclectic than those used in the training of pigeons), has become a legitimate and widely accepted form of treatment; it may not work, but the evidence that it does is about as good as it is for other forms of psychotherapy.

There is not a single process having to do with the social expression of the emotions—and not a single behavior considered in this book—that is not subject to some degree of operant conditioning. Under most circumstances, when people we approach reward us in some way, we will approach them again and again; and when people we approach punish us, we avoid them.

Many other learning processes are known in animal behavior and are also applicable to human beings. Habituation, which has been a focus of ethological research and more recently of neurophysiology, consists of the gradual waning of an unconditioned reflex; or more precisely, a narrowing of the class of stimuli that will evoke the reflexive response. A frog will at first strike with its tongue at any small black object that goes past, but will gradually come to ignore nonfood wind-borne debris. A person will startle at thunder at the beginning of a storm, but the response will gradually habituate and dampen. A woman in this day and age may well be wary of a man who approaches her with obvious sexual interest; but mere time spent in his presence without an untoward event can do a good deal to extinguish such a fear, which finds itself, like the frog's tongue, misdirected. I suspect that much of what goes on in the early part of courtship is little more than this. Habituation, in effect the converse of classical or Pavlovian conditioning, eliminates instinctual response components that prove superfluous in the facing of reality; it is perhaps the most universal and common of behavioral modification processes.

Exercise, play, and practice involve the strengthening of perceptual associations or stimulus-response sequences already in existence, whether for genetic or environmental reasons. In a sense, the interesting new process here is the association that goes on within the organism—the linking up of responses to each other, rather than to external stimuli. Smoothing of every complex behavioral sequence can occur through exercise, which presumably strengthens neural links from response to response, from response to stimulus to response, and, most interesting, over the frequently intricate neural circuitry that directs the sequence from the central nervous system.

For example, when a baby's newly matured walking ability is exercised, it is forming a series of links between the sight and feel of the floor at certain moments and the action of the legs and feet at the next; but it is also forming links between the move of the ankle and the next move of the hip; and, most impressive, it is smoothing and strengthening the neural circuit that organizes walking from the spinal cord and brain, the central system that gives the orders. Something similar is going on when we learn to play a new sonata; or, for that matter, when we become better at infant caretaking, at infantry combat, or at making love.

Observational learning has been shown in a wide variety of mammals and is likely to occur also in birds. It consists of a reduction in the time required for acquisition of a response by virtue of the subject's having had the opportunity to observe a member of its own species (preferably a familiar one) performing the same response. In humans, it is the basis of much of education and more particularly of training in many formal contexts in many societies and in many informal contexts in all of them. Observational learning, like many other learning processes, can of course produce undesirable or inadvertent results. There is a difficulty in some cases in distinguishing genuine observational learning from what is called by the ethologists social facilitation—the basis, for instance, of the wave of yawns or coughs passing through a theater audience—in which a strong motivational tendency appears to exist in advance and the observation facilitates its release, rather than eliciting what could properly be called imitation. In some well-studied cases, such as the social enhancement of overeating, or the tendency of children to pummel a large doll when they have seen a film of an adult engaged in such aggression against a similar doll, we are undoubtedly looking at intermediate points on a continuum between social facilitation and imitation.

Farther along on the same continuum is the genuine observational learning that characterizes the way Suzanne Farrell learns a new dance from Balanchine, or a medical student acquires ophthalmoscopy. According to Tinbergen and his associates, as simple an animal as the oystercatcher—an especially beautiful shoreline bird—depends for its very food supply upon such a process; for two years the young must watch more adept adults opening oysters with an intricate routine; gradually, they shape their behavior until it meets the stringent demands that make survival possible.

Most of these forms of learning are straightforward and mundane—even, seemingly, obvious. But the laboratory has quantified them exquisitely and formulated laws. More important, it has produced understandings of phenomena that are not obvious at all, and many of the resulting subtleties have found their way into this book, which is a treatise on the *biology* of the emotions. For example, we have Jay Weiss's helplessness studies in rats. Two rats in adjacent chambers are shocked, simultaneously, at the same level, for the same length of time. But one of them sees a light go on before the shock comes, and can turn the shock off. (The same act turns off the adjacent rat's shock simultaneously, so that, while the rat in control is acquiring the control response, both rats are getting shocked equally.) The behavior of the rat learning the control is being shaped by a complex sort of operant conditioning, which is known as active avoidance: The animal gets a signal and emits a behavior to avoid punitive stimuli. Meanwhile, the other rat is learning helplessness: Its natural tendency to do something decays as it realizes that doing something accomplishes nothing.

But most interesting, this latter rat, during the course of a, for it, unhappy experiment, develops significantly more stomach ulcerations, loses more weight, has higher levels of the stress hormone corticosterone in its blood, and shows greater fearfulness afterward. For the controlling rat to have avoided all these consequences—at least to some extent—makes it necessary for us to abandon the thought that a series of shocks must inevitably and always take this complex biobehavioral toll. In fact, it constrains us to presume that the relatively unscathed rat has undergone classical (Pavlovian) conditioning of a series of unknown physiological responses to the warning light, just as the dogs learned to salivate to the bell; and these conditioned physiological responses exerted a complex protective effect, at least on the stomach wall. Preceding or concurrent with this classical conditioning process must have been a simpler process of associative conditioning, linking the external stimulus of the warning light with the external stimulus of the shock. And if the rat that could not control its shock had had an opportunity to observe its fellow, we could predict that for a while at least we would see an eager form of observational learning.

Thus does one simple experiment in ordinary laboratory rats exemplify every major form of learning known in animals, including humans. But to solidify these concepts with examples from our own species: Simple habituation is at least part of what is going on when an infant makes the transition from smiling cheerily at everyone at age four months to smiling at very few people at seven months; when a child finally ceases to cry for a parent who never responds; and when a man undergoes desensitization training according to the method of Masters and Johnson for the postponement of premature ejaculation.

Simple associative conditioning is at least part of what is going on when we learn to anticipate a haughty social mien from a person with a certain carriage of the head and shoulders; when Muhammad Ali learns that a facial expression of Leon Spinks, together with some other signals, predicts with some reliability the imminent occurrence of a good right cross; and when someone we know very well inadvertently teaches us that a characteristic alteration of respiratory rhythm almost always anticipates by a few seconds the start of an orgasm.

Classical or Pavlovian conditioning is at least part of what must have gone on before a toddler reliably uses the toilet, or before a child's stomach can churn while merely talking about food—a natural version of Pavlov's famous dog study. Operant conditioning is at least part of the explanation for why one does well in school or goes to work in the morning. And observational learning is at least partly to blame when a teenage couple, out for a completely predictable evening, look like the perfect caricature of North American "masculine" and "feminine." Such processes underlying human behavior are scarcely trivial, and I cannot think of a single behavior mentioned in this book that is immune to them.

But these are only the beginning of the list of processes by which the environment can alter behavioral patterns. There are, on the fringes of the Skinnerian learning laws, a variety of forms of "special learning."

For example, there is the "one-trial learning" of the "Sauce Béarnaise syndrome"—the acquisition of a strong tendency to avoid a certain food that may follow as few as one or two experiences with nausea caused (or seemingly caused) by it. Also, there is mode-specific learning—the predictable differences in the rate of learning an association, say, between an auditory signal and nausea, as opposed to an association between a taste and nausea. Finally, there are processes such as imprinting, a term that has been used to refer to learning events ranging from the baby chick's rapid development of the response of following its mother during the first three days of life to the learning—within five minutes, by means of smell—by a mother goat of the precise identity of her newborn offspring. Events like these may not look much like what happens to a rat or pigeon in a Skinner apparatus, but they are learning—acquisition of information from the environment—even though they may follow laws of their own.

A whole separate and special category of learning processes falls under the rubric of early experience effects. Although the importance of these has become a quite controversial issue of late, it has been taken for granted by most thoughtful people throughout the history of Western civilization. Give me a child till he's seven and he'll be mine forever: Kierkegaard said this, echoing the Jesuits, but they were a few among many. This belief in what Jerome Kagan has characterized as a sort of tape-recorder metaphor for the brain—the notion that the brain faithfully records sense impressions for later advantage or disadvantage, that, as it were, nothing escapes it—has been the basis of most forms of psychotherapy, as well as of almost all modern thinking about education.

The animal laboratory studies speak with one voice on this subject. Many of them have been touched upon in this book. They do not merely show unequivocal and strong experiential effects on behavior in various animals; they show similarly impressive effects on the brain and hormonal systems that underlie, or at least may underlie, that behavior. And furthermore they show those effects to be lasting. If you close one eye of a developing rhesus monkey for a few days before the age of six months, you will get an adult monkey with poor or no depth vision; that is because depth vision depends upon certain cells in the visual part of the cerebral cortex—cells that in a normal animal respond to a flash of light on either eye. These "binocularly responsive cells" prove to be linked up to both eyes through circuitry that develops during the first six months of life (you can close one eye for years *after* that age without much effect), and the strange fact is that the two eyes are in active competition for those linkages—take one out of the competition for even a few days, and the other eye will take over the visual cortex cell completely, ending forever the chance of its responding to both eyes, integrating their slightly different information, and allowing the monkey to see depth.

These are the most elegant experiments, but they are far from being the only ones. Throughout the book I have alluded to the many laboratory studies of early social deprivation in monkeys. Rhesus monkeys raised in social isolation for the first six months of life will almost inevitably grow up to be grossly abnormal in their behavior. They will be socially and sexually inept, withdrawn, and have a tendency to be inappropriately fearful and aggressive. When the females are forcibly impregnated and give birth, they are likely to be neglectful mothers at best, fatally brutal ones at worst. Almost—not quite—every attempt to remediate this syndrome by reinstituting various forms of social contact after the initial deprivation has utterly failed.

This is of course an extreme form of social deprivation, but less extreme forms—partial isolation, rearing with peers only, rearing with mother only, and isolation for shorter periods—have also been shown to have important and lasting effects. Even an intervention as relatively minor as two separations from the mother of six days' duration during early life has measurable effects on the monkey's emotional behavior at age two years.

Although the physiological mechanisms by which these lasting psychological effects occur is by no means understood, there is now evidence that the longer and more severe forms of early social deprivation alter the pattern of dendrite branching in the nerve cells of the cortex of the cerebellum—although it is not clear that the cause in this case is really emotional deprivation, since the cerebellum is usually considered an organ of motor regulation, and the restricted subjects also have much less physical activity. But in any case there is clear evidence that these alterations of rearing condition change the brain, by whatever mechanism. There is also evidence that lasting changes in hormone mechanisms may occur in these animals.

It has now been shown many times that environmental enrichment, whether social or inanimate, and/or its inverse, impoverishment, can change the brain of the rat. The changes are most prominent in the occipital cortex, corresponding to the rear portion of the cerebral hemisphere. This region is usually thought of as having to do with vision—except that blind rats also experience changes in this "visual" area when they are reared in enriched conditions. The latter finding has occasioned some serious rethinking of the functions of that region of the cortex—parts of it may subserve more global intellective functions. The brain changes that have been seen in these studies include altered weight, thickness, number of synaptic links between nerve cells, size of those synapses, complexity of branching of the dendrites that receive incoming neural impulses, density of the spines on those dendrites (the sites where most connections occur—where most synapses are), and the activity of the enzymes associated with the processing of the important neurotransmitter acetylcholine; and, furthermore, all these changes occur in the cortex of the cerebral hemisphere, the most advanced part of the rat nervous system.

But lest it be thought that an animal needs so advanced a brain to experience such changes, there is now good evidence that in the brain of the lowly jewelfish, pyramidal neurons (the same ones that are most changed in rats) also change in response to rearing conditions—in this case, social isolation. The "listening" sites on these neurons—the dendritic spines or thorns—change in number, distribution pattern, and even shape, in response to social isolation. These changes are easily seen to be individual adaptations to experience; for example, repeated stimulation of the nerve cell by social experience makes the spine shorter and thicker, after which it affords less resistance to incoming electrical impulses. The jewelfish neurons in question are in a part of the brain called the tectum, which is an advanced brain center in fish but a primitive one in rats and in ourselves; the implication being that unknown lower regions of the human and rat brains—not just the most advanced regions—may be changing in response to experience, a possibility that has been little studied.

In the chick, the experience of imprinting—attaching to the mother hen—during the first few days of life rapidly changes in a permanent way not only behavior, but also the amount of protein production in the roof of the forebrain, the structure of nerve cells in the forebrain region known as the "hyperstriatum," and the rate of metabolism in different, highly specific brain regions, as measured by the rate of utilization of the ubiquitous cell nutrient, glucose. This line of work, which is presently very active, proves that the physical substrate of the emotions in birds is highly malleable in response to certain experiences and strongly suggests the possibility that the permanent behavioral effects of imprinting—not only the following of the mother throughout infancy, but the resulting restricted mate choice in adulthood—is explained precisely by these brain changes.

And the brain is not the only organ of behavioral modification. An extensive body of experimental work in rats in many different laboratories shows that a few minutes of stimulation or stress each day for the first three weeks of life (about half of rat "childhood") causes permanent changes in behavior. The intervention can consist of mild electric shock, or brief cooling, or being placed in a tin can with some nesting material in it and shaken gently, or even being stroked and petted solicitously in the hand of an animal caretaker (this presumedly tender intervention is evidently experienced by the rat pup in something like the way the others are). The resulting adult will be less fearful in an open-field testing situation: It will move around and explore more while defecating less. It will also grow faster, be longer and heavier in adulthood, be more difficult to kill by starvation, drowning, injected cancer tumors, and various other means, and show greater learning ability in certain situations.

Physiological studies have thrown some light on the possible mechanisms involved in some of these changes. The same early interventions were shown to have a series of effects centering on the control system—including the hypothalamus, the pituitary, and the adrenal cortex, the stress-responsive outer portion of the adrenal gland. First it was shown that the adrenal gland weighed more after stress in adulthood if the rat had *not* been stressed in infancy than if it had. This suggested the possibility that stress-responsiveness of the gland in the animals stressed in infancy had been exhausted ("toughened"?) to some extent during those early experiences, and thus expanded less during adult stress. If this were true, it might help to explain the relative calm of rats stimulated in infancy when faced in adulthood with new and possibly fearful situations.

Later it was shown that the secretory activity of the adrenal gland matures faster in early-stimulated rats, supporting the theory that activation of the gland in early life was higher, causing later lowered responsiveness of the same tissue. When it became technically possible to measure directly the amount of corticosterone—the principal adrenal cortex stress hormone in rats—directly by chemical assay, it was shown that in adulthood the rats that had been stressed in infancy secreted *less* corticosterone in the mildly stressful but basically just novel open-field test than did non-early-stimulated rats, but *more* than the latter did when both groups were given a really severe stress such as an electric shock. This suggested that the early-stressed rats were not *uniformly* less responsive to stress, but rather that they did not mobilize their hormonal resources fully until they really needed them.

Most recently, it has been shown that adrenal cortical trophic hormone (ACTH—the hormone from the pituitary that controls the production and release of corticosterone from the adrenal), and even the releasing hormone from the hypothalamus that in turn controls the pituitary's secretion of ACTH, may be changed by the early handling and stress, although it is not clear whether the change in these two controlling hormones in the system is direct or indirect. Other findings of interest: Mice can be treated in the same way in infancy as the rats were, with similar effect, and, more fascinating, the same effect in mice can be achieved by having them reared with rat "aunts"; the degree of distinction between the two halves of the rat brain ("lateralization") can be altered by the early handling procedures; and the differences in growth rate and adult body size may be due to complex interactions between corticosterone and growth hormone.

Finally, one of the most intriguing lines of research in psychopharmacology—the field responsible for developing and studying drugs that may influence behavior and mental life—shows that in many strains of laboratory mice the brain's productivity and utilization of those all-important behavioral molecules, the neurotransmitters, can be markedly changed by placing the mouse in social isolation for three weeks after weaning. There are also behavioral effects, such as the greater tendency to aggressiveness in the socially isolated males, but the relation between these and the neurotransmitter changes is at best very obscure. What can be said with certainty is that postweaning isolation of mice affects the level, turnover, production, utilization, removal, and/or related enzyme activities of many of the major neurotransmitters proven to be at work in the brains of mammals.

There are many other experimental paradigms in which early experience effects are demonstrated, but these are the best known, and they are convincing enough. In some cases the human analogue is clear, in others obscure. For example, there is a straightforward human analogue of the experiment on monkey visual deprivation of the sort in which one eye is closed. This is the condition of deviated eyes in childhood, which prevents both eyes from focusing on the same point. The condition can be corrected, but if it is not corrected early enough, the child will be able to focus both eyes on one point—it will have the appropriate muscular structures—but will not be able to enjoy the principal advantage of binocular focusing: depth perception. It is highly likely that the reason for this persistent aspect of the loss is the same as it is in monkeys; namely, that there is a critical period for the normal development of cells in the visual cortex that are supposed to become responsive, jointly, to both eyes, and that the condition of deviation makes the development impossible, almost as if one eye were closed. If the critical period passes while the two eyes are deviated, there can be no recovery of depth vision.

In the case of early social deprivation in monkeys, there is an obvious human analogue, but it is fortunately rare, at least in its extreme form. This is the condition of total childhood social deprivation in the hands of criminally neglectful parents. Children—a few— have been raised while locked in closets, and the results are psychiatrically very dire. Beyond this, it is difficult to specify precise analogues between human and monkey conditions. Are there human analogues to lesser forms of monkey social deprivation in early life, with parallel consequences? Possibly, and some of the presumed results are discussed in the chapters on love and grief, but much more needs to be learned about them, and easy generalizations are subject to many pitfalls. Are there brain changes or hormonal changes in humans in response to early social deprivation? Probably, but it will be a long time before we know what they are. As for chick imprinting and its various consequences, it is not impossible that there are human analogues, but these will be even more subtle and difficult to discover.

The analogues to the early-stimulation experiments in rats have also been difficult to establish. The first experiments were done with petting and stroking by the human caretaker, in an effort to give rat pups extra "tender loving care." When the pups grew faster and larger, that salutary result was interpreted in terms of the early need for love and physical contact. But when being placed on a block of ice or shaken up in a tin can proved to have similar effects, it began to seem that the pup was experiencing human handling as stress and not as love. It was a belief among the American Indian groups in the Great Plains region that letting a baby cry would make him tough and strong, and this is certainly consistent with the rat findings.

But there is now much better evidence than that folk belief. Psychologist Thomas Landauer and anthropologist John Whiting did a series of cross-cultural studies in which they demonstrated statistically that cultures with infant care practices that are stressful—head-binding, circumcision, ice-water baths, and the like—had adults who were fully two inches taller on the average than cultures with no such infant-care practices. Whiting, together with Sarah Gunders, later demonstrated that cultures with stressful practices in infancy also have an earlier age of first menstruation (two years earlier if maternal separation occurs in addition to the above-mentioned stresses) than those without such practices, indicating that there is a significant and large difference in the growth rate of girls.

All these studies inspired by Whiting are correlational, not experimental—that is, they are not controlled, predesigned laboratory studies—and causal propositions can never be really confirmed by correlations; too many other explanations for the same correlations are possible. But they do suggest a direction for further research, especially experimental research, that could conceivably open a new window not only on the development of human behavioral physiology, but on the process of body structural growth itself.

Finally, the studies of neurotransmitter alteration by means of postweaning social isolation in mice also have no clear human analogues. Nevertheless, it is known that the two major forms of severe mental illness—schizophrenia and affective psychosis—involve in part abnormalities of neurotransmitter metabolism. It is clear that such abnormalities can be produced by genes; but the psychopharmacology of isolated mice proves that similar neurotransmitter alterations can be produced by experience, and that, furthermore, such changes are associated with behavioral changes as well. These point clearly to the possibility that some cases of mental illness, and of mental variations in the normal range (as well as some dimension of most cases) could very conceivably be produced by the action of early experience upon the mechanisms of neurotransmitter metabolism. This possibility deserves much more attention than it has so far received.

The existence of widespread, usual, and important early experience effects in humans has not, despite common belief to the contrary, been conclusively demonstrated, at least not to the extent that it has in animals in the laboratory. Some of the reasons are obvious. Human children cannot be manipulated for experimental purposes, and therefore are usually examined in correlational studies that are subject to alternative explanations—explanations that can be ruled out only in an experimental setting by controlling all variables except those under study. Other reasons are less obvious. For example, the same experiences may affect different children in very different ways. The experience of maternal deprivation, for example, may have no effects on one child, mild effects on a second, devastating effects on a third. This is especially true when we consider the possibility that relatively rare vulnerabilities might be associated with certain genes.

For another thing, some of the effects of early experience may be very subtle—so subtle that they are not detected by the usual measures. In a study of twins by Myrtle McGraw conducted during the 1930s, one of a pair of twins was elaborately exercised in motor skills for the first few years of life while the other just watched. Throughout the early childhood period there were significant major differences in motor development and capacity favoring the exercised twin. When visited by McGraw at age twenty-two, the twins did not differ in occupation or leisure activity in such a way as to confirm the notion of a lasting effect of the early training. But before jumping to the conclusion that early experience is unimportant in later motor capacity, one must actually look at the film she made of the two adult twins performing simple activities, such as walking along a narrow bar. It is perfectly obvious to any observer that the twins differ markedly in what can only be called grace of movement—the graceful twin being the one exercised in infancy. But how do we measure grace of movement? Certainly not by any currently available psychological test. It seems quite possible that in the cognitive and emotional realms of human life, there are also differences of grace and tone undetected by the usual measures of mental capacity and personality, that would be somehow obvious to most observers.

It is easy to find no difference, easy enough so that when samples with different early experiences are compared we can be skeptical of the "no effect" conclusion. Among the many ways to find no difference when there really is one: to fail to measure the relevant outcome; to fail to look long enough; and to fail to look in situations— especially stressful ones—most likely to reveal a latent effect that has previously not been really tested. This is especially true of human creatures, who can be so successful at concealment that important difficulties—anxiety, suicidal thoughts, sleep difficulties, some phobias, some sexual problems—may be revealed to almost no one except (in the fortunate cases) to a psychiatrist.

Many of the mechanisms of alteration of the physiological substrate of behavior have been studied *in vitro*—"in glass"—in the laboratory. In these studies, a slice of brain or a single nerve or a piece of an endocrine gland from an animal is isolated and kept alive so that it can be closely studied both chemically and structurally under the microscope. Such studies remove all doubt about the plasticity of these systems, and they point very specifically to the sorts of mechanisms that are probably acting, on a larger scale, in the animal and human studies described above.

Nerve cells can respond to repeated stimulation with structural, functional, and chemical changes, many of which have been mentioned. They grow new connections, and modify old ones in a variety of ways, including changes in the size and shape of dendritic thorns and the size and structure of synapses. They increase their production of key enzymes involved, in turn, in the production of neurotransmitters. They change the chemistry of their membranes, upon which depends all electrical conduction over them—and this is what nervous system activity consists of. They change, indeed, in many ways, the characteristics of that electrical activity, as measured by the most advanced and sensitive electronic devices. And they change the nature of their chemical relations with non-neural cells around them, including those that are necessary for their life support—the glia. These too may play a role in learning.

Finally, nerve cells die, and they are never, alas, born again. Unlike most cells in the body, which "turn over"—die and are replaced—every few days, every few weeks, or at least every few months, nerve cells cannot be replaced after birth in humans, and no new ones are born by means of cell division, with the possible exception of one or two groups of very tiny "granule" cells. Perhaps this is why we are able to record experience and use it, adapting to our environments; like few other cells in the body, nerve cells are with us throughout this life, and are exactly as old as we are, ticking forward like the grandfather clock in the song. But not all of them. An estimated fifteen thousand die every day, never to be replaced. Considering that there are ten to a hundred billion, this is a small number; but as neuroanatomist Walle Nauta often says in lecture, after a certain age one starts to wonder if they aren't adding up. Each day a tiny death of the brain, an infinitesimal "stroke," an unknown loss of structure, possibly function. The thought is chilling.

But another neuroanatomist, Paul Yakovlev, sees hope in it. He presumes that the death of nerve cells is not random, that it is the least used ones that die. Consequently, the nervous system, by means of slow death, is actually sculpting itself, adapting itself daily to what he has called "the pathos of life experience." Because of this, perhaps, we become smoother in our actions, and difficult ones become easy—until we lose too much. Because of this, too, we may develop a certain inflexibility. It is an intriguing notion, and one that deserves more attention from people who study the neural basis of learning and individual adaptation; these investigators, of a much younger generation than Yakovlev's, have focused almost exclusively on the physiology of individual nerve cells, frequently losing sight of the forest that is the nervous system. And that larger picture can only be understood by means of the difficult, classical process of studying the anatomy of that system.

Nerve cells are not the only cells that change. Glands, including those that secrete behavioral molecules, can become larger or smaller in response to use, and they have at their disposal a means that the nervous system does not: the potential for producing new cells by cell division. They may not be as structurally elegant as the nervous system, but they are certainly as active, and their secretory products can regulate some aspects of nervous system function. Moreover, an individual gland cell's functional and chemical characteristics can also be changed through use.

Such capacities for adaptation go way beyond the endocrine glands. The skin forms calluses in response to frictional pressure, and similar processes may go on in the wall of the gut. Muscles hypertrophy (get larger) in response to use, and their tendinous insertions get longer and stronger. Even bone—tedious, reliable, uninspiring bone—responds to the stress of use with a major intricate functional and structural florescence, so that under the microscope a sliver of bone from a jogger's leg is noticeably more complex in its living structure and blood supply than the bone of a nonjogger the same age and sex— a tribute to the plasticity not just of the nervous system but of the body.

What then of those famous genes? Have they been forgotten? What about all those countless studies that demonstrate their powerful effects?

Some of those studies are good, but even the good ones may need reinterpreting. One of the major sources of difficulty with behavior-genetic studies (and in fact, of genetic studies in general) is the phenomenon of the statistical interaction effect. This is not like the common-parlance sense of gene-environment interaction, the notion that the gene and the environment influence each other; that is certainly true, but the statistical interaction effect is a much subtler, somewhat more difficult concept to grasp, and one that is well worth a bit of attention.

Suppose we have the simplest Mendelian situation, say the control of the height of pea plants by a single gene. Let us say that the gene "Tall" produces plants averaging 12 inches in height, and the gene "Short" produces plants 4 inches shorter. Suppose further that we have a new fertilizer, and that when we try it on "Short" we get 12-inch-high plants—we have abolished the difference between "Short" and "Tall" by means of the fertilizer. We then proceed to predict that "Tall" will respond to the fertilizer by growing to a height of 16 inches. Or if we are very clever, we presume that the fertilizer may work not by adding a fixed amount to the height of plants but by adding a fixed percentage, in this case 50 percent. We cagily predict an increase for "Tall" of between 4 and 6 inches to a height of from 16 to 18 inches, and we advise farmers accordingly.

Alas, we should have done the next experiment, instead of theorizing. We have not looked properly before leaping. We have failed to take into account the possibility that those same genes "Tall" and "Short" that produced so much difference in initial height, by unknown chemical means, may also produce a completely different reaction to the new fertilizer. The farmers who buy the fertilizer and use it on their "Tall" plants get 10-inch-high plants—the shortest of all—and we lose our job at the agricultural institute.

This fanciful instance aside, there is much evidence that such gene-environment interaction effects are important in nature. In plain language, the effects of an environmental intervention on one gene or set of genes can often not be used to predict the effects of the identical environmental intervention against a different genetic background, and the effects of genes and environment are not additive. Equally important is that we do not conclude from our sad experience that "Tall" is insusceptible to increase in height by fertilizers, lest we lose our next job as well, ceding it to a competitor who, realizing that the next new fertilizer has to be tried on "Tall" on its own merits, gets a 3-foot-high pea plant for his effort.

There are many real examples of this phenomenon. One that is often referred to by Richard Lewontin, a severe critic of behavior genetics, is an experiment in the laboratory of the great geneticist Theodosius Dobzhansky. Fruit flies were incubated at 16.5°C, 21°C, and 25°C, and the length of time they survived was measured. The genetic strain the flies came from proved as important as the temperature in predicting survival.

But what you didn't have was some strains that outsurvived others at all temperatures. On the contrary, three strains survived best at the high temperature, less well at the intermediate one, and worst at the low temperature; seven strains did the opposite, decreasing in likelihood of survival with temperature increases; seven strains did not respond to temperature changes at all, but survived equally well at all temperatures; four strains survived better at the low and high temperatures than they did at the middle temperature; and two strains survived best at the middle temperature and worse at the extremes. In other words, the seemingly sensible question, How do fruit flies respond to temperature changes, and which is the best temperature for them? is, after the experiment, a foolish one. Because of the large statistical interaction effect, the prediction must be made not for fruit flies in general, but strain by strain.

This seems an irrelevant subtlety until we realize that most of what has been written about human behavioral genetics, especially the genetics of intelligence, has assumed the nonexistence of such interaction effects. All the calculations that lead to every estimate of the heritability of intelligence, most of which come from twin studies, are subject to this possible error. But the most egregious example, as Lewontin has pointed out, came at the end of Arthur Jensen's 1968 monograph attempting to demonstrate race differences in intelligence.

Claiming to have shown that known race differences in intelligence were genetically based (he had not shown this), Jensen irrelevantly and dangerously went on to conclude that intervention programs in schools and preschools are pretty useless. Indeed, the very title of the paper, "How Much Can We Boost IQ and Scholastic Achievement?" implied this unwarranted conclusion. But worst of all, he drew a graph (graphs are sometimes more dangerous than words, because people more often believe them) showing the races as separate lines, increasing in intelligence in response to environmental enrichment. At the origin of the graph, the lines were joined, suggesting that under conditions of total environmental impoverishment the races would be equally low in intelligence. But with enrichment, the lines diverged; both increased in this fantasy world as the environment improved, but one of the lines increased much faster, so that the better the environment got, the bigger was the difference between the two.

Jensen thus invented out of whole cloth, not citing a shred of evidence, the idea of a specific gene-environment interaction effect, according to which blacks in enriched environments of the future would suffer even more by comparison with whites than they do in the poor and moderate environments of the present day. Thus Jensen mounted a frontal, deliberate assault on the efforts of decent people to intervene to improve the school performance of blacks. The evidence we now have points to a very different graph; since 1968, blacks have excelled in virtually every enriched environment they have been placed in, most of which they were previously barred from, and this in only the first few years of more or less equal opportunity. It is quite likely in fact that the real curves for the two races will one day be superimposable on each other.

What about evolution? Can we rely at least on the relationship of evolutionary change to the genes? Not entirely. In fact there is now much evidence that important characteristics of individuals, especially but not exclusively in the realm of behavior, can be passed on from generation to generation in a quite stable way outside of the genes. Several examples of this mechanism—song-sparrow dialects in California, potato washing in Japanese monkeys, and status in rhesus monkey groups—were discussed in an earlier chapter. The oyster-catchers mentioned in this chapter are another example, and the tool making observed among wild chimpanzees, already described, is yet another. In the laboratory, Victor Denenberg, famous for work on infant stress in rats, has shown that the behavior of those animals is influenced by the experience their grandmothers had as infants, even if these grandmothers are only foster-grandmothers. His paper about it, "Nongenetic Transmission of Behavior," should be required reading for everyone who thinks of the evolution of behavior only in terms of genes.

I happen to know a descendant of Charles Darwin's. She admires him, but knows not much more about what he had to say than the average intelligent person on the street. I on the other hand teach his ideas and write about them year in and year out. I also happen to know a descendant of Ralph Emerson's. She finds him unreadable, whereas I have read his essays at some of the darkest times of my life, and taken comfort from them. Who are the real descendants of Darwin and Emerson? Well, *they* are, of course, if you ask about hair color or red-blood-cell surface antigens, or even, in fact, if you ask about native intelligence. But if you consider another aspect of their phenotype, the things they said and wrote and considered very important, I am the one who is, more than a hundred years later, repeating them, and in addition gaining advantage from doing so; different descendants, and indeed different modes of inheritance, for different characteristics of individuals.

In the early days of what is now called sociobiology, when it first became common to talk about "genes for altruism," I used to try to entertain students with the following countertheory. I invented a hormone, "altruin," which I postulated as causing altruistic behavior in a hypothetical bird species by crossing the blood-brain barrier into the limbic system. (This was ludicrous, but at least as plausible as a "gene for altruism.") According to my theory, a compound known as proaltruin was contained in certain foods; it was eaten by the bird, and then converted to altruin by the enzyme proaltruin hydrolase. Only then could it cross the blood-brain barrier and do its work. It was removed from the brain by conversion to altruic acid (this required the enzyme altruin oxidase) and excreted in the urine.

Now, it was clear from this that a gene could affect altruistic behavior by altering the structure of one of the two enzymes (proaltruin hydrolase or altruin oxidase), which is just the sort of thing genes do best. Suppose a gene mutation occurs, by means of DNA miscopying, and the gene coding proaltruin hydrolase now produces a slightly different enzyme. Suppose further that the affected individual experiences a 10 percent increase in proaltruin hydrolase activity, a 7 percent increase in altruin in the brain, and a corresponding 7 percent increase in altruism, which may be advantageous or may not.

Unfortunately for simplicity, however, soon after the mutation appears, a new fruit-bearing bush colonizes the bird's ecological niche. Eating this berry, which some of the birds do, turns out to be inadvertently advantageous, since it has aphrodisiac qualities that increase reproductive success. However, it contains no proaltruin, yet is rapidly replacing the former berry, which contained ample amounts of proaltruin. The resulting decrease in the available precursor for altruin synthesis causes a decrease in altruin level in the blood, despite the gene that works the other way. This gene is still slightly favored, however, and over the course of several hundred generations has replaced the former gene, which coded for less active proaltruin hydrolase. But the new berry is also replacing the old berry, much more rapidly in fact, and the net change in the level of altruin in the blood (and of altruistic behavior) is a decrease of 15 percent, despite a mutation to increased altruism that has been favored by natural selection.

Meanwhile, another mutation occurs at the same gene locus, causing a whopping 50 percent increase in the activity of the same altruin-synthesizing enzyme. Like the first, it causes altruism that is distributed specifically to genetic relatives, preferentially according to relatedness, and so can be selected for according to the usual kin selection mechanisms. But unfortunately for the elegance of theory, a glacier is advancing on the niche. Ambient temperature decreases three degrees (over the course of many generations). This cooling has the effect of changing the birds' thermoregulatory physiology in such a way as to increase the ionization of altruin in the blood, thus reducing by 30 percent its ability to cross the blood-brain barrier. This ionization also happens to promote more efficient removal of altruin by altruin oxidase—premature removal, in fact—reducing total altruin in the brain by another 5 percent. The net change since the first mutation in the total amount of altruistic behavior observed in the bird population is zero.

The point of this exercise was not to deny the possible influence of genes on complex behavior—indeed, it assigns to them more powerful influences than many thoughtful people would allow. Neither does it suggest that natural selection—and its subsumed process, kin selection—cannot change the incidence of genes controlling complex behavior in a given higher species; this in fact happens in the example. What it suggests is something subtler and quite different;

namely, that in the real world, the nongenetic sources of variation in behavior may be so large as to swamp any effects of the genes.

This does not mean that the genetic change is not occurring or is without effect. It just means that it is slow and small compared to other forces, and that it will therefore be unhelpful to us in our effort to explain what we see and predict what will happen next. In this example, the nongenetic effects were large enough to equal and cancel the effects of the gene changes. But suppose the real nongenetic forces are much larger than that? Ten times, a hundred, a thousand times larger? What use would there be in taking the genetic change into account? What chance would there even be of detecting it? In the private words of a famous geneticist, if the nongenetic forces are large enough compared to the genetic ones for the time period under study, then one would no more take the genetic ones into account than one would measure and be concerned about the force exerted on a rocket fired from Cape Canaveral by the gravitational field of a distant star. In other words, a real force, a predictable force, but an utterly negligible one.

It is not a trivial issue. Consider the probable fact that in the year 1900 perhaps 10 percent of the human species (I am guessing) exhibited the behaviors of reading and writing, while in the year 2000 perhaps 90 percent of the species will exhibit the same behaviors; that is, in one century (three generations), the species will have changed in a major way its mode of behavioral adaptation. Or consider the fact that the average number of children per female lifetime for the same species is at the present time somewhere in the vicinity of four, whereas a hundred years from now it will be somewhere in the vicinity of two; another major change in adaptation in three generations.

Now, one can in fact mention the genes. One can do some handwaving of the sort that says, "It is the genes that make people seize the advantage afforded by reading and writing" and "It is the genes that enable a population to lower its reproductive rate when conditions require it." These are true, but they say virtually nothing about the intimate details of the two very intriguing processes mentioned. One can even refer to genes in a more specific way—for example, to people who for genetic reasons are dyslexic, or people who continue to win at reproductive competition by churning out twenty children while the species drops its birth rate. These are real effects, interesting in the abstract, but for practical purposes, in relation to the questions at hand, in the time period under study, totally trivial—like the term that is dropped out in a mathematical derivation because it complicates things more than it is worth and it is really small enough to be safely ignored.

To the question, How could these two changes in the phenotype of the species occur in only one hundred years? the genes have nothing to say. That question can only be answered in terms of the conventional and rapidly developing knowledge of behavioral and social science: the laws of learning, the laws of cognition, the laws of social psychology, the laws of economics, the laws of culture change. That the genes underlie all these laws is a high-minded, useless sociobiological truism; for this question, that truism will help us not at all. Which is to say that it will not help us in a substantive way to solve two of the major challenges facing the human species at the present time.

But biology may nevertheless tell us a good deal about how *not* to solve them, and many other problems as well. It may serve to make us a little more cautious in our meddling. And it may steer us away from certain varieties of "human engineering" disaster, simply by giving us some notion of the raw material we are working with.

Consider the following parable: It is about a hundred years ago, and a practical gentleman is about to design the longest bridge in the world, to be made of steel. He has the good luck to be on an ocean cruise with a metallurgist, who makes an excellent living exploring the properties of steel. The designer has visions of sunlit days on the upper deck playing shuffleboard and lounging and smoking cigars, all the while drinking deeply of his interlocutor's knowledge of steel, and in the evenings going back to his cabin and the drafting table.

But he finds himself getting nowhere. All his inquiries produce rhapsodic locutions about how steel is getting better all the time; about how past slanderers have underestimated its potential; about how poor present knowledge of the physics of solids is limiting steel's tensile strength and temperability; about how in this gentleman's own laboratory experiments are going on which may one day increase the weight-support potential of current girders by 8 percent. The designer's efforts to get some practical information that may be of use to him end in a frustrating shambles. Finally he shouts in exasperation, "But steel, man! Present-day steel! I'm going to build a bridge, don't you see? I have to know the properties of steel!"

Many modern conversations between social planners on the one hand and behavioral or social scientists on the other take a similar tack, and a similar sour turn. The latter simply do not want to say anything about the limitations of human potential, even with respect to a short time course. But the planners cannot do their work without some knowledge of those limitations, at least in the short run. While we are waiting for human beings to be transformed by some combination of science and magic and the very best of will into the beautiful raw material we all want them to be, we may lose our last chances to take action of practical value that will ensure that people are around long enough for that ultimate transformation to come over them. Recognizing the limitations of human nature, and the evil in it, is a necessary prerequisite to designing a social system that will minimize the effects of those limitations, the expression of that evil. That too, paradoxically, is a means of modification of human behavior.

PART FOUR

HUMAN NATURE AND THE HUMAN FUTURE

Woe unto them that call evil good, and good evil; that put darkness for light, and light for darkness; that put bitter for sweet, and sweet for bitter!

Woe unto them that are wise in their own eyes, and prudent in their own sight!

Woe unto them that are mighty to drink wine, and men of strength to mingle strong drink:

Which justify the wicked for reward, and take away the righteousness of the righteous from him!

Therefore as the fire devoureth the stubble, and the flame consumeth the chaff, so their root shall be as rottenness, and their blossom shall go up as dust. . . .

Therefore is the anger of the Lord kindled against his people, and he hath stretched forth his hand against them, and hath smitten them: and the hills did tremble, and their carcasses were torn in the midst of the streets. For all this his anger is not turned away, but his hand is stretched out still.

—Isaiah 5:20–25

17

THE PROSPECT

This is a present from a small distant world, a token of our sounds, our science, our images, our music, our thoughts and our feelings. We are attempting to survive our time so we may live into yours. We hope someday, having solved the problems we face, to join a community of galactic civilizations. This record represents our hope and our determination, and our good will in a vast and awesome universe.

—President Jimmy Carter,
Voyager 2 Spacecraft
Message, 1977

EDITORIAL

This morning the *Galaxy Times* learned from Interstellar Lasernews of yet another "bottle message" from a remote island planet. This one, carried in the hulk of an ingenious if crude vehicle, managed to drift halfway across the Galactic Federation before it was intercepted by the debris patrol. It was about two hundred thousand years old.

The geographic unit of the *Times*'s bubble library reported more than we cared to know about the primitive planet, but by the third request the report was down to hearable proportions. The planet, which was named by the early geographers, with their fine sense of language, "The Blue Drifter," followed a now familiar pattern in planetary genesis. Intelligent life on The Blue Drifter entered its lightspeed signal phase of development about one lifetime before the bottle message. Intelligent life there extinguished itself about three lifetimes later, by a process that was completely typical—it was well understood even then—and that is recounted, using other examples, on every child's history-tape.

As usual, lightspeed signals over The Blue Drifter's surface were recorded by our early geographers with compulsive diligence. These billions of signals, machine-sifted, catalogued, and edited for noise and repetition, became the grist for a great number of archeological and geographic dissertations. One of these, the pride and hope of a now long-dead young scholar, was titled "The First Sublightspeed Interstellar Message from 'The Blue Drifter,' Third Planet of Star 868-2893-41162-33: A Study in Contrasts."

The "contrasts" are hardly new; they were not new even then. But they are so vivid and stunning that they seem to bear an almost endless examination. Some of them are trivial. For example, here were intelligent creatures sending a message at a tiny fraction of lightspeed to an interstellar community of civilizations with a vastly more advanced technology. A little thought might have revealed to them that if we were so advanced we would be detecting and unscrambling their lightspeed signals, and that in about ninety years we would have the message from their descriptions of it to each other; this two hundred thousand years before their spacecart could cross the galaxy. Once within the Galactic Federation (which the casters of this "bottle" imagined with surprising accuracy), what could it do but pose a slight, inadvertent threat to spaceliners in interstellar corridors? So strong, evidently, is the impulse to shout "I am here!" as to obscure completely the uselessness of sublightspeed messages in bits of ancient hardware.

But there are larger contrasts. The dissertation follows the standard procedure, examining systematically the contents of the message as a selection from the world of The Blue Drifter. Nothing was new in it, even then. Sounds of atmospheric conditions and nonintelligent creatures, well known to the era's geographers, were included and were innocent enough. But the representations of intelligence, including the "message" part of the message, were nothing but half-truths and lies. The scholar notes in his conclusion:

> These creatures expect us to take at face value their expressions of goodwill and cheerful greeting. Members of a community

approaching the throes of extinction, they do not report the almost continual mutual slaughter they practice on an ever larger scale; nor the widespread starvation on a lush planet; nor the perpetual fouling of the little sphere with chemical excreta; nor the incessant hoarding of wealth by the few, who use it primarily to prepare for and promote their mutual slaughter. The political module responsible for the message exists in a world of utter unreality. This module, with 5 percent of the population, consumes more than half the planet's resources. Its members' hopes for material comfort are completely out of proportion to what the planet has to offer at this time; thus the inevitability of further conflict. Their self-indulgence, irresponsibility, and decadence beggar description. But lest it be thought that this tendency is restricted to one political module, it must be noted that almost all others on the planet show similar tendencies, especially among the dominating sectors of their populations.

We may carp at the young scholar's arch hyperbole: Had he been older, he would undoubtedly have been more compassionate; these creatures, after all, were on their way to a sad end and were doing the best they knew how. But we must ask, with him, What were these creatures doing sending rockets into space? This was a moment when all energies should have been turned to the sciences of education, mental illness, interpersonal conflict, population reduction, ocean cultivation, photon harvest, and waste control. Here they were voyaging around a barren interplanetary wasteland, while they failed to take seriously enough the other, nearer explorations that might have saved them.

On the basis of previous experience with such planets, and of his analysis of all the relevant lightspeed signals from The Blue Drifter, the scholar predicted "protocivilizational terminus in approximately 2.2 lifetimes." He was too pessimistic by almost a lifetime, but otherwise discouragingly right. And the most poignant thing, as always in these cases, was that they were so close; it is always only those last three or four lifetimes that make the difference between exodus and terminus.

A familiar story, on all the schooltapes, as expected by now as death, taxes, and adolescent sullenness. But perhaps we may read in The Blue Drifter's crude gesture a deeper message—about the limits of what we are pleased to call intelligence. Instead of simply mocking or ignoring these creatures' dilemma, we might take occasion to pause and review possible flaws in our own sentient condition. Smugness, now as then, is ever the enemy of survival.

> As a rule the philosopher is a kind of mongrel
> being, a cross between scientist and poet, envious of both.
> —Gustave Flaubert

Flaubert wrote these words in 1846 in a letter to the poet Louise Colet. His opinion of philosophers is something that I have often felt about many (not all) behavioral and social theorists. They are immune to criticism: When their facts or logic are challenged, they hide behind a cloak of humanism; and yet they expect to be taken much more seriously than poets (at least in the United States) because they are, after all, not delivering themselves of mere opinion borne in pretty words but presume to draw on a large body of scientific information. This is a pretty treacherous middle ground. It is clear that some behavioral and social theorists have negotiated the shoals about it very well, and they are justly admired for that, including—as is evident in many places in this book—by me and by others taking biological approaches to behavior.

Nevertheless, the last few years have seen moments of dire confrontation between biological and behavioral or social scientists over certain issues in the biology of behavior. The social and behavioral science of the last hundred years has made great progress in data-gathering and analysis, but its theoretical progress has been meager by comparison. There are small theories to explain restricted bodies of behavioral and social data—for example, the law of distributed versus massed practice in learning, or the theory of demographic transition—but there are no grand conceptions. Or, to be more precise, the grand conceptions are left over from the nineteenth century.

Biological approaches are considered threatening for several reasons. First, they have been shown to be politically misused and dangerous in some societies. Second, proper evaluation of them requires a large body of difficult knowledge, and few behavioral and social scientists are willing to undertake the mastery of that knowledge. Third, they might provide the sorts of grand conceptions that social scientists, for all their protestations to the contrary, know they lack.

This should help us to understand why at the present time behavioral and social scientists are responding with the most vigorous possible protest to the efforts of ethologists, behavioral geneticists, sociobiologists, and other behavioral biologists to contribute something of importance to our common understanding of human and animal behavior. But there is a more important reason for the confrontation: It is that the present contributions of biologists undermine the philosophical structure of behavioral and social science as it has existed for at least a hundred years. This structure rests upon two pillars, neither of which is set in solid ground. Both, in fact, are matters of faith rather than knowledge, poetry rather than science. Each is beautiful, but each is wrong.

The first is a metaphor, according to which society is an organism. (This idea goes back much farther than the nineteenth century.) The units are individuals and, like the cells of the body, are built up into tissues, organs, finally into the whole itself, all devoted to one purpose: survival. Signs of derangement can be considered pathological and can be corrected by restoring the system to balance. In its everyday functioning, the healthy society is no different from the healthy individual: a collection of cooperative units with a single end. This metaphor is simply and demonstrably wrong, because it requires that society be a plausible unit of natural selection, which, at least in animals like ourselves, it has never yet been shown to be. Precisely in contrast to the purposes of the cell, which evolution has stripped of its independence and which is consequently devoted entirely to the survival and reproduction of the organism of which it is a part, the purposes of the individual are wedded to the survival and reproduction of society only transiently and skeptically; indeed, the same process of evolution has designed the individual with a full complement of independence and a canny ability to subvert, or at least try to subvert, the purposes of society to its own. Every time a human being

≡ 413 ≡

gets fed up with his or her society or church or club or even family, and voluntarily changes affiliation, we have another factual disproof of the central metaphor of social and political science.

The second pillar is merely a simple article of faith, which I like to call, rather unkindly, the "tinker theory" of human behavior and experience. According to the tinker theory, human behavior and experience are basically good and decent and healthy and warm and cooperative and intelligent, but something has gone a bit wrong somewhere. A fuse has blown in the child-rearing process or a tube has overheated in the psyche or an evil madman has taken over the controls or some blunderer has ordered the wrong grade of concrete for the foundation of the economy (or, at the very least, the wrong glass for the windows). All we need do is some tinkering: Change the teaching apparatus or administer the right kind of psychotherapy or kick out the king and queen or institute socialism or at least print less money, and then everything will be just fine. If you can do more than one of these things and, preferably, get rid of your present wife at the same time, you will not only be just fine, you will stumble upon paradise on earth.

I am not concerned to discredit any of these estimable varieties of tinkering. I have seen convincing evidence that any of them can make things better in some cases. What I am concerned to discredit is the twofold act of faith that makes people overestimate consistently both the percentage of times these strategies will make things better and the degree of improvement that will result from them. These misestimates are perilous because they ruin the accuracy of the risk-benefit analysis that must be the basis of all intelligent action. Behavioral and social scientists of various fields and schools encourage people to make these misestimates, using very similar means, for very similar reasons, and with similarly disappointing results as are to be found in commercial advertising. I am not now talking about charlatanism—that is too easy to decry; I am talking about the everyday, ubiquitous, often pernicious exaggeration that is commonly resorted to by almost every person who happens upon a possible solution to a human problem.

Everything will not be just fine. After we make the change, even if it improves us, we will still be full of the flaws of the human condition. We will still be weakly responsive to the needs of others around us. We will still be beset by motives that are not always necessary, that we do not properly comprehend, and that are sometimes dangerous. We will still be wary of external dangers. We will still have to do things we do not like to do. We will still get bored too easily with things that should make us happy. And of course we will still be dying.

No behavioral or social tinkerer goes to any trouble to deny any of these truths. But neither do they make much mention of them. They don't have to. They know perfectly well that they can rely on the internal denial mechanisms of their listeners to sweep such matters under the rug. They are selling hope, and the people are taking their money out, and the rule of the market is let the buyer beware.

To be fair to them, they are in the main not cynics; they are merely reluctant to face these things, just as the average person is. That is why they are not good poets. Good poets not only face them, they dwell upon them in order to show us how to live in spite of them. In view of a tendency on the part of most people to identify the biologist's view of human nature as a relatively new departure from the venerable tradition of social theory, we may do well to remind ourselves that there is another tradition, the tradition of classical literature, which is much more consonant with the biological view.

In the Greek tragedies, for instance, we have such a clear, consistent view of the dark side of human life that when the chorus says it is better to die than to live, and best of all never to have been born, it scarcely causes a ripple in our emotions. Yes, we think, of course. In Shakespeare, the same tradition is carried forward and developed. In the famous Hamlet soliloquy, in Macbeth's "sound and fury" speech, in the lines about the Ages of Man in *As You Like It*, in Lear's ramblings and in the lucid pronouncements of his fool we have the same story of human chaos and foolishness and despair repeated in many different mouths, all of it totally inconsistent with the fundamental faith of all the tinkerers. And we have the evidence of the *Sonnets*, in which the poet speaks in his own voice:

> Tired with all these, for restful death I cry,
> As, to behold desert a beggar born,

And needy nothing trimm'd in jollity,
And purest faith unhappily forsworn,
And gilded honor shamefully misplaced,
And maiden virtue rudely strumpeted,
And right perfection wrongfully disgraced,
And strength by limping sway disabled,
And art made tongue-tied by authority,
And folly, doctor-like, controlling skill,
And simple truth miscalled simplicity,
And captive good attending captain ill.

. . . .

For Henry James, life was "a slow advance into enemy territory."
He wrote:

Life *is*, in fact, a battle. Evil is insolent and strong; beauty
enchanting, but rare; goodness very apt to be weak; folly very
apt to be defiant; wickedness to carry the day; imbeciles to be in
great places, people of sense in small, and mankind generally
unhappy. But the world as it stands is no illusion, no phantasm,
no evil dream of a night; we wake up to it again for ever and
ever; we can neither forget it nor deny it nor dispense with it.

For Goethe, speaking through the pen of that sad figure Werther,

All the highly learned schoolmasters are agreed that a child does
not know why he wants something; but that adults, too, like
children, stagger about on this earth of ours and do not know
where they come from or where they are going; that they act just
as little in accordance with true purpose and are governed just
as much by biscuits and cake and birch rods—no one wants to
believe that, and yet it seems to me that this is palpably so.

And for André Malraux, "grown-ups do not exist." On the opening
page of his *Antimémoires,* he tells the story of running into an old
friend he had been through the war with. The friend had spent
fifteen years as a country priest. The man of letters asked the man of
the cloth, in solemn humility, what he had learned from fifteen years

of hearing confessions, and the latter replied, after some thought, that he had learned two things:

> ". . . First, people are much more unhappy than one imagines . . . and then . . ."
> He raised his lumberjack's arms into the night full of stars:
> "And then, the bottom of everything, is that grown-ups do not exist . . ."

Let us invite these, as it were, artists of the soul to a cocktail party. On one side of the room are a group of tinkerers arguing cheerfully about various strategies for making everything just fine. On the other side, a group of biologists are discussing, rather glumly, the unchanging facts of human nature. Which group would they join?

One could go on almost endlessly with such quotations. My purpose is not to clobber the reader with a litany of literary *mots*, but to dwell on them long enough so that the mist of familiarity is dispersed, and we really look again at what they say. When we have done so we get the unmistakable impression that the great literary figures, past and present, have had much more in common with the perspective on human nature taken by modern biologists than with the perspective on human potential taken by most modern behavioral and social scientists. Thus it is almost as amusing as it is unjust for the latter to decry biologists as technicians while they try to hide behind the cloak of humanism; for them, it is a tattered cloak, affording scant cover, and, in the long term, no safe place to hide.

Lest we pull out once again the old saw that artists are fundamentally reactionaries, one should hasten to add that despite their lack of optimism about human nature, most (not, to be sure, all) of the people who wrote these things were seriously engaged in criticism—sometimes dangerous criticism—of the societies they lived in and even of the governments that ran them. They were just skeptical of most proposals for change. Their natural insight into human character made them less sanguine than some of us about how much change is possible—and thus not very susceptible to the tinker theory.

"Adults, too, like children, stagger about . . ." "Grown-ups do not exist." Like children, indeed, in our motives, in our confused yet pointed arousals, in our willful working out of our personal chaos upon the world. But unlike children, who stumble endearingly over themselves before they wreak much havoc, we do the real-world work of our besotted, arcane emotions after slower deliberation, in loftier grandeur, using subtler indirection, out of a deeper, more vengeful vein of selfishness, and with more power.

> The dream of reason produces monsters.
> —Goya, *Caprichos*

Human behavioral genetics is the most dreadfully controversial of all pursuits in behavioral biology, as well it should be. Skeptics are right to be frightened. It is only yesterday that an explicitly genetic theory of human behavior resulted in, or at least strongly supported, the ghettoization, deportation, concentration, enslavement, and finally mass extermination of millions of helpless victims guilty of absolutely nothing resembling the theoretical behavior-genetic taint they were accused of having. Any thoughtful person must take pause at this specter—arising from decades of behavior-genetic fairytales—and recognize the possibility of yet another similar scenario, at some unknown time in the future. Should this possibility not be enough in itself to keep us from meddling in such theories?

Unfortunately for dwellers in the last part of the grim twentieth century, rejection of behavior-genetic theories has proved to be no genuine guard against the terrors of authoritarian violence. Deportation, imprisonment, virtual enslavement, and direct or indirect slaughter of millions of Soviet citizens over the course of several decades was based on a complete rejection of the transgenerational, stable effects of genes, not only on the mind but on the body. As the Jewish victims of Hitler were transported and worked to death or murdered because of their presumed spiritual defects, due to unchangeable genes, so the Soviet victims of Stalin were transported and worked to death or murdered in order to change them, through "reeducation," or at least to change other people around them. As the lies of the anti-Semitic "behavior geneticists" (they really knew not the first thing about behavior genetics) justified the one, so the lies of Lysenko and other antigeneticists (ignorant of the real intellectual basis for environmentalism) justified the other. The Jew-free Europe and the New Soviet Man proved to be attainable through not dissimilar means, despite the fact of their irreconcilable provenance.

And just to bring our various fears up to date, we have seen, in the 1970s, some attempts to use behavior genetics to establish the intellectual inferiority of American blacks, with the effect that their victimization by the order of things could be ignored more guiltlessly; and, in the formerly peaceable kingdom of Cambodia, also in the 1970s, a program of deportation and mass extermination that, by some estimates, is equal to a third of that accomplished by the Nazis—quite an achievement for a technologically backward country—based entirely on a theory of the extreme plasticity of human behavior.

So, alas, there is no morally safe haven, if there ever was. The political experience of this century convincingly proves that almost any scientific theory about behavior can be bent to the purposes of evil, and used by someone to support his wicked, selfish, occasionally psychotic acts, up to and including wholesale slaughter. This experience exactly parallels the ubiquitous bending of religious ideologies to similarly wicked purpose for dozens of centuries before our own. The answer must be that the origin of large-scale wickedness does *not* lie in the minds of social theorists of one stripe or another—however misguided they may be, however they may sometimes, wittingly or unwittingly, prostitute themselves to evil purpose.

It is simply not true that recognizing some important genetic influence on human behavior must be inimical to change. And to insist that sociobiology, ethology, and behavioral genetics are inherently reactionary or conservative in a political sense is to tar thousands of dedicated scientists with a brush that should be reserved for only a few of them. It is the worst sort of guilt by gossip and association.

In many cases, the detection of a genetic basis for a human problem is compatible with or even essential to the correction of that problem. With my eyeglasses on I have excellent vision, despite the fact of my rather myopic genes. Diabetes is in part genetically caused, but insulin, appropriately used, can keep the damage those genes can cause at bay. And mental retardation resulting from phenylketonuria is a condition caused by a simple genetic defect, affecting only one enzyme, that has an *environmental* solution—the removal of phenylalanine from the diet. Yet that environmental solution could never have been arrived at unless prior knowledge of the genetic determination of the enzyme defect had been arrived at first.

Consider the following three arguments, each setting off from a specific biological determinist standpoint, and each resulting in a suggestion for policy.

1. Women and men differ in their tendency to commit acts of violence, for biological reasons attributable finally to the genes, as well as for other reasons. It should be possible but quite difficult to eliminate this difference by reducing men's aggressiveness (there is no reason why it should not be tried), and perhaps easier but probably undesirable to eliminate it by raising that of women. In the meantime, one simple, practical policy tending to reduce worldwide violence would be to replace men with women in positions of military and diplomatic power, in a strategic effort to dampen some of the irrational sources of violent conflict.

2. Some, not all, perhaps not even many, but some individuals of low normal intelligence are severely limited in their performance at school and work because of genetic reasons. They have gene variants that are not properly considered defects, perhaps, but that nevertheless directly limit their potential. Only research into the genetics of intelligence can offer them the hope of one day being free from those limitations. Yet many well-intentioned, liberal intellectuals are of the opinion that research on the genetics of intelligence should stop. They would never dream of suggesting a halt to research on the genetics of myopia or the genetics of diabetes; but the very phrase "genetics of intelligence" suggests a tampering with the human spirit, and is to them unacceptable. Such critics would deprive genetically unintelligent individuals of a research program vigorously pursuing a solution to their problem; whatever high-minded language it is couched in, it is a policy devoid of foresight and compassion. The opposite policy is in fact indicated; if we have a national institute devoted to alcoholism, or drug abuse, or mental health, or communicative disorders, we can have one devoted to learning disability, and it can be allowed to recognize the sometimes critical role of the human genes.

3. In all societies with hierarchical social structures, some people rise to positions of wealth and power over others because of their own

abilities and character traits. Some of these traits, such as intellect, cooperativeness, and compassion, may be good, while others, such as a tendency to authoritarian violence, are indisputably bad. Some degree or other of the basis of the traits that caused the rise to the top will be genetic, but not all. Yet we know from a great deal of data and theory that individuals will attempt to protect the wealth and power of their families even if their offspring show none of the traits that made their parents successful, or worse, show only the negative ones. Therefore, strenuous efforts should be made to prevent those with wealth and power from protecting their children from the normal course of genetic competition. A logical solution in a society such as ours at the present time would be an almost completely confiscatory inheritance tax. If the children of the rich cannot succeed on the basis of all the advantages they have when their parents are alive, that is evidence enough that they have not inherited their parents' abilities, and they should be thrown on their own resources, ceding power to those more able if they must.

Whether I do or do not subscribe to these arguments is not the point here. Neither is the question of how convincing they are to anyone else. The point is that they are arguments arising from the facts and theory of biological determinism, yet can scarcely be called politically conservative. The recent practitioners of ethology, sociobiology, and even behavior genetics have, in their overwhelming majority, done little or nothing to justify the charge that they are politically reactionary. With few exceptions, they are trying to find out the truth. That truth is not only usable by progressive causes, it is absolutely necessary to the success of such causes.

Nevertheless, one must not be too sanguine about new proposed solutions, wherever they come from. In Goya's series called *Caprichos*, there is a wonderfully strange etching showing a man — obviously an intellectual—asleep over his writing desk. In a whirlwind-shaped cloud coming out of his head emerge as horrendous-looking a collection of bizarre and frightening figures as ever were drawn on paper. And the caption reads, *"El sueño de la razón produce monstruos."* The dream of reason produces monsters.

This enigmatic sentence has at least three meanings. In the first, Reason is allegorical, personified in the man, and it sleeps at times, and its dreams produce monsters. In another, reasoning as a process is a type of dreaming, and that type of dreaming is always nightmarish. In the third meaning, it is the "hope" or "wish" or "prayer" sense of the word "dream"; here it is the possibility of reason that is a dream, a vain hope, which in its inevitable failure produces monsters, ones perhaps more terrible than any ever engendered by mere passion.

Joan Didion, in a review of a recent book by V.S. Naipaul, called attention to what she saw as their common suspicion that ideas are overrated by most of us most of the time: "that sense of the world," she put it, "as a physical fact without regret or hope, a place of intense radiance in which ideas may be fevers that pass." And Leo Tolstoy wrote in his private notebook, the one in which he set down meticulously the details of his life, "As soon as man applies his intelligence and only his intelligence to any object at all, he unfailingly destroys the object."

It seems to me that so far we have applied our intelligence, and only our intelligence, to the ordering of human life on earth. It's not that I don't believe in the sheer power of intelligence; I do, more, I would guess, than Goya, Tolstoy, or Didion. It's that everywhere I turn in the world of science and scholarship I encounter people who believe in it much more than I do; people who serve it as if it were a god. Increasingly, nearly every day, I have to remind myself of the words Brecht provided for his Galileo: "The aim of science is not to open the door to everlasting wisdom, but to set a limit on everlasting error."

We are going to be hearing, you and I, an almost endless train of ideas about the nature of human experience and the solutions to human problems, ideas that are the products of human intelligence. In his great book *An Introduction to the Study of Experimental Medicine*, Claude Bernard wrote: "Man is by nature metaphysical and proud. He has gone so far as to think that the idealistic creations of his mind, which correspond to his feelings, also represent reality." If this was true of ideas about physiology, how true must it be of ideas about behavior? And how easy it would be if I could tell you, with confidence, that the ideas we hear during the next couple of decades, concerning human behavior and experience, will all be wrong. They will not. Some of them will be right; we will need those, and I hope that we will know them when we see them.

In the meantime, if you ask me how to set your sail in the storm of claim and counterclaim, of fact and lie and theory, of warning and prophecy and judgment and exhortation, I do have a bit of advice that I earnestly believe in, which can be summarized in the one-word injunction, Doubt.

> Placed on this isthmus of a middle state,
> A being darkly wise and rudely great
>
> . . . . ,
> He hangs between . . .
> In doubt to deem himself a God, or Beast . . .
> —Alexander Pope,
> *Essay on Man*

In the ape house at the Bronx Zoo in New York City, among the highest primates, where it appropriately must be—taxonomically, that is—within the wider range of mammals, there is a sign that says "The Most Dangerous Animal in the World." Having learned already that the fearful-looking gorilla is not very dangerous, much less the chimpanzee or orangutan, the puzzled zoo visitor leans forward to discover which cousin of these relatively benign creatures merits such a plainly ominous label. Above the sign is a set of ordinary cage bars, and behind the set of cage bars is a mirror.

It is too set up, and too much of a cliché, to engender much of a shock of recognition. "Of course," one thinks. "Still, clever." Nevertheless, there is something about the vision of one's familiar image above that particular sign and—however illusorily—behind bars, that somehow does not fail to give pause.

The most frequently recurring theme throughout this book has been the problem of human destructiveness, including self-destructiveness, and its rather discouraging intractability. If I have seemed at times to let it slip into synonymy with the simpler "sister" problem of human violence, let me now take occasion to distinguish them. The human propensity to violence is there, is inborn, is—up to a point—enhanceable or reducible by experience, is serious, and is, in a word, bad. But it is only one part, and probably a minor part, of the problem of human destructiveness, which is made up of much else besides.

At the end of the section called "The Modification of Behavior," I argued that biological explanations of various sorts have little to say about certain major transformations now under way in our species: for example, the remarkable progress from nearly universal illiteracy to nearly universal literacy, one of the most rapid and profound behavioral changes any species has ever undergone in so small a number of generations. This would seem to belittle the importance of such explanations for the human future.

But there are other challenges facing us, and about some of them sociobiology and behavioral genetics have much to say. For example, although it can pretty safely be predicted that the world's population will stabilize within a century—a conclusion due to "demographic transition theory," although it is really less a theory than a generalization from past experience in industrializing, modernizing countries—this good news will not come soon enough. In the interim, we will be at constant risk for international and civil conflict due to one to two more doublings of the world's population, with an attendant movement of peoples and the inevitable struggles over resources.

More important, more lasting, and potentially more damaging than simple population growth, however, is the continually expanding wants or needs (the boundary between these two categories of human motives undergoes a sea change during modernization) of the already existing population. Although this will be small consolation to the millions who will starve during the coming century, there is reason to believe that sheer food productivity will not be a lasting problem.

But the vision of people thrown into armed conflict over scraps of food in a starving world is at once naive and optimistic; naive because it proposes an eventuality that will probably not occur in that form, and optimistic because it presumes that people have to be deprived of food to be willing to enter into a bellicose confrontation. It has been rare indeed for starving people to make war. People make war not because they are starving, but because they are paying more for gasoline, or because their national honor has been offended, or because they think it has, or because they want to prevent someone else from making war on them. And as for starvation, grain rots in the storage silos now while millions starve in . . . somewhere. Can we suppose that when the green revolution contrives to provide us a glut, we will automatically get it efficiently distributed to those who need it? Oh, when the war comes, to be sure, men will be men and women, women, we will rise to the occasion, we will cover ourselves with glory. Haven't we always? History offers us an endless confirmation of such courage in the midst of the flood, in the very eye of the hurricane.

But can we rise to the occasion of the call of human decency, when that call seems very faint and we hear it every day, when even to stop and cock an ear seems to risk a slip on whatever ladder we're mounting? Can we cease to think of our own selves even long enough to hear that the call comes from a multitude and is anguished?

On the beach at Malibu there are miles of tinsel mansions that are precisely as we have imagined them, precisely as they might appear in the rocking-chair dreams of an English schoolmarm. Until they were built, the French had no perfect use, I think, for their tired old phrase "newly rich." The verandas are high on stilts above the beach, to evade the water. Most of them are empty, even in summer, since their inhabitants have other mansions, at Nice, in Manhattan, in Riyadh, in Beverly Hills. One can peek in some of the windows— from a proper distance, of course—and see the glitter. The decor is plasticky palatial. It is said that in one of the homes an original Rembrandt drawing hangs in a bathroom.

On the beach the gulls are mottled, drab, as if to offset the opulence. A pair of teenage lovers runs through the dusk, angry, shouting, possibly breaking up, in any event at terrible odds with one another. The empty bottle on the beach is not Coke, but Mumm's champagne.

Every once in a while—it happened a few years ago—the sea rises up and slaps them down, those houses. No rational person would suppose such an event to be the sea's response to human arrogance, any more than a decent person would take comfort from such destruction. Nevertheless, one can scarcely escape the metaphor: Here are structures that embody in a reified real world the whole effortful chaos of human motive, of human hunger and arousal and desire and fear run wild, cast in an earthly form and held up for the world to see, so that all may gaze and hope and wish, and even hurt for wanting, so that even the very well-to-do may compare themselves and feel poor, and the *petit bourgeois* may eat out his heart with envy. And as for the poor, whether in Brooklyn or Nairobi or Laredo or Calcutta, they may go to the movies and dream of going to bed with a favorite star in one of the houses in Malibu; or look at pictures of it in a magazine they cannot afford and think . . . well, whatever.

As for the people who live, even occasionally, at Malibu, they might feel guilty, or at least ashamed; perhaps they do. But they know that even all their wealth carved up and given out among the dreaming millions would not make a dent in the problems of the world. And if they should feel so ashamed as to be distressed, they have special doctors to give them back the world as it really must be, just as kings had priests to render a similar service. And most of us, I think, would be the same way in their shoes; they are merely our own puzzled selves writ large.

But this is not a lecture on global civics; it is a meditation at the close of a long, difficult exercise in the attempt to understand human nature. There is such a thing, and it is not entirely tractable. Its most ominous elements are a deep vein of violence, perhaps attendant on a too-great sense of fright; a weakly developed capacity for material satisfaction, perhaps also partly due to that same sense of fright; a tendency to misjudge the difficulties of life as difficulties arising from a specified cause; and a sort of affectional inertia that puts a drag on generosity outside of a small circle of friends and kin.

We dwell in the midst of an energetic getting and spending, and not just in the realm of buyable things. Our motives are laced with a froth of anger that can easily churn and roil. When someone distant suffers, we have a feeling that is called pity; only when it is close is the feeling grief. "That is only natural," say the words of the wise cliché. But in most lives there is evidently enough grief so that pity's a poor clarion to action. This situation, although never exactly admirable, was workable for most of human history, when we all lived in small, face-to-face groups. But over the last ten thousand years we have piled ourselves into vast aggregates, and the same set of motives and limitations has brought us to a condition in which, with regularity, we commit the most despicable acts in the whole long record of life on earth; and, without blushing, in our respites from mutual slaughter, we prepare ourselves to try to commit more.

In Chaim Grade's beautiful novel *The Yeshiva*, about the Talmudic tradition of the Jews of Poland and the people who tried to follow it, the hero's first sermon says, "Man is evil from birth. But his nature prevents him from finding the evil in his supposedly good deeds. That is why the Torah was given to us—to teach us to lead an ethical life." This idea, in one form or another, is at the core of the Judaic and Christian traditions, and of many other belief systems besides. It is an idea more compatible with the recent discoveries of human behavioral biology than with the body of social science of the last hundred years.

I would paraphrase it this way: Human beings are irrevocably, biologically endowed with strong inclinations to feel and act in a manner that their own good judgment tells them to reprehend—that is, if they are in the least capable of sympathy with the suffering of other human creatures, or if they have any sense of the joy and order and beauty of life. The judgment, the sympathy, the sense of joy and order and beauty—all these evolved for other purposes than to save the human species from a protracted, dissolute destruction. Yet there they are. Can we not turn them now to this latter purpose?

According to "The Hollow Men," this is the way the world ends, not with a bang, but a whimper. But suppose it were not about to end, either in fire or in ice, either suddenly or morbidly, during any near time. Suppose I were to tell you that I have just consulted an oracle, and the world will go on just as it has for the last few hundred years, an unbroken extension of the past into the future, forever, or for as long as we please. Would that in itself not be reason enough to despair?

The hero of Grade's novel comes into grievous difficulties because of his failure to recognize that the human heart and human nature are not purely evil, that man is good as well as evil from birth. His foil in the novel, a rabbi named for the patriarch Abraham, tries to teach him to fight evil by drawing out good. The pupil fails, because he ignores good while insisting upon a relentless fight against evil.

The English geneticist C.H.Waddington, a few years before his death, wrote:

> It has been argued that the choice of an ethical system is like the choice of a set of axioms on which to found mathematics. There is something in this. But though in mathematics we are free to

choose whether to build up our geometry on Euclidian axioms or on some set of non-Euclidian axioms, when we need to deal with the world of objects that are about the size of our own bodies, we find that it is the Euclidian axioms which are by far the most appropriate. They are so appropriate, indeed, that we almost certainly have some genetic predisposition to their adoption built into our genotypes—for example, the capacity of the human eye to recognize a straight line.

Something of the same kind is probably true of ethical axioms. If we wish to develop an ethical system which we can apply to human life as we know it, there are probably some ethical axioms which we are almost forced to incorporate. They would be the common ground which we find between all the major ethical systems of different religions and groups of mankind—such values as truth, respect for self, respect for others, and respect for something larger and more embracing than one's own immediate experience . . . a built-in predisposition towards certain ethical values which have the same degree of general relevance to human society as do the Euclidian axioms of geometry to the material world.

And so let us leave it. Who knows what good may not yet lurk in the hearts of men? In the hope of discovering it, in the hope of bringing it forth to the light, in the hope that some mechanism of sublunary nurturance may yet cause it to thrive and grow, we may well set our hearts and minds to a most momentous task. And, as a sort of amulet, a good-luck charm of tradition, to speed us on our difficult way, we may well repeat with the Psalmist, "Break thou the arm of the wicked; and as for the evil man, search out his wickedness, till none be found. . . . Lord, Thou hast heard the desire of the humble: Thou wilt prepare their heart, Thou wilt cause thine ear to hear; to right the fatherless and the oppressed, that man who is of the dust of the earth may be terrible no more."
Amen. Selah.

PART FIVE

THE TANGLED WING

. . . Then beauty is nothing
But the start of a terror we're still just able to bear
And the reason we love it so is that it blithely
Disdains to destroy us . . .
—Rainer Maria Rilke,
"The First Elegy"

18

THE DAWN OF WONDER

The most beautiful experience we can have is the mysterious. It is the fundamental emotion which stands at the cradle of true art and true science.
—Albert Einstein, "The World As I See It"

One of the most fascinating and least discussed discoveries in the study of the wild chimpanzees was described in a short paper by Harold Bauer. He was following a well-known male chimpanzee through the forest of the Gombe Stream Reserve in Tanzania when the animal stopped beside a waterfall. It seemed possible that he had deliberately gone to the waterfall rather than passing it incidentally, but that was not absolutely clear. In any case, it was an impressive spot: a stream of water cascading down from a twenty-five-foot height, about a mile from the lake, thundering into the pool below and casting mist for sixty or seventy feet; a stunning sight to come upon in the midst of a tropical forest.

The animal seemed lost in contemplation of it. He moved slowly closer, and began to rock, while beginning to give a characteristic round of "pant-hoot"calls. He became more excited, finally beginning to run back and forth while calling, to jump, to call louder, to drum with his fists on trees, to run back again. The behavior was most reminiscent of that observed and described by Jane Goodall in groups of chimpanzees at the start of a rainstorm—the "rain dance," as it has been called. But this was one animal alone, and not surprised as the animals are by sudden rain—even if he had not deliberately sought the waterfall out, he certainly knew where it was and when he would come upon it.

He continued this activity long enough so that it seemed to merit some explanation, and did it again in the same place on other days. Other animals were observed to do it as well. They had no practical interest in the waterfall. The animals did not have to drink from the stream or cross it in that vicinity. To the extent that it might be dangerous, it could be easily avoided, and certainly did not interest every animal. But for these it was something they had to look at, return to, study, watch, become excited about: a thing of beauty, an object of curiosity, a fetish, an imagined creature, a challenge, a communication? We will never know.

But for a very similar animal, perhaps ten million years ago, in the earliest infancy of the human spirit, something in the natural world must have evoked a response like this one—a waterfall, a mountain vista, a sunset, the crater of a volcano. the edge of the sea—something that stopped it in its tracks and made it watch, and move, and watch, and move, and watch again; something that made it return to the spot, though nothing gainful could take place there, no feeding, drinking, reproducing, sleeping, fighting, fleeing, nothing *animal*. In just such a response, in just such a moment, in just such an animal, we may, I think, be permitted to guess, occurred the dawn of awe, of sacred attentiveness, of wonder.

The human infant, for its first few months of life, is all eyes, in a way that no other animal infant quite is. It isn't just that its eyes are good, that it does a lot of looking; it's that it does so little else, really. It can suck, of course, and swallow, but the rest of what it does is very primitive, except for the functions of attentiveness. Even in the adult brain, one-third of all incoming signals come through the eyes. In the infant, looking and seeing are way ahead of most other functions in development, with the possible exception of listening and hearing. The infant is not a passive figure, nor an active one either, but what might be called an actively receptive one—eagerly, hungrily receptive, famished for sights and sounds, no vague, fuzzy intelligence in a blooming, buzzing confusion, but a highly ordered, if simple, mind with a fine sense of novelty, of pattern, even of beauty. The light on a leaf outside the window, the splash of red on a woman's dress, the shadow on the ceiling, the sound of rain—any of these may evoke a rapt attention not, perhaps, unlike that of the chimpanzee at the waterfall.

For most people, as they grow, that sense of wonder diminishes in frequency, becoming at best peripheral to the business of everyday life. For some, it becomes the central fact of existence. These follow two separate paths: Either the sense of wonder leads them down an analytic path, or it leads them to simple contemplation. Either way the sense of wonder is the first fact of life, but the paths are completely different in every other way. The analyst, or scientist, moved to reveal by explaining, breaks apart the image, and the sense of wonder, focusing sequentially on the pieces. The contemplator, or artist, moved to reveal by simply looking, keeps the image and the sense of wonder whole. The artist contrives to keep the attention riveted without fragmentation, by means of high trickery. This trickery involves transmuting the image into human speech—whether a literary, plastic, or musical form of speech—thus fixing in place forever the sense of wonder.

There is a photograph that has by now been seen by most people living in civilized countries. It was taken from an ingenious if crude vehicle traveling many thousands of miles per hour, across a vast expanse of space empty of air, by men who had devoted their lives, courageously and at great personal cost, to the mastery of nature through machinery. This photograph cost perhaps a billion dollars, and in one sense it is worth every penny.

It shows an almost spherical object poised against a backdrop of black. The object is partly colored a deep, warm, pretty blue, with many broken, off-white swirls drawn across it. It looks at first like a mandala, a strange symbol woven on black cloth. It looks whole, somehow, and rather small. But as we study it (it draws us in almost mysteriously), some red-brown shapes obscured among the swirls of white take on before our eyes the unmistakable images we first saw and memorized as children encountering the geography of the continents. If the space program accomplished nothing else (and I am often at pains to discern what it did accomplish), we must be grateful to it for producing that photograph.

"Got the earth right out our front window," said Buzz Aldrin. A medium-size mammal from a middling planet of a middle-aged star in the arm of an average galaxy, gazing at home. There was no excess of poetry on that mission. There was, of course, the stark poetry of aeronautics gobbledygook and the arch, well-prepared, historic *mot* of Neil Armstrong setting foot on the Sea of Tranquillity, but "Beautiful, beautiful," "Magnificent sight out here," and "Got the earth right out our front window," was about the level at which these unique first views of the natural world were transmuted to human speech. This was no fault of Armstrong or Aldrin; they were chosen for other talents, which they had in full measure. But it is intriguing that such spontaneous poetry as there was was evoked by the machinery. "The Eagle has wings," one of them said as the lunar landing vehicle separated, after some difficulty, from the orbiting command station. *The eagle*, bold symbol of human hope on the North American continent and, beyond that, of the hope of humanity in the mission, *has wings*, has the means to transcend technical difficulty and to emerge, having mastered natural law.

But this stepping off the earth is an illusion. The mastery of natural law has proceeded no further than the grasp of some elementary laws of physics. Compared with the uncharted, infinitely more intricate laws of biology and behavior that govern the human spirit, this mastery is trivial, a mere conjurer's trick. The mastery of physical law can no longer save us while we are grounded in a tangle of ignorance of the natural laws that govern our behavior. In this sense, the eagle does not have wings.

When I was a young man in college, a professor took me to the American Museum of Natural History, not to the exhibits, which I had often seen, but into the bowels of the place, among the labyrinths of storage cabinets of bones and skins and rocks and impossibly ancient fossils. I was very much impressed by this chance to see the museum the way insiders, professionals, saw it.

There I met a man who had devoted most of his life to the study of the skeletal remains of archaeopteryx—the earliest tetrapod with feathered wings—embedded in a Mesozoic rock. I was introduced to him, awed by him, impressed with his intelligence and wisdom. It was obvious that he wanted to impart to me some piece of genuine, useful knowledge gained from the countless hours of squinting over that crushed tangle of bone and rock.

What he finally said was that he thought archaeopteryx was very much like people. This of course puzzled me, as it was calculated to do, and when I pressed him to explain, he said, "Well, you know, it's such a transitional creature. It's a piss-poor reptile, and it's not very much of a bird." Apart from the shock of hearing strong language in those relatively hallowed halls, there was an intellectual shock to my young mind that fixed those phrases in it permanently.

The dinosaurs ruled this planet for over a hundred million years, at least a hundred times longer than the brief, awkward tenure of human creatures, and they are gone almost without a trace, leaving nothing but crushed bone as a memento. We can do the same more easily and, in an ecological sense, we would be missed even less. What's the difference? seems an inevitable question, and the best answer I can think of is that we *know*, we are capable of seeing what is happening. We are the only creatures that understand evolution, that, conceivably, can alter its very course. It would be too base of us to simply relinquish this possibility through pride, or ignorance, or laziness.

It seems to me we are losing the sense of wonder, the hallmark of our species and the central feature of the human spirit. Perhaps this is due to the depredations of science and technology against the arts and the humanities, but I doubt it—although this is certainly something to be concerned about. I suspect it is simply that the human spirit is insufficiently developed at this moment in evolution, much like the wing of archaeopteryx. Whether we can free it for further development will depend, I think, on the full reinstatement of the sense of wonder. It must be reinstated in relation not only to the natural world but to the human world as well. At the conclusion of all our studies we must try once again to experience the human soul as soul, and not just as a buzz of bioelectricity; the human will as will, and not just a surge of hormones; the human heart not as a fibrous, sticky pump, but as the metaphoric organ of understanding. We need not believe in them as metaphysical entities—they are as real as the flesh and blood they are made of. But we must believe in them as entities; not as analyzed fragments, but as wholes made real by our contemplation of them, by the words we use to talk of them, by the way we have transmuted them to speech. We must stand in awe of them as unassailable, even though they are dissected before our eyes.

As for the natural world, we must try to restore wonder there too. We could start with that photograph of the earth. It may be our last chance. Even now it is being used in geography lessons, taken for granted by small children. We are the first generation to have seen it, the last generation not to take it for granted. Will we remember what it meant to us? How fine the earth looked, dangled in space? How pretty against the endless black? How round? How very breakable? How small? It is up to us to try to experience a sense of wonder about it that will save it before it is too late. If we cannot, we may do the final damage in our lifetimes. If we can, we may change the course of history and, consequently, the course of evolution, setting the human lineage firmly on a path toward a new evolutionary plateau.

We must choose, and choose soon, either for or against the further evolution of the human spirit. It is for us, in the generation that turns the corner of the millennium, to apply whatever knowledge we have, in all humility but with all due speed, and to try to learn more as quickly as possible. It is for us, much more than for any previous generation, to become serious about the human future, and to make choices that will be weighed not in a decade or a century but in the balances of geological time. It is for us, with all our stumbling, and in the midst of our dreadful confusion, to try to disengage the tangled wing.

NOTES AND REFERENCES
INDEX

NOTES AND REFERENCES

CAVEAT: THE DANGERS OF BEHAVIORAL BIOLOGY

The contents of this book are known to be dangerous.

I do not mean that in the sense that all important ideas are potentially dangerous; that would be merely tendentious and self-serving. I mean to say something much more precise. In contrast to most other ideas in biology and psychology, those concerning the biological basis of behavior have proved at least to encourage, and perhaps to be involved in the causation of, political and social tendencies and movements that, after they were over, were later regretted by all decent people and universally condemned in school histories. Why, then, purvey such ideas?

Because *some* ideas in behavioral biology are true. At least, the ones in this book are, to the best of my knowledge; and the truth is essential to logical action. That, however, does not mean that these ideas cannot be easily distorted so that they still sound true but are false; nor does it mean that false and evil acts cannot arise from them even if they are left undistorted. I doubt, in fact, that what I say can prevent such eventualities, and indeed I strongly suspect that political and social movements arise primarily from political and social causes, and then seize whatever congenial ideas are at hand. Nonetheless, I am not comfortable in the company of scientists who are content to search for the truth and let the consequences go hang. I therefore recount here a few pieces of the dismal, indeed shameful history of the misuses of behavioral biology, in some of which, at least, scientists were willing participants.

The first distinctive episode is recounted in William Stanton's *The Leopard's Spots: Scientific Attitudes Toward Race in America, 1815–59* (Chicago: University of Chicago Press, 1960). Such names as Samuel George Morton, George Robins Gliddon, and Josiah Clark Nott mean little to present-day students of anthropology, but in the politically heady decades between the death of Jefferson and the start of the War Between the States, they founded the American School of Anthropology, which dedicated itself to proving the inevitable separate status of the races and to placing white supremacy on a foundation of scientific study of crania and their internal capacity, together with some "obvious" observable facts of behavior and custom; "niggerology," as one of them privately called it (Stanton, *The Leopard's Spots*, p. 161). In its more dignified guise it was called "polygen-ism" by way of reference to the supposed separate evolutionary origins of various races. Two of the three (Morton and Nott) were physicians, but their conjectures were based on so little and such silly "evidence" that it is puzzling how they succeeded. Yet succeed they did. When they came on the scene in the early part of the century the views of Samuel Stanhope Smith, according to which mankind had a single origin and a single biological plan, held sway. By the 1850s the unity of mankind was an idea effectively dislodged from favor, linked to atavistic, religious, antiscientific sentimen-talism. Miscegenation was viewed as a threat to civilization, and slavery the logical lot of the Negro. Now no one would suppose the Civil War to have been caused by a few anthropologists; but they were highly respected and popular writers and lecturers, and it cannot be doubted that they deceived many. Meanwhile, their counterparts in Britain, France, and Germany laid a foundation for scientific racism that would stand firm for about a hundred years (Marvin Harris, *The Rise of Anthropological Theory* [New York: Thomas Y. Crowell, 1968], chapter 4).

The second episode has to do with Social Darwinism, some of which was in fact pre-Darwinian. It is recounted by George Stocking, in chapter 6, "The Dark-Skinned Savage: The Image of Primitive Man in Evolutionary Anthropology," of *Race, Culture and Evolution: Essays in the History of Anthropology* (New York: Free Press, 1968) and by Marvin Harris in chapter 5, "Spencerism," in *The Rise of Anthropological Theory*. In the latter part of the nineteenth century, most social theory was evolutionary, but in a way that has little to do with modern evolutionary theory. The leaders of social and cultural anthropology, Lewis Henry Morgan and Edward Tylor, al-though they greatly admired the "primitive" tribes and races, nevertheless viewed them hierarchically, with the "less developed" or "less complex" groups being essentially frozen relics of past epochs. Marx and Engels took over this view from Morgan, and made little attempt to conceal their patronizing attitude toward the "relics." Darwin (see Stocking, *Race, Culture and Evolution*, p.113) and his evolutionist predecessor Charles Lyell (see Harris, *Anthropological Theory*, p. 113) both predicted the extermina-tion of the "savage" races by the civilized ones, and did not seem to shed any tears over this process; this in an era when some of their readers were doubtless attempting to prosecute that very extermination. Morgan and Tylor's hierarchical arrangements of social and cultural forms were accompanied by explicit presumptions of a corresponding hierarchy of mental capacity; the more complex the civilization, the greater the native intelligence of its members. Progress through improvement was the inexorable motive force, and the pinnacle of progress was the civilization of Victorian England.

How comforting these ideas must have been to the distinguished representatives of that (and related) civilizations who were just then engaged in the difficult work of subduing, enslaving or, where necessary, exterminating those "primitive" peoples. Can they be blamed for being easily convinced, despite the absence of convincing evidence? Herbert Spencer, the leading exponent of social evolutionism, cuts a rather tragic figure against this background. Always claiming to be a friend of the poor, abhorring war and the greedy rape of the underdeveloped world, Spencer was viewed by many contemporaries, as well as by later scholars, as an apologist for the worst that was going on. He—not Darwin—coined the phrase "survival of the fittest" and justified the exploitation of the weak by the strong on the grounds that the inevitable march of progress is only interfered with by humane intervention in the struggle for existence. Spencer explicitly apologized for the most unrestrained forms of capitalism, and opposed socialism and all forms of social welfare. It is not difficult to imagine his words in the minds of the Robber Barons or of the legislators who voted against child labor laws. The progress of human decency in the nineteenth century was no doubt a complex matter, but it is not farfetched to suggest that ideas about the biology of behavior retarded that progress. (Harris proceeds with the details of later evolutionist social theory in his *Anthropological Theory*, chapters 6 and 7. For a complementary critique of evolutionary theories of social behavior and their consequences in the nineteenth and twentieth centuries, see Stephan Chorover, *From Genesis to Genocide* [Cambridge, Mass.: MIT Press, 1979], chapter 5).

The third episode takes place on both sides of the Atlantic between the beginning of World War I and the end of World War II. The American side of the episode is recounted in the first two chapters of Leon Kamin's *The Science and Politics of I.Q.* (Potomac, Md.: Erlbaum, 1974), in Chorover's *Genesis*, chapter 3, and in Stocking's *Race, Culture and Evolution*, chapter 11. Although Alfred Binet, the Frenchman who originated IQ testing in 1905, had intended it as a device for identifying children who needed mental improvement through training, it began to be used in the United States, a decade or so later, for very different purposes. Under the auspices of Lewis Terman of Stanford and Robert Yerkes of Harvard—two of the deans of American psychology—it was explicitly used to separate genetic gold—as it were—from genetic dross. Both these men, on the basis of little evidence, believed that the cause of IQ was largely genetic, and saw an opportunity to provide a then much needed social service—giving the U.S. government a good excuse to stem the tide of immigration, which was growing ever higher. In addition, the behavior-genetic notions of the nineteenth century had then recently crystallized in the formation of a clear eugenics movement in the United States. With the approval, indeed encouragement of distinguished psychologists, compulsory sterilization laws were passed by the state legislatures of Pennsylvania, Indiana, New Jersey, Iowa, California, and Washington, providing for the "unsexing" of an impressive range of undesirables. In upholding the California law, the attorney general of California used the language of behavioral biology: "Degeneracy means that certain areas of brain cells or nerve centers of the individual are more highly or imperfectly developed than the other brain cells, and this causes an unstable state of the nerve system, which may manifest itself in insanity, criminality, idiocy, sexual perversion, or inebriety"; and he went on to include "many of the confirmed inebriates, prostitutes, tramps, and criminals, as well as habitual paupers" in this class, all of whose members were potentially eligible for legal castration. The *Harvard Law Review* of December 1912, by which time all these state laws had been passed, argued that they would be constitutional, but only in the case of "born criminals" (Kamin, *I.Q.*, pp. 11–12).

Retrospective opprobrium directed at these lawyers and government officials has been great, justifiably, but it should be realized that they were somewhat at the mercy of psychologists, anthropologists, biologists, and physicians who were giving them a completely false picture of the facts. These "experts" provided what seemed to be definitive statements in a context fraught with uncertainty. They held out false hopes for great improvements in human welfare through eugenics, and rang loudly the false alarms of racial degeneracy and eugenic disaster in the event that their advice was not followed.

Given these remarkable intellectual and legal developments in the United States, the existence of parallel movements in Germany and elsewhere in Europe seems a bit less stunningly unnatural. The ideas of eugenics and racial hygiene (*Rassenhygiene*) became respectable and firmly established in German academic and medical discourse while Hitler was still a child. In 1895 the physician Alfred Ploetz wrote *The Excellence of Our Race and the Protection of the Weak*; in 1903 Wilhelm Schallmeyer won a national prize (offered by the Krupp armaments family) for his *Inheritance and Selection in the Life-History of Nationalities: A Sociopolitical Study Based upon the Newer Biology*; two important scholarly journals concerned with eugenics and racial purity, *Politisch-Anthropologische Revue* (Political-Anthropological Review) and *Archiv für Rassen und Gesellschaftsbiologie* (Archive for Racial and Social Biology) began publication in 1902 and 1904 respectively; in 1920 a distinguished jurist, Karl Binding, and a distinguished psychiatrist, Alfred Hoche, published *The Release and Destruction of Lives Devoid of Value*, advocating large-scale, eugenically motivated euthanasia.

It is critical to realize how very respectable these ideas were. They have nothing to do with brown shirts, breaking glass, goose-step marches, or diabolically energized mass rallies. They have only to do with respectable scientists, physicians, and lawyers communicating soberly with one another through the usual means of discourse. Long before the foundation of the Nazi party it was widely agreed that then recent discoveries in social biology constrained scholars to believe that civilization was the result of genetic determinants, and that its continuance depended on racial purity and the relentless elimination of the psychologically unfit from the gene pool. Furthermore, this was not a national but an international phenomenon. In 1923, a year before the publication of *Mein Kampf*, a director of health in Zwickau wrote to the German minister of the interior, urging the enactment of a program of eugenic sterilization: "What we racial hygienists promote is not at all new or unheard of. In a cultured nation of the first order, the United States of America, that which we strive toward was introduced and tested long ago." Still skeptical, the interior minister pursued the matter through the German Foreign Office, and after receiving an extensive report, became convinced. Through the example of the United States, eugenics became respectable government business in Weimar Germany (Chorover, *Genesis*, p. 98).

Ideas about the role of the Jews in what might be called "genetic history" were also current in international discourse. The English historian Houston Stuart Chamberlain had argued, in such works as *Foundations of the Nineteenth Century* and *Race and Nation* (the first was originally published in German at the turn of the century), that the fall and rise of nations could best be understood by reference to the introduction and removal of Jews, respectively. Chamberlain's work was widely discussed among German students from the time it was first published. (See Lucy S Dawidowicz, *The War Against the Jews, 1933–1945* [New York: Holt, Rinehart and Winston, 1975] for discussion and references on the influence of Chamberlain.) Alfred Rosenberg, an important adviser to Hitler during the early years of the Nazi movement, called Chamberlain's work "the strongest positive impulse in my youth," and prepared excerpts of *Foundations of the Nineteenth Century* (*Grundlage des Neunzehn Jahrhunderts*) for Hitler's easy study, (Dawidowicz, *War*, p. 20). Heinrich Himmler, later and throughout the war the head of the SS and a key figure in all concentration and killing operations, read *Race and Nation* (*Rasse und Nation*) at the end of 1921, and wrote of it in his diary: "It is true and one has the impression that it is objective, not just hate-filled anti-Semitism. Because of this it has more effect. These terrible Jews" (Dawidowicz, *War*, p. 95). The last sentence is almost poignant; it makes clear, I think, that the reading of Chamberlain gave Himmler an additional measure of genuine conviction. Are such things as the scribblings of intellectuals about behavioral biology really important in the causation of great social movements? We don't know; but we know enough, I think, to say that the truth is poorly served by the smug persuasion that they are not, and that we have here the grist for a great deal of milling by good intellectual historians.

Many people wonder why the Jews did not try to get out. Of course, they did, in much larger numbers than were able to do so. The rising tide of immigration to the United States after World War I was in part due to the realization of Jews and other Europeans that there were ominous signs on the horizon. American behavioral biologists, particularly psychologists, played, as mentioned before, a key role in stemming this tide. Terman, Yerkes, and others, referring to ludicrously poor research, involved themselves in the perpetration of falsehoods that laid the foundation for a much more restrictive immigration policy, as formulated in the Immigration Act of 1924 and other laws. Among the frequently quoted findings was Henry Goddard's report, based on IQ testing of immigrants at Ellis Island, that 83 percent of the Jews, 80 percent of the Hungarians, 79 percent of the Italians, and 87 percent of the Russians were "feeble-minded" (Kamin, *I.Q.*, p. 16), findings due primarily to sloppy testing and formidable language barriers. Robert Yerkes published the results of similarly poor, "confirmatory" research, under the auspices of the United States National Academy of Sciences, in 1921. The actual work of convincing Congressmen was done by others, but the result for immigration policy was formidable. Because of the views of American psychologists and other behavioral biologists about the genetics of mental competence, many Jews and other potential immigrants were trapped in Europe, later to become Nazi victims. (The definitive work on these events in Europe remains Raul Hilberg, *The Destruction of the European Jews* [Chicago: Quadrangle, 1961; republished with a new foreword in New York: Franklin Watts, 1973].)

Incidentally, after 1920 the role of American anthropology in these intellectual currents became a very different, indeed heroic one. (See Stocking's *Race, Culture and Evolution*, chapter 11, for details.) Franz Boas had established a new and completely different "American School" of anthropology, the main thrust of which was to break decisively with the racist and evolutionist past. He and his students (among them Alfred Kroeber, Ruth Benedict, and Margaret Mead) rejected all notions of cultural and social hierarchy, and Boas's book *The Mind of Primitive Man* laid to rest the notion that mental function was correlated with civilizational complexity. The Boas school, in a major paradigm shift, placed the concepts of culture and cultural relativism at the center of anthropology, stressing the dignity and independent validity of all known cultures. In the arguments over IQ, race, and eugenics that raged during the 1920s and 1930s they stood firmly opposed to the psychological testers and eugenicists, stressing their mounting evidence for the importance of cultural conditioning in all dimensions of ethnicity and for the universal validity of the most important human mental functions. Traveling to all the corners of the earth for evidence, sifting and organizing it into a new science, which they created against great odds and in a short period of time, they won the day. "In the long run, it was Boasian anthropology—rather than the racialist writers associated with the eugenics movement—which was able to speak to Americans as the voice of science on all matters of race, culture, and evolution—a fact whose significance for the recent history of the United States doubtless merits further exploration" (Stocking, *Race, Culture and Evolution*, p. 307). If American anthropologists today, all greatly influenced by Boas, are resisting the new currents of biological determinism, that is not only understandable but also, in my view, healthy.

What of these new currents? Are they likely to lead to, or at least to become complicit in, further disasters of social policy? The indications are not all encouraging. Konrad Lorenz, who shared the Nobel Prize in medicine and physiology in 1973 for his work in behavioral biology, and who remains an active and distinguished investigator, provides an uncomfortable link with the past. As noted by Leon Eisenberg (in "The *Human* Nature of Human Nature," *Science* 176 [1972], pp. 123–28), and by Chorover (*Genesis*, pp. 104–05, Lorenz wrote an article in a scholarly journal in 1940— quite a late date—decrying miscegenation and racial impurity as leading to degeneracy in the genetically determined aspects of behavior and character, and explicitly praising the Nazi state for its accomplishments against this danger. Of course, Lorenz has deeply regretted and retracted these statements, and he should not be hounded to his grave about them when others who did much worse things have been more or less forgiven. Yet the watchword should not be "forgive and forget" but "forgive and remember."

Statements made by Arthur Jensen, William Shockley, and other investigators in the late 1960s and early 1970s about race and IQ or social class and IQ rapidly passed into currency in policy discussions. Some of these statements later proved to be wrong, but they had already influenced some policymakers, and that influence is very difficult to retract. It is a phenomenon that needs much better study.

The last few years have seen the beginnings of an attempt to use the ideas of the sociobiology of the late 1970s in support of neofascist movements. It must be said that there is nothing specific or new about these ideas that has been seen as useful by neofascists; merely the highly visible statement that genes influence behavior, combined with a renewed emphasis on the strict evolutionary sense of "fitness." The National Socialist youth movement in Britain has adopted a sort of quasisociobiological cant, quoting or referring to E.O. Wilson, Richard Dawkins, and others. To be sure, they have little understanding of what they read; yet they find it useful. A recent exchange of letters in *Nature* on this point, between Steven Rose and Richard Dawkins, English arch rivals in the sociobiology controversy, is of interest (S. Rose, *Nature* 289 [1981], p. 335; R. Dawkins, ibid., p. 528). Rose points with obvious smugness to the misuse of Dawkins's views by the neofascists, calling on Dawkins to dissociate himself publicly from them and saying, pretty explicitly, I told you so. Dawkins responds by dissociating himself, and expressing amazement that anyone could have so misconstrued his views as to make use of them in a neofascist cause; he says, quite explicitly, that it never crossed his mind that this could happen. Now, Rose is certainly guilty of bad manners; and one wonders whether he expects other scientists to conceal their findings when they turn out to be susceptible of misuse. But Dawkins's naïve amazement is also distressing.

A few years ago an article appeared in *Time* magazine on sociobiology that included a brief, innocuous, rather favorable quotation from me, among many others. I simply pointed out that not only bad human traits, but also good ones such as altruism were part of our evolutionary endowment. I did not mention race or individual differences, and the rest of the article said little or nothing about either. I received, shortly thereafter, a long, poignant letter from a woman who identified herself as black, and who, despite being quite articulate, was beset by a variety of thoughts and feelings that indicated a need for psychiatric treatment. Among other things she discoursed at length upon the genetic and moral inferiority of blacks, attributing many of her own and other black people's problems to this "theory." My point in mentioning it is that I had said nothing that I could visualize as related to her letter in any significant way, yet she had interpreted my statement about altruism as support for her theory. She was writing in a spirit of colleaguial and mutual congratulation.

In my view anyone who investigates or writes about behavioral biology without recognizing the potential for grave misuse of it, proven many times in the last two centuries, is either a dangerous charlatan or a dangerous fool. But to the person who thinks such investigations should stop, I say this: Closing one's eyes to the truth cannot make it go away, or prevent other people from distorting it. Their efforts to distort are indeed enhanced by such suppression.

I think of modern behavioral biology as a powerful, dangerous physic, potentially healing if used appropriately, potentially poisonous if not. The vast majority of it has no bearing on the great questions of race and social class, except insofar as it may help us to understand and expose the irrational behavior of oppressors. Yet I know that other, false claims will be made for it—claims that will echo the worst errors of the nineteenth and twentieth centuries. Hence, this caveat, a sort of "package insert" for the book, warning of the known dangers of improper use of this kind of knowledge. I would not purvey such medicine if I did not think that the human species were in a critically ill condition, needing every kind of knowledge it can get. Strong maladies require judiciously applied strong remedies.

A PREFATORY INQUIRY

Page

xvi cheaper to rediscover: Sheldon White, personal communication, 1967.

xvii BBC-TV science programs: Produced in 1978 under the title, "Spaceships of the Mind." See companion volume, same title, by Nigel Calder (London: British Broadcasting Corp., 1978).

xx "Truth is the child . . .": Bertolt Brecht, *Collected Plays*, vol. 5, ed. Ralph Manheim and John Willett (New York: Pantheon, 1972), p. 35.

xx "One of the main reasons for the poverty . . .": Brecht, ibid., p. 64.

CHAPTER 1: THE QUEST FOR THE NATURAL

This chapter uses the !Kung San as one example of the hunting-gathering adaptation that is known to have played a central role in human evolution. Excessive emphasis on the !Kung has been criticized by some anthropologists, and rightly so: Many other hunting-gathering adaptations have existed or still exist, and some of these are quite different from that of the !Kung. But none of them have been nearly as well studied. Critics would therefore do well to put their energies into investigations of comparable excellence on other hunting-gathering groups, while the latter are still around to be studied. The chapter draws primarily on the works of Lee and DeVore (*Kalahari Hunter-Gatherers*), Marshall (*The !Kung of Nyae Nyae*), Lee (*The !Kung San*), Howell (*Demography of the Dobe !Kung*), and Shostak (*Nisa: The Life and Words of a !Kung Woman*), as well as on the author's own experience and research. These and other relevant books and papers are cited fully below.

No writing on the !Kung can omit mention of their present situation. After centuries of oppression at the hands especially of whites but also blacks in southern Africa, they now find themselves choosing either near-serfdom on Bantu farms, or dependency with restricted freedom on white-run racist reservations in Namibia (South-West Africa), or near-impressment into the South African Army to kill and die in a war they do not understand, as their traditional way of earning a living is made impossible by the selfishness and violence of other people around them. We who use them to help us understand human nature must not forget that they are human beings in the throes of a grave historical crisis. For the most accurate information see Lee's *The !Kung San*, and Willcox, "The Bushmen in History," cited below. John Marshall's documentary film *N!ai, The Story of a !Kung Woman*, shown several times on national public television (cited below) dramatically illustrates the events of the late 1970s. Lee, who is professor of anthropology at the University of Toronto, keeps abreast of current developments, and should be contacted by those concerned about the plight of the !Kung and other San people.

Page

3 Rousseau was not the first: Jean Jacques Rousseau, *The Social Contract*, trans. G.D. Cole (New York: Dutton, 1938).

4 the archeological record: For the full rationale for the use of hunter-gatherer studies as an aid to archeological interpretation, see Richard B. Lee and Irven DeVore, eds. *Man the Hunter* (Chicago: Aldine, 1968). For an important complementary (and more up-to-date) view see Frances Dahlberg, ed., *Woman the Gatherer* (New Haven: Yale University Press, 1981). It includes a chapter on the Agta of the Philippines, the only known case of systematic hunting by women. There may be others.

5 Marshall family: See Lorna Marshall, *The !Kung of Nyae Nyae* (Cambridge, Mass.: Harvard University Press, 1976); Elizabeth Marshall Thomas, *The Harmless People* (New York: Knopf, 1959); and John Marshall's various films, including *The Hunters, Bitter Melons,* and *N!ai, The Story of a !Kung Woman* (aired on PBS-TV, 1980–81). Available through D.E.R. Films, 5 Bridge Street, Watertown, Massachusetts.

5 Lee-DeVore expeditions: See Richard B. Lee and Irven DeVore, eds., *Kalahari Hunter-Gatherers* (Cambridge, Mass.: Harvard University Press, 1976); Richard B. Lee, *The !Kung San: Men, Women and Work in a Foraging Society* (Cambridge, Engl.: Cambridge University Press, 1979); Nancy Howell, *Demography of the Dobe !Kung* (New York: Academic Press, 1979); and Marjorie Shostak, *Nisa: The Life and Words of a !Kung Woman* (Cambridge, Mass.: Harvard University Press, 1981). These four works constitute the major ethnographic product of the Lee-DeVore expeditions in book form. Together with Lorna Marshall's book, they will undoubtedly constitute the core of the permanent definite account of !Kung life, supplemented by numerous scholarly articles, past and future.

I was privileged to be part of the Lee-DeVore expeditions, living with and learning from the !Kung for twenty months in 1969–71 and for five months in 1975. The following papers describe some of the research I did during those two periods of fieldwork. Most are discussed further later in this book. The papers are: Melvin J.

Konner, "Aspects of the Developmental Ethology of a Foraging People," in *Ethological Studies of Child Behavior*, ed. Nicholas Blurton Jones (Cambridge, Engl.: Cambridge University Press, 1972); "Relations Among Infants and Juveniles in Comparative Perspective," in *Friendship and Peer Relations*, ed. M. Lewis and L. Rosenblum, vol. 3 of *The Origins of Behavior* (New York: John Wiley, 1975) and reprinted in *Social Science Information* (Paris) 15:2 (1976), pp. 371–402; "Maternal Care, Infant Behavior and Development Among the !Kung," in *Kalahari Hunter-Gatherers*, ed. Lee and DeVore; "Infancy Among the Kalahari Desert San," in *Culture and Infancy*, ed. P.H. Leiderman, S. Tulkin, and A. Rosenfeld (New York: Academic Press, 1977); "Evolution of Human Behavior Development," in *Handbook of Cross-Cultural Development*, ed. Robert L. Monroe, Ruth H. Monroe, and Beatrice B. Whiting (New York: Garland Press, 1981); "Biological Bases of Social Development," in *Primary Prevention of Psychopathology: Social Competence in Children*, ed. J. Rolfe, M. Whalen, and J. Joffe (Hanover, N.H.: University Press of New England, 1979); and "Biological Aspects of the Mother-Infant Bond," in *Development of Attachment and Affiliation Processes*, ed. Robert Emde and Robert Harmon (New York: Plenum, 1982). Also see Melvin J. Konner and Carol Worthman, "Nursing Frequency, Gonadal Function and Birth Spacing Among !Kung Hunter-Gatherers," *Science* 207 (1980), pp. 788–91; Nicholas Blurton Jones and Melvin J. Konner, "Sex Differences in Behavior of Two-to-Five Year-Olds in London and Among the Kalahari Desert Bushmen," in *Comparative Ecology and Behavior of Primates*, ed. R.P. Michael and J.H. Crook (London: Academic Press, 1973); Irven DeVore and Melvin J. Konner, "Infancy in Hunter-Gatherer Life: An Ethological Perspective," in *Ethology and Psychiatry*, ed. N.F. White (Toronto: University of Toronto Press, 1974); Nicholas Blurton Jones and Melvin J. Konner, "!Kung Knowledge of Animal Behavior," *Kalahari Hunter-Gatherers*, ed. Lee and DeVore; Mary M. Katz and Melvin J. Konner, "The Role of the Father: An Anthropological Perspective," in *The Role of the Father in Child Development*, ed. M. Lamb (New York: John Wiley, 1981).

5–8 Depiction of the !Kung San: For extensive ethnographic descriptions of !Kung San life see Marshall, *The !Kung of Nyae Nyae*, Lee, *The !Kung San*, and Shostak, *Nisa*.

For an historical survey of the San in Southern Africa see A. Willcox, "The Bushmen in History," R. Inskeep, "The Bushmen in Prehistory," and P. Tobias, "Introduction to the Bushmen or San," in *The Bushmen*, ed. Phillip Tobias (Cape Town, South

Africa: Human and Rousseau, 1978). For a more detailed archeological perspective on the !Kung, see John Yellen, *Archeological
Approaches to the Present: Models for Reconstructing the Past* (New
York: Academic Press, 1977). This book also contains valuable
information on !Kung material culture and land use in the present
(as of 1970).

8 "solitary, poor . . .": Thomas Hobbes, *Leviathan*, ed. C.B. Mac-
Pherson (New York: Penguin, 1968), p. 186. The remark was
made in relation to the life of the North American natives at the
time of Hobbes's writing.

8 "the original affluent society": Marshall Sahlins, *Stone Age Economics* (London: Tavistock, 1974), chapter 1.

10 ". . . I thought that one should return . . .": Guillaume Apollinaire, in his preface to *Les Mamelles de Tirésias* (Paris: Éditions du
Belier, 1946), p. 10. ". . . j'ai pensé qu'il fallait revenir à la nature
même, mais sans l'imiter à la manière des photographes.

   "Quand l'homme a voulu imiter la marche, il a créé la roue qui
ne ressemble pas à une jambe . . ." (translation by the author).

CHAPTER 2: ADAPTATION

An easy-to-read popular introduction to recent concepts of adaptation, especially in the realm of behavior, is Richard Dawkins's *The Selfish
Gene* (New York: Oxford University Press, 1976), and a more advanced
brief treatment is Williams's *Adaptation and Natural Selection*, cited below.
E.O. Wilson's *Sociobiology*, cited below, is the best-known comprehensive
advanced text, but it has been widely criticized for certain poorly founded
speculations; nevertheless, it is well worth reading. A more sober text with
the same range but somewhat different emphasis appeared at the same time:
Jerram Brown, *The Evolution of Behavior* (New York: W.W. Norton, 1975);
I suspect that the book would have (and believe it should have) gotten more
attention if it had not been published almost simultaneously with *Sociobiology*.

No one should undertake to criticize a new scientific approach without
becoming familiar with the original papers that have convinced its followers
of its power. In this field they are collected together in T. Clutton-Brock
and P. Harvey, eds., *Readings in Sociobiology* (San Francisco: W.H. Freeman, 1978). The papers of W.D. Hamilton and Robert L. Trivers are
especially noteworthy.

Darwin's *Origin of Species* is perhaps the only major work of nineteenth-century science that continues to be of more than historical interest. The edition introduced by Mayr (cited below) is authoritative.

For a valuable critique of the excesses of some theories of adaptation see Richard Lewontin, "Adaptation," *Scientific American*, Sept. 1978. This whole issue of *Scientific American* was devoted to evolution, and is an authoritative, up-to-date introduction to many facets of the subject, with readable articles by a number of leading figures. For the definitive work on the interface between theories of adaptation and theories of learning, see Martin Seligman and Joanne Hager, *Biological Boundaries of Learning* (New York: Meredith, 1972).

For a brief and eloquent account by a distinguished psychiatrist of the role of evolutionary perspective in the understanding of human behavior, see David A. Hamburg, "Emotions in the Perspective of Human Evolution," in *Expression of the Emotions in Man* (New York: International Universities Press, 1963). This and other writings of Hamburg helped set the tone for a generation of interdisciplinary research in anthropology, psychiatry, psychology, evolutionary biology and brain science, and were an important source of inspiration for this book.

And for the most up-to-date account of the theory and method of ethology, see Konrad Z. Lorenz, *Foundations of Ethology* (New York: Springer-Verlag, 1981).

Page

12–13 Pre-Darwinian and Darwinian thought: Loren Eiseley, *Darwin's Century* (New York: Doubleday, 1958); Ernst Mayr, introduction to Charles Darwin, *The Origin of Species: A Facsimile of the First Edition* (Cambridge, Mass.: Harvard University Press, 1966).

13 *Origin:* Darwin, ibid. Original edition: London: John Murray, 1859.

13 Solution of the species problem: Ernst Mayr, *Animal Species and Evolution* (Cambridge, Mass.: Harvard University Press, 1963). The solution involved explaining the necessary transition from two interbreeding populations of a species to two separate species for which viable offspring are unlikely; this almost always requires the emergence of a geographic barrier to gene flow.

13 Attack on group selection theory: George C. Williams, *Adaptation and Natural Selection: A Critique of Some Current Evolutionary Thought* (Princeton: Princeton University Press, 1966). An excellent advanced introduction to the process of natural selection as it is now viewed by most evolutionary biologists.

14 "a few words on . . . Sexual Selection": Darwin, *Origin*, pp. 88–90.

15 Trivers on sexual selection: Robert L. Trivers, "Parental Investment and Sexual Selection," in *Sexual Selection and the Descent of*

Man, 1871–1971, ed. Bernard G. Campbell (Chicago: Aldine, 1974), pp. 136–79. This updating of sexual selection theory is one of the most frequently cited papers in modern behavioral ecology. It is a model of clarity, and surprisingly accessible to the nonexpert reader.

16 Wilson's book: E.O. Wilson, *Sociobiology* (Cambridge, Mass.: Harvard University Press, Belknap Press, 1975). This much maligned book is really an innovative, extraordinarily thorough, well-written, and beautifully illustrated textbook of animal behavior and its evolution. For access to the at least somewhat valuable debate it engendered, see Arthur L. Caplan, ed., *The Sociobiology Debate: Readings on Ethical and Scientific Issues* (New York: Harper & Row, 1978).

17 "Whatever the cause may be . . .": Darwin, *Origin*, p. 170.

18 Adaptation as Procrustean bed: Richard C. Lewontin, "Adaptation." Lewontin has been a vigorous and distinguished critic of sociobiology in all its manifestations. Like many of its critics, he is highly regarded in his own field (population genetics) but has not personally done research on the evolution of behavior.

18 flights of fancy: Desmond Morris, *The Naked Ape* (New York: McGraw-Hill, 1967) on breasts and buttocks; A. Zahavi, "Mate Selection—A Selection for a Handicap," *Journal of Theoretical Biology* 53 (1975), pp. 205–14; and Wilson, *Sociobiology*, on nonreproduction.

19–20 !Kung San infants: Melvin J. Konner, "Aspects of the Developmental Ethology of a Foraging People," in *Ethological Studies of Child Behavior*, ed. N. Blurton Jones (Cambridge, Engl.: Cambridge University Press, 1972).

20 Darwin's voyage: See Eiseley, *Darwin's Century*.

21 fit of an organism to its environment: This usage of the word "fit" is frequently confused with at least two other usages. One is the health-club sense of "fit," which has no place in discussions of evolution; the other is the strict, scientific definition of "fitness," which is nothing more nor less than a ratio of an individual's number of offspring to the population mean for the generation.

21 Lamarck's theory, and Darwin's Lamarckian lapses: Eiseley, *Darwin's Century*. See also Ernst Mayr's introduction to the facsimile edition of the *Origin*.

22 Rhesus monkey dominance: Donald S. Sade, "Determinants of Dominance in a Group of Free-Ranging Rhesus Monkeys," in *Social Communication Among Primates*, ed. S. Altmann (Chicago: University of Chicago Press, 1967).

22 Japanese monkey potato washing: M. Kawai, "New Acquired

Precultural Behavior of the Natural Troop of Japanese Monkeys on Koshima Islet," *Primates* 6 (1965), pp. 1–30.

22 White-crowned sparrow song transmission: Peter Marler, "A Comparative Approach to Vocal Learning: Song Development in White-crowned Sparrows," *Comparative and Physiological Psychology* 71 (1970), pp. 1–25.

23 the Baldwin effect: For discussion see Ernst Mayr, "Behavior and Systematics," in *Behavior and Evolution*, ed. A. Roe and G.G. Simpson (New Haven: Yale University Press, 1958); but Mayr expresses skepticism about the Baldwin effect in his later work, *Animal Species and Evolution*, pp. 604–12.

23–24 Waddington experiment: C.H. Waddington, "Canalization of Development and the Inheritance of Acquired Characteristics," *Nature* 150 (1942), pp. 563–65.

25 ". . . the capacity to learn . . .": From Julian Huxley, *Essays of a Humanist* (New York: Harper & Row, 1965), as quoted by Seligman and Hager in *Biological Boundaries*, p. xiv.

25 Skinner's major early work: B.F. Skinner, *The Behavior of Organisms* (New York: Appleton-Century-Crofts, 1938).

26 a series of papers: See Seligman and Hager, *Biological Boundaries*, pp. 8–9, for a summary of this history, and chapters 1–3 for reprints of the Garcia papers.

26–28 The key experiment: John Garcia and Robert A. Koelling, "Relation of Cue to Consequence in Avoidance Learning," *Psychonomic Science* 4 (1966), pp. 123–24, reprinted in Seligman and Hager, *Biological Boundaries*, pp. 10–14.

27 "genetically coded hypothesis": Ibid.

28 "Those findings are no more likely . . .": Seligman and Hager, *Biological Boundaries*, p. 15.

28 general laws of learning: John Garcia, Brenda McGown, and Kenneth F. Green, "Biological Constraints on Conditioning," in *Classical Conditioning*, vol. 2, *Current Research and Theory*, ed. A.H. Black and W.F. Prokasy (New York: Appleton-Century-Crofts, 1972), reprinted in Seligman and Hager, *Biological Boundaries*, pp. 38–41.

29 "Sauce Béarnaise phenomenon": Seligman and Hager, *Biological Boundaries*, p. 8.

29 golden hamster behavior patterns: S.J. Shettleworth, "Reinforcement and the Organization of Behavior in Golden Hamsters: Hunger, Environment, and Food Reinforcement," *Journal of Experimental Psychology and Animal Behavior Processes* 1 (1975), pp. 56–87.

29–30 ice cream aversion: I.L. Bernstein and M.M. Webster, "Learned

Taste Aversion in Humans," *Physiology and Behavior* 25 (1980), pp. 363–66.

30 human clinical phobias: Martin Seligman, "Phobias and Preparedness," *Behavior Therapy* 2 (1971), pp. 307–20.

30 "In the distant future . . .": Darwin, *Origin*, p. 488.

CHAPTER 3: THE CRUCIBLE

My favorite books on human evolution are by Bernard G. Campbell: *Humankind Emerging* (Boston: Little, Brown, 1979), an introductory account of the fossil and archeological evidence, and *Human Evolution*, 2nd ed. (Chicago: Aldine, 1974), a more technical but highly readable book focused on the functional meaning of the anatomical changes during evolution (this focus makes it for me the most intellectually satisfying of all such books). A recent advanced account of the fossil record is G.E. Kennedy, *Paleoanthropology* (New York: McGraw-Hill, 1980). For two popular, if slightly solipsistic and somewhat contradictory accounts of recent findings, see Richard Leakey and Roger Lewin, *Origins* (New York: Dutton, 1977), and Donald C. Johanson and Maitland A. Edey, *Lucy: The Beginnings of Humankind* (New York: Simon and Schuster, 1981). John E. Pfeiffer's book *The Emergence of Culture* (New York: Harper & Row, 1982) on the great cultural advances of the late Paleolithic is a valuable and readable synthesis.

Page

32 General principles on hunter-gatherers: Richard B. Lee and Irven DeVore, eds., *Man the Hunter* (Chicago: Aldine: 1968); and M.G. Bicchieri, *Hunters and Gatherers Today: A Socio-Economic Study of Eleven Such Cultures in the Twentieth Century* (New York: Holt, Rinehart and Winston, 1972).

32 Baboons as ancestor models: Sherwood L. Washburn and Irven DeVore, "The Social Life of Baboons," *Scientific American* 204 (1961), pp. 62–71; and Irven DeVore and Sherwood L. Washburn, "Baboon Ecology and Human Evolution," in *African Ecology and Human Evolution*, ed. F. Clark Howell and François Bourliere (New York: Wenner-Gren Foundation for Anthropological Research, 1963).

32 Chimpanzees as ancestor models: Jane van Lawick Goodall, "The Behavior of Free-Living Chimpanzees in the Gombe Stream Reserve," *Animal Behavior Monographs* 1 (1968), pp. 161–311.

33 The *substantia nigra*: Harvey B. Sarnat and Martin G. Netsky,

Evolution of the Nervous System (Oxford: Oxford University Press, 1974), p. 263.

34 comparative study of higher primates: Irven DeVore, ed., *Primate Behavior: Field Studies of Monkeys and Apes* (New York: Holt, Rinehart and Winston, 1965); Alison Jolly, *The Evolution of Primate Behavior* (New York: Macmillan, 1972); and Hans Kommer, *Primate Societies: Group Techniques of Ecological Adaptations* (Chicago: Aldine, 1971).

34–35 Primate social structure: H.H. Crook and J.S. Gartlan, "Evolution of Primate Societies," *Nature* 210 (1966), pp. 1200–1203; and J.F. Eisenberg, N.A. Muckenhirn, and R. Rudran, "The Relation Between Ecology and Social Structure in Primates," *Science* 176 (1972), pp. 863–74.

35–37 *Aegyptopithecus* . . . a small apelike monkey: Elwyn L. Simons, "The Earliest Apes," *Scientific American* 217 (1967), pp. 28–35.

36 "the skull of a monkey equipped with the teeth of an ape": Simons, ibid., p. 35.

37–38 Molecular evidence: V. Sarich, "The Origin of the Hominids: An Immunological Approach," in *Perspectives on Human Evolution*, vol. 1, ed. S.L. Washburn and P. Jay (New York: Holt, Rinehart and Winston, 1970).

38–39 Seed-eating hypothesis: Clifford Jolly, "The Seed Eaters: A New Model of Hominid Differentiation Based on a Baboon Analogy," *Man* 5 (1970), pp. 5–26.

39–40 baboon social behavior: Irven DeVore and Sherwood L. Washburn, "Baboon Ecology and Human Evolution."

40 Controversial defense pattern: For a quantitative critique of DeVore's concept of organized troop defense, see Stewart Altmann, "Baboon Progressions: Order or Chaos? A Study of One-Dimensional Group Geometry," *Animal Behavior* 27 (1979), pp. 46–80. Such controversy may in fact be unearthing more intergroup variation in response to different conditions—for example, different principles may govern social order in a declining as opposed to a stable or growing population.

41 Fossil footprints: Mary D. Leakey and R.L. Hay, "Pliocene Footprints in the Laetolil Beds at Laetolil, Northern Tanzania," *Nature* 278 (1979), pp. 308–12; and Timothy D. White, "Evolutionary Implications of Pliocene Hominid Footprints," *Science* 208 (1980), pp. 175–76.

41–43 Lucy: Donald C. Johanson and Timothy D. White, "A Systematic Assessment of Early African Hominids," *Science* 203 (1979), pp. 321–30.

42 Evolution of women: For one of the first serious modern treat-

ments of this subject see Sarah Blaffer Hrdy, *The Woman That Never Evolved* (Cambridge, Mass.: Harvard University Press, 1981). When the facts are known it is difficult indeed to sustain the picture of man's nurturing, coy and self-effacing helpmeet that is conventional in certain kinds of glancing back at evolution.

43 Indirect evidence that Lucy used tools: Jane van Lawick Goodall, "Continuities Between Chimpanzee and Human Behavior," in *Human Origins: Louis Leakey and the East African Evidence*, ed. Glynn Ll. Isaac and Elizabeth R. McCown (Reading, Mass.: W.A. Benjamin, 1976).

43 Other studies of chimpanzee tool use: W.C. McGrew and Caroline E.G. Tutin, "Chimpanzee Tool Use in Dental Grooming," *Nature* 241 (1973), pp. 477–78; C. Jones and J. Sabater Pi, "Sticks Used by Chimpanzees in Rio Muni, West Africa," *Nature* 223 (1969), pp. 100–101; and A. Suzuki, "On the Insect-Eating Habits Among Wild Chimpanzees Living in the Savanna Woodland of Western Tanzania," *Primates* 7 (1966), pp. 481–87.

43 model of a leopard: Adriaan Kortlandt, "Experimentation with Chimpanzees in the Wild," in *Progress in Primatology*, ed. D. Starck, R. Schneider, and H.J. Kuhn (Stuttgart: Fischeri, 1967).

44 Lucy's male counterpart: Johanson and White, "A Systematic Assessment of Early African Hominids."

44 difference in body size: Joseph L. Popp and Irven DeVore, "Aggressive Competition and Social Dominance Theory: Synopsis," in *The Great Apes*, ed. David A. Hamburg and Elizabeth R. McCown (Reading, Mass.: Benjamin/Cummings, 1979).

45 Lake Turkana: Alan Walker and Richard Leakey, "The Hominids of East Turkana," *Scientific American* 239 (1978), pp. 54–66.

45 butchering of a carcass: John E. Pfeiffer, *The Emergence of Man*, 3rd. ed. (New York: Harper & Row, 1978), p. 100; and Isaac and McCown, eds., *Human Origins*, p. 521.

46 hinted at by Darwin: Charles Darwin, *The Descent of Man* (London: John Murray, 1871).

46 Made more explicit by Engels: Friedrich Engels, "The Part Played by Labor in the Transition from Ape to Man," in Friedrich Engels, *The Origin of the Family, Private Property and the State* (New York: International Publishers, 1972).

46 Tool use and brain evolution: Sherwood L. Washburn, "Tools and Human Evolution," *Scientific American* 203 (1960), pp. 3–15. See also J.B. Lancaster, "On the Evolution of Tool-Using Behavior," *American Anthropologist* 70 (1968), pp. 56–66.

46 Range of skull variation: Walker and Leakey, "The Hominids of East Turkana."

47 Cranial capacity: Ralph L. Holloway, "The Casts of Fossil Hominid Brains," in *Human Ancestors: Readings from Scientific American* (San Francisco: W.H. Freeman, 1979).

47 "capable man": Louis Leakey, P.V. Tobias, and J.R. Napier, "A New Species of the Genus *Homo* from Olduvai Gorge," *Nature* 202 (1964), pp. 7–9.

48 transitional forms: G.G. Simpson, lecturing in a graduate course on evolutionary theory, department of biology, Harvard University, Fall 1966.

48 The rest of the story: For a good summary of the last million years, see William W. Howells, *Evolution of the Genus Homo* (Reading, Mass.: Addison-Wesley, 1973).

49 reorganization is fundamental: Ralph L. Holloway, "Cranial Capacity and Neuron Number: A Critique and Proposal," *American Journal of Physical Anthropology* 25 (1966), pp. 305–14.

49 A six-year-old juvenile: Raymond Dart, "*Australopithecus Africanus*: The Man Ape of South Africa," *Nature* 115 (1925), pp. 195–99.

50 Fire, under human control: D.R. Black, P. Teilhard de Chardin, C.C. Young, W.C. Pei, *Fossil Man in China: The Choukoutien Cave Deposits, with a Synopsis of Our Present Knowledge*, Memorial Geological Survey of China, Series A, no. 11 (1933), as cited by Campbell, *Humankind Emerging*.

50 "Look not too long . . .": Herman Melville, *Moby Dick*, chapter 96, "The Try-Works" (New York: Hendricks House, 1952), p. 422.

50–51 Huts with hearths: Henry de Lumley, "A Paleolithic Camp at Nice," *Scientific American* 220 (1969), pp. 42–50.

51 brutal big-game hunting: F. Clark Howell, *Early Man* (Chicago: Time-Life, 1973).

51 Earliest specimens of *Homo sapiens*: Howells, *Evolution of the Genus Homo*.

52 the first Neanderthal: Actually, there were previous finds of Neanderthal remains in 1829 and 1843, but these were ignored. See G.E. Kennedy, *Paleoanthropology* (New York: McGraw-Hill, 1980), for discussion.

52 Near Eastern Neanderthals: For an authoritative treatment of Neanderthal skeletal remains, see the works of Erik Trinkhaus, for example "Hard Times Among the Neanderthals," *Natural History* 87 (1978), pp. 58–63; and Erik Trinkhaus and William W. Howells, "The Neanderthals," *Scientific American* 241 (1979), pp. 118–33.

52–53 slender pelvis: Erik Trinkhaus, "The Morphology of European and Southwest Asian Neanderthal Pubic Bones," *American Journal of Physical Anthropology* 44 (1976), pp. 95–103.

53 Shanidar: Trinkhaus, "Hard Times."

53–54 The Mousterian stone-tool industry: F. Bordes, *The Old Stone Age* (New York: McGraw-Hill, 1968).

54 Cave of Witches, "lair of dragons," bear cults, burials: Bordes, *Old Stone Age*, and Johannes Maringer, *The Gods of Prehistoric Man* (New York: Knopf, 1960).

54 cultish pursuit in Faulkner's story: William Faulkner, "The Bear," in *The Portable Faulkner*, ed. Malcolm Cowley (New York: Viking, 1946).

55 Shanidar flower burial: Ralph S. Solecki, *Shanidar, The First Flower People* (New York: Knopf, 1971).

56 Cro-Magnon man: Bordes, *Old Stone Age*; Michael Day, *Guide to Fossil Man* (Cleveland: World, 1965), pp. 48–51.

56–57 Altamira, Font de Gaume, Trois Frères: Abbé H. Breuil, *Four Hundred Centuries of Cave Art* (Montignac, France: Centre d'Études et de Documentation Préhistoriques, 1953).

57 "a paleolithic Sistine Chapel": Fernand Windels, *The Lascaux Cave Paintings* (New York: Viking, 1950).

57 a kind of theater: Pfeiffer, *The Emergence of Culture*.

57–58 Other explanations for cave painting: Ann Sieveking, *The Cave Artists* (London: Thames and Hudson, 1979).

58 ". . . a language for which we have no vocabulary": Ibid., p. 209.

58 "The purpose of painting . . .": Attributed to Auguste Renoir by Phoebe Pool, in *The Impressionists* (New York: Praeger, 1969).

58 "To our distant ancestors . . .": Windels, *Lascaux Cave Paintings*, epigraph.

CHAPTER 4: THE FABRIC OF MEANING

Good books on the nervous system now number in the hundreds, and I can do no more than mention a few authoritative brief accounts of various facets of the subject: Raymond Carpenter, *Human Neuroanatomy*, seventh edition (Baltimore: Williams and Wilkins, 1976), a definitive introduction to structure; Gordon Shepherd, *The Synaptic Organization of the Brain*, second edition (New York: Oxford University Press, 1979), a brief, cogent account of nerve cell and circuit function; and Jack R. Cooper, Floyd E. Bloom, and Robert H. Roth, *The Biochemical Basis of Neuropharmacology*, third edition (New York: Oxford University Press, 1978). Other treatments are much more highly technical, but even those mentioned above will be rocky going for the reader with no background in biology. There is no easy way to become familiar with the nervous system, but, on the other hand, it is perfectly accessible to anyone willing to invest a substantial amount of time. Perhaps the single best place to start is the *Scientific American* issue of September 1979, which was devoted entirely to brain structure and function.

Page

60–61   Deprived rat pups: Mark R. Rosenzweig, "Effects of Environment on Development of Brain and Behavior," in *The Biopsychology of Development*, ed. E. Tobach, L.R. Aronson, and E. Shaw (New York: Academic Press, 1971); and Mark R. Rosenzweig, Edward Bennett, and Marian C. Diamond, "Brain Changes in Response to Experience," *Scientific American* 226 (1972), pp. 22–29.

61–62   Tay-Sachs: Dominick P. Purpura, "Pathobiology of Cortical Neurons in Metabolic and Unclassified Amentias," in *Congenital and Acquired Cognitive Disorders*, ed. Robert Katzman (New York: Raven Press, 1979); and Dominick P. Purpura and K. Suzuki, "Distortion of Neuronal Geometry and Formation of Aberrant Synapses in Neuronal Storage Disease," *Brain Research* 116 (1976), pp. 1–21.

62   Even elderly rats: J.R. Conner, S.E. Beban, B. Hansen, P. Hopper, and M.C. Diamond, "Dendritic Increases in the Aged Rat Somatosensory Cortex," *Society for Neuroscience Abstracts* 10 (1980), 248.2.

62   not just sit back passively watching: Rosenzweig et al., "Brain Changes," p. 27. Furthermore, the rats have to have both social stimulation *and* interaction with inanimate objects for significant brain changes. Rosenzweig, "Effects of Environment," p. 334.

63   Remark of Michelangelo: See H.W. Janson, *History of Art* (Englewood Cliffs, N.J.: Prentice-Hall, 1962), pp. 10–11.

64   Brain evolution "a packaging problem": Harry Jerison, *Evolution of the Brain and Intelligence* (New York: Academic Press, 1973); for a brief, simpler treatment see his "Paleoneurology and the Evolution of Mind," *Scientific American* 234 (1976), pp. 90–101.

64   jewelfish: Richard G. Coss and Albert Globus, "Spine Stems on Tectal Interneurons in Jewel Fish Are Shortened by Social Stimulation," *Science* 200 (1978), pp. 787–90.

66–67   Human brain facts: See for example Raymond Carpenter, *Human Neuroanatomy*.

67   "the posture of the internal milieu": Walle Nauta, neuroanatomy lectures to medical students in the Harvard-MIT Joint Program in Health Sciences and Technology, 1975.

68 brains of the lamprey and the shark: Alfred S. Romer, *The Vertebrate Body* (Philadelphia: W.B. Saunders, 1962); and Harvey B. Sarnat and Martin G. Netsky, *Evolution of the Nervous System* (New York: Oxford University Press, 1974).

68 ". . . a sinful orchid . . . ": This was a personal communication to the author at the Yakovlev Collection, Armed Forces Institute of Pathology, Washington, D.C., but he has said it to others on other occasions. At eighty-six, he spends his days (and many evenings) with the collection he designed and stocked, containing over a quarter of a million serial sections of human brains. This, the world's largest and most complete collection of the kind, continues to yield up to him discoveries about brain structure and function. As one might guess, it is aging in the brain that holds his fascination most at present.

69 Turn-of-the-century embryology: See Stephen Jay Gould, *Ontogeny and Phylogeny* (Cambridge, Mass.: Harvard University Press, 1977), for an excellent historical account.

69 continuing light microscope description: Paul Flechsig, *Meine Myelogenetische Hirnlehre mit Biographischer Einleitung* (Berlin: Springer, 1927); J. Leroy Conel, *The Postnatal Development of the Human Cerebral Cortex*, 6 vols. (Cambridge, Mass.: Harvard University Press, 1939–1963); and Paul Yakovlev and André Roch-Lecours, "Myelogenetic Cycles of the Regional Maturation of the Brain," in *Regional Maturation of the Brain in Early Life*, ed. A. Minkowski (Oxford: Blackwell, 1967).

70 Consider what must be accomplished: Marcus Jacobson, *Developmental Neurobiology* (New York: Plenum, 1978) is the standard advanced text on neuroembryology. For a brief introduction see W. Maxwell Cowan, "The Development of the Brain," *Scientific American* 241 (Sept. 1979), pp. 112–33.

71 Functions of myelin sheath: Stephen G. Waxman, "Conduction in Myelinated, Unmyelinated and Demyelinated Fibers," *Archives of Neurology* 34 (1977), pp. 585–89.

71 autoradiography: Richard Sidman, "Autoradiographic Methods and Principles for Study of the Nervous System with Thymidine-H³," in *Contemporary Research Techniques of Neuroanatomy*, ed. S.O.E. Ebbesson and Walle Nauta (New York: Springer, 1970).

71–72 Tritiated thymidine method: Tracing of cell division with heavy hydrogen, or tritium. Tritium is merely the radiochemical label, a radioactive isotope of hydrogen, that plays a role in thymidine just as if it were hydrogen itself. Thymidine, one of the bases of DNA, and thus a critical building block of the gene, is the interesting part of the story. The trick is to inject the labeled thymidine and then examine the developing nervous system of the embryo. The label will be found concentrated in the DNA-laden nuclei of some cells, and it will be those cells that divided during the period shortly following the injection. The reason for the certainty is twofold: First, only DNA, and not RNA—the other major component of the cell nucleus—contains thymidine; second, the only way for an externally introduced, labeled thymidine molecule to get into the DNA—the gene—is for it to be taken up by a DNA molecule that has split along its long spiral axis, and is in the process of reproducing—taking up bases from the immediate chemical environment to form the long spiral of base pairs. This process takes place only during cell division; thus a search for labeled nerve cells a few months after injection gives you only those that were being born at the time just following the injection.

72 reeler mutant mouse: Verne S. Caviness, Jr., and Pasko Rakic, "Mechanisms of Cortical Development: A View from Mutations in Mice," in *Annual Review of Neuroscience* 1 (1978), ed. W.M. Cowan, Z.W. Hall, and E.R. Kandel, pp. 297–326.

72–73 cell birthdays: Verne S. Caviness and Richard Sidman, "Time of Origin of Corresponding Cell Classes in the Cerebral Cortex of Normal and Reeler Mutant Mice: An Autoradiographic Analysis," *The Journal of Comparative Neurology* 148 (1973), pp. 141–52.

73 Cell-cell recognition in the nervous system: A. Zimmerman and M. Schachner, "Central Nervous System Antigen (NS-5) and Its Presence During Murine Ontogenesis," *Journal of Supramolecular Structure* 5 (1976), pp. 417–29.

75 amoeboid, migrating nerve cells: Such movements are the stock and trade of most of the cells of the body's immune system—like the lymphocytes as well as of the amoeba, so they are no great shock to see, except that in the embryo many more kinds of cells can accomplish them, and *in toto* they are orders of magnitude more complicated than the convergence of lymphocytes on a wound, or the approach of an amoeba to an unfortunate piece of protozoan prey.

75 long, slow climb: Pasko Rakic, "Mode of Cell Migration to the Superficial Layers of Fetal Monkey Neocortex," *Journal of Comparative Neurology* 145 (1972), pp. 61–83.

75–76 the weaver's "guide" fibers: Pasko Rakic and Richard Sidman, "Weaver Mutant Mouse Cerebellum: Defective Neuronal Migration Secondary to Abnormality of Bergmann Glia," *Proceedings of the National Academy of Sciences, USA,* 70:1 (1973), pp. 240–44.

76 exploration of the chemical gradients: For example, in the laboratory of Perry Karfunkel (formerly of the Department of Biology at Amherst College and now practicing medicine in New York), cell cultures were used to provide migrating cells with chemical

gradients. It was known that different embryonic cells have different sugar-metabolizing enzymes on their surfaces—an example of the genetically coded cell-surface molecules mentioned earlier. Karfunkel reasoned that gradients of complex sugars, providing different substrates for these cell-surface enzymes, might be a key to early cell migration. He in fact demonstrated that different embryonic cells (heart and nerve cells) have different patterns of migration over different underlying cell sheets in the petri dish (the sheets consisted of nerve, heart, or limb cells, also taken from embryos of chicks). More important, these patterns could be altered by adding various complex sugars to the underlying cell sheet. Perry Karfunkel, Gary Giorgi, Gary Horbar, and Jeffrey Wolk, "Aggregate Outgrowth on a Cellular Substratum," *Zoon* 6 (1978), pp. 69–74.

76 How does the axon growing move: This first question has been provisionally answered in a series of experiments and an elegant theoretical model provided by Dennis Bray, of the Laboratory of Molecular Biology at Cambridge University. His work has focused on the growth cone, a complex microscopic structure at the tip of the outgrowing axon. He has discovered or proposed a number of similarities between the way the growth cone is extended and the way cells carry out a number of fundamental functions. For example, growth-cone extension seems basically similar to cell movement itself. The latter apparently can involve actual new growth of the cell on one side, with absorption of the old cell structures on the other; a seemingly inefficient, yet successful way to move. For the process to change from movement to extension, all that is needed is for the absorption to take place just behind the growth cone, at a slower rate than the growth going on at the tip. The difference can be made up by the cell body itself, providing energy and materials for construction and sending them down the axon to the growth cone. Some of these materials are vesicles—little globular structures within the cell that have surfaces similar to cell membranes. These are pulled along the inside of the cell membrane itself by a process not unlike the attraction of complex proteins that constitutes the basis of muscle contraction. When the vesicles reach the growing tip, they merge with the cell membrane and make the tip longer. The axon does not stretch or add to itself in the middle, but is slowly built at the tip, in the manner of the building of a railroad. Dennis Bray, "Model for Membrane Movements in the Neural Growth Cone," *Nature* 244 (1973), pp. 93–96.

76 forces were mechanical: For a discussion of this theory, known as "contact guidance," and the controversy surrounding it, see Mar-

cus Jacobson, *Developmental Neurobiology* (New York: Plenum Press, 1978), pp. 160 ff.

76–77 chemical affinities: R.W. Sperry, "Chemoaffinity in the Orderly Growth of Nerve Fiber Patterns and Connections," *Proceedings of the National Academy of Sciences* 50 (1963), pp. 703–10.

It must be said that chemospecificity is not on a one-to-one cell-by-cell basis. Recent extensions of Sperry's experiments over a period of months rather than weeks show, for example, that if half the retina is removed in these animals the remaining half will eventually fan out its connections to take over the central brain territory vacated by the missing half. These are wrong connections in Sperry's sense. The situation is obviously very complex. See M. Edds, Jr., ed., "Specificity and Plasticity of Retinotectal Connections," *Neuroscience Research Program Bulletin* 17:2 (1979), pp. 245–359.

77 Evidence in favor of chemical labels: Such regeneration experiments did not of course prove that the process by which axons find their way in the normal developing embryo is similar. In fact, it is possible that the specificity of mutual recognition observed by Sperry is secondary to the establishment of circuits. That is, circuits initially connect up mechanically, but then influence one another chemically, so that when severed they find each other by chemospecificity. Recent studies in cell culture, however, have shown that chemical gradients can play a role even at early stages. Nerve growth factor ("NGF"), for example, long known to promote the growth of nerves by increasing growth rate, has now been shown to have a "chemotaxic" effect as well; that is, if all nerve cells in a culture are provided with a background level of NGF, and then more of this specific protein is applied microscopically to one part of the field, all cell processes will send their growth cones forward at approximately the same rate, but the ones in the neighborhood of the extra NGF will turn toward it. As in the case of Karfunkel's experiments on cell migration over gradients of complex sugars, this line of work on the chemical direction of axon growth traffic brings us closer to a grasp of the way genes direct the building of nerve circuits. R.W. Gundersen and J.N. Barrett, "Neuronal Chemotaxis: Chick Dorsal-Root Axons Turn Toward High Concentrations of Nerve Growth Factor," *Science* 206 (1979), pp. 1079–80.

77 timing of growth: D.I. Gottlieb and W.M. Cowan, "Evidence for a Temporal Factor in the Occupation of Available Synaptic Sites During the Development of the Dentate Gyrus," *Brain Research* 41 (1972), pp. 452–56.

78 Mature connections in the absence of use: Pat G. Model, Murray

B. Bornstein, Stanley M. Crain, and George D. Pappas, "An Electron Microscopic Study of the Development of Synapses in Cultured Fetal Mouse Cerebrum Continuously Exposed to Xylocaine," *The Journal of Cell Biology* 49 (1971), pp. 362–71.

79 ". . . . specific interneuronal contacts . . .": Ibid., p. 369.

79 impoverishing or enriching the environment: Rosenzweig, Bennett, and Diamond, "Brain Changes in Response to Experience."

79 Jewelfish reared in isolation: Coss and Globus, "Spine Stems on Tectal Interneurons in Jewel Fish."

79 Mice reared in light or darkness: Francisco Valverde, "Rate and Extent of Recovery from Dark Rearing in the Visual Cortex of the Mouse," *Brain Research* 33 (1971), pp. 1–11; and "Apical Dendritic Spines of the Visual Cortex and Light Deprivation in the Mouse," *Experimental Brain Research* 3 (1967), pp. 337–52.

80 The question, How?: A significant and widely read statement of this distinction was by Anne Anastasi, "Heredity, Environment and the Question 'How?'" *Psychological Review* 65 (1958), pp. 197–208.

CHAPTER 5: THE SEVERAL HUMOURS

Behavior genetics is one of the few fields of behavioral biology that has really, in recent years, generated more heat than light. It is much easier to find literature on both sides of the controversy that is tendentious and useless than it is to find the kernels of wheat among the chaff. A responsible summary of the field is Lee Ehrman and Peter Parsons, *The Genetics of Behavior* (Sunderland, Mass.: Sinauer, 1976). Its intellectual pitfalls are cogently summarized by Richard C. Lewontin, "Genetic Aspects of Intelligence," *Annual Review of Genetics* 9 (1975), pp. 387–405. Its ethical aspect, related to but separable from its intellectual accomplishments and pitfalls, is discussed in chapter 17 and in the section at the beginning of the notes entitled "Caveat: The Dangers of Behavioral Biology," which draws heavily on Leon Kamin's *The Science and Politics of I.Q.* and Stephan Chorover's *From Genesis to Genocide*.

Page

82 "In a period of thirty-five years . . .": John McCormick and Mario Sevilla Mascoreñas, *The Complete Aficionado* (Cleveland: World, 1967). For further information on the breeding and training of *toros bravos*, see José María de Cossio, *Los Toros: Tratado Técnico e Histórico*, Tomo I (Madrid: Espasa-Calpe, 1943), the definitive—

indeed encyclopedic—work. The most helpful work in English remains Ernest Hemingway's *Death in the Afternoon* (New York: Charles Scribner's Sons, 1932).

84–87 Dog behavior genetics: John Paul Scott and John L. Fuller, *Genetics and the Social Behavior of the Dog* (Chicago: University of Chicago Press, 1965). It is true that Scott and Fuller's methods did not meet the most rigorous standards of current behavior genetics, and some of their interpretations were rather naïve. Nevertheless, they pioneered the study of this most interesting and comprehensible animal, and their work is part of the canon of behavior-genetic research (see, for instance, Ehrman and Parsons, *The Genetic Analysis of Behavior*, pp. 94–100).

86 Two genes in control of playful aggression: Scott and Fuller, *Social Behavior of the Dog*, p. 270.

87–88 phenylketonuria: Charles R. Scriver and Carol L. Clow, "Phenylketonuria: Epitome of Human Biochemical Genetics," *New England Journal of Medicine* 303 (1980), pp. 1336–42, 1394–1400.

88 phenylalanine hydroxylase: This enzyme, when it is normal, carries out its function by the act of putting a hydroxyl radical—an oxygen-hydrogen group—on a molecule of phenylalanine, specifically on the six-carbon ring beside another hydroxyl group already there. This changes the phenylalanine to tyrosine, a compound that goes on to be made into other compounds critical for neural and endocrine function. Two of these—dopamine and norepinephrine—serve as neurotransmitters, both in the central, the latter also in the peripheral nervous system. Epinephrine (adrenaline), another product of phenylalanine via tyrosine, is a stress hormone secreted by the adrenal gland; and thyroid hormone, yet another, is the secretion of the thyroid gland that promotes growth and maintains normal metabolism in many parts of the body. One's initial suspicion is that all the above neurotransmitters and hormones might be lacking in an individual with an abnormality of phenylalanine hydroxylase. This, however, is fortunately not the case, because tyrosine does not come only from phenylalanine—it too is an amino acid, and we can get enough of it by eating it.

88–89 Beta-galactosidase syndrome: Dominick P. Purpura, "Pathobiology of Cortical Neurons in Metabolic and Unclassified Amentias," in *Congenital and Acquired Disorders*, ed. Robert Katzman (New York: Raven Press, 1979), p. 55.

91 "everything in the brain . . .": Benzer recounted this experience in a lecture at MIT in a symposium entitled "The Neurosciences: Paths of Discovery" (October 29–30, 1973), which later became

the subject of a book of the same title edited by Frederick G. Worden, Judith P. Swazey, and George Adelman (Cambridge, Mass.: MIT Press, 1975).

91 the common, well-studied fruit fly: Seymour Benzer, "Genetic Dissection of Behavior," *Scientific American* 229 (1973), pp. 24–37.

92 Among the other single-gene mutants: It has been possible in some cases to follow the emergence of the behavioral defect in anatomic and physiological detail from the early embryo to the final adult form, and even manipulate the expression of the defect. Best studied perhaps is the *hyperkinetic* mutant. Unrelated to the syndrome in human children that goes by the same name, it is identified when the fruit fly is anesthetized and, unlike the average fly, it shakes its legs vigorously. Composite or mosaic flies can be created in which only some of the legs are affected, and mapping of the trait on the early embryo shows that the defect emerges in the cells destined to become the ventral (abdomenside) nervous system. Studies of the electrical function of cells in that system in the adult confirm that they are the cause of the shaking.

92 "early birds" and "night owls": Benzer, "Genetic Dissection of Behavior," p. 30.

93 serotonin, norepinephrine, and dopamine: Oakley S. Ray and Robert J. Barrett, "Behavioral, Pharmacological and Biochemical Analysis of Genetic Differences in Rats," *Behavioral Biology* 15 (1975), pp. 391–417.

93 alcohol dehydrogenase: D.A. Rogers, G.E. McClearn, E.L. Bennet, and Marie Herbert, "Alcohol Preference as a Function of Its Caloric Utility in Mice," *Journal of Comparative and Physiological Psychology* 56 (1963), pp. 666–72.

93–94 susceptibility to seizures: K. Schlesinger and B.J. Griek, "The Genetics and Biochemistry of Audiogenetic Seizures," in *Contributions to Behavior-Genetic Analysis: The Mouse as a Prototype*, ed. G. Linzey and D.D. Thiessen (New York: Appleton-Century-Crofts, 1970), pp. 219–57.

94 sensitivity to androgens: Thomas E. McGill and G. Richard Tucker, "Genotype and Sex Drive in Intact and Castrated Mice," *Science* 145 (1964), pp. 514–15.

94 differ . . . only in their genes: A brief review of the literature up to 1970 concluded, "Past studies, with monotonous regularity, have confirmed the heritability of many forms of emotional behavior, and no evidence to the contrary has been found." Jan H. Bruell, "Heritability of Emotional Behavior," in *Physiological Correlates of Emotion*, ed. Perry Black (New York: Academic Press, 1970).

95 twin studies . . . by chance: John C. Loehlin and Robert C. Nichols, *Heredity, Environment and Personality: A Study of 850 Sets of Twins* (Austin: University of Texas Press, 1976), p. 2.

95 some famous studies: S. Scarr-Salapatek, "Environmental Bias in Twin Studies," *Eugenics Quarterly* 15 (1968), pp. 34–40; and Leon Kamin, *The Science and Politics of I.Q.* (Potomac, Md.: Erlbaum, 1974).

95 literature on heritability: In addition to that of Scarr-Salapatek, who found that twin concordances—and therefore heritability—are different in different social classes, two important statistical points have been made about IQ heritability. First, the inability to randomize the distribution of genotypes with respect to environments gives rise to a genotype-environment correlation whose magnitude cannot be estimated; see David Layzer, "Heritability Analyses of I.Q. Scores: Science or Numerology?" *Science* 183 (1974), pp. 1259–66. Second, because of the same methodological limitation of human studies, it is impossible to estimate the magnitude of the genotype-environment interaction term in the summation of variance; see Richard C. Lewontin, "Genetic Aspects of Intelligence," *Annual Review of Genetics* 9 (1975), pp. 387–405. These points cannot be discussed at length here, but they are important, and constitute a crucial and mathematically sophisticated challenge to all generalizations made from twin studies.

95 reluctant historian: L.S. Hearnshaw, *Cyril Burt, Psychologist* (Ithaca, N.Y.: Cornell University Press, 1979).

96 Genes and schizophrenia: James Shields, Leonard L. Heston, and Irving I. Gottesman, "Schizophrenia and the Schizoid: The Problem for Genetic Analysis," in *Genetic Research in Psychiatry*, ed. R.R. Fieve, D. Rosenthal, and H. Brill (Baltimore: Johns Hopkins University Press, 1975).

96–97 an elegant and conclusive study: S.S. Kety, D. Rosenthal, P.H. Wender, and F. Schulsinger, "The Types and Prevalence of Mental Illness in the Biological and Adoptive Families of Adopted Schizophrenics," in *The Transmission of Schizophrenia*, ed. D. Rosenthal and S.S. Kety (Oxford: Pergamon, 1968), pp. 345–62; and S.S. Kety, D. Rosenthal, P.H. Wender, F. Schulsinger, and Bjørn Jacobsen, "Mental Illness in the Biological and Adoptive Families of Adopted Individuals Who Have Become Schizophrenic: A Preliminary Report Based on Psychiatric Interviews," in *Genetic Research in Psychiatry*, ed. Fieve, Rosenthal, and Brill.

98 Hallucinogens produced by the brain: Edward F. Domino, "Indole Alkyl Amines as Psychotogen Precursors—Possible Neurotransmitter Imbalance," in *Neurotransmitter Balances Regulating Behav-*

ior, ed. Edward F. Domino and J.M. Davis (Ann Arbor: Domino and Davis, 1975); and Russell E. Dill and Katherine M. Campbell, "3-Methoxytyramine: A Possible Endogenous Toxin of Psychosis," *Research Communications in Chemical Pathology and Pharmacology* 6 (1973), pp. 975–82.

98 Poisoning the cells of pleasure and reward: Larry Stein, "Neurochemistry of Reward and Punishment: Some Implications for the Etiology of Schizophrenia," *Journal of Psychiatric Research* 8 (1971), pp. 345–61.

99 activity of MAO: R.J. Wyatt, D.L. Murphy R. Belmaker, C. Donnelly, S. Cohen, and W. Pollin, "Reduced Monoamine Oxidase Activity in Platelets: A Possible Genetic Marker for Vulnerability to Schizophrenia," *Science* 179 (1973), pp. 916–18.

99 DMT and schizophrenic delusions: Richard J. Wyatt, Juan M. Saavedra, and Julius Axelrod, "A Dimethyltryptamine-Forming Enzyme in Human Blood," *American Journal of Psychiatry* 130 (1973), pp. 754–60.

100 DBH activity up or down?: The patients in the first study were chronic schizophrenics, so the apparent contradiction between it and the second study is probably not real. One can visualize a situation in which chronic schizophrenics "exhaust" their DBH activity so that it is low when measured after death, while acute patients are on a sort of roller coaster of DBH activity associated with, and perhaps causing, their psychotic breaks. (DBH in the acute patients was measured in the peripheral nervous system, and could conceivably be just an effect of stress.) C.D. Wise and L. Stein, "Dopamine-beta-hydroxylase Deficits in the Brains of Schizophrenic Patients," *Science* 181 (1973), pp. 344–47; and Seymour Rosenblatt, W.P. Leighton, and J.D. Chanley, "Dopamine-beta-hydroxylase: Evidence for Increased Activity in Sympathetic Neurons During Psychotic States," *Science* 182 (1973), pp. 923–24. It must be noted that some investigators have been unable to detect the suggested changes in brain enzyme levels, while others have found evidence that such changes may be due to drugs taken chronically by the patients rather than to the illness itself. This issue requires more investigation. See Solomon Snyder, "Dopamine Receptors, Neuroleptics, and Schizophrenia," *American Journal of Psychiatry* 138 (1981), pp. 460–64.

100 DBH activity is heritable: Richard M. Weinshilboum et al., "Inheritance of Very Low Serum Dopamine-beta-hydroxylase Activity," *American Journal of Human Genetics* 27 (1975), pp. 573–85.

101 a single-gene recessive defect that alters an enzyme: This enzyme,

steroid 21-hydroxylase, merely adds an oxygen-hydrogen group to the carbon designated as number 21 in the standard arbitrary numbering system for the carbon atoms in the steroid molecule. Here, as in neurotransmitter synthesis, small changes can make a big difference. The adrenogenital syndrome, resulting in females with a defect in this enzyme, is discussed in the next chapter. David A. Hamburg, "Genetics of Adrenocortical Hormone Metabolism in Relation to Psychological Stress," in *Behavior-Genetic Analysis*, ed. J. Hirsch (New York: McGraw-Hill, 1967), p. 164.

101 aggressive behavior in childhood: Anke A. Ehrhardt, "Maternalism in Fetal Hormonal and Related Syndromes," in *Contemporary Sexual Behavior: Critical Issues in the 1970's*, ed. J. Zubin and J. Money (Baltimore: Johns Hopkins University Press, 1973); and Susan W. Baker, "Psychosexual Differentiation in the Human," *Biology of Reproduction* 22 (1980), pp. 61–72.

101–02 Gene on chromosome 6: L.R. Weitkamp, H.C. Stancer, E. Persad, C. Flood, and S. Guttormsen, "Depressive Disorders and HLA: A Gene on Chromosome 6 That Can Affect Behavior," *New England Journal of Medicine* 305 (1981), pp. 1301–06.

104 ". . . that what moves us is moods": Walle Nauta lecturing in Neuroanatomy, Harvard-MIT Joint Program in Health Sciences and Technology, Fall 1974.

CHAPTER 6: THE BEAST WITH TWO BACKS

The definitive treatment of the behavioral dimensions of gender is Eleanor Emmons Maccoby and Carol Nagy Jacklin, *The Psychology of Sex Differences* (Stanford: Stanford University Press, 1974). Margaret Mead's *Male and Female* (New York: Morrow, 1949) remains an important document on the anthropological perspective, supplemented by the following more recent works on women's status and roles cross-culturally: M.Z. Rosaldo and L. Lamphere, eds., *Woman, Culture and Society* (Stanford: Stanford University Press, 1974); Naomi Quinn, "Anthropological Studies on Women's Status," *Annual Review of Anthropology* 6 (1977), pp. 181–225; and Carol Ember, "A Cross-Cultural Perspective on Sex Differences," Judith K. Brown, "Cross-Cultural Perspectives on the Female Life Cycle," and R.L. Monroe, R.H. Monroe, and J.W.M. Whiting, "Male Sex-Role Resolutions," all in *Handbook of Cross-Cultural Development*, ed. Robert L. Monroe, Ruth H. Monroe, and Beatrice B. Whiting (New York: Garland Press, 1981). Of all the anthropological studies I have seen, Ember makes the most serious attempt to integrate her cross-cultural findings with up-to-date knowledge in the psychology and biology of sex differences.

As of this writing the most authoritative and up-to-date information on biological aspects of sex differentiation, including sex differentiation of brain and behavior, is an entire issue of *Science* (March 20, 1981) devoted to this subject. Edited by Frederick Naftolin and Eleanore Butz under the title "Sexual Dimorphism," it includes new summaries by a number of leading authorities. *Science* 211 (1981), pp. 1263–1324.

Page

108 seven exotic, remote societies: Mead, *Male and Female.*

108 "The Tchambuli people": Ibid., p. 54.

109 "These robust, restive people": Ibid., pp. 53–54.

109 !Kung San homicides: Richard B. Lee, *The !Kung San* (Cambridge, Engl.: Cambridge University Press, 1979), chapter 13.

109 weapon making: Roy D'Andrade, "Sex Differences and Cultural Institutions," in *The Development of Sex Differences*, ed. Eleanor Emmons Maccoby (Stanford: Stanford University Press, 1966), p. 178.

109 modern Israel or nineteenth-century Dahomey: D'Andrade, "Sex Differences and Cultural Institutions," pp. 178–79.

109–10 a study of dreams: Ibid., p. 198.

110–11 a major book: Maccoby and Jacklin, *Psychology of Sex Differences.*

111 the realm of cognitive abilities: Ibid., especially chapter 3.

111 the realm of aggressive behavior: Ibid., especially pp. 227–47.

112 "nurturance and affiliation": Maccoby, ed., *Development of Sex Differences.*

112–13 Six Cultures study: Beatrice Blyth Whiting and John W.M. Whiting, *Children of Six Cultures* (Cambridge, Mass.: Harvard University Press, 1975); and Beatrice Blyth Whiting and Carolyn Pope Edwards, "A Cross-Cultural Analysis of Sex Differences in the Behavior of Children Aged Three through Eleven," *Journal of Social Psychology* 91 (1973), pp. 171–88.

113 efforts to *train* gender roles: Herbert Barry III, Margaret K. Bacon, and Irvin L. Child, "A Cross-Cultural Survey of Some Sex Differences in Socialization," *Journal of Abnormal and Social Psychology* 55:3 (1957), pp. 327–32.

113 look at younger children separately: Maccoby and Jacklin, *Psychology of Sex Differences*, especially pp. 227–47.

113 !Kung San children: Nicholas Blurton Jones and Melvin J. Konner, "Sex Differences in Behavior of London and Bushmen Children," in *Comparative Ecology and Behaviour of Primates*, ed. Richard Michael and John Crook (New York: Academic Press, 1973).

113–14 At three weeks of age: Howard Moss, "Sex, Age, and State as

Determinants of Mother-Infant Interaction," *Merrill-Palmer Quarterly* 13 (1967), pp. 19–36.

114 Even among higher primates: Sarah Blaffer Hrdy, *The Langurs of Abu* (Cambridge, Mass.: Harvard University Press, 1978); and Jane B. Lancaster, "Play-Mothering: The Relations Between Juvenile Females and Young Infants Among Free-Ranging Vervet Monkeys (*Cercopithecus aethiops*)," *Folia Primatologia* 15 (1971), pp. 161–82.

114 dressed in pink or blue: J.A. Will, P.A. Self, and N. Datan, "Maternal Behavior and Perceived Sex of Infant," *American Journal of Orthopsychiatry* 46 (1976), pp. 135–39; Caroline Smith and Barbara Lloyd, "Maternal Behavior and Perceived Sex of Infant: Revisited," *Child Development* 49 (1978), pp. 1263–65.

114 tape recording: M.K. Rothbart and Eleanor Emmons Maccoby, "Parents' Differential Reactions to Sons and Daughters," *Journal of Personality and Social Psychology* 4 (1966), pp. 237–43.

114 Sex differences in newborns: Annelise Korner, "Neonatal Startles, Smiles, Erections, and Reflex Sucks as Related to State, Sex, and Individuality," *Child Development* 40 (1969), pp. 1039–53; and "Sex Differences in Newborns with Special Reference to Differences in the Organization of Oral Behavior," *Journal of Child Psychology and Psychiatry* 14 (1973), pp. 19–29.

114 Skin sensitivity and barrier behavior: R. Bell and N.S. Costello, "Three Tests for Sex Differences in Tactile Sensitivity in the Newborn," *Biologia Neonatorum* (Basel) 7 (1964), pp. 335–47; R. Bell, G.M. Weller, and M.F. Waldrop, "Newborn and Preschooler: Organization of Behavior and Relations Between Periods," *Monographs of the Society for Research in Child Development* 36 (1971), pp. 1–145.

115 Castration and aggressiveness: For review see A.F. Dixon, "Androgen and Aggressive Behavior in Primates: A Review," *Aggressive Behavior* 6 (1980), pp. 37–68.

115 the monthly cycle: For a review of the physiology see Griff T. Ross and Raymond L. Vande Wiele, "The Ovaries," chapter 7 in *Textbook of Endocrinology*, ed. Robert H. Williams (Philadelphia: W.B. Saunders, 1974), pp. 368–422.

116 Steroid hormone action on DNA: Lawrence Chan and Bert M. O'Malley, "Mechanism of Action of the Sex Steroid Hormones," *New England Journal of Medicine* 294 (1976), pp. 1322–28, 1372–81, and 1430–37.

116–17 Estradiol in rat sexual posturing: Bruce McEwen, Paula Davis, Bruce Parsons, and Donald Pfaff, "The Brain as a Target for Steroid Hormone Action," *Annual Review of Neuroscience* 2 (1979), pp. 65–112.

117 Testosterone and *stria terminalis*: K.M. Kendrick and R. F. Drewett, "Testosterone Reduces Refractory Period of Stria Terminalis Neurons in the Rat Brain," *Science* 204 (1979), pp. 877–79.

117–18 In songbirds: A.P. Arnold, F. Nottebohm, and D.W. Pfaff, "Hormone-Concentrating Cells in Vocal Control and Other Areas of the Brain of the Zebra Finch (*Poephila guttata*)," *Journal of Comparative Neurology* 165 (1976), pp. 487–512. Androgen effects on motor nerves have now also been found in mammals: M. Sar and W. Stumpf, "Androgen Concentration in Motor Neurons of Cranial Nerves and Spinal Cord," *Science* 197 (1977), pp. 77–79.

118 Sensitivity of the pelvic nerve: Donald Pfaff, *Estrogens and Brain Function: Neural Analysis of a Hormone-Controlled Reproductive Behavior* (New York: Springer-Verlag, 1980).

118 Durkheim's dictum: See Marvin Harris, *The Rise of Anthropological Theory* (New York: Thomas Y. Crowell, 1968), pp. 472–73.

118 human menstrual cycle: Alice Rossi and Peter Rossi, "Body Time and Social Time: Mood Patterns by Menstrual Cycle Phase and Day of the Week," *Social Science Research* 6 (1977), pp. 273–308.

119 Rossi on sex differences and the family: See, for example, Alice Rossi, "A Biosocial Perspective on Parenting," *Daedalus* 106 (1977), pp. 1–31; "Parenting, Kinship and Adult Development: A Research Agenda to Test Kin Selection Theory," paper presented to the Plenary Session on Family and Socialization, American Sociological Association, New York, Aug. 27, 1980; and "The Biosocial Side of Parenthood," *Human Nature* 1:6 (1978), pp. 72–79.

119 when two groups of monkeys fight: Robert Rose, Irwin Bernstein, and Thomas Gordon, *Psychosomatic Medicine* 34:1 (1975), pp. 50–61. The intricate relations of testosterone and aggression are considered more fully in chapter 9.

119 Testosterone and age at first arrest: Leo Kreuz and Robert Rose, "Assessment of Aggressive Behavior and Plasma Testosterone in a Young Criminal Population," *Psychosomatic Medicine* 34 (1972), pp. 321–32.

119 male juvenile delinquents: D. Kedenburg, N. Kedenburg, and A. Kling, unpublished manuscript of the Department of Psychiatry, Rutgers University School of Medicine, 1978.

120 Gender differences in fat, muscle mass: Frank Falkner and James Tanner, eds., *Human Growth*, vol. 2, *Postnatal Growth* (New York: Plenum, 1978).

120–21 Isolated rhesus monkeys placed with infants: Arnold Chamove, Harry Harlow, and Gary Mitchell, "Sex Differences in the

Infant-Directed Behavior of Preadolescent Rhesus Monkeys," *Child Development* 38 (1967), pp. 329–35.

121–22 male and female brains differ: G. Raisman and P.M. Field, "Sexual Dimorphism in the Neuropil of the Preoptic Area of the Rat and Its Dependence on Neonatal Androgen," *Brain Research* 54 (1973), pp. 1–29.

121 Hormones given at birth and castration at birth: June Mackover Reinisch, "Fetal Hormones, the Brain, and Sex Differences: A Heuristic Integrative Review of the Literature," *Archives of Sexual Behavior* 3 (1974), pp. 51–90; Bruce McEwen, "Sexual Maturation and Differentiation: The Role of the Gonadal Steroids," in M.A. Corner et al., *Progress in Brain Research*, vol. 48, *Maturation of the Nervous System* (North Holland: Elsevier, 1978).

121 "pseudo-hermaphrodite" monkeys: Robert Goy, "Experimental Control of Psychosexuality," *Philosophical Transactions of the Royal Society of London* B. 259 (1970), pp. 149–62.

122 brain slices in petri dishes: Dominique Toran-Allerand, "Sex Steroids and the Development of the Newborn Mouse Hypothalamus and Preoptic Area in Vitro: Implications for Sexual Differentiation," *Brain Research* 106 (1976), pp. 407–12.

122 sexual differentiation in birds: Christine Martinez-Vargas, Douglas Gibson, Madhabananda Sar, and Walter Stumpf, "Estrogen Target Sites in the Brain of the Chick Embryo," *Science* 190 (1975), pp. 1307–08.

123 Adrenogenital syndrome and "tomboyism": Anke A. Ehrhardt, "Prenatal Hormonal Exposure and Psychosexual Differentiation," in *Topics in Psychoendocrinology*, ed. Edward Sachar (New York: Grune and Stratton, 1975); and Susan Baker, "Psychosexual Differentiation in the Human," *Biology of Reproduction* 22 (1980), pp. 66–72.

123–25 Dominican gender changes: Julianne Imperato-McGinley et al., "Androgens and the Evolution of the Male Gender-Identity among Male Pseudohermaphrodites with 5α-reductase Deficiency," *New England Journal of Medicine* 300:22 (1979), pp. 1233–37.

125 "These subjects demonstrate . . .": Ibid., p. 1233.

125 "Our data show . . .": Ibid., p. 1236.

125 Brain control of song in male songbirds: Fernando Nottebohm and Arthur Arnold, "Sex Dimorphism in Vocal Control Areas of the Songbird Brain," *Science* 194 (1976), pp. 211–13.

125–26 Striking sex differences in the brain: R. Gorski, J. Gordon, J. Shryne, and A. Southam, "Evidence for a Morphological Sex Difference Within the Medial Preoptic Area of the Rat Brain," *Brain Research* 14 (1978), pp. 333–46.

126 policy implication: It would be disingenuous to suggest that there are not those who would draw very different conclusions from the facts outlined above. Such people must be resisted on the basis of intelligent policy and a sense of justice as to the distribution of opportunity. They cannot be resisted on the basis of untruth; and the idea of intrinsic, complete psychological equipotentiality of the two genders will soon fall into that category—if it has not done so already.

CHAPTER 7: THE WELL OF FEELING

An excellent, readable, and well-illustrated introduction to the neurobiology of the emotions may be found in Neil R. Carlson, *The Physiology of Behavior* (Boston: Allyn & Bacon, 1979), which also covers material pertinent to learning and memory. J.R. Smythies, *Brain Mechanisms and Behavior* (New York: Academic Press, 1970), gives a more specialized account directed to the goal of establishing psychiatry on a neurological foundation. Karl H. Pribram, ed., *Brain and Behavior*, vol. 4, *Adaptation* (Baltimore: Penguin, 1969) collects many of the classic papers referred to in this chapter. For summaries by distinguished neuroanatomists currently at work on these structures and functions see Walle Nauta and V.B. Domesick, "Neural Associations of the Limbic System," in *Neural Substrates of Behavior*, ed. A. Beckman (New York: Spectrum, 1980) and Paul D. MacLean, *A Triune Concept of Brain and Behavior* (Toronto: University of Toronto, 1973).

Page
128 philosophers of this century: Bertrand Russell, *Philosophy* (New York: W.W. Norton, 1927); *Human Knowledge: Its Scope and Limits* (New York: Simon and Schuster, 1948). G.E. Moore, *Principia Ethica* (Cambridge, Engl.: Cambridge University Press, 1903). A.J. Ayer, *The Central Questions of Philosophy* (New York: Holt, Rinehart and Winston, 1973). Gilbert Ryle, *The Concept of Mind* (London: Hutchinson, 1949).

128 Aristotle on mind and soul: Bertrand Russell, *A History of Western Philosophy* (New York: Simon and Schuster, 1964), chapter 19.

128 "The soul experiences sensation . . .": Epicurus, *Letters, Principal Doctrines and Vatican Sayings* (New York: Howard W. Sams, 1964), p. 24.

129 Lucretius: Russell, *History*, pp. 248–51 and Lucretius, *De Rerum Natura a Libri Sex*, trans. R.F. Latham (Harmondsworth, Engl.: Penguin Classics, 1951).

129 a lone voice: Russell, *History*, chapter 17.

129–30 a "prudent theory": Ayer, *Central Questions*, p. 129.

130 Freud's neuropsychology: Karl H. Pribram, "The Foundation of Psychoanalytic Theory: Freud's Neuropsychological Model," in *Brain and Behavior*, vol. 4, *Adaptation*, ed. Karl H. Pribram. Pribram, a neurophysiologist, has made a major contribution to our understanding of Freud's neurological writings.

130–31 Freud on aphasia: Sigmund Freud, *On Aphasia: A Critical Study*, trans. E. Stengel (New York: International Universities Press, 1953). Freud's competence and confidence in this difficult subfield of neurology are obvious. He refers not only to the era's aphasiologists but to many other major figures of neuroanatomy and neurophysiology. Unlike most of Freud's psychoanalytic writings, which are accessible to any intelligent reader, this paper is unreadable without a neuroscience background.

131 localization of language: Carl Wernicke, "Die Neueren Arbeiten über Aphasie," *Fortschritt der Medizin*, 1886, pp. 371–463.

132 "Different amounts . . .": Hughlings Jackson, as quoted by Freud, *On Aphasia*, p. 52.

133 the mature Freud's canon: *The Standard Edition of the Complete Psychological Works of Sigmund Freud*, trans. and ed. James Strachey (London: Hogarth Press, 1953–1964). For a brief explanation of the theory of personality, see Sigmund Freud, *A General Introduction to Psychoanalysis*, trans. Joan Riviere (London: Allen and Unwin, 1922). For a recent scholarly study of Freud as a biological thinker, see Frank Sulloway, *Freud: The Mind of a Biologist* (New York: Harper & Row, 1979). Sulloway's viewpoint is primarily evolutionary and complements the one taken here, which is closer to Pribram's.

133–36 four years later: Sigmund Freud, "Project for a Scientific Psychology," in *The Origins of Psychoanalysis: Letters to Wilhelm Fliess, Drafts and Notes* (New York: Basic Books, 1954).

134 The neuron doctrine and the role of the synapse: For a history of the ideas of this period see Judith P. Swazey, *Reflexes and Motor Integration: Sherrington's Concept of Integrative Action* (Cambridge, Mass.: Harvard University Press, 1969), chapter 2.

136–38 Freud's fellow physician: William James, *Principles of Psychology*, 2 vols. (New York: Holt, 1890).

137–38 *"The feeling, in the coarser emotions, . . ."*: William James, *Psychology: Briefer Course* (New York: Crowell-Collier, 1962), p. 377.

138 "Stated in this crude way . . .": James, *Briefer Course*, p. 378.

138 "with some trepidation": Walter B. Cannon, "The James-Lange Theory of Emotions: A Critical Examination and an Alternative Theory," *American Journal of Psychology* 39 (1927), pp. 106–24.

139 "The processes going on . . .": Cannon, "James-Lange Theory," p. 114.

140 "I find singularly little . . .": W. R. Adey, personal communication quoted in J.R. Smythies, *Brain Mechanisms and Behavior* (New York: Academic Press, 1970), p. 10. The emphasis on subcortical structures is proper insofar as it indicates that there is somewhat more evidence for specific localization of function in the cortex itself; however, even at these higher levels the interaction among centers through fiber tracts, both within the cortical level and beyond it to subcortical brain organs, is critical to the understanding of function.

141 *"the peculiar quality of the emotions . . ."*: Cannon, "James-Lange Theory," p. 120.

141 a fairly obscure physician-neuroanatomist: James W. Papez, "A Proposed Mechanism of Emotion," *Archives of Neurological Psychiatry* 38 (1937), pp. 725–43.

142 "In this way the sensory excitations . . .": Ibid., p. 729.

142 "Is emotion a magic product . . .": Ibid., p. 743.

143 biology has thrown down: Ernst Mayr, personal communication, 1979.

143 Darwin . . . addressed emotion: Charles Darwin, *The Expression of the Emotions in Man and Animals* (Chicago: University of Chicago Press, 1970; orig. 1872).

144 major American students of animal psychology: See, for example, Frank A. Beach, "The Snark Was a Boojum," *The American Psychologist* 5 (1950), pp. 115–24; and R. Lockhard, "Reflections on the Fall of Comparative Psychology: Is There a Message for Us All?" *American Psychologist* 26 (1971), pp. 168–79.

145 Spencer's "overflow of nerve-force": Darwin, *Expression of Emotions*, p. 71.

146–47 "the limbic system": Paul D. MacLean, "Psychosomatic Disease and the 'Visceral Brain': Recent Developments Bearing on the Papez Theory of Emotion," *Psychosomatic Medicine* 11 (1949), pp. 338–53.

147 frontal lobes and the limbic system: Paul D. MacLean, "Some Psychiatric Implications of Physiological Studies on Frontotemporal Portion of Limbic System (Visceral Brain)," *EEG Clinical Neurophysiology* 4 (1952), pp. 407–18.

147 "the neocortex of the limbic system": This outlook is elaborated in Walle Nauta, "The Problem of the Frontal Lobe: A Reinterpretation," *Journal of Psychiatric Research* 8 (1971), pp. 167–87.

147–48 "the triune brain": MacLean, *A Triune Concept of Brain and Behavior*.

148 MacLean's hamster studies: M.R. Murphy, P.D. MacLean, and S.C. Hamilton, "Species-Typical Behavior of Hamsters Deprived from Birth of the Neocortex," *Science* 213 (1981), pp. 459–61.

149–50 exploring the physiology of the emotions: Paul D. MacLean, "Effects of Lesions of Globus Pallidus on Species-Typical Display Behavior of Squirrel Monkeys," *Brain Research* 149 (1978), pp. 175–96.

150 smiling in greeting: For extensive discussion see Melvin J. Konner, "Biological Aspects of the Mother-Infant Bond," in *Development of Attachment and Affiliation Processes,* ed. Robert Emde and Robert Harmon (New York: Plenum, 1982).

CHAPTER 8: LOGOS

Of the many books on the nature of language the most influential for my thinking has been Eric Lenneberg's *Biological Foundations of Language* (New York: John Wiley, 1967), a treatise that remains the most comprehensive and eloquent statement of the biological approach. Norman Geschwind's "Language and the Brain," *Scientific American* 226 (1972), pp. 76–83, is a concise, readable statement of the anatomical essentials.

Roger Brown's *A First Language: The Early Stages* (Cambridge, Mass.: Harvard University Press, 1973) is a classic account of language acquisition. The works of Noam Chomsky, including *Syntactic Structures* (The Hague: Mouton, 1957) and *Aspects of the Theory of Syntax* (Cambridge, Mass.: MIT Press, 1965) have become an important part of the basis of most investigators' thinking about language, and Charles Hockett's accessible article "The Origin of Speech," *Scientific American* 203 (1960), pp. 88–111, has influenced the outlook of most anthropologists. For a still valuable traditional presentation of the viewpoint of anthropological linguistics see Edward Sapir, *Language* (New York: Harcourt, Brace and World, 1949).

Page

152 "The development of human speech . . .": E.O. Wilson, *Sociobiology* (Cambridge, Mass.: Harvard University Press, 1975), p. 556.

152 "In the beginning was the Word . . .": John 1:1.

152 The naming of the animals: Gen. 2:19–20.

152–53 the tower of Babel: Gen. 11:1–9.

153 "language is no longer . . .": F.G. Patterson, "The Gestures of a Gorilla: Language Acquisition by Another Pongid," *Brain and Language* 12 (1978), pp. 72–97.

153 "Language is a purely human . . .": Sapir, *Language*, p. 8.

154 Hockett's definition: Hockett, "The Origin of Speech."

155 *Colorless green ideas*: Noam Chomsky, *Syntactic Structures*, p. 15.

156 language is a fundamental feature of human biology: Lenneberg, *Biological Foundations of Language*.

157–58 the first specific piece of evidence: Paul Broca, *Bulletin of the Society of Anatomists* (Paris) 36 (1861), p. 330. For a brief review of this history, see Geschwind, "Language and the Brain."

158 Lesion on the left side: Geschwind, "Language and the Brain."

158–59 Wernicke's aphasia: Carl Wernicke, *Der Aphasische Symptom-Complex. Eine Psychologische Studie auf Anatomischer Basis* (Breslau: Cohn and Weigert, 1874).

159–60 this outlook has held up rather well: Geschwind, "Language and the Brain"; and Albert Galaburda, Marjorie LeMay, Thomas Kemper, and Norman Geschwind, "Right-Left Asymmetries in the Brain," *Science* 199 (1978), pp. 853–56.

160 Bilateral asymmetries: Geschwind, "Language and the Brain"; and Galaburda et al., "Rigth-Left Asymmetries."

160 Witelson: Sandra F. Witelson and Wazir Pallie, "Left Hemispheric Specialization for Language in the Newborn: Neuroanatomical Evidence of Asymmetry," *Brain* 96 (1973), pp. 641–46.

160 Wada: Alan E. Davis and Juhn A. Wada, "Hemispheric Asymmetries in Human Infants: Spectral Analysis of Flash and Click Evoked Potentials," *Brain and Language* 4 (1977), pp. 23–31.

160 "Why do children . . . begin to speak . . .": Lenneberg, *Biological Foundations*, p. 125.

161 Brown reviews cross-cultural evidence: Roger Brown, *A First Language: The Early Stages* (Cambridge, Mass.: Harvard University Press, 1973), pp. 70 ff.

161 Deaf children acquiring signs: E. Klima and U. Bellugi, *The Signs of Language* (Cambridge, Mass.: Harvard University Press, 1979). Remarkably, it has also been shown that deaf children who are *not* exposed to sign language will invent a manual sign language and impose it upon their parents, during the age period corresponding to that of normal language acquisition (Susan Goldwin-Meadow and Heidi Feldman, "The Development of Language-like Communication Without a Language Model," *Science* 197 (1977), pp. 401–03. This is one of the most convincing new items of evidence regarding the biological basis of language development.

161 Normal hearing children with deaf parents: Lenneberg, *Biological Foundations*, pp. 155–58.

161 Mongoloids and dwarfs: Eric H. Lenneberg, "A Biological Per-

spective of Language," in *New Directions in the Study of Language*, ed. Eric H. Lenneberg (Cambridge, Mass.: MIT Press, 1966).

162 Language Acquisition Device: Lenneberg, *Biological Foundations*.

162 distinctive features: Stephen Jay Gould, *Ontogeny and Phylogeny* (Cambridge, Mass.: Harvard University Press, Belknap Press, 1977).

162–63 Work of Conel on maturation of cortex: Lenneberg, *Biological Foundations*, p. 162; and J. Leroy Conel, *The Postnatal Development of the Human Cerebral Cortex*, vol. 3 (Cambridge, Mass.: Harvard University Press, 1947).

163 early part of this century: Paul Flechsig, *Anatomie des Menschlichen Gehirns und Rückenmarks auf Myelogenetischer Grundlage* (Leipzig: Georg Thieme, 1920).

163–64 Roch-Lecours and the anatomical LAD: André Roch-Lecours, "Myelogenetic Corrclates of the Development of Speech and Language," in *Foundations of Language Development*, vol. 1 (New York: Academic Press, 1975).

164 Myelination responsive to experience: C.P. Wendell-Smith, "Effects of Light Deprivation on the Postnatal Development of the Optic Nerve," *Nature* 204 (1964), p. 707

164 Linguistic Society of Paris: Hockett, "The Origin of Speech," p. 88.

164–65 Neanderthal people incapable of certain vowel sounds: Philip Lieberman, *On the Origins of Language* (New York: Macmillan, 1975); and Philip Lieberman, Edmund S. Crelin, and Dennis H. Klatt, "Phonetic Ability and Related Anatomy of the Newborn and Adult Human, Neanderthal Man, and the Chimpanzee," *American Anthropologist* 74 (1972), p. 3.

165 letter written to a scientific journal: John H. Fremlen, "The Demese ef the Ne'enderthels: Wes Lengege e Fecter?" *Science* 187 (Feb. 21, 1975), p. 600.

165 fossil endocasts: Ralph L. Holloway, "The Casts of Fossil Hominid Brains," *Scientific American* 229 (1974); and Ralph L. Holloway, "Endocranial Volumes of Early African Hominids, and the Role of the Brain in Human Mosaic Evolution," *Journal of Human Evolution* 2 (1973), pp. 449–59.

166 Film of chimpanzees: Peter Marler, *Communication in Wild Chimpanzees*, Rockefeller University Films, 1968.

166 the gorilla Koko: Patterson, "The Gestures of a Gorilla."

167 Washoe talks to herself: Beatrice T. Gardner and R. Allen Gardner, "Comparing the Early Utterances of Child and Chimpanzee," in *Minnesota Symposia on Child Psychology*, vol. 8, ed. A. Pick (Minneapolis: University of Minnesota Press, 1974). For a

detailed account of Washoe's grammatical capacity see Beatrice T. Gardner and R. Allen Gardner, "Evidence for Sentence Constituents in the Early Utterances of Child and Chimpanzee," *Journal of Experimental Psychology* 104 (1975), pp. 244–67.

167 Sherman and Austin conversing: E. Sue Savage-Rumbaugh, Duane M. Rumbaugh, and Sally Boysen, "Symbolic Communication Between Two Chimpanzees (*Pan troglodytes*)," *Science* 201 (1978), pp. 641–44. A subsequent attempt to produce a conversation between two pigeons simulating this one was amusing, but not more convincing than the speech of parrots. Still, see Robert Epstein, Robert Lanza, and B.F. Skinner, "Symbolic Communication Between Two Pigeons (*Columbia livia domestica*)," *Science* 207 (1980), pp. 543–45.

167 Washoe coins "water birds" and "rock berry": Roger S. Fouts, "Language: Origins, Definitions, and Chimpanzees," Journal of *Human Evolution* 3 (1974), pp. 475–82.

167 Lana: Duane M. Rumbaugh and Timothy V. Gill, "Language, Apes, and the Apple Which-Is Orange, Please," *Symposium of the Fifth Congress of the International Primate Society*, 1974, pp. 247–57; and Duane M. Rumbaugh, Timothy V. Gill, Ernst von Glaserfeld, Harold Warner, and Pier Pisani, "Conversations with a Chimpanzee in a Computer-Controlled Environment," *Biological Psychiatry* 10 (1975), pp. 627–41. For another computer-based approach to chimpanzee language see David Premack, *Intelligence in Ape and Man* (Hillsdale, N.J.: Erlbaum, 1976), or Ann James Premack and David Premack, "Teaching Language to an Ape," *Scientific American* 227 (1972), pp. 92–99.

167 Lucy coins "cry hurt food": Fouts, "Language," p. 379.

167 a leading skeptic: Brown, *A First Language,* pp. 32–51.

167 Orangutan brains: Marjorie LeMay and Norman Geschwind, "Hemispheric Differences in the Brains of Great Apes," *Brain Behavior and Evolution* 11 (1975), pp. 48–52.

168 Nim Chimpsky: H.S. Terrace, L.A. Pettito, R.J. Sanders, and T.G. Bever, "Can an Ape Create a Sentence?" *Science* 206 (1979), pp. 891–902. For a more popular treatment see Terrace's *Nim* (New York: Knopf, 1979).

169 ape-turned-human: Franz Kafka, "Report to an Academy," in *Selected Short Stories* (New York: Random House, 1952), p. 178.

169–70 "Strether sat there . . .": Henry James, *The Ambassadors* (New York: W.W. Norton, 1964), p. 307.

170 the aesthetic achievement is similar: For a comprehensive and beautiful account of !Kung San oral traditions see Marguerite Anne Biesele, "Folklore and Ritual of !Kung Hunter-Gatherers," 2 vols. (Ph.D. dissertation, Harvard University, 1975). For a

briefer treatment see her "Aspects of !Kung Folklore," in *Kalahari Hunter-Gatherers*, ed. Richard B. Lee and Irven DeVore (Cambridge, Mass.: Harvard University Press, 1976).

172 "Hello, Mr. Dinosaur": John Gottman and Jennifer Parkhurst, "Developing May Not Always Be Improving: A Developmental Study of Children's Best Friendships," paper presented at the 1977 Biennial Meeting of the Society for Research in Child Development, New Orleans, La., March 20, 1977,

CHAPTER 9: RAGE

A major contribution to the understanding of the evolution of human aggressiveness was made by David Hamburg, a distinguished psychiatrist who became interested in evolutionary and anthropological approaches to this problem. His series of papers on aggressiveness in wild chimpanzees and baboons, and its relationship to problems of human conflict, are classics in this field. They appeared during the 1970s and are cited below.

Two useful collections of readings are Charles H. Southwick, ed., *Animal Aggression* (New York: Van Nostrand, 1970), and Ralph L. Holloway, ed., *Primate Aggression, Territoriality and Xenophobia* (New York: Academic Press, 1975). Vernon H. Mark and Frank R. Ervin's *Violence and the Brain* (New York: Harper & Row, 1970) was a one-sided perspective provided by a psychosurgeon and his psychiatrist associate; it is mainly of interest for the extremes toward which allegedly responsible commentary in this area may tend (see Stephan Chorover, *From Genesis to Genocide,* and Elliot S. Valenstein, *Brain Control,* both cited below, for criticism).

An introductory ethological account of the subject is Konrad Lorenz, *On Aggression* (New York: Harcourt Brace Jovanovich, 1966). Joseph Popp and Irven DeVore provide a sociobiological perspective in their "Aggressive Competition and Social Dominance Theory: Synopsis," in *The Great Apes*, ed. David A., Hamburg and Elizabeth R. McCown (Reading, Mass.: Benjamin/Cummings, 1979).

Although not the viewpoint taken in this book, the thesis that human aggression is purely learned or environmental in origin remains perfectly respectable. For an eloquent recent defense of this thesis see Ashley Montagu, *The Nature of Human Aggression* (New York: Oxford University Press, 1976).

Page

175 Initial report of killing of Bonnie Jean Garland: Ronald Smothers, "Yale Senior Slain in Scarsdale; Boyfriend Surrenders to Priest," *The New York Times*, July 9, 1977, pp. 1 and 30.

175–76 Trial of Richard James Herrin: Facts of the case from the following sources: Ronald Smothers, "Mother Testifies at Son's Trial in Murder of Student," *The New York Times*, June 6, 1978, section 2, p. 8; Ronald Smothers, "Defendant Takes Stand in White Plains Murder Trial," *The New York Times*, June 7, 1978, section 2, p. 5; Ronald Smothers, "Herrin Jury Recalls Tortuous Path It Took Trying to Reach a Verdict," *The New York Times*, June 22, 1978, section 4, p. 18; Ronald Smothers, "Herrin Given Maximum Jail Term in Bludgeoning Death in Scarsdale," *The New York Times*, July 28, 1978, pp. 1 and 10.

176 "I could not live without her": Richard Herrin quoted in Smothers, "Herrin Given Maximum Jail Term."

176 "Even under the stress . . .": Judge Daronco quoted in Smothers, "Herrin Given Maximum Jail Term."

176 "totally inconsistent . . .": Jack Litman quoted in Smothers, "Herrin Given Maximum Jail Term."

176–77 Trial of Wang Yungtai: All quotes are from Barrie A. Chi and Emile C. Chi, "Trial of Wang Yungtai," *The New York Times Magazine*, Oct. 7, 1979, p. 48.

181 walk and chew gum: At around the time Gerald Ford became President, many standard news sources attributed this barb to Lyndon Johnson, as a commentary on Ford's intellectual capacity. It was supposed to have been said quite a few years earlier.

182 Mammalian brain in humans: Paul D. MacLean, "Some Psychiatric Implications of Physiological Studies on Frontotemporal Portion of Limbic System (Visceral Brain), *EEG Clinical Neurophysiology* 4 (1952), pp. 407–18; and Paul D. MacLean, "Psychosomatic Disease and the 'Visceral Brain': Recent Developments Bearing on the Papez Theory of Emotion," *Psychosomatic Medicine* 11 (1949), pp. 338–53.

182 The streams of action, feeling, and thought: James W. Papez, "A Proposed Mechanism of Emotion," *Archives of Neurological Psychiatry* 38 (1937), pp. 725–43.

183 The anatomical seat of consciousness: Wilder Penfield, *The Mystery of the Mind: A Critical Study of Consciousness and the Human Brain* (Princeton: Princeton University Press, 1975).

184 "killing bite": Konrad Lorenz and Paul Leyhausen, "On the Funtion of the Relative Hierarchy of Moods," in *Motivation of Human and Animal Behavior: An Ethological View* (New York: Van Nostrand Reinhold, 1973).

185–86 Brain stimulation, rage, and "sham rage": J. Flynn, H. Venegas, W. Foote, and S. Edwards, "Neural Mechanisms Involved in a Cat's Attack on a Rat" in *The Neural Control of Behavior*, ed. R.F.

Whalen, M. Thompson, M. Verzeano, and N. Weinberger (New York: Academic Press, 1970).

186 What causes . . . behavior?: Niko Tinbergen, "On the Aims and Methods of Ethology," *Zeitschrift für Tierpsychologie* 20 (1963), pp. 410–33.

188 violent epileptic fits: For a recent assessment of violent epileptic events, which are quite rare, see Antonio V. Delgado-Escueta et al., "The Nature of Aggression During Epileptic Seizures," *New England Journal of Medicine* 305 (1981), pp. 711–16, and the accompanying editorial by Jonathan Pincus, "Violence and Epilepsy," pp. 696–98.

189 lesions of the hypothalamus: W.R. Ingram, "The Hypothalamus," *Clinical Symposia* 8 (1956), pp. 117–56.

189 Removal of the temporal lobe: Heinrich Klüver and Paul C. Bucy, "Preliminary Analysis of the Temporal Lobes in Monkeys," *Archives of Neurological Psychiatry* 42 (1939), pp. 979–1000.

189 "removal of the amygdala alone": James A. Horel, E. Gregory Keating, Louis J. Misantone, "Partial Klüver-Bucy Syndrome Produced by Destroying Temporal Neocortex or Amygdala," *Brain Research* 94 (1975), pp. 347–59.

189 Septal lesions: J.V. Brady and Walle Nauta, "Subcortical Mechanisms in Emotional Behavior: Affective Changes Following Septal Forebrain Lesions in the Albino Rat," *Journal of Comparative and Physiological Psychology* 46 (1953), pp. 339–46.

190 Hypothalamic regulation: J.R. Smythies, *Brain Mechanisms and Behavior* (New York: Academic Press, 1970), chapter 3.

190 way stations in the midbrain: John T. Flynn et al., "Neural Mechanisms."

190 Treatment in Japan and Argentina: Elliot S. Valenstein, *Brain Control: A Critical Examination of Brain Stimulation and Psychosurgery* (New York: John Wiley, 1973), pp. 234–48.

190–91 destroy large portions of the amygdala: Ibid., pp. 209–33.

191 Suffering of patients, families, and physicians: A similar statement is made in Nauta's foreword to Valenstein's *Brain Control*.

191 the danger of misuse: Stephan Chorover has been a vocal and thoughtful critic of psychosurgery for years, and probably has been personally responsible for the prevention of much potential misuse of it. His excellent treatment of its past offenses in his book *From Genesis to Genocide* (Cambridge, Mass.: MIT Press, 1979) does not encourage the outlook that psychosurgeons should be left to decide these things for themselves.

191 Fighting and uptake of norepinephrine: Bruce L. Welch, Edith D. Hendley, and Ibrahim Turek, "Norepinephrine Uptake into

Cerebral Cortical Synaptosomes After One Fight or Electroconvulsive Shock," *Science* 183 (1974), pp. 220–21.

191–92 Isolation-induced fighting: Luigi Valzelli, *Psychopharmacology: An Introduction to Experimental and Clinical Principles* (Flushing, N.Y.: Spectrum, 1973), pp. 79–83.

192 mouse-killing by rats: For review see Gordon A. Barr, Judith L. Gibbons, and Wagner H. Bridger, "Neuropharmacological Regulation of Mouse Killing by Rats," *Behavioral Biology* 17 (1976), pp. 143–59.

192 "fight or flight": Walter B. Cannon, *Bodily Changes in Pain, Hunger, Fear, and Rage* (New York: Harper & Row, 1963; orig. 1915).

193 testosterone injections: Robert M. Rose, Irwin S. Bernstein, Thomas P. Gordon, Sharon F. Catlin, "Androgens and Aggression: A Review of Recent Findings in Primates," in *Primate Aggression, Territoriality and Xenophobia*, ed. Ralph L. Holloway (New York: Academic Press, 1975). Most of these studies have used castrated males subsequently injected with testosterone. It is difficult to increase the aggressive behavior of a normal male by injecting the hormone. Thus, testosterone may be a necessary but not sufficient condition for sustained aggressive action.

193 Monkey losers and winners: Robert M. Rose, Thomas P. Gordon, Irwin S. Bernstein, "Plasma Testosterone Levels in the Male Rhesus: Influences of Sexual and Social Stimuli," *Science* 178 (1972), pp. 643–45.

193 Harvard wrestling team: Michael Elias, "Serum Cortisol, Testosterone, and Testosterone-Binding Globulin Responses to Competitive Fighting in Human Males," *Aggressive Behavior* 7:3 (1981), pp. 215–24.

194 Dominance hierarchy and stress hormones: K. Manogue, A. Leshner, and D. Candland, "Dominance Status and Adrenocortical Activity to Stress in Squirrel Monkeys (*Saimiri sciureus*)," *Primates* 16 (1975), p. 457; M. Golub, E. Sassenrath, and G. Goo, "Plasma Cortisol Levels and Dominance in Peer Groups of Rhesus Monkey Weanlings," *Hormones and Behavior* 12 (1979), p. 50; Robert Sapolsky, "Stress and the Single Baboon," lecture at Wellesley College Biology Department, March 17, 1981.

194 Performance on skilled tasks: M. Frankenhaeuser, "Experimental Approaches to the Study of Catecholamines and Emotion," in *Emotions: Their Parameters and Measurement*, ed. L. Levi (New York: Raven Press, 1975).

195–96 Southwick: Charles H. Southwick, "Genetic and Environmental Variables Influencing Animal Aggression," in *Animal Aggression:*

Selected Readings, ed. Charles H. Southwick (New York: Van Nostrand Reinhold, 1970).

196–97 pain, irritation, frustration, and fear: J. Dollard, L.W. Doob, N.E. Miller, O.H. Mowrer, and R.R. Sears, *Frustration and Aggression* (New Haven: Yale University Press, 1939).

197 "redirected threat": Robert A. Hinde, *Animal Behavior: A Synthesis of Ethology and Comparative Psychology* (New York: McGraw-Hill, 1966), pp. 287–88.

197 Social isolation in mice: Valzelli, *Psychopharmacology*.

197–98 Aggression training of animals in the laboratory: Howard Rachlin, *Behavior and Learning* (San Francisco: W.H. Freeman and Co., 1976), pp. 138–40.

198 human children: Albert Bandura and R.H. Walters, *Social Learning and Personality Development* (New York: Holt, Rinehart and Winston, 1963).

198–99 Social isolation in rhesus monkeys: G.L. Arling, G.C. Ruppenthal, and G.D. Mitchell, "Aggressive Behavior of the Eight-Year-Old Nulliparous Isolate Rhesus Monkey," *Animal Behavior* 17 (1969), pp. 109–13.

199 dominance ranking in monkeys: Donald Sade, "Determinants of Dominance in a Group of Free-Ranging Rhesus Monkeys," in *Social Communication Among Primates*, ed. Stuart A. Altmann (Chicago: University of Chicago Press, 1967).

199 rats reared with mice: Victor H. Denenberg, R.E. Paschke, and M.X. Zarrow, "Killing of Mice by Rats Prevented by Early Interaction between the Two Species," *Psychonomic Science* 11 (1968), p. 39.

199–200 !Kung San: Richard B. Lee, *The !Kung San* (Cambridge, Engl.: Cambridge University Press, 1979); and Melvin J. Konner, "Aspects of the Developmental Ethology of a Foraging People," in Nicholas Blurton Jones, *Ethological Studies of Child Behavior* (Cambridge, Engl.: Cambridge University Press, 1972).

200 Maternal behavior alters aggressive behavior: Southwick, "Genetic and Environmental Variables."

201 Aggression and other emotions in wild chimpanzees: David A. Hamburg, "Psychobiological Studies of Aggressive Behaviour," *Nature* 230 (1971), pp. 19–23; "Aggressive Behavior of Chimpanzees and Baboons in Natural Habitats," *Journal of Psychiatric Research* 8 (1971), pp. 385–98; and "An Evolutionary and Developmental Approach to Human Aggressiveness," *The Psychoanalytic Quarterly* 42 (1973), pp. 185–200.

201 function of aggressive behavior: Konrad Lorenz, "What Aggression is Good For," in *Animal Aggression: Selected Readings*, ed.

Charles H. Southwick (New York: Van Nostrand Reinhold, 1970).

202 Baboons and homicide: E.O. Wilson, *Sociobiology: The New Synthesis* (Cambridge, Mass.: Harvard University Press, Belknap Press, 1975), pp. 246–47.

202 "competitive infanticide" in Indian monkeys: Sarah Blaffer Hrdy, *The Langurs of Abu* (Cambridge, Mass.: Harvard University Press, 1977). For an excellent summary of the evidence for competitive infanticide not only in langurs but in a wide variety of primates and other animals, see Hrdy's "Infanticide Among Animals: A Review, Classification, and Examination of the Implications for the Reproductive Strategies of Females," *Ethology and Sociobiology* 1 (1979), pp. 13–40.

203 Aggression is for the individual, not the group: George C. Williams, *Adaptation and Natural Selection* (Princeton: Princeton University Press, 1966).

203 Chimpanzee homicide: Jane van Lawick Goodall, "Life and Death at Gombe," *National Geographic Magazine* 155:5 (1979), pp. 592–621.

204 the least violent end of the human cultural spectrum: Elizabeth Marshall Thomas, *The Harmless People* (New York: Knopf, 1959).

204 !Kung homicide rate: Richard B. Lee, *The !Kung San*, chapter 13.

204 ". . . not one instance of murder . . .": Robert Knox Dentan, *The Semai: A Nonviolent People of Malaysia* (New York: Holt, Rinehart and Winston, 1968).

204–05 "People do not often hit their children . . .": Ibid., p. 58.

205 ". . . such an unwarlike people . . .": Ibid., pp. 58–59.

205–06 ". . . the Semai seem bemused . . .": Ibid., p. 59.

206 husband-wife intimacy: John Whiting and Beatrice Blyth Whiting, "Aloofness and Intimacy Between Husbands and Wives," *Ethos* 3 (1975), pp. 183–207.

206 when men get together: Lionel Tiger, *Men in Groups* (New York: Random House, 1969).

207 no cultural training: The viewpoint I express here is not, by any means, universally accepted. For an eloquent statement of the diametrically opposite view, see Montagu, *The Nature of Human Aggression*.

CHAPTER 10: FEAR

The most comprehensive overall treatment of this subject I know of is Jeffrey A. Gray, *The Psychology of Fear and Stress* (New York: McGraw-

Hill, 1971). It is out of date in some concepts of evolutionary biology, but has the great virtue of attempting a grand synthesis of all aspects of biological and behavioral science pertinent to fear. As such it is also a good practice run for what I believe should be done for all the major categories of human emotion and behavior. For a particularly sensitive and comprehensive treatment of the fears of childhood, see John Bowlby, *Attachment and Loss*, 3 vols. (New York: Basic Books, 1970–1980).

Page

210 *releasing stimuli*: Irenäus Eibl-Eibesfeldt, *Ethology* (New York: Holt, Rinehart and Winston, 1975).

210 *fixed action patterns*: Konrad Lorenz, *Evolution and Modification of Behavior* (Chicago: University of Chicago Press, 1965).

211 *intention movements*: Niko Tinbergen, "On Appeasement Signals," in *The Animal in Its World*, vol. 2, *Laboratory Experiments and General Papers* (Cambridge, Mass.: Harvard University Press, 1972; orig. 1959), chapter 14.

212 squirrel monkey genital display: Paul D. MacLean, "Effects of Lesions of Globus Pallidus on Species-Typical Display Behavior of Squirrel Monkeys," *Brain Research* 149 (1978), pp. 175–96.

213–14 appeasement signals inherited through the second most dominant animal: Lack makes this point in the context of an eloquent frontal assault on the theory of group selection in behavioral ecology. David Lack, *Population Studies of Birds* (Oxford: Clarendon Press, 1966), p. 284.

214 Darwin: Charles Darwin, *The Expression of the Emotions in Man and Animals* (Chicago: University of Chicago Press, 1965).

214 Cross-cultural uniformity of facial expressions: Irenäus Eibl-Eibesfeldt, "Vorprogrammierung im Menschlichen Sozialverhalten," *Mitteilungen a.d. Max-Planck-Gesellschaft* 5 (1971), pp. 307–38; Paul Ekman, E.R. Sorenson, and W.V. Friesen, "Pan-Cultural Elements in Facial Displays of Emotion," *Science* 164 (1969), pp. 86–88.

215 Sympathetic arousal: See chapter 7 and Walter B. Cannon, *Bodily Changes in Pain, Hunger, Fear and Rage*, 2nd ed. (New York: Harper & Row, 1963; orig. 1929).

215 Weak and strong stimulation of the amygdala: H. Ursin and B.R. Kaada, "Functional Localization with the Amygdaloid Complex in the Cat," *Electroencephalography and Clinical Neurology* 12 (1960), pp. 1–20.

216 Amygdala and septal-hippocampal balance: See chapter 9.

216–17 Aggression, fear, and catecholamines: D. Funkenstein, "The Physiology of Fear and Anger," *Scientific American* 192 (1955), pp. 74–76; and M. Frankenhaeuser, "Experimental Approaches to the Study of Catecholamines and Emotion," in *Emotions: Their*

Parameters and Measurement, ed. L. Levi (New York: Raven Press, 1975).

217 Situational effects: Stanley Schachter and J.E. Singer, "Cognitive, Social and Physiological Determinants of Emotional State," *Psychological Review* 69 (1962), pp. 379–99.

217 Testosterone, fear and aggression: H. Ursin, E. Baade, and S. Levine, *Psychobiology of Stress: A Study of Coping Men* (New York: Academic Press, 1978). See also chapter 9 of this book.

218 Fear in the open field: See Gray, *The Psychology of Fear and Stress*, chapter 4, for review of the genetic studies.

219 withdrawal (nociceptive) reflex: L. Carmichael, "The Onset and Early Development of Behavior," in *Carmichael's Manual of Child Psychology*, vol. 1, ed. P.H. Mussen, 3rd ed. (New York: John Wiley, 1970).

219 a toddler named Albert: John B. Watson, *Behaviorism* (New York: W.W. Norton, 1924).

219 Pavlov's famous experiment: I.P. Pavlov, *Conditioned Reflexes* (New York: Oxford University Press, 1927).

220 Fears in infant chimpanzees: Donald O. Hebb, "On the Nature of Fear," *Psychological Review* 53 (1946), pp. 259–76.

220 innate releasing mechanism: For summary and references, see Irenäus Eibl-Eibesfeldt, *Ethology* (New York: Holt, Rinehart and Winston, 1975), pp. 87–88.

220–21 fear because of discrepancy: Wolfgang M. Schleidt, "Die Historische Entwicklung der Begriffe 'Angeborenes Auslösendes Schema' und 'Angeborener Auslösemechanismus,' " *Zeitschrift für Tierpsychologie* 21 (1962), pp. 235–56; cited in Eibl-Eibesfeldt, p. 88.

221 the edge of a cliff: R.D. Walk and E.J. Gibson, "A Comparative and Analytical Study of Visual Depth Perception," *Psychological Monographs* 75 (1961), pp. 1–44.

222 infant social behavior: Mary D. Salter Ainsworth, Mary C. Blehar, Everett Waters, and Sally Wall, *Patterns of Attachment: A Psychological Study of the Strange Situation* (Hillsdale, N.J.: Erlbaum, 1978).

222–23 Variation and uniformity in infant separation protest: Jerome Kagan, "Emergent Themes in Human Development," *American Scientist* 64 (1976), pp. 186–96; Melvin J. Konner, "Biological Aspects of the Mother-Infant Bond," in *Development of Attachment and Affiliation Processes*, ed. Robert Emde and Robert Harmon (New York: Plenum, 1982).

223 Myelination studies: Paul Flechsig, *Meine Myelogenetische Hirnlehre mit Biographischer Einleitung* (Berlin: Springer, 1927); J.

Leroy Conel, *The Postnatal Development of the Human Cerebral Cortex*, 6 vols. (Cambridge, Mass.: Harvard University Press, 1939–1963); and Paul Yakovlev and André Roch-Lecours, "Myelogenetic Cycles of the Regional Maturation of the Brain," in *Regional Maturation of the Brain in Early Man*, ed. A. Minkowski (Oxford: Blackwell, 1967).

223 "reptilian brain": Paul D. MacLean, "The Triune Brain, Emotion, and Scientific Bias," in *The Neurosciences: Second Study Program*, ed. F.O. Schmitt (New York: Rockefeller University Press, 1970).

224 intermediate in discrepancy: Kagan has written extensively on this subject, but a good introduction may be found in the following: Jerome Kagan, "Do Infants Think?" *Scientific American* 226 (1972), pp. 74–82.

224 cat experiments: Ursin and Kaada, "Functional Localization."

225 Hippocampus in comparing: John O'Keefe and Lynn Nadel, *The Hippocampus as a Cognitive Map* (New York: Oxford University Press, 1978).

225 the capacity to *feel*: Konner, "Biological Aspects of the Mother-Infant Bond."

226 early-experience effects: Victor H. Denenberg, "Effects of Exposure to Stressors in Early Life upon Later Behavioural and Biological Processes," in *Society, Stress and Disease*, vol. 2, *Childhood and Adolescence*, ed. L. Levi (New York: Oxford University Press, 1975), pp. 269–81.

226 Rats handled in infancy: Seymour Levine, Gary C. Haltmeyer, George C. Karas, and Victor H. Denenberg, "Physiological and Behavioral Effects of Infantile Stimulation," *Physiology of Behavior* 2 (1967), pp. 55–59.

226–27 "pituitary-adrenocortical axis": P. Samuel Campbell, M.X. Zarrow, and Victor H. Denenberg, "The Effect of Infantile Stimulation upon Hypothalamic CRF Levels Following Adrenalectomy in the Adult Rat," *Proceedings of the Society for Experimental Biology and Medicine* 142 (1973), pp. 781–83.

227 Isolation-reared monkeys: Stephen J. Suomi and Harry F. Harlow, "Social Rehabilitation of Isolate-Reared Monkeys," *Developmental Psychology* 6 (1972), pp. 487–96.

227 effects of short separations: Robert A. Hinde and Yvette Spencer-Booth, "Effects of Brief Separation from Mother on Rhesus Monkeys," *Science* 173 (1971), pp. 111–18.

227–28 Effects of fear experienced by pregnant mothers: W.R. Thompson, "Influence of Prenatal Maternal Anxiety on Emotionality in Young Rats," *Science* 125 (1957), pp. 698–99.

228 Later results of fear *in utero*: Justin M. Joffe, *Prenatal Determinants of Behavior* (Oxford: Pergamon Press, 1969).

229 problem of childhood autism: Elisabeth Tinbergen and Niko Tinbergen, "Early Childhood Autism: An Ethological Approach," *Advances in Ethology* (Supplements to *Zeitschrift für Tierpsychologie*) 10 (Berlin: Parey, 1972), pp. 1–53. For a condensed version see Niko Tinbergen, *The Animal in Its World*, vol. 2.

229–32 analysis of Hans: Sigmund Freud, "Analysis of a Phobia in a Five-Year-Old Boy," in Sigmund Freud, *Collected Papers*, vol. 3, trans. Alix and James Strachey (New York: Basic Books, 1959).

230–31 ". . . he was perfectly well . . .": Sigmund Freud, "Analysis of a Phobia," p. 288.

232 "The anxiety in zoöphobia . . .": Sigmund Freud, *The Problem of Anxiety* (New York: W.W. Norton, 1963), pp. 62–63.

233 Valium: John F. Tallman, Steven M. Paul, Phil Skolnick, and Dorothy W. Gallager, "Receptors for the Age of Anxiety: Pharmacology of the Benzodiazepines," *Science* 207 (1980), pp. 274–81.

233 wines, beers, and spirits: J.N. Nestoros, "Ethanol Specifically Potentiates GABA-Mediated Neurotransmission in Feline Cerebral Cortex," *Science* 209 (1980), pp. 708–10.

233 American alcoholics: George E. Vaillant, "Alcoholism and Drug Dependence," in *The Harvard Guide to Modern Psychiatry*, ed. Armand M. Nicholi, Jr. (Cambridge, Mass.: Harvard University Press, Belknap Press, 1978).

233 a battlefront staple: See John Keegan, *The Face of Battle* (London: Jonathan Cape, 1976).

233 vodka consumption in the Soviet Union: *Time* magazine, special issue on the Soviet Union, June 23, 1980, p. 75.

235 looking about wildly: A paraphrase of the last line of the James Wright poem quoted at the head of this chapter. James Wright, *Collected Poems* (Middletown, Conn.: Wesleyan University Press, 1971).

CHAPTER 11: JOY

Joy remains the most poorly studied of all human emotions; perhaps this only means it is as elusive for investigators as it is for everyone else. Particular views of how it is constituted may be found in Sigmund Freud's *Beyond the Pleasure Principle* and Karl Marx's *Economic and Philosophic Manuscripts of 1844* (both cited below); these are useful but flawed in ways that will be obvious to most readers.

Robert Fagen has provided a superb overview of the subject of play in animals, with an analysis of its evolutionary meaning, in *Animal Play Behavior* (New York: Oxford, 1981). Modern psychology has gone far in explaining another aspect of joy—brain self-stimulation and neurological reward systems; James Olds, whose work is cited below, gives an authoritative summary.

Page

238 neural circuitry: For a good discussion of this concept see Robert A. Hinde, *Animal Behaviour: A Synthesis of Ethology and Comparative Psychology* (New York: McGraw-Hill, 1966), chapter 12; and Elliot S. Valenstein, *Brain Stimulation and Motivation* (Chicago: Scott-Foresman, 1973).

238 "In the theory of psychoanalysis . . .": Sigmund Freud, *Beyond the Pleasure Principle* (London: Hogarth Press, 1950), p. 1.

239 "the terrible war . . .": Ibid., p. 9.

240 Freud's conception of humor: Sigmund Freud, *Jokes and Their Relation to the Unconscious*, trans. and ed. James Strachey (London: Routledge, 1960).

240 "Then beauty is nothing . . .": Rainer Maria Rilke, "The First Elegy," in *Duino Elegies*, ed. and trans. J.B. Leishman and Stephen Spender (New York: W.W. Norton, 1939), p. 20. (Translated by author.)

241 G.T. Fechner and "aesthetic indifference": Freud, *Beyond the Pleasure Principle*, p. 3.

241–42 "smile of recognitory assimilation": Jean Piaget, *The Origins of Intelligence in Children* (New York: W.W. Norton, 1963), p. 72; Jerome Kagan, *Change and Continuity in Infancy* (New York: John Wiley, 1971), chapter 7; Philip R. Zelazo, "Smiling and Vocalizing: A Cognitive Emphasis," *Merrill-Palmer Quarterly of Behavior and Development* 18 (1972), pp. 349–65; Philip R. Zelazo, "Smiling to Social Stimuli: Eliciting and Conditioning Effects," *Developmental Psychology* 4 (1971), pp. 32–42; and Philip R. Zelazo and M. Joan Komer, "Infant Smiling to Nonsocial Stimuli and the Recognition Hypothesis," *Child Development* 42 (1971), pp. 1327–39.

242 Hebb's fear theory: Donald O. Hebb, "On the Nature of Fear," *Psychological Review* 53 (1946), pp. 259–76.

242 Fechner's exact language: As quoted in Freud, *Beyond the Pleasure Principle*, p. 3.

243 estrangement or alienation: Karl Marx, *The Economic and Philosophic Manuscripts of 1844* (Moscow: Foreign Language Publishing House, 1959).

243–44 "smile of recognitory assimilation": Daniel N. Stern, "Mother and Infant at Play: The Dyadic Interaction Involving Facial, Vocal, and Gaze Behaviors," in *The Origins of Behavior*, vol. 1, ed. M. Lewis and L. Rosenblum (New York: John Wiley, 1973).

244 "response-contingent stimulation": John S. Watson, "Smiling, Cooing, and 'The Game,' " *Merrill-Palmer Quarterly* 18 (1972), p. 327.

245 aware teaching and learning: A.S. Neill, *Summerhill: A Radical Approach to Child Rearing* (New York: Hart, 1961); John Holt, *How Children Fail* (New York: Pitman, 1964), and *How Children Learn* (New York: Pitman, 1967).

245 the "open classroom" movement: Joseph Featherstone, "The Primary School Revolution in Britain," *The New Republic*, Aug. 10, Sept. 2, and Sept. 9, 1967; and *Schools Where Children Learn* (New York: Liveright, 1971).

246 Play and intelligence in mammals: R.F. Ewer, *Ethology of Mammals* (London: Elek, 1968).

246–47 Learning by observation: See, for example, P. Chesler, "Maternal Influence in Learning by Observation in Kittens," *Science* 166 (1969), pp. 901–03.

247 drudgery into the lives of children: For a full discussion and references, see Melvin J. Konner, "Evolution of Human Behavior Development: An Integrative Review," in *Handbook of Cross-Cultural Development*, ed. Robert L. Monroe, Ruth H. Monroe, and Beatrice B. Whiting (New York: Garland Press, 1981).

247 *Homo ludens:* Johan Huizinga, *Homo Ludens: A Study of the Play-Element in Culture* (London: Routledge, 1949).

248 Milner: James Olds and Peter Milner, "Positive Reinforcement Produced by Electrical Stimulation of Septal Area and Other Regions of Rat Brain," *Journal of Comparative and Physiological Psychology* 47 (1954), pp. 419–27.

248–50 a late and masterly review: James Olds, "Behavioral Studies of Hypothalamic Functions: Drives and Reinforcements," in *Biological Foundations of Psychiatry*, vol. 1, ed. R.G. Grenell and S. Gabay (New York: Raven, 1976). For a more recent review see Aryeh Routtenberg, *Biology of Reinforcement: Facets of Brain-Stimulation Reward* (New York: Academic Press, 1980).

250 "A patient who had just attempted . . .": Elliot S. Valenstein, *Brain Control* (New York: John Wiley, 1973), p. 73.

251 an embarrassment to her: Ibid., pp. 74–75.

251 Brain stimulation with hunger, castration, and hormones: Olds, "Behavioral Studies."

251 one human patient: Valenstein, *Brain Control*, p. 74.

251 Valenstein: Elliot S. Valenstein, V.C. Cox, and J.K. Kakolewsky, "Reexamination of the Role of the Hypothalamus in Motivation,"

Psychological Review 77 (1970), pp. 16–31. See also Valenstein, *Brain Control,* chapter 1.

252 REM deprivation and self-stimulation: S.S. Steiner and S.J. Ellman, "Relation Between REM Sleep and Intracranial Self-Stimulation," *Science* 177 (1972), pp. 1122–24.

252 "Woe to you . . .": Sigmund Freud, *Cocaine Papers* (New York: Stonehill, 1974), p. 10.

252–53 "Über Coca": Ibid., 47–73.

253 "divine plant . . .": Ibid., p. 50.

253 ". . . signs of happy excitement . . .": Ibid., p. 57.

253 ". . . exhilaration and lasting euphoria . . .": Ibid., p. 60.

254 "I feel as if something pleasant had just happened to me": Richard B. Resnick, Richard S. Kestenbaum, and Lee K. Schwartz, "Acute Systemic Effects of Cocaine in Man: A Controlled Study by Intranasal and Intravenous Routes," *Science* 195 (1977), p. 697.

254–55 "the drug was almost exclusively chosen . . .": Thomas G. Aigner and Robert L. Balster, "Choice Behavior in Rhesus Monkeys: Cocaine Versus Food," *Science* 201 (1978), p. 535.

255 "I feel more relaxed": Resnick et al., "Effects of Cocaine," p. 698.

255 Abolishing the capacity for pleasure: Larry Stein and C. David Wise, "Possible Etiology of Schizophrenia: Progressive Damage to the Noradrenergic Reward System by 6-Hydroxydopamine," *Science* 171 (1971), pp. 1032–36.

255 Monkey syndrome resembling human depression: D.E. Redmond and A. Kling, "Behavior of Free-Ranging Macaques After Intraventricular 6-Hydroxydopamine," *Science* 181 (1973), pp. 1256–58.

255–56 Brain chemicals known as peptides: Dorothy T. Krieger and Anthony S. Liotta, "Pituitary Hormones in Brain: Where, How, and Why?" *Science* 205 (1979), pp. 366–72; Solomon H. Snyder, "Opiate Receptors and Internal Opiates," *Scientific American*, March 1977, pp. 44–56; and Avram Goldstein, "Opioid Peptides (Endorphins) in Pituitary and Brain," *Science* 193 (1976), pp. 1081–86.

256 "the opiate receptor": See, for example, Candace B. Pert, A.M. Snowman, and Solomon H. Snyder, "Localization of Opiate Receptor Binding in Presynaptic Membranes of Rat Brain," *Brain Research* 70 (1974), pp. 184–88; and Snyder, "Opiate Receptors and Internal Opiates."

256 mimic the effects of morphine on pain: Roger Guillemin, "Peptides in the Brain: The New Endocrinology of the Neuron," *Science* 202 (1978), pp. 390–402.

256 tiny doses of opioid peptides: Floyd Bloom, David Segal, Nicholas Ling, and Roger Guillemin, "Endorphins: Profound Behavioral Effects in Rats Suggest New Etiological Factors in Mental Illness," *Science* 194 (1976), pp. 630–32; and Yasuko F. Jacquet and Neville Marks, "The C-Fragment of B-Lipotropin: An Endogenous Neuroleptic or Antipsychotogen?" *Science* 194 (1976), pp. 632–35.

256–57 how we view the future: Lionel Tiger, *Optimism: The Biology of Hope* (New York: Simon and Schuster, 1979). For laboratory evidence that seems to offer support for Tiger's outlook, see J.C. Willer, H. Dehen, and J. Cambier, "Stress-Induced Analgesia in Humans: Endogenous Opioids and Naloxone Reversible Depression of Pain Reflexes," *Science* 212 (1981), pp. 689–91.

258–59 lifetime findings on these men: George E. Vaillant, *Adaptation to Life* (Boston: Little, Brown, 1977).

258 "Woe to the man . . .": Joseph Conrad, quoted in ibid., p. 284.

258 ". . . Campanella seemed a greater man . . .": Ibid., p. 239.

259 ". . . most outstanding mature adults . . .": Jean MacFarlane, quoted in ibid., pp. 299–300.

259 "It is not stress that kills us . . .": Ibid., p. 374.

259 "There is more happiness . . .": Eugene O'Neill, as quoted in *Eight Great Tragedies*, ed. Sylvan Barnet, Morton Berman, and William Burto (New York: Mentor, 1957).

260 "Hamlet and Lear are gay . . .": All quotes here are from W.B. Yeats, "Lapis Lazuli," in *The Variorum Edition of the Poems of W.B. Yeats*, ed. Peter Allt and Russell Alspach (New York: Macmillan, 1940), pp. 565–66.

CHAPTER 12: LUST

The emotion of lust has proved surprisingly accessible to scientific study and there is a rich literature on all its facets. An excellent introduction to the evolutionary dimensions of the subject is Martin Daly and Margo Wilson, *Sex, Evolution and Behavior* (North Scituate, Mass.: Duxbury Press, 1978). The physiological psychology of sex is summarized in G. Bermant and J. Davidson, *Biological Bases of Sexual Behavior* (New York: Harper & Row, 1974). A recent cross-cultural perspective is given by Gwen J. Broude, "The Cultural Management of Sexuality," in *Handbook of Cross-Cultural Development*, ed. Robert L. Monroe, Ruth H. Monroe, and Beatrice B. Whiting (New York: Garland Press, 1981). The reports by Alfred Kinsey and his colleagues on *Sexual Behavior in the Human Male* and *Sexual Behavior in the Human Female* (Philadelphia: W.B. Saunders, 1953) remain the best-documented accounts of average sexual practices in the United States. They apply to the United States of the 1940s, of course, but we still await equally solid work on more recent sexual habits—a major current gap in our knowledge. Finally, no literate person who has the slightest interest in sex should fail to become acquainted with William H. Masters and Virginia E. Johnson's *Human Sexual Response* (Boston: Little, Brown, 1966), a precious source of crucial information and a turning point in the history of sex research.

Page

261–63 Control systems theory in social behavior: For an account of the application of such a model to the specific case of mother-infant relations, see John Bowlby, *Attachment and Loss*, vol. 1, *Attachment* (London: Hogarth Press, 1969), chapters 1, 5, and 13. Although it does not convince me, it is very elegant, and gives many interesting references to applications of control theory to behavior. (I discuss my problems with control theory in chapter 15.) Fortunately, Bowlby's control theory is not really essential to his evolutionary model of mother-infant relations, to which I basically subscribe (see chapters 13 and 14).

265 ". . . a gene's way of making another gene": For a simple and straightforward account of this viewpoint, see Richard Dawkins, *The Selfish Gene* (New York: Oxford University Press, 1978).

266–67 "one vast breeding experiment": Irven DeVore, personal communication. For a summary of other views, see George C. Williams, *Sex and Evolution* (Princeton: Princeton University Press, 1975).

267 Male care of the young: Mary M. Katz and Melvin J. Konner, "The Role of the Father: An Anthropological Perspective," in *The Role of the Father in Child Development*, 2nd edition, ed. M. Lamb (New York: John Wiley, 1981).

267–68 In elephant seals: Burney LeBoeuf and R.S. Peterson, "Social Status and Mating Activity in Elephant Seals," *Science* 163 (1969), pp. 91–93.

267–69 "tournament species": Robert L. Trivers, "Parental Investment and Sexual Selection," in *Sexual Selection and the Descent of Man, 1871–1971*, ed. Bernard G. Campbell (Chicago: Aldine, 1972).

269–70 "all the males follow . . .": Michael D. Beecher and Inger Mornestam Beecher, "Sociobiology of Bank Swallows: Reproductive Strategy of the Male," *Science* 205 (1979), p. 1284.

270 ". . . attempt to fight off . . .": Ibid.

270–71 ringdove: Daniel S. Lehrman, Philip N. Brody, and Rochelle P. Wortis, "The Presence of the Mate and of Nesting Material as Stimuli for the Development of Incubation Behavior and for Gonadotropin Secretion in the Ring Dove (*Streptopelia risoria*),"

Endocrinology 68 (1961), pp. 507–16; Daniel S. Lehrman, "The Reproductive Behavior of Ring Doves," *Scientific American* 211:5 (1964), pp. 48–54; Daniel S. Lehrman, "The Physiological Basis of Parental Feeding Behavior in the Ring Dove," *Behaviour* 7 (1955), pp. 241–86.

270–71 Leon Eisenberg on ringdoves: Eisenberg made this point in a lecture to the Department of Anthropology at Harvard in 1978.

271 Rejection of females: Patricia G. Zanone, M. Eleanor Sims, and Carl J. Erickson, "Male Ring Dove Behavior and the Defense of Genetic Paternity," *The American Naturalist* 114 (1979), pp. 615–26. Other aspects of this pattern were discussed by Erickson in a lecture at Harvard University in 1977.

271 Redwing blackbird hormone levels: Cheryl F. Harding and Brian K. Follett, "Hormone Changes Triggered by Aggression in a Natural Population of Blackbirds," *Science* 203 (1979), pp. 918–20.

271 Redwing blackbird vasectomies: O.E. Bray, J.J. Kennelly, and J.L. Guarino, "Fertility of Eggs Produced on Territories of Vasectomized Red-winged Blackbirds," *Wilson Bulletin* 87 (1975), pp. 187–95.

271–72 Female attack and defense in Wilson's phalarope: E.O. Hohn, "Observations on the Breeding Biology of Wilson's Phalarope (*Steganopus tricolor*) in Central Alberta," *Auk* 84 (1967), pp. 220–44; E.O. Hohn, "The Phalarope," *Scientific American* 220 (1969), pp. 104–11.

273–74 polygyny: Daly and Wilson, *Sex, Evolution and Behavior*, chapter 9; based on data in George Peter Murdock, *Ethnographic Atlas* (Pittsburgh: University of Pittsburgh Press, 1967).

274 exchange of goods: Murdock, cited in Daly and Wilson, *Sex, Evolution and Behavior*.

274 Kinsey reports: Alfred C. Kinsey, Wardell B. Pomeroy, Clyde E. Martin, and Paul H. Gebhard, *Sexual Behavior in the Human Female*.

274 Among the !Kung San: Richard B. Lee, *The !Kung San* (Cambridge, Engl.: Cambridge University Press, 1979), chapter 13.

274–75 Among the Yanomamo, "the fierce people": Napoleon A. Chagnon, *Yanomamo: The Fierce People* (New York: Holt, Rinehart and Winston, 1968).

274–75 Xavante Indians: F.M. Salzano, J.V. Neel, and D. Maybury-Lewis, "Further Studies on the Xavante Indians. I. Demographic Data on Two Additional Villages; Genetic Structure of the Tribe," *American Journal of Human Genetics* (1967), pp. 463–89.

276 Savannah baboon monthly genital swelling: Thelma E. Rowell,

"Female Reproductive Cycles and the Behavior of Baboons and Rhesus Macaques," in *Social Communication Among Primates*, ed. S.A. Altmann (Chicago: University of Chicago Press, 1967).

276 Squirrel monkey annual cycle: Leonard A. Rosenblum, "Reproduction of Squirrel Monkeys in the Laboratory," in *Breeding Primates*, ed. W.I.B. Beveridge (Basel: S. Karger, 1972), pp. 130–43.

276 pineal gland: René Descartes, *Les Passions de L'Âme*, trans. E. Haldane and G. Ross, in *A Source in the History of Psychology*, ed. Richard Herrnstein and Edwin Boring (Cambridge, Mass.: Harvard University Press, 1965), pp. 205–10.

276 Pineal the seat of annual breeding rhythms: Richard J. Wurtman, "The Effects of Light on Man and Other Mammals," *Annual Review of Physiology* 37 (1975), pp. 467–83.

278 female lordosis response: R.L. Moss and S.M. McCann, "Action of Luteinizing Hormone-Releasing Factor (LRF) in the Initiation of Lordosis Behavior in the Estrone-Primed Ovarectomized Female Rat," *Neuroendocrinology* 17 (1975), pp. 309–18. What formerly was called "Luteinizing Hormone Releasing Factor" (LRF) now is called "Luteinizing Hormone Releasing Hormone" (LHRH), a tribute to its recent removal from the realm of the chemically unknown.

278 nasal spray: O. Bendert, R. Jordan, H.G. Dahlen, H.P.G. Schneider, and G. Gammel, "Sexual Impotence: A Double Blind Study of LHRH Nasal Spray *versus* Placebo," *Neuropsychobiology* 1 (1975), pp. 203–10. The nasal spray route permits much more direct delivery to the pituitary and the brain.

278 Pituitary-brain relations a two-way street: Richard M. Bergland and Robert B. Page, "Pituitary-Brain Vascular Relations: A New Paradigm," *Science* 204 (1979), pp. 18–24.

279 Testosterone in female sexual response: H.L. Judd and S.C. Yen, "Serum Androstenedione and Testosterone Levels During the Menstrual Cycle," *Journal of Clinical Endocrinology and Metabolism* 36 (1973), pp. 475–81.

279 Testosterone around the time of birth: See chapter 6 for discussion.

279 Increase of sexual interest in Americans and !Kung: J.R. Udry and N.M. Morris, "Distribution of Coitus in the Menstrual Cycle," *Nature* 220 (1968), pp. 593–96; Carol Worthman, "Psychoendocrine Study of Human Behavior" (Ph.D. diss., Harvard University, 1978). Udry and Morris also found, for their sample, a smaller increase during menses.

280 Stimulation of the lateral hypothalamus: Elliot S. Valenstein,

V.C. Cox, and J.W. Kakolewski, "Reexamination of the Role of the Hypothalamus in Motivation," *Psychological Review* 77 (1970), pp. 16–31.

280 forward portion of the midbrain: T.K. Clark, Anthony R. Caggiula, R.A. McConnell, and Seymour M. Antelman, "Sexual Inhibition Is Reduced by Rostral Midbrain Lesions in the Male Rat," *Science* 190 (1975), pp. 169–71.

280–81 stria terminalis: Donna E. Every and Benjamin D. Sachs, "Copulatory Behavior in Male Rats with Lesions in the Bed Nucleus of the Stria Terminalis," *Physiology and Behavior* 17 (1976), pp. 803–06.

281 studies of epileptics: Dietrich Blumer, "Changes of Sexual Behavior Related to Temporal Lobe Disorders in Man," *The Journal of Sex Research* 6 (1970), pp. 173–80.

281–82 Neurotransmitters and sex: B.J. Everitt, K. Fuxe, T. Hokfelt, and G. Jonsson, "Role of Monoamines in the Control by Hormones of Sexual Receptivity in the Female Rat," *Journal of Comparative and Physiological Psychology* 89 (1975), pp. 556–72; P.B. Gradwell, B.J. Everitt, and J. Herbert, "5-Hydroxytryptamine in the Central Nervous System and Sexual Receptivity of Female Rhesus Monkeys," *Brain Research* 88 (1975), pp. 281–93.

282 Parkinson's disease: M. Sandler and G.L. Gessa, eds., *Sexual Behavior: Pharmacology and Biochemistry* (New York: Raven Press, 1975), pp. 117–28.

282–83 consumption of foods: See, for example, Richard J. Wurtman and J.D. Fernstrom, "Effects of the Diet on Brain Neurotransmitters," *Nutrition Reviews* 32 (1974), pp. 193–200; Richard J. Wurtman and John H. Growdon, "Dietary Enhancement of CNS Neurotransmitters," in *Neuroendocrinology*, ed. D.T. Krieger and J.C. Hughes (Stamford, Conn.: Sinauer, 1980).

283 Courtship in the fruit fly: Seymour Benzer, "Genetic Dissection of Behavior," *Scientific American* 229 (1973), pp. 24–37.

283 Stickleback courtship displays: Desmond Morris, "The Reproductive Behaviour of the Ten-Spined Stickleback (*Pygosteus pungitius* L.)," *Behaviour*, Supplement 6 (1958).

283 Olfactory signals in rat: F. Bronson, "Pheromonal Influences on Mammalian Reproduction," in *Perspectives in Reproduction and Sexual Behavior*, ed. Marian C. Diamond (Bloomington: Indiana University Press, 1968).

283–84 Sex-attractant cocktail: Richard P. Michael and E.B. Keverne, "A Male Sex-Attractant Pheromone in Rhesus Monkey Vaginal Secretions," *Journal of Endocrinology* 46 (1969), pp. xx–xxi.

284 same five fatty acids: Richard P. Michael, "Human Vaginal

Secretions: Volatile Fatty Acid Content," *Science* 186 (1974), p. 1217.

284 Mid-month secretions "less unpleasant": R. Doty, M. Prety, M. Ford and G. Huggins, "Changes in the Intensity and Pleasantness of Human Vaginal Odors During the Menstrual Cycle," *Science* 190 (1975), pp. 1361–62. It previously had been shown that women's sensitivity to musklike odorants in perfume (musks are often sexual signals in mammals) varies with the monthly reproductive cycle: Jacqueline Scola Vierling and John Rock, "Variations in Olfactory Sensitivity to Exaltolide During the Menstrual Cycle," *Journal of Applied Physiology* 22 (1967), pp. 311–15. This paper also reviews studies showing that women in general are much more sensitive to these odors than are men or prepubertal individuals of either sex.

284 human vaginal secretions rise and fall with the monthly cycle: J. Sokolov et al., "Isolation of Substance from Human Vaginal Secretions Previously Shown to Be Sex Attractant Pheromones in Higher Primates," *Archives of Sexual Behavior* 5 (1976), pp. 269–74.

284 stumptailed monkey: David A. Goldfoot, Stanley J. Wiegard, and Guenther Scheffer, "Continued Copulation in Ovariectomized Adrenal-Suppressed Stumptail Macaques (*Macaca arctoides*)," *Hormones and Behavior* 11 (1978), pp. 89–99. Goldfoot and his colleagues also have challenged the importance of this phenomenon in rhesus monkeys, where it originally was described. See David A. Goldfoot, M.A. Kravetz, Robert W. Goy, and S.K. Freeman, "Lack of Effect of Vaginal Lavages and Aliphatic Acids on Ejaculatory Responses in Rhesus Monkeys: Behavior and Chemical Analyses," *Hormones and Behavior* 7 (1976), pp. 1–27.

285 "homosexual rape" in flatworms: Lawrence G. Abele and Sandra Gilchrist, "Homosexual Rape and Sexual Selection in Acanthocephalan Worms," *Science* 197 (1977), pp. 81–83.

285 "the ultrasonic postejaculatory song": Ronald J. Barfield and Cynetta A. Geyer, "Sexual Behavior: Ultrasonic Postejaculatory Song of the Male Rat," *Science* 176 (1972), pp. 1349–50.

285 rhesus monkey sexual development: Harry F. Harlow, "Lust, Latency and Love: Simian Secrets of Successful Sex," *The Journal of Sex Research* 11 (1975), pp. 79–90.

286 "Of the five males who reached sexual maturity . . .": Roger K. Davenport, "Some Behaviorial Disturbances of Great Apes in Captivity," in *The Great Apes*, ed. David A. Hamburg and Elizabeth R. McCown (Reading, Mass.: Benjamin/Cummings, 1979), p. 356.

287 Chicago middle-class families: This study remains the best systematic comparison of American child-training methods with a fully representative range of other cultures. John W.M. Whiting and Irvin L. Child, *Child Training and Personality* (New Haven: Yale University Press, 1953).

287–89 Masters and Johnson: William H. Masters and Virginia E. Johnson, *Human Sexual Response*. Their work on the treatment of impotence and frigidity has come in for some criticism of late, but there is no question that they have opened a new path for the study and amelioration of these and other sexual disorders.

289 "density-stat": Jeffrey A. Gray, *The Psychology of Fear and Stress* (New York: McGraw-Hill, 1971), p. 73.

289 male gestures of courtship: Niko Tinbergen, "Einige Gedanken über Beschwichtigungs-Gebaerden," *Zeitschrift für Tierpsychologie* 16 (1959), pp. 651–55. The translation, "On Appeasement Signals," can be found in Niko Tinbergen, *The Animal in Its World*, vol. 2 (Cambridge, Mass.: Harvard University Press, 1972).

289 genital display: Paul D. MacLean, "Effects of Lesions of Globus Pallidus on Species-Typical Display Behavior of Squirrel Monkeys," *Brain Research* 149 (1978), pp. 175–96.

289 mounting him from behind: Irven DeVore, "Male Dominance and Mating Behavior in Baboons," in *Sexual Behavior*, ed. Frank Beach (New York: John Wiley, 1965).

289 rape: John MacKinnon, "The Orang-utan in Sabah Today," *Oryx* 11:2–3 (1971), pp. 141–91; Biruté M.F. Galdikas, "Orangutan Adaptation at Tanjung Puting Reserve: Mating and Ecology," in *The Great Apes*, ed. Hamburg and McCown.

289–90 electric shock: Benjamin D. Sachs and Ronald J. Barfield, "Copulatory Behavior of Male Rats Given Intermittent Electric Shocks," *Journal of Comparative and Physiological Psychology* 86 (1974), pp. 607–15. See chapter 9 for discussion of shock-induced fighting.

290 removal of a female: M.P. Rathbone, P.A. Stewart, and F. Vetrano, "Strange Females Increase Plasma Testosterone Levels in Male Mice," *Science* 189 (1975), pp. 1104–06. A more recent study showed that luteinizing hormone (LH) follows the same pattern: It rises in response to a female, then fails to rise as the same female is reintroduced. Presentation of a strange female causes it to rise again. Since LH controls testosterone secretion, this second study may provide a link in the chain from brain to gonads. Arthur Coquelin and F.H. Bronson, "Release of Luteinizing Hormone in Male Mice During Exposure to Females: Habituation of the Response," *Science* 206 (1979), pp. 1099–1101.

290 Male violent sexual fantasies: Robert May, *Sex and Fantasy: Patterns of Male and Female Development* (New York: W.W.

Norton, 1980); Nancy Friday, *Men in Love: Men's Sexual Fanta-sies: The Triumph of Love over Rage* (New York: Delacorte, 1980).
290 caring for young: See, for example, I.C.T. Nisbet, "Courtship-Feeding, Egg-Size and Breeding Success in Common Terns," *Nature* 241 (1973), pp. 141–42.

CHAPTER 13: LOVE

As will be apparent from the body of the chapter, the love that is best understood at the moment is that occurring on either side of the parent-offspring bond; which will be just as well if it turns out that, as some observers believe, this relationship is the prototype for all others. Especially important contributions to our understanding of this relationship have come from the pens of Konrad Lorenz, Harry F. Harlow, and John Bowlby, whose major works are cited below and described in the text.

Evolutionary theory has made major contributions to the explanation of this phenomenon, in an attempt to explain how any individual can be favored by natural selection for expending energy on behalf of someone else. Theorizing in this area usually goes under the rubric of explaining "altruism" and "cooperation" in a universe viewed as relentlessly dog-eat-dog. The key initial contribution was by W.D. Hamilton, "The Genetical Evolution of Social Behavior, I, II," *Journal of Theoretical Biology* 7 (1964), pp. 1–52. An elegant recent extension of this approach to include the evolution of cooperation among nonrelatives, who sometimes, it turns out, have more to gain by not fighting than by fighting, is given by R. Axelrod and W.D. Hamilton, "The Evolution of Cooperation," *Science* 211 (1981), pp. 1390–96. With this article Hamilton completes, in a sense, the work he began in 1964—explaining the known varieties of animal altruism and cooperation without departing from the basic theoretical stance of individual selection through individual advantage; that is, without resort to group selection theory.

Page
294 "The Companion in the Bird's World": Konrad Lorenz, "Der Kumpan in der Umwelt des Vogels," *Journal für Ornithologie* 80:2 (1935). Trans. "Companions as Factors in the Bird's Environment," in his *Studies in Animal and Human Behavior* (Cambridge, Mass.: Harvard University Press, 1970), pp. 101–258.
294–95 Eiffel Tower analogy: Konrad Lorenz, *Evolution and Modification of Behavior* (Chicago: University of Chicago Press, 1966), p. 27.
295 The more it follows . . . the more it wants to: Eckhardt Hess, *Imprinting* (Chicago: University of Chicago Press, 1974).

295 Confirmed Lorenz's observations: Hess, *Imprinting*; and Patrick Bateson, "The Characteristics and Context of Imprinting," *Biological Review* 41 (1966), pp. 177–220.

295–96 the brain changes during imprinting: Patrick Bateson, S. Rose, and G. Horn, "Imprinting: Lasting Effects on Uracil Incorporation into Chick Brain," *Science* 181 (1973), pp. 576–78.

296–97 ". . . that very archaic heritage . . .": John Bowlby, *Attachment and Loss*, vol. 2, *Separation: Anxiety and Anger* (New York: Basic Books, 1973), p. 86.

297 "The first of the affectional systems . . .": Harry F. Harlow, *Learning to Love* (San Francisco: Albion, 1971), pp. 2–4.

298 Zebra finches' mate choice: K. Immelman, "Zur Irreversibilität der Prägung," *Naturwissenschaft* 53 (1966), p. 209.

298–99 "What does the rhesus really see in its mother?": Harry F. Harlow, "The Nature of Love," *American Psychologist* 13 (1958), pp. 673–85.

299 nursing and oral gratification: Sigmund Freud, *An Outline of Psycho-analysis*, in *The Standard Edition of the Complete Psychological Works of Sigmund Freud*, trans. and ed. James Strachey (London: Hogarth Press, 1940).

299 blast of cold air: Leonard A. Rosenblum and Harry F. Harlow, "Generalization of Affectional Responses in Rhesus Monkeys," *Perceptual and Motor Skills* 16 (1963), pp. 561–64; and Hess, *Imprinting*.

299–300 Inept monkey mothers: Gerald C. Ruppenthal et al., "A 10-Year Perspective of Motherless-Mother Monkey Behavior," *Journal of Abnormal Psychology* 85 (1976), pp. 341–49.

300 Play with peers essential: Harry F. Harlow, "Age-mate or Peer Affectional System," in *Advances in the Study of Behavior*, vol. 2, ed. D.S. Lehrman, Robert A. Hinde, and E. Shaw (New York: Academic Press, 1969).

300 species differences in response to social deprivation: Gene P. Sackett, Richard A. Holm, and Gerald C. Ruppenthal, "Social Isolation Rearing: Species Differences in Behavior of Macaque Monkeys," *Developmental Psychology* 12 (1976), pp. 282–88.

300 males can provide "mothering": William Redican and G. Mitchell, "Play Between Adult Male and Infant Rhesus Monkeys," *American Zoologist* 14 (1974), pp. 295–302.

300 rocking the cloth surrogate: William A. Mason and Gershon Berkson, "Effects of Maternal Mobility on the Development of Rocking and Other Behaviors in Rhesus Monkeys: A Study with Artificial Mothers," *Developmental Psychobiology* 8:3 (1975), pp. 197–211.

300 Rehabilitation of isolation-reared infants: Stephen J. Suomi and

Harry F. Harlow, "Social Rehabilitation of Isolate-Reared Monkeys," *Developmental Psychology* 6 (1972), pp. 487–96; Stephen J. Suomi, Harry F. Harlow, and William T. McKinney, "Monkey Psychiatrists," *American Journal of Psychiatry* 128 (1972), pp. 927–32; and William A. Mason and M.D. Kenney, "Redirection of Filial Attachments in Rhesus Monkeys: Dogs as Mother Surrogates," *Science* 183 (1974), pp. 1209–11. It must be noted, however, that subsequent studies have shown that the rehabilitation achieved in these cases is not complete, and that lower levels of social behavior can be observed in rehabilitated isolates at age three years, the time of attainment of sexual maturity in rhesus monkeys. Mark S. Cummins and Stephen J. Suomi, "Long-term Effects of Social Rehabilitation in Rhesus Monkeys," *Primates* 17 (1976), pp. 43–51.

301–04 !Kung infants: The next few pages summarize the author's work on this subject. For further information see the papers referred to in chapter 1.

303 Mothers respond in six seconds: Melvin J. Konner, "Aspects of the Developmental Ethology of a Foraging People," in *Ethological Studies of Child Behavior*, ed. Nicholas Blurton Jones (Cambridge, Engl.: Cambridge University Press, 1972).

304 weaning from being carried: Pat Draper, "!Kung Bushman Childhood" (Ph.D. diss., Harvard University, 1972).

304 Specific behavior patterns of attachment: John Bowlby, *Attachment and Loss*, vol. 1, *Attachment* (London: Hogarth Press, 1969); Mary D. Salter Ainsworth, Mary C. Blehar, Everett Waters, and Sally Wall, *Patterns of Attachment: A Psychological Study of the Strange Situation* (Hillsdale, N.J.: Erlbaum, 1978); and Mary D. Salter Ainsworth, Silvia Bell, and Donelda F. Stayton, "Infant-Mother Attachment and Social Development: Socialisation as a Product of Reciprocal Responsiveness to Signals," in *The Integration of the Child into a Social World*, ed. M.P.M. Richards (Cambridge, Engl.: Cambridge University Press, 1974).

305 Psychoanalytic "secondary drive" theory of attachment: For an excellent review, see the appendix to Bowlby, *Attachment*.

306 Function of attachment in healthy adult behavior: John Bowlby, "Maternal Care and Mental Health," *Bulletin of the World Health Organization* 3 (1951), pp. 355–534.

306 early attachment to a nurturant caretaking figure: Bowlby, *Attachment and Loss*; Freud, *An Outline of Psycho-Analysis*; and Erik H. Erikson, *Childhood and Society* (New York: W.W. Norton, 1950).

306–07 "unspoiling": Dr. Benjamin Spock, *Baby and Child Care* (New York: Simon and Schuster, 1976), pp. 223–29.

307 No unfortunate consequences of multiple-caretaking: Margaret

Mead, "A Cultural Anthropologist's Approach to Maternal Deprivation," in Bowlby, *Maternal Care and Mental Health*, and Bowlby, *Deprivation of Maternal Care* (New York: Schocken, 1966).

307 major review of cross-cultural studies: Robert LeVine, "Cross-Cultural Study in Child Psychology," in *Carmichael's Manual of Child Psychology*, ed. P.H. Mussen (New York: John Wiley, 1970).

308 Milk composition and suckling in "carrier" species: Nicholas Blurton Jones, "Comparative Aspects of Mother-Child Contact," in *Ethological Studies of Child Behavior*, ed. Nicholas Blurton Jones (Cambridge, Engl.: Cambridge Univesity Press, 1972).

308 Four feedings an hour: Melvin J. Konner and Carol Worthman, "Nursing Frequency, Gonadal Function and Birth Spacing Among !Kung Hunter-Gatherers," *Science* 207 (1980), pp. 788–91.

308–09 *non*-hunting-gathering human societies: For review, see Melvin J. Konner, "Evolution of Human Behavior Development," in *Handbook of Cross-Cultural Development*, ed. Robert L. Monroe, Ruth H. Monroe, and Beatrice B. Whiting (New York: Garland Press, 1981).

309 Sleeping distance in 90 societies: H. Barry III and L. Paxson, "Infancy and Early Childhood: Cross-Cultural Codes 2," *Ethnology* 10 (1971), pp. 466–508.

310 Bedtime protest and night-waking: Judith Bernal, "Night Waking in Infants During the First Fourteen Months," *Developmental Medicine and Child Neurology* 20 (1973), p. 760.

310 Child-care patterns astounding to read of: Lloyd deMause, ed., *The History of Childhood* (New York: Harper & Row, 1974), and David Hunt, *Parents and Children in History: The Psychology of Family Life in Early Modern France* (New York: Basic Books, 1970).

310–11 ". . . a sensible way of treating children . . .": John B. Watson, *Psychological Care of Infant and Child* (New York: W.W. Norton, 1928), pp. 83–87.

311–12 "It's hard on the kindhearted parents . . .": Spock, *Baby and Child Care*, pp. 227–29.

312–13 "Summoned from a dream . . .": Jill Hoffman, "Rendezvous," in *Mink Coat* (New York: Holt, Rinehart and Winston, 1973), p. 38.

313 studies of preschool-age children: Nicholas Blurton Jones and Melvin J. Konner, "Sex Differences in Behavior of Two-to-Five Year-Olds in London and Among the Kalahari Desert Bushmen," in *Comparative Ecology and Behavior of Primates*, ed. R.P. Michael and J.H. Crook (London: Academic Press, 1973).

313 "basic trust": Erikson, *Childhood and Society*.

313 major review of the literature: Eleanor Emmons Maccoby and John Masters, "Attachment and Dependency," in *Manual of Child Psychology*, ed. P.H. Mussen (New York: John Wiley, 1970).

313–14 Mary Ainsworth and her colleagues: Ainsworth et al., *Patterns of Attachment*.

314 Toddlers close to mothers: L. Alan Sroufe and Everett Waters, "Attachment as an Organizational Construct," *Child Development* 48 (1977), pp. 1184–99.

315 Memories of childhood sexual play: Marjorie Shostak, *Nisa: The Life and Words of a !Kung Woman* (Cambridge, Mass.: Harvard University Press, 1981). This book is the most intimate window we have on the life of the !Kung, and one of the most revealing personal narratives from any nonindustrial society.

316 "trial marriage": Bertrand Russell, *Autobiography*, vol. 2 (Boston: Little, Brown, 1968), pp. 333–65; *Marriage and Morals* (New York: Liveright, 1929).

316 "To me that man . . .": Sappho, *Lyrics in the Original Greek*, trans. Willis Barnstone (New York: New York University Press, 1965), p. 11.

317 affiliative behavior of monkeys can be abolished: Arthur Kling and Horst Steklis, "A Neural Substrate for Affiliative Behavior in Nonhuman Primates," *Brain, Behavior and Evolution* 13 (1976), pp. 216–38.

317–18 Male parental physiology: Daniel S. Lehrman, "The Reproductive Behavior of Ring Doves," *Scientific American* 211:5 (1964), pp. 48–54; and Daniel S. Lehrman, "The Physiological Basis of Parental Feeding Behavior in the Ring Dove," *Behaviour* 7 (1955), pp. 241–86.

318 Maternal behavior in the virgin female rat: Howard Moltz, M. Lubin, M. Leon, and M. Numan, "Hormonal Induction of Maternal Behavior in the Ovariectomized Nulliparous Rat," *Physiology and Behavior* 5 (1971), pp. 1373–77.

318 hooked up the circulatory systems: Joseph Terkel and Jay S. Rosenblatt, "Humoral Factors Underlying Maternal Behavior at Parturition: Cross Transfusion Between Freely Moving Rats," *Journal of Comparative and Physiological Psychology* 80 (1972), pp. 365–71.

318 "medial preoptic area": Michael Numan, Jay S. Rosenblatt, and Barry R. Komisaruk, "Medial Preoptic Area and Onset of Maternal Behavior in the Rat," *Journal of Comparative and Physiological Psychology* 91 (1977), pp. 146–64.

318–19 Priming virgin female mice: Elaine Noirot, "The Onset of Maternal Behavior in Rats, Hamsters, and Mice: A Selective Review," *Advances in the Study of Behavior* 4 (1972), pp. 107–45.

319 Priming rats: Jay S. Rosenblatt, "Nonhormonal Basis of Maternal Behavior in the Rat," *Science* 156 (1967), pp. 1512–14.

319 Priming hamsters: M.P.M. Richards, "Some Effects of Experience on Maternal Behavior in Rodents," in *Determinants of Infant Behavior*, vol. 4, ed. B.M. Foss (London: Methuen, 1965).

319 Testosterone antagonistic to maternal behavior: M.X. Zarrow, Victor H. Denenberg, and Benjamin D. Sachs, "Hormones and Maternal Behavior in Mammals," in *Hormones and Behavior*, ed. Seymour Levine (New York: Academic Press, 1972).

320–21 a dilute form of . . . affection: This view underlies the incest prohibition theories advanced by both Lewis Henry Morgan and Edward Westermarck (for discussion, see Marvin Harris, *The Rise of Anthropological Theory* [New York: Thomas Y. Crowell, 1968], pp. 198–99). For a much more sophisticated, and currently widely accepted, view of the functions of human kinship systems see Claude Lévi-Strauss, *The Elementary Structures of Kinship* (Boston: Beacon Press, 1969); it is a translation of his *Les Structures Élémentaires de la Parenté*, the most important work on the subject of human kinship in this century.

321 structural theorists: A radical statement of this approach to the study of social organization may be found in Edmund R. Leach, *Rethinking Anthropology* (New York: Humanities Press, 1966). For an authoritative viewpoint on human kinship and marriage systems that is more compatible with biology (and, in my opinion, much more down to earth), see Robin Fox, *Kinship and Marriage: An Anthropological Perspective* (Baltimore, Penguin, 1967), as well as chapters 3, 4, and 5 of his *Encounter with Anthropology* (New York: Harcourt Brace Jovanovich, 1973), and especially his most recent book, *The Red Lamp of Incest* (New York: E.P. Dutton, 1980), a fascinating attempt by an authority on human kinship and marriage to integrate his knowledge with new developments in evolutionary theory.

321 Haldane: See Richard Dawkins, *The Selfish Gene* (New York: Oxford, 1976).

322 if two people look into each other's eyes: Irven DeVore, personal communication, 1969.

322 a universal flirtation display: Irenäus Eibl-Eibesfeldt, "Human Ethology: Concepts and Implications for the Sciences of Man," *Behavioral and Brain Sciences* 2 (1979), pp. 1–57.

323 "What he could have best borne . . .": Henry James, *The Golden Bowl* (New York: Penguin, 1966; orig. 1904), pp. 182–83.

324 "Twenty-One Love Poems": Adrienne Rich, *The Dream of a Common Language* (New York: W.W. Norton, 1978).

CHAPTER 14: GRIEF

The Harvard Guide to Modern Psychiatry, edited by Armand M. Nicholi (Cambridge, Mass.: Harvard University Press, 1978), includes several chapters pertaining to the causes and consequences of feelings of loss and depression. Robert Burton's *The Anatomy of Melancholy* (cited below), one of the largest selling books of the seventeenth century, although somewhat more wide-ranging in subject than its title suggests, is of great historical interest and demonstrates the long-standing concern that people have had to explain depression. John Bowlby's *Attachment and Loss*, repeatedly cited in this chapter and the previous one, gives a crucial modern perspective while acting as a guide to much earlier psychoanalytic literature. A. Alvarez, in *The Savage God* (New York: Random House, 1970), provides an exceptionally literate, eloquent, and sensitive view of suicide.

Page

325–26 Divorce ceremonial and suicide clubs: Tracie Rozlion, "Divorce Ceremony for Children's Sake," and AP wire, "California Group Plans to Publish a Guide to Suicide," both in *The New York Times*, August 15, 1980.

326 percentage of divorced women: George Masnick and Mary Jo Bane, *The Nation's Families* (Cambridge, Mass.: Joint Center for Urban Studies, 1980), pp. 34–35.

326 as a percentage of those ever married: Ibid., p. 36.

326 Suicide rates: Morton Kramer, Earl S. Pollack, Richard W. Redick, and Ben Z. Locke, *Mental Disorders and Suicide*, Vital and Health Statistics Monographs, American Public Health Association (Cambridge, Mass.: Harvard University Press, 1972).

326–27 "prefer chloroform to cancer": Charlotte Perkins Gilman, quoted in *Charlotte Perkins Gilman Reader*, ed. Ann J. Lane (New York: Pantheon, 1980).

327 to face up to death: Elisabeth Kübler-Ross, *On Death and Dying* (New York: Macmillan, 1969).

327 a theory of human behavior: Ernest Becker, *The Denial of Death* (New York: Macmillan, 1973). See also: Sigmund Freud, *Civilization and Its Discontents*, trans. James Strachey (New York: W.W. Norton, 1961); Norman O. Brown, *Life Against Death: The Psychoanalytical Meaning of History* (New York: Viking, 1959); Herbert Marcuse, *Eros and Civilization: A Philosophical Inquiry into Freud* (Boston: Beacon Press, 1966).

327–28 "the sickness unto death": Søren Kierkegaard, *The Sickness Unto Death*, published together with *Fear and Trembling* (New York: Anchor Press, 1954).

328 death of one member: Konrad Lorenz, *Studies in Animal and*

Human Behavior, vol. 1, trans. by Robert Martin (Cambridge, Mass.: Harvard University Press, 1970), pp. 215–16.

328 Endangered goslings: Ibid., pp. 184, 276.

328 Mother and anesthetized infant: Leonard A. Rosenblum and Kenneth P. Youngstein, "Developmental Changes in Compensatory Dyadic Response in Mother and Infant Monkeys," in *The Effect of the Infant on Its Caregiver*, ed. M. Lewis and Leonard A. Rosenblum (New York: John Wiley, 1974).

328 animal grief: Charles Darwin, *The Expression of the Emotions in Man and Animals* (Chicago: University of Chicago Press, 1965).

329 "Whatever the reasons . . .": Jane van Lawick Goodall, *In the Shadow of Man* (New York: Dell, 1971), pp. 240–41.

330 the fears of infancy: René Spitz, *The First Year of Life* (New York: International Universities Press, 1965).

320–32 Bowlby on loss: John Bowlby, *Attachment and Loss*, vol. 1, *Attachment* (London: Hogarth Press, 1969); vol. 2, *Separation: Anxiety and Anger* (New York: Basic Books, 1973); vol. 3, *Loss* (New York: Basic Books, 1980).

331 four stages of grief: Bowlby, *Separation*, chapter 1.

331 Ainsworth experiment: Bowlby, *Loss*, chapter 10.

332 effects of prolonged separation: Harry F. Harlow, "Love in Infant Monkeys," *Scientific American*, June 1959, pp. 1–8.

332–33 Bonnet monkey vs. pigtail monkey: Leonard A. Rosenblum, "Infant Attachment in Monkeys," in *The Origins of Human Social Relations*, ed. R. Schaffer (New York: Academic Press, 1971).

333 Further systematic study: Gene P. Sackett, Richard A. Holm, and Gerald C. Ruppenthal, "Social Isolation Rearing: Species Differences in Behavior of Macaque Monkeys," *Developmental Psychology* 12 (1976), pp. 283–88.

333 Grieving reactions in human children: Bowlby, *Separation* and *Loss*; James Robertson, *Young Children in Hospital* (London: Tavistock, 1958).

334 Response to the mother's return: Leonard A. Rosenblum, "Affective Maturation and the Mother-Infant Relationship," in *The Development of Affect*, ed. M. Lewis and L. Rosenblum (New York: Plenum, 1979).

334–35 physiological monitoring: Martin Reite, I. Charles Kaufman, J. Donald Pauley, and A.J. Stynes, "Depression in Infant Monkeys: Physiological Correlates," *Psychosomatic Medicine* 36 (1974), pp. 363–67.

335 "the greatest medical treatise . . .": Sir William Osler quoted in Robert Burton, *The Anatomy of Melancholy* (New York: Random House, 1977), introduction, p. xi.

335 "a kind of dotage . . .": Ibid., pp. 169–70.

335–36 four-page synoptic chart: Ibid., pp. 126–29.

337 "Acute onset . . .": Max Day and Elvin V. Semrad, "Schizophrenic Reactions," in *The Harvard Guide to Modern Psychiatry*, ed. Armand M. Nicholi, Jr. (Cambridge, Mass.: Harvard University Press, 1978), p. 220.

337 ". . . a normal part of the human condition": Gerald L. Klerman, "Affective Disorders," in *The Harvard Guide to Modern Psychiatry*, ed. Nicholi, pp. 254–55.

337 ". . . impairments of body functioning . . .": Ibid., p. 255.

338 ". . . depressed mood . . .": Ibid.

338 all mood swings as symptoms: Ronald Fieve, *Moodswing: The Third Revolution in Psychiatry* (New York: Morrow, 1975).

338 "severe affective disorder": Klerman, "Affective Disorders," p. 269.

338–39 family and twin studies: Ibid., p. 270; E.S. Gershon et al., "Genetic Models of the Transmission of Affective Disorders," *Journal of Psychiatric Research* 12 (1975), pp. 301–17; Patricia McBroom, *Behavioral Genetics*, NIMH Science Monograph 2 (Rockville, Md.: National Institute of Mental Health, 1980).

339 Gene on chromosome 6: L.R. Weitkamp, H.C. Stancer, E. Persad, C. Flood, and S. Guttormsen, "Depressive Disorders and HLA: A Gene on Chromosome 6 That Can Affect Behavior," *New England Journal of Medicine* 305 (1981), 1301–06.

339 remote environmental influences: Aaron T. Beck, *Depression: Clinical, Experimental, and Theoretical Aspects* (New York: Harper & Row, 1967).

339 Rhesus response to separation: Laurens Young, Stephen J. Suomi, Harry F. Harlow, and William McKinney, "Early Stress and Later Response to Separation in Rhesus Monkeys," *American Journal of Psychiatry* 130 (1973), pp. 400–405.

339–40 Catecholamine theory: For an early statement of the theory, see Joseph J. Schildkraut, "The Catecholamine Hypothesis of Affective Disorders: A Review of Supporting Evidence," *American Journal of Psychiatry* 122 (1965), pp. 509–22.

340 Monoamine oxidase inhibitors: Ross J. Baldessarini, "Chemotherapy," in *The Harvard Guide to Modern Psychiatry*, ed. Nicholi.

340 Amphetamine and related compounds: Klerman, "Affective Disorders," pp. 274–75.

340 "tricyclics": David C. U'Prichard, David A. Greenberg, Peter P. Sheehan, and Solomon H. Snyder, "Tricyclic Antidepressants: Therapeutic Properties and Affinity for Alpha-Noradrenergic Receptor Binding Sites in the Brain," *Science* 199 (1978), pp. 197–98.

340 electroconvulsive shock therapy: Bruce L. Welch, Edith D.

Hendley, and Ibrahim Turek, "Norepinephrine Uptake into Cerebral Cortical Synaptosomes After One Fight or Electroconvulsive Shock," *Science* 183 (1974), pp. 220–21.

340 lithium: For a recent review of lithium treatment of affective psychoses, see Ross J. Baldessarini, *Chemotherapy in Psychiatry* (Cambridge, Mass.: Harvard University Press, 1977).

340 depression in monkeys: D.E. Redmond, Jr., R.L. Hinrichs, J.W. Maas, and A. Kling, "Behavior of Free-Ranging Macaques After Intraventricular 6-Hydroxydopamine," *Science* 181 (1973), pp. 1256–58.

340–41 findings relating to serotonin: Clause de Montigny and George K. Aghajanian, "Tricyclic Antidepressants: Long-Term Treatment Increases Responsivity of Rat Forebrain Neurons to Serotonin," *Science* 202 (1978), pp. 1303–05.

341 Two chemically different depressive disorders: J. Mass, "Biogenic Amines and Depression—Biochemical and Pharmacological Separation of Two Types of Depression," *Archives of General Psychiatry* 32 (1975), pp. 1357–61.

341 "Our tools are so crude . . .": Walle J. Nauta, address at the Presidential Symposium of the Third Annual Meeting of the Society for Neuroscience, San Diego, California, November 1973.

342 postpartum depression: David A. Hamburg, Rudolph H. Moos, and Irvin D. Yalom, "Studies of Distress in the Menstrual Cycle and the Postpartum Period," in *Endocrinology and Human Behavior*, ed. R.P. Michael (London: Oxford University Press, 1968).

342–43 Progesterone withdrawal irritability: Hamburg et al., "Distress in the Menstrual Cycle," pp. 3–5, 22.

343 cortisol secretion: Edward J. Sachar, "Neuroendocrine Abnormalities in Depressive Illness," in *Topics in Psychoendocrinology*, ed. Edward J. Sachar (New York: Harcourt Brace Jovanovich, 1975), pp. 136–46.

343 "it would be correct . . .": Edward C. Senay, "General Systems Theory and Depression," in *American Association for the Advancement of Science* (1973), p. 242.

343 Separation causes depression: Stephen J. Suomi, "Depressive Behavior in Adult Monkeys Following Separation from Family Environment," *Journal of Abnormal Psychology* 84 (1975), pp. 576–78.

343 Intrinsic and extrinsic depression: Hagop S. Akiskal and William T. McKinney, Jr., "Depressive Disorders: Toward a Unified Hypothesis," *Science* 182 (1973), pp. 20–29.

343–44 Psychological stresses and physical illness: Herbert Weiner, *Psychobiology and Human Disease* (New York: Elsevier, 1977); David

V. Sheehan and Thomas P. Hackett, "Psychosomatic Disorders," in *The Harvard Guide to Modern Psychiatry*, ed. Nicholi.

344–45 "learned helplessness": Martin Seligman and S. Maier, "Failure to Escape Traumatic Shock," *Journal of Experimental Psychology* 74 (1976), pp. 1–9; Martin Seligman, *Helplessness* (San Francisco: W.H. Freeman, 1975).

344 Norepinephrine in learned helplessness: Jay Weiss, H.I. Glazer, and L.A. Pohorecky, "Coping Behavior and Neurochemical Changes in Rats: An Alternative Explanation for the Original 'Learned Helplessness' Experiments," in *Animal Models in Human Psychobiology*, ed. George Servan and Arthur Kling (New York: Plenum Press, 1976). For an account of the original gastric ulcer studies, see Jay Weiss, "Psychological Factors in Stress and Disease," *Scientific American* 226 (1972), pp. 104–13.

345 children who were dying: S.B. Friedman, P. Chodoff, J.W. Mason, and David A. Hamburg, "Behavioral Observations on Parents Anticipating the Death of a Child," *Pediatrics* 32 (1963), pp. 610–25. For follow-up studies and interpretation, see David A. Hamburg, "Coping Behavior in Life-Threatening Circumstances," *Psychotherapy and Psychosomatics* 23 (1974), pp. 13–25.

345–46 "As the disease progressed . . .": Hamburg, "Coping Behavior," p. 21.

346 victims of polio and disfiguring burns: H.M. Visotsky, David A. Hamburg, M.E. Goss, and B.Z. Lebovits, "Coping Behavior Under Extreme Stress: Observations of Patients with Severe Poliomyelitis," *Archives of General Psychiatry* 5 (1961), pp. 423–48; David A. Hamburg, B. Hamburg, and S. De Goza, "Adaptive Problems and Mechanisms in Severely Burned Patients," *Psychiatry* 16 (1953), pp. 1–20; and David A. Hamburg et al., "Clinical Importance of Emotional Problems in Care of Patients with Burns," *New England Journal of Medicine* 248 (1953), pp. 355–59.

346 five phases or stages of response: Kübler-Ross, *On Death and Dying*.

346 *All That Jazz*: Bob Fosse, *All That Jazz* (Los Angeles: 20th Century-Fox, 1979).

347 "Do not go gentle . . .": Dylan Thomas, *Collected Poems* (New York: New Directions, 1953), p. 128.

347–48 ". . . People everywhere experience grief . . .": Paul C. Rosenblatt, R. Patricia Walsh, and Douglas A. Jackson, *Grief and Mourning in Cross-Cultural Perspective* (New Haven: Human Relations Area Files, 1976), p. 124.

348 ghost beliefs: Ibid., p. 65.

348–49 !Kung San healers: Richard B. Lee, "The Sociology of !Kung Bushman Trance Performances," in *Trance and Possession States*, ed. Raymond Prince (Montreal: F.M. Bucke Memorial Society, 1966); and Richard Katz, *Boiling Energy: Community Healing Among the Kalahari !Kung* (Cambridge, Mass.: Harvard University Press, 1982).

349 "death instinct": Also called "thanatos"; Freud, *Civilization and Its Discontents*.

349 "anger turned inward": For discussion, see Beck, *Depression*, p. 248.

349 !Kung vendettas: Richard B. Lee, *The !Kung San* (Cambridge, Engl.: Cambridge University Press, 1979), chapter 13.

350 Sacred dream time: A.P. Elkin, *The Australian Aborigines* (Garden City, N.Y.: Doubleday, 1964).

351 "The hostile forces . . .": Claude Lévi-Strauss, *Tristes Tropiques*, trans. John Russel (New York: Atheneum, 1965), p. 224.

351 Isoma and infertility: Victor W. Turner, *The Ritual Process: Structure and Anti-Structure* (Harmondsworth, Engl.: Penguin, 1974), chapter 1.

351 Children view death: Ned H. Cassem, "Treating the Person Confronting Death," in *The Harvard Guide to Modern Psychiatry*, ed. Nicholi, p. 588.

351 Adolescent suicide: Leon Eisenberg, "Adolescent Suicide: On Taking Arms Against a Sea of Troubles," *Pediatrics* 66 (1980), pp. 315–20.

352 ". . . the torture and extremity . . .": Burton, *The Anatomy of Melancholy*, p. 431.

352 "The logical culmination . . .": Isaiah Berlin, *Two Concepts of Liberty*, an Inaugural Lecture at Oxford University (London: Oxford University, 1958), p. 25.

352 lifetime risk: Kramer, et al., *Mental Disorders and Suicide*, p. 197.

352 most common methods: Ibid., p. 216.

353 Suicide rates by sex: Myrna M. Weissman and Gerald L. Klerman, "Sex Differences and the Epidemiology of Depression," *Archives of General Psychiatry* 34 (1977), pp. 98–111.

353 Durkheim knew: Émil Durkheim, *Le Suicide* (Paris: Felis Alean, 1912).

353 Ethnic differences: Kramer et al., *Mental Disorders and Suicide*, p. 179.

353 Scandinavian suicide: H. Hendrin, *Suicide and Scandinavia* (New York: Grune & Stratton, 1965).

353 Suicide trends in this century: Kramer et al., *Mental Disorders and Suicide*, p. 203.

353 "What youthful mother . . .": from William Butler Yeats, "Among School Children," in *The Variorum Edition of the Poems of*

W.B. Yeats, ed. Peter Allt and Russel K. Alspach (New York: Macmillan, 1940), p. 444.

353 to paraphrase Eliot: T.S. Eliot, "The Love Song of J. Alfred Prufrock," in *The Complete Poems and Plays (1909–1950)* (New York: Harcourt, Brace & World, 1952).

354–55 "Death is the mother of beauty . . .": Wallace Stevens, "Sunday Morning," in *The Palm at the End of the Mind*, ed. Holly Stevens (New York: Vintage, 1972), p. 7.

355 "Why should she give her bounty to the dead? . . .": Ibid., p. 5.

355 "Is there no change of death . . .": Ibid., p. 7.

356 "Supple and turbulent . . .": Ibid.

CHAPTER 15: GLUTTONY

A major collection of papers on the physiology of hunger and satiety is D. Novin, W. Wyrwicka and G. Bray, eds., *Hunger: Basic Mechanisms and Clinical Implications* (New York: Raven Press, 1976). An excellent recent review of the problem of what makes an animal (or person) stop eating is provided by Gerard Smith and James Gibbs, "Postprandial Satiety," in *Progress in Psychobiology and Physiological Psychology*, vol. 8, ed. J.M. Sprague and A.N. Epstein (New York: Academic Press, 1979).

The psychology of obesity is treated by Stanley Schachter and Judith Rodin, eds., *Obese Humans and Rats* (Potomac, Md.: Erlbaum, 1974), and the clinical aspects of the problem by George Bray, *The Obese Patient* (Philadelphia: W.B. Saunders, 1976).

For a view of what life is like in societies where the maximization of wealth is not the principal goal, see Marshall Sahlins, *Stone Age Economics* (Chicago: Aldine, 1972).

Page

359 Food delivered into stomach: M.M. Berkun, M.L. Kessen, and N.E. Miller, "Hunger-Reducing Effects of Food by Stomach Fistula Versus Food by Mouth Measured by a Consummatory Response," *Journal of Comparative and Physiological Psychology* 45 (1952), pp. 550–54.

359 "sham-eating": H.D. Janowitz and M.I. Grossman, "Some Factors Affecting the Food Intake of Normal Dogs and Dogs with Esophagostomy and Gastric Fistule," *American Journal of Physiology* 159 (1949), pp. 143–48.

359–60 Mechanical filling of the stomach: H.D. Janowitz and F. Hollander, "Effect of Prolonged Intragastric Feeding on Oral Ingestion," *Federation Proceedings* 12 (1953), p. 72.

360–61 "glucostatic" theory: Jean Mayer, "Regulation of Energy Intake and the Body Weight: The Glucostatic Theory and the Lipostatic Hypothesis," *Annals of the New York Academy of Sciences* 63 (1955), pp. 15–43.

361 Poisoning hypothalamic glucose receptors: Jacques Le Magnen, "Interactions of Glucostatic and Lipostatic Mechanisms in the Regulatory Control of Feeding," in *Hunger*, ed. Novin et al.

361 Lipostatic theory: R. Liebelt, C. Bordelon, and A. Liebelt, "The Adipose Tissue System and Food Intake," in *Progress in Physiological Psychology*, ed. E. Stellar and J. Sprague (New York: Academic Press, 1973). For a summary of the two major theories of feeding regulation see Jacques Le Magnen, "Interactions of Glucostatic and Lipostatic Mechanisms in the Regulatory Control of Feeding," in *Hunger*, ed. Novin et al.

361 Diet loaded with precursors of neurotransmitters: John Growdon, Edith Cohen, and Richard J. Wurtman, "Treatment of Brain Disease with Dietary Precursors of Neurotransmitters," *Annals of Internal Medicine* 86 (1977), pp. 337–39; Madelyn Hirsch and Richard J. Wurtman, "Lecithin Consumption Increases Acetylcholine Concentrations in Rat Brain and Adrenal Gland," *Science* 202 (1978), pp. 223–24. This approach, although still preliminary, may revolutionize the way we think about how diet affects brain and behavior, both in the short and the long run.

362 Glucose detection by liver: Mauricio Russek, "Semi-Quantitative Simulation of Food Intake Control and Weight Regulation," in *Hunger Models: Computable Theory of Feeding Control*, ed. D.A. Booth (New York: Academic Press, 1978). For less technical earlier treatments see Mauricio Russek, "A Hypothesis on the Participation of Hepatic Glucoreceptors in the Control of Food Intake," *Nature* (London) 197 (1963), pp. 79–80; Mauricio Russek, "Hepatic Receptors and the Neurophysiological Mechanisms Controlling Feeding Behavior," in *Neurosciences Research*, vol. 4, ed. S. Ehrenpreis (New York: Academic Press, 1971).

362–63 gut hormones in satiety: Gerard Smith and James Gibbs, "Cholecystokinin and Satiety: Theoretic and Therapeutic Implications," in *Hunger*, ed. Novin et al.; R.D. Myers and M.D. McCaleb, "Feeding: Satiety Signal from Intestine Triggers Brain's Noradrenergic Mechanism," *Science* 209 (1980), pp. 1035–37.

363 taste for variety: Jacques Le Magnen, "Hyperphagie provoquée chez le rat blanc par altération du méchanisme de satiété périphérique," *Comptes Rendus des Séances de la Société de Biologie* 150 (1956), p. 32.

363 social factors: See, for example, Wanda Wyrwicka, "The Problem of Motivation in Feeding Behavior," in *Hunger*, ed. Novin et al.

For a general account of obese people's demonstrably greater responsiveness to external (as opposed to visceral) stimulus cues relating to food and eating rituals, see *Obese Humans and Rats*, ed. Schachter and Rodin.

363–64 Stress-induced eating: N.E. Rowland and S.M. Antelman, "Stress-Induced Hyperphagia and Obesity in Rats: A Possible Model for Understanding Human Obesity," *Science* 191 (1976), pp. 310–12; this phenomenon may be mediated in part by "the brain's own morphine—or lack of it—discussed in chapter 11; see also John Moreley and Allen Levine, "Stress-Induced Eating Is Mediated Through Endogenous Opiates," *Science* 209 (1980), pp. 1259–61.

364 Similarities between humans and rats: *Obese Humans and Rats*, ed. Schachter and Rodin; Stanley Schachter, "Some Extraordinary Facts About Obese Humans and Rats," *The American Psychologist* 26 (1971), pp. 129–44.

365 "The incidence of obesity coincides . . .": *Merck Manual of Diagnosis and Therapy*, 13th ed., ed. Robert Berkow and John H. Talbott (Rahway, N.J.: Merck, Sharp and Dohme, 1977), p. 1177. For a general account of obesity, see Jean Mayer, *Overweight: Causes Cost and Control* (Englewood Cliffs, N.J.: Prentice-Hall, 1968). For a more technical, clinical treatment, see Bray, *The Obese Patient*, or *Obesity: Comparative Methods of Weight Control*, ed., George Bray (Westport, Conn.: Technomic, 1980).

365–66 rich German men: A. Stunkard, "Environment and Obesity: Recent Advances in Our Understanding of Regulation of Food Intake in Man," *Federation Proceedings* 27 (1968), pp. 1367–73.

366 "fat is beautiful": For a brief account (with before and after photographs) of a fattening ceremony in preparation for marriage see L.W.G. Malcolm, "Note on the Seclusion of Girls Among the Efik at Old Calabar," *Man* 25 (1925), pp. 113–14.

366–67 Women who could not lose weight: D.S. Miller and Sally Parsonage, "Resistance to Slimming: Adaptation or Illusion?" *Lancet*, April 5, 1975, pp. 773–75.

366 ". . . among a group of would-be slimmers . . .": Ibid., p. 773.

367 reduced energy use at the cellular level: Mario De Luise, George Blackburn, and Jeffrey Flier, "Reduced Activity of the Red-Cell Sodium-Potassium Pump in Human Obesity," *The New England Journal of Medicine* 303 (1980), pp. 1017–22.

368 Subsistence in 186 societies: G.P. Murdock and D.R. White, "Standard Cross-Cultural Sample, *Ethnology* 8 (1969), pp. 329–69.

368–70 Diet in nonindustrial societies: This entire discussion of diet in nonindustrial societies is indebted to Marjorie Whiting, "A Cross-

Cultural Nutrition Survey" (Ph.D. diss., Harvard School of Public Health, 1958).

371 "the original affluent society": Sahlins, *Stone Age Economics*. To be more fair to Sahlins, here is an argument of his that I agree with: It is probable that at the time—say twenty thousand years ago—when all the world's people were hunting and gathering for a living, a smaller percentage of all human beings went to bed hungry than do so today.

371–72 Studies of !Kung life in the 1960s: Richard B. Lee, "What Hunters Do for a Living, or How to Make Out on Scarce Resources," in *Man the Hunter*, ed. Richard B. Lee and Irven DeVore (Chicago: Aldine, 1968); Richard B. Lee and Irven DeVore, eds., *Kalahari Hunter-Gatherers* (Cambridge, Mass.: Harvard University Press, 1976). See chapter 1 for further references.

372 Mild caloric deficiency: Stuart Trusswell and J.D.L. Hanse, "Medical Research among the !Kung," in *Kalahari Hunter-Gatherers*, ed. Lee and DeVore.

372–73 Seasonal undernourishment and weight loss: Edwin Wilmsen, "Seasonal Effects on Dietary Intake in Kalahari San," *Federation Proceedings* 37 (1978), pp. 65–71. Lee replies to Wilmsen, criticizing his conclusions, in *The !Kung San* (Cambridge, Engl.: Cambridge University Press, 1979), pp. 440–41.

373 slow population growth: Nancy Howell, *Demography of the Dobe !Kung* (New York: Academic Press, 1979).

373 Body fat and infertility: Rose Frisch, "Population, Food Intake and Fertility," *Science* 199 (1978), pp. 22–30. Frisch recently has shown that exercise plays a role in limiting fertility, another factor of probable importance to !Kung population growth. Rose Frisch, Grace Wyshak, and Larry Vincent, "Delayed Menarche and Amenorrhea in Ballet Dancers," *New England Journal of Medicine* 303 (1980), pp. 17–19. For a third probable mechanism see Melvin J. Konner and Carol Worthman, "Nursing Frequency, Gonadal Function and Birth Spacing Among !Kung Hunter-Gatherers," *Science* 207 (1980), pp. 788–91.

374 life of a !Kung woman: Marjorie Shostak, *Nisa: The Life and Words of a !Kung Woman* (Cambridge, Mass.: Harvard University Press, 1981).

375 bloodthirsty killers: See the end of chapter 9 for discussion and references.

377 "We had one maid . . ." Robert Coles, *Children of Crisis*, vol. 5, *Privileged Ones: The Well-Off and the Rich in America* (Boston: Atlantic–Little, Brown, 1977), p. 384.

378 the very source of life's plenty: A recent letter to *The New York*

Times from a busboy in "a moderately priced, high cholesterol establishment that specializes in prime rib and lobster tails" read in part: "The number of overweight people who frequent this restaurant is simply amazing (and I am sure that busboys in restaurants across the country witness the same phenomenon).

"People are overweight for a variety of reasons, many of which are truly unfortunate. But what is the significance of all this excess flesh? It is evidently indicative of serious personal problems but, more importantly, it is indicative of problems of social consequence: misguided and wasted energy, the inequitable distribution of food and resources and thus the striking contrast between the overfed and the underfed. And it signifies a collective hunger emanating more from the spirit than from the flesh." *The New York Times*, January 25, 1981, section E, p. 20.

CHAPTER 16: CHANGE

For an intermediate-level exposition of the laws of learning and the facts we have to support them, see Howard Rachlin, *Behavior and Learning* (San Francisco, W.H. Freeman, 1976). An excellent brief summary of how these principles apply to research and practice in the learning of human children is Michael Howe's *Learning in Infants and Young Children* (Stanford: Stanford University Press, 1975). The recent emphasis upon cognition and linguistics in psychology, and upon evolution, genetics, and fixed action patterns in animal behavior studies, has led to a corresponding decrease of emphasis on traditional and classical studies of learning, such as grew up under the leadership of Pavlov and Skinner. This shift of emphasis is undoubtedly largely faddish, and also in part due to prior excessive claims for the explanatory power of learning psychology. It is to be hoped that the near future will see a giving way of fruitless controversy to a much more useful and generative synthetic approach. For a valuable first attempt to integrate ethology and learning psychology see Robert A. Hinde, *Animal Behavior: A Synthesis of Ethology and Comparative Psychology*, 2nd ed. (New York: McGraw-Hill, 1976).

To a large extent the study of the effects of early experience on behavior and development is a subdiscipline separate from that of traditional learning theory, but equally committed to the view that more important influences come from the environment than from the genes. Victor H. Denenberg's *The Development of Behavior* (Stamford, Conn.: Sinauer, 1972) is an indispensable collection of sixty-five key papers in this field, introduced by a leading practitioner. For the contributions of anthropology to various questions concerning the effects of experience on development, see the comprehensive *Handbook of Cross-Cultural Development*, ed. Ruth H. Monroe, Robert L. Monroe, and Beatrice B. Whiting (New York: Garland Press, 1981).

Page

382–83 Pavlov's dogs: I.P. Pavlov, *Conditioned Reflexes* (New York: Oxford University Press, 1927).

383 operant conditioning: B.F. Skinner, *The Behavior of Organisms* (New York: Appleton-Century-Crofts, 1938). See also his *Verbal Behavior* (New York: Appleton-Century-Crofts, 1957), which attempts to understand language learning by means of the same principles. Incidentally, this was also the year of publication of Noam Chomsky's *Syntactic Structures* (The Hague: Mouton, 1957), a landmark contribution to linguistics that focused on precisely that aspect of language least responsive to Skinnerian analysis. Chomsky later reviewed Skinner's book, pointing out the difficulties posed for learning theory by advances in linguistics: "A Review of B.F. Skinner's *Verbal Behavior*," *Language* 35 (1959), pp. 26–58.

383 less consistent reinforcement: Skinner, *The Behavior of Organisms*.

383–84 Behavioral psychotherapy: Alan Goldstein and Edna B. Foa, *Handbook of Behavioral Interventions* (Somerset, N.J.: John Wiley, 1979); S. Turner, K. Calhoun, and H. Adams, *Handbook of Clinical Behavior Therapy* (Somerset, N.J.: John Wiley, 1980).

384 Habituation: W.H. Thorpe, *Learning and Instinct in Animals* (London: Methuen, 1956).

384–85 Smoothing of complex behavioral sequences: For a theoretical discussion with zoological examples—for instance, the acquisition of swimming in seals and sea lions—see Konrad Lorenz, *Evolution and Modification of Behavior* (Chicago: University of Chicago Press, 1966).

385 social enhancement of overeating: Wanda Wyrwicka, "The Problem of Motivation in Feeding Behavior," in *Hunger: Basic Mechanisms and Clinical Implications*, ed. D. Novin, W. Wyrwicka, and G. Bray (New York: Raven Press, 1976).

385 pummel a large doll: Albert Bandura and R.H. Walters, *Social Learning and Personality Development* (New York: Holt, Rinehart and Winston, 1963).

385–86 Prolonged learning in oystercatchers: Michael Norton-Griffiths, "The Organization, Control and Development of Parental Feeding in the Oystercatcher (*Haematopus ostralegus*)," *Behaviour* 34 (1969), pp. 55–114.

386–87 Helplessness and ulcers in rats: Jay Weiss, "Psychological Factors in Stress and Disease," *Scientific American* 226 (1972), pp.

104–13. See chapter 14 for further discussion and references.

387 Desensitization training in premature ejaculation: William H. Masters and Virginia E. Johnson, *Human Sexual Inadequacy* (Boston: Little, Brown, 1970).

388 "one-trial learning" of the "Sauce Béarnaise syndrome": See chapter 1 for full discussion and references.

388 Give me a child till he's seven: This paraphrases a passage in his journal; see Alexander Dru, ed., *The Journals of Kierkegaard* (New York: Harper Torchbooks, 1959), p. 170.

388 tape-recorder metaphor for the brain: Jerome Kagan, *The Growth of the Child* (New York: W.W. Norton, 1978).

388–89 Closing one eye of a rhesus monkey: David Hubel, Torsten Wiesel, and Simon LeVay, "Plasticity of Ocular Dominance Columns in Monkey Striate Cortex," *Philosophical Transactions of the Royal Society of London* B 278 (1977), pp. 377–409.

389 Rhesus monkeys raised in social isolation: See chapter 13 (pp. 332–35) for discussion and references.

389 Two six-day separations: Robert A. Hinde and Yvette Spencer-Booth, "Effects of Brief Separation from Mother on Rhesus Monkeys," *Science* 173 (1971), pp. 111–18.

389–90 Social restriction and the cerebellar cortex: Mary Kay Floeter and William T. Greenough, "Cerebellar Plasticity: Modification of Purkinje Cell Structure by Differential Rearing in Monkeys," *Science* 206 (1979), pp. 227–29. The authors stress their view that the effects of social restriction seem to operate through decreased opportunity for motor learning in this experimental situation. That view is supported by internal evidence in their experiment, as well as by another experiment showing a similar effect in mice as a result of varying physical activity without varying social contact: J.J. Pysh and G.M. Weiss, "Exercise During Development Induces an Increase in Purkinje Cell Dendritic Tree Size," *Science* 206 (1979), pp. 230–32.

390 Environmental enrichment and the occipital cortex: See chapter 4 (pp. 60–61, 79) for discussion and references.

390–91 The brain of the jewelfish: Richard Coss and Albert Globus, "Spine Stems on Tectal Interneurons are Shortened by Social Stimulation," *Science* 200 (1978), pp. 787–90.

391 Effects of imprinting on bird brains: P. Bateson, G. Horn, and S. Rose, "Effects of Early Experience on Regional Incorporation of Precursors into RNA and Protein in the Chick Brain," *Brain Research* 39 (1972), pp. 449–65; S. Kohsaka, K. Takamatsu, E. Aoki, and Y. Tsukuda, "Metabolic Mapping of Chick Brain After Imprinting Using ^{14}C-Deoxyglucose Technique," *Brain Research* 172 (1979), pp. 539–44.

391 a few minutes of stimulation or stress: See the chapters by Victor H. Denenberg in any of the following three books: *Early Experience and Behavior*, ed. G. Newton and S. Levine (Springfield, Ill.: Thomas, 1968); *Miami Symposium on the Prediction of Behavior, 1968: Effects of Early Experience*, ed. M.R. Jones (Coral Gables, Fla.: University of Miami Press, 1970); *Minnesota Symposia on Child Psychology*, ed. John Hill (Minneapolis: University of Minnesota Press, 1969).

391–92 Adrenal gland "toughened": S. Levine and R. Mullins, "Hormonal Influences on Brain Organization in Infant Rats," *Science* 152 (1964), pp. 1585–86.

392 Early-stressed rats mobilize when they need to: S. Levine, G. Haltmeyer, G. Karas, and Victor H. Denenberg, "Physiological and Behavioral Effects of Infantile Stimulation," *Physiology and Behavior* 2 (1967), pp. 55–59.

392 Change in the controlling hormones: M.X. Zarrow, P. Samuel Campbell, and Victor H. Denenberg, "Handling in Infancy: Increased Levels of the Hypothalamic Corticotropin Releasing Factor (CRF) Following Exposure to a Novel Situation," *Proceedings of the Society for Experimental Biology and Medicine* 141 (1972), pp. 356–58, and "The Effect of Infantile Stimulation Upon Hypothalamic CRF Levels Following Adrenalectomy in the Adult Rat," *Proceedings of the Society for Experimental Biology and Medicine* 142 (1973), pp. 781–83.

392 Rearing of mice with rat aunts: Victor H. Denenberg, K.M. Rosenberg, R. Paschke, and M.X. Zarrow, "Mice Reared with Rat Aunts: Effects on Plasma Corticosterone and Open Field Activity," *Nature* 221 (1969), pp. 73–74.

392 Early handling alters "lateralization": Victor H. Denenberg, J. Garbanati, G. Sherman, D.A. Yutzey, and R. Kaplan, "Infantile Stimulation Induces Brain Lateralization in Rats," *Science* 201 (1980), pp. 1150–52.

392 interactions between corticosterone and growth hormone: For review, see Thomas K. Landauer and John W.M. Whiting, "Correlates and Consequences of Stress in Infancy," in *Handbook*, ed. Monroe, Monroe, and Whiting.

392–93 Postweaning isolation and neurotransmitters: L. Valzelli, *Psychopharmacology* (New York: Spectrum, 1973), pp. 79–83. For a recent review of similar phenomena in rats, see P. Brain and D. Benton, "The Interpretation of Physiological Correlates of Differential Housing in Laboratory Rats," *Life Sciences* 24 (1979), pp. 99–115.

393 Depth perception in children: M.S. Banks, R.N. Aslin, and R.D.

Letson, "Sensitive Period for the Development of Human Binocular Vision," *Science* 190 (1975), pp. 675–77.

394 fully two inches taller: Thomas K. Landauer and John W.M. Whiting, "Infantile Stimulation and Adult Stature of Human Males," *American Anthropologist* 66 (1964), pp. 1007–28. A parallel effect was later shown in comparing the stature of individuals vaccinated in infancy with that of individuals vaccinated later (the vaccination of infants and the discomfort following it being viewed as stressful) in longitudinal growth studies in the United States: John W.M. Whiting, Thomas K. Landauer, and T.M. Jones, "Infantile Vaccination and Adult Stature," *Child Development* 39 (1968), pp. 59–67. It was further shown that mother-infant separation had an effect similar to the other kinds of stress: Sarah M. Gunders and John W.M. Whiting, "Mother-Infant Separation and Physical Growth," *Ethnology* 2 (1968), pp. 196–206. For a recent review of the human studies see Landauer and Whiting in *Handbook*, ed. Monroe, Monroe, and Whiting.

394 Earlier first menstruation: John W.M. Whiting, "Menarcheal Age and Infant Stress in Humans," in *Sex and Behavior*, ed. F.A. Beach (New York: John Wiley, 1965).

395–96 One twin elaborately exercised: Myrtle McGraw, *Growth: A Study of Johnny and Jimmy* (New York: Appleton-Century-Crofts, 1935). The follow-up at age twenty-two years is illustrated in a film by McGraw, presented by her at the Department of Psychiatry, Boston Children's Hospital, 1975.

397 "the pathos of life experience": The phrase appears in print in Paul I. Yakovlev and André Roch-Lecours, "Myelogenetic Cycles of the Regional Maturation of the Brain," in *Regional Development of the Brain in Early Life*, ed. A. Minkowski (Oxford: Blackwell, 1967). But it has often been used by Yakovlev in lectures and in personal communications.

399–400 a severe critic of behavior genetics: Richard C. Lewontin, "Genetic Aspects of Intelligence," *Annual Review of Genetics* 9 (1975), pp. 387–405.

400 Temperature and survival in fruit flies: Theodosius Dobzhansky and B. Spassky, "Genetics of Natural Populations. XI. Manifestation of Genetic Variants in *Drosophila pseudoobscura* in Different Environments," *Genetics* 29 (1944), pp. 270–90.

400–401 IQ and scholastic achievement: Arthur Jensen, "How Much Can We Boost IQ and Scholastic Achievement?" *Harvard Educational Review* 39 (1969), pp. 1–123.

401 Rats influenced by their grandmothers' experiences: Victor H. Denenberg and Kenneth M. Rosenberg, "Nongenetic Transmis-

sion of Information," *Nature* 216 (1967), pp. 549–50. *One-generational transfer of experiential effects has also been shown, for both behavioral and physiological characteristics: Victor H. Denenberg and Arthur E. Whimbey, "Behavior of Rats Is Modified by the Experiences Their Mothers Had as Infants," *Science* 142 (1963), pp. 1192–93, and N. Skolnick, S. Ackerman, M. Hofer, and H. Weiner, "Vertical Transmission of Acquired Ulcer Susceptibility in the Rat," *Science* 208 (1980), pp. 1161–63. This latter paper raises the clear specter of familial effects in certain disease conditions that may not be genetic in origin. The reader may also have guessed that these findings should have caused some discomfort in the ranks of evolutionary biologists, for whom the inheritance of acquired characteristics is forbidden almost by decree. In fact, they have taken little notice of them as yet, probably because there are no evolutionary models for the handling of such phenomena.

CHAPTER 17: THE PROSPECT

Amid much heated argument during the last decade, *Scientific American* has published three balanced and authoritative multiauthored collections of articles on the human population in relation to the available resources of this planet: "The Human Population," published as the September 1974 issue, "Food and Agriculture" (September 1976), and "Economic Development" (September 1980). An important additional point is made by Nathan Keyfitz in "World Resources and the World Middle Class," *Scientific American* 235 (1976), pp. 28–35, where attention is given not merely to sheer numbers of people but also to their aspirations. These three volumes and the Keyfitz article are essential reading for anyone beginning to think seriously about the fundamental determinants of the human future.

Page
412 Louise Colet: Gustave Flaubert, in *The Letters in Gustave Flaubert*, ed. Francis Steegmuller (Cambridge, Mass.: Harvard University Press, 1979), p. 79.
415–16 "Tired with all these . . .": William Shakespeare, *Sonnets*, 66, ed. George Lyman Kittredge (Waltham, Mass.: Blaisdell, 1966).
416 "Life *is* . . . a battle . . .": Henry James, as quoted in *The Portable Henry James*, ed. Morton D. Zabel (New York: Viking, 1951), introduction, p. 27.
416 "All the highly learned schoolmasters . . .": Johann Wolfgang von

Goethe, *The Sufferings of Young Werther*, ed. and trans. Harry Steinhauer (New York: Bantam. 1962), pp. 42–45.

416–17 "grown-ups do not exist . . .": André Malraux, *Antimémoires* (Paris: Gallimard, 1967), p. 1. Translated by the author.

422 "that sense of the world . . .": Joan Didion, "Without Regret or Hope," a review of Naipaul, *New York Review of Books* 27 (June 12, 1980), p. 24.

422 "As soon as man applies his intelligence . . .": Leo Tolstoy, 1865, quoted in Henri Troyat, *Tolstoy*, trans. Nancy Amphoux (New York: Doubleday, 1967), p. 297.

422 "the aim of science . . .": Bertolt Brecht, *Collected Plays*, vol. 5, ed. Ralph Manheim and John Willett (New York: Pantheon, 1972), p. 64.

422 "Man is by nature metaphysical and proud . . .": Claude Bernard, *An Introduction to the Study of Experimental Medicine* (New York: Macmillan, 1927), p. 27.

424 "demographic transition theory": Ansley J. Coale, "The History of the Human Population," *Scientific American* 231 (1974), pp. 41–51.

426–27 Talmudic tradition in Poland: Chaim Grade, *The Yeshiva*, trans. Curt Leviant (New York: Bobbs-Merrill, 1976), p. 12.

427 this is the way the world ends: T.S. Eliot, "The Hollow Men," in *The Complete Poems and Plays 1909–1950* (New York: Harcourt, Brace and World, 1962).

427–28 "It has been argued . . .": Conrad H. Waddington, *Biology, Purpose and Ethics* (Worcester, Mass.: Clark University Press, 1971), p. 42.

428 "Break thou the arm of the wicked . . .": Psalms 10:15–18.

CHAPTER 18: THE DAWN OF WONDER

Page

431 chimpanzee ceremony at waterfall: Harold Bauer was kind enough to provide me with an unpublished manuscript describing this phenomenon. It has also been seen by other observers at the Gombe Stream Reserve, and additional information was provided in personal communications from Barbara Smuts and Irven DeVore. The interpretation placed on it here is not necessarily that of these investigators.

433–34 comments of Apollo 11 astronauts: Norman Mailer, *Of a Fire on the Moon* (Boston: Little, Brown, 1970), chapters 6 and 7.

INDEX